商贸汉语高级读本

Business Chinese

An Advanced Reader

崔颂人

Songren Cui

The Chinese University Press

Business Chinese : An Advanced Reader
  By Songren Cui

© The Chinese University of Hong Kong 2004

All Rights Reserved. No part of this publication may
be reproduced or transmitted in any form or by any
means, electronic or mechanical, including photocopying,
recording, or any information storage and retrieval
system, without permission in writing from
The Chinese University of Hong Kong.

ISBN: 962–996–009–5

Published by The Chinese University Press,
  The Chinese University of Hong Kong,
  Sha Tin, N.T., Hong Kong.
  Fax: +852 2603 6692
      +852 2603 7355
  E-mail: cup@cuhk.edu.hk
  Web-site: www.chineseupress.com

Printed in Hong Kong

To A. Ronald Walton

目 录

前　言
PREFACE

With the rapid development of China's economy, the teaching and learning of Chinese language as a second/foreign language is booming. One emerging dimension is business Chinese, a language course that purports to help students further improve their Chinese proficiency beyond the intermediate level, and in the meantime, offers some basic knowledge in business fields such as import-export trade, banking, insurance, investment, etc. *Business Chinese: An Advanced Reader* (商贸汉语高级读本) is an attempt to meet such needs. It is designed for students who have had at least three years of formal study of Chinese at college, and have an interest in further developing their Chinese language skills through the study of subject matters in business, primarily import-export trade.

There are three guiding principles in the development of this textbook. First of all, this is a language textbook rather than a business one although the content focuses on import-export matters. Users of this textbook, both students and teachers alike, should bear in mind that it is for the purpose of learning the Chinese language in a business context that this book was developed. They should try their best to strive for a balance of both CHINESE and BUSINESS, if we all agree that the two represent both ends of a continuum, so to speak. Secondly, it is not my intention to simply write a textbook that would build up students' business-related vocabulary for reading about business and conducting business. What I hope is that students will be able to learn "how to catch fish" actively instead of just "having fish" passively, that is, to apply the knowledge and skills gained in this textbook to other contexts, be it science or technology, economics or politics, and to further improve their Chinese proficiency. In addition, I hope this textbook will help students deal intelligently and sensitively with situations where the vocabularies and expressions are used. Last but not least, I believe that advanced level text materials should not be simply longer texts with more new words compared with those at the intermediate level. They should, on the contrary, include knowledge and skills in every linguistic modality that ought to be learned in the due process of Chinese language acquisition at the post-intermediate level. These may include, among other things:

1. The literal, core meaning of some commonly used Chinese morphemes and characters, and the basic word-formation rules in association with other words or characters.

2. Ways of contraction/expansion of words and phrases to meet the needs of the context.

3. The use of synonyms and antonyms, as well as word-forming, vocabulary-building techniques using synonyms or antonyms.

4. The ability to distinguish commendatory/derogatory sense of words and phrases.

5. The ability to distinguish colloquial/written usage and words of different styles.

6. An understanding of the logical relations of the clauses in various complex sentences and the correct usage of connectives.

7. Knowledge of how Chinese works at the discourse level. This means an understanding of the logical relations between groups of sentences, paragraphs, and the cohesive devices to connect them.

8. An understanding of the basic rhetorical structures and organization of a text, being able to group paragraphs centered on a theme, and the ability to use a short sentence or a phrase to summarize the main idea of each section of a text that may go beyond a paragraph in length.

9. An understanding of the merits and limitations of various sentence forms (句式), such as short sentences versus long sentences, passive sentences versus active sentences, and affirmative sentences versus negative sentences when expressing a similar idea, and knowing when to use what.

10. Knowing how to use Chinese punctuation correctly.

This textbook is, therefore, a product of the effort to materialize these skills within a business context. New words and expressions in each lesson are presented with explanations in Chinese whenever it is possible, in addition to their *pinyin* pronunciation, parts of speech, and English explanations, a common practice among most textbooks. This may help students develop the habit of consulting a Chinese-Chinese dictionary and rely more on their comprehension in Chinese instead of English translations. Moreover, for words like nouns, verbs, and adjectives, etc. certain frequently used collocations such as verb-object, verb-complement, or modifier-modified are provided. If it is a morpheme, some commonly used words that make use of such a morpheme will be included. It is hoped that this will help students understand how words are formed in Chinese, and in the process expand their vocabulary. In addition, the style of some words (colloquial versus written) is marked, and synonyms or antonyms are also given if possible. There are 1,057 new words and expressions (including supplementary ones) in this textbook. Among them, 48 (4.54%) belong to Category A (甲级词) words of the *HSK Vocabulary List* (汉语水平考试常用词汇表), and 261 (26.58%) words fall into Category B (乙级词). While Category C words (丙级词) number 188 (17.79%) and Category D words (丁级词) account for 211 (19.96%). In addition, there are 349 words that are not included in the *HSK Vocabulary List*. Among them, 12 (1.14%) are proper names of places or product brands, while 108 words (10.22%) are special terms related to international trade and business. The remaining 229 (21.67%) are uncategorized, but most of them are words and phrases derived from Categories C or D vocabulary, including 17 idioms or set phrases. This proportion of new words and expressions, in terms of their degree of difficulty, should be about right for students at this evel.

By the same token, the section of *Explanations to Words and Phrases with*

Examples that highlights the usage of some words or phrases students may have difficulty with, follows a similar distribution. With a total number of 122 words and phrases, 7 of them (5.74%) are Category A words, and 39 (31.97%) are identified as Category B, 32 (26.23%) as Category C, and still 29 (23.77%) as Category D. The rest 15 (12.29%) are basically either Categories C or D by inference according to their primary components or synonyms in the *HSK Vocabulary List*. This part offers explanations in both Chinese and English as to the usage of the words and phrases, compares the subtleties of similar expressions, and gives warnings about potential pitfalls.

Although students did learn quite a number of complex sentences, usually as sentence patterns, here and there at the beginning and intermediate levels, they seldom have had an opportunity to be introduced to complex sentences systematically, even at the advanced level. This textbook tries to fill in the gap by summarizing various complex sentences according to the logical relationships they express, and the relevant connectives to be used. Meanwhile, it shows that these logical relationships exist not only at the sentence level, but also at the discourse level. Some people may think that it is not necessary to teach such basic linguistic phenomena as attributives, numeration, and punctuation, presuming that students have learned them during the elementary and intermediate levels. The fact is that, however, students still have difficulties in arranging the order of attributives, particularly when there are multiple ones. Likewise, they may be able to deal with numbers under one hundred thousand, but will be puzzled by larger integers beyond one hundred thousand, or fractions, decimals, and multiples, etc. While most students seem to know how to use commas, full stops, or question marks, they have a vague idea of other punctuation marks, let alone their distinctions in use between Chinese and English, and the correct usage of the Chinese punctuation system. These are, therefore, also included in the textbook as a remedy for what has been lacking in most students' training before the advanced level.

With the aim to improve the communicative effect of using Chinese, the section on *Rhetoric* gives a brief introduction to basic Chinese rhetoric such as sentence forms (for example, the conversion of a regular sentence and an inverted sentence, the use of passive voice vs. active voice), the styles of language (written vs. spoken), contraction of words and phrases, the choice of commendatory and derogatory words, etc. It is hoped that these will help improve students' reading comprehension as well as their writing skills.

To reinforce what has been introduced, different kinds of exercises are included, with each targeted at a specific grammatical item or skill in each lesson. For example, there are multiple-choice exercises for distinguishing subtleties and word-formation; there are tasks such as searching for a specific kind of complex sentence from the text, or writting a complex sentence based on the information expressed in several simple sentences. The exercises for *Rhetoric* include distinguishing commendatory/derogatory terms, converting written language to spoken, or vise versa, giving synonyms or antonyms to the listed words, etc. As a comprehensive exercise, there are three short paragraphs in English to be translated into Chinese in each lesson. Feedback from students who used the field-test version indicates that this is the most helpful exercise. In addition, the textbook includes seven activities of business letter writing and one of resume writing.

Since most advanced Chinese classes at the fourth year level have three contact hours a week only, the nurture and development of self-study skills is the key to success for students' Chinese learning. When using this textbook, therefore, students are required to study seriously before coming to class. By design, this textbook has provided detailed explanations in both English and Chinese, hoping that students will, at least, have some basic conceptual control of the materials after they have read the text. To facilitate reading comprehension, each lesson will begin with three to five questions. These questions have a dual function: 1) is to prompt students to think about what the text is about based on their world knowledge; 2) is to serve as an indirect hint to students how thematic sections in the text may be divided according to their main ideas. If a student can answer these questions correctly after reading the text, he or she will have successfully summarized the main ideas of the text and grouped the related paragraphs accordingly. The text is in a rather formal, written Chinese style (书面语). It is believed that students at the advanced level should be exposed to more formal, written language, and expository essays. It is more convenient and natural for them to switch to colloquial Chinese in discussions and conversations rather than the other way around when they are required to write. After each text, there are several comprehension-check questions. These questions, in addition to the main ideas, ask for supporting details to see how well students have comprehended the text. Students are also required to divide the text into several larger sections according to a central idea, and summarize the main idea of each section. This works hand in hand with the questions at the beginning of the lesson and will help students to process and comprehend longer sections of written texts in the future.

As for teachers, their job will be leaning more toward organizing discussions, helping students test their hypotheses, providing feedback, and answering questions to clarify misunderstandings.

Although this textbook is entitled *Business Chinese: An Advanced Reader*, and is primarily focused on reading and writing, it does not mean that listening and speaking as well as colloquial expressions should be excluded. The author believes that at the advanced level of language learning all linguistic modalities interact with each other and reinforce each other, unlike the beginning level at which only the receptive skills help the productive skills in early language acquisition. Hence, all activities in class should be conducted in Chinese. Oral activities such as discussion, role-play, and presentation should have their own place. Even though this textbook is replete with a rich variety of content and exercises, it is not necessary to finish every single one of them if the situation does not permit. From my own limited experience, it seems "better to have more than less", just like most Chinese hosts who prepare a banquet for guests. As a user, or to use a similar analogy, as a customer who goes to dine in a buffet restaurant, one can always eat selectively to his or her own satisfaction and leave other dishes alone.

The writing of this textbook has been a remarkable learning experience. I am very grateful to my colleagues and friends who have given me help and support. Particularly, I own a great deal to Mr. Huang Yongpo and Ms. Gao Yuan who supplied the authentic Chinese business documents. I am indebted to Professor James Hargett, and Dr. Scott McGinnis, Ms. Liang Xia, and Ms. Dai Xiaoxue, who did the editorial and proofreading work, and provided invaluable suggestions. My heartfelt-gratitude goes to Dr. Steven K. Luk, Director of the Chinese University Press, Hong Kong, and his colleagues Mr. Fung Yat-Kong and Ms. Esther Tsang, who worked so hard to make the publication of this textbook possible, in particular to edit and proofread meticulously the manuscript several times. I would also like to thank Mr. Mark Lenhart, who arranged field-testing of this textbook in CET's Beijing, Harbin and Nanjing programs. Last but not least, I am thankful to the students of the University of Massachusetts at Amherst, Oberlin College, and the teachers and students in CET programs who participated in the field-test of the early version of this textbook and have given me their important feedback.

I understand that there are still flaws and mistakes in this textbook despite my efforts. All criticisms and comments are welcome. I will try my best to improve my work, and in the meantime, take full responsibility for any errors and mistakes that remain.

语法术语缩写及符号

Adj.	Adjective	形容词
Adv.	Adverb	副词
Aux.	Auxiliary Verb	助动词
Colloq.	Colloquialism	口语
Conj.	Conjunction	连词
Idm.	Idiom/Idiomatic Expression	成语、俗语或惯用语
Intjn.	Interjection	叹词
MW	Measure Word	量词
Mph.	Morpheme	语素
N.	Noun	名词
NP	Noun Phrase	名词短语
Num.	Numeral	数词
Partcl.	Particle	助词/小品词
Prep.	Preposition	介词
Pr.N.	Proper Noun	专有名词
Pron.	Pronoun	代词
V.	Verb	动词
Vi.	Intransitive Verb	及物动词
Vt.	Transitive Verb	不及物动词
VO	Verb Object Construction	动宾结构
VP	Verb Phrase	动词短语
L-1	Lesson 1	第一课
l-14	Lines 14 in the text	课文中的第十四行
~	The morpheme/word used in examples	
	出现在例词或例句中的有关语素或词	
✘	Incorrect/Inappropriate use	
	不正确或不规范的用法	

?   The sentence is questionable

有争议或有疑问的句子

[i.e. "belong to"] Hints about words to be used in translation exercises but may not be indiomatic or grammatical in English.

在英译汉练习中提示用引号内的词，但该词在原英语句子中可能不符合英语语法或表达习惯。

(and)   Words used for the sake of English grammar but may or may not be necessary in Chinese.

括号里的词主要是为了照顾英语的表达习惯或语法，但在翻译成汉语时可以省略。

<>   Antonym   所列词条的反义词

〔正〕   正式   Formal in style

〔书〕   书面语   Written or literary language

〔口〕   口头语   Colloquialism

建立业务关系

✎ **思考下面的问题，然后带着这些问题去阅读课文：**

一、从事国际贸易要做些什么准备工作？

二、为什么要进行市场调查？做市场调查要注意什么问题？

三、可以通过哪些途径跟客户建立业务关系？

课文：建立业务关系

任何一家公司要做进出口生意，从事国际贸易，必须进行一定的准备工作。这些工作主要包括：进行市场调查，了解对方的贸易制度和市场所在地的法律，建立与客户的业务关系等。

由于市场经常变动，各国各地的情况不一，因此，为了保证生意的成功，首先要做好市场的调查研究工作。对出口业务来说，应当调查商品对市场的适销情况，了解市场的供求关系，分析市场动向，以便选择适当的销售市场。对进口业务来说，则要注意研究价格的变动，选择合适的交易对象，掌握好各项交易条件。另外，对于进出口市场所在地的贸易惯例、关税制度、进出口管制条例和规定、港口及运输条件等也都应有充分的了解。这样才能真正做到"知己知彼"。 10

与客户建立业务关系，是进行国际贸易的必要条件之一。建立业务关系有各种不同的途径。例如，可以通过拜访外国驻本国大使馆的商务处，请他们介绍自己国家的经济贸易情况和法律制度，提供有关公司的信息，并帮助与这些公司取得联系。此外，也可以通过银行、商会、其他贸易公司等，了解有关公司的业务范围和资信情况，或请 15

他们介绍推荐，与有关的公司取得联系。还可以自己从广告、报刊杂志上得到有关厂商的信息(主要是业务范围、地址、电话、网页、电邮地址以及传真号码等)，直接写信与对方联系。

20　　写信与客户建立业务关系时，首先应当告诉对方自己是通过什么途径了解到他们的公司和地址的，然后自我介绍，说明自己公司经营的范围，表达希望与对方进行业务往来的兴趣或合作的意向。信中最好能附上介绍本公司的小册子，例如产品说明书或商品目录等材料，以及有关部门负责人的名片等。这样将有助于互相了解，为今后的进出口业务打下良好的基础。

25　　除此以外，如有机会，还可以参加一些外国的商品展览会或者交易会，与有关公司的代表当面洽谈，直接建立业务联系。

✎ **根据课文内容回答下列问题：**

1. 从事国际贸易，应当做些什么准备工作？

2. 为什么要做市场调查？

3. 市场调查要注意什么问题？

4. 可以通过哪些途径得到外国厂商的有关信息？

5. 写信与客户直接联系，一般应当包括什么内容？

6. 写自我介绍的信件时附上本公司的材料，有什么好处？

7. 除了写信以外，还有什么途径可以与客户直接联系？

✎ **根据意思，给课文划分层次(不是自然段)并写出每个层次的大意。**

生词和用法

建立	jiànlì	*V.*	开始成立；设立：大使馆、公司、制度。开始产生；形成：关系、联系、感情。 to establish; to set up.
务	wù	*Mph.(N.)*	事情：事~、业~、商~、公~、财~、家~、国~。 matter; business.
业务	yèwù	*N.*	本行业、本职的事务；本职工作：发展~；进出口~：~水平、~能力、~范围。 business; profession.
任何	rènhé	*Pron.*	不管什么。　any; whichever; whatever.
口	kǒu	*N.*	出入通过的地方：门~、窗~、港~、关~、出~、入~。 opening; mouth; entrance.
进口	jìnkǒu	*N./V.*	把货物从外地买来并运进本地。 import.
出口	chūkǒu	*N./V.*	把货物从本地卖出并运到外地。 export.
进出口	jìnchūkǒu	*NP*	=进口+出口；例：中小学、青少年、男女生、
生意	shēngyì	*N.*	商业经营、买卖：做~、谈~；~兴隆、~成功、~失败。　trade; business.
从事	cóngshì	*V.*	〔正〕参与做、致力于(某种事情)：~进口业务、~青年工作、~写作。 to be engaged in [doing sth.].
际	jì	*Mph.(N.)*	彼此之间：人~关系、校~交流、班~比赛、洲~导弹。　inter-.
国际	guójì	*Adj.*	国与国之间：~关系、~贸易、~政治、~交流。 international.
贸易	màoyì	*N./V.*	〔正〕交易；买卖：做~、从事~、进行~；进出口~、国际~；Cf. 生意。　trade.
进行	jìnxíng	*V.*	〔正〕从事(某种正式、持续的活动)：~工作、~调查、~研究、~分析、~了解。 to conduct; carry out/on.

调查	diàochá	V./N.	为了了解情况进行考察：~情况、~问题、~市场、~案件。 to investigate; investigation.
了解	liǎojiě	V.	打听、调查：~情况、~看法、~意见。 to find out; to understand.
市场	shìchǎng	N.	商品交易的场所或销售的地区：国际~、国内~、自由~；打进~、争夺~。 market.
制度	zhìdù	N.	预设的规则：社会~、关税~、政治~、法律~。 system:
法律	fǎlǜ	N.	立法机构或政府设定的规则：制定~、根据~、遵守~；~地位。 law
包括	bǎokuò	V.	包含（或列举各部分）。 to include; to consist of.
客户	kèhù	N.	厂商、律师或经纪人对顾客的称呼。 client; customer.
对方	duìfāng	Pron.	另一方：＜＞我方。 the other party;
变动	biàndòng	V./N.	（社会现象等的）改变：市场~、价格~、形势~；Cf. 变化、改变。 to change; alternation.
保证	bǎozhèng	V./N.	担保做到。 to guarantee.
成功	chénggōng	Adj./N.	达到预期的效果：＜＞失败。 to succeed; success.
首先	shǒuxiān	Adv.	第一（用来列举事项）：＜＞最后。 first of all.
商品	shāngpǐn	N.	市场上出售的物品：Cf. 货物。 commodity; goods.
情况	qíngkuàng	N.	情形：健康~、市场~、学习~；了解~、调查~。 circumstances; situation.
动向	dòngxiàng	N.	活动和发展的方向：发展~、市场~、了解~、分析~、掌握~。 trend; tendency.
供求	gōngqiú	N.	供=供应；求=需求：~关系、~变化。 mostly as modifier supply and demand.

分析	fēnxī	V./N	仔细了解：~问题、~动向、~形势、化学~、语法~。 to analyze; analysis.
选择	xuǎnzé	V./N.	挑选：~地点、~时间、~条件、~对象。 to select; to choose.
适	shì	Mph.(Adj.)	合适；适合：~用、~合、~当、~时、~口、~中、~量、~销。 suitable; fit,
适当	shìdàng	Adj.	合适、妥当。 suitable, appropriate.
适销	shìxiāo	N./Adj.	适合销售的；适合市场需要的。 salable; marketable.
交易	jiāoyì	N.	买卖商品：做~、进行~、达成~。 deal; transaction; trade.
销售	xiāoshòu	V./N.	〔正〕卖出（货物）：~价格、~情况、~市场。 to sell; to market.
则	zé	Adv.	〔书〕表示后一种情况与前一种情况形成对比，有"却"的意思。 but; on the other hand.
对象	duìxiàng	N.	行为或思考时作为目标的事物：调查~、销售~、合作~。 target; object; partner.
掌握	zhǎngwò	V.	了解事物，因而能充分支配和利用：~知识、~情况、~技术。 to know well; to control.
项	xiàng	MW	宗或件：数字+~+N.（条件、内容、任务、工作、业务）。 Measure word for things classified by items.
条件	tiáojiàn	N.	影响事物发生、发展的因素：交易~、工作~、自然~、有利~、身体~。 condition.
例	lì	Mph.(N.)	用来帮助说明或证明的事物：~子、~如、举~。 example; instance.
惯例	guànlì	N.	一向的做法：贸易~、国际~、打破~、按照~。 convention; usual practice.
条例	tiáolì	N.	定下的规章：交通~、安全~。 rules; regulations.

关税	guānshuì	N.	海关对进出口物品所收的款项。
			custom duty; tariff.
管制	guǎnzhì	V./N.	强行管理：交通~、外汇~、进出口~。
			to control.
规定	guīdìng	V./N.	对事情作出决定，多带宾语：遵守~、按照~。
			to stipulate; to set rules and regulation.
		N.	所规定的内容。 regulation; rules.
港口	gǎngkǒu	N.	河、海等岸边可供船只停靠的地方。
			port; harbor.
运输	yùnshū	V./N.	用交通工具把人或物品从一个地方载到另一个地方：~工具、~公司、~条件、公路~。
			to transport; transportation; carriage.
充分	chōngfèn	Adj.	足够(多用于抽象事物的+ N)：~了解、~准备；~的条件、~的理由。 sufficient.
知己	zhī jǐ	Idm.	知=知道，己=自己，彼=对方→对自己和对方的情况都十分了解。
知彼	zhī bǐ		
			To know oneself and one's opponents well.
必要	bìyào	Adj./N.	不可缺少的：~的说明、~的准备、~的条件、~的时候。 indispensable; necessary.
途径	tújìng	N.	(多用于比喻)管道、路径：合法~、外交~。
			(mostly used in analogy) way; channel.
通过	tōngguò	Prep./V.	through; by means of; to pass through.
拜访	bàifǎng	V.	〔敬辞〕访问：~亲友、~贵公司。
			to pay a visit to; to call on (somebody).
驻	zhù	V.	停留/住在执行职务的地方：美国驻华大使馆、中国驻纽约领事馆。
			to stay; to be stationed.

大使馆	dàshǐguǎn	N.	外交使节驻在外国首都的办公机关。
			embassy.
大使	dàshǐ	N.	由一个国家派驻另一个国家的最高外交代表。
			ambassador.
商务	shāngwù	N.	商业上的事务。 commercial affairs; business affairs.
			商务处＝(大使馆内)负责商业事务的部门。
经济	jīngjì	N./Adj.	economy; economical.
提供	tígōng	V.	供给(意见、条件、物资、信息等)。
			to supply; to furnish.
有关	yǒuguān	V.	关＝关系，有关系的：~公司、~部门、~方面、~信息、~途径。 related; relevant.
公司	gōngsī	N.	经营商品的生产或销售的工商业组织：贸易~、运输~、工业~、汽车~。
			company; corporation.
信息	xìnxī	N.	有关事物的消息和材料：提供~、了解~、取得~。 information.
取得	qǔdé	V.	(通过努力)得到：~联系、~经验、~好成绩、~联系。 to obtain; to acquire; to achieve.
联系	liánxì	V.	彼此接上关系：保持~、取得~、失去~。
			to contact; to be in touch:
商会	shānghuì	N.	商人为进行商业活动而成立的组织。
			chamber of commerce.
范围	fànwéi	N.	scope; range: 工作~、业务~、活动~、经营~。
资信	zīxìn	N.	资＝资产，信＝信誉。assets and credit.
推荐	tuījiàn	V.	向别人介绍并希望接受或任用。
			to recommend.
广告	guǎnggào	N.	通过报纸、电视、电台等介绍商品或服务的一种形式：商业~、汽车~、服装~、饮料~；打~、做~。 advertisement; commercial.

报刊	bàokān	N.	报纸、杂志的总称；不加个体量词。 newspapers and periodicals; journals
杂志	zázhì	N.	定期或不定期的刊物，也叫期刊。 magazine
厂商	chǎngshāng	N.	工厂和商店、公司。 manufacturers and companies
地址	dìzhǐ	N.	(人、团体)居住或通信的地点。 address.
传真	chuánzhēn	N.	fax, facsimile: 发~、接收~、~机、~号码。
号码	hàomǎ	N.	表示事物次第或代表事物的数目字：电话~、传真~、房间~。 number (of phone or room, etc.)
直接	zhíjiē	Adj.	不经过中间事物的：~原因、~关系、~了解、~联系；＜＞间接。 direct; immediate.
自我	zìwǒ	Pron.	自己(加在双音节动词前表示动作从自己发出)：~介绍、~分析、~教育、~批评。 self (+ disyllabic V.) indicating a self-directed action toward oneself.
说明	shuōmíng	V.	解释明白。 to explain; to illustrate.
		N.	解释的话。 explanation; illustration.
说明书	shuōmíngshū	NP	关于物品使用、性能等方面的文字或图片介绍。 manual.
经营	jīngyíng	V.	筹办、计划并管理。 to deal in/with; to manage.
往来	wǎnglái	V.	〔正〕互相之间的交往(可用于个人、团体、国家之间)：业务~、贸易~、友好~。Cf. 来往(多用于个人之间)。 come and go; contact.
合作	hézuò	V./N.	为了共同的目的互相配合、一起工作：经济~、技术~、互助~。 to cooperate.
意向	yìxiàng	N.	意图、目的。 intention; purpose.

附上	fùshàng	VP	附带、加上。	to attach; to add.
小册子	xiǎocèzi	N.	装订好的小本子。	brochure; pamphlet.
目录	mùlù	N.	按一定次序排列的事物名目：商品~、图书~。 catalog; list.	
材料	cáiliào	N.	资料：参考~、调查~、第一手~。 data; material.	
部门	bùmén	N.	机构的一部份：业务~、研究~、有关~。 department; section.	
负责	fùzé	V./Adj.	担负责任。 例：负责人、负责部门。	to be responsible for; be in charge of.
名片	míngpiàn	N.	印有自己名字、职位、地址、电话号码的卡片。	business card.
有助于	yǒuzhùyú	VP	〔正〕对…有帮助。	to be conducive to.
良好	liánghǎo	Adj.	〔正〕好的、令人满意的：~的习惯、~的关系、~的成绩、~的基础。 good; favorable; positive.	
基础	jīchǔ	N.	事物发展的根本或起点：经济~、政治~、物质~、~知识、~工业、~课。 base; basis.	
机会	jīhuì	N.	时机、恰好的时候：发展~、工作~、错过~、抓住~。 opportunity; chance.	
展览	zhǎnlǎn	V./N.	陈列出来给人们观看：展览会、商品~、邮票~、汽车~、图书~。 to display; to exhibit; exhibition.	
代表	dàibiǎo	N./V.	抽出来作榜样：业务~、学生~、妇女~。 representative; to represent.	
当面	dāngmiàn	Adv.	面对面（做某事）：~说清楚、~证明、~洽谈。 to somebody's face; in someone's presence.	
洽谈	qiàtán	V.	接洽商谈：业务~、商业业务~、友好业务~。 to talk something over with somebody; to hold a talk with somebody.	

补充词

领事	lǐngshì	*N.*	由一个国家政府派驻外国某个城市的外交官员。 consul.
领事馆	lǐngshìguǎn	*N.*	一个国家派驻外国某个城市的外交办公机关。 consulate.
参赞	cānzàn	*N.*	由一国派驻另一国的外交官员，负责办理某方面的事务：商务~、文化~。 counselor; attache.
总	zǒng	*Adj./Adv.*	为首的；领导的；概括全部的：~统、~理、~领事。 chief; head; general.
副	fù	*Adj.*	职务上居第二位的：辅助的（区别于'主''正''总'）：~总统、~总理、~厂长。 deputy; vice; assistant.
董事长	dǒngshìzhǎng	*N.*	商业、企业、学校、团体等机构的最高领导人：公司~、副~。 president/chairperson of the board of directors.
总裁	zǒngcái	*N.*	某些政党或商企业团体机构最高领导人的名称：副~、业务~、银行~。 president/chairman (of a party, a company); the chief executive officer.
经理	jīnglǐ	*N.*	某些商业、企业部门的负责人：总~、副~、出口部~、银行~。 manager
机构	jīgòu	*N.*	泛指机关、团体或其他工作单位：政府~、商务~、管理~。 organization.
海关	hǎiguān	*N.*	对出入境的人员、物品和运输工具进行检查、征收关税、查禁走私的国家机关。 Customs Service
口岸	kǒuàn	*N.*	港口：通商~、入境~。 port.
国境	guójìng	*N.*	一个国家行使主权的领土范围。 national territory.

| 征收 | zhēngshōu | V. | 政府依照法律向人民或所属机构收取(税款、公粮等)。
to levy; to collect; to impose (taxes). |

词语例释

一、任何……都/也…… (any; whatever; whichever; whoever)

l-1. <u>任何</u>一家公司要做进出口生意，从事国际贸易，必须进行一定的准备工作。

　　1. <u>任何</u>国家都不能没有法律。

　　2. 他对<u>任何</u>运动都感兴趣。

　　3. 你<u>任何</u>时候去找她，她都能回答你的问题。

　　"任何"修饰名词时一般不带"的"，除了"人"，"事"以外，不修饰单音节名词。

When "任何" modifies a Noun, it does not go with "的" generally. Except for "人" or "事", it does not modify monosyllabic nouns.

二、进行＋(表示正式、持续性活动的) Verb (to carry out/on; to conduct)

l-1. 任何一家公司要做进出口生意，从事国际贸易，必须<u>进行</u>一定的准备工作。

　　1. 这个研究还在<u>进行</u>，要过几个月才会有结果。

　　2. 我们对市场的动向<u>进行</u>了分析，决定扩大出口的范围。

　　3. 他们对这些情况已经<u>进行</u>深入的了解，不会有什么问题的。

1) 位于"进行"后的宾语，表示所从事的活动的词不能是单音节的。例如：

The object after "进行" indicating the activity which the subject is engaged in, cannot be monosyllabic. For example,

进行调查(✗进行查)　　进行比较(✗进行比)

2) 用作"进行"的宾语的动词，不能再带宾语。如果再语义上要求受事，表示受事的名词可用介词"对"引进，但必须在"进行"之前。例如：

> The Verb which serves as the object of "进行" cannot take another object. However, the Preposition "对" can be used to introduce another object for this Verb if there is such a need. For instance,

大家对他进行了帮助。(✘大家进行了帮助他。)

3) "进行"用于比较正式 (formal)、庄重的活动，不用于非正式的或短暂的活动。用了"进行"的语体比较正式。例：

> "进行" is used for formal and serious activities, rather than for casual activities, or those which last for a short duration only. When "进行" is used, the text becomes more formal in style although the meaning may be the same.

他们比较了两国的贸易制度。
〔正〕他们对两国的贸易制度进行了比较。
✘进行开玩笑，✘进行吃饭。

4) "进行"可带"了"，但一般不能带"着"或"过"。例：

> "进行" can appear with the Particle "了", but seldom with a "着" or "过", for example:

双方进行了长时间的讨论，可是还没有结果。

三、Clause 1, 以便 Clause 2　(so that; in order that; so as to)

l-6. 对出口业务来说，应当调查商品对市场的适销情况，……以便选择适当的销售市场。

1. 你准备点零钱，以便买车票。
2. 现附上本人的地址和电话号码，以便今后联系。
3. 我们公司派了几个人去北京，以便了解新产品的适销情况。

"以便"用在第二个分句的前头，表示有了前面提到的情况或条件，后面的目的就容易实现了。

"以便" is used at the beginning of the second clause, indicating that the goal mentioned later is easy to realize when the situation or condition in the first clause occurs or exists.

四、……，则……　　(then; whereas)

l-7. 对于进口业务来说，则要注意研究价格的变动，……掌握好各项交易条件。

1. 这种商品，在国内买的人不多，在国外则很受欢迎。
2. 他对小事很马虎，对大事则非常认真。
3. 王经理对欧洲市场很熟悉，对拉美的情况则不太了解。

1) "则"作副词，表示后面的情况与前面的形成对比，有"却"的意思，多用于书面语。

When "则" is used as an Adverb, it indicates a contrast between the situation in the second part and the one in the first part of the sentence, bearing the meaning of "却" (but; to the contrary). It is mostly used in written Chinese.

2) "则"作连词，用在后一分句前头，表示根据前面所说的情况，可以得出后面的结论。有"那就""那么就"的意思。

不了解市场情况，则无法取得生意的成功。

建立了良好的业务关系，则为以后的交易打下了基础。

When "则" is used as a Conjunction in the second clause, it indicates the conclusion reached or result obtained is based on the previously mentioned situation. It has a meaning similar to "那就" "那么就" (then; such that).

五、知己知彼　　(to know oneself and one's opponent well)

l-10. 这样才能真正做到"知己知彼"。

1. 人们常说，商场就象战场，只有知己知彼，才能百战百胜。

2. 虽然大家都知道<u>知己知彼</u>的重要，但是能真正做到的却不多。

3. 这个球队的教练总是要求他的队员努力做到<u>知彼知己</u>，所以他们比赛经常能够取得好成绩。

成语"知己知彼"表示对自己和对方的情况都非常了解，也可以说为"知彼知己"。

The idiom "知己知彼" means that one knows himself very well and the situation he is in, as well as his opponent. It is sometimes written as "知彼知己".

六、例如　(for example, for instance)

l-12. 建立业务关系有各种不同的途径。<u>例如</u>，可以通过拜访外国驻本国大使馆的商务处，……并帮助与这些公司取得联系。

1. 她会说好几国外语，<u>例如</u>德语、法语、日语、西班牙语等。

2. 要知道对方的业务范围很容易，<u>例如</u>，你可以直接给他们写信，或者向其他公司打听。

3. 搞进出口贸易必须做一定的准备，<u>例如</u>，进行市场调查，了解有关国家的贸易制度，建立与客户的业务关系等等。

"例如"作连词，引出所举的例子；后面有停顿。

"例如" is a Conjunction, introducing a number of examples. There is usually a pause after it.

七、通过 Noun/Noun Phrase + Verb Phrase　(through; by means of)

l-12. 例如，可以<u>通过</u>拜访外国驻本国大使馆的商务处，请他们介绍自己国家的经济情况和法律制度，……并帮助与这些公司取得联系。

1. 我们<u>通过</u>银行介绍，跟那家公司建立了联系。

2. 因为他不会西班牙语，所以要<u>通过</u>翻译才能交谈。

3. <u>通过</u>市场调查，他们了解到很多新情况。

4. <u>通过</u>电视广告，我们公司的产品很快就打开了市场。

"通过"作介词，引进动作的媒介或手段。"通过"可用在主语前，有停顿。

> When "通过" is used as a Preposition, it introduces a media or a means by which the action is carried out. It can be placed in front of the subject, with a pause.

八、(……)此外，……　　(besides; in addition; moreover)

1-14. <u>此外</u>，也可以通过银行、商会、其他贸易公司等，了解有关公司的业务范围和资信情况，……与有关公司取得联系。

　　1. 这家公司经营电视、电脑，<u>此外</u>，还进口电话、传真机和音响。

　　2. 我们给贵国大使馆发了传真，写了信。<u>此外</u>，我们总经理还亲自拜访了商务处的代表。

　　3. 小关只喜欢打球、游泳，<u>此外</u>再也没有其他爱好了。

"此外"作连词，表示除了前面所说的，还有另外的一些什么，或者再也没有别的什么了。"此外"也可以变成短语"除此之外"。

> "此外" is a Conjunction, which either states there is something else in addition to whatever has been mentioned before, or there is nothing else except what has been mentioned. "此外" can also be expressed as "除此之外".

九、……有助于……　　(to be conducive to; contribute to)

1-23. 这样<u>有助于</u>互相了解，为今后的进出口业务打下良好的基础。

　　1. 常看中文电视<u>有助于</u>提高听力。

　　2. 了解世界各地的贸易惯例、关税制度和港口条件<u>有助于</u>出口业务的发展。

　　3. 中美两国的文化交流和贸易往来<u>有助于</u>两国人民的相互了解。

动词短语"有助于"多用于书面语或正式场合，为正常的"主—谓—宾"词序。口语里一般较少使用，注意口语的"……对……有帮助/有好处"在词序上的不同。

The Verb Phrase "有助于" is generally used in written Chinese or in a formal context. It follows the regular word order of "Subject-Verb-Object" and is seldom used in colloquial Chinese. Please note the difference between the word order of "……对……有帮助/有好处" in spoken Chinese and "有助于".

词义辨析

一、供应　供给　提供

　　动词"供应"、"供给"和"提供"，译成英语，都可以是 supply，但是使用的范围不同。"供应"的使用范围较窄，一般多指物资，如水电、食物、日用品、材料等，但不可用于钱财或其他抽象事物。"供给"的使用范围较宽，可以是物资，也可以是钱财或资料等。"提供"的使用范围更广，除了具体的事物如物资、钱财、资料等以外，还可用于抽象事物，如帮助、意见、条件、经验等等。

　　The Verbs 供应, 供给 and 提供 can mean "to supply" when translated into English. The Objects they take respectively, however, are quite different. While 供应 mostly refers to objects such as utility, food, articles of everyday use, materials, etc., 供给 covers a wider range, which also includes money, data, and/or reference material. In addition to all the above-mentioned Concrete Nouns, 提供 takes Abstract Nouns as its Object such as assistance, opinion, condition, and experience.

二、必须　必需　必要

　　虽然"必须"、"必需"和"必要"都有同一个词素"必"字，并有时都可译成英语 must, (highly) necessary，但是这三个词的词性是不同的。"必须"是副词，一般用在动词或形容词前（大致相当于英语的助动词），意思着重在"非这样不可"。否定式为"不必"或"无须"。"必需"是动词，意思着重在"一定得有"、"必不可少"。"必需"一般不用在动词前，常用在"(不)是必需的"结构，作谓语用，也可充当定语，修饰名词或名词短

语，其说明对象多数是表示事物的词语，像原料、物品、时间、人力
等。"必需"不受程度副词修饰，不能说"很必需"或"非常必需"。"必要"
是形容词，除了有"非有不可"的意思外，还有"非这样不行"的意思。
"必要"的适用范围较广，凡是物品、方法、条件等在人们的生活中感觉
非有不可的东西，都可以用。"必要"作谓语时，它前面的主语一般是表
示某种动作或做法的动词性词语。

Although the three terms 必须, 必需, 必要 share the same Morpheme 必, and may be translated as "must", "(highly) necessary" sometimes, they belong to different Parts of Speech. 必须 is an Adverb, and primarily precedes Verbs or Adjectives (similar to the Auxiliary Verbs in English to some extent). It means that "it got to be this way", or "it won't do if not …", and its negation form is 不必 or 无须. 必需 is a Verb, meaning "absolutely necessary", "indispensable". It seldom goes before any Verbs, but is usually used in the collocation (不) 是必需的 and serves as a Predicate of a sentence. It can also function as an Attributive to modify a Noun or Noun Phrase, referring to words such as raw materials, things, time, manpower, etc. 必需 is not modified by Adverbs of Degree such as 很 or 非常.

必要 is an Adjective. In addition to the meaning of "must have", it also means "it won't do if not this way". It is used rather broadly — applicable to almost everything that is felt indispensable in all human activities. When 必要 is used as a Predicate of a sentence, the Subject that precedes it is a Verb or Verb Phrase indicating some kind of action or practice in general.

三、变　变化　变动

动词"变"、"变化"、"变动"英语都有change的意思。"变"的基本意
思是"变化、改变，跟原来不同"，强调脱开原形。"变"可以作不及物
动词和及物动词（带宾语），可带"了、过"，常作谓语，比"变化"更常
用于口语。"变"作不及物动词时，前面可用"有点儿、完全"修饰，
如：他的声音有点儿变了。作及物动词时，"变"可重叠，带名词宾
语。例如：

Verbs 变, 变化 and 变动 can all mean "change" in English. The core meaning of 变 is "to change; to be different from before", and the emphasis is on "deviation from the original one". 变 can be both an Intransitive Verb (not taking an Object) and a Transitive Verb (followed by an Object), and go with particles such as 了 or 过. When it functions as a Predicate of a sentence, 变 is more common in colloquial Chinese than 变化. As an Intransitive Verb, 变 can be modified by 有点儿, 完全, etc. for example, 他的声音有点儿变了. When it is used transitively, 变 can be reduplicated and take Nouns as its Object, for example,

1) 饭菜可以多变变花样。

2) 老这样不行，得变个办法试试。

有些事物起了变化，可在"变"的前面或后面，下面两种句式的意思基本相同：

Occasionally, when changes have taken place in something (certain Nouns only), the Noun can go either before or after 变, and the meaning of the phrases in the following remains the same basically:

样子变了——变了样子／颜色变了——变了颜色／主意变了—变了主意。当一种性质或状态转换为另一种不同的性质或状态时，"变"后面往往要加上"成"或"为"，强调变的结果。例如：

When referring the change of nature or status from one to a different one, 成 or 为 usually follows 变, emphasizing the result of change. For example,

小渔村变成了大城市。／他们把荒山变成了果园。

有时"变"后面可直接带名词、动词或形容词作宾语，如：

Sometimes, a Noun, Verb, or Adjective can go directly after 变, serving as its Object. For instance,

一个变两个／坏事变好事／落后变先进

书面语常用"变……为……"的格式，表示"使……变为……"，如：

In the written language, the above are often expressed in the pattern 变……为……, similar to the meaning of 使……变为…… (to turn … into …). For example,

变废为宝（使废物变为宝物）/变后进为先进（使后进变为先进）

变坏事为好事（使坏事变为好事）。

"变化"一般只作不及物动词，不带宾语，强调事物与以前不同，成为另外的样子，可用于自然现象和社会现象。另外，"变化"也可是名词，作其他动词的宾语，例如：

变化 is primarily an Intransitive Verb, not taking any Object. It emphasizes that things are no longer the same as before, and have taken different looks. This is applicable to both natural phenomena and social events. In addition, 变化 is also a Noun, serving as an Object of other Verbs. Note the following examples,

要注意市场的变化；发生了变化；有了很大的变化。

"变动"多用于社会现象，并且强调"动"，通常涉及事物的地位、顺序、位置等的移动，可带宾语。例如：

变动 is mostly used for social changes, and focuses on the "motion", referring to a shift of position, hierarchy, location or order. It can take an Object. For instance,

变动一下会议的日程；价格的变动。

四、建立 成立 设立

及物动词"建立"除了有创建、成立的含义外，还有"开始产生、开始形成"的意思，适用范围较广，可用于具体的事物（如组织、机构等），也可用于像"友谊、感情、信心、关系"等抽象事物。

In addition to the meaning of "to establish, to build, to found", the Transitive Verb 建立 also indicates "beginning to bring about/taking shape". It can refer to both Concrete Nouns such as an organization or an institution, as well as Abstract Nouns such as friendship, feeling, confidence, and relationships.

"成立"表示"筹备成功，开始存在"，常与国家、政府、党派、组织、机构等词语搭配，也可以带宾语，但不可用于"友谊、感情、信心、关系"等抽象事物。另外，"成立"还有"站得住、有根据"的意思，主要指理论、观点、意见等，例如：

成立 often goes with words like country, government, party, organization, or institution, when it means "having prepared/setup successfully, and beginning to exit". It can take a Noun as its Object, but not Nouns like 友谊、感情、信心、关系 with an abstract sense. 成立 can also mean "to be tenable", "to hold water" when referring to a theory, a point of view, or an opinion. For example,

这种说法根本不成立.　(This kind of saying is totally unfounded.)

"设立"是及物动词，带宾语，其含义侧重在某个现存的组织机构设置建立另一个(下属的)组织或机构。

设立 is a Transitive Verb, and takes an Object. It emphasizes the establishment of/setting up an organization or a department, usually subordinated to an existing organization or institution.

语 法

一、单句与复句　Simple Sentences and Complex Sentences

句子是语言实际运用的单位。它能表达一个相对完整的意思或感情，独立完成一定的社会交际功能或思想交流的任务。根据结构形式，句子可以分为单句和复句两大类。

A sentence is a unit of language in use. It can express a complete meaning or some kind of feeling, and serve a certain purpose in communication by itself. Sentences, in accordance with their structures, can be divided into two categories — simple sentences and complex sentences.

(一)单句 **Simple Sentences**

单句由词或词组构成,是语言实际使用的基本单位。在表述功能上,单句有相对的独立性和完整性。小于单句的单位,是词或词组。在孤立、静态时,词或词组没有表述上的完整性,也没有独立完整的语调。例:

A Simple Sentence is composed of words or phrases. It is a basic unit of language in action. In terms of its expressive function, a Simple Sentence is independent and complete. Words or phrases are units smaller than simple sentences. When they are in isolation, they do not have the completeness in inexpression, nor an independent intonation. For example:

〔词和词组〕Words and phrases: 开始、美国、大量、市场、进入、中国商品、近年来

〔句子〕A sentence: 近年来,中国商品开始大量进入美国市场。

由词组构成的单句结构比较单一,基本上可分成主语、谓语、宾语、补语、定语、状语等成分。主语和谓语是句子的主要成分。如果谓语是及物动词,谓语后面就要带宾语,但是每个单句不一定都有补语、定语、状语等成分。例:

Simple Sentences that are composed of phrases are unitary in structure, and their components are basically subject, predicate, object, complement, attribute, adverbial, etc. A subject and a predicate are the major components of a sentence. If the predicate contains a Transitive Verb, an object is to follow the Verb. However, every Simple Sentence will not necessarily have elements such as a complement, an attribute or an adverbial. Here are some examples:

1. 他／来了。

　〔主〕〔谓〕

2. 我／写了／一封长／信。

　〔主〕〔谓〕　〔定〕〔宾〕

3. 市场调查／工作／已经／做／好了。

　〔定〕　　〔主〕〔状〕〔谓〕〔补〕

单句可以单独完成一定的社会交际、思想交流的任务，但是它的表意容量，要比复句的小。

A Simple Sentence alone may serve certain purposes of communication, but the content which it can express is limited in comparison with a complex sentence.

(二) 复句　Complex Sentences

两个或两个以上的单句，通过关联组合，构成双重或多重的逻辑关系，表达比较复杂的意思，并且取得统一的语调，就是复句。构成复句的各个单句，叫做分句。

A Complex Sentence consists of two or more Simple Sentences. They are joined by correlatives such as Conjunctions or Adverbs to form dual or multiple logical relations, and can express a considerably more complex meaning with a consistent intonation. Simple Sentences within a Complex Sentence are called clauses.

复句有以下的特点：

Complex sentences are characterized by the followings:

1. 构成复句的各个分句，在意思上必须有一定的联系。这种联系往往通过某种连词或关联副词来表示。例如：

There must be a certain connection in meaning between each clause in a complex sentence. Such connection is usually indicated by some Connectives such as Conjunctions or Adverbs. For instance:

<u>因为</u>他们只学过一年汉语，<u>所以</u>还看不懂中文报纸。

<u>虽然</u>我们还没有正式的业务关系，<u>但是</u>已经从其他公司多次听到过贵公司。

做出口生意要进行一定的准备，从事进口贸易<u>也</u>要做准备工作。

2. 复句内的各个分句之间，一般都有较短的语音停顿，书面上多用逗号或分号表示。单句与单句之间的停顿则较长，书面上用句号、问号或感叹号表示。简单的单句，成分之间一般没有什么语音停顿，因此不用标点符号。复杂的单句，成分之间有的有停顿，有的没有。

Normally, there is a pause in speaking between each clause in a Complex Sentence, which is marked with a comma or a semi-colon in writing. The pause between Simple Sentences, as compared to the pause between clauses in a Complex Sentence, is longer and thus is indicated by a full stop, a question mark, or an exclamation mark in writing. As there is no pause between each element in a typical Simple Sentence, no punctuation is used in writing. However, in some long Simple Sentences with considerable complexity, there may or may not be pauses between sentence components.

3. 复句是由有一定相对独立性的分句组成的，因此，复句的一个分句不能是另一个分句的某一句子成分，如主语、宾语或者状语等。下面的句子，只是较为繁杂的单句，而不是复句。

A Complex Sentence is composed of clauses that are independent; therefore, a clause within a Complex Sentence cannot be an element of another clause, such as a subject, an object or an adverbial, etc. The following sentences are by no means Complex Sentences but Simple Sentences with considerable complexity only:

这些工作主要包括：进行市场调查，了解对方的贸易制度和市场所在地的法律，建立与客户的业务关系。（划线部分是"包括"的宾语。）

与客户建立业务关系，是进行国际贸易的必要条件之一。（划线部分是句子的主语。）

你们写信给新华银行时，顺便了解一下大同公司的资信情况。（划线部分是句子的状语。）

(三) 复句的类型 Types of Complex Sentences

复句可以分成两大类：联合复句和偏正复句。如果复句的各个分句之间在语法上是平等的，不互相修饰或说明，这种复句叫做联合复句。例如：

There are two types of Complex Sentences, Coordinate Complex Sentences and Subordinate Complex Sentences. If each clause in a Complex Sentence is independent in grammatical structure, and one does not modify nor describe one and the other, such a Complex Sentence is a Coordinate Complex Sentence. For example:

她不但会说日语，而且会说法语。

我现在跟朋友联系，不是打电话，就是发电子邮件，不写信了。

他们先自我介绍，然后就谈起生意来了。

如果复句有两个分句，其中一个分句修饰、限制另一个分句，这样的复句就是偏正复句。偏正复句中被修饰、限制的分句是正句，另一个起修饰、限制作用的分句是偏句。例如：

If a Complex Sentence contains two clauses, one of which modifies or restricts the other, such a Complex Sentence is a Subordinate Complex Sentence. The clause that is modified or restricted in a Complex Sentence is the main clause, whereas the one that modifies or restricts the other is the subordinate clause. For example:

为了保证生意的成功，必须做好市场的调查工作。

如果寄信来不及，你可以给我发传真。

只有掌握好汉语，才能更好地研究中国的经济情况。

根据各个分句之间的意义关系，联合复句又可分为选择复句、并列复句、解说复句、递进复句、承接复句等五种；偏正复句又可再分为因果复句、条件复句、目的复句、转折复句、假设复句、取舍复句等六类。

According to the syntactic relations between clauses, Coordinate Complex Sentences can be further classified into five categories. They are: Alternative, Coordinative, Elaborative, Progressive, and Successive Complex Sentences. Likewise, Subordinate Complex Sentences can be categorized into six more types: Cause and Effect, Conditional, Purpose, Adversative, Hypothetical, and Preference Complex Sentences.

二、因果复句　Complex Sentences of Cause and Effect

分句之间所表示的关系是原因/理由和结果/结论的关系，这种复句叫因果复句。因果复句又分两种，说明因果复句和推断因果复句。

The relation between clauses is one of cause and effect, reason and conclusion. Complex sentences of cause and effect can be further broken down into two subcategories, illustration and inference.

1. 说明因果复句 —— 一个分句（偏句）说明原因，另一个分句（正句）说明结果。常用的关联词语有：

Complex Sentences of Illustration of Cause and Effect — While the subordinate cause presents the cause or reason, the main clause states the effect or result of the premise. The correlatives commonly used are:

"因为……所以……"、"由于……（所以）……"、"……，因此……"、"……因而……"、"之所以……，是因为/由于……"、"……，以致……"等。例如：

因为这家公司十分注意市场的动向，所以业务发展得非常快。
我给他打了几次电话都打不进去，因为他在用电脑收发电子邮件。
由于市场经常变动，各国各地的情况不一，因此，为了保证生意的成功，首先要做好市场的调查研究工作。

有的因果复句虽然不用关联词语，但因果关系也仍然很清楚。例如：

Sometimes, although no Connective is used, the relation of cause and effect is self-explanatory:

我不太了解那家公司的情况，就没有答应他们。
你不在，那位小姐留下名片就走了。

2. 推断因果复句 —— 偏句提出一个既定事实，正句表示由这个事实作出的推断。常用的关联词语是：

Complex Sentence of Inference of Cause and Effect — The subordinate clause states a fact, and the main clause draws an inference from such a fact. The common correlatives are:

"既然……就……"、"……，那就……"。

既然你有兴趣跟中国做生意，我可以介绍你认识商务处的陈先生。

既然贵公司的产品这样受欢迎，为什么不多出口一些呢？

修 辞

一、什么是修辞　What Is Rhetoric

修辞是一门研究提高语言表达效果的方法和技巧的学科，也是在合乎语法和逻辑的基础上，根据"题旨"和"语境"，运用不同的表现手法，对语言进行调整加工的语言活动。修辞不只局限于文字的修饰、词句的选炼，拘泥于辞格的套用，它还涉及到话语篇章的结构、句群段落的组织、文体的风格等问题。既然思想感情的表达和信息的交流基本是在句子以上的话语、篇章层面上进行的，要取得最佳的表达效果，就必须从整体考虑，按全局安排。好的文章，除了用词得当，语句通顺外，还要主题突出、结构合理、层次分明、逻辑性强、合乎语境、风格得体、前后连贯照应、句式变化多样、表达准确生动。

学习修辞，掌握一定的修辞方法和技巧，不但可以提高写作能力，而且有助于提高阅读欣赏水平，懂得从全段、全篇的角度来分析语言的实际运用，了解文章的各部分的相互联系，因而能更好地理解文章表达的确切意思。

Rhetoric is the study of using language effectively in speaking and writing. It is also an art and activity of applying various skills to manipulate the language to fine tune words and expressions on the basis of grammaticality and logicality, in accordance with the intended topic and the context. Rhetoric is not merely limited to polishing words, selecting phrases, and applying techniques of artistic arrangement on sentences. It deals with matters such as the structure of an essay, the organization of paragraphs, and the style of texts. Since expression of feelings and information exchange take place primarily on a discourse level which is beyond the sentence level, we should consider the overall organization of a text, and arrange its components accordingly so as to achieve the best result of communication. In addition to the appropriate use of words, smooth reading of sentences and being grammatically correct, a good essay should give prominence to the theme, be appropriate in style for the context, with sound logic and reasonable structure. Moreover, it should have coherence in the text organization and a variety of sentence forms, so that it can express ideas accurately and vividly.

Rhetoric does not only improve our writing but it is also helpful in our reading comprehension. It enables us to analyze the use of language from the perspectives of a paragraph and a whole essay, and to know the interrelation of each part, which in turn helps us better to understand the pertinent ideas conveyed through the text.

二、句式　Sentence Forms

句式指的是句子的结构形式。同样的意思可以用不同的句式来表达，但是它们所表现的语气、情调、风格等都有所不同，都与一定的语言环境，包括说写的对象，交际的场合以及上下文有密切的关系。譬如，请别人把门关上，从语气上考虑，就可以有不同的说法：

Sentence Forms denote the constructions and forms of sentences. A similar idea can be expressed in various sentence forms, but the tone, the mood, the emotion, and the style etc., may be different. Each of these aspects is related to the particular environment in which the language is used, including the audience or readers, the situation where the communication takes place, and the discourse context. For instance, there are several ways to ask someone to close the door, depending on the tone:

1. 关门！
2. 把门关上。
3. 把门关上吧。

4. 请你把门关一下。

5. 请把门关上，好吗？

又如，收到别人的来信后，过了一段时间才回信，从语体风格上看，也有口语和书面语之分：

To give another example, when one has received a letter and replied after some delay, there is a distinction between colloquial and literary style, as shown in the following examples:

1. 来信已经收到了，这么久才给你回信，实在是很对不起。

2. 慧书已悉，迟复为歉。

因此，选择适当的句式，使它适合于具体的语言环境，在语义、语体、情调、风格上取得一致，以达到最佳的表达效果，是修辞的一项重要内容。

Therefore, it is an important part of learning rhetoric to select the right sentence form, so that it is appropriate for the context and enables one to obtain the best effect with a harmony in meaning, genre, mood and style.

三、短句与长句   The Use of Short/Long Sentences

修辞上的短句和长句是从句子的长短来讲的。短句是指字数少、形体短、结构比较简单的句子；长句是指字数多、形体长、结构比较繁杂的句子。

In rhetoric, Short Sentences and Long Sentences, are distinguished by their length. Short sentences are those which contain fewer characters, are short in appearance, and thus, are relatively simple in structure. Long Sentences are those that contain more characters and are considerably complex in structure.

(一)短句   Short Sentences

短句除了简短的单句外，也包括复句中字数少、结构简单的分句。短句的特点是短小精悍，生动活泼，结构单纯，节奏明快，因此常见于文艺语体，特别是文学作品、戏剧、诗歌等。日常会话、讲演、报告等场合也多用短句，这样使语言自然流畅，简明易懂。例如：

In addition to free-standing sentences, Short Sentences include some clauses in Complex Sentences which have fewer characters and are simple in structure. The distinguishing features of Short Sentences are that they are short and pithy, vivid and expressive, simple in structure, and rhythmically lively. Hence, they are usually used in literature and the performing arts, especially in literary works, drama, poetry, etc. They are also very common in daily conversation, speeches and presentations, thus making language sound more natural, smooth, succinct and easy to comprehend. For example:

"找乐子"，是北京的俗话，也是北京人的"雅好"。北京人爱找乐子，善找乐子。这"乐子"也实在好找得很。养只靛颏儿（diànkér ——一种鸟，身体大小和麻雀相似，羽毛褐色，雄的叫声很好听。）是个"乐子"。放个风筝是个"乐子"。一碗酒加一头蒜也是个"乐子"。（陈建功《找乐》）

人感到寂寞时，会创作；感到干净时，即无创作，他已经一无所爱。

创作总归于爱。

杨朱无书。

创作虽说抒写自己的心，但总愿意有人看。

创作是有社会性的。

但有时只要有一个人看便满足：好友，爱人。（鲁迅《小杂感》）

(二) 长句　Long Sentences

长句有结构繁杂、字数多、形体长的单句，也包括由关系密切的几个分句组成的多重复句。其中有些层次多、信息容量大，能够比较准确严密地表达丰富的思想内容。长句一般多用于书面语，尤其在政治评论、科技文献、法律条文等类文件中用得较多。例如：

Long Sentences include both simple sentences with complex structures and have more characters. They may be complex sentences composed of several clauses that are closely linked with multiple relations. Long Sentences are noted for their complexity in structure, arrangement with multiple levels, capacity for abundant information, and expression of ideas with relative accuracy and coherence. Long Sentences are usually used in the written language, particularly in political essays, science and technology writings, and legal documents. Here are some examples:

> 签证是指一国主管机关在本国或外国公民所持的护照或者其他旅行证件上签注、盖印，表示准其出入本国国境或者过境的手续。

> 交易的一方在接到一项发盘后，不能完全同意该项发盘的条件，但仍有兴趣进行交易，为了进一步洽商，于是针对该项发盘的内容提出不同的建议，这种口头或书面的表示，在国际贸易中称为还盘，也就是习惯上说的还价。

> 短句和长句各有特点，用处和表达效果也不同。我们应当根据不同的内容、对象和文体，恰当地选用。口语里多用短句，书面语一般是长句和短句交错着用，互相配合，互相补充。短句和长句用得好，可以使文章生动活泼，节奏分明，富有表现力。

Short Sentences and Long Sentences are unique in their own ways, and are different in their use and effect. We should choose them properly according to content, audience/readership, and style. In general, Short Sentences are used in spoken language while Long Sentences are coordinated with Short Sentences in the written language. When both short sentences and long sentences are used appropriately, an essay can be vivid, rhythmic, and forceful.

练习

一、用线将意思相同的词和词语连起来：

国家与国家之间的事情	人际关系
大学各个系之间的篮球比赛	适销产品
人与人之间的关系	地铁出口
地铁站让人出去的地方	海口
家庭日常生活的事务	国际事务
两条路交叉相会的地方	业务
海湾内的港口	系际篮球赛
个人或某个机构的专业工作	适量
所卖的商品是大家都想买的	十字路口
数量正合适，不多也不少	家务

二、用括号里的词或词组改写下列句子，但不改变其基本意思，必要时可替换某些词或对词序作一定的调整：

1. 不论什么进口商品，海关都会检查。　（任何、进行）

2. 老师故意说得很慢，为的是让大家都能听懂。　（以便）

3. 懂中文对了解中国的市场是有帮助的。　（有助于）

4. 我从一家英国银行那儿了解到建业公司的经营范围。除了这个以外，经过美中商会的介绍，我还认识了他们的董事长。　（此外、通过）

5. 做进出口生意，必须了解市场所在地的情况。比方说，法律制度、贸易惯例、关税制度等等。　（例如）

6. 这种商品的价格最近不断变动，出口商十分高兴，进口商却非常担忧。　（则）

7. 电视台的记者向他打听这些水果卖出的情况。　（了解、销售）

8. 只有对最近和对方的各种情况都非常清楚，才能在生意上得到预期的效果。　（知己知彼、取得成功）

9. 因为有足够的准备，他们很快就了解并且学会了怎样利用这项新技术。　（充分、掌握）

10. 按照一向的习惯做法，我们公司给客户各种方便。　（惯例、提供）

三、选择最合适的词填空：

1. 这个学校每年都给学生 _____ 大量的奖学金。
   a. 供给　　　　b. 供应　　　　c. 提供

2. 由于下雨过多，最近市场的蔬菜 _____ 比较紧张。
   a. 供给　　　　b. 供应　　　　c. 提供

3. 办理进口手续，_____ 你亲自去。
   a. 必须　　　　b. 必要　　　　c. 必需

4. 这是我朋友在美国驻北京大使馆的电话号码，_____ 时可以给他打电话，不过如果是一般的问题就不要麻烦他了。
   a. 必须　　　　b. 必要　　　　c. 必需

5. 你一个人去外国留学，要时常注意天气 _____，穿够衣服。
   a. 变　　　　b. 变化　　　　c. 变动

6. 这几天市场的价格有很大的 _____ 。
   a. 变　　　　b. 变化　　　　c. 变动

7. 经过友好谈判，两国决定 _____ 外交关系。
   a. 建立　　　　b. 成立　　　　c. 设立

8. 我们这个学习小组是上个月 _____ 的。

   a. 建立　　　　　b. 成立　　　　　c. 设立

四、判别下列句子是单句还是复句：

1. 老王刚开始做生意的时候，什么都不懂。

2. 要是你觉得今天晚上不方便，我们可以明天再定个时间。

3. 商店里人太多，商品又太少。

4. 生词多、句子长、语法难，是这些课文的特点。

5. 总经理叫我们研究一下怎样打开非洲市场的问题。

6. 不了解市场的动向，就很难做好进出口贸易工作。

7. 董事长不太高兴，因为关副经理忘了向他报告市场变动的情况。

8. 这家银行不算大，但业务范围很广。

9. 他们参加了法国的商品展览会，与邦达公司的总裁见了面，很快就
建立了业务关系。

10. 我们跟这个商号的业务来往已经有许多年了，因此非常了解他们的
资信情况。

五、找出课文里的因果复句。

六、用括号里的连词把下列句子改成因果复句：

1. 昨天晚上的练习很多。小张很晚才睡觉。　　（因为）

2. 我没有收到她的传真。我不知道她已经回日本了。　　（所以）

3. 今天下大雪。图书馆提早关门了。　　（因此）

4. 双方都有兴趣进行合作。他们的洽谈很成功。　　（由于……所以……）

5. 电子邮件比长途电话便宜。电子邮件在大学生中使用得非常普遍。
（因而）

6. 他们没有做市场调查。他们进口的商品都卖不出去。　　（以致）

7. 她病了。她应该好好休息。　　（既然……就……）

七、阅读下列句子，用简短的句子回答问题，把长句改成短句：

1. 这是中国西安飞机公司与美国波音公司共同研究和合作生产的一种短程民用客机。

   a. 这是一种什么飞机？

   b. 谁和谁做了什么？

   c. 这种飞机是什么公司研究、生产的？

2. 要跟外国公司建立业务关系，除了可以通过外国驻本国的大使馆，请他们提供有关公司的资料以外，还可以通过银行或商会，请他们推荐或介绍，帮助与这些公司联系。

   a. 要跟外国公司建立业务关系，可以通过什么人？

   b. 可以请他们做些什么？

3. 海关是有关国家设立在各个口岸，对出入国境的人员、物品和运输工具进行检查、征收关税、查禁走私的国家机关。

   a. 海关是什么？

   b. 海关设在哪儿？

   c. 海关检查什么？

   d. 海关还做些什么事情？

八、把下列句子翻译成汉语：

1. We have conducted a thorough investigation, (and) have found out that China is a suitable [selling] market for our goods. In addition, the condition of the Shanghai port is pretty good. We have selected China's Da Tong Company as our trade partner. In doing so, it is helpful for the export of our goods.

2. Any company that wants to establish a business relationship with American manufacturers and firms may directly contact the Office of Commercial Affairs at the US Embassy in China. The office can provide a variety of information about American companies that are interested in doing business in China such as their addresses, telephone numbers and fax numbers. In addition, it has also prepared some brochures, newspapers and periodicals, so that people [i.e. "everyone"] can understand the trading conventions and the legal system of the United States.

3. First of all, let me introduce myself. I am Tianming Ma, Sales Manager of the (National) Light Industry Import and Export Company of China, Guangdong Branch. I have got information about your corporation through Mr. King, who has been your customer for years. We are very interested in doing business with you and would like to develop a cooperative relationship in the future.

九、根据《文化与商贸背景知识》中名片的格式和中国外贸机构组织的信息，给自己设计一张名片。

文化与商贸背景知识

✎ 名片

名片是一种身份的说明方式，也是加深彼此印象和相互了解，方便今后联系，收集资料的重要手段。因此，接递名片在商贸活动中，是必不可少的。

一般来说，如果双方初次见面，客人（来访者）应主动先把名片拿出来递给主人（被访者）。收下名片后，主人（被访者）应对客人递送名片表示谢意，并送上自己的名片作为回报。假如身上没带名片，应当表示歉意。

对别人递来的名片，应用双手去接，表示尊重。同时要仔细地把名片看一遍，必要时可以说一些客气话，如"贵公司非常有名"、"先生是某方面的权威，久仰久仰"、"您年轻有为，前途无量"、"幸会幸会"等等。然后慎重地把名片放进上衣袋中。当我们递名片给对方时，应恭敬地用双手或右手递上，报上自己的姓名，并说一句"初次见面，请多关注"、"请多多指教"、"冒昧打扰，请多原谅"之类的话。

YUECAL INTERNATIONAL INC.
粵加國際有限公司
JEFFREY M. LI
CHAIRMAN
李　覺　民　董事長

Subsidiaries:
Soon Lim Yuen Trading Corp. ● Han-Li International Group

333 Hegenberger Rd.　　　　　Tel: (415) 638-0590
Suite 615　　　　　　　　　　Fax (415) 638-0591
Oakland, CA 94621　　　　　　Telex 650 3362350 MCI

新資訊科技事業股份有限公司
NEW INFORMATION TECH, ENTERPRISE CO., LTD.

鄧　有　立

中華卡通製作股份有限公司　　董事長

台北縣新店市寶中路47號6樓
6F, No. 47 Pao Chung Road, Hsin Tien, Taipei, R. O. C.
TEL: 886-2-2914-0158．2935-4383　FAX: 886-2-2913-4694
E-mail: nite@ms2.hinet.net

富龍首飾有限公司
FLORENCE JEWELERS LIMITED

Chen Xiao Shan　　　陳　小　山
Director　　　　　　　董事
General Manager　　　總經理

香港九龍紅磡鶴園東街4號，恒藝珠寶大廈501-502室
Rm. 501-502 Heng Ngai Jewelry Centre,
4, Hok Yuen Street East, Hunghom, Kowloon, Hong Kong.
電話 Tel.: 363-9828　　電報 Cable: BIGAPPLE
圖文傳眞 Fax: 764-2039

國光國際有限公司

許　國　風

董事總經理

香港德輔道中 287-291 號長達大厦 20 字樓
電話：851-8966 (4線)　　　電傳：79643 GGRC HX
傳眞：850-7919　　　　　　電掛：GUOGCANG
國光貿易公司　　美國加州域克維爾市

中國人民保險公司
廣東省分公司國際保險部

余　　　正　副經理

地址，中國廣州廣衛路2號　　　電傳：44462 PICCG CN
電話：3324567　3356783—0511　電掛：42001
郵政編碼：510030　　　　　　傳眞：3324566

廣東省紡織品進出口(集團)公司
花紗布公司

余　揚　帆
副經理

地址：中國廣州市文明路六十三號
電掛：CANTEX 或 0093
電傳：44371 KTTEX CN
電話：331750
圖文傳眞：336356

深圳市貿易發展局　局長助理
進出口處　　　　　　處　長

劉　廣　琪

地址：深圳上步中路八號市政府第二辦公大樓405室
電話：2243843, 2223211-4095　　傳眞：2243803
郵政編碼：518006

文橋出版社

社長　總編輯
蘇建文

地址：台北市民生東路3段113巷25弄6號2樓
統一編號：12358762
電話：(02) 712-8536．717-2631　專線：(02) 717-2629
傳眞：(02) 712-8509
電子信箱：Lanbridg@ms15.hinet.net

✐ 中国主要的对外贸易机构组织

中国国际贸易促进委员会

China Council for the Promotion of International Trade

中国人民保险公司

The People's Insurance Company of China

中国进出口商品检验总公司

China Inspection Company of Import and Export Commodities (Head Office)

中国粮油食品进出口总公司

China National Cereals, Oil and Foodstuffs Import and Export Corporation

中国土产畜产进出口总公司

China National Product and Animal By-Products Import and Export Corporation

中国纺织品进出口总公司

China National Textiles Import and Export Corporation

中国工艺品进出口总公司

China National Arts and Crafts Import and Export Corporation

中国轻工业品进出口总公司

China National Light Industrial Products Import and Export Corporation

中国化工进出口总公司

China National Chemicals Import and Export Corporation

中国机械设备进出口总公司

China National Machinery and Equipment Import and Export Corporation

中国五金矿产进出口总公司

China National Metals and Minerals Import and Export Corporation

中国仪器进出口总公司

China National Instruments Import and Export Corporation

中国医药保健品进出口总公司

China Medicine and Health Production Articles Import and Export Corporation (Head Office)

中国煤炭进出口总公司

China National Coal Import and Export Corporation (Head Office)

中国技术进口公司

China National Technical Import Corporation

中国航空技术进出口总公司

China National Aero-Technology Import and Export Corporation

中国电子技术进出口总公司

China National Electronics Technology Import and Export Corporation

中国种子进出口总公司

China National Seed Corporation

中国种畜进出口总公司

China National Breeding Stock Import and Export Corporation

中国冶金进出口总公司

China National Metallurgical Products Import and Export Corporation

中国新型建筑材料公司

China National New Building Materials Corporation

中国航空器材总公司

China National Air Materials Corporation

中国林木进出口总公司

China National Timber Import and Export Corporation

中国农机进出口联合公司

China Agricultural Machinery Import and Export Corporation

中国丝绸公司

China National Silk Corporation

中国图书进出口公司
China Books Import and Export Corporation

中国国际书店
China Publication Center

中国电影输出输入公司
China National Films Import and Export Corporation

中国国际信托投资公司
The China International Trust and Investment Corporation

中国对外贸易仓储公司
China National Foreign Trade Storage Corporation

中国出口商品包装公司
China National Export Commodities Packing Corporation

中国对外贸易运输公司
China National Foreign Trade Transportation Corporation

中国外轮代理公司
China Ocean Shipping Agency

中国远洋运输公司
China Ocean Shipping Company

中国外轮理货公司
China Ocean Shipping Tally Company

中国石油公司
China National Petroleum Corporation

中国外贸咨询与技术服务公司
China Foreign Trade Consultation and Technical Service Corporation

中国北方工业公司
China Northern Industrial Corporation

国际贸易的一般交易程序

✎ **思考下面的问题，然后带着这些问题去阅读课文：**

一、国际贸易的交易洽商主要包括哪些环节？

二、什么是询盘？询盘一般包括哪些内容？

三、什么是发盘？什么是还盘？

四、什么是接受？为什么要签订合同？

五、哪些是达成交易最基本的环节？

课文：国际贸易的一般交易程序

　　国际贸易的一个重要阶段，就是交易洽谈。从开始进行业务接洽到达成交易，一般包括询盘、发盘、还盘、接受、签订合同等五个环节。这五个环节就是交易的一般程序。

　　询盘，在中国的对外贸易习惯上，又称为询价，即交易的一方向另一方询问购买或出售某种商品的各项交易条件。询问的内容有　　5
繁有简，一般可包括：商品的品质规格、包装、数量、价格、支付方式、装运、交货期等。买卖双方只有对各项交易条件取得一致意见以后，交易才可达成。因此，询盘作为交易洽商的一环，具有投石问路，了解另一方的交易条件的功能。

　　发盘，又称作报盘或报价。它是交易洽商中必不可少的重要环　　10
节。所谓发盘就是交易的一方有意购买或出售某项商品，向另一方提出该项商品的各项交易条件，并希望按照这些条件达成交易，订立合同。在国际贸易中，从法律的责任来分析，发盘可分为有约束

力的发盘和无约束力的发盘。根据中国的贸易习惯，前者叫做"实

15 盘"，后者称为"虚盘"。

还盘，指的是交易的一方在接到一项发盘以后，不能完全同意
该发盘的条件，但仍有兴趣进行交易，为了进一步洽商，于是针对
该项发盘的内容提出不同的建议。这种口头或书面的表示，在国际
贸易中称为还盘，也就是习惯上说的还价。但是还盘不一定只限于

20 还价。对支付方式、数量或交货期等交易条件提出不同的建议，也
都属于还盘的性质。还盘实际上也是发盘，从法律的含义来看，是
一方针对另一方的发盘而提出的一项新发盘。

接受，就是交易的一方在接到另一方的发盘或还盘后，对其提
出的所有交易条件，表示完全同意，没有任何的不同意见或保留。

25 这种表示，无论是口头的还是书面的，都是一种有效的承诺。在国
际贸易中，称之为接受。如果一方在表示接受时，对原发盘中的某
些交易条件提出了修改或者附加了保留条件，这种行为不应作为接
受——因为它只是一项还盘，真正的交易还没有达成。

买卖双方经过洽商，一方的发盘或还盘被另一方接受以后，交

30 易立即达成，双方就要承担各自的法律责任。为了明确各方的权利
和义务，交易双方用书面的形式，把双方都接受的交易条件确定下
来，双方签字后，各执一份，据以执行，相互监督。这种行为就是
签订合同。

以上的五个环节是交易的一般程序。但是具体的每一笔交易，

35 未必都经过所有的五个环节。例如有的交易是由一方主动发盘而开
始洽商的，询盘的这一环节自然就不存在；又如有的交易在一方发
盘后，立刻被另一方所接受，还盘这一环节也就不需要了。与此相
反，有的交易，双方要经过多次谈判，反复还盘，才能达成交易。
这样的洽商过程也就较为复杂。但是无论洽商的过程是简单还是复

40 杂，发盘和接受都是达成交易必不可少的两个最基本的环节。

✎ **根据课文内容回答下列问题：**

1. 国际贸易中的交易洽商主要包括哪些环节？

2. 什么是询盘？它一般包括哪些内容？

3. 什么是发盘？发盘可以分为哪几种？

4. 什么时候会提出还价？还价是否只讨论价格？

5. 接受指的是什么？口头表示算不算有效的接受？

6. 为什么要签订合同？

7. 在交易洽谈中，哪些环节是最基本的？为什么？

✎ **根据意思，给课文划分层次(不是自然段)并写出每个层次的大意。**

生词和用法

一般	yībān	Adj.	普通；通常：~人、~情况、~关系、~条件，<>特殊。 general(ly), ordinal(ly)
程序	chéngxù	N.	事情进行的先后顺序：工作~、法律~、会议~、交易~。 procedure; sequence
阶段	jiēduàn	N.	事物发展过程中的不同段落：准备~、发展~、合作~、最后~。 stage; phrase; period
洽	qià	Mph. (V.)	跟人联系，交换意见：接~、~商、~借、~谈。 to consult with; to discuss
接洽	jiēqià	V.	与别人商量相互有关的事，希望得到解决：洽谈、面洽、电洽、函洽、再洽。 to consult with; to take up the matter with
洽商	qiàshāng	V.	接洽商量、共同讨论。 to discuss; to consult with
达成	dáchéng	V.	达到、得到(商谈后大家都同意的结果)：~协议、~交易。 to reach (agreement)

询	xún	Mph. (V.)	问；打听：询问、查询。 to ask about; to inquire
盘	pán	N.	指商业行情：开~、收~、询~、报~、发~。 price or condition in trading
询盘	xúnpán	VO	询问价钱和其他交易条件；=询价。 to inquire (terms)
发盘	fāpán	VO	报价；报盘。 to offer (terms)
还盘	huánpán	VO	还价。 to counter offer
即	jí	V.	〔书〕就是；表示判断，需带宾语。 that is; i.e.
方	fāng	N.	活动所涉及的方面：我~、你~、对~、贵~、双~。 part; party
订	dìng	V.	经过研究或商量后立下(合同、条约、计划、章程等)：~货、~购、~立、~约、~计划、制~、签~。 to conclude; to draw up; to agree on
订立	dìnglì	V.	双方或多方经过商谈后用书面形式把大家同意的(合同、条约)肯定下来。 to conclude, to make (a contract)
签订	qiāndìng	V.	订立(合同、条约)并在上面签字。 to conclude and sign(a contract or treaty)
签	qiān	V.	在文件上亲手写上自己的名字：~字、~名、~合同。 to sign(one's name)
合同	hétóng	N.	双方或多方为做某事一起订立、共同执行的文件：销售~、运输~、交易~。 contract
环节	huánjié	N.	许多互相关联的事物中的其中一个：主要~、销售~、装运~、中心~。 link; component
购	gòu	Mph. (V.)	买：订~、采~、抢~、邮~、洽~、电~；<>销。 to buy

| 购买 | gòumǎi | V. | 〔正〕买；＜＞销售、出售。 |
| | | | to purchase; to buy |

| 售 | shòu | V. | 卖：~货、~票、零~、销~、预~、出~。；＜＞购、买。 |
| | | | to sell |

| 出售 | chūshòu | V. | 〔正〕把东西拿出来让别人买走、卖；＜＞购买。 |
| | | | to sell |

| 繁 | fán | Adj. | 繁多、繁杂、繁琐；＜＞简。 |
| | | | numerous; miscellaneous; many and diverse |

| 品质 | pǐnzhì | N. | 物品的好坏、质量。 |
| | | | quality; (moral)character |

| 规格 | guīgé | N. | 产品质量的标准，如大小、长短、轻重、性能等。 specifications; standards |

| 包装 | bāozhuāng | N./V. | packing; package; to pack：商品~、精美的~。 |

| 数量 | shùliàng | N. | 事物的多少。 amount; quantity; number |

| 价格 | jiàgé | N. | 商品价值的货币表现：提高~、降低~、合理的~、批发~、零售~、优惠~。 price |

| 支付 | zhīfù | V./N. | 〔正〕交钱、付款；＜＞收取。 |
| | | | to pay; payment |

| 方式 | fāngshì | N. | 说话做事所用的方法和形式：生活~、支付~、运输~、调查~。 |
| | | | mode; way; fashion |

| 装运 | zhuāngyùn | V./N. | 装载（上交通工具）并运输：~时间、~地点、~条件。 |
| | | | to load; to ship; loading; shipment |

| 交货 | jiāohuò | VO | 把货物交付给买方：~期、~地点；＜＞收货、提货。 to deliver(goods); delivery |

| 一致 | yīzhì | Adj. | 没有不同（意见、看法、观点、说法、立场）。 |
| | | | identical; the same; unanimous (in opinion, view, etc.) |

| 具有 | jùyǒu | V. | 〔正〕有（多用于较抽象方面的东西：如意义、品质、信心、精神、本领、力量、能力等）。 |

			to possess; to have; to be of (certainquality)
投	tóu	V.	向一定的目标扔去或放进去：~球、~弹、~票、~资。 to throw; to cast; to put in
投石问路	tóushí wènlù	Idm.	（夜间）走路时心里有怀疑和顾虑，先扔块石头看看有什么反应。比喻在采取某一行动前，先探虚实。 to throw a stone to test the situation for safety before making a final move (usually at night)
功能	gōngnéng	N.	事情或方法所起的特定作用。 function
报价	bàojià	N./VO	一方向另一方提出交易的条件。 (to) offer (a quote)
必不可少	bì bù kě shǎo	Idm.	必需的、不可缺少的。 indispensable; essential; necessary
所谓	suǒwèi	Adj.	所说的。 so-called
有意	yǒuyì	VO	有心思、有意愿，常与其他动词连用；< > 无意。 to intend; be inclined to
责任	zérèn	N.	份内应做的事。 responsibility
约束	yuēshù	V.	限制使不超出范围。~力=约束的能力。 to restrain; to keep in bound the power; to constrain; constraints
虚	xū	Adj.	虚假：~名、~岁、~数、~盘，< > 实。 false; nominal
虚盘	xūpán	N.	没有约束力的发盘，一般内容不太明确、完整或带有一定的保留条件；< > 实盘。 offer without engagement
实	shí	Adj.	真实：~话、~物、~数、~盘；< > 虚。 true; real; factual

实盘	shípán	N.	有约束力的发盘，内容明确、完整，不带任何保留条件，在有效期间内，发盘人不得更改该发盘的内容；＜＞虚盘。 offer with engagement; firm offer
于是	yúshì	Conj.	〔书〕（就）这样。 hence; therefore; as a result
针对	zhēnduì	V./Prep.	对准：~人或事。 to be directed against (at); to pinpoint at
建议	jiànyì	V./N.	向别人提出自己认为合理的主张、看法。 to suggest; suggestion
口头	kǒutóu	Adv.	用说话方的式来表达的：~建议、~报告、~表达、~翻译；＜＞书面。 oral; verbal
书面	shūmiàn	Adv.	用文字来表达的：~通知、~材料、~形式；＜＞口头。 written; in writing
不一定	bùyīdìng	Adv.	未必、并不是必然的。 not necessarily; not definitely
限于	xiànyú	V.	受条件或情况的限制，局限在一定的范围。 to be limited to
属于	shǔyú	V.	归某方或某一方面所有。 to belong to; to be part of
性质	xìngzhì	N.	一种事物区别于另一种事物的特征。 nature; characteristic
实际	shíjì	Adj./N.	确实：~含义、~价值、~情况。 real; practical; reality
含义	hányì	N.	词句所含有的意义。 meaning; implication
其	qí	Pron.	〔文〕他（她、它、他们）的，他（她、它、他们）。 his; her; its; their; him; her; them
意见	yìjiàn	N.	对事情的看法和想法：提~、有~、接受~、保留~。 opinion; point of view
保留	bǎoliú	V.	（对某种意见、做法不完全同意，但）留下、不

			想说出来。 to reserve, to keep back (one's opinion)
无论	wúlùn	*Conj.*	不论，表示条件不同而结果不变＝不论、不管〔口〕。 no matter what/how; regardless
有效	yǒuxiào	*Adj.*	能达到预期的目的，有效果：～(的)方法、～(的)行动、～期、～的承诺；＜＞无效。 valid; effective
承诺	chéngnuò	*V./N.*	〔书〕对某件事情答应照办。 promise to undertake; acceptance of offer
某	mǒu	*Pron.*	指一定的或指不定的人或事物：～人、～地、～事、～天、～些、～个。 certain; some
修改	xiūgǎi	*V.*	对文件、文章、计划所作的改动。 to modify; to alter; to change
附加	fùjiā	*V.*	额外加上、附带的：～说明、～税、～条件。 to add; to attach
行为	xíngwéi	*N.*	行(动)＋(作)为。非法～、不法～。 behavior; action; deed.
承担	chéngdān	*V.*	担负；担当：～责任、～费用、～后果。 to bear, to undertake
权利	quánlì	*N.*	理应享有的利益。＜＞义务。 Cf. 权力 (power) right.
义务	yìwù	*N.*	理应担当的责任＜＞权利。 responsibility, duty, obligation.
形式	xíngshì	*N.*	事物的形状结构、办事的方法程序：口头～、书面～。 form; shape
确定	quèdìng	*V.*	(使事情)明确和肯定：～时间、～地点、～内容、～条件、～责任。 to finalize; to define; to fix
		Adj.	明确而肯定：～的答复、～的数量。 definite
执	zhí	*Mph. (V.)*	拿着：～笔、明火～仗。 to hold; to grasp
执行	zhíxíng	*V.*	实行、实施：～法律、～计划、～命令、～规

			定、~合同。	to carry out; to implement
据	jù	Prep.	按照；依据：~报导、~说。	according to; on the ground of
监督	jiāndū	V.	察看并督促。	to supervise; to monitor
相互	xiānghù	Adv.	互相、彼此：~作用、~监督、~关系。	mutual; each other; reciprocal, (less common than互相)
具体	jùtǐ	Adj.	特定的，细节很明确的；<>抽象。	specific; concrete
笔	bǐ	MW/N.	用于与钱有关的事物：一~钱、那~款、三~帐、一~生意/交易。	a measure word for things related to money
未必	wèibì	Adv.	不一定；<>必定。	not necessarily; may not
主动	zhǔdòng	Adj.	不等待外力推动而行动：~联系、~帮助、~关心、~提供、~介绍；<>被动。	initiative
自然	zìrán	Adv./Adj..	表示理所当然。	naturally; of course
相反	xiāngfǎn	V. /Conj.	opposite; on the contrary.	
反复	fǎnfù	Adv./V.	一次又一次重复做同样的事情：~建议、~检查、~修改。	repetitively; again and again
谈判	tánpàn	V./N.	对有待解决的重大问题进行会谈：边界~、关税~、贸易~、价格~。	to negotiate; negotiation
过程	guòchéng	N.	事情发生或发展所经过的程序：发展~、运输~、谈判~、交易~。	process; course
复杂	fùzá	Adj.	(事物的种类、头绪)多而杂；<>简单。	complicated; complex
基本	jīběn	Adj.	主要的；根本的：~条件、~任务、~内容。	basic; fundamental; essential

补充词

大型	dàxíng	Adj.	形状或规模大的：~企业、~工厂、~歌剧、~计算机、~运输机。 large scale; large (used as modifier only)
外资	wàizī	N.	外国资本：~企业、~公司、~银行、~工厂。 foreign capital; foreign investment
企业	qǐyè	N.	从事生产、购销、运输或服务性活动的经济单位：如工厂、商店、贸易公司、铁路等。 enterprise
财务	cáiwù	N.	有关财产的管理或经营以及现金计算、保管、出纳等事务：管理~、~工作、。 financial affairs
审计	shěnjì	V./N.	对财务收支进行全面系统的审查，以确定其是否正确和合乎有关规定：~制度、~账目。 to audit
深圳	Shēnzhèn	N.	中国改革开放初期组建的四个经济特区之一，在广东省，毗邻香港。 a city in Guangdong Province adjacent to Hong Kong, one of the special economic zones in China
学历	xuélì	N.	学习的经历；指在那个学校毕业或肄业：填写~。 education; record of formal schooling
专业	zhuānyè	N.	大学里设置的学业门类：中文~、英语~、经济~、会计~。 specialization; major (at college)
会计	kuàijì	N.	管理财务的工作；担任会计工作的人：~师、~事务所。 accounting; accountant
会计师	kuàijìshī	N.	担任会计工作的人：专业~。 accountant

| 主计员 | zhǔjìyuán | NP | 主要负责某一方面的会计师。 |
| | | | chief accountant |

| 学士 | xuéshì | N. | 大学毕业时所得最低的学位。 |
| | | | Bachelor (degree) |

| 硕士 | shuòshì | N. | 学位的一级，高于学士，低于博士：管理学~、文学~、计算机科学~。 |
| | | | Master (degree) |

| 博士 | bóshì | N. | 最高的一级学位：数学~、经济学~。 |
| | | | Ph.D. |

| 专攻 | zhuāngōng | VP | 专门学习某种课程：~税务、~国际贸易、~市场学。 |
| | | | to concentrate on; to specialized in (a major/subject) |

| 主修 | zhǔxiū | VP/N. | 集中学习某方面课程：~企业管理、~会计、~中文、~电脑、~化学；＜＞副修。 |
| | | | to major in; to specialized in (a major/subject) |

| 副修 | fùxiū | VP/N. | to minor in (an area of study /a subject)：~英文、~经济。 |

| 持 | chí | V. | 拿着、带有：~刀、~不同意见、~证。 |
| | | | to hold; to grasp |

| 持证 | chízhèng | VO | 有合格的证书，可以从事某方面的专业工作：~会计、~律师、~翻译。 |
| | | | to be certified; to have a license (to engage in certain job) |

| 颁发 | bānfā | V. | 由有关部门给予；授予：证书、奖品。 |
| | | | to issue, to grant |

| 合格 | hégé | Adj. | 合乎规定，符合标准：质量~、~产品、~证书。 |
| | | | qualified |

| 证书 | zhèngshū | N. | 由机关、学校、团体等发的证明合格或权力等的文件：毕业~、学位~、结婚~、合格~。 |
| | | | certificate |

管理	guǎnlǐ	V./N.	管辖、负责处理、保管、料理：~学校、~生产、企业~、财务~、图书~。 to manage, to administer, to run, to look after
经历	jīnglì	N./V.	亲身遇到过、做过或参加过 (的事情)：工作~、生活~、各种~。　experience; to experience
稽查	jīchá	V.	检查：~账目、~部门。 to check; to audit; to examine
主任	zhǔrèn	N.	某个部门的主管：稽查~、财务~、系~。 director
助理	zhùlǐ	Adj./N.	协助主要负责人办理的：~教授、~经理、~主任；协助主要负责人办事的人：研究~、部长~。 assistant
分	fēn	Mph.(N.)	分支、部份：~公司、~行、~会。 branch; division
事务所	shìwùsuǒ	N.	某些办事机构，如律师~、会计师~等。 a (law/accounting) firm
半职	bànzhí	Adj.	兼职的、不是正式的、全职工作人员。 part-time; half-time (employee)
旅游	lǚyóu	V./N.	旅行游览。　to travel; to tour
技能	jìnéng	N.	掌握和运用专门技术的能力。　skill
荣誉	róngyù	N.	光荣的名誉。　honor; credit
奖励	jiǎnglì	N./V.	对作出成绩的人用荣誉、财物表示赞扬鼓励。 award; reward
秘书	mìshū	N.	管理文书和协助领导人处理日常工作的人。 secretary
基金会	jījīnhuì	N.	foundation：福特~、蒋经国~、诺贝尔~。
奖学金	jiǎngxuéjīn	N.	作为奖励，给某些学生提供的一笔钱。 scholarship

协会	xiéhuì	*N.*		association; society
备	bèi	*Mph.(V.)*	准备：~索、~用、~查。	to provide, to be prepared for; be ready to
索	suǒ	*Mph.(V.)*	要；讨取：~取、~赔。	to ask for; to demand

词语例释

一、(1) Subject（在……上/中），称为/称作/叫做……　（to be called/named as ...）

l-4. 询盘，在中国的对外贸易习惯上，又<u>称为</u>询价，……

l-10. 发盘，又<u>称作</u>报盘或报价。

l-14. 根据中国的贸易习惯，前者<u>叫做</u>"实盘"，后者<u>称为</u>"虚盘"。

1. 用电脑收发的信件，<u>称为</u>"电子邮件"。

2. 这条在历史上把中国和西亚、欧洲连接起来，促进了中外贸易和友好往来的道路，<u>称作</u>"丝绸之路"。

3. 移动电话，又<u>叫做</u>"手机"或"大哥大"，使用起来非常方便。

(2) Subject 被(somebody) 称为/称作/叫做……　（to be called/named as ... [by somebody]）

1. 黄河<u>被称为</u>"中华民族的摇篮"。

2. 文化大革命的时候，知识分子<u>被称作</u>"臭老九"。

3. 她因为很喜欢指手画脚，要别人做这做那，<u>被同事们叫做</u>"老板娘"。

　　虽然(1)和(2)在形式上有主动和被动之分，但是在意思上都是被动的。(1)可以看成是"被"字的省略，尤其是有"又、也、都"等副词时。

Although there is a distinction between the active and passive forms in(1)and (2), they actually share the same meaning, both are passive. 被 can be omitted in(1), especially when adverbs such as 又、也、都 are used.

(3) Subject 把……称为/称作/叫做……　(Subject called/s ... as...) Cf. A 管B 叫……

1. 这几年他常常跑中国，对中国的情况十分了解，朋友们都<u>把</u>他<u>称为</u>"中国通"。
2. 美国人<u>把</u>纽约<u>称作</u>"大苹果"。
3. 八十年代后，中国人<u>把</u>经商做生意<u>叫做</u>"下海"。

(4) Subject 称……为……　(Subject called/s ... as...) Cf. A 管B 叫……

1. 北京人<u>称</u>有钱人<u>为</u>"大款"或者"款爷"。
2. 大家都<u>称</u>他<u>为</u>"活字典"。
3. 人们<u>称</u>香港<u>为</u>"东方之珠"。

有一种更通俗的说法，就是"A 管B 叫……"，意思和 (3) (4) 相同。实际上，"称"就是"叫、叫做"的意思。"为"原是古汉语常用词，现在多用于书面，有"作为、当作"的意思。注意在词序上(4) 和(3) 以及"A 管B 叫……"的区别。

There is a more colloquial way to express the same idea as (3)and (4), which is "A 管B 叫...". As a matter of fact, 称 means 叫, 叫做. "为" was a commonly used word in literary Chinese. It is now mostly used in written Chinese, meaning 作为、当作. Please note the difference in word order of (4) and (3) as well as "A 管B 叫...".

(5) Noun Phrase ……，Subject 称之为……　(Noun Phrase, Subject called/s it as ...)

l-26. 这种表示，无论是口头的还是书面的，都是一种有效的承诺。在国际贸易中，<u>称之为</u>接受。

1. 芝加哥常常刮大风，所以人们<u>称之为</u>"风城"。

2. 由于这种发盘没有法律的约束力，发盘人没有明确表示要按一定的条件进行交易并且承担责任，在国际贸易中<u>称之为</u>"虚盘"。

3. 篮球明星迈克尔·乔丹球技高超，上篮时好像飞一样，球迷们<u>称之为</u>"飞人"。

"之"是古汉语代词，相当于"他、它"的意思。(5)一般多用于书面语。

之is a Pronoun in literary Chinese, which means 他、它. (5) is usually used in written Chinese.

二、……(Noun Phrase 1) 即……(Noun Phrase 2)（NP1 is/means NP2）

l-4. 询盘，在中国的对外贸易习惯上，又称为询价，<u>即</u>交易的一方向另一方询问购买或出售某种商品的各项交易条件。

1. 还盘，<u>即</u>习惯上说的还价，并非是达成交易必不可少的环节。

2. 电子计算机，<u>即</u>电脑，已逐步进入了中国人的家庭。

3. 春节，<u>即</u>农历新年，是中国人最重要的传统节日。

"即"是书面语，"就是"的意思，后面带宾语，常用来对前面的名词或短语作出解释、说明。

即 is from literary Chinese, meaning "that is, namely". It is followed by a Noun Phrase, which usually explains the previous Noun Phrase.

三、只有……才…… （only and if only..., then...）

l-7. 买卖双方<u>只有</u>对各项交易条件取得一致意见以后，交易<u>才</u>可达成。

1. <u>只有</u>优良的品质，商品在市场上<u>才</u>有竞争力。

2. 出口商<u>只有</u>了解了市场的动向，<u>才</u>能取得生意的成功。

3. <u>只有</u>家长和学校共同努力，<u>才</u>能教育好孩子。

"只有"后面表示唯一条件，非此不可。如果没有这个条件，就不可能出现"才"后面的情况。

The phrase after 只有 indicates the only condition that will lead to the situation after 才.

四、 对……取得一致意见/看法 （to reach a consensus on something; to agree upon something）

l-7. 买卖双方只有对各项交易条件<u>取得一致意见</u>以后，交易才可达成。

1. 虽然已经过多次还盘，但是双方对价格条款还没有<u>取得一致看法</u>。
2. 经过谈判，两国政府就双边贸易问题<u>取得了一致的意见</u>。
3. 对这个问题，如果大家还不能<u>取得一致的意见</u>，那就没有必要继续谈下去了。

由于"取得"后面已有宾语"一致意见/看法"，因此必须用介词"对"来引进另一个宾语，表示有关某方面事物的看法。由"对"引进宾语，也可以位于句首，在主语的前面，如句3。

As there is already an object after 取得, the Preposition 对 must be used to introduce another object, which indicates an opinion on a certain matter. The object after 对 can go at the beginning of a sentence and before the subject, such as in Sentence 3.

五、 作为……，Subject +Verb Phrase （As NP..; Being NP..）

l-8. 因此，询盘<u>作为</u>交易洽商的一环，具有投石问路，了解另一方的交易条件的功能。

1. <u>作为</u>出口商，应当随时注意市场的动向。（泛指）
2. <u>作为</u>合同，签订以后就不能随便更改了。（泛指）
3. <u>作为</u>哥哥，你要关心弟弟妹妹，主动帮助他们。（特指）
或：你<u>作为</u>哥哥，要关心弟弟妹妹，主动帮助他们。

"作为"表示以某种身份或资格来做某事，或从某个角度来作出判断，其后面必须带名词宾语。泛指一般情况时（如句1和2），"作为"位于句首，后面借用"作为"的宾语作句子的主语，不再重复。特指某人或某事时（如句3），主语（多数是人称代词或人名）不能省，可出现在"作为"前边或后边。

作为 indicates one does something in a certain position, or judges something from a certain perspective. When it refers to a general situation, 作为 appears at the beginning of a sentence, and the Noun Phrase after 作为 functions as the subject of the sentence (as in Sentences 1and 2). When it refers to a specific person or thing, the subject (normally a Personal Pronoun or a Personal Name) of the sentence CANNOT be omitted (as in Sentences 3). It may either occur before 作为 or after 作为.

六、 Subject 具有……　(to possess; to have)

1-8. 因此，询盘作为交易洽商的一环，<u>具有</u>投石问路，了解另一方的交易条件的功能。

1. 中国是<u>具有</u>极大潜力的市场。
2. 贵国总统对我国的访问，对于发展两国的友好关系<u>具有</u>深远的意义。
3. 本公司的产品质量优良，我们<u>具有</u>足够的信心和能力打开欧美市场。

"具有"后面的宾语，多用于抽象的事物，如信心、意义、能力、作用、功能、精神、传统、品质、特征、力量等。

The objects after 具有 are usually abstract such as confidence, significance, competence, function, spirit, tradition, quality, potential, a feature, ora characteristic.

七、 ……可分为……　(can be divided into/as...; can be categorized as...)

1-13. 在国际贸易中，从法律的责任来分析，发盘<u>可分为</u>有约束力的发盘和无约束力的发盘。

1. 国际贸易<u>可分为</u>进口、出口、和转口贸易三种。

2. 外语能力<u>可分为</u>听、说、读、写、译等。

3. 中学生<u>可分为</u>初中生和高中生两类。

在这个动词短语中，"可"是"可以"的简略形式，"为"是"成为、变为"的意思。"可分为"后面多数是更详细的分类或是前面名词的组成部份。

In this Verb Phrase, 可 is the contraction of 可以 whereas 为 means 成为、变为. Usually, a more detailed classification or some components of the previous Noun follows 可分为.

八、……，于是……　　(thus; therefore; as a result)

l-17. ……为了进一步洽商，<u>于是</u>针对该项发盘的内容提出不同的建议。

1. 她本来不打算上中文课，但是听说商贸汉语很有用，<u>于是</u>就选了这门课。

2. 开始我们学校只买了十台这种电脑，后来发现不错，<u>于是</u>，又买了二十台。

3. 我们公司很早就想进口这种产品了，因为缺乏有关的资料，没有成功。最近国内市场的需求不断增加，<u>于是</u>，我们拜访了美国驻华大使馆的商务处，请他们帮助我们与有关的公司取得了联系。

"于是"连接两个分句或句子，表示后一事是前一事的自然结果。"于是"一般用于后一分句或句子的开头，后面可以有停顿。"于是"也可说成"于是乎"。

于是 is used to link up two clauses or sentences, indicating whatever goes after 于是 is a natural outcome of the previous event. Normally, 于是 occurs at the beginning of the second clause or sentence, and may be followed by a pause. 于是 can also be said as 于是乎.

九、 无论(是)……都/也……　　(no matter...; regardless ...)

l-25. 这种表示，<u>无论</u>是口头的还是书面的，都是一种有效的承诺。在国际贸易中，称之为接受。

l-39. 但是<u>无论</u>洽商的过程是简单还是复杂，发盘和接受都是达成交易必不可少的两个最基本的环节。

　　1. <u>无论</u>什么人都必须遵守法律。

　　2. 这些条件，<u>无论</u>你们接受与不接受，请尽早告诉我们。

　　3. <u>无论</u>从事进口还是出口业务，都要搞好市场调查。

　　这个句型表示在任何条件或情况下，结果或结论都不变。"无论"后面有任指的疑问代词"谁、什么、哪儿、怎么"或者选择关系的并列词语（还是、V.不V.），常与"都、也"呼应。"无论"也可说成"不论"，多用于书面，口语里一般用"不管"。因此，"无论、不论"后面可以跟"如何、是否、与否"等有文言色彩的字眼，"不管"则不行。另外，"不管"后可直接跟"形容词＋不＋形容词"短语，用"无论、不论"时，一般要在形容词前加上"还是、跟、与"。

　　This pattern indicates that under whatever circumstances or no matter what happens, the result or conclusion remains the same. Following 无论 there is an Interrogative Pronoun 谁、什么、哪儿、怎么, or a parallel phrase of choice（还是、V.不V.), with the following phrase often containing 都 or 也. 无论 can be 不论 also, and is usually used in written Chinese. It is more common to use 不管 in colloquial Chinese. Therefore, words like 如何、是否、与否 that have literary Chinese connotations cannot go with 不管 but can appear with 无论、不论. In addition, phrases such as "Adj. +Adj." can directly follow 不管; however, when appearing with 无论、不论, 还是、跟、与 should be added before the Adjective Phrase.

十、 未必＋Verb Phrase（not necessarily; may not）

l-35. 但是具体的每一笔交易，<u>未必</u>都经过所有的五个环节。

　　1. 发亮的<u>未必</u>都是金子。

2. 老师也<u>未必</u>认识这几个字。

3. 还盘<u>未必</u>只限于还价。

副词"未必"是"不一定、也许不"的意思，表示委婉的否定。作为回答，可以单独成句。

未必 is an Adverb, meaning 不一定、也许不. It is used to express euphemistic negation. It can be used independently as an answer to a question.

十一、跟/与……相反 (opposite to; contrary to)

1-37. <u>与此相反</u>，有的交易，双方要经过多次谈判，反复还盘，才能达成交易。

1) 1. 这种新产品与公司主管们想的<u>相反</u>，在市场上的销售情况并不好。

2. 我们的看法跟他们的正好<u>相反</u>。

3. 你们提供的消息与我们了解的情况完全<u>相反</u>。

"相反"是形容词，表示事物互相矛盾、互相对立或互相排斥。可用介词"与、跟、同"等引进宾语，表示与主语对立。

相反 is an Adjective, which means "opposite; contrary" A preposition 与、跟 or 同 can be used to introduce an object to contrast with the subject.

2) 1. 你这样做不但不能帮助他，相反，还会给他带来麻烦。

2. 李老师听了这些话以后，并没有生气，相反，她还谢谢大家给她提出这些意见。

3. 老刘不喜欢打电话，<u>相反</u>，他喜欢写信。

"相反"也可作连词，插入两个句子或分句之间，起递进或转折的作用。"相反"前的分句或句子多数是否定形式，后面的分句或句子与前面的否定句互相对立。"相反"可被"正好、完全、恰恰"等词修饰，后面有停顿。

相反 can also be used as a Conjunction, inserted between two sentences or clauses. The sentence or clause before 相反 is usually in the negative form, while the sentence or clause after 相反 is contrary to the previous one. It can be modified by 正好、完全、恰恰, etc., and followed by a pause.

词义辨析

一、程序　过程　阶段

"程序"、"过程"、"阶段"都是名词，在意思和用法上各有侧重。"程序"主要指的是事情进行的先后次序，在中国，也可指电脑软件执行的一系列指令。在句子中可作主语、宾语、定语，或跟"按照"、"根据"、"把"等配合，构成状语。

"过程"强调经过，使用范围广，可用于口语和书面语，表示各种事情的进行或事物发展变化的经过，常带定语作句子成份。

"阶段"指的是事物发展过程中划分的段落，较多用于书面语或正式的场合，常带定语作句子成份。注意"阶段"与"时期"的区别："时期"强调的是某个时候或时间段落，而"阶段"着重于过程而非时间的某一段落。

Each of the Nouns 程序、过程、and 阶段 emphasizes a different aspect in meaning. 程序 refers to the priority or sequence of doing things; however, it also means "computer program" in China. It can function as a Subject, an Object or an Attributive in a sentence, or an Adverbial when in collocation with 按照、根据、把, etc.

过程 primarily emphasizes a process or the individual stages of development within a process. It often takes an Attributive or a Modifier in a sentence, and is used in both the spoken and the written Chinese.

阶段 indicates the stages or phases of a project, and is mostly used in writing or formal context, modified by an Attributive. Please note the differences between 阶段 and 时期: while the word 时期 focuses on a certain period of time, 阶段 emphasizes a stage or a phase in a process.

二、 有　具有　所有

　　动词"有"、"具有"、"所有"译成英语，都可以是 to have/to possess。"有"是通用于口语、书面语和各种场合的常用词，表示"领有"的意思，后面一般直接跟名词或名词性词组（作宾语），否定时用"没（有）"或"无"。

　　"具有"强调掌领着，有郑重的色彩，意思比"有"稍重，多用于书面语，一般不带表示具体事物的名词作宾语，而多用于"意义、信心、爱好、风格、本领、意识、品质、水平、特点、作用、功能"等方面以及"资源、领土"等较抽象而且量大的东西。否定是用"不"。"有"可带"了"、"着"、"过"等体态助词，而"具有"不能。另外，"有"可以构成连动词组，如"有人找你"，而"具有"不能。

　　"所有"作动词时，通常用在"属于/归/为（某人）所有"等短语，是书面语。"所有"带"的"字时，可作形容词，意思与"一切"相近，用于修饰名词或名词词组，表示某一（较小）特定范围内事物的全部，如"屋子里所有的东西都是新的。"（不可用"一切"代替"所有"。）但"一切"不限于某个范围，而指某个事物所含的全部类别或泛指全部事物。"一切"是代词，可单独作宾语，如"不顾一切/把一切献给祖国"，但"所有"不能这样用。

These Verbs all mean "to have/to possess" in English, but vary in their usage. The most commonly used one is 有, and it appears in almost all situations, speaking or writing. It proceeds a Noun or Noun Phrase, and uses 没（有）or 无 in its negation. 具有 is a formal word and is more significant in meaning. It is primarily used in written Chinese, and seldom takes Nouns referring to concrete things as its Object. It usually collocates with abstract Nouns such as 意义、信心、爱好、风格、本领、意识、品质、水平、特点、作用、功能, or Nouns like 资源、领土 that imply a large volume. Its negation is 不 instead of 没（有）. While 有 can take 了, 着, or 过, 具有

cannot. In addition, 有 can form Pivot Sentences such as 有人找你, 具有 cannot either.

When used as a Verb, 所有 is usually associated with Phrases such as 属于/归/为（某人）所有, and is used in written Chinese. When 所有 is paired with 的, it is an Adjective. It is close to 一切 in meaning, especially as a Noun Modifier, indicating the "entireness of something within a certain (usually rather small) scope. For example, 屋子里所有的东西都是新的. In this case, 一切 cannot serve as substitute for 所有. However, 一切 is not limited to merely "a certain scope" but can refer to all categories of something or even everything. 一切 is a Pronoun, which is possible to function as an Object of a sentence, as in 不顾一切 (to have no regard for anything) /把一切献给祖国 (to give one's all to the country), whereas 所有 cannot.

三、因此　所以　于是

连词"因此"，按字面的意思，就是"因为这样"，只能出现在表示原因或前提的句子或分句的后面，表示重复前面提及的原因或前提。"因此"一般与"由于"而不与"因为"呼应，且较多用于书面语。

"所以"也是连词，多用于表示因果关系的复句或语段中，通用于口语和书面语。

"所以"可与"由于"或"因为"呼应。当表示原因的分句出现在后面时，"所以"可跟在主语后，位于复句的句首。

连词"于是"主要表示两事前后相承，后一事与前一事有密切的联系，按事理的自然发展但不一定是前者引起的必然结果或结论。它可以出现在主语前或主语后，口语常用作"于是乎"。注意下面句子的区别：

(1) 大家都说喝绿茶对身体有好处，<u>于是</u>我也开始喝绿茶，不喝咖啡了。
(2) 昨晚我喝了太多茶，<u>所以/因此</u>很晚都没睡着。（✘于是）

第一句用"于是"，表示"我喝绿茶"是由"大家都说有好处"引起的，如果用"所以"，则表示一种因果关系，即根据上述的原因，得出下面的结果或结论。而第二句说明的是纯因果关系，不可用"于是"来代替"所以"或"因此"。

因此 is a Conjunction, which means 因为这样 in its literal sense. It can only follow a sentence or clause that shows a reason, cause or premise, indicating repetition of what has mentioned previously. In general, 因此 follows a sentence/clause with 由于 but not 因为, and is used more in written Chinese.

Like 因此, the Conjunction 所以 indicates a cause and effect relationship in a Compound Sentence or a discourse, but it can go with either 因为 or 由于. It is widely used in both spoken and written Chinese. When the clause indicating a reason or a cause appears at the second part of a Compound Sentence, 所以 can appear at the beginning of a sentence right after the Subject.

Although 于是 is also a Conjunction, it does not express a cause-effect relationship.

四、方式　方法　形式

这三个都是名词。"方式"用于说明做事所采取的方法和形式，常带"生活、生产、思维"等定语作句子成份。"方法"表示(成为系统的)一套办法，着重于一定的门路、程序，但不表示做事的形式。"形式"主要指事物的形态、结构，可用于具体和抽象事物。"方法"强调应能合理地认识现象和处理矛盾，用于较正式的场合，常与"工作、学习、教学、研究、领导、解决、思想、分析"等词组合连用，但不可直接作动词"想"的宾语(✘想方法)。

The three Nouns over lap somewhat in meaning. While 方式 refers to both the method, way and form of doing things, and often follows Attributives such as 生活, 生产, 思维. The word 方法 primarily means "method" or "methodology" but does not include the arrangement and the formality. 形式 focuses on the form, shape or the structure, and is applicable to things either concrete or abstract. 方法 is often used in formal situations, and is associated with words like 工作、学习、教学、研究、领导、解决、思想、分析, etc.

as its modifier. However, 方法 cannot be the Object of the Verb 想. It is incorrect to say: 想方法.

五、义务　责任

"义务"作名词时，着重指法律规定应做的或道义上应做的事情，与"权利"相对。"义务"还可作定语形容词，修饰名词或动词，表示"不要报酬的"意思，如"义务劳动"、"义务演出"等。"责任"只能作名词，表示"本份"内应做的事情，多用于本职工作和形势要求完成或上级布置的工作。

As a Noun, 义务 means "ligation" or "duty", that is, one is obliged to do something because of law, moral pressure, or promise, etc. It is the opposite of 权利 (right). 义务 can also function as an Attributive Adjective to modify a Noun or a Verb, meaning "to provide voluntary service" or "(doing something) for free" For example, 义务劳动 (volunteer work) or 义务演出 (benefit performance). 责任 is a Noun only, which is similar to "responsibility" in meaning. Generally speaking, it is the business related to a job that one is responsible for, and must care for because of the position he or she is in.

六、权利　权力

"权利"和"权力"同音而且都是名词。"权利"是单意词，指每一个公民或组织成员依法享受的、不容侵犯的权力和利益，和"义务"相对。"权力"是多意词，可指政治上的权柄和力量，也可指有一定地位、在某些职责范围内享有的支配权和指挥权。"权利"常被"合法、民主、人身"等词修饰，并多作"维护、保护、享受、剥夺、侵犯"等动词的宾语。"权力"常被"统治、最高、国家、社会、无限、部份"等词修饰，一般作"行使、利用、拥有、得到、夺取"等动词的宾语。

These are homonyms and can easily cause confusion. 权利 has a single meaning only. It is often translated as a "right", a proper claim to something or the authority to do things as a citizen or a member of an organization. It is the opposite of 义务. However, 权力 is a multi-meaning word, similar to "power" and "authority" particularly in terms of politics and social status. 权利 is usually modified by 合法、民主、人身, etc., and functions as the Object of verbs such as 维护、保护、享受、剥夺、侵犯. Common modifiers of 权力 are 统治、最高、国家、社会、无限、部份, etc., and verbs like 行使、利用、拥有、得到、夺取 often take 权力 as their Object.

语法

一、条件复句　Conditional Complex Sentences

　　一个分句（偏句）提出条件，另一个分句（正句）说明在这种条件下产生的结果。表示这种关系的复句，叫做条件复句。条件复句又可分为两种：特定条件复句和无条件复句。

This type of complex sentence contains two clauses. One clause (the subordinate clause) puts forward a condition, while the other clause (the main clause) shows the result brought about by that condition. Conditional complex sentences can be further divided into definite conditional sentences and unconditional sentences.

（一）特定条件句　Definite Conditional Sentences

　　正句表示结果，偏句提出实现这个结果所需的条件。常用的关联词语有：

In this type of complex sentence, the main clause states the result while the subordinate clause indicates the condition that is necessary for such a result. The commonly used correlatives are:

"只有……才……、只要……就……、除非……才……".
只有学过三年中文的学生，才能上这门课。

只<u>要</u>你跟大使馆商务处联系，他们<u>就</u>会给你提供有关的信息。

<u>除非</u>我们能够提出更好的条件，这家公司<u>才</u>会跟我们合作。

句型"只要……就……"指出所需要的条件，一旦有了这个条件，就会产生正句所说的结果。"只有……才……"和"除非……才……"指出得到结果的唯一条件，没有这个条件，就不可能产生正句所说的结果。

The pattern 只要……就……sets the necessary condition. Once the condition exists, it will lead to the result stated in the main clause. 只有……才…… and 除非……才……, on the contrary, specify the only condition that will produce the result. Without such a condition, it is absolutely impossible to have that result.

(二) 无条件句　Unconditional Sentences

这种复句表示在任何条件下都会产生正句所说的结果。常用的关联词语有：

This type of complex sentences indicates that the result stated in the main clause will happen under all circumstances. The following Connectives are often found in unconditional sentences：

无论……也/都……、不论……也/都……、不管……也/都……

<u>无论</u>困难有多大，我<u>都</u>要把中文学好。

她<u>不论</u>多么忙，每天<u>都</u>要运动半小时。

<u>不管</u>是白猫还是黑猫，能抓老鼠的<u>就</u>是好猫。

"无论、不论"多用于书面语，"不管"多用于口语。"不管"后一般不用"如何、是否、与否"等有文言色彩的词。

While 无论、不论 are usually used in the written language, 不管 is more common in the spoken language. Thus, words such as 如何、是否、与否 that have a literary Chinese flavor are seldom associated with 不管.

二、文言词(1)   Literary Chinese Words (1)

文言词是古汉语遗留下来，至今仍在现代汉语，尤其是在书面语里使用的词语。恰当地使用文言词，不但可以使语言表达丰富多彩，而且可以表示庄重、严肃的感情，或者表示讽刺的意义。文言文里的某些代词和虚词，在现代汉语的许多特殊结构中，使用得也比较多。这里介绍的，是几个常见的文言词。

The term "Literary Chinese" refers to the written language used by the court and government in ancient China for all official written business. Expressions drawn from Literary Chinese survive in Modern Chinese, particularly in the written language. They can, not only enrich expressions, but also show emotions of solemnity and seriousness, or used satirically sometimes. Some of the pronouns and function words in literary Chinese are rather common in their structures. The following are examples usually seen in Modern Chinese.

（一）者 zhě

(1) 用在动词、形容词、名词后，构成名词，表示从事某种工作、有某种特性或具有某种信仰的人：

者 is used after Verbs, Adjectives, and Nouns to form Nouns, which refer to people who are engaged in certain work, or have certain characteristics or believe in acestain religion/ideology:

作~、编~、译~、读~、记~、学~、听~、消费~、执行~、投资~、成功~;
强~、弱~、老~、长~、勇~;
笔~、教育工作~、爱国主义~、自然主义~、女权主义~、无神论~、工商业~。

(2) 用在"前、后"或个位数词如"二、三"后，构成名词，指事物或人：

When it is used after 前、后 or a single digit Numeral such as two or three to form a Noun which refers to a person or an object, meaning "the ... one(s)"

前~、后~、二、三~、两~。

（二）此 cǐ

(1) 表示近指，相当于"这、这个"，与"彼"相对。常用于固定词组，或作词素构成合成词。"此"后面一般不加量词：

Opposite of 彼, 此 refers to something that is closer in terms of time and space and is similar to "this". It is usually used in some fixed expressions or in word compounds as a morpheme. Normally, no Measure Word is necessary after 此：

~人、~时、~地、~事、~次、~刻、~处、因~、如~、为~、彼~、~致、~路不通、由~可知、顾~失彼。

(2) 指当时、当地：

Referring to a specific time or place, 此 can mean "now, then, here" or "there"

从~以后、到~结束、就~告别、由~往东。

（三）其 qí

(1) 表示"他/她/它/的；他（她、它）们的"的意思，在句子中作定语：

Serving as an attribute, "其" bears the meaning of "his, her, its; their" as in the following:

~条件、~结果、~原因、如闻~声、如见~人、莫明~妙、自食~果、自圆~说

(2) 表示"他、她、它、他（她、它）们"的意思，在句子中作兼语，后面必须跟动词或动词词组：

其 functions as a pivot in a sentence; that is, an object of the first verb and the subject of the second verb. It is similar to "it, him, her" in meaning. For example:

任~发展、　　促~早日实现、　　听~自然。

(3)表示"这、那"的意思，在句子中作定语：

Here, 其 refers to "this, that" and is used as an attribute in a sentence.

~中＝那里面、不乏~人＝这样的人并不少、

~间＝那中间、确有~事＝的确有那么一回事。

(四) 之 zhī

(1) 代替人或事物，意思相当于"他、她、它、他们、她们、它们"，只作宾语：

之 refers to a human or a thing. It is similar to "him, her, it, them" in meaning and is used as an object only.

换言~、总而言~、听之任~、求~不得、取而代~、

(2) 意思大致相当于"的"，用于修饰语和中心语之间。有的场合虽可用"的"，但习惯上往往用"之"，尤其是下列的固定格式：

Frequently 之 is quite similar to 的 in its use. Between a modifier and the Head Noun, 之 is the preference by convention, especially in the following instances:

北京~夜、少年~家、星星~火、无价~宝；

原因~一、三分~二、百分之七、十~八九；

谈判~前、签约~后、两国~间、五天~内、千里~外、调查~中；

(某些事物) 如：电脑~类、

(某个有代表性的人物，含贬义) 如：四人帮~流；

品种~多、价格~高、范围~广、速度~快；

非常~＋双音节形容词(困难、合适、重要、正确、及时)。

(3)虚用，不代替实际事物，只用在某些固定词语：

"之" does not stand for anything specific in these fixed expressions, but is just a "filler" used in some fixed expressions.

久而久~、这次考试，你的成绩最好，小李次~。

（五）该 gāi

指前面说过的人或事物，意思相当于"这、那"，多用于公文：

该 is mostly used in formal documents, and refers to a person, a party, or a matter that has been mentioned previously. It is similar to "this; that; the above-mentioned" in translation:

~厂、~校、~公司、~客户、~合同、~报价、~项工作。

（六）无 wú

(1) 动词，相当于"没有"，与"有"相对，多带宾语：

无 is a verb, meaning "do not have" which negates 有. It takes an object in most cases:

~色、~味、~生命、~条件、~希望、~目的、毫~保留。

(2) 用在名词＋名词、或名词＋动词前，构成名词词组：

It is used before a Noun+Noun, or Noun+Verb structure to form a Noun Phrase. For example:

~线电话、~轨电车、~烟商场、~名英雄、~效劳动、~偿贷款。

(3) 与单音节词素组合，构成形容词或动词：

It can also combine with a monosyllabic morpheme to form an Adjective or a Verb, as in:

~理、~声、~效、~限、~数、~情、~法、~关、~意、~知。

修辞

缩略语　Contractions

现代汉语中有些词组，特别是表示事物特征意义的词组，有时可以抽出其中某些成分，构成意思相同，但结构更为简单紧凑的形式。这种形式的词组，就叫做缩略语。

常见的缩略形式有以下几种：

In modern Chinese, some words or phrases, particularly those that refer to characteristics of objects, can have contracted forms that bear the same meaning yet are shorter and simpler in structure. These are contractions in Chinese. The usual ways of word/phrase contraction are as follows:

一、 分合式缩略　Merging

两个词各有独立的意义，但都有相同的词素，合用时省去词素相同的其中一个，就是分合式缩略词组。例如：

Merging takes place when two words that are independent in meaning but share a similar morpheme go together for which one of the shared morphemes is dropped. For instance:

进口和出口＝进出口、青年和少年＝青少年、男生和女生＝男女生、工业和商业＝工商业、优点和缺点＝优缺点、原料和材料＝原材料、上午和下午＝上下午、节日和假日＝节假日。

二、 抽取式缩略　Extracting

两个或两个以上的词连用时，抽取各个词的核心词素（通常为第一个字），组成一个双音节或三音节结构，就是抽取式缩略词组。这类缩略法生成能力强，因而使用得也最多。例如：

This type of contraction is formed by extracting a core morpheme (usually the first character) from each word of the original phrase to create a two or three syllable structure. Since extracting is very convenient in forming contractions, it is the most commonly used. Note the following examples:

老师和学生＝师生、经济和贸易＝经贸、科学与技术＝科技、供应和需求＝供求、中国共产党中央委员会＝中共中央、广州中国出口商品交易会＝广交会、商业事务办事处＝商务处、奥林匹克运动会＝奥运会、外事办公室＝外办、对外贸易＝外贸、外国资本＝外资、台湾商人＝台商、商品检验＝商检、北京大学＝北大、高等教育＝高教、邮政编码＝邮编、公共关系＝公关、外籍劳工＝外劳、商品展览＝商展、联合运输＝联运、电影明星＝影星、调查研究＝调研、遥远控制＝遥控、增加生产＝增产、拒绝接收＝拒收。

三、局部替代式缩略　Part Referring to Whole

这种缩略方式是用一个词语的一部份，甚至一个词的某个字来代替整个词语或词的意思。这类缩略语相对来说，字数少、节奏快。特别是后一种，在书面语中使用得相当多。如：

These contractions use a word from the original phrase, or even a character of the original word to stand for the entire phrase or word. They are, comparatively speaking, fewer in numbers, and faster in rhythm. The second group in particular are quite common in the written language. For example:

1) 清华大学＝清华、复旦大学＝复旦、宽银幕电影＝宽银幕、喷气式飞机＝喷气式、上海大众汽车公司生产的桑塔那汽车＝桑塔那、美国联合航空公司＝联航;

2) 因为＝因、如果＝如、虽然＝虽、但是＝但、并且＝并、或者＝或、凡是＝凡、可以＝可、能够＝能、应该＝应、需要＝需、已经＝已、仍然＝仍、曾经＝曾、例如＝如、按照＝按、根据＝据、经常＝常、比较＝较、以前＝前、大约＝约。

四、数字概括式缩略　To Highlight with a Number

在内容上有关联，有两项或两项以上的词组并且其中的某个词素相同，有时可以用一个数词加在相同的词素前，以概括的形式，代替这几个词组所表示的内容。这类缩略语，一般多用于政治或学术方面。如：

Sometimes, there are phrases that contain two or more items, each of which is relevant in content and shares a similar morpheme or word. In this case, a number (representing the number of items) may be used before the shared morpheme or word to form a contraction. The number and the shared morpheme or word jointly highlight the ideas expressed in the long phrase. Such contractions are usually used in political propaganda. These are some typical examples:

两个文明＝物质文明、精神文明，

双百方针＝百花齐放、百家争鸣，

三好学生＝学习好、工作好、身体好的学生，

三民主义＝民族主义、民权主义、民生主义，

四个现代化＝工业现代化、农业现代化、科技现代化、国防现代化，

四美＝心灵美、语言美、行为美、环境美，

五讲＝讲文明、讲礼貌、讲卫生、讲秩序、讲道德，

五爱＝爱祖国、爱人民、爱劳动、爱科学、爱护公共财物。

练习

一、 用线将意思相同的词和词语连起来：

当面商谈	开盘
约定购买货物	销售
向另一方提出有关商品的交易条件	订货
通过电话或电子邮件等商量某事	邮购
卖出（货物）	抢购
在商店里卖商品的工作人员	电洽
交易市场开始营业	制订计划
抢着去买	发盘
用邮寄的方式买东西	面洽
对交易另一方的发盘提出不同的建议	售货员
接洽商谈	还盘

一起商量创制、拟订计划　　　　　　　　洽谈

二、 用括号里的词或词组改写下列句子，但不改变其基本意思，必要时可替换某些词或对词序作一定的调整：

1. 合同签订后，不管是买方还是卖方，都不可以随便修改自己答应了的交易条件。 （无论、承诺）

2. 这个报盘有特别的意义，你不一定知道，但张经理心里很清楚。 （具有、未必）

3. 经过一次又一次的谈判，双方都改变了自己原来提出的价格条款。 （反复、各自）

4. 你是经理，必须实行董事会决定的计划。 （作为、执行）

5. 他一天到晚都在搞电脑，什么事都说可以用电脑，就这样，大家都叫他"电脑迷"。 （于是、称之为）

6. 还盘，就是买方针对卖方的报盘提出的新的交易条件。如果卖方不接受，就不会达成交易。 （即、只有……才）

7. 在这个问题上，我们和你们的意见基本相同。 （一致、我方、贵方）

8. 按照海关规定，进口商必须交百分之二十的关税。 （据、支付）

三、 选择最合适的词填空：

1. 这件事我们一定会按照法律_____来处理，请你放心。
   a. 阶段　　　　b. 过程　　　　c. 程序

2. 如果在交货_____出现什么问题，保险公司会负责赔偿。
   a. 阶段　　　　b. 过程　　　　c. 程序

3. 这种商品的包装_____中国的民族特色。
   a. 具有　　　　b. 所有　　　　c. 有

4. "虚盘"都没_____法律约束力。

     a. 具有   b.所有   c. 有

5. 去年他中文考试考得不好，本来打算不再学了。后来，大家都鼓励
   他，帮助他，_____他又恢复了信心。

     a. 因此   b.所以   c. 于是

6. _____这么多人迟到，是因为今天一早下大雪。

     a. 因此   b.所以   c. 于是

7. 在国际贸易中，有不同的支付_____。

     a. 方式   b.形式   c. 方法

8. 如果你们对合同有不同意见，请用书面_____提出来。

     a. 方式   b.形式   c. 方法

9. 在美国，只要你工作并有一定的收入，就得交税，这是每个人的
   _____。

     a. 义务   b. 责任   c. 权利

10. 每个人都有上学受教育的_____。

     a. 义务   b. 责任   c. 权利

四、 找出课文里的条件复句和因果复句。

**五、 用文言词替代下列句子中的划线部份，必要时可替换某些词或对词序
     作一定的调整。**

1. 按这个规定，卖方装运的那天，就是交货的时候。

2. 感兴趣的人，请在这里等候。

3. 这个盘是虚盘，它的交易条件不完备，因此是没有约束力的发盘。

4. 他们要打开亚洲的市场。为了这个，他们必须做好市场调研，修改他
   们的计划，使它适应亚洲的贸易惯例。

5. 美中商会向我们推荐了两家银行——美洲银行和远东银行。前一家在纽

约，与我方<u>没有</u>任何业务联系；后<u>一家</u>在旧金山，<u>它的</u>董事长是<u>这个</u>商会<u>的</u>主要负责人，和我们也有过来往。

6. 买卖双方都是<u>执行合同的人</u>，也是<u>监督对方执行合同的人</u>。<u>那方和这方</u>的责任相同。

六、完成下列句子：

1. 不论是买方还是卖方，都……

2. 只有签订了合同，……才……

3. 不管我怎么说，她都……

4. 除非大家都同意，小高才……

5. 无论谁提出建议，董事长都……

6. 只要你不怕麻烦，就……

7. 只有经过洽商，问题才……

8. 无论什么时候，……都……

七、缩略下列句子的划线部分，但不改变其意思：

1. <u>按照</u>合同规定，买方<u>应该</u>在本月十日<u>以前付款</u>，<u>但是</u>我们目前<u>仍然</u>未收到。

2. <u>根据报导</u>，<u>中国和美国</u>两国政府谈判<u>已经</u>结束，<u>并且</u>签订了<u>经济贸易</u>合作协定。

3. 我们的报价<u>虽然</u>高，<u>但是</u>产品的品质也<u>比较</u>好，<u>如果</u>贵方对我方产品的质量有疑问(doubt)，<u>可以</u>与<u>商品检验</u>部门联系。

4. <u>因为市场调查研究没有做好，不了解供应和需求的</u>变化，去年那家公司的<u>进口出口</u>都受到一定的影响。

5. 他<u>常常</u>去<u>中学和小学</u>，向<u>青年、少年</u>介绍<u>科学技术</u>知识，受到<u>老师和学生</u>们的热烈欢迎。

八、 根据意思，重新安排下列两组句子的顺序并加上标点符号，使它们成 为文句通顺、合乎逻辑的两段话：

（一）1. 中国国际贸易促进会，简称贸促会

2. 并常在国外举办商品展览会或交易会

3. 外商可以在参观商展时，与中国的外贸公司洽谈订货

4. 主要是为了促进中国和世界各国的经济和贸易关系

5. 贸促会在北京、上海、天津、广州以及各省、区都有分会

6. 贸促会成立于 1952 年

（二）1. 广州中国出口商品交易会，又叫广交会

2. 以后每年举办两次，分别在春、秋季举行

3. 这样的交易会，义务范围广，货源充足，选择性广，不论什么样 的生意都可以做，非常方便

4. 到目前已经举办了几十届了

5. 是综合性的大型交易会

6. 广交会上，集中了全国各进出口总公司和有关企业、单位，组织 了各种出口商品货源

7. 展（览）销（售）结合，进出口结合，当面看样(look at the samples)， 洽谈成交

8. 中国从 1957 年开始在广州举办这样的大型交易会

九、把下列句子翻译成汉语：

1. If one party intends to sell, and the other party agrees to buy, and both parties have reached a consensus on all the trading conditions, a deal is reached. Thus, signing a contract is the essential procedure [i.e. "indispensable link"]. This is called "acceptance" in foreign trade.

2. The content of a contract includes the name of the commodity, its quality,

specification, price, terms of payment, amount, packing, shipment, the date of delivery, etc. As a legal document, a contract contains certain constraints [i.e. "binding power"]. After signing the contract, no matter what happens, both parties must carry out the contract, and cannot change its content.

3. Only when the buyer has promised to pay will the seller then deliver the goods. Analyzing from the information provided by the bank, the buyer has not made the payment yet. Contrary to what you have said, the responsibility should fall on [i.e. "belong to"] the buyer. There is no indication [i. e. "no such problem exists"] that we have not carried out the contract.

十、 按照中文履历表的格式，写一份关于你自己的履历表。

文化与商贸背景知识

✐ 个人履历表

　　个人履历表主要用于申请工作或入学。履历表要简单明确，客观地反映个人的学历、工作经历及特长。因此，履历表不宜太长，一般一、两页即可。一些与申请目的关系不大的个人情况，如年龄、性别、出生日期、身高、体重、健康情况、婚姻状况等，可以不提。记住：最重要的是根据你自己的实际情况和你要申请的工作或者学校，突出你自己的优点和特点，让对方一看就有一个比较好的印象。下面是以申请工作为目的的个人履历表格式和范例。

1. 姓名

地址
电话/传真号码
电子邮件地址

2. 意向 (可有可无、视情况而定)

简单说明自己希望申请哪方面的工作及原因。

3. 学历

a. 专业 (证书) 职称。
b. (大学、研究所名称) 最高学位，(系名称) 专业，修业起止时间。
c. (大学名称) 次高学位，(系名称) 专业，修业起止时间。
d. 其他与所申请的工作有关的培训班，学习班，学习起止时间。

4. 经历

a. 与所申请的工作关系最密切的工作经历和经验，工作单位名称，所
   担任的职务，工作的性质，工作起止时间。
b. 其他工作经历和经验，工作单位名称，所担任的职务，工作的性
   质，工作起止时间。(可顺时序排列或逆时序排列。)

5. 荣誉和奖励 (可有可无、视情况而定)

简单说明自己何时何地获得的有关荣誉和奖励。

6. 其他技能 (可有可无、视情况而定)

简单说明自己具备的电脑、外语或其他有关的专业技能。

7. 出版著作 (可有可无、视情况而定)

按时间顺序列举自己的著作，出版日期，著作名称/登载刊物名称及页
码，出版者名称等。

8. (专业) 组织成员 (可有可无、视情况而定)

自己参加的有关专业团体、组织名称，所任职务等。

9. 其他个人资料 (可有可无、视情况而定)

10. 有关推荐人或查询单位 (可有可无、视情况而定)

随时备索

伍雪丽 Shirley A. Wood

美国麻州波士顿阿灵顿街 240 号
邮政编码：MA 02115
电话/传真：(617)987-6543
电子邮件：resume@aol.com

意向

在华大型外资企业财务审计工作，最好在上海、深圳、或广州等地。

学历

专业会计硕士，专攻税务（1995年6月）。

　　波士顿大学—美国麻州波士顿（1993年9月至1995年6月）。

持美国麻州颁发合格证书的会计师（1987年10月）。

经济企业管理学学士，主修：经济；副修：中文（1987年6月）。

　　布兰代斯大学—美国麻州波士顿（1983年9月至1987年6月）。

经历

稽查主任，美国麻州波士顿阿门—格丁—匹列司戈暨史密斯公司

　　（1995年7月至今）。

研究助理，美国麻州波士顿大学专业会计硕士班，华德·杰克逊教授

　　（1994年6月至1995年6月）。

主计员，美国纽约国家通讯公司训练系统分公司

　　（1990年12月至1993年7月）。

高级稽查员，美国麻州波士顿威尔森—分维克会计事务所

　　（1988年10月至1990年11月）。

稽查员，美国麻州波士顿威尔森—分维克会计事务所

　　（1987年10月至1988年10月）。

半职职员，汤马斯—库克旅遊公司　　（1985年5月至1987年3月）。

其他技能

汉语：中级会话能力；西班牙语：能流利地进行听说读写。

荣誉和奖励

荣誉会计学秘书　（1996年）。

企业暨专业妇女基金会奖学金　　（1994年）。
布兰代斯大学校长奖学金　　（1984年9月至1985年5月）。

专业组织成员

　　美国持证合格会计师协会(AICPA)会员
　　美国麻州持证合格会计师学会 (波士顿分会) 会员

推荐人或查询单位资料

　　随时备索

第三课

询盘和发盘

✏ **思考下面的问题，然后带着这些问题去阅读课文：**

一、 什么是询盘？询盘主要通过哪些方式进行？

二、 是不是买方和卖方都可以发盘？

三、 发盘有几种？它们有些什么区别？

四、 发盘有哪些方式？

课文：询盘和发盘

进出口贸易中每一笔生意的成交，如同日常生活中一般商品的买卖，总是由一方先主动与另一方联系，表达要购买或出售某种商品的意愿，提出自己的或了解对方的交易条件而开始的。这就是国际贸易中所谓的询盘，或习惯上所说的询价。

询盘可以用口头的方式，当面或以电话提出，也可以用书面 5
的方式，通过信函、电报、传真、电子邮件以及邮寄固定格式的询价单进行。询盘仅仅是一种邀请洽商的表示，它本身对买卖双方并无法律约束力。但是如果一笔交易是从询盘开始，经过双方洽商，最后成交的话，询盘就可能成为达成这笔交易的不可缺少的文件，其内容对确定双方的责任将可能有一定的法 10
律约束作用。

发盘是国际贸易洽商过程中必不可少的环节。实际上，有很多交易都是以发盘开始的。发盘可由买方发出，习惯上称为买方发盘或递盘，但多数发盘是由卖方发出的，因此也叫卖方发盘。

15   发盘有两种：有约束力的发盘和无约束力的发盘，也就是所谓
的实盘和虚盘。有约束力的发盘（实盘）是指发盘人明确地、肯定地
表达了订立合同的意图。在一项发盘的有效期限内，一般不能撤销
或修改该盘的内容。一旦受盘人作出有效的接受，交易立即达成。
发盘人对该盘的内容，不得更改或反悔，否则将要承担违约的后
20   果。反之，无约束力的发盘（虚盘）是指发盘人没有明确表示肯定要
订立合同的意图，因而不受该项发盘的约束，即使受盘人作出了有
效的接受，发盘人也不承担任何法律责任。那么，怎样辨别一项发
盘是实盘还是虚盘呢？一般认为，实盘必须是一项明确要订立合同
的建议，其各项交易条件必须是明确的、完整的、毫无保留条件
25   的。所谓"明确的"，是指发盘的内容清楚确切，没有含糊的、模棱
两可的词句；所谓"完整的"，是指主要的交易条件是完备的，包括
商品名称、品质规格、包装、数量、交货期、价格、支付方式等
等；所谓"无保留条件的"，是指发盘人愿意按自己提出的各项交易
条件同受盘人订立合同，除此之外，没有任何其他的保留条件。如
30   果一项发盘具备了以上的三项基本要求，就是实盘；反之，凡是不
具备这三项基本要求的发盘，都应视为虚盘。因此，所谓的"虚"和
"实"都是以发盘人是否明确表示愿意对其发盘承担订立合同的法律
责任而言的。

           无论是发虚盘还是发实盘，都必须根据实际情况来决定。例如
35   卖方一时对市场情况不明，需要作一定的试探时，就可以发虚盘。
又如买方询盘很急而卖方供货有限时，或为了争取更好的成交条件
同时向几个客户发盘，都可以使用虚盘。发虚盘时，一般都加上
"以我方最后确认为准"的条件，以避免发生误解和引起不必要的争
议或纠纷。

40   对外发盘时，除了一般的函电或口头方式外，还可以采用其他
的固定书面格式，如报价单、价格表、形式发票等。

✎ **根据课文内容回答下列问题：**

1. 询盘可以用哪些方式进行？

2. 询盘本身有没有法律约束力？为什么？

3. 发盘是否全部是由卖方发出的？不是由卖方发出的发盘叫什么？

4. 发盘人在对方接受了其发出的实盘以后，能否再修改这个发盘？为什么？

5. 如果一项发盘的价格是"参考价"，或该发盘有"数量视我方供货的可能而定"的词句，这样的发盘是实盘还是虚盘？

6. 实盘和虚盘最主要的区别是什么？

7. 在什么情况下可以发虚盘？发虚盘时怎样避免可能发生的误解？

✎ **根据意思，给课文划分层次(不是自然段)并写出每个层次的大意。**

生词和用法

如同	rútóng	*V.*	好像；像。	similar to, as
日常	rìcháng	*Adj.*	平时的：~生活、~工作、~用品。	everyday; daily
表达	biǎodá	*V.*	表示（思想、感情、意思等）。	express
意	yì	*Mph.(N.)*	意思；愿望、心愿：~愿、~图、~向、~见。	meaning; wish; desire
意愿	yìyuàn	*N.*	愿望、心愿。	desire; wish; aspiration
函	hán	*N.*	〔书〕信件：公~、信~、~电。	letter; mail
电报	diànbào	*N.*	telegram：发~、收~、打~。	
电子邮件	diànzǐ yóujiàn	*NP.*	用电子计算机收发的信：发~、收~。	e-mail; electronic mail

固定	gùdìng	*Adj.*	不变动或不移动的：~格式、~价格、~职业、~人口：<>流动、移动。
			fixed; formulated
格式	géshì	*N.*	一定的规格式样：公文~、书信~、电报~。
			form; pattern
仅仅	jǐnjǐn	*Adv.*	表示只限于某个范围。　merely
邀请	yāoqǐng	*V.*	请人到某个地方或做某事。
			to invite
约束	yuēshù	*V.*	限制使不超出范围。
			to restrain; to bind
约束力	yuēshùlì	*NP.*	限制、约束的能力和效力。
			binding force
缺少	quēshǎo	*V.*	人或物数量的不足：~人手、~工具、~雨水、~资金：<>拥有。
			to lack; to be short of
文件	wénjiàn	*N.*	公文、信件。　document, files, mail
确	què	*Adv.*	牢固、坚定：~立、~定、~认、~信。
			firm; definite.
		Mph.	符合事实的，真实的：的~、~实、明~、正~、准~。　accurate; true
定	dìng	*V.*	约定，预定：~货、~价、~期、~时、~票、~量。　to agree on; to settle
		Mph.(V.)	用在动词后，表示固定、确定、坚定等，不会改变：法~、规~、决~、肯~、确~、商~、~、约~、指~。　to settle; to secure
递	dì	*V.*	（用手把东西）传递：~交、~送、~盘。
			to hand over; to pass; to give
递盘	dìpán	*VO.*	买方主动提出交易的条件，也叫买方发盘。
			to bid
指	zhǐ	*V.*	指点、表示　to indicate; to refer to

明确	míngquè	Adv.	清楚明白而确定不变：态度~、目标~、分工~： <＞含糊。　　　　clear and definite
		V.	使明确：~责任、~交货期。 　　　　　　　　　　to make clear
肯定	kěndìng	V.	承认事物的存在或事物的真实性：~成绩、~进步：<＞否定。　　to affirm; to regard as true
		Adj.	一定、没有怀疑的：~的回答、~的态度。 　　　　　　　positive; affirmative
意图	yìtú	N.	希望达到某种目的的打算。 　　　　　　　　intention; intent.
项	xiàng	MW.	量词，用于分项目的事物：一~交易/报盘/内容。　　measure word for things categorized by items
期限	qīxiàn	N.	限定的一段时间或所限时间的最后界限：~三天、~已到、~很短。 　　　　　　　deadline; the allocated time
限	xiàn	V.	指定范围，不得超过：~定、~度、~量、~制。 　　　　　to set a limit; to restrict
		N.	指定的范围、数量、时间等：期~、年~、局~、有~、无~、上~、下~。 　　　　　　　limit; bounds
内	nèi	Lclz.	里头：~部、~衣、国~、室~、年~：<＞外。 　　　　　　inside; within
撤销	chèxiāo	V.	取消：~合同、~职务、~处分。 　　　to cancel; to rescind; to withdraw
改	gǎi	V.	改变；更改；改正：修~、~动、~订~、进、~革、~期、~正、~用、~写。 　to change; to revised; to alter; to correct
该	gāi	Pron.	〔书〕指上文说过的人或事：~地、~校、~公司、~合同、~经理。　　this.

一旦	yīdàn	Adv..	不确定的时间词，表示有一天；天。
			once; someday
	N.		一天之间（形容时间短）
			a day, a short time
更改	gēnggǎi	V.	变换；改动：~日期、~决定、~地址、~内容、~电话号码、~计划。
			revision; change; alter
反悔	fǎnhuǐ	V.	对以前承诺的事后悔、不承认；＝翻悔。
			to go back on one's word
否则	fǒuzé	Conj.	如果不是这样；（要）不然。
			otherwise
否	fǒu	Adv.	〔书〕表示不同意，相当于口语的"不"：~定、~认、~决。 not
	Partcl.		用在问句，相当于口语的的"吗"、"么"可~、来~、能~、是~、知~。
			Used to form a question
违	wéi	Mph.(V.)	不遵守、不依从：~反、~背、~法、~规：
			to violate; to disobey
违约	wéiyuē	VO.	违反合约。＜＞守约。
			to break a contract; to violate a treaty
后果	hòuguǒ	N.	将来产生的结果（多用于坏的方面）
			consequence
反之	fǎnzhī	Conj.	相反；从相反的方面／角度来看、来说。
			conversely; on the contrary
即使	jíshǐ	Conj.	表示假设和让步；Cf.〔口〕哪怕；就算；就是。
			even if; even though
辨别	biànbié	V.	根据不同事物的特点，在认识上加以区别：~是非、~真假、~方向。
			to distinguish; to differentiate
完整	wánzhěng	Adj.	具有或保持着应有的各部分，没有损坏或残

			缺：＜＞残缺。	complete; comprehensive
确切	quèqiè	*Adj.*	准确、恰当：用字~、~的回复。	exact; precise
毫	háo	*Adv.*	一点儿（只用于否定）：~不、~无。	in the least; (not) at all
含糊	hánhú	*Adj.*	不明确、不清楚：＜＞明确。	ambiguous; vague
模棱 两可	mólīng liǎngkě	*Idm.*	（态度、意见等）含糊、不明确；不肯定也不否 定。	equivocal; ambiguous
完备	wánbèi	*Adj.*	应该有的都有了：手续~、材料~、工具~。	complete; perfect
备	bèi	*V.*	具有；具备；准备：筹~、后~、齐~、预~、完 ~、自~。	to possess; to have; to prepare.
具备	jùbèi	*V.*	具有、齐备：~条件、~本领：＜＞欠缺、缺乏。	to possess; to have.
名称	míngchēng	*N.*	事物的名字（也可以用于人的集体）：公司~、商 品~、职务~。	name; title
视	shì	*Mph.(V.)*	看：~力、~线、~觉、近~。	to look; to see; to view
视为	shìwéi	*VP.*	把……看成……	to be considered; be treated as
言	yán	*Mph.(N./V.)*	话：语~、~行、~辞；说：言之有理、对……而 言 Cf. 对……来说。	words; remarks; to say; to speak
一时	yīshí	*Adv./N.*	短时间、暂时的：＜＞长期。	for a while; temporarily
试探	shìtàn	*V.*	用含义不很明确的话或举动来了解对方的反应 和意见。	to probe; to explore
供货	gōnghuò	*VO*	供＝供应，货＝货物。	supply of goods
有限	yǒuxiàn	*Adj.*	有一定的限度；数量不多：＜＞无限。	

limited; finite

争取	zhēngqǔ	V.	力求得到：~机会、~主动、~客户、~时间。 to strive for, to attempt to gain	
确认	quèrèn	V.	明确承认（事实、原则、约定的条件或时间等）。 to confirm; to finalize	
避免	bìmiǎn	V.	想办法不让某种情况发生；防止出现：~错误、~纠纷、~事故。 to avoid; to refrain from	
误解	wùjiě	V.	理解得不正确。 to misunderstand.	
		N.	不正确的理解：引起~、避免~、消除~。 misunderstanding	
争议	zhēngyì	V./N.	争论：引起~、避免~、还有~。 to dispute; to controvert	
纠纷	jiūfēn	N	争执的事情。 dispute; controversy	
采用	cǎiyòng	V.	认为合适并且加以利用：~先进技术、~新方法；Cf. 用。 to adopt; to use; to utilize	
报价单	bàojiàdān	NP.	卖方向买方开出的单子，上面有货物的名称和价格。 quotation sheet	
价格表	jiàgébiǎo	NP.	列有货物名称和单价的表格。 price list	
发票	fāpiào	N.	商业单据，上面常有商品名称、数量、价格等：开~、写~。 invoice; receipt	
形式发票	xíng shìfāpiào	NP.		pro-forma invoice

补充词

赞扬	zànyáng	V.	称赞表扬，常带宾语：~她的品德；~新产品的性能。也可作"受到、加以"的宾语：＜＞贬斥。 to praise; to commend
贬斥	biǎnchì	V.	贬低并排斥，常带宾语：~别人：＜＞赞扬。

			to denounce
虚伪	xūwěi	*Adj.*	不诚实；不实在；作假：~的政治骗子、这个人很~：＜＞诚实、真诚。 hypocritical; dishonest; false
贪心	tānxīn	*Adj.*	贪得无厌，不知满足：~的商人、他真~：＜＞廉洁。　　　greedy; avaricious
		N.	贪得的欲望：~不足。　　greed; avarice
狡猾	jiǎohuá	*Adj.*	不老实；耍花招：~的敌人、狐狸很~：＜＞老实。　　crafty; cunning; sly
愚蠢	yúchǔn	*Adj.*	头脑迟钝，行为愚笨：~的家伙、这样做很~：＜＞聪明。　　stupid; foolish
优惠	yōuhuì	*Adj.*	比一般的优厚：~价格、~条件、~待遇。 favorable
竞争	jìngzhēng	*V./N.*	为了自己的利益与别人争胜：自由~、激烈的~、~性、~力。　　to compete; competition
有竞争力	yǒujìngzhēnglì	*VP.*	有跟别人争胜的能力。　competitive
吸引	xīyǐn	*V.*	把物体、力量、或人的注意力引到某一方面来：互相~、~力：＜＞排斥。 to attract
有吸引力	yǒuxīyǐnlì	*VP.*	有能力吸引到别人。attractive
合理	hélǐ	*Adj.*	合乎道理或事理：价格~、~安排、~分配：＜＞无理。　　　reasonable
仪器	yíqì	*N.*	用于实验、计量、观测、绘图等较精密的器具或装置。　　instrument; apparatus
合计	héjì	*V.*	加在一起计算；总共。to add up to; to amount; total
批发	pīfā	*V.*	成批地出售商品：~价格、~商品、~服务：＜＞零售。　　wholesale
零售	língshòu	*V.*	把商品直接卖给消费者：~价格、~商店：＜＞批发。　　retail

编号	biānhào	V./N.	按顺序编排（的）号数。	serial number
品名	pǐnmíng	N.	商品的名称，也叫货名。	name of commodity
单位	dānwèi	N.	计算事物标准量的名称，如斤、尺、秒等：重量~、长度、时间~。	unit
盖章	gàizhāng	VO	打上印章。	to seal; to stamp (with aseal)
填写	tiánxiě	V.	在表格、单据等空白处按规定要求写上文字或数字：~报价单、~申请表、~表格。	to fill out (a form)

词语例释

一、……如同…… （NP1 to be as NP2; to be like; to be similar）

l-1. 进出口贸易中每一笔生意的成交，<u>如同</u>日常生活中一般商品的买卖，总是由一方先主动与另一方联系，……

1. "商场<u>如同</u>战场"。从事对外贸易，必须了解市场的动向，掌握好时机，才能取得生意的成功。
2. 他们俩从小在一起，十分要好，<u>如同</u>亲兄弟一样。
3. 国庆节晚上，广场上灯火通明，<u>如同</u>白昼。

"如同"作为及物动词，须带宾语，用作比喻，意思相当于口语的"像、好像"。

如同 is a Transitive Verb and must take an object. It is used in a metaphor, similar to 像、好像 in colloquial Chinese.

二、以 Noun Phrase +Verb Phrase （Verb with NP.; to use/take NP. to do...）

l-5. 询盘可以用口头的方式，当面或<u>以</u>电话提出，……

l-13. 实际上，有很多交易都是<u>以</u>发盘开始的。

1. 目前在进出口贸易中<u>以</u>电子邮件发盘已经相当普遍了。
2. 这笔生意最后<u>以</u>三百万美元成交。

3. 这虽然是一件小事，但是她还是<u>以</u>认真的态度来对待，使外商非
　常满意。

　　介词"以"有"用、拿、凭借"的意思，表示行为动作的方式或手段。
常与名词结合，组成介词词组作状语，多用于书面语。

The Preposition 以 means 用、拿、凭借, indicating the means or
manner of an action. It often goes with a Noun to form a Preposition Phrase,
functioning as an adverbial in a sentence. It is used primarily in the written
language.

1-38. 发虚盘时，一般都加上"<u>以</u>我方最后确认为准"的条件，以避免发生
　　误解和引起不必要的争议或纠纷。　(according to; in the line with)

1. 我们将<u>以</u>对方的报价作为参考，讨论以后再还盘。
2. 我方将<u>以</u>贵方的规定为标准，生产、包装这批货物。
3. 这台电脑会<u>以</u>邮件到达先后为序，分别给对方回信。

　　同"为"配合使用，构成"以……为……"的格式，表示"按照、根
据"，或"把……作为……"的意思。

It often goes with 为 to form a structure of 以……为……, with a meaning
of "according to, in line with", or "taking as ..." etc.

三、……Verb Phrase 1；以 Verb Phrase 2　　(in order to; in order that)

1-38. 发虚盘时，一般都加上"以我方最后确认为准"的条件，<u>以</u>避免发生
　　误解和引起不必要的争议或纠纷。

1. 公司最近派她去上海，<u>以</u>调查个人电脑的销售情况。
2. 他决定到中国去留学，<u>以</u>进一步提高自己的汉语水平。
3. 买卖双方就交易条件取得一致意见后，必须签订合同，<u>以</u>明确各
　方的权利和义务。

　　"以"在这里是连词，表示目的，相当于"为了、为的是"的意思。可
以连接两个动宾词组或分句，用于书面语。

"*以*" is a Conjunction here, and indicates the purpose of an action. It is similar to "*为了*、*为的是*" in meaning. It can link up two Verb-Object Compounds or two clauses, and is used in the written language.

四、 Subject 由 Somebody +Verb Phrase （to be Verb+ed by somebody）

l-13. 发盘可由买方发出，习惯上称为买方发盘或递盘，但多数发盘是由卖方发出的，因此也叫卖方发盘。

1. 这批货物将由卖方负责装运。
2. 合同必须由双方签字后才具有法律效用。
3. 由我国驻英国大使馆商务处介绍来的客商已经到了。

"由"是介词，用来引进动作的执行者（施动者）。代表动作接受者（受动者）的名词，可在"由"字前作句子的主语，也可在动词后作宾语。

As a Preposition, 由 introduces the executor (Agent) of an action. The Noun that stands for the receiver (the Patient) of an action can either appear before 由 as the subject of the sentence, or as an object after the Verb.

注意"由"和"被"的区别："被"主要用于被动句，除了引进动作的施动者外，还可以在不披露施动者的情况下，说明受动者所受到的处置、待遇，或受外来动作的影响，发生了什么情况。也就是说，在"被"字句"被"字句里，施动者可以出现，也可以不出现。"被"字句常述的行为，多数有主语（受动者）不希望发生或受到损害的含义，而"由"字结构却没有这种含义。另外，"被"字句可以有其否定形式，而"由"一般都只以肯定形式出现。下列句子只可用"被"，不可用"由"：

Please note the differences between 由 and 被. In addition to introducing an Agent of an action in a sentence in the passive voice, 被 is able to show what has happened to the subject of the sentence, i.e. the Patient of the Verb, without mentioning the Agent. In other words, the Agent may or may not be mentioned in a sentence with 被, yet it is obligatory with 由. While in most cases the 被 structure has a negative connotation that there is some sort of loss, misfortune or inconvenience to the subject of the sentence (the Patient) who is reluctant to receive the action, there is no such connotation with 由. Moreover, 被 may be negated, but 由 is generally in the positive form only. 被 is the only choice in the following sentences:

她的钱包被偷走了。　　　　　小王没被董事长骂了一顿。

✘她的钱包由偷走了。　　　　　✘小王没由董事长骂了一顿。

✘她的钱包由人偷走了。　　　　✘小王没由骂了一顿。

五、……（是）指……　　(to be referred to ... as...; to indicate ...)

l-16. 有约束力的发盘(实盘)<u>是指</u>发盘人明确地、肯定地表达了订立合同的意图。

l-20. 反之，无约束力的发盘(虚盘)<u>是指</u>发盘人没有明确表示肯定要订立合同的意图，……

1. 还盘<u>是指</u>一方接到一项发盘后，因为不完全同意该发盘的某些内容而提出修改的建议。

2. "模棱两可"<u>是指</u>一个人对事情的态度不明确，不说好也不说不好，不肯定　也不否定。

3. 在中国，"下海"<u>是指</u>去当个体户做生意。

"指"是及物动词，带宾语，相当于"意思上指着、表示"的意思，常和"是"配合使用。

指 is a Transitive Verb and thus must take an object. It usually is paired with 是, meaning "to refer to, to mean, to indicate" etc.

六、一旦……就……　　(once..., then...; whenever..., ...would/will... ; in the event of)

l-18. <u>一旦</u>受盘人作出有效的接受，交易立即达成。

1. <u>一旦</u>签订了合同，买卖双方就要承担各自的法律责任。

2. 住在加州的人都习惯自己开车，<u>一旦</u>没有汽车，就会觉得很不方便。

3. 这个港口非常先进，<u>一旦</u>出现问题，电脑系统就会立刻作出适当的处理。

"一旦"原是名词，"一天之间"的意思，形容时间很短。这里是副词，表示"要是有一天"的意思，常常和"就"配合，有时放在动词前，有时放在句首。用于假设，还没有发生的事情。多用于书面语。

一旦 is a Verb by origin, meaning "Within a day". It is an Adverb here, and means "someday, if someday". Sometimes it appears before the Verb, sometimes at the beginning of a sentence. It usually is paired up with 就 and refers to something that has not happened yet. It is normally used in the written language.

七、 不得＋双音节/多音节 Verb Phrase (must not; not allowed to...)

l-19. 发盘人对该盘的内容，<u>不得</u>更改或反悔，否则将要承担违约的后果。

1. 合同签订后，双方都<u>不得</u>随意更改其内容。
2. 仓库重地，未经许可，<u>不得</u>入内。
3. 车多路窄，<u>不得</u>超速行驶。

助动词"得"通常以否定形式出现，表示"不允许、不许可"的意思，多用于公文、法令、广告之类。

The Auxiliary Verb 得 usually appears in the negative form, indicating "not allowed, not permitted". It is normally used in official documents, decrees or bulletins.

"得"可以有双重否定，表示客观情况迫使必须这样做。例如：

得 may have double negation, indicating an action is forced because of the circumstances. For example:

1. 由于天气不好，<u>不得不</u>坐火车。
2. 因为价格太高，我们<u>不得不</u>减少订货。

八、……，否则……　(...otherwise; if not, or else ...)

l-19. 发盘人对该盘的内容，不得更改或反悔，<u>否则</u>将要承担违约的后果。

1. 从事进出口义务，必须随时了解市场的变化，<u>否则</u>就不能取得生意的成功。

2. 学习外语应该经常练习，<u>否则</u>很难学好。

3. 发虚盘时，一般都加上"以我方最后确认为准"或"参考价"等条件，<u>否则</u>会引起误解或争议。

连词"否则"有"不然、要不、如果不是这样"的意思。用在复句后一分句的开头，连接两个分句，表示是前一分句推论的结果，或者提供另一种选择。"否则"后面有时可跟"的话"，但要有停顿。注意"否则"和"不然"的区别。"否则"只作连词，"不然"还可有形容词的用法，可作谓语，或用于句首，否定对方的话。如：

As a Conjunction, 否则 is similar to 不然、要不、如果不是这样 in meaning. It appears at the beginning of the second clause of a Complex Sentence serving to link up the two clauses, showing the inference in accordance with the previous clause, or suggesting another option. Sometimes, it can be followed by 的话, but there must be a pause afterwards. Note the distinction between 否则 and 不然. 否则 is used as a Conjunction only, while 不然 can also be an Adjective, functioning as a predicate. Moreover, it can be placed at the beginning of a sentence to negate the remarks made by the other party, but 否则 cannot. For example:

他以为商贸汉语很难，其实<u>不然</u>。

<u>不然</u>，事情没那么简单。

九、(……)反之，……　(conversely; on the contrary; otherwise)

l-20. <u>反之</u>，无约束力的发盘(虚盘)<u>是指</u>发盘人没有明确表示肯定要订立合同的意图，……

l-30. 如果<u>一</u>项发盘具备了以上的三项基本要求，就是实盘；<u>反之</u>，凡是

不具备这三项基本要求的发盘，都应视为虚盘。

1. 如果商品供不应求，价格就会上涨；<u>反之</u>，商品供过于求，价格就会下降。

2. 商品质量好，价格合理，自然就畅销；<u>反之</u>，商品质量差，再便宜也没有人买。

3. 教育水平和经济地位有密切的关系。一般来说，教育水平越高，经济地位越高；<u>反之</u>，教育水平越低，经济地位也越低。

连词"反之"是书面语，有"与此相反、反过来说"的意思。表示前后情况相反，用在两个分句、句子或段落中间，起转折作用，引出同上文相反的另一个意思。"反之"后面有停顿，前后两个句子或分句是并列成分。

反之 is a Conjunction, meaning 与此相反、反过来说. It is used between two clauses, two sentences, or two paragraphs to indicate the two matters in the former and the latter parts are opposite of each other. There is a pause after 反之, and the two sentences or clauses on either side of it are coordinative in their relationship to each other.

十、(……)因而……　(therefore; hence)

l-21. 无约束力的发盘(虚盘)是指发盘人没有明确表示肯定要订立合同的意图，<u>因而</u>不受该项发盘的约束，……

1. 他们加强了市场调研，及时掌握了市场的动向，<u>因而</u>产品的出口额大增。

2. 这个报盘没有注明交货期，<u>因而</u>是不完整的，应该是个虚盘。

3. 我方的产品品质优良，价格合理，<u>因而</u>在国际市场上很有竞争力。

连词"因而"基本上与"因此"意思相同，用在因果复句中的后一个分句，表示结果或结论。注意"因而"和"所以"的区别："所以"可以和"因为"配合使用，"因而"不行；"所以"可位于第一个分句的开头，"因而"则不行。

Similar to 因此 in meaning, 因而 is used in the second clause of a Complex Sentence of Cause and Effect, indicating a result or conclusion. Note the differences between 因而 and 所以: While 所以 can be associated with 因为, 因而 cannot. In addition, 所以 can appear at the beginning of the first clause, while 因而 cannot.

十一、即使……' 也……　（even if; even though）

l-21. 即使受盘人作出了有效的接受，发盘人也不承担任何法律责任。

1. 你说吧，即使说错了也不要紧。
2. 这种货即使有恐怕也不多了。
3. 即使在十二月，大连港也不结冰。

连词"即使"表示假设兼让步，可用在主语前或后。用"即使"的复句，前后两个分句分别指有关的两件事情。前面常表示一种假设情况，后面表示的结果或结论不受这种情况的影响。有时也可以表示一种极端的情况，如句 3。前后两部分只有一个主谓结构，后一部分是名词或介词短语(只限于"在……""对……""跟……")。"即使"和"即便"多用于书面语，口语里常用"就算、就是、哪怕"。注意："虽然"和"即使"都可表示让步，但"虽然"所说的情况是已然的事实，而"即使"表示的一般是假设的未然情况。

即使 is a Conjunction that denotes hypothesis and concession. It can go before or after the subject of a sentence. In a Complex Sentence that uses 即使, the two clauses refer to two relevant matters: the first one presents a hypothetical situation, and the second one states the result or conclusion regardless of the hypothesized situation. It can also be used in an extreme case, such as in example 3. In such a sentence, there is only one subject — predicate structure in the whole sentence, the second part is a Noun or Prepositional Phrase (only used with 在……、对……、跟……). 即使 and 即便 are mostly used in the written language, while it is more common for 就算、就是、哪怕 to be used in the colloquial language. Although both 虽然 and 即使 can express a concession relation, the situations 虽然 refers to are situations that are primarily facts that have materialized, whereas the ones that 即使 refers to are generally hypotheses.

十二、凡是……都……（every single one; all; any）

l-30. 凡是不具备这三项基本要求的发盘，都应视为虚盘。

1. 凡是进出口的货物，都必须经过海关的检查。
2. 凡是学中文的人都知道中文的声调很难，但也很重要。
3. 凡是愿意和我们做生意的，我们都欢迎。

副词"凡是"用在主语前，统括一定范围内的一切。"凡是"通用于口语和书面语，"凡"多用于书面语。

The Adverb 凡是 appears before the subject, covering every single one within a scope referred by the subject. It is applicable to both the written and the spoken languages, but 凡 is more common in written Chinese.

十三、模棱两可（equivocal; ambiguous）

l-25. 所谓"明确的"，是指发盘的内容清楚确切，没有含糊的、模棱两可的词句……

1. 他是个老好人，从来都不想得罪人，所以在很多事情上，都采取模棱两可的态度。
2. 因为不了解情况，所以她只好说了一些模棱两可的话。
3. 这个问题关系到公司的前途，你是主管，对这件事绝对不能含糊、模棱两可。

"模棱两可"是成语，表示含含糊糊、态度或主张不明确的意思，用来形容人遇事态度暧昧，也作"摸棱两可"。

This is an idiom, which means ambiguity, lack of clarity, and equivocalness of one's stand or point of view. It can also be 摸棱两可.

十四、是否　（whether...; if ...）

1-32. 因此，所谓的"虚"和"实"都是以发盘人<u>是否</u>明确表示愿意对其发盘承担订立合同的法律责任而言的。

1. 除了这个办法之外，<u>是否</u>还有别的办法？

2. 这次谈判，<u>是否</u>总经理也参加？

3. 我不知道他们<u>是否</u>会接受这个报盘。

4. 这种产品在非洲市场<u>是否</u>适销，还要再作进一步的市场调研。

副词"是否"是书面语，相当于口语"是不是"的意思。表示商量、怀疑或不确定的语气，可用于直接问句（句1，2）或陈述句中的间接问句（句3，4）。

"是否" is an Adverb, and is used in the written language. Its equivalent in colloquial speech is "是不是". It carries a tone of consulting, skepticism, or uncertainty. It may be used in direct questions, such as sentences 1 and 2, or in indirect questions, such as sentences 3 and 4.

词义辨析

一、意愿　意图　意向

这三个名词都有同一个词素"意"字，是"心愿、愿望"的意思。"意愿"可以说是"意"的双音节同义词，常带褒义性的定语，作"怀着、实现、表达、违背"等动词的宾语。"意图"是"意愿"和"图谋、策划"的结合，表示"希望达到某种目的、打算"的意思。常带限制性的定语或表示性质(可以是贬义)的定语，在句子中作定语或宾语。"意向"是中性的，指的是带有一定倾向性的意图或目的。

These three Nouns share a Morpheme 意, which means "desire, wish, aspiration". It is possible to say that 意愿 is a disyllabic synonym of 意, and often follows Attributive with a commendatory sense, functioning as Objects of Verbs such as 怀着、实现、表达、违背, etc. 意图 is the combination of "aspiration" and "conspiracy", meaning "the wish to achieve certain purpose". It usually takes a Restrictive Attributive or an Attributive that indicates some kind of nature (may be derogative), and functions as an Attributive or Object in a sentence. The word 意向 is neutral in meaning, referring to some sort of wish or goal with certain inclination.

二、确认　确定　确切

　　动词"确认"是"明确认定"的意思，常带"原则、事实、合同、条款"等抽象名词作宾语，也可带主谓词组作宾语。"确定"是多意词，作动词时，表示"明确地决定下来"的意思，强调把事物从某种非正式、不稳定或不明确的状态固定下来，使它不会改变或转移。如：确定交货日期，确定恋爱关系。"确定"作形容词时，有"明确而肯定"的意思。"确切"是形容词，有两重意思：一是表示"真确可靠"，强调真切，符合事物的本质或事实，多用于修饰"理解、表述、名称"等；二是"准确恰当"的意思，可作定语 (确切的说法)，补语 (描述得很确切) 或状语 (确切地理解)等。

The Verb 确认 refers to "hold or declare clearly and definitely", and often takes abstract Nouns 原则, 事实, 合同, 条款, etc. or a Clause as its Object. 确定 has multiple meaning and functions. When used as a Verb, it emphasizes the sense to make something that is uncertain or unclear fixed or settled so that it will not change again. Typical examples are: 确定交货日期 (to determine the date of delivery), and 确定恋爱关系 (to settle the relationship of boyfriend and girlfriend with somebody). When 确定 is used as an Adjective, it means "clear and definite". Unlike the other two, 确切 is an Adjective. It has two usages. The first one is "true and reliable", which stresses truthfulness, agreeing to a fact, and is mostly used to modify 理解、表述、名称, etc. The second usage is "accurate and appropriate". It can function as Attributive, Complement, or Adverbial, etc. as in the following:

确切的说法　　　(a precise expression)
描述得很确切　　(to describe accurately), and
确切地理解　　　(to understand exactly).

三、 有限　无限　期限

语素"限"表示"指定(的)范围"的意思，可与不同的语素组合，构成不同意思的词。"有限"是形容词，指"有一定的限度"，可作定语或状语。"无限"也是形容词，是"有限"的反义词，即"没有一定的限度"的意思。名词"期限"既可是"限定的一段时间"的意思，也可表示"所限时间的最后界限"的意思，如：合同的期限就要到了。

The character 限 indicates "to set a limit" or "the limit", and can form words with different Morphemes to mean different things. The Adjective 有限 is "limited" and can function as Attributive or Adverbial. Its Antonym is 无限, which means "unlimited". 期限 is a Noun. It can be "the time limit, the allotted time" or "deadline" as in 合同的期限就要到了 (the deadline of the contract is approaching).

四、 决定　商定　肯定

动词"商定"的意思比较单纯，即"经过商量，作出决定"。"决定"既是动词，也是名词。当作动词表示"对如何行动作出主张"时，一般不带动态助词"了"或"着"，如"他们决定报离岸价"。当表示"一事物对其他事物构成先决条件，起主导作用"时，常带动态助词"了"。如"市场的情况决定了价格的高低。""决定"还可作名词，意思是"决定的事项"，常带定语作句子成分，但是不可被程度副词修饰(✘很决定)。"肯定"是多意词，作动词表示"正面承认"的意思，强调同意或愿意作出决定的态度。常带宾语或补语，也可作"予以"、"加以"、"得到"等的宾语。"肯定"作形容词时，表示"承认的、正面的、确定的、明确的"意思，可以被程度副词"十分、非常、很"等修饰。"肯定"加上"地"，可以作状语，修饰动词或形容词，表示"一定、无疑"的意思，但是"肯定"不可作名词用。

The meaning of the Verb 商定 is rather straightforward, i.e. "to decide after discussion". 决定 is both a Noun and a Verb. When functioning as a Verb, meaning "to decide", it normally does not take 了 or 着, as in 他们决定报离岸价. (They have decided to bid F.O.B.). However, when it means "to determine", it often takes the Particle 了 as in the sentence: 市场的情况决定了价格的高低. (The market situation determines the price). When 决定 functions as a Noun, it means "decision". It often goes with an Attributive, but cannot be modified by an Adverb of Degree. It is ungrammatical to say 很决定. 肯定 has several meanings. When it is a Verb, it means "to affirm, to approve", and often takes an Object or a Complement. It can also function as the Object of words like 予以、加以、得到, etc. When it is an Adjective, it means "positive, affirmative, definite", and can be modified by Adverbs such as 十分、一定、无疑. It cannot, however, function as a Noun.

五、修改　更改　改动

　　虽然这三个动词都带同一词素"改"，但侧重各有不同。"修改"着重就文章的文字或计划的安排作出改动，主观上使之效果更好。"修改"可以大改，也可小改；可能会改好，也可能会改坏。"改正"主要指把错误的改成正确的，但不仅限于文章和计划。"更改"是"改换、变动"的意思，对象多为"日期、计划、决定、方案、路线"等，也可作"有(所)、作、进行"等动词的宾语。及物动词"改动"，主要用在文字、项目、次序等方面，带上定语后，可活用为名词，如："这些文字上的改动更好地体现了原作的意思。"

Although these Verbs all share the character 改, each has a different focus. 修改 emphasizes the revision of an essay or modification of a plan, with the intention to make it better. While the revision or change may be minor or significant, the result may be either better or worse. 改正 means "to correct or rectify", and is not limited to essays or plans. 更改 means "to alter, to change", and often takes 日期、计划、决定、方案、路线, etc. as its Objects. It can also follow Verbs like 有(所), 作 or 进行. The Transitive Verb 改动 is primarily used with Nouns such as 文字、项目、次序. It can function as a Noun when adding an Attributive before it. For example:

这些文字上的改动更好地体现了原作的意思。

(The change of wording has given a much better expression to the original work.)

六、 具备　完备　预备　准备

动词"具备"除了"具有、存在"的意思外，还有"完备、齐备"之意。"具备"的使用范围比较窄，一般只限于具体的"条件、技能、本领、素质"等。"完备"可作形容词，表示"齐全、应有尽有"，一般多用于形容事物，可受程度副词"十分、非常"等修饰。此外，"完备"也可作及物动词带宾语或补语作谓语，表示"使完备、使齐全"的意思。"预备"是动词，有"预先准备"之意，着重于事先筹办、准备，以供将来使用。"预备"也指进入正式阶段前的筹划，可直接修饰名词，如"预备会议"、"预备会员"。"预备"强调的是时间性，一般不受其他名词的修饰，也不跟在动词"作"的后面当宾语。"准备"则强调针对性或目的性，着重按照一定的要求或需要事先创造条件，常受"物质、思想、心理、精神"等名词的修饰，也可以作动词"作"的宾语。

In addition to the meaning of "to have, to exist", the Verb 具备 also indicates that something is "complete, all ready". It is used specifically with 条件、技能、本领、素质, etc. 完备 is an Adjective, meaning "have everything that one expects to find, all is available". It is primarily used to describe objects, and can be modified by Adverbs of Degree such as 十分、非常. In addition, 完备 can be a Transitive Verb that takes an Object or a Complement, indicating "to complete, to make everything available". The Verb 预备 is "to prepare" in meaning, and it stresses "to get ready in advance". It can also mean "the arrangement before the formal start of something", modifying a Noun directly, as in 预备会议, and 预备会员. 预备 emphasizes "timeliness". It is not modified by any Nouns in general, nor does it follow 作 as its Object. Another Verb 准备, which means "to prepare" in its English translation, is goal oriented and is focused on creating conditions beforehand according to certain requirements or needs. It is usually modified by Nouns such as 物质、思想、心理、精神. Moreover, it can also follow 作 as its Object.

语法

一、选择复句 Alternative Complex Sentences

选择复句是联合复句的一种。它包含两个或两个以上的分句，分别提出不同的事情，要从中选择一个。叙述句的选择复句常用以下的关联词语：

An Alternative Complex Sentence is a subcategory of Coordinate Complex Sentences. It contains two or more clauses, providing two or more options to choose from. The following Connectives are commonly used in the declarative forms of Alternative Complex Sentences:

"（或者）……或者……"、"……，或……"、"要么……要么……"、"要就是……要就是……"、"不是……就是……"。

每一笔生意的成交，总是由一方先主动与另一方联系，表达要购买或出售某种商品的意愿，提出自己的或了解对方的交易条件而开始的。

或者发电子邮件，或者发传真，他们都能收到。

现在美国卖的这类产品，不是中国出口的，就是韩国出口的，很少有美国自己生产的。

这是我方最后的一次报价，请你们认真考虑。要么就按这些条件成交，要么就谈到这儿为止，我们的报价不可能再低了。

选择复句的疑问形式，不论是直接问句还是间接问句，关联词都是用"（是）……还是……"。如：

The question form of an Alternative Complex Sentence, whether it is a direct or indirect question, uses the correlative（是）……还是……. For example:

怎么辨别一项发盘是实盘还是虚盘呢？

小杨还没决定到底学医好还是学商好。

二、定语 (1)　Attributive (1)

(一) 定语和中心语　Attributive and Head

定语是在句子中修饰或限制主语和宾语（多数是名词，但不只限于名词。）的句子成份。被修饰的词语叫中心语。除特殊情况外，汉语的定语总是在中心语的前面。注意下列词组在词序和意思上的区别：

An Attributive is the part that modifies or restricts the subject and object (mostly Nouns but not necessarily all Nouns) in a sentence, and the part to be modified is called the Head. An Attributive always precedes the Head in Chinese, except in rare, special occasions. Note the differences in word order and meaning in the following:

定语＋中心语		定语＋中心语	
小陈的	照片	照片上的	小陈
左边的	桌子	桌子的	左边

正确了解定语和中心语的位置和关系，对于清楚地准确地理解原文的意思，特别是处理有多层修饰关系的复杂长句，提高汉语的阅读能力和写作能力，都有非常重要的实际意义。在阅读时，尤其要留意汉语的习惯，注意汉语和英语有关定语词序上的区别。

It is vitally important to understand correctly the positions of the Attributive and the Head, and their relationship. Such understanding is very helpful for comprehending the meaning of authentic texts with clarity and accuracy, particularly in dealing with long complicated sentences with multiple modifiers. In reading, special attention should be paid to the distinction between Chinese and English in terms of the word order and customs in the use of Attributive.

(二) 定语的分类　Categories of Attributive

按照定语和中心语在意义上的关系，定语可分为两大类：限制性的定语和描述性的定语。

In accordance with the relationship between the Attributive and the Head with respect to meaning, Attributives can be divided into two types: Restrictive Attributive and Descriptive Attributive.

1. 限制性的定语——限制性的定语是从数量、时间、处所、归属和范围等方面来说明中心语的定语。它主要指明中心语是"哪一个"，以区别于和它同时存在的人或事物。例如：

   Restrictive Attributive — A Restrictive A ttributive is the one that explains the Head in terms of amount, time, location, ownership, scope, etc. Its function is primarily to show "which one" is the Head, so as to distinguish others that co-occur with it. For example:

   a. 数量：我要写<u>几封</u>信。

      <u>很多</u>公司都感兴趣。

   b.时间：经过<u>两个星期的</u>谈判，他们才达成了协议。

      谁拿了<u>昨天的</u>报纸？

   c. 处所：任何人也不能动<u>总经理办公室里的</u>东西。

      <u>合同上的</u>交易条件写得很清楚。

   d. 归属：台湾是<u>中国领土的</u>一部分。

      领属：黄小姐是<u>吴董事长的</u>秘书。

   e. 限定范围：根据<u>海关关于进口物品的</u>规定，你们必须交百分之三十的税。

      <u>他们中间</u>的几位都是学经济的。

2. 描写性的定语——描写性的定语是从性质、状态、特徵、用途、质料、职业等方面来描写中心语的定语。它着重指明中心语是"什么样的"，而不太在乎其他同类的人或事物是否同时存在。例如：

   Descriptive Attributive — A Descriptive Attributive is the one that describes the Head with respect to its nature, status, usage, material, occupation, etc. It highlights "what" or "how" the Head is, but is not so concerned as to whether there exists anyone or anything with the Head simultaneously. For instance:

　　　　a. 性质：这是一项<u>没有法律约束力的</u>发盘。

　　　　　　　　无论是<u>口头的或书面的</u>接受，都是一种<u>有效的</u>承诺。

　　　　b. 状态：他把那辆<u>修好了的</u>车开走了。

　　　　　　　　中国是一个<u>发展中的</u>国家。

　　　　c. 特徵：实盘的内容清楚明确，没有<u>含糊的、模棱两可的</u>词句。

　　　　　　　　我们老板是个<u>矮矮、胖胖的</u>老头儿。

　　　　d. 用途：这是一种<u>专门接送孩子们上学的</u>汽车。

　　　　　　　　他们要订五千个<u>比赛用的</u>足球。

　　　　e. 质料：我看用<u>纸</u>箱包装就可以了。

　　　　　　　　山上有一所<u>石头</u>房子。

　　　　f. 职业：她毕业后在一家<u>会计</u>事务所工作。

　　　　　　　　<u>汉语</u>老师不一定都是中国人。

(三) 可作定语的词语和 "的" 字的使用　Words and Phrases Used as Attributives and the Use of "的"

　　可以作定语的词语，主要有数量词、名词 (短语)、代词、形容词 (短语)、动词 (动宾/动补短语)、主谓短语 (小句)、固定 (联合、偏正、介词) 短语等。一般来说，定语后常带有"的"字，但不是所有的定语都要带"的"字作为它的形式标志。请注意下列的句子和说明。

　　The words and phrases that can serve as Attributives are: Numerals and Measure Words, Nouns (Noun Phases), Pronouns, Adjectives (Adjective Phrases), Verbs (Verb Phrases such as Verb-Object/Verb-Complement Phrases), clauses, fixed (Coordinate, Endocentric, Prepositional) phrases, etc. In most cases, there is a 的 after an Attributive, but not all Attributives need a 的 as the marker of an Attributive. Please note the distinctions and illustrations of the following:

1. 数量词作定语　Numerals as Attributives

必须用"的"字	不必用"的"字
表示描写关系（什么样的）： 在美国，21岁以下的青少年 不许买酒。 我要买四张六毛钱的邮票。	表示描写关系（哪一个）： 那几本书是她借的。
表示"满"的意思： 看你这一头的汗。	表示具体的数量（多少）： 今天收到了上百份订单，赶快找两个人来帮忙处理。
分数、百分数后： 那个学校三分之一的学生都 不会游泳。 这个工厂百分之七十的工人 都是女的。	量词重叠： 他说的种种情况都是可能的。 小王学习用功，门门功课都是五分。
数词"一"与量词构成的短语重叠： 这里建起了一座一座的新工厂。	非具体数量： 她喝了一些/很多茶，睡不着。

2. 名词作定语　Nouns as Attributives

必须用"的"字	不必用"的"字
表示领属关系： 这是图书馆的书，别弄脏了。 楼下传来了孩子们的笑声。	表示人或事物的性质（原料或职业）： 不用买玻璃杯，塑料杯就可以了。 他爸爸是个电影演员。
表示时间： 下学期的时间表已经出来了。	合成词组： 业务关系、电子邮件、法律制度、研究生宿舍
表示处所： 中间的椅子比较舒服。	专名和固定词组： 首都机场、长城饭店、邮政编码、电视新闻

3. 代词作定语　Pronouns as Attributives

必须用"的"字	不必用"的"字
强调亲属关系时： 他是我的儿子，也是你的儿子！	表示亲属关系： 我母亲、她妹妹、你老师
表示领属关系（中心语多为事物）： 这儿有你的信。 我不太了解她的学习情况。	表示所属的单位： 他们公司、你们学校、我国
表示处所： 那儿的气候怎么样？	"什么、多少"： 什么时候/地方、多少钱/时间
表示方式、式样： 我们也有这样的电脑。 老胡不是那样的人。	"这、那"表示限制、特指： 那笔交易怎么样了？ 这三份合同、那几个月

4. 形容词作定语　Adjectives as Attributives

必须用"的"字	不必用"的"字
双音节形容词，特别是修饰单音节名词时： 舒服的床、宁静的夜、谦虚的人	单音节形容词： 好学生、老朋友、新书、大碗
重叠形容词： 红红的脸、蓝蓝的天、高高的个子、干干净净的房间、斯斯文文的举止	固定词组： 老实人、正经事、糊涂虫、马虎眼、一般情况、重大问题、关键时刻、优良品质
表示强调/对比的单音节形容词： 你用这台新的电脑，我用那个旧的。	形容词短语： 很多时候、好多客户、不少国家、少量样品

5. 动词作定语　Verbs as Attributives

必须用"的"字	不必用"的"字
单音节动词，尤其区别于动宾结	双音节动词和时间、地点、方式、

构的： 吃的东西、穿的衣服、学的课文、开的车	方法、手段、现象、问题、情况等名词的组合： 开会时间、交货地点、支付方式、学习方法、迟到现象、运输问题、合作情况、考试成绩、促销手段
主谓词组： 双方签订的合同、小张唱的歌	
动宾词组： 戴眼镜的老师、说台湾话的商人	
动补词组： 做不完的工作、洗干净的毛巾	

6. 固定短语/句子作定语　Fixed Phrases, Idioms and Sentences as Attributives

固定短语或句子作定语，都要加"的"字。例如：

When a fixed expression or a sentence functions as an Attributive, 的 must be added before the Head. For example:

1) 介词短语 (Prepositional Phrase)：
> 这是对我们有利的条件。
> 跟赵经理一起出国的小田病了。
> 你看到从上海发来的传真没有？

2) 成语、惯用语、四字词组 (Idioms, Four-Character Fixed Expressions)：
> 讨价还价的人、　模棱两可的词句、　马马虎虎的态度

3) 句子、复句 (Clauses/Complex Sentences)：
> 她两天就看完了这本妈妈花了几个星期才借回来的书了。
> 不但了解自己，而且知道对方的情况的商人做生意一般都比较成功。
> 老杨把这个因为交易条件写得不清楚而造成了误解的报盘拿出来给大家来讨论。

修辞

词义的褒贬　The Commendatory and Derogatory Meaning of Words

汉语中有些词明显地带有肯定、赞扬、喜爱的感情色彩，像"发展、努力、伟大、温暖、可爱、干净、女强人"等，这类词叫褒义词。相反，有些词在没有上下文的情况下也带有否定、贬斥、憎恶的感情色彩，比如"落后、虚伪、贪心、狡猾、自私、愚蠢、母老虎"等，这类词就叫贬义词。处在这两类词中间，既没有褒义又没有贬义色彩的词，叫中性词。很多表示物件或颜色的词，都是中性词，例如"桌子、椅子、课本、字典、红、黄、蓝、白、黑"等。有不少词，需要在一定的语境或加上其他成份才能显出褒义或贬义来，像"出卖（朋友）"、"做（作）"、"（奸）笑"、"（说话）随便"、"（皮包）公司"、"（经济）动物"、"（不是个）东西"等。

In Chinese, there are words with distinct emotional features such as approval, appraisal, and the like. Take the words 发展、努力、文明、温暖、可爱、干净、女强人 for example, they are called Commendatory Terms. In contrast, there are words that indicate negative, denouncing, and abhorrent meanings even without clear context. For example, words like 落后、虚伪、贪心、狡猾、自私、愚蠢、母老虎 are some of them. These words are called Derogatory Terms. Words that carry neither commendatory nor derogatory meaning are called Neutral Terms. Many words that represent objects and colors are neutral terms, such as 桌子、椅子、课本、字典、红、黄、蓝、白、黑. Quite a lot of words will have a positive or negative connotation only in a certain context or when associated with other elements. Examples are: 出卖（朋友）、做（作）、（奸）笑、（说话）随便、（皮包）公司、（经济）动物、（不是个）东西, etc.

因此，我们学生词时，除了要知道一个词字面上的意思，还要了解这个词的感情色彩，褒贬的含义和使用的场合。尤其要注意不要只看英语的词义翻译。因为有的词在英语中可能是中性或者是褒义的，但在汉语却可能是贬义的，反之亦然。例如，英语的"个人主义者

(individualist)"、"特务/间谍 (agent)"、"骄傲 (proud)"并没有什么不好的意思，但是在汉语里却会有贬义的含义。相反，汉语的某些常用词，像"宣传 (propaganda)"、"爱人('wife' or 'lover' literally)"、"聪明 (clever; intelligent)"等完全是褒义词，英语的翻译就可能有贬义的含义。

Hence, when we learn a new word, we should understand the emotional flavor, the positive or negative connotation of the word, and the context of its use, in addition to knowing the literal meaning of the word. We should be cautious with the English translation/interpretation of words in textbooks, and not rely totally on the English translation. The reason is that some of the words are neutral or positive in English but may have a negative connotation in Chinese, or vise versa. For instance, there is no negative connotation in English in these words such as "individualist"（个人主义者）, "agent"（特务/间谍）or "proud"（骄傲）. However, their Chinese counterparts do carry a derogatory meaning. Likewise, words like 宣传 (propaganda), 爱人 (wife or 'lover' literall), or 聪明 (clever) are commendatory or neutral in Chinese, but this is not the case in English.

练习

一、用线将意思相同的词和词语连起来：

表示心意和愿望	改正
对别人达到某种目的的打算知道得不清楚	确认
把原定的时间从某一天改为另一天	期限
把错误改为正确的	公函
数量不多；有一定的限度	确信
指定的时间，不许超过	表达意愿
明确认定	更改日期
毫不怀疑、确实相信	函(邮)购
通过写信来买东西	不了解意图
公家而不是私人的信件	有限

二、 用括号里的词或词组改写下列句子，但不改变其基本意思，必要时可对词序作一定的调整：

1. 任何人都不可以用公司的传真机发私人信件，要不然就会受到处罚。
   　　　　　　　　　　　　　　　　　　　　　（不得、以、否则、将）

2. "知彼知己，百战百胜"说的是必须充分了解对方和自己的情况，才能取得成功；相反，如果对自己和对方的情况都不明，就会失败。
   　　　　　　　　　　　　　　　　　　　　（是指、只有、反之）

3. 商场就好像战场一样，有时哪怕只慢了一分钟，生意也会受损失。
   　　　　　　　　　　　　　　　　　　　　　　（如同、即使）

4. 买方已口头接受了这个报价，他们一反悔，就会被看成是违约。
   　　　　　　　　　　　　　　　　　　　　　　（一旦、视为）

5. 我不喜欢对方那种不说肯定也不说否定的态度，与他们合作，我一点兴趣也没有。　　　　　　　　　　（模棱两可、本人、毫无）

6. 对大多数客户来说，我们的商品都是非常有竞争力的。只要跟我们做过生意的，都会觉得我们的报价是合理的。　　　（而言、凡是）

7. 通常说的"知己知彼"，是不是"了解自己也了解别人"的意思？
   　　　　　　　　　　　　　　　　　　　　　（所谓的、是否）

8. 这种产品目前在国际市场上的销售情况，他短时间也很难了解，就这样，他就报了个虚盘。　　　　　　　（一时、因而）

三、 选择最合适的词填空：

1. 对方的_____很简单，就是等我方降价以后，大量订货，然后控制当地的市场。
   a. 意愿　　　　　b. 意向　　　　　c. 意图

2. 建立一个全国性的大型销售网，是王董事长退休前的_____。
   a. 意愿　　　　　b. 意向　　　　　c. 意图

3. 我们是不是_____一个时间，进一步讨论交货期和支付等条件。
   a. 确定   b. 确认   c. 确切

4. 因为对方还没有_____他们的报价，这份合同先不要做。
   a. 确定   b. 确认   c. 确切

5. 这个计划是董事会讨论_____的，怎么会随便改变呢？
   a. 商定   b. 肯定   c. 决定

6. 老师充分_____同学们的进步，同时也指出了大家还存在的问题。
   a. 商定   b. 肯定   c. 决定

7. 时间_____，请你赶快给他发一个传真。
   a. 期限   b. 无限   c. 有限

8. 如果买方到了支付_____还不付款，就是违约。
   a. 期限   b. 无限   c. 有限

9. 她写信总是喜欢_____一下再寄出。
   a. 改动   b. 更改   c. 修改

10. 我们最近搬了家，所以要_____一下原来的电话号码。
    a. 改动   b. 更改   c. 修改

11. 他们是个小公司，现在还不_____生产这种高科技产品的条件。
    a. 具备   b. 完备   c. 预备

12. 这批货物的进口手续_____，不会有什么问题。
    a. 具备   b. 完备   c. 预备

四、 找出课文里的选择复句。

五、 用括号里的选择复句完成下列对话：

1. 甲：这批货……？   （是……还是……）
   乙：报虚盘或者报实盘都可以。

2. 甲：哎，那本《汉英字典》上哪儿去了？

　　乙：　　　　　（不是……就是……）

3. 甲：我已经大学二年级了，可是还没选专业，你看我学什么好呢？

　　乙：……，赶快决定吧。　（要么……要么……）

4. 甲：怎样跟他们联系呢？

　　乙：……都行。(或者……或者……)

5. 甲：为什么小张今天没来上课？

　　乙：　　　　　（不是……就是……）

6. 甲：你想喝什么？我有茶，也有咖啡。

　　乙：只要不麻烦，……(……或者……)

7. 甲：陈经理，这份合同我下星期才交给你，可以吗？

　　乙：不行，……（要么……要么……）

六、 连接左边定语和右边的词或词组，看哪些能构成合乎逻辑的偏正关系名词短语。注意哪些要用"的"字，哪些不用"的"字：

1.	新	客户	产品	报价
2.	美国	大使馆	车	答复
3.	很多	朋友	衣服	交易
4.	两种	学生	情况	后果
5.	她	哥哥	桌子	意愿
6.	王经理	律师	计算机	看法
7.	装运		货物	方式/期
8.	北京	人	马路	春天
9.	模棱两可		词语	态度
10.	口头		语	承诺/形式
11.	必不可少	太太	文件	条件/环节

12.	法律	代表	问题	程序/约束力
13.	前面	银行	港口	内容
14.	高		山	水平
15.	有限	公司	地方	帮助/时间
16.	干干净净	手	房间	习惯
17.	非常简单		电脑	包装
18.	电子	狗	邮件	科技
19.	邀请参观	一方	信函	办法
20.	一般	进口商	字典	关系

七、 找出下列句子的定语和中心语，然后删去所有的定语，再对比删改前后句子之间的差别：

1. 会说几国外语的周文静小姐是我们公司最年轻的副总经理。

2. 那个成立不到半年的中外合资企业目前还没有你说的这种免费服务。

3. 关董事长要见的那位可以帮助我们在南美洲推销中国布鞋的巴西华侨商人已经来了。

4. 家在农村，父母没有上过中学，自己连北京、上海这样的大城市都没去过的小莫明天就要到英国最有名的大学去留学了。

5. 从天津学习回来的几位有经验的师傅正在教这些刚进厂的新工人用电脑检验产品质量的先进技术。

6. 今年才二十六岁、还在念博士的研究生孙晓亮在老师的帮助下，把这个数学界几十年来都没有解决的难题一下就解决了。

八、 改正下列句子中的错误：

1. 去年他们进口了很多新美国的电脑。

2. 那个城市每年都举办这样两次的出口的商品展览会。

3. 有约束力和无约束力的发盘，也就是所谓的实盘和虚盘。

4. 因为没有足够时间，所以小黄没去拜访那位的老先生。

5. 如果方便，请给我们寄有关一些你们的公司的资料。

6. 方明妈妈是我好的朋友小学的老师。

7. 我问了她几个问题有关日本市场情况，可是她只给了我一个模棱两可回答。

8. 即使80多岁老人，也会打国际长途的电话。

9. 我们已收到贵公司的传真邀请我方参加交易会明年春天。

10. 西门子是一个德国的非常的有名的大公司。

九、 区别下列词语意义的褒贬，用（＋）表示褒义，用（－）表示贬义，用（0）表示中性：

帮派（　　）　　标榜（　　）　　标致（　　）　　好为人师（　　）

假扮（　　）　　假冒（　　）　　不凡（　　）　　花言巧语（　　）

小康（　　）　　多事（　　）　　高傲（　　）　　沉鱼落雁（　　）

俗丽（　　）　　小心眼（　　）　　说大话（　　）　　嬉皮笑脸（　　）

笑面虎（　　）　　帮倒忙（　　）　　笨鸟先飞（　　）　　大手大脚（　　）

十、把下列句子翻译成汉语：

1. Once the general manager has decided to sell a certain kind of goods, she will explicitly [i.e. "clearly"] express her idea [i.e. "intention"], without any [i.e. "not a bit"] ambiguity. Sometimes, even though she knows there may be serious consequences, she won't change her plan.

2. This contract is short of one item in its content; therefore, it is incomplete. We don't know whether the seller can revise the contract within 3 days. Otherwise, we cannot sign it and have to cancel this contract.

3. Please do not misunderstand my intent. By proposing "an offer without engagement", it is meant that we are not going to settle a deal immediately. Whenever I am not sure momentarily whether it is the best price, I will make "an offer without engagement". In this way, I can take initiative, (so as) to avoid unnecessary trouble.

4. Accepting a spoken offer, like a written offer, is viewed as a valid promise. Thus, it has the same legal binding power [i.e. "restrictions"]. No matter whether it is the seller or the buyer, no party can go back on his word once they have accepted the trade conditions.

文化与商贸背景知识

✎ 敬辞与谦辞

(一) 敬辞

　　敬辞是对别人表示尊敬的言辞。比如问对方姓名，会用"贵姓"或"尊姓大名"；请别人来，会说"敬请光临"或"请赏光"；请别人原谅会说"请海涵"等。敬辞一般都含有第二人称代词的意思，所以用起来不再加"您"或"你"。下面是一些常见的敬辞：

1. 贵＋名词（尊称对方和对方有关的人或事物。）
   贵姓？（问姓氏）　贵庚？（问同辈年龄）　贵国（称对方的国家）
   贵方（称对方）贵校（称对方的学校）　贵府（称对方的家）　贵公司（称对方的公司）

2. 令（"美好"、"善"的意思，后接名词，称对方的家人。）
   令尊（你父亲）　令堂（你母亲）　令妻（你太太）　令兄（你哥哥）
   令妹（你妹妹）　令郎（你儿子）　令爱（你女儿）

3. 尊（"敬重"的意思，后接名词，称对方有关的人或事物。）
   尊姓大名？（问对方姓名）　尊府（您家）　　尊亲（您父母）

尊意（您的意见、想法）　尊夫人（您太太）　悉听尊便（随您的便；听您的）

4. 敬＋动词（表示尊敬、恭敬，用于自己对别人的行为。）

敬请（恭敬地请）　敬告（恭敬地告知对方）　敬奉（恭敬地接受）　敬候（恭敬地等候）　敬祝（恭敬地祝愿对方）

敬谢不敏（"不敏"即"不聪明，没有才能"的意思，用来推辞做某事的客气话。）

5. 惠＋动词（表示对方加惠于自己，对自己有好处，用于对方对自己的行为。）

惠临（对方来）　惠顾（对方向自己买东西）　惠存（请对方收下留念）　惠复（对方给自己复信）　惠鉴（请对方看自己写的信）　惠赐（对方给自己东西）

（二）谦辞

谦辞是自己表示谦虚的言辞。在交际中，汉语的习惯是说话人常把自己或与自己有关的人或事物有意降低其地位或等级，表示谦虚和客气。谦辞可在不少场合见到，如：别人夸奖自己时，一般都予以否认，说"哪里哪里"或者"过奖过奖"、"不敢当"；别人感谢自己时，可以说"举手之劳，不足挂齿"；向对方提出请求或说出自己的意见时，会加上"冒昧"、"提出个人的浅见"或"不成熟的意见"；在别人面前展示自己的技艺时，说"献丑"、"见笑"；给别人送礼时说"薄礼一份，不成敬意"；请别人吃饭作客说"没有什么菜"、"招待不周"等等。

另外，称呼自己家、家人或自己的东西时，也会加上一些带贬义的字眼。比如称自己家为"寒舍"、"舍下"；称自己的妻子为"贱内"、"内子"；称自己的丈夫为"外子"；称自己的儿子为"犬子"；如果自己比对方的年纪大，称自己为"愚兄"、"愚姐"；称自己写的文章为"拙作"等等。

敬辞和谦辞一般在公文信件中使用得较多，但是在知识分子（特别是老年知识分子）的口语以及一些较正式的社交场合也比较常见。正确地使用敬辞和谦辞，不但对别人的尊重，而且也可以表现一个人的学识和修养。但是使用时要注意对象和场合，千万不要乱用。

✐ 报价单、价格表、形式发票

报价单是卖方事先印好的固定格式，其中包括商品名称、规格、数量、单价等项目，供卖方发盘时具体填写。报价单多适用于规格复杂或花色品种繁多的商品，特别是汽车零件、机器配件、小工具、日用轻工业品等。报价单可以是实盘，也可以是虚盘。

价格表也叫价目表，一般都有固定格式，其中包括商品名称、品质、规格、单价等项目。价格表多适用于日用轻工业品的交易，由出口人定期寄送给客户，供客户参考。价格表一般不属于实盘性质。

形式发票也叫做预开发票，一般都有固定格式。亚非地区某些国家，为了管制进口和控制外汇支出，常明文规定，进口商必须凭外国供货人提供的形式发票才能申请进口许可证。形式发票的格式同正式发票相类似，主要内容包括：抬头人的名称和地址、商品的名称、规格、包装、数量、单价、总值、交货期以及支付方式等项目。此外，在形式发票中，一般还规定有效期，并列有"以我方最后确认为准"或"仅供申请进口许可证之用"等文句。

东 方 科 学 仪 器 进 出 口 公 司
THE ORIENTAL SCIENTIFIC INSTRUMENTS IMPORT & EXPORT CORPORATION

中国 · 北京西城区三里河路52号

52 San-Li -He Road, Beijing, China

Tel: 2614983

Telex: 20063 OSIC CN

Fax: 8512412

报 价 单
Q U O T A T I O N

Messrs.

No. 92641423

LEGEND TECHNOLOGY LTD.

Date. Apr 28, 1992

FLAT A.14/F., SUMMIT INSUSTRIAL BLDG. 9 SUN YIP STREET,

CAI WAN Hong Kong

Your Ref.

货 名 及 规 格 Name of Commodity & Specification	数量及单位 Qty & Unit	单 价 price	合 计 Amount
COMPUTER SYSTEM	1	2075.00	2075.00

经 最 后 确 认 为 准
SUBJECT TO OUR FINAL CONF IRMATION

东 方 科 学 仪 器 进 出 口 公 司
THE ORIENTAL SCIENTIFIC INSTRUMENTS IMPORT & EXPORT CORPORATION

中国 · 北京西城区三里河路52号

52 San-Li -He Road, Beijing, China

Tel: 2614983

Telex: 20063 OSIC CN

Fax: 8512412

报 价 单
Q U O T A T I O N

Messrs.	No. 92641423
HEAL TH INTERNAT IONAL LIMITED	Date. Apr 28, 1992
RIVEBANK HOUSE PUTNEY BRIDGE APPROACH LONDON	
SW6 3JD U.K.	Your Ref.

货 名 及 规 格 Name of Commodity & Specification	数量及单位 Qty & Unit	单 价 price	合 计 Amount
SHUI NIU JIAO POWDER	20	9.50	190.00
			190.00

经 最 后 确 认 为 准
SUBJECT TO OUR FINAL CONF IRMATION

報 價 單

1998年批發專用 (本報價不含5%税金)

產品編號	品名規格	單位	單價	產品編號	品名規格	單位	單價
003P	30MM 紫晶光圓球	個	650	237	牛 65MM	頭	850
004P	40MM 紫晶光圓球	個	980	237-1	臺灣水牛 90MM	頭	1300
005P	50MM 紫晶光圓球	個	1700	237-2	牛轉乾坤 70MM	個	900
013-0	30MM 透明切面球	個	340	237-4	牛伯伯 80MM	個	1100
014-3	40MM 透明切面球	個	600	237XL	進寶牛 (大) 160MM	個	7000
015-3	50MM 透明切面球	個	1500	238N	老虎 (新) 100MM	隻	800
016-1	60MM 透明切面球	個	1900	239	公雞 70MM	隻	900
201	鳳梨 50MM	個	700	240	鯉魚	條	850
202	大象 65MM	隻	750	241	母雞 55MM	隻	850
204	玩具熊 50MM	隻	750	242	小雞 35MM	隻	480
207	天鵝	隻	600	243A	水晶麒麟獎座 (單)	個	2200
208	貓頭鷹 60MM	隻	600	243B	水晶麒麟獎座 (雙)	個	4100
211	小兔子 50MM	隻	430	244	小伯恩狗 45MM	隻	480
214	鱷魚	隻	500	245	大伯恩狗 70MM	隻	900
215	立馬	隻	650	246	駱駝	隻	1100
217	無角立馬 70MM	隻	650	247	神燈 90MM	個	1400
219	小狗 40MM	隻	450	248	狼狗 65MM	隻	800
220	大狗 60MM	隻	550	249	土狗 60MM	隻	800
221	獅頭魚身	個	700	250	12 生肖木制禮盒裝	套	9500
222	大袋鼠 80MM	隻	500	251	聚寶盆	個	1800
224	大烏龜	隻	650	252	迷你咖啡壺	個	450
225	大兔子 70MM	隻	700	252-01	迷你杯子	個	250
227	大鹿	隻	750	252-02	迷你咖啡研磨機	個	450
228	豬 60MM	隻	750	252-03	迷你香水瓶	個	350
228A	進寶豬	個	420	252-04	迷你水壺	個	350
228B	母子豬	對	1200	252-05	迷你油燈	盞	300
229	彌勒佛	個	950	252-06	迷你香檳杯	個	300
230	躍馬	匹	1000	252-07	迷你椒鹽罐	個	580
231N	山羊	隻	850	252-08	迷你晚餐鈴	個	250
232	龍	條	900	252-09	迷你台燈	盞	400
233	猴子 65MM	隻	700	253	無尾熊 75MM	隻	850
234	蛇 60MM	條	600	254	椰子樹 (單株)	棵	950
235	鼠 50MM	隻	800	255	椰子樹 (隻株)	棵	950

1998年8月15日修訂　　　　捷越實業有限公司　TEL: (02)798-6830　FAX: 798-0711

南方罐头食品进出口公司

产品批发价格表

品 名	规 格	货 币	单 价
(一) 水果制品			
糖水荔枝	15盎斯罐装	港币	120港元/每打
糖水龙眼	15盎斯罐装	港币	130港元/每打
甜芒果干	8盎斯袋装	港币	80港元/每打
蜜桔片	15盎斯罐装	港币	100港元/每打
糖水桃片	12盎斯罐装	港币	90港元/每打
石榴汁	15盎斯罐装	港币	110港元/每打
蜜饯果脯	10盎斯盒装	港币	80港元/每打
(二) 蔬菜制品			
清水蘑菇	15盎斯罐装	港币	60港元/每打
玉米笋	15盎斯罐装	港币	50港元/每打
鲜嫩竹笋	1磅罐装	港币	60港元/每打
四川榨菜	12盎斯罐装	港币	50港元/每打
去皮番茄(淡)	2磅罐装	港币	70港元/每打
酸辣小黄瓜	12盎斯罐装	港币	50港元/每打
(三) 调味品			
特级酱油	22盎斯瓶装	港币	84港元/每打
厨用米酒	22盎斯瓶装	港币	90港元/每打
蒜蓉辣椒酱	13盎斯瓶装	港币	90港元/每打
甜豆瓣酱	10盎斯瓶装	港币	50港元/每打
高级餐用香醋	15盎斯瓶装	港币	84港元/每打

　　本价格表所列价格均为香港船上交货价。由于以上商品的市场价格随成本价浮动，所以成交时的交货价也随之有相应变化。如对出口包装有特别要求，敬请另洽商定。

PRO-FORMA INVOICE
形 式 发 票

RECEIVER'S ADDRESS
收 件 人 地 址

DESCRIPTION OF GOODS
品 名

REASON FOR SENDING
发 件 用 途

COUNTRY OF ORIGIN
发 件 地

NUMBER OF PACKAGES
数 量

VALUE

(If of no <u>commercial</u> value, please give

<u>Value for the Customs Purposes Only</u>)

价 值

(若无<u>商业价值</u>，请填上报关价值)

SIGNATURE OR COMPANY STAMP
签 字 或 盖 章

(PRO-FORMA INVOICE MUST BE IN ENGLISH, AND ALL VALUE IN U. S. DOLLARS)
(形式发票须用英文填写，价值须换成美元)

价格谈判

✎ **思考下面的问题，然后带着这些问题去阅读课文：**

一、什么是价格谈判？

二、价格通常指什么？国际贸易中的价格还包含什么？

三、国际贸易中有哪些常见的价格术语？

四、做进出口贸易一般怎样选择不同的价格条款？

课文：价格谈判

　　无论做小额生意还是大宗交易，价格始终是买卖双方洽商的一个重要内容。买方力争降低商品的价格，以便尽量节省开支；卖方则力图提高商品的价格，希望更多地赚取利润。这就是俗话所说的"讨价还价"，在进出口业务中叫做"价格谈判"。

　　价格通常是指商品出售的单价，即商品的每一个计量单位以某 5 一种货币表示的价钱。在国际贸易中，价格的含义却比这复杂得多。由于买卖双方在地域上的距离，货物从卖方所在地运交买方，往往需要经过多次装卸，长途运输；需要办理保险报关等多项手续；需要支付各种费用，承担各种可能遭受的风险。因此，买卖双方在洽谈商品的价格时，除了商定单价以外，还要明确双方在货物 10 交接过程中， 各自应当承担的费用和风险。一种商品价格的高低，不但取决于这个商品本身的价值，而且也取决于买方或卖方在交货过程中所承担的工作和费用的多少。如果卖方承担的工作和费用较多，价格就会相应提高；相反，如果买方承担的工作和费用较

15　多，价格就会相应降低。

　　国际贸易中所用的各种价格术语，就是为了解决货物从卖方交付给买方的过程中，各种手续费用以及风险由哪方负责的问题。其中最常见的价格术语是："船上交货（装运港）价"(Free on Board, 简称F.O.B.)，"成本加保险及运费（目的港）价"(Cost, Insurance, and
20　Freight, 简称 C.I.F.)，以及"成本加运费（目的港）价"(Cost and Freight, 简称 C. & F.)等。

　　"船上交货（装运港）"价格术语，习惯上叫做"离岸价格"。使用这种价格术语时，应当标明装运港名称，例如：F.O.B.上海。这个价格术语表明卖方在上海港把货物装上买方指定的（一般由买方租订）的船只[1]，并负担货物装上船为止的一切费用和风险。"成本加保
25　险及运费（目的港）"价格术语，简称"到岸价格"。使用这一价格术语时，必须注明目的港名称，例如：C.I.F.纽约。这个价格术语表明卖方负责租船订舱，按期将合同规定的货物装船运往双方约定的目的港（纽约），同时负责办理保险手续并支付运费和保险费。值得注意的是，卖方承担的风险，与 F.O.B. 价格术语的一样，只是货物
30　在装运港上船以前发生的风险，而不是承担货物自装运港运抵目的港所发生的一切风险（这些风险按险别由保险公司负责）。"成本加运费（目的港）"价格，又称作"离岸加运费价格"。使用这个价格术语时，同样必须在 C. & F. 后注明目的港名称，例如：C. & F. 旧金山。这一价格术语是指卖方负责将合同规定的货物装上开往指定目
35　的港（旧金山）的船只，支付运费，并且负担货物装船以前的各项费用和风险。C. & F. 价格术语的性质与C. I. F. 基本上是一致的，唯一的差别是卖方不负责办理保险手续和支付保险费。

1　美国、加拿大和一些拉丁美洲国家使用的 F.O.B. 价格术语与一般国际贸易中通用的含义不太相同。对这些国家使用 F.O.B. 价格术语时，必须在 F.O.B. 和装运港之间加上 "Vessel" 字样，否则卖方可能只负责在城内交货，而不负责把货物交到港口的船上。

40　　　　不同的价格术语代表了买卖双方应该承担的不同责任、费用和风险。交易双方在谈判时，都会选择对自己最有利的价格条款。一般来说，做进口贸易的商人倾向于采用 F.O.B.。因为租船订舱、办理保险都是自己负责，所以比较主动，也可以节省开支。做出口贸易的，由于自己负担联系租船、办理保险的工作和费用，这样不但在安排交货、组织装运上比较方便，而且可以多赚钱，因此比较倾

45　　向于 C. I. F. 价格条款。

✐ **根据课文内容回答下列问题：**

1. 为什么价格是买卖双方谈判的一个主要内容？

2. 价格一般指什么？国际贸易中的价格还包括什么？

3. 为什么国际贸易中会有各种不同的价格术语？

4. 国际贸易中商品价格的高低取决于什么？

5. "离岸价格"应当注明什么？买卖双方的责任是什么？

6. "到岸价格"应当注明什么港口名称？卖方的责任是什么？

7. "成本加运费"价格与"到岸价格"有什么不同？

8. 做出口贸易时，一般选择什么价格条款？为什么？做进口贸易呢？

✐ **根据课文内容，在下面的表格里写上"买方"或者"卖方"：**

价格术语	风险	手续		费用	
	哪方承担货物装上船后的风险	哪方办理订舱手续	哪方办理保险	哪方支付到目的港的运费	哪方支付保险费
F.O.B.					
C.&F.					
C.I.F.					

✐ **根据意思，给课文划分层次(不是自然段)并写出每个层次的大意。**

生词和用法

额	é	*Mph.(N.)*	规定的数目：贸易~、成交~、名~、定~、超~。 a specified number or amount
小额	xiǎo é	*Adj./N.*	数量不大：~交易、~生意：＜＞巨额。 a small amount
宗	zōng	*MW*	量词：一~心事（交易、货物、款项、案件）。
大宗	dàzōng	*Adj./N.*	数量很大：~商品、~交易、~货物、~产品。 a large amount; a large quantity of
始终	shǐzhōng	*Adv./N.*	始＝开始，终＝终结，从开始到终结。 from beginning to end
力争	lìzhēng	*V.*	极力争取：~上游、~成功、~完成。 to do all one can to, to strive for
力图	lìtú	*V.*	尽力追求、希望得到；＝力争：~恢复、~提高、~取得、~降低。 to try hard to; to strive for
降低	jiàngdī	*V.*	下降；使下降：~价格、~要求、~水平、~标准：＜＞提高。 to reduce; to lower; to cut down
尽量	jǐnliàng	*Adv.*	力求在一定范围内达到最大限度：~争取、~提早、~降低、~避免、~节省。 to the best of one's ability; as far as possible
节省	jiéshěng	*V*	使可能被用掉的时间或物品不被用掉：~时间、~资金、~人力、~材料：＜＞浪费。 to save up; to economize.
开支	kāizhī	*V./N.*	付出（钱）；支出的费用：节省~、~很大。 to pay (expenses); expenditure
赚	zhuàn	*V.*	获得利润：~钱、~取利润；＜＞赔。 to make profit; to make money; to gain

利润	lìrùn	N.	商品生产或交易的赢利：~很高、<>成本。 profit
俗语	súyǔ	N.	通俗而广泛流行的定型语句，简练而形象化；〔口〕俗话。 common saying; proverb
讨价 还价	tǎojià huánjià	Idm.	做买卖时反复讨论价钱，买卖双方各不相让，常用来表示谈判或接受任务时提出各种条件，斤斤计较。 to bargain; to haggle
计量	jìliàng	V.	用一个规定的标准作为已知量比较、计算出一个暂时未知的量。 to measure; to calculate
单位	dānwèi	N.	计算事物多少的标准量：长度~、时间~、重量~、温度~、计量~。 unit
货币	huòbì	N.	代表商品价值的特殊物品，可以购买或交换任何商品。 money; currency
却	què	Adv.	but; yet; however; whereas：＝倒、可〔口〕。
地域	dìyù	N.	面积相当的的一块地方。 region; district; territory
距离	jùlí	N./V.	在时间或空间上相隔，相隔的长度。 distance; to be away from
物	wù	Mph.(N.)	东西；物件：动~、植~、生~、货~、食~、药~、~质、~价。 object; thing
货物	huòwù	N.	在市场上出售的物品。 commodity; goods
装卸	zhuāngxiè	V.	装到运输工具上或从运输工具上卸下来。 to load and unload
办理	bànlǐ	V.	处理(事务)：~手续、~案件。 to conduct; to handle
保险	bǎoxiǎn	V./N.	to insure; insurance：~费、~手续、汽车~、医疗~、人寿~、财产~、火灾~。
		Adj.	稳当可靠：~的做法、~柜、<>危险。 safe; secure

报关	bàoguān	VO	报＝申报，关＝海关；货物、行李或船只等进出口时，向海关申报，办理进出口手续。 to declare something at the Customs
手续	shǒuxù	N.	（办事的）程序：入学~、报名~、保险~、报关~、提货~。 procedures; formalities
费用	fèiyòng	N.	花费的钱；开支。 expenses; cost; expenditure
费	fèi	N.	费用：学~、水电~、运~、保险~、邮~、药~、小~。 fee; cost
遭受	zāoshòu	V.	受到不幸或损害：~损失、~失败、~打击、~风险。 to suffer; to incur (a disaster or a loss)
风险	fēngxiǎn	N.	可能发生的危险：政治~、经济~、战争~、冒~。 risk; hazard, venture
商定	shāngdìng	V.	商＝商量，定＝决定；交换意见后决定。 to decide upon (after discussion)
取决	qǔjué	V.	由某方面或某种情况决定（后面多跟"于"字）。 to depend upon, to be determined by
价值	jiàzhí	N.	value: ~极大、很有~、使用~、毫无~。
相应	xiāngyìng	V./Adv.	互相呼应、互相适应：~提高、~改变、~发展、~的办法。 to correspond; corresponding; accordingly
术语	shùyǔ	N.	专门学科中的专门用语：医学~、外贸~、军事~。 terminology; technical terms
交付	jiāofù	V.	交给：~定金、~费用、~任务、货物~：＜＞收取。 to pay; to hand over; to deliver
装运港	zhuāngyùngǎng	NP	把货物装上船的港口。 port of loading
目的港	mùdìgǎng	NP	想要到达的港口。 port of destination
成本	chéngběn	N.	生产一种产品所需的全部费用：生产~、节约

			~：＜＞利润。　　　cost
岸	àn	N.	江河湖海等水边的陆地：海~、口~、沿~、离~价格、到~价格　shore; coast
标明	biāomíng	V.	做出记号或写出文字使人知道：~价格、~期、~地址、~收货人。　to mark clearly; to indicate properly
负担	fùdān	V./N.	承担（责任、工作、费用等）；工作~、学习~、经济~、~很重、减轻~。　to bear; burden
订舱	dìngcāng	VO	租订舱位。　to book shipping space
值得	zhídé	V.	指这样做会有好处、有价值、有意义：~研究、~学习、~注意、~买。　to be worth; to deserve
按	àn	Prep.	依照：~时、~规定、~期、~合同、~险别。　according to
抵	dǐ	Mph.(V.)	〔书〕到，抵达＝到达　运抵＝运到。　to arrive
别	bié	Mph.(N.)	类别：性~、类~、级~、职~、险~。　categorization, distinction
险别	xiǎnbié	N.	保险的类别。　coverage; the different categorizations of insurance
唯一	wéiyī	Adj.	只有一个、独一无二；＝惟一：~的办法、~的希望、~的条件。　only; sole
差别	chābié	N.	形式和内容上的不同：年龄~、品质上的~、明显的~、~不大。　difference; disparity
条款	tiáokuǎn	N.	文件或合约上的条目：价格~、装运~、包装~。　clause, article
倾向	qīngxiàng	V.	偏于赞成（对立的事物中的一方）。　to be inclined to
安排	ānpái	V./N.	有条理、分先后地处理（事物）；适当地安置（人员）：~装运、~工作、~学习、~生产；人力

			~、合理~。	to arrange; to plan; arrangement
组织	zǔzhī	V./N.	安排分散的人或事物使其有一定的系统性或整体性：~人力、~晚会、~装运；青年~、学生~、参加~。	to organize; organization

补充词

展销会	zhǎnxiāohuì	N.	展＝展览，销＝销售，同时进行展览和销售的会。	an exhibition fair; a trade show
成千上万	chéng qiān shàng wàn	Idm.	形容数量极多。	thousands and thousands; numerous; countless
市民	shìmín	N.	城市居民。	the residents of a city; citizens.
外地	wàidì	N.	本地以外的地方：~人、~话、去~：＜＞本地。	part of the country other than where one is
好家伙	hǎo jiāhuǒ	Intjn.	表示赞叹或惊讶。	(for exclamation) good lord; good heaven
停车	tíngchē	VO	把汽车停下来，使其停止前进或后退。	to park a car; to stop; to pull up
停车场	tíngchēchǎng	NP	给公众停车的地方：免费~、公共~。	parking lot; garage
满	mǎn	Adj.	全部充实，达到容量的极点：装~、放~、停~、坐~：＜＞空。	full; filled; packed
赶紧	gǎnjǐn	Adv.	表示抓紧时机，不拖延：~回家、~准备、~上车。	in a hurry; lose no time; quickly
礼物	lǐwù	N.	为表示友好、尊敬或庆贺而送的物品。	gift; present.
丝绸	sīchóu	N.	用蚕丝或人造丝织成的织品的总称。	silk; silk cloth

旗袍	qípáo	N.	中国妇女穿的一种长袍，原为满族服装。
			a close-fitting women's dress with high neck and slit skirt
称谓	chēngwèi	N.	人们为了表示相互之间的某种关系，或为了表示身份、职务、地位的区别而使用的一些称呼。
			appellation; title.
空…格	kònggé	VO	把每段第一行的起头缩进去几格。
			to indent
正文	zhèngwén	N.	书信、文章的本文。
			the body of a letter or an article
套语	tàoyǔ	N.	文章、书信中套用的习惯用语。
			set phrase; polite formal expressions in a letter/document
祝颂	zhùsòng	V.	表示良好的愿望和赞颂。
			to express good wishes or praise
祝颂语	zhùsòngyǔ	N.	书信、公文里表示良好的愿望和赞颂语句。
			expressions of good wishes or praise in letters or documents
附言	fùyán	N.	书信等写完之后另加上的话，也可说"附、又及"。 postscript
职务	zhíwù	N.	规定、担任的工作。
			title; position
事由	shìyóu	N.	〔公文用语〕公文的主要内容。
			matters concerned; content
起首	qǐshǒu	N.	书信、公文开头的地方。
			the beginning of a letter or a document
署名	shǔmíng	V./N.	把自己的名字写在书信、文件等上面。
			to sign; signature

词语例释

一、始终 + Verb Phrase （from beginning to end; always）

l-1. 无论做小额生意或大宗交易，价格始终是买卖双方洽商的一个重要
内容。

1. 王经理始终十分注意分析市场的动向。
2. 她始终不明白为什么对方没有接受这个发盘。
3. 虽然我们给那个公司写过信，发过传真，但是他们始终没有跟我
们联系过。

"始终"表示某种情况、状态从开始到最后都是一样，没有发生变
化。"始终"的意思与"一直"相似，但"一直"后的动词可带时间状语，也
可以用在将来，而"始终"只能指过去和现在。作副词时，能用"始终"的
地方，都可用"一直"，但能用"一直"的地方，不一定都能用"始终"。
"始终"后面必须跟表示特定状态或结果的动词短语，并且多用于否定
式。下面的句子都是错误的：

始终 indicates that a situation or status remains the same from the beginning
to the end without changes. While it is similar in meaning to 一直 and refers to
the past or present time frame, the Verb after 一直 can take an adverbial of time,
and may also be used in the future. This is not the case in 始终. When 始终 is
used as an Adverb, 一直 can always replace 始终, but it is not necessarily the
other way around. There must be a Verb Phrase denoting a specific state or
result after 始终, and it is mostly in the negative form. The sentences below are
all wrong:

✘ 她虽然很累，但是开会的时候始终听，没有睡觉。　　（听＋着）
✘ 那天我始终等到 12 点。　　　　（一直）
✘ 他打算在这儿始终工作下去。　　（一直）

另外，"始终"有名词的用法，如"贯彻始终"，"一直"没有。而
"一直"可以表示顺着一个方向不变的意思，如"一直走"，"始终"则不
行。

In addition, the word 始终 can function as a Noun, such as in 贯彻始终, but 一直 cannot. However, while 一直 has the meaning of going along in the same direction, as in 一直走, it is not true with 始终.

二、讨价还价 （to bargain; to haggle）

l-4. 这就是俗话所说的"讨价还价"，在进出口业务中叫做"价格谈判"。

1. 老张买东西很爽快，从来不讨价还价。

2. 我们的报价已经相当低了，不必再讨价还价了。

3. 这是学校，不是市场，你怎么可以在学习成绩上跟老师讨价还价？

"讨价还价"是成语，多作谓语或定语。指买卖双方商量、争执商品的价钱。当比喻谈判或接受某项工作时讲条件，斤斤计较时，含贬义。

The idiom 讨价还价 is primarily used as a predicate or an attributive. It refers to the buyer and the seller discussing or arguing about the price of the commodity. When it is used metaphorically to indicate someone bargaining on condition and is preoccupied with one's personal gain and loss when taking a job, it has a derogatory connotation.

三、Clause 1, Subject 却＋Verb Phrase （but; yet; however; whereas）

l-6. 在国际贸易中，价格的含义却比这复杂得多。

1. 买东西讲价钱也许可以省一点钱，有时却要花很多时间。

2. 这种车价钱便宜，质量却不一定比贵的差。

3. 他觉得自己已经说得很清楚了，但是大家却不知道他说了些什么。

副词"却"用在后一分句的主语后、谓语前，表示转折，可以与"但是、可是、然而"等连用，多用于书面语。口语里可用"倒、可"。

The Adverb 却 is used after the subject before the predicate in the second clause to indicate a contrary relation. It can go with 但是、可是、然而 etc., and is mostly used in written Chinese. Its colloquial counterpart is 倒、可.

四、各自 + Verb Phrase （each; respectively）

l-11. 因此，买卖双方在洽谈商品的价格时，除了商定单价以外，还要明确双方在货物交接过程中，<u>各自</u>应当承担的费用和风险。

1. 在美国，和朋友上街吃饭，一般都<u>各自</u>付钱。

2. 打完球以后，大家就<u>各自</u>回宿舍去了。

3. 合同签订以后，买卖双方<u>各自</u>保留一份，互相监督对方执行的情况。

人称代词"各自"指各人自己或各方面自己的一方，所称代的对象一般在前文出现过。"各自"常跟在名词或代词后，构成复指词组作主语，如例3。"各自"也可单独或构成词组作定语，常常带"的"字——各自的 + 名词短语。例如：

The Personal Pronoun 各自 refers to one's own self or each single one of the party on one's side. The person(s) it stands for has appeared previously in the context. 各自 often follows a Noun or a Pronoun to form a phrase referring to the same Noun, as in Example 3. Moreover, it is also possible for 各自 to act alone or as an Attribute of a Noun Phrase, usually followed by a 的, as in the structure –各自的 + Noun Phrase (each; one's Noun). For example:

L.2, l-30　　……一方的发盘或还盘被另一方接受以后，交易立即达成，双方就要承担<u>各自的</u>法律责任。

4. 很多父母都只管忙着<u>各自的</u>工作，没有时间关心孩子的学习。

5. 他们都坚持<u>各自的</u>意见，不肯作一点让步。

6. 服务员叫大家保管好<u>各自的</u>行李。

五、取决于 （to depend upon; to hinge on; to be decided by）

l-12. 一种商品价格的高低，不但<u>取决于</u>这个商品本身的价值，而且也<u>取决于</u>买方或卖方在交货过程中所承担的工作和费用的多少。

1. 产品的销路主要<u>取决于</u>它的品质和销售服务。

2. 我们要订多少货<u>取决于</u>贵方什么时候能够交货。

3. 一个人的学习成绩常常<u>取决于</u>他的努力程度。

动词"取决"表示由某种因素或条件决定，常用介词"于"引出决定的条件或因素，多用于书面语。

The Verb 取决 indicates that something is determined by a certain factor or condition which is usually introduced by the Preposition 于. It is mostly used in written Chinese.

六、 相应(的/地) + Verb　 (corresponding; relevant; accordingly)

l-14. 如果卖方承担的工作和费用较多，价格就会<u>相应</u>提高；相反，如果买方承担的工作和费用较多，价格就会<u>相应</u>降低。

1. 这几年，随着美国经济的稳定发展，买房子的人也<u>相应</u>增加了。
2. 现代科学技术发展很快，我们必须努力学习，使自己的工作能力有<u>相应</u>的提高。
3. 市场的情况变了，公司的经营方式也要<u>相应</u>地改变。

"相应"是动词，表示互相呼应或照应，相适应，相符合。不带宾语，如：文章首尾相应。在这里，"相应"作状语和定语，后面带"的"或"地"。

相应 is an Intransitive Verb which means two parts work in concert, and coordinate with each other. In the sentences referenced above, 相应 functions as an adverbial and attribute, followed by 的 or 地.

七、 同时　 (at the same time; in the meantime; meanwhile)

l-29. 这个价格术语表明卖方负责租船订舱，按期将合同规定的货物装船运往双方约定的目的港(纽约)，<u>同时</u>负责办理保险手续并支付运费和保险费。

1. 中国改革开放以来，大力发展进出口贸易，<u>同时</u>也积极引进外国的先进科学技术。
2. 她选了这门课，希望进一步提高自己的中文水平，<u>同时</u>，也学一些有关做生意的知识。

3. 这个公司的主管想了各种办法，力图赚取更多的利润，<u>同时</u>，尽量节省开支，降低成本。

"同时"可作名词，表示"同一时候"的意思，可单独作状语，如课文的句子1-29。"同时"也可作连词，表示进一层，有"并且"的意思。经常用在分句、句子或段落的开头，与"也"、"又"等配合表示并列关系，或与"不但……也／又／还……"等词语搭配，表示分句之间的递进关系。

When 同时 is used as a Noun, it means "at the same time" and can function as an adverbial by itself. The sentence in Line 29 of the text is an example. 同时 can be a Conjunction also, indicating an additional relation, and bears the meaning of "moreover" or "furthermore". It usually appears at the beginning of a clause, a sentence or a paragraph and goes with 也 or 又 to form a parallel coordinate relation. It may, in addition, pair up with 不但……也／又／还……to indicate a progressive relation between clauses.

八、（只）是……，而不是…… (it is only ...., but not ... ; instead of ..., it is merely...)

l-30. ……卖方承担的风险，与 F.O.B. 价格术语的一样，<u>只是</u>货物在装运港上船以前发生的风险，<u>而不是</u>承担货物自装运港运抵目的港所发生的一切风险……。

1. 他<u>只是</u>提醒你，请你注意这方面的问题，<u>而不是</u>批评你，说你做错了。

2. 老师<u>只</u>希望我们知道一下国际贸易的一般知识，<u>而不是</u>要求大家真的去跟中国人做生意。

3. "形式发票"<u>只是</u>为了帮助某些国家的进口商向政府申请进口许可证的一种预开发票，<u>而不是</u>真正的商业发票。

这个句型用于表示对比关系，强调肯定前一分句，否定后一分句。

This pattern expresses a contrastive relationship, and emphasizes the first clause and negates the second clause.

九、 一般来说　（generally speaking; in general）

l-40. <u>一般来说</u>，做进口贸易的商人倾向采用 F.O.B.。

1. <u>一般来说</u>，大公司的资信情况都比较好。

2. 合同签订以后，<u>一般来说</u>，都不会有什么大的改动。

3. <u>一般来说</u>，学生都比较关心自己的学习成绩。

词组"一般来说"是插入语，可出现在句首或句中，表示所说的事情或现象有一定的普遍性，也可以说成"一般说来"。

The expression 一般来说 is an insertion, and can appear at the beginning or in the middle of a sentence. It indicates that a thing or phenomenon is a rather common one. An alternate version of this expression is 一般说来.

十、 倾向 (于) ＋ Verb/Noun Phrase　（to be inclined to; to prefer）

l-41. 一般来说，做进口贸易的商人<u>倾向</u>采用 F.O.B.。

l-44. 做出口贸易的，由于自己负担联系租船、办理保险的工作和费用，这样不但在安排交货、组织装运上比较方便，而且可以多赚钱，因此比较<u>倾向于</u>C. I. F. 价格条款。

1. 陈经理<u>倾向</u>立刻接受这个报盘，而马经理则<u>倾向于</u>继续进行价格谈判。

2. 这件事我<u>倾向</u>暂时不告诉她，等收到传真以后再说。

3. 虽然大多数人都同意第一种意见，但我还是比较<u>倾向于</u>第二种。

"倾向"在这里是及物动词，须带宾语，表示偏于赞成对立事物中的一方。"倾向"也常以介词"于"构成的介宾词组作补语。

The Verb 倾向 here is a Transitive Verb and should take an object. It means that the speaker is leaning toward one side of two contrasting opinions. 倾向 often forms a complement with the Preposition 于.

词义辨析

一、价钱　价格　价值

　　"价钱"和"价格"虽然都指某种商品以特定的某种货币在一定时间内体现的价值，而且英语都是 price，但在含义和使用上，两者仍有一定的区别。"价钱"着重某种货币的一定数量，多用于口语，可直接受形容词"好"、"大"的修饰。"价格"含有一定的高低水平或尺度的意味，适用于正式场合，只被"高"、"低"修饰。"价值"是体现在商品里的社会劳动，指的是物品本身的代价。"价值"一般较为稳定，而"价钱"和"价格"是用货币表现出来的商品的价值，可因市场的不同而变动。"价值"除了在经济方面，还可指商品以外的人或事物的用途或重要意义，常同动词"有"、"没有"或形容词"（重）大"、"小"等搭配。"价格"只能表示某一具体商品值多少钱，不用于抽象事物。

　　Both 价钱 and 价格 mean "price" in English, but there are differences in their Chinese implications and usage. The word 价钱 stresses a certain amount of a specific currency, and is used mostly in spoken Chinese. It can be modified by Adjectives such as 好 or 大. 价格 indicates a certain level or scale in terms of fluctuation, and is primarily formal. Its modifiers are basically 高 and 低.

　　价值 is "value", which is considerably stable compared with 价钱 and 价格, which can fluctuate with the market situation. In addition to the economic sense, 价值 can also refer to the use or significance of people or things. It often associated with Verbs 有, 没有, or Adjectives such as （重）大 or 小. However, 价格 is used for how much a specific commodity is worth but not for abstract things.

二、受　接受　遭受

　　单音节动词"受"是"接受、容纳"的意思，强调某种外在的行为或事情加及到自己身上，是一种被动的承受关系。"受"所带的动词性宾语，多是双音节的，如"教育、重视、表扬、批评、影响"等；而名词性的宾语，则多是单音节的，如"伤、罪、苦、难、礼"等。"接受"表示对事物的领受、容纳而不拒绝。它的使用范围较广，可以是具体事物，也可以是抽象事物，但不表示被动的关系。"接受"可以是名词，也可以是动词。它带的宾语，较常见的有"任务、教育、教训、帮助、批评、检查、赔偿、意见、要求、建议、礼物、遗产、奖金"等。"遭受"是贬义词，表示不是出于自愿地受到不幸或损害。常与"打击、失败、痛苦、不幸、灾难、损失"等贬义词搭配使用。

The monosyllabic Verb 受 means 接受 (to receive), 容纳 (to hold), stressing a passive, receptive relationship. Verbs that follow 受 are mostly disyllabic, such as 教育、重视、表扬、批评、影响, etc. However, When Nouns function as its Object, they are primarily monosyllabic, such as 伤、罪、苦、难、礼, etc. 接受 means "to accept, to admit without rejection. It can be used for both concrete and abstract things, but does not indicate a passive relationship. It can function as a Noun and a Verb. The Objects that 接受 takes are usually words like 任务、教育、教训、帮助、批评、检查、赔偿、意见、要求、建议、礼物、遗产、奖金, etc. The term 遭受 has a derogative sense, which mean "to meet with a misfortune or suffer from a loss". It is often associated with derogative words such as 打击、失败、痛苦、不幸、灾难、损失, etc.

三、　处理　办理　整理

"处理"含有"治理、料理、办理、清理、做"等意思，着重在"安排事情、解决问题"，对象可以是人或物，可指具体事物和抽象事物，通常用于口语、书面语和各种场合。"办理"除了强调"做某件事情或处理某种事务"外，还有郑重的意味，多用于正式场合，常带宾语或补语。"整理"表示改变原来不好的状况，使之整齐、有条理的意思。多用于"思想、材料、资料、内务、环境"等方面而不用于人。

处理 has multiple meanings such as "harness, take care of, handle, process, dispose, do" etc. Its focus is on "arrangement making and problem solving". It deals with human or object, applying to both concrete and abstract things in various situations, and is widely used in spoken and written Chinese. While 办理 emphasizes "handling some kind of business, or doing something", it implies a sense of seriousness, and is used mostly in formal situations. It often takes an Object or a Complement. 整理 refers to "putting in order, sorting, straighten out things". It is not used with human beings, but primarily with words like 思想、材料、资料、内务、环境, etc.

四、相应 相当 相反

"相应"是不及物动词，不带宾语，表示"互相呼应或照应，互相适应、符合"的意思，可作谓语或状语。如：

As an Intransitive Verb, 相应 means "to fit, correspond, appropriate(ly)" and it does not take any Object. For example,

这篇文章的首尾不相应。

The ending of this article doesn't fit its beginning.

由于市场情况发生了变化，进口商品的价格也相应提高了。

With the change of the market situation, the price of imported goods has increased correspondingly.

"相当"作形容词，是"适当、合适"的意思，常作定语，修饰名词，如"有相当的基础"，"找不到相当的人来代替"。"相当"也可作副词，表示程度高、但是还不到"很"的地步，多用于口语，后面一般不带"地"字，在形容词前面作状语。"相反"作为不及物动词，表示"事物的两个方面互相矛盾，互相排斥"。"相反"多作谓语，有时也带"的"字作定语。"相反"还可受"恰恰"、"正好"等副词修饰，用在后一分句或句子的开头，表示同上文的意思对立或对比，起转折或递进作用。有时可以加上"地"字，在句子中作独立成分。

When 相当 is an Adjective, it usually functions as an Attributive to modify a Noun, meaning "suitable" or "appropriate" as in 相当的基础 (with certain foundation) and 找不到相当的人来代替 (cannot find a suitable person as a substitute). When it functions as an Adverb, 相当 indicates "a relatively high degree" but not to the extent of 很. It is mostly used in spoken Chinese to modify an Adjective, and no 地 is needed after it. 相反 is an Intransitive Verb, which means "to contradict". It is primarily used as a

Predicate, but sometimes can be used as an Attributive without the marker 的. Moreover, 相反 may be modified by Adverbs such as 恰恰 or 正好, appearing at the beginning of a sentence or a second clause to contrast with the previous one. Sometimes, it can take the character 地, and function as an Independent element in a sentence.

五、使用　利用　采用

　　这三个都是动词，同时共有语素"用"字。"使用"主要指"使人员、器物、资金等为某种目的服务"，对象主要是物品或资金、技术等。"利用"有两重意思，一是使人或物充分发挥效能；二是用手段使人或物为自己服务，含贬义。"采用"强调"认为合适而有选择地使用"，常带宾语，如"（新）技术、（新）方法、优良品种、建议、方案"等。

　　These three Verbs share a Morpheme 用, and they may mean "to use" in certain context. 使用 refers to "employing people, utensils, money, etc. to serve a certain purpose" and its targets are mainly articles, money, technology, etc. 利用 has duel meanings. The first one is "to make full use of", or "to maximize the effect of a person or a thing." The second meaning is "to take advantage of someone or something for one's own benefit" and is a derogative term. 采用 emphasizes" to utilize (selectively because of it is appropriate. 采用 usually takes an Object, such as （新）技术、（新）方法、优良品种、建议、方案, etc.

语法

一、目的复句　Purposive Complex Sentences

　　一个分句（偏句）提出要达到的某个目的，另一个分句（正句）说明为达到这个目的所采取的行动，这种复句就是目的复句。下列的关联词语，通常用于偏句在前，正句在后的句式：

　　A Purposive Complex Sentence contains one clause (the subordinate clause), which indicates a purpose while the other clause (the main clause) shows the action that leads to that purpose. The following Connectives are normally used in Purposive Complex Sentences with a subordinate clause appearing first and followed by a main clause:

为、为了、为着、为了……起见……。

以下的关联词语则只用于主句在前，偏句在后的句式：

The Connectives below are usually used in Purposive Complex Sentences where the main clause goes first and the subordinate clause goes next:

为的是、以、以便、以免、免得、省得。

"为"、"为了"、"为着"、"为的是"、"以"、"以便"这些关联词语一般表示从积极方面去达到目的；而"以免"、"免得"、"省得"则表示从消极方面避免某种情况的发生。例如：

While the Connectives 为、为了、为着、为的是、以、以便 etc. express the idea of achieving a purpose or result from a positive standpoint; Connectives such as 以免、免得、省得 indicate taking actions to avoid the occurrence of a negative situation. For example:

1. 为了找到更好的工作，很多人都在努力学习外语和计算机技术。
2. 他每天都看中文电视，为的是提高自己的汉语听力水平。
3. 为了方便起见，商务处准备了一些关于中国对外贸易情况和法律制度的资料。
4. 最近公司请了一批会汉语的职员，以扩大在中国的业务。
5. 对于出口业务来说，应当调查商品对市场的适销情况，了解市场的供求关系，分析市场动向，以便选择适当的销售市场。
6. 发虚盘时，一般都加上"以我方最后确认为准"，以免发生误解引起不必要的争议或纠纷。

二、 标点符号(1)点号 Punctuation (I)

标点符号是用来表示停顿、语气以及词语的性质和作用的。它帮助文字准确地记录实际语言的使用、信息的交流、思想感情的表达，是书面语言重要的有机组成部分。因此，必须重视标点符号的使用。句号、问号，叹号、逗号、顿号、分号和冒号统称点号。点号一般占一个字的位置，通常不出现在一行之首。

Punctuation is used to signify pauses, the tone of a speech, and the nature and functions of expressions. It helps the writing to record accurately the actual use of language, to communicate, and to express ideas and emotions. It is an important organic component of the written language. Hence, we must pay close attention to the use of punctuation. Full Stops, Question Marks, Exclamation Marks, Commas, Listing Marks, Semicolons, and Colons are all called **diǎnhào** (literally "pause marks") in Chinese. A "pause mark" generally takes up the same amount of space as a character, and is not supposed to appear at the very beginning of a line.

(一) 句号 (。)　**Full Stop**

句号表示陈述句完了以后的停顿。它是一个空心的圆点，不是英语的实心圆点。陈述句一般是用来说明事实或表达意见的。例如：

A Full Stop indicates the pause after the completion of a declarative sentence. It is a hollow circle instead of a black round dot as in English. A declarative sentence is used to state a fact or to express an opinion. For instance:

1. 本公司经营各类食品的进出口业务。
2. 我觉得对方的报价过高，但他却认为十分合理。
3. 如果一方在表示接受时，对原发盘中的某些交易条件提出了修改或者附加了保留条件，这种行为不应作为接受——因为它只是一项还盘，真正的交易还没有达成。

祈使句用来要求听话人做某件事情，结尾一般用叹号，但语气和缓的祈使句，末尾也可用句号。例如：

An imperative sentence is used to request someone to do something and normally ends with an Exclamation Mark. However, in a soft-tone, mild imperative sentence, it is possible to use a Full Stop. For example:

4. 请稍等一下。

5. 时候不早了，你先回去吧。

(二)问号(？)　　Question Mark

问号表示一个疑问句完了以后的停顿。疑问句一般用来提出问题。例如：

A Question Mark signifies the pause after the completion of an interrogative sentence. Interrogative sentences are used to ask questions in general. For instance:

1. 你能不能给我们寄几本最新的商品目录？

2. 她报的是实盘还是虚盘？

3. 请问中国黄豆 F.O.B.（青岛）多少钱一吨？

反问句：Rhetorical Questions:

4. 难道买东西不用付钱吗？

5. 你不是会说日语吗？

有的句子虽然有疑问词"谁"、"什么"、"怎么"、"哪儿"等，但如果整个句子不是疑问句时，句末不用问号。如：

Occasionally, some sentences contain question words such as 谁、什么、怎么、哪儿. If these sentences are not a question at all by nature, no Question Mark should be used at the end. For example:

6. 谁也不知道那是什么。

7. 你可以问问她飞机几点到。

(三)叹号(！)　　Exclamation Mark

叹号表示感叹句完了以后的停顿。感叹句是用来抒发某种强烈感情的。例如：

An Exclamation Mark is used to indicate the pause after the completion of a exclamatory sentence. Exclamatory sentences are used to express certain strong emotions. For example:

1. 太棒了！

2. 自己开公司当老板，多好啊！

3. 我哪儿有时间休息！

语气强烈的祈使句、反问句、或者叹词、呼语后面都可以用叹号。如：

Imperative sentences, rhetorical sentences or interjections and terms of address with a strong tone may also take an Exclamation Mark. For example:

4. 快起来！房子着火了！

5. 糟糕！我的护照不见了。

6. 奶奶！您放心吧，您的话我们都记住了。

(四) 逗号 (，)　Comma

逗号表示一个句子内部的停顿，行文中间用得最多。它可以在单句里表示句子成分之间 (主谓语之间、结构复杂的宾语或较长的状语等) 的停顿，也可以表示复句里分句之间，甚至分句里某些成分之间的停顿。比如：

A Comma shows pauses within a sentence, and is used most in writing. It can be used to indicate the pauses among sentence elements (between a subject and predicate, an object with complex structures, or a long adverbial, etc), and it can signify a pause between clauses within a Complex Sentence or even a pause between certain components in a clause. For example:

1. 喝杯茶吧，老王。

2. 这种口头或书面的表示，在国际贸易中称为还盘，也就是习惯上说的还价。

3. 范经理告诉过我们，实盘的各项交易条件都必须是明确的、完整的、毫无保留的。

4. 明天签合同的时候，你再问问他。

5. 无论做小额生意还是大宗交易，价格始终是买卖双方洽商的一个主要内容。

6. 国际贸易中所用的各种价格术语，就是为了解决货物从卖方交付
   给买方的过程中，各种手续费用以及风险由哪方负责的问题。

(五) 顿号（、） **Listing Mark**

顿号多用于列举事物，表示句子中并列词语之间的停顿。它表示的
停顿时间比逗号短，用来隔开并列的词或短语。如果并列词语之间用了
"和"、"或"、"与"、"及"、"而"等连词，就不再使用顿号。如下面例子
中的后两句：

A Listing Mark is used to separate the people or things listed, indicating a
pause between parallel words or phrases. The pause is shorter than that of a
Comma, and is used to separate parallel words or phrases. However, if
Conjunctions such as 和、或、与、及、而 are used between the parallel words
or phrases, it is not necessary to use a Listing Mark. Examples can be found in
the last two sentences below:

1. 询问的内容有繁有简，一般可包括：商品的品质规格、包装、数
   量、价格、支方付式、装运、交货期等。
2. 另外，对于进出口市场所在地的贸易惯例、关税制度、进出口管
   制条例和规定、港口及运输条件都应有充分的了解。
3. 合同的制作是一件严肃而认真的工作。

(六) 分号（；） **Semicolon**

分号表示复句中并列分句之间的停顿。它表示的停顿时间比逗号
长，较多用来隔开结构相同或相似的并列分句。例如：

A Semicolon signifies the pause between coordinate clauses in a Complex
Sentence. The time of pausing is longer than that of a Comma, and it is mostly
used to separate the Coordinative Clauses that have the same or similar structures.
For instance:

1. 买方力争降低商品的价格，以便尽量节省开支；卖方则力图提高
   商品的价格，希望更多地赚取利润。

2. 按前者进行的交易，叫做"凭卖方样品买卖"；按后者进行的交易，叫做"凭买方样品买卖"。

3. 我国年满十八周岁的公民，不分民族、种族、性别、职业、家庭出身、宗教信仰、教育程度、财产状况、居住期限，都有选举和被选举权；但是依照法律被剥夺政治权利的人除外。

(七) 冒号（：）　**Colon**

冒号表示提示语或总括语之后的停顿，用来提起下文。书信和发言稿中的称呼语是提示语；"例如"、"比如"等引出具体例子或说明的，也是提示语，后面要用冒号。有些句子（如并列复句表示总分关系的、解说复句）的前一部分提出总说，然后再提出具体的说明，在总说分句后面，也要用冒号。另外，在引出直接引语的"说"、"写道"等后面，也要用冒号。例如：

A Colon shows the pause after a phrase of prompt or a phrase of summary, which signals the up-coming paragraph. Terms of address in letters and phrases such as "for example" and "for instance" that introduce specific examples and illustrations, are phrases of prompt, and a Colon should be used afterwards. Some sentences (such as Coordinate Complex Sentences denoting a general-specific relation, and Elaborative Complex Sentences) contain two parts. The first part is a general statement and the second part provides detailed illustration. A Colon should be used after the first clause. In addition, before a direct quote following words like 说、写道, a Colon should be used also. For example:

1. 各位来宾、各位朋友：
   你们好！欢迎参加我们的商品展览会。
2. 国际贸易中最常见的有：船上交货价 (F.O.B.)，成本加保险及运费价 (C.I.F.)，以及成本加运费价 (C. & F.) 等。
3. 他高兴地说："我毕业了！"

修辞

同义词　Synonyms

　　同义词是指词义相同或相近的词。正确使用同义词，可以避免用词重复、呆板，使语言生动活泼，增强表现力。但是，在意义和用法上完全相等，在任何语境中都可以相互替换的同义词，如"电脑/电子计算机"、"旅店/旅馆"、"报价/报盘"是不多的。大部分的同义词，只是在一定的程度上相同或接近而已。因此，选用同义词时，必须注意它们在以下各方面的差别：

Synonyms are words that have the same meaning or are close in meaning. Using Synonyms correctly can achieve the result of avoiding simple repetition and monotone, making the language more vivid and more expressive. However, Synonyms that are exactly equal in meaning and usage and are interchangeable in all contexts are rare, such as 电脑/电子计算机、旅店/旅馆、报价/报盘. The majority of Synonyms are, to some extent, similar or close in meaning. Therefore, it is necessary to pay close attention to the following distinctions when choosing Synonyms:

1. 对象和使用范围的差别　Distinctions in Target and Scope of Use

　　有些同义词核心意义相同或基本相同，有时甚至有相同的词素或发音，但是适应于不同的对象和范围。例如"会见/会面"都有"相见"的意思，但"会见"是指地位或辈份较高的人与地位或辈份较低的人相见，有郑重的色彩；而"会面"是指人们一般交往的见面。可以说，前者是大词，后者是小词。又如"具有/有"都表示存在，但是"具有"多用于抽象事物，像"条件、本领、技能、意义、价值"等，使用的范围较窄；而"有"既可用于具体事物又可用于抽象事物，使用范围较宽。下面的同义词，都要注意这方面的差别：

Some Synonyms basically overlap in the core meaning or are close in the core meaning, and some even share a similar morpheme or pronunciation. However, the scope of and contexts within which they can apply may differ. For instance, both 会见 and 会面 share the meaning of "meeting", but 会见 refers to meetings of people who enjoy a higher status or seniority with those who have a relatively lower status or seniority, and is usually rather formal in nature. In contrast, 会面 simply means meetings among ordinary people. It may be true that the former is a "big word" whereas the latter is a "small word". To take another example, both 具有 and 有 indicate "to exist". However, 具有 is used mostly with abstract things, such as 条件、本领、技能、意义、价值, and its scope of use is relatively narrow. As for 有, it can be used with both abstract and concrete things, with a wider scope. The following synonyms all have a similar distinction which require special attention:

改变——改正　意思——意义　美丽——华丽　失去——丧失

伟大——高大　使用——采用　方式——方法　质量——品质

2. 词义褒贬的差别　Distinctions between Commendatory and Derogatory Meaning

有些同义词的差别在于词义褒贬的对立，或者是中性词于褒义、贬义的对立。例如"教员"是个中性词，它的褒义词是"老师"或"先生"，贬义词是"教书匠"。又如"老头儿"含有亲热的意思，是褒义词，而"老头子"则含有厌恶的意思，是贬义词。与两者相对的中性词是"老汉"。当然，不是所有的同义词都有褒和贬或者和中性意义对立的。下面的同义词，要注意褒义和贬义的差别：

Sometimes, distinctions of Synonyms lie in the contrast between a commendatory versus a derogatory meaning or a neutral meaning versus the commendatory or derogatory meaning. For example, 教员 is a neutral term; its commendatory counterpart is 老师 or 先生, and the derogatory one is 教书匠. Likewise, 老头儿 has a sort of affectionate flavor, and is a commendatory term. However, 老头子 bears an abominable meaning and is a derogatory term. The neutral term is 老汉. Of course, it is not true that all Synonyms have counterparts in positive, negative and neutral lexical forms. Please note the distinctions of the following in terms of their commendatory and derogatory meanings:

保护——庇护　　理想——幻想　　倾向——偏向　　节俭——吝啬
结果——后果　　顽强——顽固　　讲究——挑剔　　推销——兜售
充满——充斥　　匆匆忙忙——慌慌张张　　侃侃而谈——夸夸其谈
计划——阴谋　　能言善辩——花言巧语　　悔人不倦——好为人师

3. 语义轻重和感情色彩的差别　Distinctions of the Intensity of Meaning and Emotions

有些同义词同属褒义或贬义，但在表达的语气和感情上有轻重之分。如"优异"和"优良"都是褒义词，但说"成绩优异"的肯定程度就显然高于"成绩优良"。同样，"懊悔"比"后悔"比"后悔"的感情色彩就更重一些。下面的同义词都有这样的差别：

Some synonyms are of the same category in terms of their commendatory or derogatory sense, but there are still differences in the intensity of the mood or emotions they carry. Take 优异 and 优良 for example. Although both 优异 and 优良 are commendatory in meaning, it is definitely more positive to say 成绩优异 than 成绩优良. Similarly, the emotional strength of 懊悔 is stronger than 后悔. The following Synonyms warrant attention in this regard:

悲伤——悲痛　　忘记——忘却　　时间——光阴　　远看——遥望
害怕——恐惧　　请求——恳求　　生气——愤怒　　祝贺——庆贺
过失——错误　　匆忙——仓促　　困难——艰难　　知道——了解

4. 语体风格的差别　Distinctions of Types of Text Style

同义词在语体风格上的差别，主要表现在口语和书面语上。比如口语说"要紧"，书面语是"重要"。书面语用"然而"，口语却常说"但是"或"可是"。下面列举的是一些用于不同语体的同义词：

The distinctions of types of text style are primarily in colloquial and written discourse. Here are some common examples: While 要紧 is often found in spoken and 重要 in written Chinese, 然而 is seen in more formal, literary contexts, while 但是 or 可是 is heard more frequently in colloquial language. Please note the differences of the following in style:

卖——销售　　到——抵达　　看一遍——过目　　付钱——付款

打听——询问　　不同——差异　　不一定——未必　　要是——倘若

也——亦　　　　知道——得悉　　急迫地——亟　　许多——诸多

生——出生　　　死——死亡　　　开(车)——驾驶　　用——使用

5. 集体和个体概念的差别　Distinctions of Collectivity and Individuality

有些同义词指的都是同一类事物，但有的是集体概念，有的是个体概念。当表示事物的具体数量时，只能在个体概念的名词前加上数词和量词，不能在表示集体概念的名词前加数量。比如，可以说"一个人"，但是不能说"三个人口"。下面的同义词，都要注意这方面的差别：

Although some Synonyms refer to the same entity; some are in the generic sense and are collective in concept, while others are specific and individual conceptually. When it is used to indicate specific amounts, only Nouns of individual sense can be preceded with numerals and measure words, and Nouns in collective sense cannot. For instance, it is possible to say 一个人, but it is grammatically incorrect to say 三个人口. Please pay attention to the distinction of the following synonyms in this aspect:

树——树木　　船——船只　　车——车辆　　河——河流

书——书籍　　纸——纸张　　药——药品　　布——布匹

信——信件　　菜——蔬菜　　花——花卉　　人——人民

6. 词性和语法功能的差别　Distinctions of Parts of Speech and Grammatical Functions

有些同义词虽然意思相同，但是因为词性不同，或虽然词性相同，但语法功能不同，在句子中只能充当某种句子成分，所有用法也不同。例如，"够"和"足够"都表示"数量上可以满足需要"的意思，但"足够"是形容词，而"够"是动词。我们可以说"买这本书，五十块钱够了/足够了"。但是不能说"我有够钱买这本书"而一定要说"我有足够的钱买这本书"。因为"够"不是定语形容词，不能修饰名词而只能当谓语或补语。又如，"变动"和"变化"都是动词，都表示"出现新情况，和以前不一样"的意思。但是，由于前者是及物动词，后者是不及物动词，所有像"变动一下计划"这样的句子，就只能用"变动"而不能用"变化"。下面的几组同义词、近义词，在词性或语法功能上都有差别，使用时要特别注意：

Sometimes, some Synonyms may share the same meaning, but due to the differences in their parts of speech, or in their grammatical functions despite their similarity in parts of speech, they may only appear in certain part of a sentence, and have different usages. For instance, both 够 and 足够 mean "can satisfy the need in quantity" but the former is a Verb and the latter is an Adjectives. However, why it is possible to say 买这本书，五十块钱够了/足够了, it is incorrect to say 我有够钱买这本书, and only the following is possible: 我有足够的钱买这本书? It is because 够 is not an Attributive Adjective and cannot modify a Noun and can only function as a Predicate or Complement. Look at another example. Both of the Verbs 变动 and 变化 mean "the occurrence of a new situation, different from the past" Because the former is a Transitive Verb and the latter is an Intransitive Verb, in the sentence of 变动一下计划, only 变动 can be used but not 变化. Special attention should be paid to the distinctions in their parts of speech and their grammatical functions in the following:

1. 及物动词与不及物动词 Transitive versus Intransitive Verbs:
   认识——相识　降低——下降　帮助——帮忙　发展——进展

2. 动词与形容词　Verbs versus Adjectives:
   适合——合适　必需——必要　害怕——可怕　庆幸——幸运

3. 动词与名词　Verbs versus Nouns:
   标志——标记　限期——期限　战胜——胜利　花费——费用

4. 形容词与名词　Adjectives versus Nouns:
   年青——青年　友好——友谊　特别——特点　荣幸——荣誉

5. 形容词与副词　Adjectives versus Adverbs:

所有——都　急忙——赶忙　迅速——立刻　自私——私自

6. 形容词/副词与副词　Adjectives/Adverbs versus Adverbs only:

相互——互相　特别——尤其　永久——永远　专门——特地

练习

一、 用线将意思相同的词和词语连起来：

买卖双方达成交易的数目	讲价
规定生产的数量	运费
货币票面的数目	食物
某种商品出售时的价格	降低物价
因为价钱太高而另外提出愿意出的价钱	小费
买卖双方商议价钱	成交额
托运货物的费用	价钱
不收费用；不用付钱	礼物
顾客给旅馆、饭馆等服务人员另外多付的钱	免费
使商品的价钱比以前更便宜	还价
为了表示友好、尊敬或庆贺而送的物品	面额
吃的东西	生产定额

二、 用括号里的词或词组改写下列句子，但不改变其基本意思，必要时可对词序作一定的调整：

1. 这批货物什么时候运到目的港，完全要看下个月的天气。

（抵、取决于）

2. 卖方办理的事务和程序越多，货物的价格就会跟着提高。

（手续、相应）

3. 今年我们公司赚的钱和去年没有什么不同。　（利润、差别）

4. 她总是在一些小事上跟别人讲价钱，在其他大问题上倒一声不吭。

（讨价还价、却）

5. 我比较赞成后一种意见，这样我们承担的费用就可以降低百分之五。

（倾向于、负担）

6. 那个国家的出口商品一直以咖啡为数量最大。（始终、大宗）

7. 你们要尽量不花或少花时间，极力争取在一个星期内完成这项工作。

（节省、力争）

8. 因为货物要经过远距离运输，为了避免可能受到的损失，所以买方或卖方都会买一定的保险。（长途、遭受）

三、 选择最合适的词填空：

1. 这件衣服样子又好看，_____又便宜，多买两件吧。

    a. 价格   b. 价钱   c. 价值

2. 我不反对节省成本，但是别忘了时间的_____。

    a. 价格   b. 价钱   c. 价值

3. 你们要做进出口生意，就要熟悉各种_____术语和它们的内容。

    a. 价格   b. 价钱   c. 价值

4. 由于他们作了充分的准备，所以_____的损失不是很大。

    a. 受   b. 接受   c. 遭受

5. 美国银行的总裁_____了我们的邀请，下个月将要访问我国。

    a. 受   b. 接受   c. 遭受

6. 这种情况我也是第一次见，不知道怎样_____。

    a. 整理   b. 办理   c. 处理

7. 这批出口货物的报关手续，请你_____一下，好吗？

    a. 整理   b. 办理   c. 处理

8. 她在港口工作过几年，对运输业务_____了解。

　　a. 相当　　　　　b. 相应　　　　　c. 相反

9. 因为今年夏天特别热，所以电风扇、空调机的进口也_____增加了。

　　a. 相当　　　　　b. 相应　　　　　c. 相反

10. 老师说的跟字典上写的完全_____，这是怎么回事？

　　a. 相当　　　　　b. 相应　　　　　c. 相反

11. 我们这种产品_____最先进的技术，因而速度更快，质量更好。

　　a. 使用　　　　　b. 采用　　　　　c. 利用

12. 这种机器_____方便，只要一看说明书，就马上会用了。

　　a. 使用　　　　　b. 采用　　　　　c. 利用

四、 找出课文里的目的复句。

五、 用目的复句完成下列句子：

1. 现在，我提议：为_____干杯！

2. 很多外国学生暑期去中国，为的是_____。

3. 为了_____，他们决定自己租船订舱，办理保险手续。

4. 你到了以后，马上给家里打个电话，省得_____。

5. 这一点最好在合同上说明，以免_____。

6. 为了_____起见，他们把船停在港口外边不远的地方。

7. 大使馆商务处准备了中英文的资料，以便_____。

8. 请大家把开会时间写下来，免得_____。

六、 给下面的短文在适当的地方加上标点符号，然后分段：

　　　　最近　中国国际贸易促进会在我们的城市举办了一个商品展销　会因为这是中国第一次在我们这儿举办这样的大型展销会　所以吸引了成千上万的加拿大人　除了本市的市民以外　还有不少从外地来的人　昨

天一早我就到了展销会的地方　好家伙　没想到停车场早就停满了车了　这时　一位工作人员走过来　问　先生　您要停车吗　前面那儿还有些地方　我谢了他以后　赶紧把车开过去停好　展销会展出的东西可真多　吃的　穿的用的什么都有　我想给女朋友买一件礼物　可是不知道买什么才好　吃的　不知道她喜欢不喜欢　用的　又好像有点儿大　带起来不方便　最后我选了一件中国的丝绸旗袍　我想　她穿了一定特别漂亮　她肯定会喜欢

七、 给下面的词写出同义词，并注意它们之间的差别：

1. 价格——	8. 合适——	15. 根据——	22. 购买——
2. 母亲——	9. 交易——	16. 由于——	23. 销售——
3. 功能——	10.节省——	17. 无论——	24. 进入——
4. 星期——	11.使用——	18. 如果——	25. 信函——
5. 办法——	12.取得——	19. 答应——	26. 纸张——
6. 美丽——	13.拜访——	20. 一直——	27. 抵达——
7. 一般——	14.改变——	21. 观看——	28. 邀请——

八、 把下列句子翻译成汉语：

1. Insurance has always been a high-profit business. No matter when, there are people who want to travel, and goods need to be transported. Thus there are possibilities of incurring danger. In general, going through [i.e. "to handle"] the insurance procedures is not very complicated; meanwhile, you don't need to bargain. Therefore, many people have bought different kinds of coverage in the insurance.

2. Since goods will arrive at the port of destination at the same time, I prefer organizing shipments together. Yet, she wants to arrange the reservation of shipping space respectively. Of course, it may be more convenient to pay for the expenses, but the cost will increase accordingly. The only way to solve this problem is that we sit down and negotiate again.

3. Generally speaking, people who like to bargain pay relatively more attention to economize (their) spending. The difference between people who really know how to save and those who like to bargain is that the former buy things when they need to buy rather than when things are cheap. In other words, whether they buy or not depends on their needs but not the price. I think this kind of practice [i.e. "the way of doing"] is worth learning.

文化与商贸背景知识

✎ 商业信函格式

中文商业信函基本上有两种形式：传统式和新型通用式。

(一) 传统式

传统式主要由以下部分组成：1. 收信人姓名称谓、2. 信首套语、3. 正文、4. 信尾祝颂套语、5. 署名、6. 日期。如果写完信后还有事情要补充，可以在信的末尾加上 7. 附言。

1. 收信人姓名称谓

和私人信件一样，商业信函的开头一定要写清楚收信人的姓名称呼。称呼必须在信纸的第一行顶格开始写，后面要加冒号（：），而不是英语的逗号（，），表示下面有话要说。对收信人的称呼要看彼此的关系、亲密程度、社会地位和辈份。一般来说，如果双方已经认识，平常有所来往，写信时就按平时的称呼。如果是初次联系，最好用比较正式的称呼 (详见第六课的"文化与商贸背景知识")。注意，除了对家人或比较要好的朋友，中国人一般都不只用收信人的名 (不带姓) 称呼对方。另外，"亲爱的"也只用于家人、关系特别密切的好友，对其他人，特别是业务方面的来往，都不使用。

2. 信首套语

　　在收信人姓名称谓的下一行，是表示问候、想念、感谢或道歉之类的客套话，或者是对收到对方来信的回答。这类客套话有一定的格式（详见第五课的"文化与商贸背景知识"）并且都在信的开头，所有叫信首套语。但在进出口业务的信件中，这类套语不是必要的，有时也可省去。信首套语要空两格，即在第三格开始写。

3. 正文

　　正文是书信的主要部分，也就是要告诉对方的具体内容。正文要另起一行，前面空两格，即从第三格开始写。如果内容较多，就要分段。每一段都要另起一行，前面要空两格。虽然商业信件比较简短，但也要注意内容要有层次，尽量不要一段写到底。

4. 信尾祝颂套语

　　正文结束后，是信尾祝颂套语，即对收信人表示敬意、祝愿或希望的话，有时也可请收信人向另外一个人或另一些人转达问候（详见第五课的"文化与商贸背景知识"）。祝颂套语一般分两行写，前半部分的"此致"、"祝你"之类多数在正文的下一行，前面空两格（即在第三格开始写），后面不加标点符号。接下来的后半部分要另起一行，顶格写（即不空格）。如果这部分只有两三个字，如"敬礼"、"成功"等，后面可以不加标点符号，但如果是个句子，则可在句末加上句号或叹号（详见后面各课的"商业信函"范例。）。

5. 署名

　　写信人的姓名要写在信的右下方（竖写格式是在左下方），单占一行，不加标点符号。署名的方法取决于写信人和收信人的关系。业务来往信件，要写全名，也可加上职称（"经理、董事长等"），以表示郑重。有时为了表示尊重，可以在名字后（空一格）加上"敬上"、"敬启"、"谨启"等。

6. 日期

传统式信函日期的位置与英文书信的不同，不在信首右上方，而在信尾写信人署名的下方。要另起一行，不加标点符号，要先写年，再写月，最后写日。

---

1. (顶格) 收信人姓名称谓：_____

    2. (空 2 格) 信首套语 (可有可无、视具体情况而定)

    3.1 (空 2 格) 正文   正文

正文   正文

    3.2 (每段开始都空 2 格) 正文   正文

正文   正文

    4. (空 2 格) 信尾祝颂套语

4. (顶格) 信尾祝颂套语

           5. 写信人署名

           6. 日 期

7. (顶格) 附言 (附：/ 又及：)

  (空 2 格) (可有可无、视具体情况而定)

---

7. 附言

信写完后，有时想起来还有事情要补充，可以加上附言。附言一般写在日期后面隔一行或两行。顶格写"附"或"又及"(P.S.)，后面加冒号（：），表示还有事情补充。附言的内容要写在"附"或"又及"下，另起一行，空两格 (即在第三格开始写)。写完后不必再署名和写日期。

传统式商业信函可以横写，也可以竖写。横写时从左到右，竖写时从右到左。现在一般都用横写形式。

(二) 新型通用式

由于英文书信在国际上的广泛通行和历史的影响，其格式广为大家所熟悉。近年来，中国国内也开始接受，并逐渐发展出下面的这种新型通用格式。

1. 发信人的信件编号

2. 收信人地址

3. 收信人所在机构

4. 收信人姓名职务

                                                    5. 日   期

                        6. 信件名称或标题

                    (事由：××××××)

7. 收信人姓名称谓：

8. 正文 (空 2 格)   8.1 起首语

    正文 (每段开始都空 2 格)   8.2 发函者的意见

    正文 (空 2 格)   8.3 结束语

                                            9. 发信人署名

                    页码 (如不止一张信纸时)

这种格式的信一律采用横写。除正文部分和署名与传统式大致相同外，新型通用式有以下的特点：

甲、第一页的左上方有

1. 发信人的信件编号（顶格写）；空一两行后，是 2. 收信人地址和 3. 收信人所在机构名称；以及 4. 收信人姓名职务。

乙、写信日期跟在收信人地址、姓名后，另起一行，在信纸的右边（与英文书信相同）。

丙、接下来是 6. 信件名称或标题，通常用"事由："来说明这封信的主要内容或目的。

一般写在一行的中央，有时为了引起对方的注意，可以在信件名称或标题下加上横线。

丁、正文部分与传统式基本相同。起首语和结束语可套用传统式的信首套语和祝颂套语，但结束语多数写在一行上。

新型通用式有两大好处，一是格式固定，不易遗漏；二是顶端有编号、收发地址（公用信笺上多数都印有机构名称和地址）、发信日期、信件名称或标题，方便存档查阅。

不论使用传统式还是新型通用式，写信时都要注意不要用红笔或铅笔，否则会被认为不礼貌。

(三) 信封书写格式

中文信封有横写和竖写两种格式。横写时，收信人地址姓名要写在信封的中央。收信人地址在上，收信人姓名在下。发信人地址和姓名在收信人姓名的右下方。竖写时，收信人地址写在信封的右上侧，收信人姓名写在信封中间，发信人的地址姓名写在信封的左下侧。

中文地址的写法是单位从大到小，即先写国名，然后是省、市、区（县）、街道、门牌号码和单位名称，如：

中国北京市海淀区复兴路丙12号

中国人民建设银行

如果还有楼层和房间号码，可按收信人的习惯，在单位名称前或后加上。如果地址比较长，可分两到三行写。

收信人的姓名后面，按中国人的习惯，一般都加上称谓，如"总经理"、"先生"、"小姐"、"老师"、"同志"等。在称谓后还可加上"收"、"启"、"展"等。业务信函，收信人所在单位一般都用全称，不用简写或缩写。

甲、横式

收信人邮政编码	邮票
收信人地址 ＿＿＿＿＿＿＿	
收信人姓名 ＿＿＿＿＿＿＿	
	发信人地址
	发信人邮政编码

乙、竖式

邮票

收信人地址

收信人姓名

发信人地址

✏ **商业信函(1)**

中国上海
维康医疗器械进出口公司
进口部

经理先生：

　　我们从中国驻波恩大使馆商务处得悉贵公司的地址，并了解到贵公司是中国主要的医疗器械进口商。所以特发此函，希望与贵公司建立业务关系。

　　本公司专营医疗器械产品的出口多年，在欧美市场上享有很高的声誉，在全世界拥有众多的客户。我们非常高兴地看到，随着中国的改革开放和经济发展，中国与世界的交往日益增加，中国的医学科技水平不断提高。中国是一个极有潜力的市场。我们真诚地希望能够与你们合作，在贵国市场上推销我们的产品。

　　现随函附上我方最新的商品目录和两本样品说明书，相信你们会对其中的某些商品感兴趣。我们保证向你们提供质量可靠的产品，并报最优惠的价格。盼早日回复。

　　此致

敬礼

　　　　　　　　　　　　　　　德国克劳尔兄弟公司
　　　　　　　　　　　　　　　董事总经理

　　　　　　　　　　　　　　　冯卓平
　　　　　　　　　　　　　　　×××年×月×日

通函第123号

京华电子技术公司
北京复兴门外大街 567号
邮政编码：北京 100204

京华电子技术公司
总经理

×××× 年3月16日

事由：询问XX技术转让事宜

总经理先生：

　　本公司产销XX方面的产品已达十八年(关于本公司历史，参见附件《通达电子公司历史简介》)之久。最近得悉贵公司XX技术寻求转让，我们对此新技术的开发极感兴趣，唯对贵公司的历史、业务范围、XX技术及其转让细节了解不多，难以向本公司董事会提交详尽而有说服力的建议和计划，故恳请贵公司尽可能提供下列资料：

　　1. 有关贵公司组织、业务和历史的简介；
　　2. 有关XX技术的主要特点、效益及所需设备的说明；
　　3. 该技术转让的条件；
　　4. 购买专利权的条件。

如蒙惠复，不胜感激。

香港通达电子有限公司
技术开发部经理

刘世才

商品的品质

✎ **思考下面的问题，然后带着这些问题去阅读课文：**

一、为什么说品质是商品的生命？

二、品质通常指什么？合同中的品质条款有什么作用？

三、在国际贸易中，主要有哪些表示品质的方法？具体又分为哪几种？

四、使用品质表示方法要注意什么？

课文：商品的品质

　　一种商品在市场上的地位，在很大的程度上取决于它的品质。品质的好坏不但关系到价格的高低，而且影响到商品的销售情况和竞争能力。可以说，品质是商品的生命。因此，商品的品质是买卖双方都十分关注的问题，也是合同中必须明确的主要交易条件。

　　通常所说的商品品质是指商品的内在质量和外观形态，例如其　5
化学成分、物理或机械性能、生物学特征以及造型、结构、色泽、味觉等技术指标或要求。合同中的品质条款，是货物交接时的重要依据。如果卖方所交的货物品质不符合合同的规定，买方有权撤销合同并要求赔偿损失。

　　由于国际贸易中商品的种类繁多，特点各异，所以表示商品品质　10
的方法也不尽相同。这些方法主要可以分为两大类：一是用样品表示，二是用文字或图样表示。在后一种方法中，又可再分为凭规格、等级、标准；凭商标、牌号；凭产地名称以及凭说明书和图样等等。

交易双方以样品作为买卖和交货品质的依据，称为"凭样品买
15 卖"。样品通常由卖方提供，有时也可由买方提供。按前者进行的
交易，叫做"凭卖方样品买卖"；按后者进行的交易，叫做"凭买方
样品买卖"。不论按哪一种方法达成的交易，卖方都必须向买方提
供与样品品质完全一致的货物。"凭样品买卖"一般适用于难以用科
学方法来表示品质，或在色、香、味和造型等方面有特殊要求的商
20 品，因此除了工艺品、服装、土特产品以外，在国际贸易中一般都
较少采用"凭样品买卖"。

较为广泛使用的是"凭规格、等级、标准买卖"。由于各种商品
品质的特点不同，因此要有不同的指标来反映这些品质的特点，如
成分、含量、长短、大小等。买卖双方通过文字说明商品的规格，
25 既方便准确，也比较客观，所以多用于农副产品和工矿产品。有的
产品像矿砂、天然橡胶等，在长期的生产和贸易过程中，已经形成
了用甲、乙、丙，一、二、三等文字、数码或符号来表示品质分类
的习惯，这就是"凭等级买卖"。双方在交易时，只要说明等级，就
可了解商品的品质规格。标准是经过政府或商业团体统一制定和公
30 布的规格或等级。例如药品、罐头食品的标准，多数由政府制定；
而棉花、小麦等，则基本上由商业团体制定。

某些商品在长期销售过程中，由于品质稳定，规格统一，并且
在市场上已建立了良好的信誉，其商标牌号已为广大消费者所熟
悉，因此在买卖这些商品时，只要说明商标牌号，品质即已明确，
35 无须再说明其规格或提供样品。比如中国的"红双囍"乒乓球、德国
的"奔驰"汽车以及美国的"耐克"球鞋，都是世界名牌，在国际贸易
中都是"凭商标牌号买卖"。

还有一些商品，特别是农副土特产品，由于受产地的自然条件
和传统生产技术的影响较大，产品的品质优良且具有一定的特色，
40 其产地名称也就成为代表该产品品质的重要标志。例如中国的"青
岛啤酒"、"张家口绿豆"和"龙口粉丝"等，都是驰名中外的产品，

所以都是用产地来表明商品品质，并"凭产地名称买卖"的。

至于机械仪器、成套设备等类商品，因为结构功能复杂，型号繁多，且安装、使用和维修时技术性强，需按一定的操作规程进行，所以除了规定牌号和规格以外，还要有详细的说明书、设计图 45 纸等，这就是所谓的"凭说明书和图样买卖"。

以上是国际贸易中常见的表示商品品质的方法。这些方法可以单独使用，也可以根据商品的特点，市场或交易的习惯，将几种方法结合使用。值得注意的是，在同时使用规格与样品时，必须明确以哪一种为准。如果以规格为准，就应注明"样品仅供参考"的字 50 样，以免日后卖方所交的货物只合规格要求而与样品不符时，产生不必要的纠纷。

✐ 根据课文内容回答下列问题：

1. 为什么说品质是商品的生命？

2. 品质通常指的是什么？

3. 为什么合同中要明确规定商品的品质？

4. 表示商品品质的方法有几类？具体又可分为哪几种？

5. "凭样品买卖"主要适用于什么商品？为什么？

6. 哪种方法在国际贸易中使用较多？为什么？

7. 哪些商品的品质标准通常是由政府规定的？

8. 为什么有些商品可以"凭商标牌号买卖"？

9. 什么商品可以"凭产地名称买卖"？

10. 哪类商品要"凭说明书和图样买卖"？为什么？

11. 在规格和样品同时使用时，应注明什么？为什么？

✐ 根据意思，给课文划分层次（不是自然段）并写出每个层次的大意。

生词和用法

质	zhì	Mph./N.	事物的根本特性，本质：实~、变~、性~、特~；质量：优~、~地、品~。
			nature; characteristic; quality
地位	dìwèi	N.	人、团体或事物在社会关系中所处的位置：经济~、政治~、国际~、学术~、领导~。
			status; position
竞争	jìngzhēng	V./N.	为了自己的利益跟别人争高低：自由~、公平~、贸易~、~激烈。
			to compete; competition
关注	guānzhù	V.	关心、重视：~局势的发展、引起~、对……十分~。 to pay close attention to
内在	nèizài	Adj.	事物本身就有的：~规律、~因素、~质量、~联系、~矛盾；＜＞外在。
			inherent; intrinsic
质量	zhìliàng	N.	产品或工作的好坏程度：教学~、工作~、检查~。 quality.
外观	wàiguān	N.	物体从外表看的样子。
			outward appearance; exterior.
形态	xíngtài	N.	事物的形状和表现。 form; shape.
化学	huàxué	N.	研究物质的组成、结构和变化规律的科学；有关化学的：~成分、~实验、~变化、~纤维。
			chemistry; chemical.
成分	chéngfèn	N.	指构成事物的各种不同的物质或因素：化学~、主要~。 component; composition; ingredient
物理	wùlǐ	N.	关于事物的内在规律的研究：~学、~变化。 physics; physical
机械	jīxiè	N.	利用力学原理组成的各种装置：~工业、~产品、运动、~化。 machinery; mechanical

性能	xìngnéng	N.	机械或其他工业制品对设计要求的满足程度：~良好、机械~、~稳定。 function; performance
生物	shēngwù	N.	自然界中由活质构成并具有生长、发育、繁殖等能力的物体：~制品、~钟、~化学。 living objects; organism
生物学	shēngwùxué	N.	研究生物的科学。 biology
特征	tèzhēng	N.	可以作为事物特点的标志、征象：性格~、面部~、基本~。 characteristic; feature; trait
造型	zàoxíng	N.	创造出来的物体的形象。 design; shape; modeling; figure
结构	jiégòu	N.	各个组成部分的搭配和排列：经济~、人体~、机械~、语音~、文章的~。 structure; composition
色泽	sèzé	N.	颜色和光泽：~鲜明、~和谐；Cf. 颜色。 color and luster
味觉	wèijué	N.	舌头与物质接触时所产生的感觉，最基本的几种是酸、甜、苦、咸、辣等。 sense of taste
技术	jìshù	N.	人类在利用和改造自然的过程中积累起来，并在生产劳动中体现出来的经验和知识，也泛指其他操作方面的技巧：科学~、~水平、提高~、~性能。 technology; technique
指标	zhǐbiāo	N.	计划中规定达到的目标：数量~、质量~、生产~、技术~。 target; index
依据	yījù	N.	根据，作为作出结论的事物或理由：科学~、有~、可靠的~。 (on the) basisof; foundation; evidence
符合	fúhé	V.	相合，达到；多指数量、形状、要求、条件等：~实际、~愿望、~要求、~规定。 to accord with; to conform with
撤销	chèxiāo	V.	取消：~合同、~职务、~原计划。

to cancel; to revoke

赔偿	péicháng	V.	因自己的行为使别人受到损失而给予（一般为金钱上的）补偿：照价~、~名誉、~损失。 to compensate; reparation
损失	sǔnshī	V./N.	没有代价地消耗或失去：遭受~、严重的~。 to lose; loss
种类	zhǒnglèi	N.	根据事物本身的性质或特点而分成的门类。 variety; kind; type
异	yì	Mph.(Adj.)	有分别；不相同：大同小异、日新月异、异口同声；＜＞同。　different; other; another
凭	píng	V./Prep.	根据、依靠：~票进场、~证供应。 to rely on; to depend on
图样	túyàng	N.	按照一定的规格和要求绘制的各种图形。 pattern; drawing
商标	shāngbiāo	N.	刻在或印在商品表明或包装上的标志、记号，使这种商品和同类的其他商品区别开来：注册~。　trade mark
牌号	páihào	N.	为某种商品专门起的名字；商标。　brand
产地	chǎndì	N.	物品出产的地方。　place of production; place of origin
特殊	tèshū	Adj.	不同于同类的事物或平常的情况的：~设备、~产品、关系~、情况~；＜＞一般。 special; particular
工艺品	gōngyìpǐn	N.	手工艺的产品。　handicraft article
土产	tǔchǎn	N.	某地出产的具有地方特色的产品。local product
特产	tèchǎn	N.	某地或某国特有的（著名产品）。 local specialty; well-known product of a country or a place
土特产	tǔtèchǎn	N.	土产＋特产。
广泛	guǎngfàn	Adj.	（涉及的）方面广、范围大；普遍：~接触、~的

			兴趣、~的交谈、~调查；＜＞狭隘、狭窄。 extensive; wide-ranging
反映	fǎnyìng	V.	反照，比喻把客观事物的实质表现出来。 to reflect; to mirror
含量	hánliàng	N.	一种物质中所包含的某种成分的数量。 content
客观	kèguān	Adj.	按照事物的本来面目去考察，不加个人偏见的：~标准、~事物、~存在；＜＞主观。 objective
矿砂	kuàngshā	N.	从矿床中挖出或经选矿加工制成的砂状矿物。 mineral ore
天然	tiānrán	Adj.	自然存在的，自然产生的：~橡胶、~景色；＜＞人造、人工。 natural
橡胶	xiàngjiāo	N.	rubber: ~轮胎、~手套、人造~。
数码	shùmǎ	N.	数字、数目。 number; figure, digital
团体	tuántǐ	N.	有共同目的、志趣的人组成的集体：商业~、~票、~活动。 group; organization
统一	tǒngyī	V.	把部分联成整体；使成为一致的：~度量衡、~行动、~祖国、~标准。 to unify
		Adj.	一致的、整体的、单一的：~的意见、~的标准。 unified
制定	zhìdìng	V.	定出（法律、计划、规程等）：~学习计划、~合同、~政策。 to formulate; to lay down
公布	gōngbù	V.	公开发布（法律、命令、规定、通知等），使大家都知道：~名单、~新规定。 to promulgate; to publish; to announce
品	pǐn	Mph.(N.)	物品：商~、药~、礼~、毒~、食~、用~、化装~。 article; product
罐头	guàntou	N.	加工后装在密封的罐子或瓶子里的食品，可放长时间而不坏：水果~、~鱼、~蔬菜、~牛肉。

			canned food
棉花	miánhua	N.	cotton
小麦	xiǎomài	N.	wheat
稳定	wěndìng	Adj.	稳固安定，没有变动： 质量~、水平~。 slable; steady
		V.	使稳定：~价格、~情绪。 to stabilize
信誉	xìnyù	N.	信用和名誉：良好的~、保持~。 credit and reputation; prestige
乒乓球	pīngpāngqiú	N.	ping pong ball; table-tennis
名牌	míngpái	N.	出名货物的牌子：~产品、~货、~手表。 name-brand; famous (product)
传统	chuántǒng	N.	世代相传、具有特点的社会因素，如风俗、道德、思想、作风、艺术、制度等。 tradition
优良	yōuliáng	Adj.	(品种、质量、成绩、作风等)十分好：~ 的传统、~的品质、成绩~；＜＞恶劣。 excellent
特色	tèsè	N.	事物所表现的独特的色彩、风格等：民族~、个人的~、有一定的~。 distinguishing feature; characteristic
标志	biāozhì	N.	表示特征的记号：明显的~、成功的~。 mark; sign; symbol
		V.	明示，常带"着"：~着达到了新的水平。 to symbolize
绿豆	lùdòu	N.	mung bean
粉丝	fěnsī	N.	用绿豆等淀粉制成的线状食物。 vermicelli made from bean starch, etc.
驰名	chímíng	V.	驰=(车、马等)跑得很快，名=名声，形容名声传播很远：远近~、~中外。 well-known, renowned

驰名	chímíng	Idm.	renowned at home and abroad
中外	zhōngwài	N.	

仪器	yíqì		科学技术上用于实验、计量、观测、检验、绘图等比较精密的器具或装置。 instrument; apparatus

设备	shèbèi	N.	进行某项工作或供应某种需要所必需的成套建筑及机器。 equipment; facilities

安装	ānzhuāng	V.	按照一定的方法、规定把机械或器材（多指成套的）固定在一定的地方：~机器、~水管、~电话。 to install

维修	wéixiū	V.	保护和修理：~房屋、~汽车。 to maintain; service

操作	cāozuò	V.	按照一定的程序和技术要求进行活动：~方法、~规程、安全~、~简单。 to operate

规程	guīchéng	N.	对某种制度、政策等所做的分章分条的规定。 rules; regulations

详细	xiángxì	Adj.	周密完备：~的报告、~地址、~研究、~了解、~调查；＜＞简略。 detailed; minute

设计	shèjì	V./N.	在正式做某项工作以前，根据一定的目的要求，预先制定方法、图样等。 (to) design; (to) plan

图纸	túzhǐ	N.	（为修建或制造而）画了图样的纸。 blueprint; drawing

单独	dāndú	Adv.	不跟别的合在一起；独自：~操作、~行动、~经营、~设计。 alone; by oneself; on one's own

结合	jiéhé	V.	人或事物间发生密切联系：理论~实际、~具体情况。 to combine; to joint

参考	cānkǎo	V.	利用有关材料帮助了解情况：仅供~、~价格。 to refer to; for reference; to consult

奔驰	Bēnchí	Pr. N.	德国汽车名，也译为"宾士"。 Mercedes Benz

		V.	跑得很快。	to run quickly; to speed; to gallop
耐克	Nàikè	*Pr. N.*	美国名牌运动鞋。	Nike
青岛	Qīngdǎo	*Pr. N.*	中国山东省的一个沿海城市，以产啤酒出名。	A coastal city in Shandong Province, China famous for its brewery which has named its beer, "Tsingtao" (Qingdao).
张家口	Zhāngjiākǒu	*Pr. N.*	中国河北省的一个城市，在北京的北面，以产绿豆出名。	A city in Hebei Province, China famous for producing mung bean
龙口	Lóngkǒu	*Pr. N.*	中国山东省的一个地方，以产粉丝出名。	A place in Shandong Province, China well-known for producing mung bean noodles.

补充词

轻工业	qīng gōngyè	*N.*	以生产生活资料为主的工业，包括食品、纺织、医药、造纸、皮革等。	light industry
主管	zhǔguǎn	*N.*	负主要管理责任的人员：公司~、~部门、~经理。	chief executive officer; person in charge
		V.	负主要责任管理。	to take (to be in) charge of
富有	fùyǒu	*V.*	大量拥有，宾语多为抽象名词：~经验、~感情、~代表性、~特色、~传统；＜＞缺乏。	to be rich in; full of
家用电器	jiāyòng diànqì	*NP*	日常生活中使用的用电器具，如电冰箱、电视机、电风扇、空调机等。	electric appliance
均	jūn	*Adv.*	全；都：一切~好、~已办好。〔书〕	all.

经销	jīngxiāo	V.	经手出售：~商品、~电器、~商。 to deal in; to sell
远期	yuǎnqī	N.	长时间：~预报、~信用证。　long term
预报	yùbào	V./N.	预先报告：天气~、气象~。 to forecast; to predict
罕见	hǎnjiàn	Adj.	非常少见。　rare; seldom seen
持续	chíxù	V.	延续不断：~高温、~增长、~上升、~半年。 to continue; to sustain
高温	gāowēn	Adj./N.	比较高的温度（取决于具体情况）。 high temperature
预计	yùjì	V.	预先计算、计划或推测。 to estimate; to calculate in advance
电风扇	diànfēngshàn	N.	利用电动机带动叶片旋转，使空气流动生风的装置，也叫电扇。　electric fan
空调机	kōngtiáojī	N.	调节空气温度、干湿的装置，也叫空调。 air conditioner; air conditioning
致	zhì	V.	给予；表示〔书〕：~电、~函、~敬、~谢、~意、~欢迎词。　to send; to express
询问	xúnwèn	V.	打听；了解；问〔书〕。 to inquire; to ask about
现货	xiànhuò	N.	现成的；可以当时交付的货物：~交易、~价格、~市场、~供应。 merchandise on hand
考虑	kǎolù	V.	思索；斟酌：~问题、~一下、认真~。 to consider; to think
互利	hùlì	Adj.	互相有利：平等~、~合作。 mutually beneficial; of mutual benefit
开端	kāiduān	N.	事情的开头：良好的~、合作的~；<>结局。 beginning; start

蒙	méng	V.	承受，敬辞〔书〕：~您指教、如~赐复、多~关照。 to receive; to meet with
赐复	cìfù	V.	给予回复，敬辞〔书〕。 to favor a reply
不胜	bùshèng	Adv.	非常；十分（多用于感情方面）：~感激、~遗憾。 very much; deeply
		V.	承受不了；不能忍受：体力~、~其烦。 cannot bear
感激	gǎnji	V.	因得到别人的帮助而产生好感和谢意。 feel grateful; to feel indebted

词语例释

一、凭(着) Noun +Verb （to be based on; to take as a basis of; to rely on ）

1-12. 在后一种方法中，又可再分为凭规格、等级、标准；凭商标、牌号；凭产地名称以及凭说明书和图样等等。

1. 这些茶叶的价格是凭它们的等级规格而定的。
2. 学外语不能只凭上课听老师讲，必须自己经常练习才行。
3. 这家公司虽然小，但是他们的产品凭着优良的品质打进了国际市场。

"凭"作为及物动词，须带宾语，有"依靠、依仗"的意思。常与助词"着"连用作状语。"凭"也可作介词，表示依靠或根据，常与名词和动词组成短语，如：

As a Transitive Verb, 凭 must take an object. It means "to rely on; to depend on" It often goes with 着 and functions as an adverbial. 凭 can also be a Preposition, followed by a Noun and a Verb Phrase, indicating "to rely on" or "in accordance with". For example:

凭常识判断；凭经验作决定。

二、 难以 ＋（Disyllabic Verb） （difficult to; hard to）

l-18. "凭样品买卖"一般适用于<u>难以</u>用科学方法来表示品质，或在色、香、味和造型等方面有特殊要求的商品，因此除了工艺品、服装、土特产品以外，在国际贸易中一般都较少采用"凭样品买卖"。

1. 很抱歉，这样的交易条件我们实在<u>难以</u>接受。
2. 由于天气的关系，他们恐怕<u>难以</u>按时交货。
3. 那个学生常常问一些连老师都觉得<u>难以</u>回答的问题。

副词"难以"有"很难；不容易"的意思，常作状语，后跟双音节动词或形容词。

The Adverb 难以 means "difficult, not easy" and isusually followed by a disyllabic Verb or Adjective, functioning as an adverbial.

三、 既……也／又…… （both ... and.../neither ... nor ...）

l-25. 买卖双方通过文字说明商品的规格，<u>既</u>方便准确，<u>也</u>比较客观，所以多用于农副产品和工矿产品。

1. 做生意<u>既</u>有赚钱的机会，<u>也</u>有亏本的风险。
2. 咱们还是用电子邮件联系吧，<u>既</u>方便<u>又</u>经济。
3. 为了推销这批货，这次我们<u>既</u>向一些客户报了实盘，<u>也</u>向一些客户报了虚盘。

副词"既"表示不止一个方面的意思，后跟"又、也、且"等，用于连接两个并列的动词或形容词成分，说明同一个主语，表示两种情况同时存在，可用于单句或复句。

The Adverb 既 indicates that there is more than one aspect of someone or something. It usually coordinates with 又、也、且 etc. in conjunction with two Verbs or Adjectives to describe a subject, showing the coexistence of two situations. It can be used in simple sentences and Complex Sentences.

"既……又……"表示同时具有两个方面的性质或情况，连接的部分往往结构和字数都相同。如：

既……又……indicates two features or situations existing at the same time, and the parts it connects are normally similar in terms of structure and number of characters. For instance:

这种包装<u>既</u>美观<u>又</u>坚固。

她<u>既</u>会开车<u>又</u>会修车。

"既……也……"的后一部分表示进一步补充说明，连接两个结构相同或相似的词语。如：

The second part of 既……也……gives an additional comment to that previously mentioned. This structure usually links up two similar structures or phrases. For example:

老师<u>既</u>肯定了我们的进步，<u>也</u>指出了存在的缺点。

他<u>既</u>没来过，我<u>也</u>没去过。

"既……且……"多用于书面语，只限于少数单音节形容词，如：

既……且……is primarily used in written Chinese, and is limited to a few monosyllabic Adjectives only. For example:

"高……大"、"杂……乱"、"深……广"等。

四、只要……就……　 (as long as... ; so long as...)

1-28. 双方在交易时，<u>只要</u>说明等级，<u>就</u>可了解商品的品质规格。

1. <u>只要</u>你们的产品能达到我们的技术指标，我们<u>就</u>可以订货。

2. 作为卖方，我们只承担货物装运上船为止的风险。<u>只要</u>货物一装上了船，发生了什么问题，责任<u>就</u>属于保险公司的了。

3. 我们已经作了充分的研究，<u>只要</u>董事会同意，这个计划<u>就</u>一定能实现。

连词"只要"用于限定条件复句，表示必要条件，常与"就、便、总"等配合。"只要"可用在主语前或后。

The Conjunction 只要 is used in definite Conditional Complex

Sentences, indicating the necessary condition to achieve the desired result. It often goes with 就、便、总 etc. and can be placed either before or after the subject.

五、为……(所)……　(to be Verb +ed [by somebody])

l-33. 某些商品在长期销售过程中，由于品质稳定，规格统一，并且在市场上已建立了良好的信誉，其商标牌号已为广大消费者所熟悉，因此在买卖这些商品时，只要说明商标牌号，品质即已明确，无须再说明其规格或提供样品。

1. 这项为青少年所喜爱的运动也慢慢地在中年人甚至老年人中普及起来了。
2. 我们非常高兴地看到，经过谈判，这些条件终于为双方所接受。
3. 今天我们来讨论一下青少年教育问题。这个问题，一直都是为大家所关心的。

　　"为"是介词，相当于"被"的意思，用于书面语。常与"所"配合使用，表示被动，可用于褒义和贬义。

为 is a Preposition which is the equivalent of 被 in written Chinese. It often associated with 所 to indicate a passive voice. The structure can be used in both commendatory and derogatory senses.

六、驰名中外　(renowned at home and abroad)

l-41. 例如中国的"青岛啤酒"、"张家口绿豆"和"龙口粉丝"等，都是驰名中外的产品，所以都是用产地来表明商品品质，并"凭产地名称买卖"的。

1. 杭州生产的龙井茶，驰名中外，已经有很多年历史了。
2. 如果不注意品质管理，即使是驰名中外的产品，也会慢慢地失去其竞争力。
3. 他们是凭什么生产出这种驰名中外的酒的呢？

"驰名"表示"名声远扬"的意思。作及物动词时，须带宾语，但数量非常有限，如：驰名中外／世界／天下／全国。如作不及物动词，可作谓语，用在"远近驰名"、"因……而驰名"，或作定语，如"驰名的＋名词"。

驰名 means to "to be known far and wide; renowned". When used as a Transitive Verb, it must take an object that is very limited in terms of possible words; for example, 驰名中外/世界/天下/全国. When it is used intransitively, it can be a predicate such as in 远近驰名, 全国驰名, 因……而驰名, or as an attributive, as in 驰名的+Noun.

七、 至于 （as for...; as to... ）

l-43. <u>至于</u>机械仪器、成套设备等类商品，因为结构功能复杂，型号繁多，且安装、使用和维修时技术性强，需按一定的操作规程进行，所以除了规定牌号和规格以外，还要有详细的说明书、设计图纸等，这就是所谓的"凭说明书和图样买卖"。

1. 货物已经装运，<u>至于</u>何时运抵目的港，就要看天气了。
2. C. & F. 的运费是由卖方支付的，<u>至于</u>保险，则要由买方自己负责。
3. 这种新产品的质量不错，<u>至于</u>价钱会不会比一般的高、高多少，目前还不太清楚。

连词"至于"用在分句或句子的开头表示另提一件事情？或一种情况，常与副词"就"或"则"配合使用。"至于"后面的名词或动词等是个新话题，后面有停顿。注意"至于"和"关于"的区别：用"关于"的句子只有一个话题，也不在原来话题之外引进另一个新话题。"关于"还可以用于书名、文章名，但"至于"不行。

The Conjunction 至于 appears at the beginning of a clause or sentence to signify switching to a new topic or mentioning a new thing. It often goes with the Adverb 就 or 则. What follows is a new topic, and there is a pause afterwards. Note the distinction between 至于 and 关于. Sentences with 关于 deal with one topic only, and will not introduce another topic. While it is possible for 关于to be used in titles of books or essays, it is not possible with 至于.

八、以……为……　　(subject to.../take ... as...)

l-50. 值得注意的是，在同时使用规格与样品时，必须明确<u>以</u>哪一种<u>为准</u>。

1. 一般来说，虚盘都注明"<u>以</u>我方最后确认<u>为准</u>"。
2. 所有的进口药物和食品，必须<u>以</u>政府有关部门制定的品质标准<u>为</u>准。
3. 这个报价，一直到本月28日下午五时有效，<u>以</u>美国东部时间<u>为</u>准。

"以"是介词，表示行为动作的手段、方式，相当于"用、拿、按"的意思。经常与"为"配合使用，表示"拿/把……作为……"的意思，用于书面语。

以 is a Preposition and is similar to "take, use, accord" in meaning. It usually pairs up with 为, meaning "to take...as", to show the means or manner of an action. It is generally used in the written language.

"以……为……"，还可以表示"比较起来怎么样、要数、要算"的意思，或者表示主观判断，含有"认为"的意思。如：

In addition, the pattern 以……为……indicates something is "more desired, better in comparison with others" It may express some kind of subjective judgement, i.e., "to consider, to deem". For example:

4. 汽车的机械性能<u>以</u>德国的"奔驰"<u>为</u>最好。
5. 这种商品<u>以</u>塑料包装<u>为</u>宜。
6. 她<u>以</u>帮助别人<u>为</u>自己最大的快乐。

九、……，以免……　　(so as to avoid...; so as not to...)

l-51. 如果以规格为准，就应注明"样品仅供参考"的字样，<u>以免</u>日后

卖方所交的货物只合规格要求而与样品不符时，产生不必要的纠纷。

1. 开车要系安全带，<u>以免</u>车祸时受重伤或发生生命危险。
2. 你最好通过银行调查一下他们的资信情况，<u>以免</u>遭受损失。
3. 请用英语再说一遍，<u>以免</u>有人没有听懂。

连词"以免"有"可以免去"的意思，表示可以避免某种不希望发生的情况，多用于目的复句后一分句的开头，主语往往可承前省略。常用于书面语，口语多数用"省得"或"免得"。

The Conjunction 以免 denotes "may be immune" indicating it is possible to avoid a certain undesired situation. It is normally used at the beginning of the second clause of a Purposive Complex Sentence, and the subject of the clause is often omitted. 以免 is normally used in writing, whereas in spoken Chinese, it is more common to use 省得 or 免得.

十、……与……相符/ 不符 （not/to conform to; not/to be correspond with）

l-51. 如果以规格为准，就应注明"样品仅供参考"的字样，以免日后卖方所交的货物只合规格要求而与样品<u>不符</u>时，产生不必要的纠纷。

1. 当地商会提供的信息<u>与</u>我们了解的情况完全<u>相符</u>。
2. 请你检查一下信用证上的条款<u>与</u>合同是否<u>相符</u>。如果发现有什么地方<u>与</u>合同<u>不符</u>，请他们按照合同的条款马上修改。
3. 对，这种新产品的外观和价格都很有吸引力，性能也很可靠，但是它<u>与</u>我们的使用条件<u>不符</u>，就是再好也没有用。

形容词"相符"是"彼此一致"的意思，前面由介词"与"引出另一个名词短语。"相符"的否定形式"不相符"常常简略成双音节的形式"不符"。

The Adjective 相符 means "mutually congruent" and is preceded with 与 which introduces a Noun Phrase. The negative form of 相符 is 不相符, but it is often shortened to 不符.

词义辨析

一、 质量　质地　品质

　　"质量"、"质地"、"品质"都可译成 quality。"质"字的本意是指"事物的本质或根本特征"。"质量"侧重于产品或工作的好坏程度。"质地"一般指某种材料的结构性质（如自衣服的布料、自做家具的木料等），也可用来指人的品质或资质（如"她质地善良。"）。"品质"主要表示某个人的行为、作风所表现的思想、认识、品性等的本质（如"这个人的道德品质很有问题。"），但也可用于物品，表示其质量的好坏。

　　As the core meaning of 质 is "the nature or fundamental trait of something", the English translation of these words can all be "quality" 质量 emphasizes the degree of goodness or worth, and usually refers to products or work. 质地 is used for the structure or properties of certain material in general, such as fabric for clothes, or wood for furniture, etc. It can refer to a person's character or natural endowments as well. For example: 她质地善良. (She is kind in nature.) 品质 primarily indicates the moral character/integrity of a person, as in 这个人的道德品质很有问题. (The moral character of this guy is questionable.). However, it can also be used to describe objects in terms of their good/poor quality sometimes.

二、 特产　特色　特征

　　"特"字的意思是"独特、特殊，不同于一般"。"特产"是指某个地方或国家特有的事物，也指某地或某国特有的著名产品。例如：龙井茶是杭州的特产。"特色"是指事物所表现的独特风格、色彩，一般多用于具体的事物。例如：那个地方的建筑很有特色。"特征"强调事物外表或外形表露出来的特有的征象、标志，可以作为该事物的特点，可用于人或具体事物。用于抽象事物时，只限于"思想"、"时代"等。"特征"是名词，不可受副词修饰，也不可单独作谓语或定语。"特点"表示事物所具有的独特的地方，它的使用范围很广，可用于具体或抽象事物，可用来指事物内在和外在的独特之处，如内容、性质、形式、外形等。

特 means "unique, special, different from the ordinary". 特产 refers to things peculiar to a place or a country, and also special products known to a certain place or country. For example,

龙井茶是杭州的特产。(Longjing tea is the special product of Hangzhou.)

特色 indicates the distinguishing feature, style, or quality of something, which is mostly used for concrete objects. For instance,

那个地方的建筑很有特色。(Buildings in that area all have distinctive features.)

特征 emphasizes the marks or symbols that something shows or reveals from its exterior or appearance, which can serve as the symbol/representative of itself. 特征 can be used for human beings or concrete objects. When it is used with abstract nouns, it is limited to words like 思想, 时代 etc. 特征 is a Noun, and it can neither be modified by an Adverb, nor can it serve as a Predicate or Attributive alone.

特点 refers to the specific characteristics of something, and it is widely used to both concrete and abstract things. It can indicate the uniqueness of the interior and exterior of almost anything, such as the content, nature, form, and appearance of things.

三、标志　标记　标准

"标"字有"标志、标号"或"榜样、准的"等意思。"标志"作名词时，指的是"表明事物特征的记号"，可用于具体事物或抽象事物。例如：

标 can mean "sign, mark, symbol" or "model, standard". When functioning as a Noun, 标志 refers to an image or object that represents a certain thing. It can be used for concrete or abstract things. For example,

龙是他们公司的标志。(The Dragon is the symbol of their company.)

"标志"作及物动词时，有"成为某事物的特征后被用来表明该事物"的意思。它常带"着"加小句或抽象名词的宾语作谓语，多用于书面语，有郑重的色彩。例如：

When 标志 is used as a Transitive Verb, it means "to mark, to symbolize". It often takes 着 with a Clause or an Abstract Noun as its Object to serve as a Predicate of a sentence. It is mostly used in written Chinese and is formal and serious. For example,

买汽车和买房子的人越来越多, 标志着经济的好转。(That more and more people are buying houses and cars indicates the recovery of the economy.)

"标记"是名词, 表示可用来记认所标明的事物或现象。一般用于具体东西所充当的记号来起标示作用的情形, 只用于具体事物, 没有严肃、郑重的色彩, 不可作动词用。

标记 is a Noun, meaning "mark or sign of an object or a phenomenon". It is normally used in situations in which concrete object functions as a mark or sign, and is for concrete things only. It does not have the sense of formalness or solemness, non can it function as a Verb.

"标准"作为名词, 意思是"衡量事物的尺度、依据或准则", 使用范围较广。"标准"还可作形容词表示事物合乎一定的准则, 可供同类事物作比较、核对。如:

As a Noun, 标准 refers to "criterion, standard" and is used in various context. In addition, 标准 can function as an Adjective as well, which means conforming to a standard. For instance,

虽然他没去过中国留学, 可是说得一口标准的普通话。(Although he has not been to China to study, he speaks native-like Mandarin Chinese.)

四、图纸　图样　图表

"图"指的是用绘画表现出来的形象。"图纸"专指为修建或制造而画了图样的纸。"图样"是按照一定的规格和要求绘制的各种图形, 说明大小、结构和形状, 供制造或建筑时做样子, 或在商业贸易中, 供订货参考用。"图表"是表示各种情况和注明各种数字的图和表的总称, 如示意图、统计表等。

图 is the image presented by drawing or painting. 图纸 refers specifically to a detailed print of a building to be constructed or a drawing of a device to be manufactured. 图样 is the various drawing of patterns or designs according to certain specifications or requirements that illustrate sizes, structures and shapes for the purposes of building, manufacturing, or for reference when making an order in trade. 图表 is the general term for charts and tables that provide information or help explaining different situations or various figures such as illustrations or statistic graphs

语法

一、并列复句　Coordinative Complex Sentences

并列复句可包含两个或两个以上的分句，分别说明或描写几种情况，几件事情，或同一事物的几个方面。并列复句有时可以不用关联词语，只靠语序排列或相同的句子结构来表示并列关系。例如：

Coordinative Complex Sentences contain two or more clauses, which refer to or describe several situations, matters or the various aspects of something. Some Coordinative Complex Sentences may not need Connectives, but simply rely on proper word order or similar sentence structures to show the coordinative relation. For example:

1. 王师傅儿子是大学生，女儿是研究生。
2. 现在电脑的速度越来越快，功能越来越多，质量越来越好。

并列复句也常用下列的关联词语来表示平行、并列的关系：

Usually Coordinative Complex Sentences use the following Connectives to indicate a parallel, coordinative relation: "也"、"又"、"同时"、"也……也……"、"又……又……"、"既……又/也……"、"一方面……，(另)一方面……"、"一边……一边……"、"一面……一面……".

3. 他这次去中国见了很多老朋友，同时也认识了不少新朋友。
4. 这种鞋既美观又舒服，买一双吧。

5. 买卖双方通过文字说明商品的品质规格、<u>既</u>方便准确，<u>也</u>比较客观，所以多用于农副产品和工矿产品。

6. 中国的大学生现在也有人<u>一边</u>念书，<u>一边</u>打工的了。

有些并列复句，分句之间的关系是一种对比的关系，在意义上是相对相反的。这种并列复句常用以下的关联词语来连接两个分句：

The relationship within some Coordinative Complex Sentences is a contrastive one, and is mutually contradictory in meaning. These Coordinative Complex Sentences often use the following to connect the two clauses: "不是……，而是……"、"是……（而）不是……"、"……则……"、"……，而……".

7. 药品、罐头食品的标准，多数由政府制定；<u>而</u>棉花、小麦等，<u>则</u>基本上由商业团体制定。

8. 买方力争降低商品的价格，以便尽量节省开支；卖方<u>则</u>力图提高商品的价格，希望更多地赚取利润。

还有一些并列复句，分句之间是一种总分关系，即前一分句提出一个总的概说，后面的分句再分别细说。总说与细说之间，有时用冒号，有时用逗号。有的不用关联词语，但是有的常用以下的关联词语来连接各个分句：

There are still other Coordinative Complex Sentences that bear a general-specific relation; that is, the first clause sets up a general statement while the second clause gives more detailed elaboration. In between the general statement and the detailed elaboration, a Colon or a Comma may be used, depending on the situation. Sometimes, no Connectives is used, but the following are commonly used to coordinate the two clauses: "……，有的……有的……，（还）有的……"、"……，一是……，二是……，三是……"、"……，一则……，二则……".

9. 放暑假了，同学们都有不同的计划，<u>有的</u>上暑期学校，<u>有的</u>工作<u>还有的</u>去旅游。

10. 表示商品品质的方法主要可以分为两大类：<u>一是</u>用样品表示，<u>二是</u>用文字或图样表示。

二、 解说复句　Elaborative Complex Sentences

　　分句之间是解释说明关系的复句叫解说复句。从功能上来说，解说复句又可再分为两种：一种是举例和比方，常用的关联词语有"比如、譬如、例如、比方说"等；另一种是解释说明，前面的分句提出一个概念、术语或事物，后面的分句从不同的角度作进一步的说明。常用的关联词语有"也就是说"、"即是说"、"即"、"换句话说"、"换言之"等。例如：

Elaborative Complex Sentences are those with a relation of illustration and elaboration between clauses. Functionally speaking, Elaborative Complex Sentences can be further divided into two groups. One group is those that give examples for which the common Connectives are 比如、譬如、例如、比方说etc. The other group is those that explain or illustrate. Normally, the first clause introduces a concept, terminology, or an issue, and the second clause gives further explanation or elaboration from a different angle. The Connectives often seen are 也就是说、即、是、说、即、换句话说、换言之 etc. Please note the following examples:

　　与客户建立业务关系有各种途径，<u>比如</u>请外国大使馆商务处介绍，请银行、商会　推荐，或者从广告、报刊上得到有关厂商的信息。

　　普通话是中国政府规定的现代汉民族规范的共同语，<u>换言之</u>，任何地方方言，广东话、上海话等都不是全汉民族统一的规范的共同语。

　　价格通常是指商品出售的单价，<u>即</u>商品的每一个计量单位以某一种货币表示的价钱。

修辞

反义词　*Antonyms*

反义词是词性相同，但意义相反或相对的一组词。例如：大/小、多/少、好/坏、来/去等等。从逻辑上说，反义词可以分成两大类。一类是表达的意义互相矛盾、互相排斥，二者必居其一，中间没有第三意义存在。如：

Antonyms are those pairs of words of the same part of speech that have opposite meaning. For instance, 大/小、多/少、好/坏、来/去, etc.. Logically speaking, there are two types of Antonyms. The first type are those contradictory to each other — mutually to exclusive ones — and there is no other meaning between the two. These are some of the examples:

生——死　动——静　战争——和平　成功——失败
男——女　真——假　主观——客观　特殊——一般

另一类是表达的意义不一定是互相矛盾、互相否定的，而是一种鲜明的对比关系，两者中间可以有其他意义存在。如：

The other type of Antonyms are those words that may not necessarily contradict or negate each other, but shows a striking contrast as a pair, and there may be other words or meanings between the two. For example:

上——下(中)　东——西(南)　前进——后退(停止)　老年——少年(青年)
黑——白(红)　冷——热(暖)　购买——出售(租赁)　增加——减少(持平)

反义词以形容词则最多，其次是动词。表示具体事物的名词(如：笔、书、字典、电话)大部分都没有反义词。在一个词的前面加上"不"字的，是否定词组，一般不看成是反义词。组成反义词的一对词基本上都属于同一意义范畴，例如：长——短，是指长度；早——晚，是指时间；开始——结束是指过程。但是有些词是多义词，因此可以在不同的意义范畴内有与其相配的反义词。例如"快"，当指速度时，反义词是"慢"；当指锋利程度时，反义词却是"钝"。另外，像"新"和"开"，也可有"老、旧、陈"和"关、闭、停"等不同的反义词。

Adjectives are the major types of Antonyms, followed by Verbs. Nouns that refer to concrete objects such as 笔、书、字典、电话 normally do not have Antonyms. A word that is preceded with a 不 is a short phrase of negation, and is not considered as an Antonym in general. A pair of words that are Antonyms normally belong to the same category. For instance, 长 and 短 are words about length; 早 and 晚 are related to time, and 开始 and 结束 describe a certain process. However, some words have multiple meanings, and may have various Antonyms in different semantic scopes. Take 快 as an example: when it refers to speed, its antonym is 慢; when it refers to the sharpness of a knife, the Antonym is 钝. Other examples are 新 and 开, which can have 老、旧、陈 and 关、闭、停 respectively as their Antonyms.

反义词在修辞上有非常重要的作用。由于反义词意义上的对立，通过反义词进行对比，可以突出事物的是非、善恶、轻重、缓急，形成鲜明的对照，使语义更加深刻有力，收到良好的表达效果。例如：

Antonyms play a important role in rhetoric. As they are contrastive or contradictory in meaning, when properly used, they can effectively project right and wrong, good and bad, degree of significance as well as the difference in pace. Thus, Antonyms can provide a sharp contrast, making expressions more vivid and forceful. Here are some excellent examples:

假作真时真亦假，无为有处有亦无。

(曹雪芹《红楼梦》第一回)

虚心使人进步，骄傲使人落后，我们应当永远记住这个真理。
(毛泽东《中国共产党第八次全国代表大会开幕词》)

我们大家辛辛苦苦为的是什么？就为的一个心愿：要把死的变成活的；把臭的变成香的；把丑的变成美的；把痛苦变成欢乐；把生活变成座大花园。

(杨朔《京城漫记》)

另外，反义词也有很强的构词功能。汉语里有许多双音节词是由一对单音节反义词构成的。例如：

Antonyms are also very powerful in forming words. As a matter of fact, a lot of words in Chinese are constructed by associating two monosyllabic Antonyms together. These are a few of them:

天地、日夜、买卖、先后、大小、呼吸、是非、反正、得失、存亡、胜负。

有不少成语也是利用反义词构成的。如：

Quite a number of Chinese idioms are formed in this fashion. For example:

出生入死、争先恐后、有名无实、口是心非、得不偿失、推陈出新、欢天喜地。

练习

一、 用线将意思相同的词和词语连起来：

人的思想或事物的本质发生了变化	性质
一种事物所具有的、区别于其他事物的特征	特点
品质优良	展品
由农业生产出来的物品	食品
用于商品推销，供人家观看或试用的物品	优质
经过加工制作后，可供食用的东西	特价
展览时给大家观看的东西	样品
研究语言的本质、结构和发展规律的学科	经济学
人或事物特殊的地方	变质
特别降低的价格	特性
研究国民经济各方面问题的学科	语言学
某种事物所特有的性质	农产品

二、用括号里的词或词组改写下列句子，但不改变其基本意思，必要时可对词序作一定的调整：

1. 我们主要根据产品的品质来决定价钱，并不是只看外表的样子。

   　　　　　　　　　　　　　　　　　　　　　　　　（凭、外观）

2. 价格我们可以进一步商量，但说到质量，我认为还是要用国际商业团体统一制定的规格来作为标准。　　（至于、以……为……）

3. 贵州生产的茅台酒，在全中国和全世界都很有名，但是却未必与外国人的口味相同。　　　　　　　（驰名中外、符合）

4. 他们不但要我们降低价格，而且还要提早交货，这笔交易看来很难达成。　　　　　　　　　　　（既……又……、难以）

5. 这是台进口的新设备，最好不要让她一个人自己操作，省得发生问题时要你负责。　　　　　　　　（单独、以免）

6. 今天我们普遍地、大规模地调查客户对我们产品的意见，将来新产品的质量就会有很大的提高。　　　（广泛、日后）

7. 公司的主管部门对这件事情十分关心，非常重视，希望你们能够提出具体、周密完备的计划来。　　　（关注、详细）

8. 如果卖方交货的数量与合同规定的不一致时，买方有权要求卖方付一些钱作为补偿。　　　　　　　（不符、赔偿）

三、选择最合适的词填空：

1. 这个人的＿＿＿＿很成问题，为了赚钱，他什么都做得出来。

   a. 品质　　　　　b. 质量　　　　　c. 质地

2. 我们生产的家具价格合理，造型美观，材料的＿＿＿＿也不错。

   a. 品质　　　　　b. 质量　　　　　c. 质地

3. 她们这次去台湾，带回来了很多当地的＿＿＿＿。

   a. 特征　　　　　b. 特产　　　　　c. 特色

4. 她虽然在法国留学，但是设计的服装都很有中国的传统_____。
   a. 特征　　　　　b.特产　　　　　c.特色

5. 我们老板的脸有着非常明显的_____，你一眼就可以认出他来。
   a. 特征　　　　　b.特产　　　　　c.特色

6. 作为老师，必须根据每个学生的_____来进行教学，才能有好的效果。
   a. 特征　　　　　b.特产　　　　　c.特点

7. 一个国家的进出口额不断增加，是这个国家经济发展的重要_____。
   a. 标记　　　　　b.标志　　　　　c.标准

8. 由于你方提供的样品达不到我们的质量_____，我方不可能跟你们订货。
   a. 标记　　　　　b.标志　　　　　c.标准

9. 因为机械设备的结构复杂，安装使用技术性强，所以要用说明书和_____来表示其品质。
   a. 图样　　　　　b.图纸　　　　　c.图表

10. 我们还没有收到这套进口设备的设计_____，所以没法安装。
    a. 图样　　　　　b.图纸　　　　　c.图表

四、 找出课文里的并列复句和解说复句。

五、 用括号里的关联词将下列句子改成并列复句：

1. 口头接受和书面接受报价都是有效的承诺。　　（也）

2. 用文字来说明商品的规格，不但方便简单，而且准确客观。
   　　　　　　　　　　　　　　　　　　（既……又……）

3. 我给对方打了电话，并发了传真。　　（还）

4. 经理叫你发实盘的时候，一起发一些虚盘。　　（同时）

5. 他想赚大钱，但是怕冒风险。　　（一方面……另一方面……）

6. 卖方希望提高价格，更多地赚取利润；买方却要降低价格，尽量节省开支。　　（则）

7. 采用C.I.F.价格条款时，卖方不负责货物从装运上船后到运抵目的港的一切风险，只负责装运上船为止的风险。　　（不是……而是……）

8. 这几天天气很不好，刮风下雨，不知道能否按时装运。

　　　　　　　　　　　　　　　　　　　（又……又……）

9. 我们除了出口美国的农产品，还进口各国的土特产。（既……也……）

10. 最近我们接到了很多要求建立业务关系的信函，有美国公司的，有日本公司的。　　（有的……，有的……）

11. 表示商品品质的方法主要有用样品表示和用文字或图样表示两大类。　　（一是……，二是……）

12. 凡是内容符合这三项要求的发盘，即各项交易条件都是明确的、完整的、毫无保留条件的，就是实盘。

　　　　　　　　　　（第一、……，第二、……，第三、……）

六、 用解说复句的形式转述下面的内容：

1. 实盘是有法律约束力的发盘，也就是说，……

2. 你可以用各种方式跟他们联系，比方说，……

3. 现在美国的商店，到处都可以看到中国货，比如：……

4. 商品的价格是根据供求情况而变动的。换句话说，……

5. 这次展览的都是名牌产品，例如：……

6. 品质是商品的生命，换言之，……

7. 英语的价格术语F.O.B.，即……

8. 用这种材料包装有很多好处，譬如：……

七、 给下面的词写出相应的反义词：

1. 大——	9. 虚——	17. 左——	25. 含糊——
2. 多——	10.异——	18. 上——	26. 肯定——
3. 高——	11. 始——	19.成功——	27. 提高——
4. 长——	12. 难——	20. 复杂——	28.一般——
5. 是——	13. 先——	21.购买——	29. 赚钱——
6. 新——	14. 远——	22. 直接——	30.客观——
7. 进——	15. 快——	23. 主动——	31. 口头——
8. 供——	16. 买——	24.有效——	32. 必须——

八、 把下列句子翻译成汉语：

1. Theirs is a name-brand product, and it is difficult for our new product to compete with theirs temporarily [i.e. "in a short time"]. However, the design of our new product is reasonable, and the structure is unique. While its operation is convenient, the maintenance is simple. With [i.e. "relying on"] its high performance and excellent quality, I believe that this new product can definitely become a famous one renowned in China and the world.

2. This is a special situation. The insurance company has been paying close attention all the way [i.e. "from the beginning to the end"] to the loss you have suffered. We will compensate your loss as long as we have investigated it clearly. As for how much to compensate, we will take the result of our investigation as the basis. We will, of course, also refer to the information provided by you and the other party. Once we combine the result of our investigation and other information, we will have a relatively objective and detailed understanding. By that time, we can announce the result to all of you.

3. The shapes of these so-called handicraft articles have neither modern characteristics nor do they conform with our tradition. If one (of them) is on

display alone, you have no idea what it is at all. I don't think they will be favored [i.e. "liked"] by people here. You'd better cancel the exhibition, so as to avoid (the situation that) no one comes to visit.

九、 商业信函练习一

1. 阅读下面的信，注意其格式和用词：

2. 根据上面这封信的内容，以总经理的名义写一封回信给美国波士顿美丽芳香公司董事长谭升易先生。回信必须包括下面的内容：

1. Acknowledge receipt of the letter and thank him.

2. Express interest of establishing business relations with Magnificence Company, and look forward to having a long term partnership.

3. Enclose the latest catalogue of your products for Mr. Tan to select the articles that may interest him.

4. Can offer at very competitive prices if Mr. Tan orders in large quantity.

5. Look forward to an early reply.

中国陶瓷工艺品进出口公司
广州陶瓷出口部
总经理

总经理先生：

　　我们从贵国驻纽约总领事馆商务处参赞马立成先生处得悉贵公司的地址，并了解到贵公司是中国陶瓷餐具的主要出口商，因此特地发函与您联系，希望能与贵公司建立业务关系。

　　本公司是美国东北部餐具及厨房用品的主要经销商，在新英格兰地区和加拿大都有很多客户。我们非常乐意与贵公司进行交易，进口你们的产品，并希望能够长期合作。如能给我们寄上贵公司的最新商品目录及有关资料，将不胜感激。

　　此致

敬礼

　　　　　　　　　　　　　　董事长

　　　　　　　　　　　　谭升易　敬上

　　　　　　　　　　　　××××年2月9日

文化与商贸背景知识

📎 书信常用套语

　　书信中常有一些比较固定的"客气话"，也就是套语。套语有两种：用在信件开头的叫"信首套语"；用在信件结尾的叫"信尾祝颂套语"。以下是一些常用的书信套语。

(一) 信首套语

　　信首套语用来向收信人表示问候、想念、感谢、道歉或告知对方寄来的邮件已收到等。注意："您"不用于复数，如果不止一个人，用"你们"而不用"您们"。

1. 您好。　　　你好。　　　你们好。

　　新年好!　　新春好!　　春节好!

　　您最近身体好吗?　　　你近来工作(学习/生活)怎么样?

2. 久未通信，不知近况如何?

　　很久没有跟您联系了，甚念。

　　分别已有半年了，非常想念你们。

3. 久未奉函致意，甚为抱歉。

　　好久没给你写信了，请原谅。

4. 十分感谢您的来信。

　　感谢你们寄来的资料，……

5. 非常高兴收到您(你们/贵公司)的来信(订单)。

　　×月×日的来信(来函/订单)已悉。

　　接到(收到)×?月×?日的来信(来函(订单)，我们……

　　得悉…+(消息)，欣闻…+(消息)，

　　据悉…+(消息)，据报…+(消息)，

　　近悉(近接)……(消息)，

　　顷奉(顷接)贵公司(贵方)来函(信/电)，

　　前接你们(贵公司)的来信，…+(消息)

(二) 信尾祝颂套语

　　信尾祝颂套语用来向收信人表示敬意、谢意、祝愿或希望，或请收信人向其他人转达发信人的问候。

1. 此致　敬礼　　　　　　　　　　　顺致崇高的敬意!

2. 谨致　衷心的谢意　　　　　　　　特此致谢

　　再次表示衷心的感谢！　　　　　　如蒙协助，不胜感激。

3. 致以良好的祝愿！　　　　　　　　谨祝贵公司生意兴隆 (繁荣昌盛)。

　　顺祝业务蒸蒸日上 (生意成功)。　预祝展出 (访美、访华或地名) 圆满成功。

　　祝合作成功 (工作顺利)。　　　　望进一步加强联系。

　　愿我们的合作愉快。　　　　　　愿今后有更广泛的合作。

4. 望进一步加强联系。　　　　　　　请保持联系。

　　望及早告知。　　　　　　　　　盼早日回复。

　　烦请早日赐复。　　　　　　　　希尽早回复为盼。

　　如蒙惠复，不胜感激。　　　　　烦请函 (电) 复。

5. 祝你工作顺利　　　　　　　　　　祝你学业进步

　　敬祝贵体安康 (身体健康)　　　　祝幸福 (愉快)

　　祝安康 (康乐)　　　　　　　　　遥祝全家平安

　　即颂春安 (春天用)　　谨祈　早日康复 (收信人在伤病中)

　　顺颂暑安 (夏天用)　　敬祝　愈安 (收信人在病愈后)

　　此颂秋安 (秋天用)　　此颂　时祺

　　谨颂冬安 (冬天用)　　谨颂　近祺

　　谨祝教安 (对老师)　　　　　　顺祝　学安 (对学生)

　　并颂俪安 (对夫妇)　　　　　　祝　安好

6. 祝新年 (圣诞/×？×？节) 快乐！　　恭贺新禧 (春节用)

　　祝新春愉快 (春节用)！　　　　万事如意 (春节用)

　　祝如意吉祥 (春节用)！

✏️ **商业信函**(2)

中国上海

中国轻工业品进出口总公司

上海分公司

主管先生：

  据中美总商会推荐，贵公司从事轻工业品进出口业务，是中国富有经验的家用电器主要出口商。

  本公司专门经营进口家用电器，美东地区的大小经销商均有销售我公司进口的各类商品。据远期天气预报，今年夏季将会提前到来，并可能出现持续高温。我们预计电风扇、空调机的需求量会大增，因此特地致函贵公司询问是否有现货供应。

  请接函后尽早给我们邮寄你们最新的商品目录及有关参考资料。如果贵方产品的品质规格符合我方的要求，且价格合理，我方将考虑大宗订货。

  我们相信有机会与贵方进行互利交易，同时希望这是今后长期合作的良好开端。

  如蒙早日赐复，不胜感激。

                                        美国海湾贸易有限公司
                                        采购部经理

                                        钱大发 敬上
                                        ××××年2月9日

✏️ **检验证书、检验申请单、产地证明书**

中 华 人 民 共 和 国
上 海 商 品 检 验 局
SHANGHAI COMMODITY INSPECTION BUREAU
OF THE PEOPLE'S REPUBLIC OF CHINA

检 验 证 书
INSPECTION CERTIFICATE

字第 号
No.

DATE 年 月 日

地　址；　上海中山东一路十三号 (正. 1)
Address;　No. 13, Zhongshan Road (E. 1), Shanghai

电报挂号；　上　海 二九一四
CABLE;　Shanghai 2914

副 本
COPY

发 货 人
Consignor

受 货 人
Consignee

品　　名
Commodity

报验数批及（试）亚批
Quantity &/or Weight
Declared

标记及号码；
Mark & Number；

检 验 结 果；
RESULTS OF INSPECTION:

中國檢驗有限公司
CHINA INSPECTION COMPANY LIMITED

香港灣仔港灣道二十六號
華潤大廈二十八樓二八〇六至七室
Rm. 2806 7, 28/F., China Resources Building
26, Harbour Road, Wan Chai, Hong Kong
Telex: 61649 HKCIC HX   Tel: 8276282
Fax: 8275081

檢驗申請單
APPLICATION FOR INSPECTION

編號
No. _____

日期
Date _____

申請人 Applicant:	

聯系人 To contact:	地址及電話 Address & Telephone:
買　方 Buyers:	賣　方 Sellers:

品名及規格 Description & Specification:

請驗數量／重量 Quantity / Weight Declared:

產地 Origin:	船名或其他運輸工具 Name of vessel or other means of transportation:

起運地及目的地 From	To

貨物堆存地點 Store place:

請驗項目及要求 Inspection items & requirements:	包裝情況及標記號碼 Packing, Mark & Number:

提供單證 Documents furnished:

需要証書份數 Copies of certificate needed:	約定工作日期 Appointed date

備　註 Remarks:

申請人簽字
Applicant's Signature:

中国国际贸易促进委员会
China Council for the Promotion of International Trade

产 地 证 明 书
CERTIFICATE OF ORIGIN

日期　　　　年　　月　　日

（Date　　　　　　　　　）

兹证明下列商品系中华人民共和国生产／制造

（This is to certify that the under-mentioned commodities were

produced/manufactured in the People's Republic of China）

标记及号码 （Mark & No.）	品　　名 （Commodity）	数　　量 （Quantity）	重　　量 （Weight）

（盖章或签字处）

产 地 证 明 书
(CERTIFICATE OF ORIGIN)

北 京
Beijing_____

兹 证 明 下 列 商 品 确 系 中 国 制 造
(This is to certify that undermentioned commodities were manufactured in China)：—

品　名 (Commodity)	
产　地 (Place of origin)	中 国 China
数　量 (Quantity)	标 记 及 号 码 (Marks & Nos.)
发 货 人 (Consignor)：	
受 货 人： (Consignee)：	
运 往 地 点 (Destination)：	

第六课

订货量与计量

✎ **思考下面的问题，然后带着这些问题去阅读课文：**

一、为什么订货量是买卖双方都十分重视的谈判内容？

二、什么是"起订量"？什么是"溢短装条款"？为什么要有这些规定？

三、国际贸易中主要有哪些计量方法和计量单位？

四、为什么越来越多国家开始采用"国际单位制"？

课文：订货量与计量

在国际贸易中，订货量是买卖双方都十分重视的谈判内容。对进口商来说，它既关系到商品的单价和成交的总金额，也关系到自己的资金周转和储存、销售能力。对出口商来说，如果订货量太小，则可能得不偿失；但订货量太大，则可能出现别的问题：一个是货源是否充足和能否按时交货的问题；另一个是商品今后的销路 5 和价格的问题。由于市场的供求关系，商品的供应量对市场价格影响很大：若供过于求，价格就会下跌；若供不应求，则会上涨。因此，双方都必须注意市场的供求变化，结合各方面的情况，慎重考虑，对订货量作出适当的选择。

为了保证获得必要的利润，卖方通常在交易谈判前，事先定出 10 一个最低的订货量，叫做"起订量"。也就是说，买方所订货物的数量，不能低于卖方规定的某一数量，否则交易无法达成。有时为了促销或进一步提高利润，卖方可能在买方的订货达到一定的数量时，适当削减商品的单价或给客户打一些折扣，来鼓励或吸引买方

15　　增加订货量。但如果买方的订货量过大，超出了卖方的供货能力
时，卖方会要求客户削减订货量，以免日后因无法按期交货而负担
违约的责任。

　　　　交易协议达成之后，卖方必须严格按照合同中规定的数量，如
期交货。若有出入，不论多少，买方都有权拒收全部货物或超额的
部分。因此，在合同中必须明确交货的数量和计量单位。有些商
20　　品，如粮食、煤炭、石油等，因其本身的特性或易受自然条件的影
响，实际交货数量往往难以符合原来合同上规定的数量。为了避免
争议，对于这类散装的货物，买卖双方通常在合同中规定出一定百
分比的偏差幅度，叫做"溢短装条款"。溢短装的幅度一般由卖方决
定，但有时在买方派船装运的情况下，也可由买方决定。

25　　　　进出口合同中数量条款的最基本内容，是交货的数量和计量单
位。由于货物的性质和形态不同，计量的方法也有多种：有按重量
计算的，如天然产品矿砂及其制品钢铁等；有按长度计算的，如金
属缆索、纺织品等；有按面积计算的，如纺织品、玻璃等；有按体
积计算的，如木材、化学气体等；也有按容积计算的，如小麦、谷
30　　类和大部分液体商品；还有按个数单位计算的，如服装、电器等一
般的日用品以及工业制品。

　　　　目前，由于各国采用的计量制度不同，进出口贸易中的计量工
作相当复杂。即使在同一计量方法中，各国的计量单位也不尽相
同，其代表的数量亦各有差异。国际贸易中较为常见的，在重量单
35　　位中，有克、公斤、盎斯、磅；在长度单位中，有厘米、米、英
寸、码；在面积单位中，有平方米、平方英尺、平方码；在体积
单位中，有立方米、立方英尺、立方码；在容积单位中，有公升、
加仑、蒲式耳；在个数单位中，有件、台、双、套、打等。

　　　　形形色色的商品货物，各种各样的计量方法，名目繁多的计量
40　　单位，加上计量单位之间的换算，不但繁琐复杂，而且给国际贸易

带来了很多麻烦。要清除这一障碍，必须有一个国际统一的计量制度。近年来，越来越多的国家开始采用"国际单位制"，也就是所谓的米制。这样不但方便了不同国家之间的贸易活动，也逐步减少了因计量问题引起的纠纷。但是，在全世界都采用统一的计量制度以前，买卖双方在洽谈交易和签订合同时，仍须明确规定使用哪一种　45
计量制度，才不致造成误会和纠纷。

✐ 根据课文内容回答下列问题：

1. 订货量对进口商来说，关系到什么？

2. 出口商对于客户提出的订货量，要考虑些什么问题？

3. 什么是"起订量"？为什么要规定起订量？

4. 卖方在什么情况下可能会削价或给买方一定的折扣？

5. 为什么有时卖方会要求买方削减订货量？

6. 买方在什么情况下可以拒收货物？

7. 什么是"溢短装条款"？

8. 国际贸易中主要有哪些计量方法？

9. 不同国家使用同一的计量方法，其计量单位代表的数量是否一定相同？为什么？(请举例说明)

10. 怎样避免交易时因计量问题可能引起的纠纷？

✐ 根据意思，给课文划分层次(不是自然段)并写出每个层次的大意。

生词和用法

量	liàng	N.	数目、数量：~重~、大~、订货~、计~、起订~、适~、过~。 quantity; amount; volume
金额	jīn'é	N.	〔书〕钱数：总~、成交~、~大小。 amount/sum of money
资金	zījīn	N.	指经营工商业的本钱：~雄厚、~短缺、筹备~。 capital; fund
周转	zhōuzhuǎn	V./N.	企业的资金从投入生产到销售产品而收回货币，再投入生产，这个过程一次又一次地重复进行，叫做周转。周转所需的时间，是生产时间和流通时间的总和：~时间、资金~、~不过来、加速~。 to turn over; to circulate
储存	chǔcún	V.	(把物或钱)存放起来，暂时不用。 to store; to stockpile; to save
得不偿失	dé bù cháng shī	Idm.	得＝得到、偿＝抵偿，得到的抵不上失去的。 the loss outweighs the gain
销路	xiāolù	N.	货物销售的出路：~广、~很好、没有~、打开~、寻找~。 market; sale
若	ruò	Conj.	〔书〕如果、要是。 if.
跌	diē	V.	摔倒、降落：~倒、~价、~落、下~；＜＞涨。 to fall; to drop
涨	zhǎng	V.	(水位)升高、(物价)提高：上~、~潮、看~、~价；＜＞跌。 to rise; to go up
源	yuán	Mph.(N.)	水源起头的地方；来源：水~、货~、电~、根~、财~、能~、资~、病~。 source; cause
货源	huòyuán	N.	货物的来源：~充足、扩大~、开辟~、组织~。 source or supply of goods
慎重	shènzhòng	Adj.	谨慎认真：~处理、~研究、~的态度；＜＞轻率。 cautious; careful

考虑	kǎolǜ	V.	思考问题，以便作出决定：再三~、慎重~、~清楚、~成熟。　　to consider
事先	shìxiān	Adv.	事情发生以前；事前：~准备、~商量、~决定、~讨论；＜＞事后。 in advance; beforehand; prior
促	cù	V.	催、推动：~销、~进、~使、~成、催~、督~。　　to urge; to promote
削减	xuējiǎn	V.	从已定的数目中减去：~开支、~人员、~费用、~订货；＜＞增加。　　to reduce; to cut down
折扣	zhékou	N.	买卖货物时，照标准价减去一个数目，减到原标价的十分之几叫做几折：打~。　discount
鼓励	gǔlì	V.	激发、勉励（某人）。　　to encourage; to urge
吸引	xīyǐn	V.	把别的物体、力量或别人的注意力引到自己这方面来：~力、互相~；＜＞排斥。　　to attract; to lure
超出	chāochū	V.	越出（一定的数量或范围），比原计划或需要的大或多：~规定、~定额、~意料、~范围。　　to exceed; to surpass
超额	chāo'é	V.	超出定额：~完成。to go beyond the quota; to surpass the target
协议	xiéyì	V./N.	协商；双方经过谈判、协商后取得一致意见：达成~、口头~、签订~。　　to agree upon; to reach an agreement
严格	yángé	Adj.	在遵守制度或掌握标准时认真、不放松：~执行、~要求、~检查、~的规定；＜＞马虎、随便。　　strict; rigorous
如	rú	Prep.	〔书〕依照、适合：~期＝按期、~数＝按照数目、~实＝按照事实、~愿＝按照意愿。　　in compliance; according to
出入	chūrù	N.	（数目、话语）不一致；不相符；有差别：有~、~不大。　　discrepancy; difference

拒收	jùshōu	VP	拒＝拒绝、收＝接收。	refuse to accept
粮食	liángshí	N.	供食用的谷物、豆类和薯类的统称。 grain; cereals; food
煤炭	méitàn	N.	＝煤。	coal
石油	shíyóu	N.		petroleum
散	sǎn	Adj.	零碎的、不集中的。 scattered, fall apart
散装	sǎnzhuāng	VP	没有用任何容器包装，零散地装运或堆放的： ~货物、~运输、~汽油；＜＞整装。 bulk, in bulk
百分比	bǎifēnbǐ	N.	用百分率来表示两个数的比例关系。 percentage
幅度	fúdù	N.	物体振动或摇摆所展开的宽度，比喻事物变动 的大小：大~、增长~、上涨~、降价~。 range; score; extent
溢	yì	Mph.(V.)	充满而流出来。	to overflow; to spill
溢装	yìzhuāng	VP/N.	实际装运的量超出应有的量；＜＞短装。 overload
短	duǎn	Mph.(V.)	缺少、欠。	to lack; to be less
短装	duǎnzhuāng	VP/N.	实际装运的量少于应有的量；＜＞溢装。 underload
计算	jìsuàn	V.	根据已知数目运用数学方法求出未知数：~人 数、~时间、~面积、~重量、~长度、电子~ 机。 to calculate; to compute; to count
重量	zhòngliàng	N.	由于地心引力的作用，物体具有向下的力，这 个力的大小叫做重量。 weight
钢铁	gāngtiě	N.		iron and steel
长度	chángdù	N.	两点之间的距离。	length
金属	jīnshǔ	N.		metal

缆	lǎn	N.	拴船用的铁索或粗绳、许多股拧成的粗绳：钢~、电~。 hawser; mooring rope; cable
索	suǒ	N.	大绳子或大链子：船~、绳~、缆~。 thick rope; cable
纺织	fǎngzhī	V./N.	把棉、麻、丝、毛等纤维制成纱或线，织成布匹、丝绸、呢绒等：~品、~公司、~工人。 spinning and weaving
纺织品	fǎngzhīpǐn	N.	用棉、麻、丝、毛等纤维经过纺织及其复制加工的产品。 textile; fabric
面积	miànjī	N.	平面或物体表面的大小。 area; space
玻璃	bōlí	N.	一种质地硬而脆的透明物体。 glass
体积	tǐjī	N.	物体所占空间的大小。 volume; bulk
木材	mùcái	N.	树木采伐后经过初步加工的材料。 timber; lumber
气体	qìtǐ	N.	没有一定形状也没有一定体积，可以流动的物体，空气、氧气等都是气体。 gas
容	róng	V.	容纳、包含：~不下、可~30人。 to hold; to contain
容积	róngjī	N.	容器或其他能容纳物质的物体的内部体积。 volume; capacity
谷类	gǔlèi	N.	稻、麦、谷子、高粱、玉米等作物的统称。 grain; cereal
液体	yètǐ	N.	有一定的体积，没有一定的形状，可以流动的物质，如水、酒、油等。 liquid
电器	diànqì	N.	electric appliance
克	kè	MW	公制重量单位或质量单位，一克等于一公斤的千分之一。 gram
公斤	gōngjīn	MW	公制重量的主要单位，一公斤等于一千克，所以也叫千克。 kilogram
盎斯	àngsī	M.W	美制重量单位，是一磅的十六分之一。 ounce

磅	bàng	MW	美制重量单位，一磅等于 0.373 公斤。 pound
厘米	límǐ	MW	公制长度单位，一厘米等于一米的百分之一，也叫公分。 centimeter
米	mǐ	MW	公制长度单位，一米为一百厘米。 meter
英寸	yīngcùn	MW	美制长度单位，一英寸是一英尺的十二分之一，等于 2.54 厘米。 inch
码	mǎ	MW	美制长度单位，一码等于三英尺，合 0.9144 米。 yard
平方	píngfāng	MW	计算面积的单位：~米、~英尺、~码。square
立方	lìfāng	MW	计算体积的单位：~米、~英尺、~码。 cube; cubic
公升	gōngshēng	MW	公制容量的主要单位，一公升等于一百毫升。 liter
加仑	jiālún	MW	美制容量单位，一加仑等于 3.785 公升。 gallon
蒲式耳	pǔshì'ěr	MW	美制谷物、粮食重量单位，一蒲式耳等于 35.238 升。 bushel
套	tào	MW	量词，用于成组的事物：一~家具、十~课本、三~衣服、一~新制度。 a set of (document furniture, garment, etc.)
打	dá	MW	量词，十二个叫一打。 dozen.
形形色色	xíngxíng sèsè	Adj.	形容事物品类繁多，各式各样。 of every hue; of all forms
名目	míngmù	N.	事物的名称：~繁多、巧立~。 names of things; items
繁多	fánduō	Adj.	种类多：花色~、品种~、名目~；＝烦多。 various
差异	chāyì	N.	差别：~很大、互有~。 difference; divergence; diversity

换算	huànsuàn	V./N.	把某种单位的数量折合成另一种单位的数量。 to convert; conversion
繁琐	fánsuǒ	Adj.	繁杂琐碎（多形容文章或说话、手续等）；＜＞简便。 tedious; with trivial details
清除	qīngchú	V.	扫除净尽，全部去掉：~积雪、~障碍、~垃圾。 to clear away with; to eliminate
障碍	zhàng'ài	N.	阻挡前进的东西：造成~、设置~、扫除~。 obstacle; obstruction
		V.	挡住道路，使不能顺利通过：~前进、~发展。 to hinder; to obstruct
逐步	zhúbù	Adv.	一步一步地：~开展、~进行、~提高、~解决。 step by step; progressively
米制	mǐzhì	N.	国际统一单位制，也称公制。 the metric system
误会	wùhuì	V.	错误理解对方的意见。 to misunderstand
		N.	对对方意见的错误理解。 misunderstanding
不致	bùzhì	VP	不会引起某种后果。 not result in; not incur

补充词

信任	xìnrèn	V.	相信而敢于托付。 to trust; to have confidence in
手织	shǒuzhī	VP	用手工编织：~毛衣。 hand-knitting
羊毛衫	yángmáoshān	NP	用羊毛纺的线编织成的上衣。 woolen sweater
质地	zhìdì	N.	某种材料的结构的性质：~上乘、~优良、~纯正。 quality of a material; texture
纯正	chúnzhèng	Adj.	纯粹，不含杂其他成分：动机~、~的发音。 pure; unadulterated
优美	yōuměi	Adj.	美好；给人以美感或快感：风景~、图案~、姿态~、~的环境。 beautiful; graceful

做工	zuògōng	N.	手工制作的质量：~精细、~讲究。 workmanship
精细	jīngxì	Adj.	精密细致：做工~、考虑得很~；＜＞粗糙。 delicate; exquisite; with great detail
享誉 全球	xiǎngyù quánqiú	Idm.	在全世界都享有很高的声誉。 to enjoy fame all over the world
逐渐	zhújiàn	Adj.	一点一点地；渐渐地：~减少、~提高、~增大； Cf. 逐步。 gradual; gradually
库存	kùcún	N.	仓库所存的现金或物资：大量的~、~不多。 stock; reservation
追订	zhuīdìng	VP	事后在原来的基础上再增加订购。 to place an additional order
遗憾	yíhàn	Adj.	不称心；大可惋惜：非常~、令人~、深感~。 to be regretted; regretful
		N.	遗恨，多指没有如愿的事：没有~、终身~。 regret
补充	bǔchōng	V.	补满不足：~营养、~货源、~一下、~说明。 to replenish; to supplement
等待	děngdài	V.	等候，期待：~时机、~亲友、~登机。 to wait; await

词语例释

一、 对 (某人/某物) 来说　　(for somebody/something..; to somebody/something...)

1-2. 对进口商来说，它既关系到商品的单价和成交的总金额，也关系到自己的资金周转和储存、销售能力。

　　1. 你们昨天的报价，对我们来说，还是高了一点。

　　2. 对现在的小学生来说，用电脑已经是一件很普通的事情了。

3. 要完成所有这些工作，<u>对</u>这台机器<u>来说</u>，只是十分钟的事，简单得很。

"对"是介词，指示动作的对象，有"向、朝"的意思。"对……来说"表示从某人、某事的角度来看，有时也说"对……说来"。

对 is a Preposition, referring to the target of an action, and has the meaning of "to, toward". The collocation 对……来说 indicates a consideration from the position of someone of something. It can sometimes be said as 对……说来.

二、 关系到　（to be significant to; to affect; to matter to）

l-2. 对进口商来说，它既<u>关系到</u>商品的单价和成交的总金额，也<u>关系到</u>自己的资金周转和储存、销售能力。

1. 学习成绩的好坏<u>关系到</u>能否找到好工作。
2. 这件事情<u>关系到</u>公司的信誉，请你认真考虑。
3. 商品的品质<u>关系到</u>价格的高低及其销路。因此，可以说，品质是商品的生命。

动词"关系"表示"关联、牵涉"，作谓语时常与"到、着"等配合，并带宾语。

The Verb 关系 indicates "to be related, involved". It is often associated with 到 or 着, and takes an object when serving as a predicate.

三、 得不偿失　（the loss outweighs the gain; the game is not worth the candle）

l-4. 对出口商来说，如果订货量太小，则可能<u>得不偿失</u>；但订货量太大，则可能出现别的问题……

1. 她这样做生意，虽然可能会很快赚点钱，但是很容易就失去信誉，实在是<u>得不偿失</u>。
2. 最近市场情况不太好，你最好赶快把这批货卖掉，以免<u>得不偿失</u>。
3. 这是一笔<u>得不偿失</u>的交易，我是不会做的。

　　"得不偿失"是成语，"得"是"得到"，"偿"是"抵补"的意思，表示得到的抵不上失去的。常作谓语或定语。

> In this idiom, 得 refers to "to get" or "the gain" and 偿 is "to compensate" or "to be equal to". It means the gain from doing something is not worth the effort. The idiom is often used as a predicate or an attribute.

四、若……就/则……　　(if ... then...)

l-7.　由于市场的供求关系，商品的供应量对市场价格影响很大：<u>若</u>供过于求，价格<u>就</u>会下跌；<u>若</u>供不应求，<u>则</u>会上涨。

　　1. 董事长来电：<u>若</u>对方降价百分之三，<u>就</u>马上签约。
　　2. C.I.F. 价格条款规定：卖方只承担货物装运上船后的风险，<u>若</u>货物在运输过程中遭受任何损失，<u>则</u>由保险公司负责赔偿。
　　3. 最近因天气关系，北美市场对空调的需求大增。<u>若</u>贵方有现货供应，我们将大量订购。

　　连词"若"是书面语，相当于"如果、假如"的意思。用在假设复句的前一分句表示假设情况，后一分句提出结果、结论或疑问。常与"就、则"配合使用。

> The conjunction 若 is used in written Chinese and means "if". It serves in the first clause of a hypothetical complex sentence to make a hypothesis. It often goes together with 就 or 则.

五、　A+(monosyllabic Adjective)于 B　　(A is more [monosyllabic Adjective] than B)

l-12.　也就是说，买方所订货物的数量，不能<u>低于</u>卖方规定的某一数量，否则交易无法达成。

　　1. 我可以保证，这批货最迟也不会<u>晚于</u>四月底就可以运抵目的港。
　　2. 我们可以给你打一些折扣，但是不能<u>多于</u>百分之五。
　　3. 这台机器的尺寸<u>大于</u>日本的而又<u>小于</u>美国的，非常合适。

这个句型多用于书面语的比较，"于"前多为单音节形容词，如大、小、多、少、高、低、难、易、长、短、早、晚、优、劣〔注：不是"好、坏"〕。

注意在词序上与普通的比较句的区别：　　A 比 B+Adjective

This expression is primarily used for comparison in written Chinese. What precedes 于 is normally monosyllabic adjectives such as 大、小、多、少、高、低、难、易、长、短、早、晚、优、劣. [N.B. not 好 or 坏]. Please note the distinction between this pattern and the one more commonly used for comparison: A 比 B+Adjective.

六、　(给某人)打(……)折扣　　(to give [someone] a discount; to sell at a discount)

l-14. 有时为了促销或进一步提高利润，卖方可能在买方的订货达到一定的数量时，适当削减商品的单价或给客户打一些折扣，来鼓励或吸引买方增加订货量。

1. 因为他是我们的老客户，所以经理决定给他打百分之十五的折扣。
2. 对不起，我们的价格已经非常优惠了，不能再给您打任何折扣了。
3. 现在都十月了，就是打五折，这些电扇也未必有人会买。

词组"打折扣"指商品降价出售，口语里常说"打(……)折"。也可作惯用语，比喻没有按原来的要求或规定去做。

The phrase denotes selling goods at a reduced price. In colloquial Chinese, it usually is expressed as 打(……)折. It can also be used as an idiom, referring to doing something without following the original requirement.

七、　因(Noun Phrase/Verb Phrase/Clause)……而(Verb)……　　(due to...; owing to...)

l-16. 但如果买方的订货量过大，超出了卖方的供货能力时，卖方会要求客户削减订货量，以免日后因无法按期交货而负担违约的责任。

1. 我们公司的产品因品质优良、价格合理而受到顾客的欢迎。

2. 这笔交易<u>因</u>对方报价太高<u>而</u>没有达成。

3. 你不能<u>因</u>自己不喜欢这种音乐<u>而</u>反对别人喜欢。

　　这个表达法常在助动词或"不"后，说明某个行为动作的原因，多用于书面语。

> This expression usually follows an auxiliary verb or a negative adverb 不, showing the cause or reason of an action. It is mostly used in written Chinese.

八、按(Noun Phrase/Clause) +Verb …… 　(according to... ; in the light of; on the basis of ...)

l-26. 由于货物的性质和形态不同，计量的方法也有多种：有<u>按</u>重量<u>计算</u>的，如天然产品矿砂及其制品钢铁等；有<u>按</u>长度<u>计算</u>的，如金属缆索、纺织品等；有<u>按</u>面积<u>计算</u>的，如纺织品、玻璃等；有<u>按</u>体积<u>计算</u>的，如木材、化学气体等；……。

1. 一般来说，我们的出口商品都是<u>按</u>美元<u>计价</u>的。

2. 商检部门将会<u>按</u>规定对这批进口药品<u>进行</u>严格的<u>检验</u>。

3. 这些服装的牌子虽然一样，但是质量不同，所有价钱也有差别，这就叫做"<u>按</u>质<u>定价</u>"。

　　"按"是介词，有"按照、依照"的意思，表示遵从某种标准去做某件事情。"按"后面不可只跟指代人的名词或代词(不可以说"按他"或"按老师")，还必须有动词。"按"和"按照"大致相同，但选用哪个与跟在后面的名词的音节有关系。"按"后面可以是单音节或双音节的词，如：按期完成、按时交货、按政策办事；但"按照"后面不能跟单音节词，如不能说："按照期完成、按照时交货"等。

> The Preposition 按 means "according to, in light of", indicating to do something in line with some standard or requirement. No nouns or Pronouns that refer to humans may follow 按 (It is ungrammatical to say 按他 or 按老师 in Chinese.) without also being followed by a Verb. 按 and 按照 are more or less the same in meaning, but the choice of which one depends on the number of syllables in the noun that follows it. A monosyllabic or disyllabic word is used after 按,

such as in 按期完成、按时交货、按政策办事; however, no monosyllabic word may follow 按照. It is wrong to say 按照期完成、按照时交货, etc.

九、　换算/把……换算成……　　（to convert ... to ...）

l-40. 形形色色的商品货物，各种各样的计量方法，名目繁多的计量单位，加上计量单位之间的换算，不但繁琐复杂，而且给国际贸易带来了很多麻烦。

1. 从八十年代起，中国政府规定：重量单位市斤一律用公制千克<u>换算</u>。
2. 按照今天的银行牌价，如果把我手上的3000美元<u>换算</u>成新台币，该是多少钱？
3. 很多人都不懂怎样把英里<u>换算</u>成公里。

动词"换算"表示把某种单位的数量折合成另一种单位的数量，可以带或者不带宾语。后面也可跟由"成"构成的补语。

换算 means to convert the amount of a certain measurement into that of another system. It can be either transitive or intransitive, and can be followed by a complement formed with 成.

十、　Clause 1，（才/就）不致＋Verb Phrase　　（ ..., not in such a way as to; not likely to ...）

l-46. 但是，在全世界都采用统一的计量制度以前，买卖双方在洽谈交易和签订合同时，仍须明确规定使用哪一种计量制度，才<u>不致</u>造成误会和纠纷。

1. 幸好我们买了保险，才<u>不致</u>遭受太大的损失。
2. 如果她在签订合同时再仔细检查一下，就<u>不致</u>发生违约的问题。
3. 你把这些计量单位记清楚，到时候<u>不致</u>换算错了。

"不致"有"不会招致、引起"的意思，常和副词"才、就"配合使用。注意与"不至于"在意思上的区别。"不至于"是"不会达到某种程度"的意思。

The verb 不致 means "won't incur; won't trigger", and is usually associated with the adverbs 才 or 就. Note the difference between 不致 and 不至于. 不至于 means "not to the extent of...".

词义辨析

一、 资本　资金　资源

"资"的原意是"货物、钱财的总称"，也可作"积蓄"解。名词"资本"是指"经营工商业的本钱，包括厂房、设备、机械、原材料等生产资料及周转的资金"，其引申的意思可以比喻"牟取某种利益的凭借"。例如：

The character 资 *per se* is a collective term for goods and money, it can also mean "savings". The Noun 资本 refers to the capital for running a business in industry or commerce, including the means of production such as factory buildings, equipment, machines, materials, etc. as well as circulation fund. The extended meaning of 资本 is "something that is used to one's own advantage". For example,

年青、美丽是她的本钱。(Being young and beautiful is her asset.)

"资金"也是名词，主要指"经营工商业的钱财"，但不包括生产资料。"资源"指的是"生活资料和生产资料的天然来源"，如自然资源、矿产资源、人力资源等。

资金 is a Noun, too. It basically refers to funds for business operation, not including the means of production. 资源 refers to "resources" in the sense of the (natural) supply of the means of livelihood and raw materials, etc., which bring a country or a person as in the examples of 自然资源 (natural resources), 矿产资源 (mineral resources), and 人力资源 (human resources), etc.

二、 超过　超出　超额

这三个都是动词，"超"字主要是"超越、胜出"的意思。"超过"的第一个意思是"某人或某物从后面赶到另一个人或物的前面",例如:中国的某些家用电器产量已经超过了日本。"超过"的另一个意思是"高出、跨过某一范围的界限,不被这个范围限制",其使用范围要比"超出"广。下面的句子就只能用"超过"而不能用"超出":

These are all Verbs, and seem somewhat similar in their English translation. The meaning of the character 超 is "to exceed". The word 超过 has duel meaning. The first one is "to overtake". For example, 中国的某些家用电器产量已经超过了日本. (The output of certain home appliances in China has already overtaken that in Japan.) Another meaning is "to surpass", "to go beyond", and is used in a wider context than 超出. Only 超过 is possible in the following sentences, but not 超出:

超过1.2米的儿童必需买票。

(Children over 1.2 meters must buy tickets.)

我们会尽快给你答复,最晚也不会超过下个星期四。

(We will give you an answer as soon as possible, and it won't be later than next Thursday.)

"超出"表示"在原范围以外,越出一定的数量或范围",强调比原计划的或需要的大或多。能用"超出"的地方,一般都可用"超过"代替。"超额"所指的范围比较窄,即"超过规定的数量",跟它搭配的,基本上是"生产"、"完成"等词。

超出 indicates that something goes beyond a certain area, and exceeds a certain amount or scope, emphasizing more than the original plan, expectation or need. In general, 超过 can substitute 超出 whenever it is used, but not the other way around. The usage of 超额 is rather limited, which refers mostly to a certain quota. It collocates primarily with words such as 生产 or 完成.

三、气体 液体 固体

这三个名词是物质存在的三种不同形态,"体"是"物体"的意思。"气体"是指没有一定的体积,也没有一定的形状,可以流动的物质。

"液体"是有一定的体积，但没有一定的形状，可以流动的物质。"固体"则是有一定的体和一定的形状，质地比较坚硬的物体。

These three Nouns share a common Morpheme 体, which means 物体 (substance). They refer to the different forms of the existence of matters, that is gas, liquid, and solid, respectively.

四、质量　数量　计量

"量"作为名词，可指"数目、限度"或"计算东西的数目的器具或标准"。"质量"表示"产品或工作的好坏程度"，而"数量"则表示"事物的多少"的意思。"计量"是指"用一个规定的标准作为已知量，计算出另一个暂时未知的量"。

As a Noun, 量 can refer to 数目 (amount)、限度 (limit) or the utensil/criterion to calculate the amount of things. While 质量 (quality) refers to the degree of goodness or worth of a product or work, 数量 indicates the quantity of things. 计量 can be a Noun and a Verb, which means "to measure", "to calculate" or "measurement", "calculation".

五、逐渐　逐步　逐个

"逐渐"、"逐步"、"逐个"都是副词，都有"逐"字在词首。"逐"主要是"依次、挨着顺序"的意思。虽然"逐渐"和"逐步"英语都是 gradually，但在使用上，侧重各有不同。"逐渐"表示事物变化、进行的延续性，多用于自然而然、较缓慢的变化，没有明显的阶段性。"逐步"，按字面的意思，就是一步一步地进行，强调的是变化或进行过程中比较明显的阶段性，多用于人所从事的有计划的活动。比较下面的句子：

With the character 逐 at the beginning, 逐渐、逐步 and 逐个 are all Adverbs. The meaning of 逐 is primarily "one by one, in an orderly fashion". Although the English translation of 逐渐 and 逐步 may be similar, each has a different emphasis. 逐渐 indicates the continuity of change or progress, and is usually used in things happening naturally and rather slowly, without noticeable stages. 逐步 in its literal sense, is "step by step" with an emphasis on noticeable stages or phases of a changing process. It is normally used in human activities in a planned way. Compare the following sentences:

一到十一月，天气就<u>逐渐</u>冷起来了。(✘逐步)

如果你们能保证质量，我们会<u>逐步</u>(逐渐)增加订货。

"逐个"强调"按次序一个一个地进行"，一般适用于能用量词"个"来计算数量的名词宾语。

逐个 focuses on "one by one in an orderly manner", and is used to modify Verbs that can take Nouns measured by 个 as their Objects in general.

语法

一、转折复句　Adversative Complex Sentences

偏句(通常是前面的分句)表达一个意思或叙述一个事实，正句(往往是后一分句)不顺着前一分句的意思说下去，而是说出一个完全相反或部分相反的意思，这样的复句叫转折复句。按语义差别的大小和语气的轻重，转折复句又可分为两种：重转句和轻转句。

An Adversative Complex Sentence contains two clauses —a subordinate clause (usually the first one) expresses an idea or states a fact, and a main clause (normally the second one) shows a completely opposite or a partially contradictory meaning that does not conform with the preceding clause. Adversative complex sentences can be further divided into two categories, according to differences in their meaning and tone. One category is the Adversative/Concessive Complex Sentence,and the other is the Reservation Complex Sentence.

两个分句的意思完全相反，语气较重的，叫重转句。常用的关联词语有：

An **Adversative/Concessive Complex Sentence** consists of two clauses that have exactly the opposite meaning, and the tone is quite serious. The commonly used Connectives are:

"虽然……但是/可是……"、"虽然……却……"、"尽管……但是/可是……""尽管……然而……"、"否则"、"然而"、"反而"、"倒"、"却"、"但是"等。

<u>虽然</u>我们的产品可能不是最便宜的，<u>可是</u>品质绝对是第一流的。

<u>尽管</u>大家都喜欢名牌货，<u>但是</u>真正什么都买名牌货的人倒不是很多。

这个公司只有几百人，<u>然而</u>它的产品畅销全国并且出口到十几个国家。

我把要买的东西都写在一张纸上，没想到出门的时候<u>却</u>忘了带来。

他们改进了商品的包装，提高了价格，销售量<u>反而</u>增加了百分之三十多。

你方的信用证必须在本月25日前开到，<u>否则</u>我们无法按时装船。

两个分句的意思部分相反，语气也较轻的，叫轻转句。常用的关联词语有："不过"、"只是"、"就是"等。

A **Reservation Complex Sentence** contains two clauses that are partially contradictory in meaning, and the tone is relatively mild. Connectives often found in these sentences are: 不过、只是、就是, etc.

老陈学过两年法文，<u>不过</u>都已经忘了。

你们的报价确实很有吸引力，<u>只是</u>交货期晚了点。

我很想跟他们联系一下，<u>就是</u>没有他们的地址和电话号码。

二、 数字表示法　Numeration

表示数目的多少 (包括整数、分数、小数、倍数和概数)，和事物的次序，除了用数词和量词外，还涉及其他的词类和表达法，下面是比较常用的数字表示法。

In addition to using numerals and measure words, other parts of speech and means of expressions are used in Chinese to express quantity and number (including integer, fraction, decimal, multiple, and approximate number) as well as the sequencing of objects. The following are the common ways of numeration.

(一) **整数** 整数是不含分数或小数的数，即零和带正号（＋）或负号（－）的自然数。

整数的表示法如下：

I. Integers Integers are numbers that do not contain fractions or decimals, including zero and any natural numbers with a positive (+) or negative (-) sign. The chart below shows the ways of expressing whole numbers.

位			数									读 法
千	百	十	亿	千	百	十	万	千	百	十	个	
								3	5	1	2	三千五百一十二
							2	4	1	0	0	二万四千一百
						1	8	0	0	0	3	十八万零三
					4	1	0	2	0	0	5	四百一十万二千零五
				6	0	3	0	0	0	1	7	六千三十万零一十七
			9	8	7	6	5	4	3	2	1	九亿八千七百六十五万四千三百二十一
		7	0	0	4	0	6	0	9	0	8	七十亿四百零六万九百零八
	3	8	1	5	0	1	7	0	6	9	4	三百八十一亿五千零一十七万六百九十四
8	0	0	3	2	5	4	9	7	0	5	0	八千零三亿二千五百四十九万七千零五十

汉语多位整数的表示法以四位为一级，即在"千"以上，还有"万"的一级（注意不是"十千"！）。每四位数为一段，每一段都是从左到右，以"千"、"百"、"十"的顺序排列。表示整数时要注意：

The numeration of multiple digit integers is based upon divisions at every four digits. Instead of dividing on the basis of 3 digit numbers as in English, there is a unit called 万 (Note the difference between Chinese and English —it is "ten thousand" in value, but cannot be expressed as 十千 in Chinese!) for units higher than "the thousands". In Chinese, every 4 digits serves as a division, with units from left to right at 千、百、and 十. Please pay close attention to the following:

1. "11—19"的读法——数目为两位数，左边第一个数是"一"(即在十位
    上)时，读数时不说"一"，如 12 读作"十二"。但如果数目是三位或
    超过三位时，在十位上的"一"必须念出来。如；"三百一十七"(317)、
    "五千六百一十四"(5614)等。

    The reading of 11-19: When the figures are in 'teens', it is not necessary to
    say 一 for the number of 10s. One may merely say "ten one, ten two..." etc. For
    example, "12" is 十二. However, if there are three digits or more in the number,
    一 must be used for the number in the 'teens'. For instance, 317 is 三百一十七,
    and 5,614 is 五千六百一十四.

2. "零"的读法——当数列中间有零，不管有几个空位，都只读一个
    零。但如果是多位数，在"万"和"亿"中间出现零时，在"万"和"亿"
    的数段上的零，连同后面的零，都要读出来。如："七十亿四百零六
    万九百零八"(7 004 060 908)、"八千零三亿二千五百四十九万七千零
    五十"(800 325 497 050)。当零在数字的末尾，不管有几个，都不读出
    来。如："二万四千一百"(24 100)、"八千零三亿二千五百四十九万七
    千零五十"(800 325 497 050)。

    The reading of zero: When multiple zeros appear within a number of less
    than 10,000, only one "zero" is read. When there are zeros in the sections of 100
    millions and 10 thousands, as well as in the hundreds and "teens", each zero
    should also be read, again only once if there are multiple zeros within a given
    section. For example, 7, 004, 060, 908 is read as 七十亿四百零六万九百零
    八，and 800, 325, 497, 050 is 八千零三亿二千五百四十九万七千零五十.
    "Zero" is silent at the end of a figure, no matter how many zeros there are in the
    number. For example, 24, 100 is 二万四千一百, and 800, 325, 497, 050 is 八千零
    三亿二千五百四十九万七千零五十.

3. "两"和"二"——数字 2 在汉语里可用"二"或"两"来表示，但两者的
    区别是：

    When to use 两 and 二: The number 2 in Chinese can be 二 or 两, and the
    differences are:

甲、"二"可以单独使用，"两"则不可，后面必须跟其他词语。

如：这是二。

✘这是两。

A. It is possible to use 二 all by itself, but not 两. There must be other words following it. A simple example is: 这是二. It is ungrammatical to say:

✘这是两。

乙、表示一位数，有量词时，必须用"两"。如：两个学生、两张纸、两次、两小时。在计量单位前，可用"两"也可用"二"。例如：两/二公斤、米。

B. 两 has to be used in a single digit with a Measure Word. For instance: 两个学生、两张纸、两次、两小时. When preceding a measure unit, it can be either 两 or 二. For example, 两/二公斤、米 etc.

丙、在三位或超过三位数，2在最左边，即最高数位（如百、千、万）时，可用"二"也可用"两"，但习惯上多用"二"。

C. When 2 is at the very beginning of a 3 or 4 digit number, such as in the hundreds', the thousands', or ten thousands' position, either 二 or 两 is possible although it is more common to use 二.

丁、其他情况都用"二"，特别是读数和数字运算中，如：一、二、三、四……；一加一等于二。当多位数千位后的数是2时，必须用"二"。如：十二(12)、二十(20)、六百二十五(625)、九千七百二十二(9722)、八万二千二百一十二(82212)。

D. In all other cases, 二 is normally used, particularly in numbering or calculation. For example, 一、二、三、四…; 一加一等于二. When there is 2 in positions after the thousands in a multiple digit number, 二 must be used such as in the following: 十二 (12), 二十 (20), 六百二十五 (625), 九千七百二十二 (9722), and 八万二千二百一十二 (82212).

戊、序数词必须用"二"，如：第二、第十二、第二十九。

E. 二 has to be used in Ordinal Numbers such as in 第二、第十二、第二十九.

(二) **分数** 分数通常用"A分之B"来表示。前面的数字 A 是分母，后面的 B 是分子。

注意读数时先说分母，再说分子，顺序与英语相反。如：1/2 二分之一、2/3 三分之二、4/5 五分之四、7/10 十分之七。分数前面有整数时，读作"A 又B分之C"，如：8 3/7 八又七分之三、10 5/12 十又十二分之五。

II. Fractions   The term A 分之 B is used to represent fractions. Note the difference between Chinese and English: The first number "A" is the **Denominator** and should be read first, and the second number "B" is the **Numerator** and should be read next, just the reverse order of English. For example, 1/2 is 二分之一、2/3 is 三分之二、4/5 五分之四、7/10 十分之七, etc. When there is an Integer before the Fraction, it reads as A 又 B 分之 C. Some examples are: 8 3/7 八又七分之三, 10 5/12 十又十二分之五.

分母为 100的 叫百分数，读作"百分之……"。如：90% 百分之九十、75% 百分之七十五、118% 百分之一百一十八。

When the denominator equals 100, it is a Percentage, and is 百分之……in Chinese. For example, 90% is read as 百分之九十, 75% is 百分之七十五, and 118% 百分之一百一十八.

分母为 1000的 叫千分数，读作"千分之……"。如：12/1000 千分之十二。

When the denominator equals 1000, it is a Number of Thousandths, and is expressed in the similar fashion as percentage except changing to 千分之……, for example, 12/1000 is 千分之十二.

分母为10000的叫万分数，读作"万分之……"。如：1/10000 万分之一。

When the denominator equals 10000, it is a Number of Ten Thousandths, and is simply 万分之……. An example is 1/10000 万分之一.

"成"是表示"十分之……"的一种特殊说法，比如：3/10 可以读作"十分之三"，也可读作"三成"。同样，如果是 65%，即 6.5/10，也可以说成是"六成五"。

A special way to express "...out of 10" is 成. For instance, 3/10 can be said as 十分之三, or 三成. Likewise, 65% is similar to 6.5 out of 10, and it is possible to say 六成五.

(三) 小数　小数通常用"A点B"来表示。"点"就是"小数点"。小数点前面的数是整数，小数点后面的数是小数，要一个一个单独地说，如：0.618 读作"零点六一八"，（不可说成"零点六百一十八"！）；3.14159 读作"三点一四一五九"（不可说成"三点一万四千一百五十九"！）。小数点前面的整数，可按整数称读或者一个个单说，如：56.7802 可读作"五十六点七八零二"或"五六点七八零二"。

III. Decimals　Decimals are expressed by A 点 B, and 点 stands for "decimal point". The number before the Decimal Point is an Integer, and those after are Decimals. Therefore, Decimals must be read individually and are different from whole numbers. For example, 0.618 is 零点六一八, but not 零点六百一十八! Similarly, 3.14159 reads as 三点一四一五九, instead of 三点一万四千一百五十九. As for the integer before a Decimal, one can say it in the normal way as in 56.7802 五十六点七八零二, or simply 五六点七八零二.

(四) 倍数　在数字后面加上量词"倍"就可以表示倍数。倍数一般用于表示比较或增加等情况。具体用法如下：

IV. Multiples　One can add the word 倍 after a certain number to express Multiples. Multiples are normally used to refer to comparison or increase. Here are the ways to express Multiples:

1. A 是 B 的 C 倍。　　　12 是/等于 3 的 4 倍。
   B 的 C 倍是 A。　　　　3 的 4 倍是/等于 12。
2. A 比 B 多/大 C-1 倍。　12 比 3 多/大 (4-1=3) 3 倍。
   A 比 B 增加/提高了 C倍。　12 比 3 增加/提高了 3 倍。

注意 1 和 2 的区别：

Please note the distinctions between groups 1 and 2:

1 表示的是"相当于"的关系，只要用A÷B=C，就可以得到相当于的倍数。如：

Group 1 denotes "equal to" and the Multiple is obtained by the formula A÷B=C, for example:

12÷3=4，4 就是 3 的倍数。

2 表示的是"多于"的关系，必须用 (A-B)÷B 或 C-1 才能得出多于的倍数。如：

Group 2 indicates "more than" and is obtained by the formula "(A-B)÷B" or "C-1". Look at the following illustration:

(12-3)÷3=3 或者 4-1=3，得出 12 比 3 多/大 3 倍。

"小于"、"减少"、"降低"或"节省"等，通常都不用倍数，而用分数来表示。

Multiples are not used to represent concepts such as "smaller", "reduced", or "to save" in general, but Fractions are. For instance:

例如：上学期学中文的学生有150人，这个学期只有100人。这个学期的中文学生比上学期减少了三分之一（或者：是上学期的三分之二）。

还有一种关于"增加……倍"的说法，就是"翻……番"。但是要注意，"翻一番"是增加一倍的意思，而"翻两番"不是增加两倍而是"增加三倍"的意思！因为：

There is another way to express the idea of "to increase ...by ...times", that is, 翻……番. Caution: "翻一番" means "to increase by 1 time", yet "翻两番" is not "to increase by 2 times" but 3 times! The reason is as follows:

翻 × 番 ＝ 增加 2^x-1 倍

翻 1 番 ＝ 增加一倍 (2^1-1) ＝ 1

翻 2 番 ＝ 增加三倍 (2^2-1) ＝ 3

翻 3 番 ＝ 增加七倍 (2^3-1) ＝ 7

（五）概数   概数就是不确定的、不是非常准确的大概数目。概数的表示法
有下列几种：

V. Approximate Numbers   Approximate numbers are indefinite or not very
accurate ones. Here are the ways to express approximate numbers:

1. 用"几、若干、一些、好些、很多、不少、大多数"等来代替具体的数
   字。另外，也可以在"十"以上的数字前后加上"几"表示概数。如：

A. Use 几、若干、一些、好些、很多、不少、大多数 to stand for specific
   numbers. In addition, use 几 after numbers of 十 or larger than 十 to represent
   approximate numbers of larger quantity.

   若干封信　　一些样品　　好些问题　　很多订单　　不少商人
   几位先生　　十几个朋友　几十本书　　几百公斤　　几千英里

2. 两个相邻的数字连用，通常数目小的在前，数目大的在后，中间不
   加标点符号。例如：

B. Use Adjacent Numbers with the smaller one going first and the larger one
   next, and add no punctuation in between the two numbers. For example:

   一两个月　　　　　三四个小时　　　十八九岁　　七八十次
   五六百种商品　　　三五百块钱*

注：除了"三五"以外，其他数字必须是紧挨着的，不可说"四六枝笔"。"九"
   和"十"不可连用来表示概数，否则会造成歧义"九十"，引起误解。

N.B. Except for 三五, all numbers must be adjacent ones. One cannot say 四六
   枝笔. Moreover, 九 and 十 are not supposed to go together to represent an
   approximate number; otherwise, it will be indistinguishable from 九十,
   and will cause misunderstanding.

3. 在数词前加"大概、约、差不多、上、成、至少、顶多"等，或在数
   词后加"多、来、左右、上下、以上、以下"等表示概数。例如：

   The addition of 大概、约、差不多、上、成、至少、顶多 etc. before
   a number or attach 多、来、左右、上下、以上、以下 after a numeral

can also express approximation. For example:

这批货物<u>约</u>两周后运抵纽约。

什么？这辆自行车要<u>上</u>千块钱！我看<u>顶</u>多就值七百块。

他们俩已经三年<u>多</u>没见面了。

这篇文章我修改了五遍<u>左右</u>。

一共有二十<u>来</u>人参加了昨天的讨论会。

这时候，进来了一位四十岁<u>上下</u>的中国人。（"上下"一般用于成年人的年龄）

十七岁<u>以下</u>少年儿童不得入场。

注意"多"和"来"的位置：The positioning of 多 and 来：

如果数词是一位数，而且后面的量词表示连续的量，即表示的单位下面还有可拆开的、更小的单位（如"年"下面有"月"和"天"；"公斤"下面有"克"等。）时，"多"和"来"一般在数词和量词的后面。如：

When a single digit number and the Measure Word that follows represents a continuum, it can be further broken down into smaller units such as "month" and "day" in "year", or "gram" in "kilogram", 多 and 来 usually go after both the Numeral and the Measure Word. For instance:

四年<u>多</u>   五本<u>多</u>书   喝了两瓶<u>来</u>啤酒   买了三斤<u>来</u>肉

如果量词不是表示连续的量的，即不可拆开、下面没有跟小的单位的，数词是一位数时，不可与"多"或"来"连用。下面的用法都是错误的：

If the Measure Word does not refer to a continuum, it cannot be further broken down into smaller units, and if the Numeral is a single digit, no 多 or 来 can be used with the number. The following are all mistaken:

✘来了七个多人   ✘养了两只多狗   ✘买了三把来椅子

如果数词是两位数或两位数以上的，不论是不是跟着表示连续量的量词，都可以和"多"或"来"连用，其位置在数词和量词之间。如：

When the Numeral has two or more digits, regardless whether the measure word that follows is a continuum, either 多 or 来 can be used with the number, and is positioned in between the number and the Measure Word. For example:

十多天　二十多个电话　六十来岁　四十来个学生　一百来份合同

相对来说，"多"、"来"、"上"、"成"、"顶多"比其他的几个词更口语化。

Relatively speaking, 多、来、上、成、顶多 are more colloquial than the others.

(六) 序数　词表示事物次序的数词叫序数词。汉语的序数词由前缀"第"加上基数词构成。序数词后面一般要跟量词。如：

VI. Ordinal Numbers　Ordinal Numbers represent sequences of objects. In Chinese, an ordinal number is formed by adding a Prefix 第 before a Cardinal Number . A measure word is generally required after an Ordinal Number.

第三天　　第七课　　第一名　　第五杯咖啡　　第二次握手

下列情况，通常用基数词或其他方法而不用序数词来表示次序：

In the following cases, Cardinal Numbers are usually used instead of Ordinal Numbers to indicate sequences:

1. 年代日期：二〇〇〇年 (读作"二零零零年")　一九九八年八月十八号
   （口语）　　　元月五日　　　　　　　　农历正月初七

2. 亲属排行：大哥、二姐、三弟、小妹、大伯、二叔、三婶、长子、
   　　　　　　次女、小儿子

3. 楼房层次：一楼 (层)　　　六楼 (层)　　　十二楼 (层)

4. 等级：　　头等　二等　（或"甲等、乙等"）　三等

5. 房间教室：一三八号房间　二号教室　五号会议室

6. 班组：   一班、二班   (第)四组

   下列方法也可以用来表示次序：

   The following are also possible ways to show order or sequence:

1. 甲、乙、丙、丁、戊、己、庚、辛、壬、癸

2. 拉丁字母，如A, B, C, D等，或阿拉伯数字1, 2, 3, 4等。

三、 文言词 (2)   Literary Chinese Words (2)

(一) 于   介词，用于书面语，后跟名词或动词，多组成介词词组在补语或
    状语。

   于 is a Preposition followed by either a Noun or a Verb to form a
Prepositional Phrase, which functions as a complement or an adverbial. It is
used in written Chinese.

1. "在、从、由"的意思，表示时间、地点、范围，可在动词前或后。
   例如：

   It means "from" to indicate a time, place, or scope, and can go before or
after a Verb. For instance:

   样品已<u>于</u>昨日收到。   本公司成立<u>于</u>一九七一年。
   会谈<u>于</u>总经理办公室进行。   熊猫产<u>于</u>中国西南。
   景德镇瓷器驰名<u>于</u>全世界。
   他做学问细致认真，常<u>于</u>无人注意之处，发现新问题。

2. "向、对、给"的意思，表示目的、方向、对象等。例如：

   In the following examples, it means "to, toward" and indicates a purpose,
direction or target of an action.

   问路<u>于</u>人。   求教<u>于</u>有经验的同事。
   嫁祸<u>于</u>人   有助<u>于</u>了解市场行情。
   从事<u>于</u>科学研究。   把成绩归<u>于</u>大家。

3. 相当于"对"的意思，表示方面、原因，常在形容词或动词后连接另
   一个动词。如：

   It is roughly similar to 对 in meaning, referring to the related aspects or cause/reason, and often follows an Adjective or Verb to link with another Verb.

   形容词后：便<u>于</u>携带　　忙<u>于</u>准备　　乐<u>于</u>接受　　急<u>于</u>出售
   动词后：　善<u>于</u>讨价还价　倾向<u>于</u>同意　敢<u>于</u>承担责任

4. "比"的意思，用于比较，多跟在单音节形容词后。一般用于书面
   语，注意与正常比较句在词序上的差别。例如：

   比 is used after some Monosyllabic Adjectives to make a comparison in the written language. Please note the difference in word order between this usage and the regular patterns of comparison.

   高<u>于</u>　大<u>于</u>　轻<u>于</u>　优<u>于</u>　宽<u>于</u>　等<u>于</u>

5. "被、受"的意思，表示被动，在动词后引出施事者。例如：

   It is similar to 被、受 in meaning in introducing the agent of an action in a passive sentence. For example,

   这个问题，限<u>于</u>目前的技术水平，还不能解决。
   一九九八年的世界杯足球赛，巴西队负<u>于</u>法国队。

(二) 以　介词、连词，用于书面语。

　　以 can be a Preposition or a Conjunction, and is primarily used in written Chinese.

1. "用、拿、按"的意思，后跟名词，组成介词短语作状语，表示行为
   的方式或手段。例如：

   It means "to use", "to take" or "to accord", and is followed by a Noun to form a Prepositional Phrase as a adverbial of means or manner.

   她<u>以</u>自己的行动教育了大家。

这样每天可以节省十块钱。如果每年<u>以</u>365天计算，一年就可以节省 3650 块钱。

这笔生意最后<u>以</u>三百万美元成交。

2. 与"为"配合，组成"以……为……"的结构，表示"把／拿……作为……"的意思。(参看第三课 (p.93)"词语例释"(二)。) 例如：

It associates with 为 to form the structure of 以……为……, which refers to "take ... as" in meaning. Please refer to Lesson 3 (p.93) 词语例释-二 for details.

最后，买方<u>以</u>对方降价百分之五<u>为</u>条件，同意把订货量增加到十万桶。

这个发盘有"<u>以</u>我方最后确认为准"的词句，不能算是实盘。

董事长要求大家<u>以</u>世界名牌<u>为</u>目标，努力提高产品的质量。

3. "由于、因为"的意思，后面常与"而"呼应，表示原因。

It means "owing to, due to, because" and is often associated with 而 to indicate a reason or cause.

桂林<u>以</u>其美丽的风景吸引着中外游客。

对方<u>以</u>市场需求量减少而取消了这批订单。

这个公司的产品<u>以</u>一流的品质成为世界名牌。

4. "给"的意思，同单音节动词组成介词词组作补语。例如：

It is similar to "to" in meaning and often teams up with a Monosyllabic Verb to serve as a complement. For example:

那件事给小张<u>以</u>极大的教育。

我向大家致<u>以</u>节日的问候。

观众们对他们的精彩表演报<u>以</u>热烈的掌声。

5. 连词，连接两个动词短语表示目的。(参看第三课 (p.93)"词语例释"(三)。) 例如：

Here it is a Conjunction, linking up two Verb Phrases to indicate the purpose of an action. Pleare refer to Lesson 3 (p.93) 词语例释-三 for detail.

他决定去中国留学，*以*进一步提高自己的汉语水平。

公司最近组织了一个小组，*以*加强市场调研工作。

这个城市决定建地铁，*以*解决日益紧张的交通问题。

(三) 而　连词，多用于书面语。

而 is a Conjunction, and is primarily used in written Chinese.

1. 把表示目的、原因、方式、结果等词语和谓语连接起来，常与"为"、"因"、"通过"等配合使用。例如：

   It connects words or phrases of purpose, cause, manner of result with the predicate, and is usually associated with 为、因、通过, etc.

   他们为建立业务关系*而*拜访了美国大使馆商务处。

   那个城市每年因交通堵塞*而*损失几百万美元。

   中国和世界各国通过经济文化交流*而*促进了相互了解。

2. 连接实词或短语，表示状态的改变，常与"由、自"等连用。例如：

   It joins content words or phrases to indicate a change of status. It often goes with 由 or 自 as in the following examples:

   那个大圆球自上*而*下，慢慢地降落下来。

   一个奇怪的声音由远*而*近传来，越来越响。

   喝了这种饮料，你会觉得由热*而*温，由温而凉，舒服极了。

3. 连接意思相对立、相反的前后两部分，表示转折，有"然而、但是"或"如果"的意思。例如：

   It links up two parts that are contrastive or contradictory in meaning, to show some kind of reverse or turn in events. It is analogous in meaning to "yet", "but" or "if". For instance:

   这种西瓜大*而*不甜。

   真正有竞争力的商品，不是靠华丽的包装*而*是优良的品质。

   去年这个时候已经可以穿单衣了，*而*今年还得穿毛衣。

（如果）学习外语<u>而</u>不经常练习是不可能学得好的。

4. 连接两个并列的同性质的形容词，相当于"又、并且"的意思。例如：

It connects two parallel Adjectives of the same nature, and is equal to "and, also" in meaning.

他说话简短<u>而</u>明确，毫不含糊。

同学们都喜欢这位严格<u>而</u>耐心的老师。

这种方法，快速<u>而</u>简单，值得推广。

(四) 由　介词，可用于口语和书面语。

由 is a Preposition, and can be used in spoken and written Chinese.

1. 引进动作的施动者（参看第三课 (p.94)"词语例释"（四））。例如：

It is used to introduce the Agent of an action in the following type of sentences. Please refer to Lesson 3 (p.94) "词语例释"（四）for details.

这批货物<u>由</u>卖方负责装运。

下面<u>由</u>陆华小姐给大家介绍本公司的情况。

这件事<u>由</u>你决定好了。

2. 表示方式、原因或来源。例如：

It shows the manner, cause/reason, or source of actions, as in the following:

采用了统一的计量制度以后，<u>由</u>计量而引起的纠纷就逐渐减少了。

委员会<u>由</u>学生和老师代表组成。

大会代表<u>由</u>民主协商、选举产生。

3. 表示处所、起点或来源，意思相当于"从、自"。例如：

It indicates the place, starting point or source in a sentence, and is similar to "from" in meaning.

她一抬头，看见了<u>由</u>图书馆出来的冯老师。

会议*由*上午九点一直开到下午三点。

日本的石油大部分*由*中东进口。

4. 表示发展、变化范围的起点。例如：

It shows the starting point of certain development or change as in the following examples:

自行车的价格*由*每辆150块钱降到132块。

这样，小何就*由*职员变成了经理了。

什么事情都有一个*由*不懂到懂的过程。

修辞

语体：口语与书面语 Style: Colloquial and Written Chinese

语体是人们为了适应不同的交际需要而逐渐形成的不同的语言风格体式。语体可以分成口语语体和书面语体两大类。

Style is ways of putting words together to express thoughts for different communicative purposes and in different situations. It can be divided into two major categories, colloquial style and written style.

口语语体主要是人们日常交谈所用的体式，在话剧、电视、电影、相声等表演艺术以及说唱文学中也常用。这种语体主要以口头形式存在，但在文艺作品中的对话或某些叙述性语言，也会用到。

The Colloquial style is the manner and mode of expression people use in everyday conversation. It is also found in drama, television, movies, "cross talks", etc. as well as in some special talking and singing performing arts and oral folk tales. Colloquial style exists primarily in speaking form, but it also used in dialogues or narratives in literature.

口语语体有以下的特点：

The following are major characteristics of colloquial Chinese:

1. 大量使用通俗易懂，与日常生活密切相关的基本词、口语词、谚
    语、惯用语、禁忌语、方言、俗语和语气词等。有时还夹杂着"这个
    这个"、"那么那么"等两次重复的"剩余成分"。

    Colloquial Chinese uses a lot of common and easy to understand basic
    vocabularies that are closely related to day-to-day life. These include idioms,
    slangs, taboos, vernacular, interjections as well as words signaling certain moods.
    Moreover, there are repetitions of "gap-fillers" or "residuals" such as 这个这
    个or 那么那么.

2. 因为口语多用于面对面的交谈，语境非常明确，还可以借助手势、
    表情、语调、实物等，所以常常省略某些句子成分，尤其是主语。
    口语里省略句多，完整句少。另外，定语用得也比较少。

    Since the spoken language is mostly used in face-to-face conversations, the
    context is very clear and gestures, facial expressions,intonation, and surrounding
    objects are all employable. Thus, omission of sentence elements, particularly the
    subject, is very common. There are more elliptical sentences, and fewer full
    sentences and attributes.

3. 口语的句子简短，较少用长句和关联词语。复句往往通过紧缩变成
    单句。由于口语对话通常是即兴而发，没有经过很周密的思考，经
    常会加进补充性的话语，因此在口语语体中，词序有较大的灵活
    性，变式句也比书面语体多。

    In colloquial Chinese, while there are more short sentences than long ones,
    Complex Sentences are often contracted into Simple Sentences and the use of
    correlatives is reduced. As speaking takes place simultaneously, and the time for
    thinking is limited, a lot of remarks come as afterthoughts, "repairing" or
    supplements to the preceding conversation. Hence, it is more flexible in word
    order and inverted sentences are much more common than in the written language.

    书面语体是在口语语体的基础上发展形成的。它主要用于政治、经
    济、文化等方面的书面形式交际。但是像正式讲演、新闻广播等，虽然
    都用口头表达，但在语体特征上还是书面语的居多。

Written style has evolved on the basis of the colloquial language. It is mostly used in written communication related to politics, economics, and culture. However, in formal speeches, or news broadcasting, while mostly transmitted by oral means, there is more written than colloquial style.

书面语体有以下的特点：

Written Chinese is characterized by the following:

1. 所用的词汇量要比口语语体的大得多。并且大量使用专门术语、文言词、成语和外来语，而像口语中常见的俗语、昵语、禁忌语、方言词、语气词等却用得比较少。书面语体除了运用口语语体中通用的单音节词外，还常常用一套与其对应的双音节词。如：

The vocabulary is much larger and broader than colloquial Chinese in writing, and special terminology, literary Chinese words, proverbs and words of foreign origin are used more extensively. In contrast with the colloquial language, the written language uses considerably less slang, taboos, vernacular expressions and interjections as well as words expressing moods. In addition to the monosyllabic words frequently used in speaking, written Chinese also employs a set of disyllabic words in the place of monosyllabic counterparts. Here are some examples:

看——观看　读——阅读　买——购买　来——到来　等——等候
治——治疗　病——疾病　好——美好　死——死亡　进——进入

书面语体还常常保留着不少古汉语成分。许多口语里已经不用的古汉语词汇和文言虚词，有时某些书面语里还口语用。例如，先秦汉语里表示被动意义的"为……所……"等句式，也常见于书面语。

The written language still retains quite a lot of elements in literary Chinese. Numerous words or function words that are no longer in use in speaking are found in written Chinese sometimes. For instance, sentence patterns such as 为……所…… which indicates passive voice and originated in the Qin and Han dynasties are rather common in written Chinese.

2. 由于书面交际不是面对面对话，语境不太明确，同时也缺乏体态手势等辅助表达条件，因而表达上要求准确、详尽、严密。句子成分的省略比较少，尤其是正式的公文或政论文章，主语较少省略，但是定语用得比较多。虽然书面语体也用短句，但较多使用陈述句、完整句和长句，而较少用祈使句、省略句、感叹句、变式句。另外，复句和关联词语的使用频率也高于口语。

As written communication does not take place in face-to-face situations, the situational context is less clear. Moreover, because supplementary means such as postures, gestures, and facial expressions are not available, it is more demanding in accuracy, detail, and organization. Therefore, there are fewer omissions of sentence elements, particularly in official and business documents, or political essays. Not only is the subject of a sentence omitted less frequently, but long, complex attributes are more frequently used. Although short sentences are also used in written Chinese, declarative sentences, full sentences, and long sentences are more common. In contrast to colloquial style, imperative sentences, elliptical sentences, exclamatory sentences, and reversed sentences are more frequently used.

3. 因为书面表达通常有比较充裕的时间准备，可以逐字逐句地反复推敲润色，所以更易于精炼、规范或富于文采。书面语体还比较讲究音节的整齐和句式的对称。

Normally there is more time for a person to produce something in writing, which allows one to weigh his or her words, and repetitively polish the writing. Therefore, the written language tends to be more succinct, accurate and with more literary grace. In addition, written Chinese pays more attention to the uniformity of syllables and parallelism in sentence structures.

书面语体还可以细分为事务语体、政论语体、科技语体和文艺语体四类。

Written style can be further classified as business style, political commentary style, science and technology writing style, and literature and art style.

练习

一、 用线将意思相同的词和词语连起来：

超过了限定的数量　　　　　　　　　　　　　　超产

数量不多不少、正好合适　　　　　　　　　　　计算

卖方规定买方必须购买的最低数量　　　　　　　资源

用一个规定的标准作为已知量，比较、计算出　　计价
一个暂时未知的量

货物的来源　　　　　　　　　　　　　　　　　起订量

把电能供给电器的装置　　　　　　　　　　　　适量

生产资料或生活资料的天然来源　　　　　　　　货源

超过规定的数量　　　　　　　　　　　　　　　超支

多于预计要生产的数量　　　　　　　　　　　　过量

支出超过了收入　　　　　　　　　　　　　　　超额

用数学方法通过已经知道的数目算出未知的数目　计量

计算商品的价格或价值　　　　　　　　　　　　电源

二、 用括号里的词或词组改写下列句子，但不改变其基本意思，必要时可对词序作一定的调整：

1. 那家公司因为经营的本钱不足，所以减少了原来决定的订货量。
（因……而……、资金、削减）

2. 我们在事情发生以前就通知过你们，样品的颜色和所交的货物可能会有一些差别。　　　　　　（事先、出入）

3. 这是一笔钱数很大的交易，请你谨慎、认真研究，以免赚得少、亏得多。　　　　　　（金额、慎重、得不偿失）

4. 买方和卖方在谈判时就取得了一致的意见，对粮食等农副产品有特别规定，允许交货的数量在一定的范围内可以多些或少些。
（达成协议、溢装、短装）

5. 这种水果存放起来非常困难，而很多人都喜欢吃，所以常常赶不上市场的需求。　　　　　　　　　　　　　（储存、供不应求）

6. 圣诞节快到了，商场里摆满了种类繁多、各式各样的货物，有的为了吸引顾客，还减价百分之二十甚至四十。　（形形色色、打……折）

7. 经理和同事们都理解错了她的意思，她只好一步一步地向他们解释。　　　　　　　　　　　　　　　　　　　（误会、逐步）

8. 这一点合同上已有说明，如果交货时比规定的数量少，也不会引起争议。　　　　（若、……Adjective ＋于……、不致）

三、 选择最合适的词填空：

1. 为了加速＿＿＿＿＿＿＿周转，苹果电脑公司决定大幅度降价出售他们的新产品。
   a. 资金　　　　　　b. 资本　　　　　　c. 资源

2. 这个国家虽小，但是拥有非常丰富的自然＿＿＿＿＿＿＿。
   a. 资金　　　　　　b. 资本　　　　　　c. 资源

3. 我是有一些钱，可是还不够作为成立一家进出口公司的＿＿＿＿＿＿＿。
   a. 资金　　　　　　b. 资本　　　　　　c. 资源

4. 到十一月底，这个工厂就可以＿＿＿＿＿＿＿完成今年的生产计划了。
   a. 超出　　　　　　b. 超过　　　　　　c. 超额

5. 已经＿＿＿＿＿＿＿时间了，他还没来，不能再等了，咱们开始吧。
   a. 超出　　　　　　b. 超过　　　　　　c. 超额

6. 这辆汽车的性能的确非常好，可是它的价格远远＿＿＿＿＿＿＿了你的支付能力，你怎能买得起？
   a. 超出　　　　　　b. 超过　　　　　　c. 超额

7. 水烧开了以后，就会变成＿＿＿＿＿＿＿，是吗？
   a. 固体　　　　　　c. 气体　　　　　　d. 液体

8. 汽油、牛奶、酒等商品是_____，它们都是按容量而不是按重量计算的。

　　a. 固体　　　　　c.气体　　　　　d.液体

四、 找出课文里的转折复句和目的复句，并注意它们的用法。

五、 试用不同的关联词语填空，把下列句子变成转折复句：

1.（　　）这些服装已经打了六折，（　　）买的人还是不多。

2. 他赚了很多钱，他的女朋友（　　）觉得还不够。

3. 越来越多的国家都开始采用"国际单位制"了，（　　）美国（　　）还继续使用自己的计量制度。

4. 今年的房子普遍都涨了价，买房子的人（　　）（　　）多起来了。

5.（　　）电脑很先进，也很聪明，（　　）出了问题还得靠人来解决。

6. 这些孩子穿的、用的都是世界名牌，（　　）他们的父母自己买的（　　）只是普通的牌子。

7. "耐克"球鞋好是好，（　　）贵了点儿。

8.（　　）双方事先已达成了协议，（　　）在执行的过程中还可能会产生纠纷。

六、 根据下面图表的信息回答下列问题：

1. 1996年中国对美国的进出口总额是多少美元？出口总额是多少？增加了百分之几？进口总额呢？

2. 1996年中国从美国进口大约占进出口总额多少？请用分数说明。

3. 如果把计算单位换成"亿美元"(hundred million dollars)，中国对日本1996年的贸易总额是多少美元？对德国呢？请用小数说明。

4. 1996年中国对美国的进出口总额是对加拿大贸易总额的多少倍？请用概数说明。

5. 1996年中国从澳大利亚的进口增加了几成？向韩国的出口呢？请用成数说明。

6. 1996年中国和哪个国家或地区的进出口贸易比1995年在各个方面都减少了？减少了多少？

7. 请按进出口总额的大小，用序数词排列中国的三个主要贸易伙伴。

中国同有关国家(地区)海关进出口总额

单位：万美元 (US$10000)

国家 (地区)	1995年			1996年		
	进出口总额	出口总额	进口总额	进出口总额	出口总额	进口总额
香港	4457414	3598343	859071	4073324 -8.62%	3290554 -8.55%	782770 -8.88%
台湾	1788200	309806	1478394	1898491 +6.17%	280268 -9.53%	1618223 +2.69
日本	5747122	2846669	2900453	6005829 +4.51%	3087448 +8.46%	2918381 +5.96/10000
韩国	1698104	668781	1029323	1999266 +17.74%	751118 +12.31%	1248148 +21.26%
澳大利亚	421074	162619	258455	510710 +21.29%	167330 +2.90%	343380 +32.86%
加拿大	421384	153252	268131	418587 -6.64/1000	161601 +5.64%	256986 -4.16%
美国	4083179	2471350	1611829	4284073 +4.92%	2668549 +7.98%	1615524 +2.29/1000
英国	476973	279767	197206	508192 +6.54%	320064 +14.40%	188128 -4.60%
法国	449020	184182	264838	414680 -7.65%	190687 +3.53%	223993 -1.54%
德国	1370931	567145	803786	1316896 -3.94%	584470 +3.05%	732426 -9.11%

摘自《中国统计年鉴-1997》中国统计出版社，北京：中国1997年。

七、 用文言词替代下列句子中的划线部份，必要时可替换某些词或对词序作一定的调整：

1. 货物将<u>在</u>本月十六日<u>从</u>上海运往纽约。

2. 这样的交易条件只<u>对卖方有利</u>，<u>但</u>对买方<u>不利</u>，他们当然不会接受。

3. 这个<u>因为</u>粗心大意造成的错误，应该<u>归</u>她自己负责。

4. 为民公司<u>把产品质量作为</u>主要目标，他们的产品<u>又</u>美观<u>又</u>耐用，很受欢迎。

5. 你们的报价<u>比</u>国际市场的价格<u>高</u>百分之三，这样<u>很难</u>推销你们的商品。

6. 每到节日，各个商场都实行大减价，<u>为了</u>吸引顾客。

7. 打骂孩子对教育孩子<u>没有</u>帮助。

8. 如果因为有风险<u>就</u>不做生意，怎么可以赚钱？

八、 判别下列句子的语体并写出与其语体相对的意思：

1. 因行情有变，故日前报价一概无效。自本日起，以此函之报价为准。

2. 虚盘者，无法律约束力之报盘也。

3. 若无意外，货物将如期运抵。

4. 做买卖，这个人是一点儿兴趣也没有。

5. 贵公司来函已悉，问及货物何时装运之事。现复如下：

6. 我们是不是要卖，完全要看他们的还价，跟你没关系。

7. 如此精美的工艺品，确实罕见，而其售价，亦高于我等所料。

8. 此事并非全然无望，唯需耐心。

9. 如蒙赐复，不胜感激。

10. 不管怎么样，一有货我就打电话告诉你。

九、 把下列句子翻译成汉语：

1. At present, the supply of computers has surpassed the demand, and the price has been falling all along. In order to promote sales, many computer dealers have given 10 to 20 percent discount to (their) customers. Some even sell computers at a price lower than the cost. If these computers can't be sold, dealers have to look for places to store them. Then, it is true that "the loss outweighs the gain".

2. There are various measures [i.e. "measuring units"]in the world. To a lot of people, the conversion among different systems is not only tedious, but also easy to create discrepancies. For example, iron ore and products of steel and iron are calculated by [i.e. "according to"] weight. However, if measured in [i.e. "according to"] the British system, a ton equals 2,240 pounds; if measured in [i.e. "according to"] the U.S. system, one ton is 2,000 pounds only. This will definitely cause a lot of misunderstandings. Therefore, more and more countries are gradually [i.e. "step by step"] adopting the Metric System.

3. The import of cigarettes may have significant impact on people's health, and we must be cautious in consideration. While the government is encouraging people to smoke less or not to smoke, it has strict regulations on cigarette imports. We should not take such risks for making money.

十、 商业信函练习二

1. 阅读下面的信，注意其格式和用词。

2. 以出口商 (金宏利) 的名义，给进口商钱大发写一封回信，内容包括：

甲) 说明来信已收到，感谢进口商对中国的电器产品感兴趣。

乙) 向对方报实盘，但改报"成本加运费及保险 (C.I.F.) 波士顿"价，每台单价为57美元。想一个理由，说明为什么不能报"船上交货 (F.O.B.) 上海"价。

丙) 如果对方增加订货量至 68,000 台，并同意在四月底以后装运，可以考虑报"船上交货 (F.O.B.) 上海"价。

丁) 报价有效期为十四天，如对方接受这个报盘，请在三月二十日前开出信用证。

美国麻州波士顿
海湾贸易有限公司
采购部经理
钱大发

中国上海
轻工进出口公司
金宏利总经理

金宏利先生：

　　您好。贵方二月十五日来函及商品目录已悉。我们从中选择了 BT-120 型清凉牌 20 英寸台式电扇，请按下列条件报优惠实盘：

商品名称：　清凉牌 20 英寸台式电扇，BT-120 型。

数量：　　　45,000 台。

包装：　　　标准出口纸板箱装。

价格：　　　船上交货 (F.O.B.) 上海。

装运：　　　××××年 4、5 月，倘若可能，请于 4 月中旬装运。

支付：　　　不可撤销即期信用证。

敬请早日回复。

钱大发

××××年 2 月 23 日

文化与商贸背景知识

✐ 汉语的常用称谓

一、 社交称谓

在社交场合，特别是正式的社交场合和业务书信来往，中国人都比较注意使用职业或职务的名称来称呼对方，以示尊重。汉语里表示职业或职务而又可作为称谓的名词，要比英语的多。除了"医生"、"教授"、"律师"、"法官"、"博士"、"船长"等与英语相同外，以下的名词都可以跟在某个人的姓或全名后面，作为一种正式的社交称谓：(赵)老师、(钱)经理、(孙)秘书、(李)会计、(周)顾问、(吴)导演、(郑)大使、(王)领事、(冯)翻译、(陈)书记、(史)教练、(卫)主任、(蒋)委员、(程)总监、(韩)老板、(杨)助理、(朱)工程师、(秦)技术员、(尤)研究员、(许)特派员

另外，几乎所有带"长"字的职务都可以作为正式的称谓。如：(调查组何)组长、(研究所吕)所长、(医院施)院长、(工厂张)厂长、(大学孔)校长、(进口科曹)科长、(外事处严)处长、(公司华)董事长、(商检局金)局长、(公安厅谢)厅长、(民航客机任)机长、(火车客车毛)列出长、(苏)县长、(范)区长、(马)市长、(方)省长、(唐)部长、(邓)总理、(刘)主席、(江)总统。

警察(民警)、司机、护士、服务员等职业，不可直接作为称谓，后面必须加上"先生、小姐或同志"，如"民警同志"、"护士小姐"等。

有几个称谓，可通用于很多场合，特别是不知道对方的身份职务或不方便直接使用时，可以考虑使用以下的称谓：

<u>先生</u>：汉语的这个称谓原无性别之分，现多用于男性。在对方身份或性别不明时，都可以使用。如果对方是老年女知识分子，也可以用。"先生"前还可以加上姓名或者职务，表示郑重。如："主管先生"、"齐大明先生"、"高教授志远先生"等。

"<u>女士</u>"：通用于所有成年女性，无论已婚未婚。如："各位女士"、"黄希平女士"、"余局长庆华女士"等。

"<u>小姐</u>"：一般只适用于年轻女性，如："孟春铃小姐"、"公关小姐"等。但对明显已上岁数的女性，基本上不用，而改用"女士"。

"<u>夫人</u>"：一般只在外交或比较正式的社交场合对已婚的女性使用。如："宋夫人"、"林素明夫人"等。注意："夫人"前面基本上不能加被称呼者本人的职称，如加上后，往往会认为是她丈夫的职务而不是她本人的，如："董事长夫人"意思相当于"董事长的夫人"，"董事长"指的是她的丈夫，而不是她本人。

"<u>同志</u>"：这个称谓在中国大陆虽然没有以前用得那么广泛，但仍然是一个无性别无级别的通用称谓，如：售货员同志、民警同志、解放军同志等。对政府机关工作人员、军人、警察等，或不知道应该如何称呼对方时，都可以用"同志"。如要找"负责人"，可称"负责同志"。

"<u>师傅</u>"：多用于口语，尤其流行于中国北方，没有年龄、性别的区别，对工商、服务行业的工人，如修理自行车或电器的、开出租汽车的、冲洗胶卷的、售货员或饭店的男性服务员（女性的多数用"小姐"）一般都适用。

二、亲友称谓

　　亲友之间的称谓，平时会话和书信来往没有太大的差别，加上亲戚朋友彼此比较熟悉，关系也较为密切，相对来说，就没有社交称谓那么讲究。下面是一些常用的亲友称谓和要注意的事项。

1. 家庭成员之间

父母称呼子女：一般只称名，不加姓（双音节的姓名例外），也可在名后加"儿"或"女儿"。如："海强"或"海强儿"（写信时）；"玉铃"、"玉铃女儿"（写信时）。有时为了表示亲密，也会称"强儿"、"小强"、"强强"；"小铃"或"铃铃"等。

子女称呼父母：不称呼姓名，只称"爸爸"、"妈妈"。写信时可称"父亲"、"母亲"。如果信是写给父母俩人的话，按中国人的习惯，男的在前，女的在后。如："爸爸、妈妈"、"父母大人"（旧）。前面可加定语"亲爱的"、"尊敬的"等。

兄弟姐妹之间：对哥哥姐姐平时一般不叫姓名，只称"哥哥"或"姐姐"。如有几个哥哥姐姐，按排行称"大哥"、"二哥"、"大姐"、"三姐"等。写信时可用同样的称呼或在名（不加姓）后加上"兄"、"哥"或"姐"，如："海强兄、海强哥、玉铃姐"等。

如果信同时写给哥哥姐姐，按习惯，也是男的在前，女的在后。如："亲爱的大哥、二姐"或"海强哥、玉铃姐"等。

对弟弟妹妹，平时一般不称名，不加姓，或者只叫"弟弟"、"妹妹"、"二弟"、"小弟""三妹"、"小妹"等。写信时大致相同，但也可用弟弟或妹妹的名，如："海平弟"或"海平"，"玉英妹"或"玉英"。如果信是同时写给弟弟妹妹的，按习惯，也是男的在前，女的在后。如："海平弟、玉英妹"或"海平、玉英"。

夫妻之间：多数只称名，不加姓（如果全名只有两个字，会有例外）。有时为了表示亲密，也常用名字的则最后一个字称呼对方，如："志诚"或"诚"，"秀云"或"云"。写信时前面可加定语"亲爱的"等。

2. 亲戚之间

长辈称呼晚辈：多数只称名，不加姓。写信时可在名后加上称呼。如："海强"或"海强孙儿"、"玉铃"或"玉铃孙女"、"海平"或"海平外甥"、"玉英"或"玉英侄女"等。

晚辈称呼长辈：平时和写信都不称名，不加姓，只用称呼。如：爷爷（写信时可用"祖父"）、奶奶（写信时可用"祖母"）、伯父/伯伯、叔父/叔叔、姨妈/姨母、婶婶、大伯、二叔、三婶、四姨等。

3. 朋友之间

一般朋友之间：平时多数互相称全名，或者以"小……""老……"称呼，
　　　　　显得比较亲切、随便。写信时，基本上与平时的称呼相同，如果
　　　　　关系比较密切，可以只写名，不加姓，或在名后加上"友"、"同
　　　　　学"等。如："张晓明"、"晓明友"、"同学"或"晓明"等。

男女朋友之间：平时互相叫名字，但写信时，多数只用名，不加姓。有
　　　　　时只用名字的最后一个字，表示亲密的关系，不同于一般人。
　　　　　如："国伟"或"伟"、"雪梅"或"梅"等。

✐ **商业信函**(3)

美国纽约市
大苹果国际贸易公司
王总经理福强先生

王福强总经理：

　　您好！××××年九月二十六日来函已悉，感谢贵公司对我们的信任并对我方产品进行大量的订货。本公司经销的"雪莲牌"手织羊毛衫质地纯正，设计优美，做工精细，多年来一直是享誉全球的名牌产品。最近天气逐渐转冷，对羊毛衫的需求大大增加，"雪莲牌"更是供不应求。目前我方的库存十分有限，无法满足贵方关于"按原报价追订1000打'雪莲牌'手织羊毛衫"的要求。对此，我们深表遗憾。

　　我们正在与厂商联系，希望能在近期内尽快补充货源。如果贵方能够等待，一旦有新消息，我们将立即向贵方重新报价。

　　此致
敬礼

　　　　　　　　　　　　天山服装纺织品进出口公司
　　　　　　　　　　　　××××年十月三日

✎ 公制与美制计量单位换算表

类别 Categories	名称 Name	汉译 Chinese	等值 Equivalent	折合公制 Metric Value
长度 Linear Measure	mile (mi.) fathom (fm.) yard (yd.) foot (ft.) inch (in.)	英里 英寻 码 英尺 英寸	880 fm. 2 yd. 3 ft. 12 in.	=1.6093 千米/公里 =1.829 米 =0.9144 米 =0.3048 米 =0.0254 米
海程长度 Nautical Measure	nautical mile (naut. m.) cable	海里 链	10 cables 720 ft.	=1.852 千米/公里 =219.45 米
面积 Square Measure	square mile (sq. mi.) acre (a.) square yard (sq. yd.) square foot (sq. ft.) squre inch (sq. in.)	平方英里 英亩 平方码 平方英尺 平方英寸	640 a. 4 840 sq. yd. 9 sq. ft. 144 sq. in.	=2.59 平方千米/公里 =4 047 平方米 =0.8361 平方米 =0.929 平方米 =0.0645 平方米
常衡重量 Avoirdupois Weight	ton (t.) hundredweight short ton (s.t.) pound (lb.) ounce (oz.) dram (dr.)	吨 英担 短吨 磅 盎司 打兰	20 cwt. 100 lb. 2 000 lb. 16 oz. 16 dr.	=45.359 千克/公斤 =0.907 公吨 =0.454 千克/公斤 =28.35 克
容量 capacity 干量 Dry Measure	bushel (bu.) peck (pk.) quart (qt.) pint (pt.)	蒲式耳 配克 夸脱 品脱	4 pk. 8 qt. 2 pt.	=35.239 升 =8.810 升 =1.101 升 =0.55 升
液量 Liquid Measure	gallon (gal.) quart (qt.) pint (pt.) gill (gl.)	加仑 夸脱 品脱 及耳	4 qt. 2 pt. 4 gl.	=3.785 升 =0.946 升 =0.473 升 =0.118 升

第七课

包装

✐ **思考下面的问题，然后带着这些问题去阅读课文：**

一、商品的包装有什么作用？

二、商品的包装可以分成几类？其中具体的又有哪几种？

三、什么是"中性包装"？常见的中性包装有哪几种？

课文：包装

　　商品流通，一般都要经过运输、装卸、分配、销售等过程。在这些过程中，多数商品都需要一定的包装。在国际贸易中，包装对于商品的保护、运输、储存、分配以及消费都有着重要的作用。坚固合理的包装，可以减少货损，节省运费；而精美华丽的包装，更能吸引顾客，有助于商品的推销，乃至于售价的提高。因此，在一定的意义上来说，包装是实现商品的价值和使用价值，并增加商品价值的一种有效手段。 5

　　当然，有些商品是不需要包装的，例如石油、煤炭、矿砂等。这些散装货可用专门设计的运输工具和装卸设备，直接散装在承载的运输工具上。还有些商品，如木材、钢材、铝锭等，由于品质比较稳定，不易受外界条件的影响，可以裸装在货舱里。然而，绝大多数商品都是离不开包装的，特别是食品、药品、轻工业品、化工产品、电器和电子产品等。没有包装，这些商品都不可能进入市场。 10

　　商品包装，根据其作用的不同，可以分为两大类： 15

　　以便于商品的运输、装卸和储存为目的的包装，叫做"运输包装"或"外包装"。这类包装可分为单件运输包装和集合运输包装两种。单件运输包装是指货物在运输过程中作为一个计件单位的包装。这种包装按照造型又可分为箱、桶、袋、包、捆等。根据需要，单件包装使用的材料也各有不同，如箱有纸箱、木箱，桶有铁桶、木桶，袋有纸袋、尼龙袋等，使包装既有防潮、防腐、防震、防盗等性能，又便于运输、装卸、储存。因此，买卖双方应根据不同的货物，在交易洽谈中商定单件运输包装的要求，并在合同中具体说明。

　　集合运输包装是指在单件运输包装的基础上，将若干件单件运输包装组合成一件大包装。这对于提高装卸效率，保护商品，节省费用都有积极的作用。目前较为广泛使用的集合运输包装有集装箱（即货柜）、集装包和集装袋、托盘等。

　　以便于商品的陈列展销、识别及使用为目的的包装，叫做"销售包装"或"内包装"。这类包装不但要造型美观大方，装潢设计能突出商品的特点，有良好的展销效果，还要方便消费者直接了解商品的外观形态，容易开启，便于携带和使用。随着超级市场的日益发展，商人们更加注重商品的包装装潢，因为精美的销售包装有利于吸引顾客，能够起到"无声推销员"的作用。

　　在国际贸易中，卖方有时可以按买方的要求，不注明商品的商标和牌号，或生产国别和厂商，这就是所谓的"中性包装"。国际市场上常见的中性包装有两种：一种是既无商标牌号，又无生产国别的"无牌中性包装"；一种是"定牌中性包装"。它有买方指定的商标，不一定注明生产国别，但有时也可以加注生产国别的标志。这些做法都是为了适应国际市场的特点，作为扩大销售的一种手段。

✐ **根据课文内容回答下列问题：**

1. 为什么大多数商品都需要一定的包装？

2. 哪些商品是不需要包装的？为什么？

3. 商品包装可以分成几类？

4. 什么叫做"外包装"？

5. 外包装可以分成几种？

6. 外包装使用些什么材料，有些什么造型和要求？

7. 集合运输包装有什么好处？

8. 内包装的目的是什么？

9. 内包装有些什么要求？

10. 什么是中性包装？它可以分为哪几种？

✐ **根据意思，给课文划分层次(不是自然段)并写出每个层次的大意。**

生词和用法

流通	liútōng	*V./N.*	流转通行、不停滞：空气~、商品~、货币~。 to circulate; circulation
分配	fēnpèi	*V./N.*	安排、分派：~劳动力、~时间、合理~、工作~。　to distribute; to allot; to assign
保护	bǎohù	*V./N.*	尽力照顾，使不受损害：~眼睛、~儿童、环境~、自我~；＜＞伤害。 to protect; protection
消费	xiāofèi	*V./N.*	为了满足生产需要和生活需要而消耗的物质财富：~品、~者、~资料、~城市。 to consume; consumption
坚固	jiāngù	*Adj.*	结合紧密，不容易破坏，牢固、坚实：结构~、

			~耐用。	solid; firm; sturdy
货损	huòsǔn	*NP*	货＝货物，损＝损失、损坏。	damage/loss of goods
精美	jīngměi	*Adj.*	精致、美好：~的台灯、包装~、设计~；＜＞粗劣。	exquisite; elegant
华丽	huálì	*Adj.*	美丽而有光彩：服饰~、包装~、~的宫殿。	magnificent; gorgeous
推销	tuīxiāo	*V.*	推广货物的销路：~商品、~广告、~员、~工作。	push the sale; to promote sales; to peddle; to market
乃至	nǎizhì	*Conj.*	甚至；用在两项以上并列成分中最后一项的前面，表示这一项最突出，也说"乃至于"。	even; to the extent of; even go so far as to
意义	yìyì	*N.*	语言文字或其他信号表示的内容：在某种~上；毫无~。	meaning; sense
			价值；作用；影响：教育~、历史~、深刻的~、伟大的~。	significance
实现	shíxiàn	*V.*	使成为事实：~目标、~理想、~自动化、~工业化。	to realize; to materialize
手段	shǒuduàn	*N.*	为达到某种目的而采取的具体手法：合法的~、支付~、不择~。	means; measure; method
专门	zhuānmén	*Adj.*	专一从事某一件事的；为某一事物特地设计的：~负责、~机构、~人才。	special; specialized
承载	chéngzài	*V.*	托着物体，承受它的重量：~能力、~量。	to bear the weight of
钢材	gāngcái	*N.*	钢锭或钢坯经过轧制后的成品，如圆钢、方钢、扁钢等。	steel products; steels; rolled steel
铝	lǚ	*N.*		aluminum

锭	dìng	N.	做成块状的金属产品：钢~、铝~、金~、银~。
			ingot
外界	wàijiè	N.	外部环境，主体以外的人或物：~条件、~影
			响、~反应；＜＞内在。
			outside; the outside/external world
裸	luǒ	Adj.	露出，没有遮盖：~露、~体、~装货。
			(nude cargo) bare; naked
裸装	luǒzhuāng	VP	（货物）没有遮盖，直接装载在运输工具上。
			goods loaded on means of transportation without any cover or packaging
然而	rán'ér	Conj.	〔书〕但是；可是。 however; nevertheless; but; yet
绝	jué	Adj.	极，最：~早、~好、~大部分、~大多数。
			extreme; most
集合	jíhé	V.	许多分散的人或物聚在一起，使集合起来：~地
			点、紧急~；＜＞分散、解散。
			to gather; to assemble
箱	xiāng	N./MW	存放物品用的方形器具，可用木头、铁皮、塑
			料、皮革或纸板等制成：木~、皮~、纸~。
			box; case; trunk
桶	tǒng	N./MW	盛东西的器具，用木头、塑料或铁皮等制成，
			多为圆形：水~、木~、铁~、汽油~。
			barrel; bucket; pail; drum; a measure word
袋	dài	N./MW	口袋：旅行~、工具~、布~。
			sack; bag; pocket
			用于装在口袋的东西：一~面粉。
			a measure word
包	bāo	N./MW	装东西的口袋：书~、背~、钱~。
			bag; sack

			用于成包的东西：三~大米、一~棉纱。	
				a measure word
捆	kǔn	*V.*	用绳子等把东西缠紧打结。	
				to tie; to bind; to bundle up
		M.W.	用于捆起来的东西：一~干草。	
				bundle; a measure word
尼龙	nílóng	*N.*		nylon
防	fáng	*V.*	防止、防备，有防止 (某种后果) 能力的：~火、~水、~雨、~毒、~潮、~腐、~震、~盗。	
				to prevent; to guard against; to resist; anti-; -proof
潮	cháo	*Adj.*	含有比正常状态下多的水分，潮湿；＜＞干、干燥。	damp; moist
腐	fǔ	*Adj.*	腐烂，变坏。	rotten; putrid; stale
震	zhèn	*V./N.*	受外力的影响而移动：地~；~荡。	
				to shock; to shake; shock; quake
盗	dào	*V./N.*	偷，未经许可私下拿别人的东西，据为己有。	
				to steal; to rob; theft
若干	ruògān	*Pron.*	〔书〕多少 (指数量或不定量)：~天、~年、~次、~地区、~批货。	a certain number or amount; several
组合	zǔhé	*V./N.*	组织成为整体：~起来、~家具。	
				to make up; to compose
效率	xiàolǜ	*N.*	单位时间内完成的工作量的大小：提高~、工作~、运输~、~很低。	
				efficiency
积极	jījí	*Adj.*	正面的、有益的、多用于抽象事物：~的影响、~的因素、~的作用；＜＞消极	
				positive

			热心于某项活动：~参加、~准备、~进行。
			active; vigorous
集装箱	jízhuāngxiāng	N.	用于装载货物的、标准尺寸大型金属制箱子，可直接吊装上下车、船等运输工具（多用于中国大陆）。
			container
货柜	huòguì	N.	＝集装箱，（多用于港台地区和海外）。
			container
托盘	tuōpán	N.	装卸和搬运货物专用的平板装置。
			tray
陈列	chénliè	V.	把商品摆出来供人观看：~品。
			to display; to exhibit
销	xiāo	V.	（把货物）卖出去：推~、展~、促~、畅~、滞~、直~；＜＞购。 to sell; to market
展销	zhǎnxiāo	V./N.	为了推销把产品拿出来陈列展览。
			show; commodity exhibition
识别	shíbié	V.	辨别；辨认：~真假、~能力、~好坏。
			to distinguish; to discern; to identify
突出	tūchū	Adj.	超过一般地好；显著的：成绩~、表现~、~的例子；＜＞一般、平常。
			outstanding; prominent
		V.	使突出：~重点、~主体。
			to give prominence to; to highlight
开启	kāiqǐ	V.	〔正〕开；打开：自动~、容易~；＜＞关闭。
			to open
便于	biànyú	Adj.	比较容易（做某事）：~携带、~计算、~使用、~开启；＜＞难以。 easy to; convenientfor
携带	xiédài	V.	随身带着：~行李、~方便。
			to carry; to take along
随着	suízhe	Prep.	表示某事物的变化以另一事物为事发前提。

along with; in the wake of; in pace with

超级 市场	chāojí shìchǎng	NP	综合的方便商场，出售水果、蔬菜、肉类等食品和其他日用品、杂货等。 supermarket	
日益	rìyì	Adv.	一天比一天：~增加、~改善、~提高、~发展。 increasingly with each passing day	
美观	měiguān	Adj.	(形式)好看，漂亮。 beautiful; artistic	
大方	dàfang	Adj.	(式样、颜色等)自然、不俗气。 natural and poised; unaffected	
注重	zhùzhòng	V.	重视：~调查研究、~产品质量、~发展农业、~按时交货。 to lay stress on; to pay attention to; to attach importance to	
装潢	zhuānghuáng	V.	装饰物品，使其美观。 to decorate	
		N.	物品的装饰。 decoration; packaging	
效果	xiàoguǒ	N.	由某种力量或因素产生的结果(多指好的)：教学~、良好的~、~不大。 effect; result	
无声	wúshēng	VO	没有声音：~电影、~手枪、~推销员；< >有声。 silent; noiseless	
注明	zhùmíng	VP	用文字明确地表示、解释：~日期、~产地、~商标。 to give clear indication of; to specify	
中性	zhōngxìng	Adj.	不带任何偏向，没有明显标志的。 neutral	
指定	zhǐdìng	V.	确定(做事的人、时间、地点等)：~目的港、~代理、~商标、~的船只。 to appoint; to assign (person in charge, time, place, etc.)	

| 适应 | shìyìng | *V.* | 适合客观条件或需要：~要求、~环境、~新情
况、~需要。　　　　　to suit; to fit; to adapt |
| 扩大 | kuòdà | *V.* | 放大范围：~生产、~影响、~市场、~面积、~
眼界；＜＞缩小。　to extend, to enlarge |

补充词

固体	gùtǐ	*N.*	有一定的体积和一定的形状，质地比较坚硬的 物体。钢、岩石、木材、玻璃等都是固体。 　　　　　　　　　　　solid
网络	wǎngluò	*N.*	电脑、电视、电话、通讯或交通运输等方面互 相连接、广泛分布的网状系统。电脑~、交通 ~、神经~。　　　　network
畅销	chàngxiāo	*Adj.*	指商品销路广，卖得快：十分~、~产品；＜＞ 滞销。　　　　　　a booming sale
		V.	在比较大的范围内很快售出：~海内外。 　　　　　　　　　　to sell briskly
直销	zhíxiāo	*V.*	直接把商品卖出去，中间不经过任何零售商。 　　　　　　　direct marketing; to sell di- 　　　　　　　rectly to consumers
发挥	fāhuī	*V.*	把内在的性质、能力和作用尽量表现出来：~特 长、~主动性、~想像力、~积极性。 　　　　　　　to bring into play; to give 　　　　　　　free rein to
想像力	xiǎngxiànglì	*NP*	对于不在眼前的事物想出它的形象的能力。 　　　　　　　　　　imagination
保障	bǎozhàng	*V.*	保护、保证；常带宾语：~供给、~人民的权 利。　　　　　to ensure; to guarantee; to 　　　　　　　safeguard
		N.	起保障作用的事物：有保障。 　　　　　　　　　　guarantee

平等	píngděng	N.	指人们在社会、政治、经济、法律等方面享有相等待遇：~权利、争取~。
			equality
		Adj.	泛指地位相等，一样：~待人、~互利、男女~。
			equal
轮椅	lúnyǐ	N.	装有轮子的坐椅，供走路有困难的人使用。
			wheel-chair

词语例释

一、……，乃至（于）…… (even; to the extent of; go so far as to)

l-5. 坚固合理的包装，可以减少货损，节省运费；而精美华丽的包装，更能吸引顾客，有助于商品的推销，<u>乃至于</u>售价的提高。

1. 这个新产品从性能、造型，<u>乃至</u>包装都有了很大的改进。

2. 为了推销产品，他们想了很多办法：举办展销会，给客户打折扣，<u>乃至于</u>请进口商吃饭，可是订货的人还是不多。

3. 现在不仅学校的老师、学生，公司的主管、职员，<u>乃至于</u>六七十岁的老人也会用电脑了。

　　连词"乃至（于）"连接并列的各种句子成分或分句，放在被连接的最后一项前，"甚至"的意思。但是"甚至"可作副词，而"乃至（于）"不可。下面的句子不可用"乃至（于）"：

　　The Conjunction 乃至（于）appears before the last one of a series of connected items to link up various parallel sentence elements or clauses, meaning "even; go so far as; to the extent of". It is similar to 甚至. However, 甚至 can function as an Adverb, but 乃至（于）cannot. The following sentence can use 甚至 only:

　　他甚至生病时还去上课。✗他乃至生病时还去上课。

二、……，然而…… (yet; but; however)

l-11. 还有些商品，如木材、钢材、铝锭等，由于品质比较稳定，不易受外界条件的影响，可以裸装在货舱里。<u>然而</u>，绝大多数商品都是离不开包装的，特别是食品、药品、轻工业品、化工产品、电器和电子产品等。

1. 精美的包装可以吸引顾客，<u>然而</u>，如果产品的质量不高，再漂亮的包装也没有什么用。

2. 这些都是美国的名牌服装，<u>然而</u>生产厂商却大部分是中国或香港的。

3. 不少国家自己采用的计量制度是国际米制，<u>然而</u>他们向美国出口的产品都使用美国的计量单位。

连词"然而"意思与"但是、可是"相同，用于句首，连接分句、句子或段落，表示转折，对上文进行限制补充或引出相反的意思。"然而"多用于书面语，一般不与"虽然"连用。"但是、可是"通用于口语和书面语，可以"虽然"与配合使用。

Similar to 但是、可是 in meaning, the Conjunction 然而 is used at the beginning of a sentence to join clauses, sentences, or paragraphs. 然而 is primarily used in written Chinese, and does not go with 虽然 normally. 但是、可是 is generally used in both spoken and written Chinese, and can team up with 虽然.

三、 A 离不开 B　（A can't do without B; A can't depart from B）

l-12. 然而，绝大多数商品都是<u>离不开</u>包装的，特别是食品、药品、轻工业品、化工产品、电器和电子产品等。

1. 国际贸易基本上不用现金交易，所以进出口公司都<u>离不开</u>银行的服务。

2. 这两家公司有着长期的合作关系，谁也<u>离不开</u>谁。

3. 他觉得自己的每一个进步都<u>离不开</u>老师的帮助。

动词"离开"表示跟人、物或地方分开。"离不开"是可能补语"离得开"的否定形式，后面可带宾语。

The Verb 离开 means the departure of a person or an object. 离不开 is the negation of the Potential Complement 离得开, and can be followed by an Object.

四、 A使B+Verb/Adjective （A makes /causes B+Verb/Adjective ）

l-21. 根据需要，单件包装使用的材料也各有不同，如箱有纸箱、木箱，桶有铁桶、木桶，袋有纸袋、尼龙袋等，<u>使</u>包装既有防潮、防腐、防震、防盗等性能，又便于运输、装卸、储存。

1. 今年夏天特别热，市场上对电风扇、空调机的需求量大增，<u>使</u>这些商品的价格大幅度上升。
2. 学校要求老师减少给学生的作业，<u>使</u>同学们有更多时间参加其他活动。
3. 她考上了这所名牌大学，<u>使</u>父母十分高兴。

动词"使"多用于书面语的使动句，相当于"让、叫、致使"的意思。不单独作谓语，须带兼语。

The Verb 使 is usually used in Causative Sentences, which is equal to 让、叫、致使 in meaning. It cannot function as a Predicate itself, and has to take an object and a Verb to form a Pivot Sentence.

五、 在……的基础上＋Verb （on the basis of ...; based on ....）

l-25. 集合运输包装是指<u>在</u>单件运输包装<u>的基础上</u>，将若干件单件运输包装组合成一件大包装。

1. 我们希望<u>在</u>平等互利<u>的基础上</u>，与各国的公司建立和发展业务关系。
2. 只有<u>在</u>提高质量<u>的基础上</u>去提高产品的竞争力，才是最有效的办法。
3. 去年这家公司<u>在</u>节省成本百分之六<u>的基础上</u>，又多赚了几百万美元。

"在……基础上"通常作状语，表示事物发展的根本、起点或先决条件。

The phrase 在……基础上 usually serves as an Adverbial, indicating the basis, starting point or precondition of the development of an event.

六、 Subject 将 Definite Object+Verb +Other Elements　（Cf. 把）

l-25. 集合运输包装是指<u>在</u>单件运输包装的基础<u>上</u>，将若干件单件运输包装组合成一件大包装。

1. 请<u>将</u>这些商品目录翻译成汉语，然后寄出去。
2. 客户要求我们<u>将</u>原来的包装改为中性包装。
3. 他仍然在考虑是否<u>将</u>这个消息告诉对方。

介词"将"相当于"把"的意思，多用于书面语，把动词涉及的对象提前，表示对人或事物的处置。

The Preposition 将 is similar to 把 in meaning and usage. It is primarily used in written Chinese, to advance the Object before the Verb, indicating what the Subject does, has done, or did to someone or something (the Object).

七、 Subject 对……有作用/Subject 起……的作用　（Subject plays a ... role in...）

l-26. 这对于提高装卸效率，保护商品，节省费用都<u>有</u>积极的<u>作用</u>。

l-34. 随着超级市场的日益发展，商人们更加注重商品的包装装潢，因为精美的销售包装有利于吸引顾客，能够<u>起</u>到"无声推销员"的<u>作用</u>。

1. 贸易对促进各国人民之间的相互了解和友好交流<u>有</u>很大的<u>作用</u>。
2. 这种进口药品对他的病一点儿也<u>不起作用</u>。
3. 虽然精美的包装对商品的推销<u>有</u>一定的<u>作用</u>，可是<u>起</u>决定<u>作用</u>的还是商品本身的质量。
4. 大使馆商务处的官员对这次展销会的举办成功<u>起</u>了非常重要的<u>作用</u>。

"作用"是名词，常与动词"有、起"等配合，组成词组，表示一事物对另一事物产生效果、效用。动词与"作用"之间可以加修饰语，说明作用的方面或程度。

> 作用 is a Noun and is often associated with Verbs such as 有 or 起 etc. to form a phrase, indicating the result or effect that one thing brings to another. A modifier may be added between the Verb and 作用, showing in which aspect or to what extent the function is.

八、 随着……，Subject Verb （along with...; in pace with...）

1-32. 随着超级市场的日益发展，商人们更加注重商品的包装装潢，因为精美的销售包装有利于吸引顾客，能够起到"无声推销员"的作用。

1. 随着中国经济的发展，世界上学汉语的人也在不断增加。
2. 商品的价格是随着市场的供求情况而变动的。
3. 随着温度的变化，水可以成为液体、气体或者固体。

"随着"在这里是介词，表示某事物的变化以另一事物为前提，可以与"而"配合使用。"随着"还可以作副词，用在动词前作状语，表示一个事物伴随另一个事物发生或紧接着发生，有"跟着、接着"的意思。如：

> 随着 is a Preposition here, indicating the change of something depends on another. It can also go with 而. 随着 can also be an Adverb, functioning as an Adverbial before a Verb. When used in this way, it means "along with, following". For example:

4. 他们自我介绍以后，随着就讨论起世界经济来了。
5. 刘副经理仔细地检查了一遍合同，随着在上面签上了自己的名字。

九、 便于 + (Disyllabic) Verb （easy to; convenient for）

1-32. ……还要方便消费者直接了解商品的外观形态，容易开启，便于携带和使用。

1. 这种机器设计合理，便于操作和维修，所以很受欢迎。

2. 我们已经把有关的资料放在电脑网络上了，这样就<u>便于</u>大家随时查找。

3. 集装箱<u>便于</u>装卸，<u>便于</u>运输，已经成为货物的主要装载工具。

动词"便于"表示做某件事情比较容易，后面跟双音节动词或多音节的动词词组。

The Verb 便于 indicates that it is quite easy or convenient to do something, and is usually followed by a disyllabic or polysyllabic Verb Phrase.

十、 Subject日益＋(Disyllabic)Verb 　(with each passing day; increasingly)

l-30. 随着超级市场的<u>日益</u>发展，商人们更加注重商品的包装装潢，因为精美的销售包装有利于吸引顾客，能够起到"无声推销员"的作用。

1. 从八十年代起，中国与世界各国的经济和文化交往都在<u>日益</u>增加。

2. 随着科学技术的发展，电脑的质量日益提高，速度日益加快，而电脑产品的价格却<u>日益</u>下降。

3. 现代社会的特征之一就是人与人之间的竞争变得<u>日益</u>激烈。

"日益"是书面语，相当于"一天比一天"的意思，表示变化程度加深或水平升降，多用在双音节动词或形容词前。

日益 is used in written Chinese, and is similar to 一天比一天 in meaning, indicating the degree or the ups and downs of changes. It is mostly used before a disyllabic Verb or Adjective.

十一、有利于 　(to be favorable to; to be advantageous to)

l-33. 随着超级市场的日益发展，商人们更加注重商品的包装装潢，因为精美的销售包装<u>有利于</u>吸引顾客，能够起到"无声推销员"的作用。

1. 采用国际统一的计量制度<u>有利于</u>各国之间的贸易，也可以减少因计量单位不同而引起的纠纷。

2. 董事长先生对我国的访问将<u>有利于</u>我们双方今后进一步的友好合作。

3. 超级市场常常打折，好像少赚了一些钱，但是却<u>有利于</u>商品的推销和资金的周转。

"有利"是褒义词，表示"有好处、有帮助"的意思，后面常跟介词"于"，引出作用的对象。否定式用"不利"或"无利"。注意与口语句型"对……有利"在词序上的区别。

As a commendatory term, 有利 means 有好处、有帮助and is often followed by Preposition 于to introduce the target of the effect. The negative form is 不利 or 无利. Please note the difference of word order between 有利于 and its colloquial equivalent 对……有利.

词义辨析

一、装运　装卸　装载　装潢

"装"字的一个意思是"把东西放进器物内"。"装运"、"装卸"、"装载"都与运输有关系。"装运"指把东西装上交通工具并运输。"装卸"是把物品装到运输工具或仓库和卸下来的统称。"装载"是用运输工具装人员或物品的意思。"装潢"虽然也含"装"字，但与运输无关。作为动词，它是"装饰物品，使其美观"的意思。作为名词，是指物品，尤其是商品的装饰。

One of the meanings of the character 装 is "to put things into a container". The words 装运, 装卸, and 装载 all concern transportation. 装运 refers to loading things onto a conveyance and ship them somewhere. While 装卸 is the term for both "loading and unloading", 装载 means "to load things or passengers onboard a vehicle". Although 装潢 also contains the character 装, it has nothing to do with transportation. As a Verb, it means "to decorate, to dress something up". As a Noun, it refers to the decoration or packaging of things, especially goods.

二、保护 保证 保险 保障

"保"字的基本意思是"保安、庇护、保持、负责或担保"。这几个词的区别主要在第二个词素。"保护"强调护卫，通过用心照顾，用较强或可靠的力量使受照顾的方面不受损害或破坏。"保护"多用于人或具体事物，但也可用于"利益、积极性"等抽象名词。

"保证"作动词时，表示"担保，负责做到"的意思，后面可带名词、动词、小句作宾语。用作名词时，指"作为担保的事物"，如：

The basic meaning of 保 is "to ensure security, to shelter, to preserve, to assure". The distinctions of these words are mostly on their second morphemes. 保护 emphasizes to protect, by strong or reliable means so that the party to be looked after won't suffer from any harm or damage. Although 保护 is primarily for human beings and concrete things, it is also used for abstract Nouns such as 利益、积极性, etc.

When 保证 is a Verb, it refers "to assure, to guarantee" and can take a Noun, Verb, or Clause as its Object. When it functions as a Noun, it stands for "a pledge, a guarantee" as in the sentence:

良好的服务是生意成功的<u>保证</u>。(Good service is the guarantee of business success.)

"保险"中的"险"字，是"遭到不幸或发生灾难的可能"的意思。可作形容词，也可作名词。作形容词时，表示"稳妥可靠"，如：这样做可能不太<u>保险</u>。"保险"作为名词，意思是集中分散的社会资金，补偿因自然灾害、以外事故或人身伤亡而造成损失的办法。例如，人寿保险、汽车保险等。

"障"就是"屏障"。当"保障"作名词时，是"像屏障一样复盖，起保护作用的事物"的意思。作动词时，着重指维护，使不受侵犯或损害的意思。其对象多是已有的抽象事物，如"生命、财产、权力、自由"等。比较下面的句子：

The character 险 in the word 保险 indicates "danger, the possibility of mishap or disaster". When 保险 is an Adjective, it means "safe and reliable", for example, 这样做可能不太保险. (It may not be safe to do so). When it is a Noun, it refers to "insurance" as in *life insurance, car insurance*, etc.

障 is "a protective screen". As a Noun, 保障 refers to something that can provide protection or covers, like a screen or a shelter. As a Verb, it emphasizes "to safeguard, to defend, to maintain", and is mostly used with abstract Nouns such as 生命、财产、权力、自由, etc. Compare these sentences:

宪法保障人民的言论自由。(The Constitution guarantees freedom of speech of the people.)

小学生要保护好自己的眼睛。(Elementary school students should take good care of their own eyes.)

三、结果 效果 后果

这三个词都共有一个词素"果"字，原意是植物的果实，引申表示事情的结局，和"因"相对。"结果"是中性词，指在一定阶段，事情发展所达到的最后状态。"结果"可作名词，也可作连词。如：

These words all share a morpheme 果, which means the fruit of a plant. Its extended meaning is the "ending, the final result", and is the opposite of the character 因. 结果 is a word of neutral sense, indicating the outcome or final result of something. It can be either a Noun or a Conjunction:

我的进步是老师和同学们帮助的结果。

(My progress is the result of the help of my teachers and classmates.)

他们改进了装潢设计，结果，这个商品比过去好卖多了。

(They have improved the design and packaging of their goods. As a result, it sells much better than before.)

"效果"强调结果是有效的，能起到应有的作用或影响。"效果"多指好的，常用来表示主观上所作所为的结局。"结果"兼指好的和坏的，可指主观上所作所为的结局，也可指客观上事物变化形成的结局。

"后果"按字面的意思，就是"最后的结果"，多用在坏的方面，常受贬义词修饰。

效果 stresses that something is effective, which refers to the outcome or impact. It normally refers to things positive, and is used to indicate some kind of ending that relates to one's subjective behavior or conduct. 结果 can refer to either good things or bad things. It can be one's subjective behavior or conduct, or the result of things that take a natural course.

According to its literal meaning, 后果 is "the final result". It is primarily used in a negative sense, usually modified by derogative words.

四、合适　适合　适当　适应

"适"字有两个意思，一是"符合、切合"，二是"恰好、恰当"，一般在口语中很少单用，如用在书面语，则常与"于"连用。

"合适"是形容词，表示"合乎实际，或符合某种客观要求"，常用于"A 对 B 合适"的句式。"适合"是动词，意思与"合适"相同，但使用频率不及形容词"合适"高，常带宾语或补语。如：他这么高，适合打篮球。

形容词"适当"是"合适"和"妥当"的结合，多作修饰语。常与名词"机会、时候、时机、办法、场合"等搭配。与动词"增加、减少、提高、降低、休息、处理、安排"等搭配时，表示要掌握在一定的数量或范围内。

动词"适应"表示"适合客观条件或需要"，常带宾语或补语，可加程度副词"很、非常、十分"，也可带名词或动词作宾语，并且可重叠。例如：

The character 适 can mean 1) to accord with, to fit in with; and 2) just right and appropriate. It is rarely used by itself in spoken Chinese, and is often associated with 于 if used in writing.

合适 is an Adjective, meaning "suitable, or to accord with certain requirements. It is usually used in the sentence pattern "A 对 B 合适". 适合 is a Verb, which is similar to 合适 in meaning. It is, however, not as frequently used as its Adjectival counterpart, and often takes an Objector Complement, for example, 他这么高, 适合打篮球. (He is so tall, and so it is fitting for him to play basketball.)

The Adjective 适当 is the combination of 合适 and 妥当, and functions primarily as a modifier. It often modifies Nouns such as 机会、时候、时机、办法、场合, etc. When it is associated with Verbs such as 增加、减少、提高、降低、休息、处理、安排, etc., it indicates that something should be within a certain amount or limit.

The Verb 适应 refers to "adapt to, adjust to", and usually takes an Objector Complement. It may be modified by Adverbs such as 很、非常、十分, and can take Nouns or Verbs as its Objects. It can be used in duplication also. For example,

产品必须适应市场的要求。(All products must conform to the needs of the market.)

你最好先适应适应一下环境。(You'd better adjust to the environment first.)

这些孩子适应得很快。 (These children have adapted quite fast.)

他对新工作还不太适应。 (He has not adjusted himself to the new job yet.)

语法

一、 递进复句 Progressive Complex Sentences

后一个分句的意思，比前一个分句的意思更进一层，即表示数量更多、程度更深、范围更广、或性质更严重等，这种复句叫递进复句。递进复句经常使用成对的关联词语，如：

Progressive Complex Sentences are those in which the second clause goes further in meaning than the first, that is, showing more in quantity, greater in degree, broader in scope, or more serious in nature, etc. Progressive Complex Sentences usually rely on Connectives in pairs, such as:

不但/不仅……而且……、不但……还……、不只/不单/不光……还……、不但（不）……反而/反到……、尚且……何况……、尚且……，更不用说……，等等。

有的关联词可以单独使用（通常在后一分句），如：而且、并且、还、更、何况、甚至（于）、乃至（于）等。但如果第一个分句用了"不但"或"不仅"，第二个分句必须用相应的关联词"而且"、"并且"、"还"等。例如：

Some of the Connectives can be used individually (normally in the second clause). Examples are 而且、并且、还、更、何况、甚至（于）、乃至（于）, etc. However, if the first clause has already taken 不但 or 不仅, the second clause must adopt the corresponding Connectives such as 而且、并且、 还. For example:

1. 商品质量的好坏<u>不仅</u>关系到价格的高低，<u>而且</u>影响到商品的销售情况和竞争能力。
2. 她<u>不只</u>帮她的朋友，<u>还</u>帮那些不认识的人。
3. 那条路经常堵车，有时走路<u>反而</u>比开车还快。
4. 这笔生意<u>不但</u>没有亏本，<u>反倒</u>赚了十几万块钱。
5. 这个语法问题老师<u>尚且</u>解释不清楚，<u>更何况</u>一个三年级的学生？
6. 这种电脑功能多，速度快，<u>况且</u>也不贵，可以多买几台。
7. 坚固合理的包装，可以减少货损，节省运费；而精美华丽的包装，更能吸引顾客，有助于商品的推销，<u>乃至于</u>售价的提高。

有时候递进复句的意思可以是多层的连续递进，因此可以连用几个关联词。如：

Sometimes, the meaning of a Progressive Complex Sentence can go further and further in succession, and several Connectives can be wsed in sequence as in the following:

8. 她这次去中国<u>不但</u>汉语有了很大的进步，<u>而且</u>交了很多朋友，<u>甚至</u>还学会了做中国菜。

9. 我们<u>不仅</u>和几家有名的大公司建立了业务关系，<u>并且</u>和两家签订了合同，<u>还</u>商定今后要进行广泛的合作。

二、 比较的方式　Comparison and Contrast

汉语中比较的方式很多，但归结起来，主要有两类：一类是比较事物的异同，一类是比较事物的差别。

Although the word 比较 in Chinese applies to both cases, in fact it covers two different acts: the comparison of similarity and dissimilarity, and the contrast of differences and disparity.

（一）比较异同　Comparison

表示人或事物相同、相似或区别事物的差异，常用下列方式：

The following are often used to compare similarity and dissimilarity of people and things:

1.　a) A 跟/和 B 一样/相同　　否定：A 跟/和 B 不一样/不(相)同

这个孩子跟他妈妈一样。现在的学生跟 20 年前的已经不(相)同了。

"一样"、"相同"前面可以用副词"完全"、"简直"、"差不多"等来修饰，有时为了强调，甚至可以说"一模一样"。否定句也可用"很"、"大"、"非常"等来修饰，如：

一样, 相同 can be modified by Adverbs such as 完全、简直 or 差不多. Sometimes, one can even say 一模一样 to emphasize. In addition, negative sentences can be modified with 很、大、非常, also. For example:

"可是"和"但是"的用法完全相同。

绿茶的包装跟红茶的差不多一样。

中国文化和美国文化很不一样。

国产电视机和进口电视机的质量差不多，但价钱大不相同。

"一样"后面可以加上形容词，进一步说明具体在哪方面的异同。但是"相同"后面不可加任何形容词。例如：

An Adjective can be added after 一样 to further specify similarity and dissimilarity in what aspect, but no Adjective can be used after 相同.

发传真跟发电子邮件一样方便。✘发传真跟发电子邮件相同方便。

这条船和那条船不一样长。　　　✘这条船和那条船不相同长。

b) A 跟 B 一样 Verb (+Obeject)

这个句型一般只用于表示喜爱、认知、意愿等非行为动作的动词，如"喜欢、爱 (好)、了解、希望"等，或在行为动词前面加上"能、会、可以、想、要"等能愿动词。例如：

This pattern is used either with non-action Verbs that indicate preference, cognition, desire, etc., such as 喜欢、爱 (好)、了解、希望 or action Verbs preceded by an Auxiliary Verb such as 能、会、可以、想、要.
For instance:

弟弟和哥哥一样喜欢踢球。

我跟你一样希望早日达成交易。

不少老外跟中国人一样会用筷子。

小孩跟大人一样都要买票。

如果是行为动词而前面没有能愿动词，必须加上状语。如：

When there is no Auxiliary Verb preceding an action Verb, an Adverbial is required. For example:

弟弟和哥哥一样常常在街上踢球。　✘弟弟和哥哥一样踢球。

c) A 跟 B+Verb 一样的 Obeject　　否定：A 跟 B+Verb 不一样的 Obeject

这个句型用于说明动作相同而宾语的异同。例如：

This pattern specifies the similarity or dissimilarity of an Object with the same action. For example:

那个公司的老板跟职员穿一样的衣服。

小潘和他的女朋友都买了一样的汽车。

他们跟我们用不一样的课本。

爸爸和妈妈给孩子们送了不一样的礼物。

2.   A 有 B 这/那么＋形容词/表示喜爱、认知、意愿等非行为动词

     否定：A没有 B 这/那么＋表示喜爱、认知、意愿等非行为
     动词

     这个句型用于比较两个事物，以 B 为标准，看 A 是否达到了 B 的
     程度。如：

     This pattern compares two people or things. While taking B as the standard,
     it measures A to see whether A has reached the point of B. Either Adjective or
     non-action Verbs indicating preference, cognition, desire, etc. are used.

     挂号信有航空信那么快。
     你爸爸有陈老师这么了解你的学习吗？
     日语语法没有汉语语法那么简单。
     吴经理没有老宋那么熟悉中东市场的情况。

3.   A 像 B   否定：A 不像 B
     A 像 B 一样/那样＋Adj.   A 不像 B 这么/那样＋Adj.

     这个句型以B为标准，表示两事物在性质、特征、状态上相像。
     "像"前可有副词"很、好、就、有点儿"等来修饰，也可以在"像"后面加
     上"一样/那么＋形容词"，表示 A 具体在哪方面与 B 相似或达到 B 的程
     度。例如：

     This pattern takes B as the standard, and shows that the two things or
     people resemble or look alike in nature, feature, or state. Adverbs such as 很、
     好、就、有点儿 can be added before 像 or as a modifier, or things like 一
     样/那么＋形容词 can follow 像 to show in what aspect or to what extent that
     A resembles B. For instance:

     他说的英文很像英国英文。
     老赵有点儿像咱们的董事长。
     她对学生就像对自己的孩子一样。

我们这儿坐地铁就像坐出租汽车那样方便。

他不像老板，倒像老师、朋友。

做进出口生意不像去商店买东西那么简单。

这种药不像进口的那样有效。

(二) 比较差别　Contrast

比较人或事物性质、状态、能力 (范围) 和程度方面的差别，常用下列的方式：

The following expressions are usually used to contrast the differences and disparity of people or things in their nature, state, ability or degree:

1. ① A 比 B+Adj./V

德国汽车比美国汽车贵。　　✗德国汽车比美国汽车很贵。

A Verb (OV) 得比 B+Adj.

他睡觉睡得比谁都晚。　　✗他睡觉睡得比谁都非常晚。

A 较 B+Adj./V (这是书面语，一般多用于同一事物不同时期的比较，B 多为时间词。)

日本今年的出口较往年有所下降。✗日本今年的出口较往年有所有一点儿下降。

注意：在带"比"字的比较句里，"很、太、特别、非常、有一点儿"等副词不可在形容词前对它进行修饰，但"还、更"则可以 (详细例子请看下面 d 处)。

N.B. In sentences of comparison with 比, Adverbs such 很、太、特别、非常、有一点儿 cannot go before and modify an Adjective, but it is possible with 更、还 and 再 (Please see ④ in the following for details).

A 比 B+Adj./V+程度/数量

新产品的包装比旧产品的轻一些。　我们班的女生比男生多七个人。

② A Verb (OV) 得比 B+Adj./V+ 程度/数量

老师解释语法解释得比课本清楚多了。　妹妹跑得比姐姐快两分钟。

在谓语动词或形容词后加上"一点儿、一些、得多、多了"或具体的数量，可以表示两者差别的程度。

The extent to which the two people or things differ from each other can be illustrated when 一点儿、一些、得多、多了, or a specific amount is put after a Verb or Adjective in the Predicate.

③ A 比 B+多／少／早／晚／先／后／难／好（易）Verb (O)

当谓语是一般动词，比较涉及动作的数量、时间、词序、或难易时，"多、少、早、晚、先、后、难、好（易）"等须位于动词前面，而动词后仍可带表示程度或数量的宾语或补语。例如：

When the Predicate is an ordinary Verb, and the comparison/contrast involves the amount, time, sequence, or difficulty and easiness of an action, words like 多、少、早、晚、先、后、难、好（易）should go before the Verb and the Verb can still take an Object or Complement that indicates the degree or the quantity. For instance:

他们比原计划多订了五十桶。

总经理请你明天（比今天）早来半小时。

由于法国的公司比我们先报了实盘，这笔生意让法国人抢走了。

西班牙语比日语好学一点儿，是吗？

④ A 比 B+更／还 Adj./Verb（一点儿／一些）

　　A 比 B Verb (OV) 得更＋Adj.（一点儿／一些）

　　A 比 B 再 Adj.（多用于假设／疑问／否定）

这几个句型通过副词"更、还、再"表示 B 已有一定的基础，在这个基础上，A 的程度更进一层。句末可以加上"一点儿、一些"或具体的数量，但不可用"得多、得了"。例如：

With Adverbs such as 更、还、再 these patterns show that on the basis of B, the degree of A is even higher. While it is possible to add 一点儿、一些 or the specific amount at the end of the sentence, it is not the case with 得多 or 得

了. For example:

（他们那样的包装不错，）我们的包装比他们的更美观一点儿。

你们的报价相当有吸引力，但是永新公司的报价每件比你们的还便宜一块钱。

"再"一般只用于表示假设、疑问或否定的句子。如：

再 is usually used in sentences of hypothesis, interrogation, or negation. For example:

你就是比老师再聪明，也要尊敬老师。　　〔假设〕

甲：没有比这再便宜的飞机票了吗？　　〔疑问〕

乙：没有比这再便宜的了。　　〔否定〕

表示比较的否定形式主要有以下几种：

The following are some common negative forms of contrast:

A 不比 B+Adj./Verb

这个句型表示 A 的程度不超过 B，可能低于或等于 B 的程度。如：

This pattern indicates that the degree of A does NOT exceed that of B, but may be equal to or lower than B. Just listen to the following simple conversation:

甲：东京比纽约大吗？

乙：东京<u>不比</u>纽约大。

A 没有 B+（这么/那么）Adj./Verb

这个句型表示 A 绝对不到 B 的程度。如：

This pattern shows that A is absolutely below the level of B. For instance:

天津新港的条件<u>没有</u>大连港的<u>那么</u>好。

A Verb (OV) 得没有 B（这么/那么）＋Adj.

这个句型表示 A 绝对不到 B 的程度。如：

This pattern shows that A can never reach the degree of B in doing something. For example:

张师傅开车开得<u>没有</u>李师傅<u>那么</u>快。

A不如/不及B

这个句型没有相应的肯定形式，表示A在总体上绝对不到 B 的程度。句末没有形容词或动词，多用于书面语。如：

This pattern indicates that A cannot match with B as a whole, and does not have an affirmative form. Normally there is no adjective or Verb at the end of the sentence, and the pattern is mostly seen in written Chinese. For example:

日本的科技水平<u>不及</u>美国。

A不如/不及B(这么/那么)＋Adj.

这个句型没有相应的肯定形式，表示 A 在具体的某方面达不到 B 的程度。如：

This pattern indicates that A cannot match B in a specific area, and does not have an affirmative form, either. For instance:

跑步<u>不如</u>打球那么有意思。

2. A+单音节 Adj.于B

这个句型一般用于书面语，作谓语的形容词或动词基本上是单音节的。后面跟介词"于"，连接作为比较标准的B，使用时要注意在词序上与"A 比 B+Adj."的区别。（参看第六课"词语例释"五。）

This pattern is used in written Chinese in general. Its Predicate is usually a monosyllabic Adjective or Verb, which follows by the Preposition 于 to link up with B that serves as the standard. Note the difference of word order comparing with the pattern A 比 B+Adj. (Please refer to 词语例释-五 in Lesson Six.).

我方的产品质量普遍<u>优于</u>同类产品。
对比：我方的产品质量普遍比同类产品的质量好。
八十年代以来，中国的经济每年都以<u>高于</u>百分之十的增长幅度发展。
对比：八十年代以来，中国的经济每年都以比百分之十还高的增长幅度发展。

3. A+Adj., B 更 Adj., C 最 Adj.

当比较的人或事物达三项或三项以上时，可以使用这个句型，但第一项有时可以省略，用"B 比 A 更＋Adj."来表示同样的意思。例如：

When there are three or more items involved in comparison/contrast, this pattern can be used. However, the first part can be omitted, and the same meaning can be expressed by using B 比 A 更＋Adj.. Please note the following examples:

印尼人口很多，印度人口更多，中国人口最多。

或：印度人口比印尼更多，中国人口最多。

打七折不错，买一送一更好，不用钱白给最好。

或：买一送一比打七折更好，不用钱白给最好。

(三) 句子成分的省略　Omission of Sentence Elements

在汉语的比较方式中，只要是语境清楚，不产生歧义，某些句子成分往往都可以省略。下面是几种常见的情况：

In Chinese comparison/contrast, some sentence elements are usually omitted as long as the context is clear and no other interpretation is suggested. The following are some omissions commonly occur in comparison/contrast:

1. <u>省略中心语</u>　如果"比"前后的成分是名词短语，而其中心语又相同，"比"后的中心语可以省略。如：

   <u>Omission of the Head Noun</u>　When the elements before and after 比 are both Noun Phrases, and they share an identical Head Noun, the one after 比 can be omitted. For instance:

   今年夏天的气温比去年(夏天的气温)高。

   她的狗跑得比我的(狗)快。

2. <u>省略定语</u>　如果"比"前后的成分有相同的定语，"比"后的定语可以省略。如：

   <u>Omission of the Attributive</u>　When there is an identical Attributive in the

elements before and after 比, the Attributive that goes after 比 can be omitted. For example:

商品的质量比(商品的)包装更重要。

他的汉语说得比(他的)英语流利。

3. 省略定语和中心语的相同部分　如果"比"前后的成分有相同的定语和中心语，其中的一个(或前或后)可以省略。如：

Omission of the Same Part in the Attributive and Head Noun　If there is an identical Attributive and Head Noun in the elements before and after 比, one of them (either before or after) can be omitted. For example:

我们公司进口的交易额比(我们公司)出口的(交易额)大。

小芳每天看电视(的时间)比(她)看书的(时间)还长。

4. 省略主谓短语中的谓语或主语　如果"比"前后的成分有相同的主谓短语，其中的一个(或前或后)可以省略。如：

Omission of the Predicate or Subject　When there is an identical phrase of Subject and Predicate before and after 比, one of them (either before or after) can be omitted. For example:

老程做进出口生意比我们(做进出口生意)都早。

她打字比(她)写字快多了。

5. 省略状语　如果比较的事物是关于时间、地点等状语时，"比"前的时间状语或地点状语可以省略。如：

Omission of the Adverbial　When an Adverbial such as time or place is involved in comparison or contrast, the Adverbial of time or place before 比 can be omitted. For instance:

陈先生(现在的)身体比前几年好多了。

小朋友们(在这儿)比在家里睡得早一点儿。

修辞

段落（自然段）　Paragraphs

　　段落即自然段。它是大于或等于句子、句群的语言单位，是文章的层次的外在表现。它标志着作者思路发展的具体步骤。段落有明显的形式标志：每个段落的开始，总是另起一行，缩进两格（即在第三格开始）书写。

　　A paragraph is a language unit larger than or equal to a sentence or a group of sentences. It is the expeicit mark of the strata, i.e. the organization of ideas in an essay, which signifies the specific steps of thought development of the writer. A paragraph bears distinct features —it always begins with a new line, and is indented by two characters (i. e. beginning at the third space).

　　一篇文章是一个完整、连贯的统一体，通常包含着几个层次。所谓层次，就是文章各部分内容的相对地位和次序，也就是意义段。意义段反映了作者思想发展过程的主要阶段，并通过段落（自然段）把其中各个步骤表现出来。有时候，一个段落就是一个意义段。在这种情况下，段落（自然段）就是篇章的直接构件。有时候，几个段落（自然段）合起来才组成一个意义段。在这种情况下，段落（自然段）是意义段的直接构件，对于整篇文章来说，它就是最小的组成部分，是文章的基本构件。

　　An article is a complete, coherent entirety, which contains several strata of ideas. By stratum, it is meant the relative position and sequence of ideas arranged in each part of a composition, namely, a Thematic Section（意义段）. The Thematic Sections in a composition mark major stages of thought development of the writer, each specific step of which is shown by means of a paragraph. Sometime, a paragraph is a Thematic Section by itself. In this case, a paragraph is a direct component of an essay. On other occasions, several paragraphs join together to form a Thematic Section. In such case, a paragraph is a direct component of a Thematic Section. It is, in regard of the entire composition, the smallest part of organization, and a basic component of the essay.

　　段落由句子或句群组成。按结构来划分，段落可分为独句段和多句段。例如：

A paragraph is composed of a sentence or a group of sentences. It can be classified as a single sentence paragraph or a multiple sentence paragraph in accordance with its structure. For instance:

1. 除此之外，如有机会，还可以参加一些外国的商品展览会或者交易会，与有关公司的代表当面洽谈，直接建立业务联系。

（第一课 lines 25–26）

2. 国际贸易中的支付方式主要有三种：信用证、托收和汇付。

（第九课 line 15）

　　以上的例子都是独句段，每段都只有一句话，例 1 是个复句，例 2 是个单句。又如：

The examples cited above are single sentence paragraphs, each of which contains one sentence only. While the first one is a Complex Sentence, the second one is a Simple Sentence. Now, take a look at other examples:

3. 任何一家公司要做进出口生意，从事国际贸易，必须进行一定的准备工作。这些工作主要包括：进行市场调查，了解对方的贸易制度和市场所在地的法律，建立与客户的业务关系。

（第一课 lines 1–3）

4. 询盘，在中国的对外贸易习惯上，又称为询价，即交易的一方向另一方询问购买或出售某种商品的各项交易条件。询价的内容有繁有简，一般包括：商品的品质规格、包装、数量、价格、支付方式、装运、交货期等。买卖双方只有对各项交易条件都取得一致意见以后，交易才可达成。因此，询盘作为交易洽商的一环，具有投石问路，了解另一方的交易条件的功能。　　（第二课 lines 4–9）

　　例 3 和例 4 为多句段。例 3 含有两个比较长的单句，而例 4 则有三个复句和一个单句。段落可长可短，结构可繁可简，层次可多可少，段落内部的意义关系有时简单有时复杂，但是所有这些，都必须根据一定的意思和逻辑关系连接在一起。这些句子、句群以及段落之间的逻辑关系，与复句的分类大致相同，基本上是并列、承接、总分、递进、转折、因果、说明、对比等几种。因此，如果我们能掌握好各类复句，理解分句与分句之间的逻辑关系和相互联系，再推而广之，把这些关系逐步扩展到句群、段落甚至意义段之间的层面上，就可以比较清楚地看到整篇文章的全貌，知道不仅是句与句之间，而且是段与段之间的关系和联系。这样，就可以更好地理解全文的意思，不断提高阅读理解能力。

Both examples 3 and 4 are multiple sentence paragraphs. In 3, there are two long Simple Sentences whereas in 4, there are three Complex Sentences and a Simple Sentence.

A paragraph can be long or short, and its structure can be complex or simple. Similarly, the arrangement of the ideas may vary in its order or hierarchy, the relations between ideas within a paragraph may be either simple or complicated. Whatever they may be, ideas and sentences should be organized and connected coherently according to some logical relations and centering around a certain topic. The logical relations between sentences, groups of sentences and paragraphs are considerably similar to those categories assigned to complex sentences. They are, basically, relations of coordination, succession, general and specifics, progression, concession, cause and effect, elaboration, comparison and contrast, etc. Thus, if we can learn all the types of Complex Sentences well, and if we can understand their logical relations and transitions, we will then be able to extend them beyond the sentence level, from groups of sentences, to paragraph level, and gradually to thematic sections. On this basis, we will be able to have a whole picture of the overall organization of a text. We not only will know the relations between sentences, but also relations between and transitions from paragraphs to paragraphs. As a result, we will be able to better understand the ideas of the entire text, and to further improve our reading comprehension.

练习

一、 用线将意思相同的词和词语连起来：

(货物) 没有任何包装，直接放在运输工具上　　　　　集装

为了方便商品的陈列展销、运输储存而在商品外
加上的装潢和保护　　　　　　　　　　　　　　　防腐

把一定数量的单件货物集中放在承载装置里，
以便于装卸运输　　　　　　　　　　　　　　　　直销

把商品摆出来陈列展览，以便推销　　　　　　　　裸装

想办法使货物卖得更多更快　　　　　　　　　　　畅销

直接把商品卖出去，中间不经过任何零售商　　　　绝早

防止物品变坏腐烂　　　　　　　　　　　　　　　防火功能

为防止别人偷东西而设计的专门装置　　　　　　　包装

有不怕火烧的作用　　　　　　　　　　　　　　　绝大多数

商品很受欢迎，卖得很快　　　　　　　　　　　　展销

非常早；早极了　　　　　　　　　　　　　　　　促销

百分之九十以上　　　　　　　　　　　　　　　　防盗设备

二、 用括号里的词或词组改写下列句子，但不改变其基本意思，必要时可对词序作一定的调整：

1. 电脑的使用越来越广泛以后，很多人的工作和学习都已经不能没有电脑了。　　　　　　　　　　　　　　　　　（随着、离不开）

2. 他们除了提高产品的质量以外，还把产量从1000辆增加到1150辆。　　　　　　　　　　　　　　　　　（在……基础上、将）

3. 这种货币的价值一天比一天下跌，甚至3000元才换1美元。　　　　　　　　　　　　　　　　　（日益、乃至于）

4. 新设计的门开启很方便，让坐轮椅的人都能自由进出。　　　　　　　　　　　　　　　　　（便于、使）

5. 这样做对降低成本当然有好处，但是也可能会影响生产效率。

(有利于、然而)

6. 几年以后，你们现在种的树对于保护环境将会产生很重要的效果和
   影响。　　　　　　　　　　　　　　　(若干、起到……的作用)

7. 这家超级市场经常用打折扣作为吸引顾客、推销商品的方法。

(以……为……、手段)

8. 为了适合业务发展的需要，他们计划在三年内使港口装卸电脑化成
   为事实。　　　　　　　　　　　　　　　　　(适应、实现)

三、 选择最合适的词填空：

1. 作为董事长，她既注重产品的质量，也重视包装_____。
   a. 装运　　　　　b. 装卸　　　　　c. 装载　　　　　d. 装潢

2. 这个港口电脑化以后，_____速度有了很大的提高。
   a. 装运　　　　　b. 装卸　　　　　c. 装载　　　　　d. 装潢

3. 合同签订以后，卖方必须按照规定及时组织货物的_____。
   a. 装运　　　　　b. 装卸　　　　　c. 装载　　　　　d. 装潢

4. 包装不光是为了好看，它还有_____商品的功能。
   a. 保护　　　　　b. 保障　　　　　c. 保证　　　　　d. 保险

5. 你放心吧，我们的产品是第一流的，_____你满意。
   a. 保护　　　　　b. 保障　　　　　c. 保证　　　　　d. 保险

6. 在所有发达国家中，美国没有健康_____的人最多。
   a. 保护　　　　　b. 保障　　　　　c. 保证　　　　　d. 保险

7. 何太太吃了这种药已经两个多星期了，可是还没有什么_____。
   a. 后果　　　　　b. 效果　　　　　c. 结果　　　　　d. 如果

8. 副总经理叫你马上把调查_____给她送去。
   a. 后果　　　　　b. 效果　　　　　c. 结果　　　　　d. 如果

9. 这样做会带来严重的_____，你能负责吗？

    a. 后果   b.效果   c. 结果   d. 如果

10. 下次报价，你可以_____给他们打一些折扣。

    a. 合适   b.适合   c. 适应   d. 适当

11. 医生说老年人不_____参加这样激烈的运动。

    a. 合适   b. 适合   c. 适应   d. 适当

12. 只有不断学习，才能_____形势的变化。

    a. 合适   b. 适合   c. 适应   d. 适当

四、 找出课文里的递进复句和目的复句。

五、 用递进复句说明下列情况：

1. 你喜欢看某个电视节目的几个原因。

2. 请老师取消期末考试，同时说明你能想出来的所有理由。

3. 你是某某产品的推销员，发挥你的想像力，尽量向你的顾客推荐这个产品。

六、 根据下面的图表，用各种比较方式回答下列问题，然后再利用有关的信息，写一篇两段的短文：

1990年和1995年中国某些主要出口商品的金额对比

亿美元

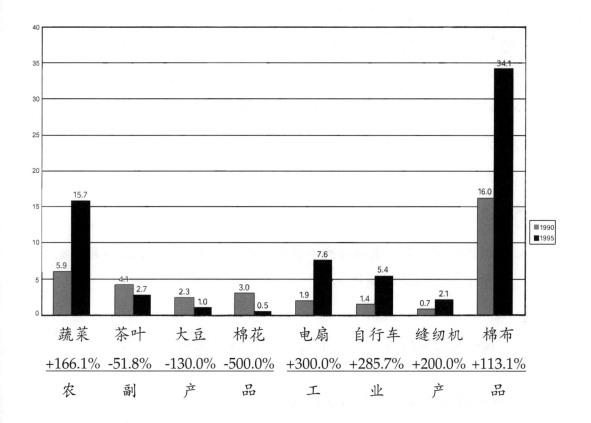

摘自《中国统计摘要－1997》中国统计出版社，北京：中国，1997年。

问题：

1. 1995年中国自行车出口的金额是多少美元？比1990年增加了多少美元？

2. 1995年中国缝纫机的出口金额是1990年的几倍？比1990年增加了几倍？

3. 与1990年相比，中国电扇的出口翻了几番？

4. 在这些出口商品中，哪个商品的出口金额最大？它的增长幅度是否大于蔬菜的增长幅度？

5. 1990年中国出口金额最大的是哪两种商品？1995年出口金额最大的商品和1990年的是否一样？

6. 1995年中国茶叶的出口比1990年减少了几成？

7. 1995年中国大豆的出口比1995年减少了多少美元？下降的幅度是否比茶叶的大？

8. 和1990年相比，什么商品的出口减少得最利害？下降的幅度是多少？

9. 1995年自行车和蔬菜的出口金额哪个大？增长幅度呢？

10. 1990年中国的出口以工业产品还是农副产品为主？1995年发生了什么变化？

七、 根据逻辑和意思，重新排列下列句子的顺序并把它们连接成段。必要时加上适当的关联词语。

*张三和李四是好朋友。

*"我女儿20岁结婚，你儿子就40岁了"，张三说。

*张三问："你儿子几岁了？"

*他的朋友李四有一个四岁的儿子。

*张三没等李四说完，就说："你的儿子四岁，我女儿才两岁，你儿子比我女儿整整大一倍"。

*两个人的孩子从小就经常在一起玩儿。

*张三听了，生气地说："那怎么行！你想让我女儿嫁给一个老头子吗？"

*"四岁了"，李四回答。

*张三有一个两岁的女儿。

*李四觉得很奇怪，就问："怎么回事？我儿子才……"

*"她25岁才嫁过去，你儿子不是已经50岁了吗？"

*有一天，李四叫张三把女儿嫁给他的儿子。

八、 把下列句子翻译成汉语：

1. Along with changes in the market situation, we have decided to expand the production scale on the basis of not increasing the cost. We will take raising (working) efficiency as a key measure to (enable us to) double the output.

2. The design of cars is becoming more and more artistic, and the competition is getting more and more intense day by day. Such competition is favorable to the improvement of product quality, and lowering of the price. It can be said that the market economy is playing a decisive role here.

3. This kind of computer is convenient to carry around, and simple to use [i.e. "operate"]. Many people often take them to work, to attend meetings, even to travel. It seems that these people cannot part with computers in their life. Yet, there is one problem with these computers, that is, they don't have any anti-theft function.

九、 商业信函练习三

　　指出下面信中所有的错误（包括标点符号），按照其意思，重新改写全信：

香港华琳进出口公司丝绸纺织品部

编号：太002号
美国加州洛杉矶
太平洋波浪公司
总经理
王万宜先生

<u>事由：丝绸手绢报盘</u>

亲爱的总经理先生，

好久不见，你好吗？最近忙不忙？

对于你们贵公司的4月5号的所来的信函中询问到我公司的中国丝绸手绢的可能性的供应量，本公司已经立刻联系了我们的制造者。以便回答你的要求，我附信寄了给你们我们公司的另类样品，就算我们的样品不同你们的来样；不过我能肯定他们的品质如同你们的样品，如果不更好。他确定相配你们的样品.我们的最近报价在下面。

花色1到4号：　一打美元28块，C.I.F.
花色5到8号：　一打美元42块，C.I.F.

要是你能够这个月开信用证，一收到信用证就我们能装运在一个月。如果你肯给现钱，我就能减价到5%。

上面的报盘是为了数量不能少过3,000打每一花色的订货，也月底有效。我们等你早点订货。

祝你好运！

你的

陈育华　经理

1997年3月10日

文化与商贸背景知识

📝 报关与商检

一、报关

报关是指进出口公司在货物装运前，向海关申报。按中国海关规定，凡是进出中国国境的货物，必须经设有海关的港口、车站、国际航空港进出，并由货物的所有人向海关申报，经海关放行后，货物才可提取或装船出运。

一般来说，如果是中方出口的货物，就由中国的出口公司填写"出口货物报关单"。必要时还要提供出口合同副本、发票、装箱单或重量单、商品检验证书及其他有关证件，向中国海关申报出口。如果是中方进口的货物，也由中国的进口公司负责填写"进口货物报关单"，向中国海关申报进口。货物、证件经海关核对查验无误后，在装货单上盖章放行，承运人方可接受装货。

二、商检

凡属中国规定必须检验，或合同规定必须由中国商品检验局检验的出口商品，在货物备齐后，出口人（中方）应填写"检验申请单"（见第五课"文化与商贸背景知识"），向商检局申请检验。"检验申请单"的内容一般包括：品名、规格、数量（或重量）、包装、产地等项。货物经检验合格，即由商检局发给检验证书。只有取得合格的检验证书，海关才准放行。

进口中国的货物也必须经过商检局检验，取得商品检验证书后，才能向海关申报。如果发现残损短缺，凭商检局出具的证书对外索赔。

除商品检验局外，中国还设立了一些专门的检验和检疫部门，管理有关专业性检验和检疫工作。例如，动植物检疫所负责进出口动物产品和植物的检疫工作；船舶检验局负责进口船舶及主要船用设备的检验工作。

✎ **装箱单、出口货物报关单、动植物检疫报检单、植物检疫证书**

东 方 科 学 仪 器 进 出 口 集 团 公 司
THE ORIENTAL SCIENTIFIC INSTRUMENTS IMPORT & EXPORT GROUP

中国·北京三里河路52号
No.52,San Li He Road
Beijing 100864,China
Tel: 2614983
FAX: 2614399

装 箱 单
PACKING LIST

逐 启 者　Messrs: S.C.WORKS CO. LTD.
地　　址　Address: 10/10-11 CHAROEN KRUNG RD..
　　　　　　　　　　BANGKOK 10200

合同号: 970EB64098TH Contract No.	发票号: 9764118 Invoice No.	日期: Aug 11, 1997 Date
发货口岸: TIANJIN Port of Loading	运输工具: SHIP Shipped Per	开航日期: Sailing on or About
到货口岸: BANGKOK Port of Discharge	交货条件: CIF BANGKOK Delivery Terms	

唛 头 Marks	货 名 Description	数 量 Quantity	净重量 N.Weight	毛重量 G.Weight	体 积 Measurement
GOLD PLATING LINE		1SET		1.04MT	4x1.05x1.4mx2CTNS 0.8X0.6X1.3mx1CTN

TOTAL: CIF BANGKOK
AMOUNT: TWENTY EIGHT THOUSANDS NINE HUNDRED AND NIGHT
US DOLLARS ONLY.

THE ORIENTAL SCIENTIFIC INSTRUMENTS
IMPORT AND EXPORT CORPORATION

....
Authorized Signature

中华人民共和国海关出口货物报关单

预录入编号：　　　　　　　　　　　海关编号：

出口口岸 天津新港		备案号		出口日期		申报日期
经营单位 东方科学仪器进出口集团公司 1102919055		运输方式 江海	运输工具名称		提运单号	
发货单位 东方科学仪器进出口集团公司		贸易方式 一般		征免性质		结汇方式 L/C
许可证号 （签章）		运抵国(地区) 泰国		指运港 罗勇		境内货源地
批准文号		成交方式 CIF	运费		保费	杂费
合同协议号 970EB6409 8TH		件数	包装种类	毛重(公斤)		净重(公斤)
集装箱号		随附单据			生产厂家	

标记唛码及备注

项号	商品编号	商品名称、规格型号	数量及单位	最终目的国(地区)	单价	总价	币制	征免
		稽康线设备	1套	泰国	USD28998.00	USD 28998.00	USD	

税费征收情况

录入员	录入单位	兹声明以上申报无讹并承担法律责任	海关审单批注及放行日期(签章)	
			审单	审价
报关员				
		申报单位(签章)	征税	统计
单位地址				
邮编	电话	填制日期	查验	放行

中华人民共和国动植物检疫

报 检 单

报检单位（盖章）_____　　　　　• 编号 _____

报检人 _____　联系电话 010-62614983　　　报检日期 _____

发货人及地址 （中英文）	东方科学仪器进出口集团公司 THE ORIENTAL SCIENTIFIC INSTRUMENTS IMPORT&EXPORT GROUP.				
受货人及地址 （中英文）	日商岩井株式会社 NISSHO IWAI CORPORATION(4-5,Akasaka 2-chome,TOKYO,JAPAN)				
品　名 （中英文）	紫云英 CHINESE MILKVETCH				
数　量	10,000kgs.	包装种类	纸箱	货物类别	标记唛码
重　量	毛重	净重 10,000kgs.			N/M
货　值	单价 USD 2.00	总价　USD 20,000.00			
产　地	湖北	启运口岸	天津新港		
到达口岸	横滨	货运终点			
运输工具名称	海运	集装箱号码			
□进☒出口性质		用　途			
□进☒出境日期		提单／运单号			合同／协议号码及订立的检疫条款
检疫审批单位		检疫审批文号			
停货地点					
备注：					

• 应缴检疫费	检　疫	检　验	监／测处理	复核及收款人	应补交项目及款额	随 附 单 证
	证　书	外出检疫	合　计		复核及收款人	
				月　日	月　日	

• 检疫记事：　　　　　　（批次数_____，是／否有报检单的附单）

需要单证种类及份数

□动检证　一正___副本
☑植检证　一正 3 副本
□熏蒸证　一正___副本
□
□检疫放行单

检疫员 _____　主管 _____

注：凡有＊者请勿填写，请在□内做出标记"✓"。
不清楚地方详见填单说明。

放行
检疫 _____　日期 ___ 年 ___ 月 ___ 日
出证　检务经办人 _____

75, 4713

中华人民共和国农业部

植 物 检 疫 证 书

正 本
ORIGINAL

PHYTOSANITARY CERTIFICATE
MINISTRY OF AGRICULTURE OF P.R.CHINA

编号 No. 970705150

发货人及地址
Name & Address of Consignor THE ORIENTAL SCIENTIFIC INSTRUMENTS IMPORT AND EXPORT CORPORATION.

受货人及地址
Name & Address of Consignee NISSHO IWAI CORPORATION (4-5, Akasaka 2-chome, TOKYO, JAPAN)

品名及数量
Name of Produce & Quantity Declared CHINESE MILKVETCH 400 GUNNY BAGS 10MTS

标记笺码 Mark & Number

N/M

产地
Place of Origin HUBEI

到达口岸
Port of Destination YOKOHAMA

运输工具
Means of Conveyance BY SEA

兹证明上述植物、植物产品,经本检疫机关于 1997 年 8 月 12 日检验,该认为不带有检疫性病虫害,并且基本不带有其他有害的病虫害,因而被认为符合进口国现行的植物检疫规定。

This is to certify that the plants or plant products described above were thoroughly examined on Aug. 12, 1997 by this service and are considered to be free from quarantine pests, and practically free from other injurious pests; and that they are considered to conform with the current phytosanitary regulations of the importing country.

除虫和/或灭菌处理 DISINFESTATION AND /OR DISINFECTION TREATMENT

日期
Date X X X

处理时间及温度
Duration & Temperature X X X

处理方法
Treatment X X X

药剂及浓度
Chemical & Concentration X X X

附加声明
ADDITIONAL DECLARATION

CBHU124272
CBHU1209044

印章
Stamp

签证日期 Date of Issue Aug. 13, 1997

检疫官 Name of Authorized Officer Zhao Longzhang

签 名 Signature

中华人民共和国动植物检疫机关及其官员或代表不承担颁发本证书的任何财经责任。
No financial liability shall attach to the animal and plant quarantine service of P.R. China or to any officer or representative of the service with respect to this certificate.

交货与装运

✎ **思考下面的问题，然后带着这些问题去阅读课文：**

一、什么是买卖双方在签订合同后的首要任务？

二、"交货"的概念在国际贸易中指的是什么？"装运"又是什么意思？

三、"装运"涉及哪些方面？具体的又包括什么内容？

四、在什么情况下可以"分批装运"或"允许转船"？

课文：交货与装运

　　成交协议达成后，买卖双方按照合同的规定各自付款、交货是义不容辞的责任。这就是俗话说的"一手交钱，一手交货"。付款与交货是买和卖的具体表现，只有在卖方收到货款而买方也收到货物之后，整个交易才算真正完成。对卖方来说，在签订合同后，其首要任务，就是按合同规定的时间、地点和方式将货物运交买方、买方代理人或指定的运输工具。 5

　　国际贸易是国与国之间的商品交易。卖方交货，并非像商店那样直接把货物交到顾客手中，而是采用装运港交货的价格术语(F.O.B., C.I.F., C. & F.)，由卖方把货物交到装运港的运输工具上，然后向承运人取得象征货物所有权的提单，再通过有关的银行把提单 10交给买方。一旦货物装上了指定的运输工具，卖方的交货任务便告完成。买方或卖方指定的承运人在运输单据上所注明的日期，即作为交货的日期，货物的装运地点(即装运港)，也就是交货的地点。因此，"装运"这个词常被用来代替"交货"的概念，国际贸易合同中的"交货条件"也常被称为"装运条件"。

　　装运和交货是一个十分复杂的问题。它涉及运输方式、装运时间、装运港和目的港等内容。

　　国际贸易中的运输方式有多种，包括海洋运输、陆路运输、航空运输、邮政运输等。如果采用两种或两种以上不同的运输方式，20　就叫联合运输。在诸多方式中，以海运最为普遍。因为海运具有运载量大、费用低廉、不受道路限制等优点，因此海运大约占了世界贸易货运总量的三分之二。然而，在具体的每一笔交易中采用哪种运输方式，还要结合商品的特点、货运量大小、自然条件、装卸港口的具体情况以及国际政治局势变化等因素来考虑，由买卖双方商25　定，选择合理的运输方式，做到"安全、迅速、准确、节省、方便"。

　　装运时间，又称作"装运期"。当采用 F.O.B., C.I.F., C. & F. 价格条款时，卖方只要在装运港把货物装上运输工具，就算完成了交货的任务。因此，货物的装运时间与交货时间是一致的，"装运期"也就30　是"交货期"。在进出口贸易中，大部分货物都属于时间性较强的商品，如果错过了销售季节，商品的价值就会大幅度降低，而买方的经济利益也将大受影响。因此，假若卖方不能如期装运，即等于不能按时交货，这样便构成了违约，买方就有权要求赔偿由此而造成的损失，甚至撤销合同。为了避免日后可能产生的纠纷，买卖双方35　都应重视合同上装运时间的规定，力求把条件订得具体、明确、合理。一般来说，在合同中应当尽量采用定期装运，也就是限于一定日期以前或者在某某季节某几个月内装运，同时避免采用"即期装运"、"立即装运"等在时间概念上含糊的术语。

　　货物的装运港和目的港除了与商品的价格有关以外，还关系到40　买卖双方各自承担的运输责任。在一般情况下，装运港要便于货物的装运，所以都由卖方在洽商时提出，经买方同意后确定；目的港要便于货物的接收或转售，所以都由买方提出，经卖方同意后确定。根据双方的需要，装运港和目的港可以分别规定为一个，例

如：装运港——高雄，目的港——旧金山；也可以分别规定为两个
或两个以上，例如：装运港——大连/天津/上海，目的港——伦 45
敦/汉堡/鹿特丹。

　　对于某些成交额较大的商品来说，有时因为受到生产能力、运输
工具、装运港口等条件的限制，卖方不能一次完成货物的装运任务。
在这种情况下，经买方同意，可以采用"分批装运"的方式。另外，假
如货物运往的目的港没有直达船或者直达船的船期不固定或很少，双 50
方在合同中也应规定"允许转船"的条款，以便于租船装运。

✐ 根据课文内容回答下列问题：

1. 一笔交易怎样才算真正完成？

2. 卖方在签订合同后的首要任务是什么？

3. "交货"在国际贸易中的概念是什么？它跟在商店买东西有什么不
   同？

4. "装运"主要包括哪些内容？

5. 运输方式有几种？哪种最普遍？为什么？

6. 在国际贸易中，为什么说"装运期"就是"交货期"？

7. 卖方不能按期装运意味着什么？为什么？

8. 为什么要尽量采用定期装运？

9. 装运港和目的港是怎样确定的？

10. 在什么情况下，可以"分批装运"或者"允许转船"？

✐ 根据意思，给课文划分层次（不是自然段）并写出每个层次的大意。

生词和用法

款	kuǎn	N.	钱，经费：货~、现~、公~、交~、借~、赔~、罚~、存~。 a sum of money; fund
义不容辞	yì bù róng cí	Idm.	道义上不容许推辞 to be duty bound; to have an unshirkable duty
首	shǒu	N.	头：~饰、~尾、~领、昂~；＜＞尾。 head.
		Adj.	第一，最高的：~次、~批、~位、~席。 first; chief
首要	shǒuyào	Adj.	摆在第一位的，最重要的：~任务、~工作、~条件、~人物；＜＞次要。 of first importance
代理	dàilǐ	V./N.	受当事人委托，代表他进行某种活动，如推销、纳税、签订合同等：~总经理、~厂长、~签订合同。 to act as an agent (or proxy, procurator)
代理人	dàilǐrén	N.	受当事人委托，代表他做某事的人。 agent
象征	xiàngzhēng	V.	用具体的事物表现某种特殊意义或代表另一事物。 to symbolize; to signify; to stand for
		N.	用来表现某种特别意义或代表另一事物的东西：和平的~、成功的~、友谊的~。 symbol; emblem; token
所有权	suǒyǒuquán	N.	集体或个人对生产资料或生活资料的占有权。 ownership
单据	dānjù	N.	收付款项或货物的凭据，如收据、发票、发货单、收支传票等：货运~、报销~、提货~。 documents attesting to the giving or receiving of money, goods, etc.

提单	tídān	N.	提=提货，单=单据；提货单。 bill of lading
告	gào	V.	宣布或表示某种情况的实现：大功~成、~一段落、~终。 to declare, announce (of the status of something)
		Mph.(V.)	表明：~别、~辞、~急、~诉、~知。 to make known.
承	chéng	V.	接受；承担，负责：~运、~办、~制、~接、~包、~保。 to undertake; to contract
承运人	chéngyùnrén	NP.	负责运输的人。 a contractor for shipping
代替	dàitì	V.	代换，替换。 to substitute; to replace; to take the place of
概念	gàiniàn	N.	concept: 基本~、抽象~、模糊~、~的形成。
涉及	shèjí	V.	牵涉到，关联到。 to involve; to relate
海洋	hǎiyáng	N.	海和洋的总称：~资源、~运输、~动物。 seas and oceans
陆路	lùlù	N.	旱路：走~、~交通、~运输。 land route
航空	hángkōng	V.	飞机在空中飞行。 to aviate; to fly
		N.	跟飞机飞行有关的：~信、~公司、民用~。 aviation
邮政	yóuzhèng	N.	邮电业务的一大部门，在中国邮政的主要业务是寄递信件和包裹、办理汇兑、发行报刊等：~局、~服务、~编码。 postal service
联合	liánhé	V./Adj.	结合在一起，共同：~举办、~企业、~行动、~运输。 to join, to unite, joint, united
联合运输	liánhé yùnshū	V./N.	不同的交通部门或分段的交通线段之间建立联系，连续运输，旅客或托运者只要买一次票或办理此手续，简称联运：水陆~、火车汽车~、国际~。 through transport, through

traffic, coordinated transport

诸多	zhūduō	Num.	〔书〕许多，好些个（只作定语，不加量词，多用于抽象事物）：~不便、~手续、~困难。 a good deal of; a lot of (to modify abstract nouns only)
运载	yùnzài	V./N.	装载和运送。 to carry, to deliver; to load; carriage; delivery.
低廉	dīlián	Adj.	（物价）便宜；＜＞昂贵。 inexpensive; cheap.
优点	yōudiǎn	N.	好处、长处；＜＞缺点。 merit; advantage; virtue.
普遍	pǔbiàn	Adj.	存在的面很广泛，具有共同性：~现象、~流行、~性、十分~。 common; popular
占	zhàn	V.	处在一定的地位或属于某种情况：~多数、~优势、~首位。 to make up; to account for; to occupy
政治	zhèngzhì	N./Adj.	politics, political: ~局势、~观点、国际~、~学。
局势	júshì	N.	（政治、军事等）一个时期内的发展情况。 situation
因素	yīnsù	N.	构成事物本质的成分，决定事物成败的原因或条件：积极~、基本~、决定~。 factor; element
安全	ānquán	Adj./N.	没有危险，不受威胁，不出事故：注意~、~生产、~到达；＜＞危险。 safe; secure; safety; security
迅速	xùnsù	Adj.	速度高，非常快：~解决、~提高；＜＞缓慢。 rapid; fast; swift
错过	cuòguò	V.	失去（时机）：~时间、~机会。 to miss; to let slip
假若	jiǎruò	Conj.	〔书〕如果，要是。 if

构成	gòuchéng	V.	形成，造成：~违约、~犯罪。 to constitute; to form; to compose
接收	jiēshōu	V.	接受（多用于具体的物件）：~信号、~来稿、~礼物。 to receive
转售	zhuǎnshòu	V.	把买进来的东西再卖出去。 to resell
高雄	Gāoxióng	Pr.N.	台湾南部的港口城市。 A harbor city in southern Taiwan
大连	Dàlián	Pr.N.	中国东北辽宁省的港口城市。 A harbor city in Liaoning Province in northeastern China
天津	Tiānjīn	Pr.N.	中国四个直辖市之一，距离北京一百多公里。 One of the four municipalities directly under the Central Government in China, about 100 kilometers to the Southeast of Beijing
伦敦	Lúndūn	Pr.N.	英国首都。 London
汉堡	Hànbǎo	Pr.N.	德国北方的港口城市。 Hamburg (Germany)
鹿特丹	Lùtèdān	Pr.N.	荷兰的港口城市。 Rotterdam (Netherlands)
限制	xiànzhì	V.	规定范围，不许超过；约束：~数量、~发展、~人数。 to restrict; to place/impose restriction; to confine
		N.	规定的范围：年龄~、速度~、没有~。 limit; restriction
任务	rènwù	N.	指定担任的工作，指定负的责任：生产~、分配~、完成~。 task; assignment; mission

批	pī	MW.	用于大宗的货物或多数的人：一~、分~、大~、整~。 batch; lot; group
分批	fēnpī	VP.	把人或物分组，按次序逐一处理或进行：~到达、~装运。 in batches; lots; in turns
直达	zhídá	V.	不必在途中转换交通工具而直接到达：~车、~船、~飞机。 through traffic; nonstop
船期	chuánqī	NP.	轮船开航的日期：错过~、~表。 sailing date
允许	yǔnxǔ	V.	许可；容许；答应。 permit; allow
转船	zhuǎnchuán	VO.	中途换船。 to transship; transshipment

补充词

事故	shìgù	N.	意外的变故或灾祸：交通~、生产~、发生~、调查~、预防~的发生。 accident; mishap
投保人	tóubǎorén	N.	向保险公司买保险的人。 the insured party
道义	dàoyì	N.	道德和正义：~之交、~上的支持。 morality and justice
燃料	ránliào	N.	燃烧时能产生热能、光能的物质：固体~、液体~、气体~、节约~、进口~。 fuel
代销	dàixiāo	VP.	代为销售：~商店、~饮料、要求~。 to sell on a commission basis
悉	xī	Mph.(V.)	〔书〕知道：得~、获~、欣~、熟~。 to know; to learn; to be informed
奔腾	bēnténg	N.	名牌电脑元件。 Pentium
		V.	奔跑跳跃：万马~；形容液体急速流动：河水~。 to gallop; to surge forward

处理器	chǔlǐqì	N.	电脑的主要元件。 processor
欣然	xīnrán	Adv.	〔书〕愉快地，多用于修饰动词：~同意、~前往、~奉告、~命笔。
			joyfully; with pleasure
奉告	fènggào	V.	〔敬辞〕无可~、改日~、~详情。
			to inform; to let other's know
指示	zhǐshì	V.	上级对下级，长辈对晚辈说明处理某个问题的原则和方法； to instruct; to give directions
		N.	上级给下级，长辈给晚辈的有关说明或指导。
			instructions; instructive
属下	shǔxià	VP.	隶属某单位或部门之下。
			to subordinate to; under
启航	qǐháng	VP.	轮船离开港口，开始航行；开船。
			to set sail
再生	zàishēng	VP.	死而复生；对废品加工，使恢复或具有新功能：~纸、~橡胶、~塑料、~纤维。
			to resurrect; to recycle and regenerate
套	tào	V.	罩在外面。 to cover with; to encase
		MW.	量词：一~单据/衣服/茶具/家具。
			a set of (document, furniture, garment, etc.)
密封	mìfēng	VP.	严密地封闭。 to seal up; to seal hermetically
塑料	sùliào	N.	plastic
单据	dānjù	N.	收付款项或货物的凭据，如收据、发票、提单等：装运~、报销~。
			payment document
副本	fùběn	N.	文件正本以外的其他本。
			copy (oforiginal document)
查收	cháshōu	VP.	检查后收下，多用于书信，表示寄上款项、物品、文件等。 please find (in a letter)

洁净	jiéjìng	*Adj.*	干净、没有污染、尘土、杂质等：＜＞肮脏。
			clean
保险单	bǎoxiǎndān	*NP.*	保险公司向被保人开出的承保证明。
			insurance policy
谨	jǐn	*Adv.*	郑重地，修饰动词：~启、~请、~望、~颂、~表谢意。
			sincerely; solemnly

词语例释

一、义不容辞 （to be duty-bound; to have an unshirkable duty）

l-2. 成交协议达成后，买卖双方按照合同的规定各自付款、交货，是<u>义不容辞</u>的责任。

  1. 老师帮助学生，<u>义不容辞</u>。
  2. 教育子女是家长<u>义不容辞</u>的责任。
  3. 事故发生后，保险公司按规定给投保人赔偿所遭受的损失，是<u>义不容辞</u>的。

  "义不容辞"是成语，表示从道义上讲不允许推辞，常作谓语或定语。

  义不容辞 is an idiom, which means that it is duty-bound morally for some one to do something. It usually functions as a Predicate or an Attributive in a sentence.

二、算＋NP./VP./Clause （to regard as; to count as; to consider）

l-4. 付款与交货是买和卖的具体表现，只有在卖方收到货款而买方也收到货物之后，整个交易才<u>算</u>真正完成。

  1. 这个港口<u>算</u>是中国北方目前最现代化的港口了。
  2. 水陆联运可能不<u>算</u>最快的，但是运费可<u>算</u>是最低廉的。
  3. 她在这么短时间内，能单独处理进出口业务的大部分问题，<u>算</u>很不错了。

　　"算"作动词时，有"认为、当作"的意思，常带动词、形容词和小句作宾语。作副词时，有"比较起来最突出"的意思。

> When 算 is used as a Verb, it is meant "to be considered as; to be regarded as" and often takes a Verb, an Adjective or a Clause as its Object. When it serves as an Adverb, it can mean "it is the most ...comparing with others".

三、并非……而是…… (instead of/rather than ... but...)

l-7. 国际贸易是国与国之间的商品交易。卖方交货，并非像商店那样直接把货物交到顾客手中，而是采用装运港交货的价格术语 (F. O. B., C.I.F., C. & F.)，……

　　1. 他们成功的首要条件并非是先进的设备和技术，而是同事之间的合作与信任。

　　2. 出口贸易的提货单并非由卖方签发而是由承运人签发的。

　　3. 我认为你刚才指出的并非是这个产品的缺点而是它的优点。

　　副词"并"用在"不、没、非"等否定词前，表示确实不是这样，起强调的作用。这个句型与"不是……而是……"大致相同。

> When the Adverb 并 is used before words of negation such as 不、没、非, it emphasizes the negation and means "indeed it is not the case". This pattern is basically similar to 不是……而是…….

四、代替 (to substitute for; to replace; to stand for)

l-13. 因此，"装运"这个词常被用来代替"交货"的概念，国际贸易合同中的"交货条件"也常被称为"装运条件"。

　　1. 假如实在没有办法，是否可以考虑用别的材料代替一下？

　　2. 老欧病了，经理请你代替他去参加明天的谈判。

　　3. 为了保护环境，他们用天然气代替汽油作汽车的燃料。

　　动词"代替"有"代换、替换"的意思，表示以甲换乙，让甲起乙的作用，多带宾语或用在被动句中。"代替"可变成"替代"，用"相互、互相、彼此"等修饰。

> The Verb N替 normally takes an Object or is used in Passive Sentences, meaning "to replace; to substitute". 代替 can be a palindrome as 替代, and modified by 相互、互相、彼此 etc.

五、 涉及(到)　(to involve; to relate to; to deal with)

l-15. 装运和交货是一个十分复杂的问题，它涉及运输方式、装运时间、装运港和目的港等内容。

   1. 他们的谈话涉及到了很多方面的问题。

   2. 海关的这次调查可能涉及到贵公司的方先生和杨小姐。

   3. 对方的来信并没有涉及装运日期，不知道你注意到了没有？

"涉及"是及物动词，须带宾语或补语。宾语常是名词性词语，如例3; 补语常用"到"加上名词词组，如例1和例2。

> 涉及 is a Transitive Verb and must take an Object or a Complement. While its Objects are usually Noun Phrases such as in sentence 3, its Complements are mostly Noun Phrases with 到 as in sentences 1 and 2.

六、 Subject 占 ＋分数／百分数／成数／比例　(to constitute; to make up; to account for)

l-20. 因为海运具有运载量大、费用低廉、不受道路限制等优点，因此海运大约占了世界贸易货运总量的三分之二。

   1. 八十年代以前，中国的出口产品中占大多数的是农副产品和工矿产品，工业产品和机械产品只占少数。

   2. 去年我们公司第四季度的出口占了全年销售总额的百分之四十。

   3. 那个学校的女生占全校人数一半以上。

动词"占"在这里表示"处于某种地位和情况"的意思，常带数词作宾语或补语。另外，也可带"优势、上风"等名词。

> The Verb 占 here means "to be in a certain position or situation", and often

takes a Numeral as an Object or Complement. It can also take Nouns such as 优
势 or 上风 as its Object.

七、 Subject 受到＋Disyllabic Verb　（to receive; to subject to; to suffer from ; to be Verb-ed)

l-20. 因为海运具有运载量大、费用低廉、不<u>受</u>道路<u>限制</u>等优点，因此海
运大约占了世界贸易货运总量的三分之二。

　　1. 因为装卸时不小心，这批货物<u>受到</u>了一定的<u>损失</u>。

　　2. 那些工人<u>受到</u>了老板的<u>批评</u>。

　　3. 她是个艺术家，当然不希望<u>受到限制</u>，<u>受到约束</u>。

　　4. 我们的产品在世界各地都<u>受到欢迎</u>。

　　5. 这个问题正在逐步<u>受到</u>政府的<u>重视</u>。

不/大/深/很＋受＋Disyllabic Verb　（to be Verb+ed in a big/profound way; to be Verb+ed tremandously）

l-31. 在进出口贸易中，大部分货物都属于时间性较强的商品，错过了销
售季节，商品的价值就会大幅度降低，而买方的经济利益也将<u>大受
影响</u>。

　　1. 由于天气的关系，那个国家的农业生产<u>大受影响</u>。

　　2. 看了这个电影，大家都觉得<u>深受教育</u>。

　　3. 小刘不喜欢在船上工作，觉得一切活动都<u>很受限制</u>。

　　"受、受到"后的宾语一般为不另带宾语或补语的双音节动词，作宾
语的动词可以是褒义，如"欢迎、表扬、关心、关注、尊敬、重视、教
育、好评、照顾、帮助"等，也可以是贬义的，如"损失、批评、破坏、
打击、处罚、污染、限制、约束"等。"受、受到"后的补语多是数量词
组。比较"受到"和"得到"："受到"着重"接受、遭到"的意思；"得到"着
重"获得"，没有"遭受"的意思。另外，"得到"可以跟名词性宾语，如：
得到＋"信息、消息、样品、传真、成绩、名片"等。"受、受到"只能跟
动词性宾语。

The Object after 受到 or 受 is normally a Disyllabic Verb without an Object nor a Complement. The Verbs can be either positive or negative in meaning. Usually, the positive ones are: 欢迎、表扬、关心、关注、尊敬、重视、教育、好评、照顾、帮助, etc.; and the negative ones are: 损失、批评、破坏、打击、处罚、污染、限制、约束, etc. The Complement after 受到 or 受 is usually a Numeral Phrase. Compare 受到 and 得到: while 受到 focus on "to receive, to suffer", 得到 emphasizes "to obtain, to achieve". In addition, 得到 can take Nouns as its Object, such as , 得到＋信息、消息、样品、传真、成绩、名片, etc., but 受到 can take Verbs only.

八、 假如/假若……，就/便…… (if..., then...)

l-31. 因此，假若卖方不能如期装运，即等于不能按时交货，这样便构成了违约，……

1. 假如我没有记错的话，这个图案就是"联合"的象征。
2. 假若该国的政治局势保持稳定，我方将继续与海星公司进行合作。
3. 假若有直达船而无须转船，这批货物便可提前一周运抵目的港。

连词"假如、假若"是"如果"的意思，有文言色彩，用于书面语的假设复句前一分句提出假设，与后一分句的"那、就、则、便"呼应。

The Conjunctions 假如 and 假如 are similar to 如果 in meaning, but has a flavor of Literary Chinese. It is often used in the first clause of a Hypothetical Complex Sentence to indicate a hypothetical situation, and coordinates with 那、就、则 or 便 in the second clause.

九、 允许 (to allow; to permit)

l-50. 另外，有时因为货物运往的目的港没有直达船或者直达船的船期不固定或很少，双方在合同中也应规定"允许转船"的条款，以便于租船装运。

1. 我们不仅应该允许别人犯错误，更重要的是帮助他们改正错误。
2. 只要条件允许，她都尽量满足孩子们的要求。

3. 虽然学校已经<u>允许</u>他过两年才毕业，但是他觉得时间不<u>允许</u>他这样做，他必须抓紧时间，赶快完成学业。

　　动词"允许"有"许可"的意思，常带动词或动词词组作宾语，可构成兼语词组作谓语。多用于同意某种要求或做法，既指别人允许，也可指客观情况、天气、时间等许可，所表达的语气比"准许、容许"轻些，和缓一些。

The Verb 允许 bears the meaning of "to allow; to permit". It often takes a Verb or a Verb Phrase as its Object, and may form a Pivot Sentence with a Noun and a Verb Phrase as its Object. It is normally used to show approval of a request or some kind of action. It works both for human permission, or for nature, a certain situation, weather, time, etc. The tone that it carries is milder than words like 准许, and 容许.

词义辨析

一、交货　送货　提货

　　在这三个动宾词组中，"货"都是"货物"的意思。"交货"是商业用语，专指卖方按照合同，在规定的时间、地点、以规定的方式，把货物（一般数量较大）运送并移交给买方、买方的代理人或买方指定的运输工具上。"送货"的使用范围较广。它可指卖方（公司、商店、或私人）把顾客购买的货物送到顾客指定的地点（办公室、仓库、私人的住宅等），而且货物的数量可大可小。另外，送货也可指负责运输者（不是卖方）把货物运送到某个地方，如：

The character 货 in these Verb-Object Constructions means "goods, commodity". 交货 is a business term and refers specifically to "delivery". That is, the seller delivers the goods (usually in a large amount) to the buyer, the buyer's agent or the means of transportation specified by the buyer in the contract. 送货 is a more general term and used more commonly. It can refer to the fact that a seller (as a company, a store, or an individual) delivers the merchandise that a customer ordered to a designated place (an office, a warehouse, or a residence), and the amount of the merchandise can be large or small. In addition, 送货 can also mean that a deliverer (not necessarily the seller) ships some goods to a certain place. For example,

请您放心，我们负责<u>送货</u>上门。

(Please don't worry, we will take care of the delivery and ship it to your door.)

这些年来我们都是请他帮助<u>送货</u>。

(We have been asking him to help deliver goods these years.)

"提货"就是提取货物的意思，即买方凭提单到存放货物的地点办理一定的手续，然后把货物取走。

提货 simply means to pick up goods, i.e. the buyer goes to the place where the goods are stored and pick up the merchandise after going through certain proper procedures.

二、代替　代理　代表

"代替"表示以甲换乙，可用于人或物，强调替换者仍能起被替换者的作用。例如：

代替 indicates to replace a person or thing with someone or something else, and stresses that the substitute has the same functions as the person or thing to be replaced. For instance,

用国产车<u>代替</u>进口车。

(To substitute imported cars with domestic cars.)

他今天有事，请你<u>代替</u>他去开这个会吧。

(He is busy today. Please attend the meeting in his place, will you?)

"代理"有两重意思，一是"暂时代人担任某单位或某部门的负责职务"，可带宾语或补语，如：

The word 代理 has dual meaning. The first one is to act on behalf of somebody in a responsible position. It can take an Object or a Complement. For example,

市长生病期间，工作由副市长代理。

(The deputy mayor will exercise the duties of the mayor when he is sick.)

经理的这个工作，她曾经代理过半年。

(She has acted for the manager for six months.)

二是"受委托，代表当事人进行某种较正式的活动"或"代表某人处理某事"的意思，其后一般跟双或多音节动词或词组，如诉讼、纳税、签订合同等。

The second meaning is to act as an agent to engage in some formal activities or to handle certain business. It usually goes before some disyllabic Verbs of Phrases such as 诉讼、纳税、签订合同.

"代表"可作动词和名词。作动词时，有两种意思。第一是代替个人或团体办事或发表意见，常带主谓词组作宾语，如：

代表 can be a Verb and a Noun. As a Verb, it means two things. One is to act as a substitute or a deputy for an individual or an organization, and often used in a Pivot Sentence as in the following:

小李代表全体毕业生在大会上发言。

(Xiao Li, representing all the graduates, will deliver a speech at the meeting.)

第二种用法是显示象征同一类事物的共同特征，如

Another meaning is to stand for or to be a symbol or equivalent of something. For example,

这些产品代表着我们公司的最高技术水平。

(These products represent the highest level of the technology of our company.)

"代表"作名词时，也有不同的意思。一个是"显示同一类特征的人或

事",如:他们的作品是那个年代摇滚乐的<u>代表</u>。另一个是由行政区、团体、组织等选举出来替选举人办事或表达意见的人,如:学生代表、工人代表、人民代表等。

When functioning as a Noun, it can mean both "things that represent something", and "person elected to represent others in a legislative body, a representative, or a deputy". For example,

他们的作品是那个年代摇滚乐的<u>代表</u>。

(Their works are the representation of the rock and roll music at that time.)

学生代表、工人代表、人民代表

(student delegate, workers delegates, people's representatives)

三、 承担　承办　承运

词素"承"的基本意思是"托着、负责"。"承担"强调"担负、担当,接受并负起责任"的意思,常带像"责任、义务、费用、任务"等宾语。"承运"是"承接运输"的缩略语,使用范围很窄。"承办"指的是承接办理,多指订货、加工、办理事务等,可带宾语,使用范围比较广。

The essential meaning of 承 is "holding, to be responsible for". 承担 emphasizes "to shoulder , to take on, to assume the responsibilities for". It usually takes a Noun like 责任、义务、费用、任务 as its Objects. 承运 is the contraction of 承接运输 which means "contract to accept transportation for (others)", and is used in a very limited area. 承办 refers to undertaking, and is primarily for business such as taking order, processing, handling business transactions, etc.

四、 限定　限制　限于

"限"字作动词解,表示"指定范围或期限,不许超过"的意思,适用于口语和书面语。"限制"可作动词,也可作名词。作动词时,强调外部力量对人或物加以约束,不得超过规定的范围,多用于人的行为或事物的发展方面,如:

When the character 限 functions as a Verb, it means "to specify a scope of time or limit, which cannot exceed." It is used in both spoken and written Chinese. 限制 can function as a Noun and also a Verb. As a Verb, it stresses to impose control and restraint on people or things, which cannot step over the boundary. It is normally used for human behavior or the development of things. For example,

老板没有权力限制工人的行动自由。

(A boss does not have the right to restrict workers' freedom of movement.)

文章的字数不受限制。

(There is no limitation on the length of the article.)

作名词时，表示"规定的、不可超越的范围"。如：

As a Noun, 限制 refers to "the stipulated limit which cannot be overstepped." For instance,

新的速度限制是每小时65英里。(The new speed limit is 65 miles an hour.)

"限定"只能作动词，不可作名词，是"在数量、时间、范围等方面加以规定"的意思，常带宾语或补语。例如：

限定 is a Verb only and cannot function as a Noun. It means "to stipulate or to set a limit with regard to amount, time, scope, etc., and often takes an Object or a Complement. For example,

限定在两个月内交货。

(It is stipulated that delivery will be made within two months.)

每次限定在50人以内。　(It is limited to 50 people every time.)
必须限定参观的人数。　(There should be a limit on admission of visitors.)

"限于"是及物动词，须带双或多音节宾语，指"受到某些条件或情况的限制，局限在一定的范围之内"的意思。如：

The Transitive Verb 限于must take a disyllabic or polysyllabic Object, when it means "because of the constraint of certain condition or situation", or "within a certain limit". Some common examples are:

限于水平、限于能力、限于人手不足、限于时间的关系，etc.

五、接收　接受　收

这三个动词都可译成英语receive，但意思侧重各有不同。"接收"主要表示接纳和收下，并且强调"吸收、收下"，多指别人送来或发来的物品、信息或组织的新成员，如：接收无线电信号、接收遗产、接收新会员等。"接收"的另一个意思，是根据法令，把原来属于某一方的机构、财产等拿过来，归为己有，如：

It is possible to translate these three Verbs as "to receive" in English, but each has a different focus. 接收 indicates "to admit and accept" primarily, and emphasizes on "to absorb, to accept". It mostly refers to receive things, information sent by others, or new members of an organization. For example, 接收无线电信号 (to receive radio signals), 接收遗产 (to receive an inheritance), 接收新会员 (to admit new members), etc. Another meaning of 接收 is "to take over (an organization or property)", For example,

这家破产的公司将由我们接收。

(We will take over this bankrupted company.)

"接受"有两重意思，一是领取别人给予的东西，宾语多为具体事物，如：接受礼物、接受奖金、接受报酬等。二是对事物容纳而不拒绝，其宾语多数是像"意见、批评、教育、帮助、要求、任务、教训、考验"等抽象事物。"接收"没有这样的意思。

接受 has two meanings. One is "to take something offered willingly", and its Objects are usually concrete Nouns such as gift, bonus, payment, etc. The other meaning is "willingly agree to something" and the Objects it takes are usually abstract Nouns such as 意见、批评、教育、帮助、要求、任务、教训、考验, etc. The Verb 接收 does not have this meaning.

收 is a versatile Verb that has multiple meanings. It usually takes an Object or a Complement. The following are some common usages and examples,

　　"收"是常用多义动词，多带宾语或补语。下面是一些常用的意思和例子：

(1) 取回属于自己的东西或自己有权取得的东西：收信、收钱、收租、收税、收回成本。

(2) 获得（经济利益）：收入、收益、收支平衡。

(3) 收获：收割、收成、收麦子。

(4) 接受、容纳：收留、收容、收徒弟、收学生。

(5) 把外面的东西拿到里面，把散开的东西聚拢起来：下雨了，快收衣服！收拾桌子。

(6) 结束、停止（工作或活动）：收工、收市、收场。

1) collect something that belongs to oneself or one is entitled to own:
收信，收钱，收租，收税，收回成本。

2) gain (profit): 收入，收益，收支平衡。

3) harvest: 收割，收成，收麦子.

4) accept, receive: 收留，收容，收徒弟，收学生。

5) take (things) in, gather (things) together: 下雨了，快收衣服！收拾桌子。

6) bring to an end: 收工，收市，收场。

语法

一、假设复句　Complex Sentences of Hypothesis

　　偏句提出一种假设情况，正句说明在这种情况下会出现的结果。表示这种关系的复句就是假设复句。假设复句又可分为两种类型：一般假设复句和让步假设复句。

　　In a Complex Sentence of Hypothesis, the subordinate clause proposes a hypothetical situation, and the main clause states what would happen under such circumstances. Complex Sentences of Hypothesis can be further divided into two types: Complex Sentences of General Hypothesis and Complex Sentences of Concessive Hypothesis.

（一）一般假设复句　Complex Sentences of General Hypothesis

一般假设复句是指假设的情况和产生的结果相符，也就是说，偏句假设一种情况存在或一个道理成立，正句表示以这假设条件为依据，产生相应的结果或结论。常用的关联词语有：

A Complex Sentence of General Hypothesis indicates the congruence of a hypothetical situation and reality. That is, the subordinate clause supposes the existence of a situation or the tenability of a proposition, while the main clause shows the outcome or conclusion that results from the hypothetical situation or proposition. It is, on the one hand, similar to the English conditional sentence, a relation between two propositions referring to the so-called real world. On the other hand, it can be imaginative —a proposition about an unreal or imagined situation, one that diverges from the real world, or counter-factual —what could have been true but was not. . The commonly used Connectives are:

要是……就……、如果……的话，那就……、假如/假若/倘若……那么/就/便……、倘若/若……就/则/便……、万一……那就……、要不是……就……。

例如：For example:

<u>如果</u>大家都同意<u>的话</u>，我们<u>就</u>按照<u>这些</u>条件制作合同了。

<u>假如</u>发现什么问题，你可以随时和我联系。

<u>倘若</u>贵方降价百分之十，我方<u>则</u>可大量订货。

还是再检查一下再签字吧。<u>万一</u>有什么差错，签字以后再改<u>就</u>很麻烦了。

<u>要不是</u>遇到台风，这批货早<u>就</u>到了。

（二）让步假设复句　Complex Sentences of Concessive Hypothesis

让步假设复句是指假设的情况和结果不符，也就是说，偏句退一步姑且承认某种假设的情况，但正句却说出与假设情况相反的结果或结论。让步假设复句偏句中提出的假设情况，一般都是虚拟的，就说话者看来，其出现的可能性极小。这种假设复句也有转折的意思，但它所表示的是一种未然的假设，而转折复句表示的是一种既成事实。

A Complex Sentence of Concessive Hypothesis refers to the discrepancy between the supposed situation and the reality. That is, the subordinate clause concedes that there exists a certain situation, yet the outcome or conclusion in the main clause contradicts with the supposed situation. Normally, there is little possibility for the realization of the supposed situation in the subordinate clause in the speaker's mind. Such Complex Sentences of Hypothesis also bears an adversative sense, but it usually refers to an imaginative hypothesis, quite similar to the Subjunctive in Western languages. On the contrary, the Adversative Complex Sentence refers to an existing fact in general.

让步假设复句常用的关联词语有：

The following Connectives are commonly used in Complex Sentences of Concessive Hypothesis:

即便……也……、即使……也/还……、纵然……也/还……、哪怕……也/都……、就算……也/都……。

例如：　For instance:

即使包装再华丽，质量不好的商品还是没有竞争力的。

你有什么就说吧，哪怕说错了也没关系。　〔口语〕

纵然对方有再多的理由，违约以后就必须承担法律责任。〔书面语〕

假设复句和条件复句有相通之处，从某种意义上来说，假设有条件的意思，而条件又有假设的意味。两者的区别是：一个侧重于假设；一个侧重于条件。

There is some resemblance between Hypothetical Complex Sentences and Conditional Complex Sentences. In a certain sense, hypothesis bears some sense of condition whereas the reverse may also be true. However, there is certain distinction: while the former emphasizes hypothesis, the later focuses on setting the condition.

二、 成语、惯用语、俗语和四字词组　Idioms, Set Phrases, Common Sayings and Four-Character Phrases

(一) 成语　Idioms

成语是汉语中一种相延习用，具有书面语色彩的固定词组或短语。大多数成语由四个字构成，在句子中一般起一个词语的语法作用，特别是以作谓语或修饰语居多。如：

Idioms are fixed phrases that have been passed down from the past and become customary and with the features of written Chinese. The majority of idioms consist of four characters. Idioms normally have a grammatical function as a word, and act as a Predicate in particular. For example:

1. 谓语：As *Predicate*:

老师帮助学生，义不容辞。

她这样做生意，虽然可能会很快赚点钱，但是很容易就失去信誉，实在是得不偿失。

2. 状语：As *Adverbial*:

孩子们正在兴高彩烈地做游戏。

他目不转睛地看着电脑上不断出现的数字。

3. 定语：As *Attributive*:

所谓"明确的"，是指发盘的内容清楚明确，没有含糊的、模棱两可的词句。

成交协议达成后，买卖双方按照合同的规定各自付款、交货，是义不容辞的责任。

成语主要来源于以下的几个方面：

Idioms are primarily from the following origins:

1. 神话寓言，如：　Myths and fables, for instance:

　　愚公移山、牛郎织女、塞翁失马、叶公好龙。

2. 历史故事，如：　Historical stories, for example:

　　望梅止渴、四面楚歌、负荆请罪、画蛇添足。

3. 诗文语句，如：　Poems and verses, such as:

　　窈窕淑女、万紫千红、温故知新、不亦乐乎。

4. 口头俗语，如：　Colloquial expressions, for instance:

　　千方百计、指手划脚、讨价还价、一干二净。

5. 外国典故，如：　Foreign allusions, for example:

　　火中取栗、盲人摸象、象牙之塔、水中捞月。

　　成语的结构主要有下面几类：

　　Idioms can be divided into several categories structurally:

1. 联合结构，如：　Coordinative structure, such as:

　　价廉物美、成千上万、千方百计、出生入死。

2. 偏正结构，如：　Modifier-Modified structure, for example:

　　斤斤计较、窈窕淑女、火中取栗、汗马功劳。

3. 主谓结构，如：　Subject-Predicate structure, for instance:

　　愚公移山、叶公好龙、百花齐放、盲人摸象。

4. 述宾结构，如：　Predicate-Object structure, such as:

　　大显身手、不计其数、平分秋色、对牛弹琴。

5. 复谓结构，如：　Dual-Verb-Phrase structure, for example:

　　知彼知己、指手划脚、画蛇添足、讨价还价。

　　成语的结构是定型的，文字是固定的，一般不能随意变换或增减。如"一日千里"不可改为"一日万里"或"一天千里"。当然，在特定的语境中，为了表达的需要，有时也可以灵活运用，如把"知难而退"改为"知难而进"，把"事半功倍"改为"事倍功半"也是可能的。

The structures of Idioms are in patterns, and the wording is fixed; thus they cannot be changed, added or deleted arbitrarily. For example, 一日千里 cannot be turned into 一日万里 or 一天千里. However, under certain circumstances, and on special occasions, it is possible to adapt or adjust flexibly according to the context. The revision of the Verb in 知难而退 to 知难而进, and the reverse of the word order of 事半功倍 to 事倍功半 are two good examples.

　　成语是经过加工提炼的语言材料，比起普通词语更精炼生动，寓意深刻得多。学习成语要在了解成语字面意思的基础上，确实弄清其实际意义，不要望文生义。另外，要注意成语褒义和贬义的区别。例如，不要把贬义的成语"好为人师"当褒义词来用，以免闹出笑话来。总之，使用成语要小心，如果没有把握，不清楚某个成语的确切意思和不确定该成语是否适用于某个语境时，宁可不用成语也不要以词害意。

Idioms are expressions that have undergone polishing and refinement, hence are more succinct and vivid, and much more profound in meaning than ordinary words and phrases. When learning Idioms, one must understand the real meaning and connotation of an Idiom, in addition to its literal meaning, and avoid interpreting the Idiom literally, based on superficial understanding. In the meantime, one should pay attention to the distinction of recommendatory and derogative connotation of an Idiom. For example, if one takes 好为人师 as an idiom with a recommendatory sense, he/she may make a fool of him/herself. Therefore, we must be careful when using Idioms. When one is not sure, or does not have a thorough understanding of the meaning and the appropriate context of an Idiom, it is wiser not to use the Idiom, rather than to cause confusion by using it inappropriately.

（二）惯用语　Set Phrases

　　惯用语是结构比较定型、常用于口语的固定词组。惯用语以三个字的居多，它所表达的意义是整体的。多数的惯用语，在使用时都已经从字面上的意义转化为一种更加深刻的抽象含义，变成一种虚指的比喻。如：

Set phrases are fixed expressions that often fall in patterns and are used in spoken Chinese. Most Set Phrases are composed of three characters. The meaning is holistic and metaphorical which deviates from the original meaning and becomes more abstract and profound. For example:

走后门儿——比喻私下利用某人的职权或非法途径，取得办事的方便条件或某种好处。

Indicating figuratively one gains benefit or advantages by using his, her or other's power or by unlawful channels.

铁饭碗———比喻非常稳固的职业或生活收入。

A metaphor referring to a secured job and a stable income.

气(妻)管炎(严)——指妻子对丈夫管得很严，引申指怕妻子的人。

By using homophones, it refers to a wife who is very manipulative and strict with her husband. It can also be extended to refer to a man who is hen-pecked.

惯用语的结构大致可分为四种类型：

Set phrases can be roughly categorized into four types:

1. 并列结构： Parallel structure:

张三李四、东家长西家短、挂羊头卖狗肉

2. 偏正结构： Modifier-Modified structure:

活字典、铁饭碗、老油条、纸老虎

3. 主谓结构： Subject-Predicate structure:

狗咬狗、天晓得、鬼画符、蜻蜓点水

4. 动宾结构： Verb-Object structure:

开倒车、开绿灯、走后门、放空炮、吹牛皮、碰钉子、磨洋工、挖墙角、炒鱿鱼、踢皮球、穿小鞋、吃大锅饭、唱对台戏、戴高帽子、打退堂鼓

惯用语和成语有一定的相似性。但是，惯用语口语色彩浓，成语书面色彩浓；惯用语含义单纯，成语含义丰富。惯用语大部分是动宾结

构，且定型性比成语弱。这种结构的惯用语，在动词和宾语之间，可以按需要加插定语而意思不变。例如：

Set Phrases and Idioms have something in common. While Set Phrases have a strong flavor of being colloquial expressions; Idioms are more literary. Set phrases are relatively simple and straight forward in meaning, but Idioms are much richer and implicative. Most of the Set Phrases are Verb-Object in structure, and they are less rigid in pattern. Usually, an Attributive can be inserted in between the Verb and the Object in a Set Phrase with a Verb-Object structure. For example:

开 (历史的) 倒车， 拍 (他的) 马屁， 碰 (了一个大) 钉子

动宾结构的成语则不可这样做。

However, it does not apply to Idioms with the similar structure.

简明生动、通俗有趣是惯用语的主要特征。

The noticeable characteristics of Set Phrases are concise and vivid, popular and witty.

惯用语虽然有部分是历史上流传下来的，但大多数是在当代，由一般词组在特定的语境中引申转化，再经人们口头相传习用而成的。有些惯用语，还带有某个行业或地方的特色，比如经贸方面的"重合同、讲信用"，"供不应求"、"平等互利，互通有无"等；方言上的"侃大山"(北京话)，"拆烂污"(上海话)，"炒鱿鱼"(广东话)等。

Quite a lot of Set Phrases have been handed down from ancient times, but the majority are formed in contemporary China, first through converting their meanings from ordinary phrases in specific context, and then spread orally. Some Set Phrases even bear features of certain occupations or locales. For example, 重合同、讲信用, 供不应求, 平等互利, 互通有无 are jargon from business, while 侃大山、拆烂污、炒鱿鱼 originated from places such as Beijing, Shanghai, and Guangdong respectively.

(三) 俗语　Common Sayings

俗语是民间广泛流传、通俗简练、形象生动的定型语句，包括谚语、惯用语和歇后语等，也叫俗话。例如："种瓜得瓜，种豆得豆"（谚）、"不知天高地厚"（惯）、"十五个吊桶打水——七上八下"（歇）。

Common Sayings are fixed expressions that are widely spread, vivid, figurative and easy to understand. They include *Adages, Set Phrases*, and Xiēhòuyǔ (a two-part allegorical saying, of which the first part always stated, is descriptive, while the second part, sometimes unstated, carries the message.). For example: 种瓜得瓜, 种豆得豆 is an *Adage*, 不知天高地厚 is a Set Phrase, and 十五个吊桶打水——七上八下 is a Xiēhòuyǔ (where usually the second part does not need to be stated. It means someone is extremely nervous and unease just as in a chaotic scene when a dozen of buckets are being used to fetch water from a well all at the same time, some going up and some going down.).

俗语和成语有相似的地方，有人有时候也把成语归入俗语，但是两者是有差别的。从风格上看，俗语比较浅易通俗，是口语性的；成语较为文雅，是书面性的。试比较下面两组意思大致相同的成语和俗语：

There are common features shared by Common Sayings and Idioms. Sometimes, Idioms are considered as part of Common Sayings, but the two are different as a matter of fact. Stylistically speaking, Common Sayings are popular, easy to understand, and are colloquial; while Idioms are more cultured and mostly in written Chinese. Compare the two groups of Idioms and Common Saying that share the same meaning:

畏首畏尾（成语）——前怕狼，后怕虎（俗语）
饮水思源（成语）——吃水不忘打井人（俗语）

从结构上看，成语定型性强，多为四字词组，而俗语定型性较弱，字数不等。如：俗语"只要功夫深，铁杵磨成针"相对的成语就是"磨杵成针"。

Structurally speaking, Idioms are more fixed, and mostly with four characters whereas Common Sayings are less structured, and the number of

character counts may vary. For instance, the counter part of the Common Saying
只要功夫深, 铁杵磨成针 is 磨杵成针 as in an Idiom.

从造句功能上看，俗语往往可以独立成句，而成语作为固定短语，
一般只充当句子成分（尤其是作谓语、补语、定语或状语）。比如，只说
成语"集腋成裘"，听者可能会觉得这句话的意思不太完整，话还没有说
完。但如果说"滴水流成河，粒米凑成箩"，别人就明白这是"积少可以
成多"的意思了。

Functionally speaking, in terms of sentence-formation, a Common Saying
can usually be a sentence by itself, whereas an Idiom serves as part of a sentence
in general (particularly as a Predicate, a Complement, an Attributive or an
Adverbial). For example, if one says the idiom 集腋成裘 only, the listener may
feel that it is not a complete sentence and the remark has not finished yet. However,
if it is substituted with its equivalent in Common Saying 滴水流成河, 粒米凑成
箩, then the listener will understand that it is meant "many a little makes a mickle".

另外，俗语多数是人们总结生活、生产的经验的口头创作，在民间
广泛流传的，大多数找不到具体的出处。而成语，特别是来源于神话、
寓言、历史典故的，基本上都可以追寻到它们的出处。

In addition, most Common Sayings have been coined orally by folks based
on their experience in everyday life. They have been spread far and wide and it
is almost impossible to trace the origin of most of them. As for Idioms, however,
it is quite possible to find out their roots in general, particularly those that have
originated from myth, fable, or legend.

下面是一些俗语的例子：

The following are some examples of Common Sayings:

1. 一手交钱，一手交货。
2. 一年之计在于春。
3. 活到老，学到老。
4. 老王卖瓜，自卖自夸。
5. 公说公有理，婆说婆有理。

6. 一口吃不成一个胖子。

7. 不管三七二十一。

8. 车到山前必有路。

(四) 四字词组 Four-Character Phrases

　　汉语中的四字词组非常发达，所以汉语的节奏性很强。在书面语里，特别是像政论文章、法令布告、文件公函、广告说明、诗歌散文等，用得都相当多。四字词组可以使语言简洁精练、形式工整对称、节奏强弱分明。比如，列举家务杂事时，我们常说"油盐酱醋"、"锅碗瓢盆"。在提到学校的全体人员时，就会用"师生员工"的说法。有时候虽然说的事物不足四项，我们也会想办法把其中的一项变成双音节词，凑足四个字，像"桌椅板凳"，就是一个例子(不会说"桌椅凳")。

　　There are a lot of Four-Character Phrases in Chinese, thus Chinese is a language with conspicuous rhythms. Four-Character Phrases are used widely in the written language, especially in political essays, legal documents and notices, business letters and papers, advertisements and manuals, poems and proses as well. By using Four-Character Phrases, the language can be more terse and succinct; texts may look more symmetric in form, and the beat of a discourse sounds more rhythmical. For example, when we list family chores, the cooking ingredients such as 油盐酱醋 or utensils 锅碗瓢盆 are used. When all the members of a school community is mentioned, the term of 师生员工 is the choice. Occasionally, when the objects mentioned are less than four, we tend to turn one of the items into a disyllabic word so that the phrase becomes a quad-syllabic one, such as in 桌椅板凳. (Note: it is odd to say 桌椅凳.)

　　常见的四字词组有以下的几种：

　　The following are several common structures of Four-Character Phrases:

1. 并列结构 Parallel structure

　　a) 把四项同类的单音节词平行并列 (多用于列举事物)，如：

　　Line up four monosyllabic words in a row(mostly used in listing things), such as:

东西南北、柴米油盐、笔墨纸砚。

b) 双音节词并列，如：

Associate two disyllabic words, such as:

平等互利、简单方便、美观大方。

2. 双谓结构　Dual-Predicate structure

把口语中正常的双音节词缩减为单音节，形成"动宾动宾"结构。如：

Omit one syllable from each disyllabic Verb and Object, forming a dual monosyllabic "Verb +Object" structure. Such as:

奉公守法、尊师爱生、按质论价。

3. 主谓结构　Subject-Predicate structure

双音节词作主语，加上双音节动词或形容词作谓语，常见于商业广告、产品说明。如：

A disyllabic word functions as the Subject and takes a disyllabic Verb or Adjective as its Predicate. This structure is often found in advertisements, or product manuals. For examples:

品质优良、质量可靠、设计新颖、外形美观、用料讲究、质地纯正、性能稳定、操作便利、维修方便、技术先进、疗效显著、价格合理。

4. 偏正结构　Modifier-Modified structure

单音节形容词或副词修饰单音节名词或动词，或是双音节形容词、副词修饰双音节名词或动词。如：

A monosyllabic Adjective or Adverb modifies a monosyllabic Noun or Verb, or a disyllabic Adjective or Adverb modifies a disyllabic Noun or Verb. For instance:

薄利多销、小心轻放、便于携带。

5. 动宾结构　Verb-Object structure

动词(单音节动词常带单音节修饰语)加上双音节宾语。如：

A Verb (a monosyllabic one usually follows a monosyllabic modifier) plus a disyllabic Object. For example:

互通有无、驰名中外、享誉世界。

英语句子比较讲究成分的齐全，如果句子的动词是及物动词，一般都要有主语、谓语和宾语。而汉语的句子比较灵活，只要不影响意思的完整，某些成分常常可以隐去。所以，不少英语的句子，都可以用四字词组来表达。学好汉语的四字词组，注意对比汉语四字词组和英语句子之间的差别，对于提高阅读、写作与翻译能力，都是非常有帮助的。但是使用四字词组时，要注意表达的需要和文体风格，不要滥用。如果一篇文章从头到尾尽是四字词组，就会显得呆板，不自然，没有变化。

In English, grammaticality generally requires the presence of all sentence elements. If the Verb is a transitive one in a sentence, then a Subject, a Verb and an Object are obligatory. Unlike English, a Chinese sentence is much more flexible. Some sentence elements can often be omitted as long as it does not affect the meaning. A lot of English sentences can be represented in Chinese with four character phrases accordingly. It is, therefore, very helpful to improve one's reading comprehension, Chinese composition and translation when he/she has a good commend of Four-Character Phrases, and knows the subtleties between Chinese Four-Character Phrases and English sentences. However, when using Four-Character Phrases, one should be cautious about the register, style and the purpose of writing, and beware of the tendency to overuse them. If Four-Character Phrases run through a composition, from the beginning to the end, it will be rigid, unnatural and monotonous. It must be kept in mind that Four-Character Phrases are used because of communication needs and for rhetorical effect, and not just for the sake of using them.

意义段　**Thematic Sections**

意义段就是文章的层次，也叫结构段、大段或部分。意义段由段落（自然段）或段组（即大于段落、小于意义段的价格单位）组成，表示一个大于（或等于）段落或段组的相对完整意思。有时候一个段落就是一个意义段；有时候几个段落组成一个意义段；有时几个段落先组成段组，再和其他段落或段组结合才构成一个意义段。

A Thematic Section is a stratum of a composition. It is also named "structural paragraph", "grand paragraph", or "part" of an essay. A Thematic Section consists of a paragraph or a group of paragraphs, expressing a relatively complete idea that is bigger than the one in a single paragraph. While a paragraph can be a Thematic Section by itself, sometimes several paragraphs work together to form a Thematic Section. Still on other occasions, it is possible that several paragraphs compose a larger unit, which in turn constitutes a Thematic Section with another paragraph or other paragraphs.

由于意义段表达的是一个相对完整的意思，因此每个意义段都有一个明确的中心。构成意义段的各段落或段组在意义上都有密切的联系，段落或段组的主要意思要围绕意义段的中心，并服从这个中心。例如，第一课的第三个意义段，中心意思是"建立业务关系的各种途径"。这个意义段由三个段落（自然段）组成，分别说明通过什么方法可以与外国公司或厂商建立业务关系，以及写信联系时要注意的问题。一般来说，论说文或说明文每个意义段的中心意思，大概与英语的主题句 (Topic Sentence) 相似。表示中心意思的句子，有的在意义段第一个段落的首句，有的在意义段的中部或尾部。汉语写作有关篇章结构的一种手法，叫"开门见山"，就是把中心意思的句子放在段首。这样做可以收到提纲挈领的效果，适合演绎的逻辑推理。如果把中心句放在段尾，先具体叙述，再总体概括，则有"水到渠成"的好处，适合于归纳法。中心句处于不同的位置，有着不同的修辞效果，所以应该根据全文的构思和意义段的实际需要而定。

As a Thematic Section expresses a complete theme, each Thematic Section holds a specific central idea accordingly. The paragraph or group of paragraphs that composes a Thematic Section cohere, with the main idea of each paragraph centering around, and subordinated to the theme of the section. Take the third thematic section in Lesson One for example. The central idea is "the various ways of establishing business relations" This Thematic Section consists of three paragraphs, and each shows different ways one may establish business relation with foreign companies or manufacturers, as well as things that need to be attended to when writing contact letters. Roughly speaking, the central idea of a political essay or an expository writing in Chinese is similar to the Topic Sentence in English composition. The sentence that represents the central idea may occur at the very beginning, in the middle, or at the end of a Thematic Section. One of the ways of organizing the rhetorical structure in Chinese composition is called "开门见山" (literally "to see the mountain as one opens the door"), which means "come straight to the point" by putting the central idea at the beginning of a paragraph. This is very effective in bringing out the essentials, and is applicable for logical reasoning. In contrast, if putting the topic sentence at the end of a paragraph, first giving substantial recounts and then making a generalization, it has the advantage of "水到渠成" (literally "where water flows, a channel is formed" meaning "success will come whenever conditions are ripe"), and is particularly suitable for induction. The placement of the topic sentence at a different position can have different rhetorical effects, depending on the organization of the entire essay and the need of each Thematic Section.

同段落一样，意义段内部上下紧邻的层次之间的意义关系，主要有并列、承接、递进、总分、转折、因果、解说等。如第二课第三个意义段（即从第 10 行到 22 行，第三、第四自然段），就是一种并列关系，而第四课第三个意义段（即从第 16 行到 38 行，第三自然段），就是一种解说关系。

Similar to a paragraph, the relations between immediate strata within a Thematic Section include the following, mainly, *Coordinative, Successive, Progressive, General to Specific, Adversative, Cause and Effect, and Elaborative Relations*, etc. For instance, in the third thematic section in Lesson Two (from lines 10 to 22, the third and forth paragraphs) is a *Coordinative* relation, while the third Thematic Section in Lesson Four (from lines 16 to 38, in the third paragraph) is an *Elaborative* relation.

意义段，特别是由几个段落或段组构成的意义段，要成为一个统一的有机体，表达一个相对完整的中心意思，必须注意内部的组织，上下段落段组的次序安排、衔接连贯和相互照应。一般说来，上下段落、段组的次序，应该按照事物的内部联系来安排，正确地反映这种内在联系。但是有时为了提高表达效果，可在不影响前后意思连贯的前提下，适当调换一下顺序。无论作什么样的安排，必须有利于上下段落之间的联系，保证前后连贯。

A Thematic Section, particularly one that consists of several paragraphs, must stress its internal organization, the arrangement of the sequence of paragraphs, as well as the coherence and cohesion among these paragraphs, so as to achieve unity and to express effectively a complete central idea. In general, the sequence of paragraphs should be arranged in light of the mutual relations among things, and to reflect their organic connection properly. Nevertheless, the sequence can be shift occasionally, on condition that such shift would not distort the meaning and jeopardize the coherence. Whatever is the arrangement, it must be for the benefit of the cohesion between paragraphs and the coherence of its meaning.

要做好意义段内部段落与段落、段组与段组之间的连接，要注意紧邻上下段落的起句与结句。在多数情况下，连接段落、段组靠的是关联词语。值得注意的是，汉语的关联词语不但可以连接分句、复句，而且还可以连接段落、段组，甚至意义段。这一点和英语有很大的不同。除了用关联词语外，相同的句式、表示平列关系的句子，也常用来关联段落或段组。意义段内部的段落或段组，还要注意内容上的呼应，前面提到的，后面要有交待，否则就会出现脱节。作为读者，大概没有什要人喜欢花时间、费脑子去猜测或填补一篇文章里作者应该说明而又没有交待的内容。

To achieve unity and coherence, we must pay close attention to the transition between paragraphs and between sections, particularly the concluding sentence of one paragraph and the beginning sentence of another paragraph. In most cases, the smooth transition lies on the correct use of Connectives. It is worth noticing that Chinese Connectives differ from the English ones significantly in that they can not only link up clauses, complex sentences, but also paragraphs and Thematic Sections. In addition to the use of Connectives, similar sentence patterns, sentences showing parallelism, are often used to connect paragraphs or Thematic Sections. Attention should also be paid to the coherence of content within a paragraph or a Thematic Section. Whatever has been mentioned previously, there must be a follow-up, otherwise, the essay will fall apart in giving a complete meaning. Most probably, readers are not so fond of spending extra time to rack their brains to guess or to fill in the gaps for whatever the author should have told his or her readers yet failed to do so.

练习

一、　用线将意思相同的词和词语连起来：

属于国家、企业、团体而非个人的钱	现款
赔偿别人受损失的钱	承担费用
可以当时就交付的钱	承包
提取并领走货物	交货
厂家或商店储存未出售的货物	托运
把货物交付给买方或其代理人	赔款
负责办理运输业务的人或公司	联运
把运来的东西再运到另外的地方去	提货
委托运输部门运送货物或行李等	存货
不同的交通部门之间建立联系，用两种或多种	
方式连续运送旅客、行李或货物	承运者
负责担负有关的花费	公款
接受并负责完成 (某项业务或工程)	转运

二、　用括号里的词或词组改写下列句子，但不改变其基本意思，必要时可
　　　对词序作一定的调整：

1. 对医生来说，治病救人是道义上不可推卸的责任。现在最重要的工
　 作，就是使病人的情况稳定下来。　　　 （义不容辞、首要）

2. 周小姐差不多是全公司工作效率最高的会计师了，大概现在还没有
什么人能够顶替她的位置。   （算、代替）

3. 我的意思不是现在就马上签合同，我是说应该再考虑这笔交易，不
然，我们可能会失去这个机会。   （并非……而是……、错过）

4. 这件事关联的范围这么广，你认为董事长会答应吗？
（涉及、允许）

5. 电子邮件在大学使用得非常广泛，其中有百分之七十是 学 生 发
的。   （普遍、占了）

6. 参加这次比赛的人，因为没有年龄、性别、学历等限制，所以超过
一半都是家庭妇女。   （不受……限制、以上）

7. 有人说蓝色代表安全。如果真是这样，蓝色的天空和海洋就不应该
有任何事故发生。   （象征、假若……便……）

8. 由于经营邮购直销的费用很便宜，这几年邮购服务增加了几倍，不
少大型商场的生意受到了很大的影响。(低廉、大受影响)

三、 选择最合适的词填空：

1. 只有交付货款以后，买方才能_____。
   a. 交货   b. 提货   c. 运货

2. 这个合同的价格条款是 F.O.B.，所以应该由买方负责组织_____。
   a. 交货   b. 提货   c. 运货

3. 国际贸易中的_____，要比在商店里买东西复杂得多。
   a. 交货   b. 提货   c. 运货

4. 除了负责订票服务以外，我们还_____行李托运的业务。
   a. 代表   b. 代理   c. 代替

5. 作为部门经理，她有权_____公司签订这个合同。
   a. 代表   b. 代理   c. 代替

6. 虽然电脑很聪明能干，但是有些事情它们还是_____不了人。
 a. 代表　　　　b. 代理　　　　c. 代替

7. 本公司_____各种大型装卸设备，欢迎来电进行业务洽谈。
 a. 承办　　　　b. 承运　　　　c. 承担

8. 他们决定进行合作，一起_____这次的出口商品展览。
 a. 承办　　　　b. 承运　　　　c. 承担

9. 这个规定只_____二十一岁以下的青少年。
 a. 限制　　　　b. 限定　　　　c. 限于

10. 这些规定不是要_____你们的自由，而是为了保证大家的安全。
 a. 限制　　　　b. 限定　　　　c. 限于

四、 从本课和第二课、第六课的课文中找出所有的假设复句。

五、 用假设复句完成下面的对话：

1. 甲：这些货物用海运，来得及吗？
 乙：（如果……的话，那就……）

2. 甲：我喝了很多茶，可是还是觉得很困。
 乙：（要是……就……）

3. 甲：进口电脑普遍都比国产的贵百分之二十到三十。
 乙：（即使……也……）

4. 甲：我们本来应该在合同上注明"不许分批装运"。
 乙：（倘若……就……）

5. 甲：听说那条船遭到了风险，我们的货受损失了没有？
 乙：还好，（要不是……早就……）

6. 甲：这次报什么价，F.O.B. 还是 C.I.F. ？
 乙：（假如……就……）

7. 甲：你已经给她发了传真和电子邮件，为什么还要寄信？

乙：(万一……就……)

8. 甲：唉，很多百货商店都在大减价，东西好便宜啊！

   乙：(就算……也……)

六、 解释下列成语、惯用语和俗语的意思，并用它们各造一句：

1. 不计其数
2. 千变万化
3. 口是心非
4. 价廉物美
5. 重合同，讲信用
6. 誉满全球
7. 供不应求
8. 耳听为虚，眼见为实
9. 独木不成林
10. 老王卖瓜，自卖自夸

七、把下列句子的划线部分改写成四字词组：

1. 丰田(Toyota)汽车，在全世界都很有名。
2. 中国景德镇瓷器，有很长的历史，品质是非常好的。
3. 我们的新产品，看起来又漂亮又大方，价格也很合理。
4. 这种电脑，用起来很简单，带起来也很方便。
5. 他听完了我的话，好像懂了又好像不懂，一点反应也没有。

八、 修辞练习：

1. 分析本课课文，看哪部分（哪几个自然段）符合下面的这种关系，并在横线下写上第几段：

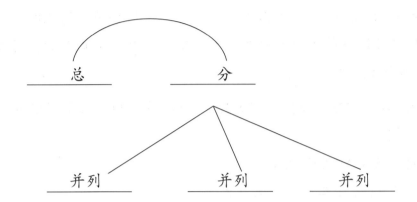

2. 你在其他课文里也能找到有类似关系的段落吗？

九、把下列句子翻译成汉语：

1. It is our unshirkable duty to guarantee the safety of our passengers. Weather like this simply does not permit (us) to set sail at all. The primary issue [i.e. "leading question"] we are concerned about is not missing the plane but your safety. If the ship suffers any hazard, not only the reputation of our coordinated transport company will be greatly affected, but your lives will be in danger.

2. This type of computer is inexpensive [i.e. "low"] at price, yet stable in performance. It basically is not subject to any limitations. It has combined various aspects of advanced technology; therefore, it is well received [i.e. "popularly welcomed"]. It has already replaced the imported brand-named products rapidly, and made up three quarters of the total sale amount this year. It is a symbol of success.

3. Foreign trade is much more complicated than ordinary business. It involves banks, transportation, the Customs, inspection, and many other parties [i.e. "departments"]. Therefore, ownership of import and export companies that belong to the government consists of over 85%. This company does not belong

to the government but to Mr. Rong and his sons. It is considered to be the largest private company in China.

十、 商业信函练习四

参考本课的"商业信函",根据下面的信息,用<u>新型通用式</u>的书信格式,以出口商美国英特尔公司的名义,给中国的长城电脑工业公司写一封有关"改期装运"的信。内容包括:

1. 受台风的影响,578号合同项下的70000个奔腾四型处理器不能照原定日期按时装运。
2. 新的装运期改在四月十九日。
3. "明珠"号可在五月二日到达天津新港。
4. 向对方道歉并希望对方谅解。

文化与商贸背景知识

✐ 送礼

对外贸易,虽然是一种公务性质的活动,但绝对不是机械呆板、不讲情谊的往来。有时给对方送一件小小的礼物,可以拉近彼此之间的距离,增进友谊,甚至建立牢固的业务关系。

中国外贸公司的代表,通常会在出国访问或接待重要的外商时,向对方送一些富有一定含义、具有中国特色或某个地方特色的礼物。譬如,一条表示"一帆风顺"的木雕小船,或者象征友谊长存、有青松图案的织锦。现在,也有些人把印有自己公司名称、标志的文具、提包等,作为礼物送给客户。这既是一件实用的礼品,又可起到广告的作用,真是一举两得。

因此,同中国人做生意、打交道,不妨也在适当的时机,特别是初次见面时(所谓的"见面礼"),或在生意做成后感谢对方的努力和合作等,向对方送一件既实用又有意义的小礼品。送给对方的礼物,不需要是非常贵重的。中国有句话，叫做"礼轻情意重"。除非是想用送礼来贿赂促成交易，否则，只要礼物符合中国的民族习惯，适合对方的爱好兴趣，比如一件工艺品、一条领带、甚至一枝笔，都会收到良好的效果。如果给对方几个人送礼，要尽量做到平等对待，不要厚此薄彼，因为中国是个讲究集体负责、共同决策的国家。另外，送礼时也可按中国人的习惯，自谦地说上两句，如"薄礼一份，请笑纳"或"一点小意思，不成敬意"等。接受礼物的中国人在吃惊的同时，一定会用这些话来回答，像"受之有愧"、"多谢、多谢，让你破费了"等。值得注意的是，中国人在接受礼物时，极少当着送礼者的面打开礼物。这样做是很失礼的，会被人认为贪心，把礼物看得比朋友更重。如果你在中国接受礼物，最好也"入乡随俗"，按中国人的习惯去做。

商业信函(4)

中国北京
长城电脑工业公司

主管先生：

　　本月九日来函已悉，感谢贵公司通过中国银行旧金山分行开来的2093号保兑、不可撤销的信用证。该信用证规定：我方578号销售合同，你方第61号订单，总值3500000美元的70000个奔腾四型处理器，应于四月二十日前交货。

　　现欣然奉告，我们已按贵方来函的装船指示，于四月十二日在旧金山将这批货物装上了中国远洋(运输集团)总公司的"明珠"号货轮。该轮于四月十四日启航，预计四月二十七日可抵达天津新港。

　　此货按合同规定，内包装为再生硬纸盒，每盒10打，另每个处理器再外套一个密封防震塑料袋。运输包装为标准出口纸板箱。

　　现随函附上有关装船单据副本壹套，请查收：
　　第S153号洁净的、已装船提单壹份
　　第7086号发票一式三份
　　第C2490号保险单壹份。
谨请提货后将收货情况及时告知我方。多谢合作。

　　　　　　　　　　　　　　　美国英特尔公司
　　　　　　　　　　　　　　　海外销售部总经理
　　　　　　　　　　　　　　　杨思文
　　　　　　　　　　　　　　　×××× 年四月十三日

✐ 发票、提单、海运出口货物委托书

东 方 科 学 仪 器 进 出 口 集 团 公 司
THE ORIENTAL SCIENTIFIC INSTRUMENTS IMPORT & EXPORT GROUP

中国·北京三里河路52号
No.52,San Li He Road
Beijing 100864, China
Tel: 2614983
FAX: 2614399

发　　票
I N V O I C E

迳 启 者　Messrs: S.C.WORKS CO. LTD.
地　　址 Address: 10/10-11 CHAROEN KRUNG RD..
　　　　　BANGKOK 10200

卖方参考号: 0763891 Seller's Ref.No.	发票号: 9764118 Invoice No.	日期: Aug 11, 1997 Date	合同号: 970EB64098TH Contract No.
发货口岸: TIANJIN Port of Loading	运输工具: SHIP Shipped Per		开航日期: Aug 26, 1997 Sailing on or About
到货口岸: BANGKOK Port of Discharge	交货条件: CIF BANGKOK Delivery Terms		买方参考号: Buyer'S Ref.No

唛头 Marks	货　名 Description	数量 Quantity	单价 Unit price	合计 Amount
GOLD PLATING LINE		1 SET	USD28998.00	USD28998.00

TOTAL: CIF BANGKOK　　　　　　　　　　　　　　　　　　USD28998.00
AMOUNT: TWENTY EIGHT THOUSANDS NINE HUNDRED AND NINETY EIGHT
US DOLLARS ONLY.

东方科学仪器进出口公司
THE ORIENTAL SCIENTIFIC INSTRUMENTS
IMPORT AND EXPORT CORPORATION

Authorized Signature

中国粮油食品进出口公司广东省粮油分公司
**China National Cereals, Oils & Foodstuffs
Import & Export Corp., Kwangtung Cereals & Oils Branch.**

INVOICE

Kwangchow

Invoice No.

Credit No.

To Messrs.　　　　　　　　　　　Contract No.

Shipped by Vessel

Destination

Marks & Nos.	Quantities & Descriptions	Unit Price	Amount

CERTIFICATE OF ORIGIN

This is to certify that the goods named herein are of Chinese Origin.

CHINA NATIONAL CEREALS, OILS & FOODSTUFFS
IMPORT & EXPORT CORPORATION
Kwangtung Cereals & Oils Branch

中国轻工业品进出口公司上海市分公司
CHINA NATIONAL LIGHT INDUSTRIAL PRODUCTS IMPORT AND EXPORT CORPORATION

SHANGHAI BRANCH

128, HUCHIU ROAD

SHANGHAI, CHINA

CABLE ADD.: INDUSTRY SHANGHAI

发票号码
Invoice Number ....

定单或合约号码
Sales Confirmation No. ....

发票日期
Date of Invoice ....

To:

目的地
To ....

装船口岸
From ....

开证银行
Issued by ....

信用证号数
Letter of Credit No. ....

唛头号码 Marks & Numbers	数量与货品名称 Quantities and Descriptions	总值 Amount

託運人
Shipper

中　國
遠洋運輸公司
CHINA OCEAN SHIPPING COMPANY

收貨人
Consignee　　　　　　　　或賬受人
　　　　　　　　　　　or assigns.

總公司 HEAD OFFICE:　北 京 BEIJING
　　　　　　　　　　广 州 GUANGZHOU
分公司 BRANCH OFFICE:　上 海 SHANGHAI
　　　　　　　　　　天 津 TIANJIN
　　　　　　　　　　青 岛 QINGDAO
　　　　　　　　　　大 连 DALIAN
電報掛號 CABLE ADDRESS: "COSCO"

通　知
Notify

提　　單
BILL OF LADING
直運或轉船
DIRECT OR WITH TRANSHIPMENT

正　本
ORIGINAL

船　名 Vessel	航次 Voy.	發貨單號 S/O No.	提單號 B/L No.

裝貨港 Port of Loading	卸貨港 Port of Discharge		
國　籍　　中 華 人 民 共 和 國 Nationality　THE PEOPLE'S REPUBLIC OF CHINA	運　費　在 Freight payable at		支付

託運人所提供的詳細情況
Particulars furnished by the Shipper

標誌和號數 Marks and Numbers	件　數 No. of Packages	貨　名 Description of Goods	毛　重 Gross Weight	尺　碼 Measurement

合 計 件 數（大 寫）
Total Packages (in words)

上列外表情況良好的貨物(另有說明者除外)已裝在上列船上並應在上列卸貨港或該船所能安全到達並能保持浮泊的附近地點卸貨。
　Shipped on board the vessel named above in apparent good order and condition (unless otherwise indicated) the goods or packages specified herein and to be discharged at the above mentioned port of discharge or as near thereto as the vessel may safely get and be always afloat.

重量、尺碼、標誌、號數、品質、內容和價值是託運人所提供的，承運人在裝船時並未核對。
　The weight, measure, marks, numbers, quality, contents and value, being particulars furnished by the Shipper, are not checked by the Carrier on loading.

託運人、收貨人和本提單的持有人茲明白表示接受並同意本提單和它背面所載的一切印刷、書寫或打印的規定、免責事項和條件。
　The Shipper, Consignee and the Holder of this Bill of Lading hereby expressly accept and agree to all printed, written or stamped provisions, exceptions and conditions of this Bill of Lading, including those on the back hereof.

運費和其他費用
Freight and Charges:

茲證明以上各節，承運人或其代理人已簽署本提單一式　　　份，其中一份經完成提貨手續後，其餘各份作廢。
　In witness whereof, the Carrier or his Agents has signed Bills of Lading all of this tenor and date, one of which being accomplished, the others to stand void.

請託運人特別注意本提單內與貨貨保險效力有關的免責事項和條件。
Shippers are requested to note particularly the exceptions and conditions of this Bill of Lading with reference to the validity of the insurance upon their goods.

簽單日期　　　　　　　　　　　在
Dated...at........................

船　長
For the Master

請閱背面條款　　See Clauses on the Back.

The following are the conditions and exceptions hereinbefore referred to:

1. **Definition.** Wherever the term "Shipper" occurs hereinafter, it shall be deemed to include also Receiver, Consignee, Holder of the Bill of Lading and Owner of the goods.

2. **Jurisdiction.** All disputes arising under and in connection with this Bill of Lading shall be determined in the People's Republic of China.

3. **Period of Responsibility.** The responsibility of the carrier shall commence from the time when the goods are loaded on board the ship and shall cease when they are discharged from the ship.

4. **Responsibilities.** The carrier shall be bound, before and at the beginning of the voyage, to exercise due diligence to make the ship seaworthy; properly man, equip and supply the ship, and to make the holds, refrigerated and cool chambers and all other parts of the ship in which goods are carried fit and safe for their reception, carriage and preservation.

The carrier shall not be liable for loss or damage arising or resulting from defects not discoverable though the carrier has exercised due diligence as aforesaid.

5. **Immunities.** Neither the carrier nor the ship shall be responsible for loss or damage arising or resulting from:

(a) Force Majeure;
(b) Dangers or accidents of the sea or other navigable waters;
(c) Fire;
(d) Military activities;
(e) Strikes, lock-outs, stoppage or restraint of labour from whatever cause, whether partial or general;
(f) Orders or acts of government authorities (seizure, arrest, quarantine, etc.);
(g) Act or ommission of the shipper, consignee or their agents;
(h) Nature and latent defects of the goods;
(i) Defects in packing not discoverable from outside;
(j) Insufficiency, illegibility or inadequacy of marks;
(k) Sickness or death of live animals;
(l) Act, neglect or default of the Master, Mariner, Pilot or any other person in the navigation or management of the ship;
(m) Saving or attempting to save life or property at sea;
(n) Any other cause arising without the actual fault or neglect of the carrier or his agents.

6. **Packing and marks.** The shipper shall have the goods properly packed accurately and clearly marked before shipment. The port of destination of the goods should be marked in letters of 5 cm high, in such a way as will remain legible until their delivery.

7. **Freight and other charges.** Advance freight together with other charges is due on shipment. If not prepaid, though stipulated, the freight and other charges shall be paid by the shipper or receiver, plus 5% interest per annum running from the date of notification for their payment.

If the cargo shipped are perishables, low cost goods, live animals, deck cargo or goods for which there is no carrier's agent at the port of destination, the freight for such cargo and all related charges shall be paid at the time of shipment.

Freight payable at destination is due on ship's arrival together with other charges. Advance freight and/or freight payable at destination shall be paid to the carrier in full, irrespective of whatever loss or damage may happen to ship and cargo or either of them.

8. **Penalty freight.** The carrier is entitled, at port of shipment and/or port of destination, to verify the quantity, weight, measurement and contents of the goods as declared by the shipper. If the weight, measurement and/or contents of such goods as stated in the Bill of Lading turned out to be inconsistent with that of the goods actually loaded, and the freight paid falls short of the amount which would have been due if such declaration had been correctly given, the carrier is entitled to collect from the shipper double the amount of difference between the freight for the goods actually shipped and that mis-stated.

The shipper shall be liable for loss of and damage to the ship and/or cargo arising or resulting from inaccuracies in stating the description, quantity, weight, measurement or contents of the goods and shall indemnify the carrier for the costs and expenses in connection with weighing, measuring and checking such goods.

9. **Lien.** The carrier shall have a lien on the goods for freight, dead freight, demurrage and any other amount payable by the cargo, and shall be entitled to sell the goods by auction or otherwise at carrier's option. If, on the sale of the goods, the proceeds fail to cover the amount due and the cost and expenses incurred, the carrier shall be entitled to recover the difference from the shipper.

10. **Notice of Claim.** When the cargo is taken delivery of by the receiver against Bill of Lading, if notice of damage or partial loss be not given in writing to the carrier at the time of the removal of the goods by the receiver, such removal shall be prima facie evidence of the delivery by the carrier of the goods as described in the Bill of Lading. If the partial loss or damage of the goods cannot be discovered under the usual way of delivery, a notice of claim shall be given in writing within three days of the delivery. However, such notice of claim is not required in case the receiver has verified the goods jointly with the carrier.

In all circumstances, the carrier and the ship shall be discharged from all liabilities in respect of loss or damage unless suit is brought within one year after delivery of the goods or the date when the goods should have been delivered.

11. **Indemnity.** The indemnity for loss of cargo shall be determined on the basis of its actual value, while the indemnity for damage to cargo shall be determined on the basis of the difference between the values of the goods before and after the damage. The value of the goods shall be determined on the basis of the market value at the port of destination on the day of ship's arrival, or, in case of nonarrival, on the day of expected arrival, or, at the carrier's option, on the basis of the market value of the goods at the port of loading on the day of departure plus other charges concerned.

The duties and expenses saved shall be deducted from the indemnity for loss of or damage to the goods.

The amount of indemnity for loss of or damage to cargo shall in no case exceed R.M.B. ¥ 700 per package or freight unit, except special agreement besides Bill of Lading has been made and extra freight paid. Should the actual value of the goods per package or freight unit exceed the declared value stated in the aforesaid agreement, the carrier's liability, if any, shall not exceed the declared value, and any partial loss or damage shall be adjusted pro rata on the basis of such declared value. Under no circumstances shall the carrier make allowances for loss of profit or loss in market value.

12. **Loading, discharging and delivery.** The goods shall be supplied and taken delivery of by the owner of the goods as fast as the ship can take and discharge them, without interruption, by day and night, Sundays and Holidays included, notwithstanding any custom of the port to the contrary and the owner of the goods shall be liable for all losses or damages incurred in default thereof.

Discharge may commence without previous notice. If the goods are not taken delivery of by the receiver from alongside the vessel without delay, or if the receiver refuses to take delivery of the goods, or in case there are unclaimed goods, the carrier shall be at liberty to land such goods on shore or any other proper places at the sole risk and expense of the shipper or receiver, and the carrier's responsibility of delivery of cargo shall be deemed to have been fulfilled.

The carrier has the right to sell the goods by public auction, if they are not taken delivery of within one month after the ship's arrival at the port of destination. Goods liable to deteriorate or those under special conditions shall be sold earlier.

13. **Lighterage.** Any lighterage in or off ports of loading or ports of discharge shall be for the account of the shipper or receiver.

14. **Forwarding, substitute of vessel, through cargo and transhipment.** If necessary, the carrier may carry the goods to their port of destination by other vessel or vessels either belonging to the carrier or other persons or by rail or other means of transport proceeding either directly or indirectly to such port, and to carry the goods or part of them beyond their port of destination, and to tranship, lighter, land and store the goods on shore or afloat and reship and forward same at carrier's expense but at shipper's or receiver's risk. The responsibility of the carrier shall be limited to the part of the transport performed by him on the vessel under his management.

15. **Deviation and changing of route.** Any deviation in saving or attempting to save life or property at sea, or any reasonable deviation and changing of route shall not be deemed to be infringement or breach of the contract of carriage, and the carrier shall not be liable for any loss or damage resulting therefrom.

16. **Dangerous cargo.** If goods of an inflammable, explosive or dangerous nature are shipped without contents being previously declared or shipped under false description, they may at any time be landed at any place or thrown overboard or destroyed or rendered innocuous by the carrier without compensation. The shipper shall be liable for all damages caused by such goods to the ship and/or cargo on board.

If any such goods shipped with such knowledge and consent shall become a danger to the ship or cargo, they may likewise be dealt with by the carrier without liability on the part of the carrier except to general average, if any.

17. **Deck cargo, plants and live animals.** Cargo on deck, plants and live animals are received, handled, carried, kept and discharged at shipper's or receiver's risk and the carrier shall not be liable for loss thereof or damage thereto.

18. **Refrigerated cargo.** Before loading cargo in any insulated space, the carrier shall, in addition to the Class Certificate, obtain the certificate of the Classification Society's Surveyor or other competent person, stating that such insulated space and refrigerating machinery are in the opinion of the surveyor or other competent person fit and safe for the carriage and preservation of refrigerated cargo. The aforesaid certificate shall be conclusive evidence against the shipper, receiver and/or any holder of Bill of Lading.

Receivers have to take delivery of refrigerated cargo as soon as the ship is ready to deliver, otherwise the carrier shall land the cargo at the wharf at receiver's or shipper's risk and expense.

19. **Timber.** Any statement in this Bill of Lading to the effect that timber has been shipped "in apparent good order and condition" does not involve any admission by the carrier as to the absence of stains, shakes, splits, holes or broken pieces, for which the carrier accepts no responsibility.

20. **Bulk Cargo.** As the carrier has no reasonable means of checking the weight of bulk cargo, any reference to such weight in this Bill of Lading shall be deemed to be for reference only, but shall constitute in no way evidence against the carrier.

21. **Heavy lifts and awkward cargo.** Any one piece or package of cargo which weighs 2000 kilos or upwards and any awkward or over length cargo must be marked with the weight and/or dimensions and/or length clearly and boldly by the shipper and shall be loaded and discharged by shore crane or otherwise at the ship's option and at the risk and expense of the shipper or receiver. If any damage, loss or liability to the ship, lighter, wharf, quay, cranes, hoisting tackle, or whatsoever or to whomever occurs owing to the lack of statement or mis-statement of weight, measurement or length, the shipper or receiver shall be responsible for such damage, loss or liability.

22. **Optional Cargo.** The port of discharge for optional cargo must be declared to the vessel's agents at the first of the optional ports not later than 48 hours before the vessel's arrival there.

In the absence of such declaration the Carrier may elect to discharge at the first or any optional port and the contract of carriage shall then be considered as having been fulfilled. Any option must be for the total quantity of goods under this Bill of Lading.

23. **Goods to more than one consignee.** Where bulk goods or goods without marks or goods with the same marks are shipped to more than one consignee the consignees or owners of the goods shall jointly and severally bear any expense or loss in dividing the goods or parcels into pro rata quantities and any deficiency shall fall upon them in such proportion as the carriers, his servants or agents shall decide.

24. **General average.** General average, if any, shall be adjusted in the People's Republic of China.

25. **War, quarantine, ice, strikes, congestion, etc.** Should it appear that war, blockade, pirate, epidemics, quarantine, ice, strikes, congestion and other causes beyond the carrier's control would prevent the vessel from safely reaching the port of destination and discharging the cargo thereat, the carrier is entitled to discharge the cargo at the port of loading or any other safe and convenient port and the contract of carriage shall be deemed to have been fulfilled.

Any extra expenses incurred under the aforesaid circumstances shall be borne by the shipper or receiver.

THE ORIENTAL SCIENTIFIC INSTRUMENTS IMPORT AND EXPORT
CORPORATION 52 SAN LI HE ROAD, BEIJING 100864, CHINA

B/L NO.
COSU371212033

Consignee
TO ORDER

Notify Party
TANIDMANSHA CO., LTD. 473, KAMO, KITAGATA-CHO,
KOTOSU-GUN, GIFU-PREF.

中国远洋运输（集团）总公司
CHINA OCEAN SHIPPING(GROUP) CO.

CABLE: COSCO BEIJING
TLX: 210740 CPC CN   ORIGINAL

Combined Transport BILL OF LADING

RECEIVED in apparent good order and condition except as otherwise noted the total number of containers or other packages or units enumerated below for transportation from the place of receipt to the place of delivery subject to the terms and conditions hereof. One of the Bills of Lading must be surrendered duly endorsed in exchange for the goods or delivery order. On presentation of this document duly endorsed to the Carrier by or on behalf of the Holder of the Bill of Lading, the rights and liabilities arising in accordance with the terms and conditions hereof shall, without prejudice to any rule of common law or statute rendering them binding on the Merchant, become binding in all respects between the Carrier and the Holder of the Bill of Lading as though the contract evidenced hereby had been made between them. IN WITNESS whereof the number of original Bills of Lading stated under have been signed, all of this tenor and date, one of which being accomplished, the other(s) to be void.

Pre-carriage by	Place of Receipt		
Ocean Vessel Voy. No.	Port of Loading		
HUA LI HE 227	TIANJIN PORT		
Port of Discharge	Place of Delivery		Final Destination (of the goods-not the ship) see Article 7 paragraph (2)
NAGOYA PORT			

Marks & Nos. Container/ Seal No.	No of containers or P kgs	Kind of Packages; Description of Goods	Gross Weight Kgs	Measurement
N/M	1000BAGS	MILK VETCH SEEDS (AS PER SALES CONTRACT NO. (97)OEDS4032JP) FOB	20500.00KGS	28.000CBM
		FREIGHT COLLET SHIPPER'S LOAD COUNT AND SEAL		

TOTAL NO. OF CONTAINERS
OR PACKAGES (IN WORDS)   TOTAL: ONE THOUSAND BAGS ONLY.

FREIGHT & CHARGES	Revenue Tons	Rate	Per	Prepaid	Collect
CRA02376912 (G75308)= 1000/CY/CY	/ 20500.00 /	28.000/20'			

天津中远经济贸运有限公司
COSCO ... INTERMODAL CO., LTD.

天津中远经济贸运有限公司
COSCO ... INTERMODAL CO., LTD.

	Payable at	Place and Date of Issue	
		TIANJIN 7 AUG 1997
No. of Original B/s)	THREE	Signed for the Carrier	

7 AUG 1997

海运出口货物委托书

合同号: 97OEB64098TH	97 年 08 月 24 日	信用证号: A139710002

委托单位	THE ORIENTAL SCIENTIFIC INSTRUMENTS I/E *CORP.* 52 SAN LI *HO* ROAD,BEIJING CHINA TEL:10-61624983	委 托 编 号	
		提 单 号	
提抬单头	To Order KRUNG THAI BANK PUBLIC COMPANY LIMITED. YAWARAJ BRANCH. 260 YAWARAJ ROAD. BANKOK 10100, *THAILAND*	装 船 期	
		结 汇 期	
被通知人 详细地址	正本: S.C. WORKS CO.,LTD. 10/10-11 CHAROEN KRUNG RD. BANKOK 10200,THAILAND. Tel:2221377	可否转船	*ALLOWED*
		可否分批	*NOT ALLOWED*
	付本:	离 岸 价 格	US$.
		货 证 情 况	

船 名:	装 货 港: Hsinkang	随 附 单 证	
目的港: BANKOK	运费支付: PREPAID	提单份数:	正 付

唛 头:	件 数:	货 名:	毛 重:	体 积:
N/M	1 SET	GOLD PLATING LINE		

特殊条款		外运记载事项	配 舱	
			到 审	
其它要次			洞 单	
			审 核	

委托单位盖章:	洞 审:	复 核:

第九课

支付

✐ **思考下面的问题，然后带着这些问题去阅读课文：**

一、什么是"支付"？

二、买卖双方在谈判时，在支付问题上首先要明确什么？应该选择什么
作为支付工具？

三、国际贸易有哪几种主要的支付方式？它们相互之间有什么不同？

课文：支付

顾客在商场购物，必须付钱后才能把商品拿走。同样，在国际
贸易中，买方在签订合同后，必须遵照合同的规定，如数、按期向
有关银行交付货款，然后才能取得代表货物所有权的凭据，待货物
运抵后，再凭各项货运单据提货。这就是"支付"。支付，相对卖方
"交货"而言——是买方执行合同的具体行动。   5

由于买卖双方分属不同的国家和地区，所用的货币制度也不
同，因此，双方在洽谈和签订合同时，必须先明确商定使用什么货
币作为支付工具：使用本国的货币，使用对方国家的货币，或者使
用第三国的货币。

无论哪一种货币，其比率在国际金融市场上都是经常变动的。为   10
了尽量减少因受币值比率波动而可能造成的损失，很多国家都尽可能
采用可以自由兑换，流通广泛，币值相对稳定的外币作为支付工具，
如：美元、英镑、欧洲一些国家通用的欧元，及日元、港币等。

国际贸易中的支付方式主要有三种：信用证、托收和汇付。

15   较为普遍使用的是信用证。信用证是银行应进口人（买方）的要
     求，开给出口人（卖方）的一种保证承担付款责任的凭证。它是一种
     银行信用，所以对买卖双方来说都是相当可靠而有利的。对卖方而
     言，信用证是收取货款的一种双重保障：一方面有买方对支付货款
     的承诺，另一方面有开证银行（一般为进口地银行）以自己的信用对
20   付款作出的保证。因此，采用信用证支付，既安全又迅速，大多数
     出口人都乐于接受。反之亦然。对买方而言，用信用证不但付款后
     即可肯定取得代表货物的单据，而且可以通过信用证的条款促使出
     口人履行合同上的有关规定。

          信用证的种类颇多，但从银行信用这一基本特征来分，最主要
25   有两种，即不可撤销信用证和可撤销信用证。不可撤销信用证是指
     信用证一经开出，在有效期内，未经受益人（一般为出口人）或有关
     当事人的同意，开证行不得片面修改或撤销已开出的信用证。可撤
     销信用证是开证行可以不经过受益人同意，在议付行（一般为出口
     地银行）议付[1]之前，随时修改或撤销信用证。由于这种信用证对出
30   口人收取货款没有什么保障，在国际贸易中较为罕用。

          从支付时间来分，信用证又可分为即期信用证和远期信用证两
     种。前者规定受益人可凭即期汇票收取货款；后者规定受益人以远期
     汇票收款。使用远期信用证时，由于付款时间的延长，受益人（出口
     人）需要承担延期收款的利息[2]，所以出口人在谈判时往往会结合客
35   户、商品、市场等因素考虑，以高于即期信用证付款的价格成交。

---

1   议付在国际贸易上一般是指出口地银行（议付行）向出口人购买其出具的汇票和货运单据，
    然后再将汇票和货运单据寄到国外开证行或其指定的付款银行办理索取代垫货款的手续。

2   这主要跟信用证支付的程序有关。进口人向银行（开证行）申请开立信用证时，只交纳押金
    或提供其他保证，并不是立即付款。出口人（受益人）收到由开证行委托的出口地银行（通
    知行）转交的信用证后，按规定装运，开出汇票，并备齐各种货运单据，送交当地银行（议
    付行）议付。议付行按信用证核对单据无误后，按照汇票金额扣除利息，把货款垫付给出
    口人，同时将汇票和货运单据寄给开证行索偿。开证行（或其指定的付款行）核对单据无误
    后，付款给议付行，然后通知进口人付款赎单。由于货款都是由议付行事先代付给出口

　　托收也是较常见的支付方式之一。托收方式是出口人在装运货物后，先填写托运委托书，开具汇票，然后把委托书和汇票，连同全套货运单据送交出口地托收银行，再通过它在进口地的分行或代理银行，向进口人收取货款。托收方式中的汇票是出口人要求进口人在限定时间内无条件支付一定金额给受款人（通常为出口人）的书面命令。由于这种汇票附有货运单据（主要包括提单、发票、保险单等），所以又称为跟单托收。根据不同的交单条件，跟单托收又分为"付款交单"、"承兑交单"[3]等几种。托收这种方式对进口人较为有利，因为它既省了开立信用证的手续，又免了交纳给开证行的押金。尤其是"承兑交单"，进口人只要向银行承认对货款有支付的责任（即所谓的"承兑"），就可取得代表货物的货运单据，到汇票到期日才付款。这种支付依靠的完全是进口人的商业信用，银行只提供服务，如果发生进口人不付款的情况，银行不负偿付的责任。所以出口人所冒的风险，远远大于信用证支付方式。除非是资信良好的老客户，或者是为了推销有大量库存、亟待处理的滞销商品，否则一般都不会轻易同意使用"承兑交单"这种支付方式。

　　汇付是指进口人将货款通过银行付给出口人。汇付有信汇、电汇、和票汇三种。但是，这种支付方式在国际贸易中比较少用，除了预付货款外，一般只用于收付佣金、样品费、赔款或交纳履约保证金等。

人，再向开证行（或其拍定的付款行）索偿的，而这与进口人最后付款总有一段时间，如果使用远期信用证，议付行收回代垫款的时间就越长，因此延期收款的利息，就由出口人来负担。

[3]　付款交单（Documents against Payment, 简称D/P）是指出口人的交单以进口人的付款为条件，即出口人将汇票连同货运单据交给银行托收时，指示银行只有在进口人付清货款以后，才能把代表货物的全套货运单据交给进口人。按支付时间的不同，付款交单又可分为即期付款交单（Documents against Payment at Sight, 简称D/P Sight）和远期付款交单（Documents against Payment after Sight, 简称D/P after Sight）两种。
承兑交单（Documents against Acceptance, 简称D/A）是指出口人的交单以进口人的承兑汇票为条件。进口人承兑汇票，即进口人向银行承认自己负有支付货款的责任，便可向银行取得代表货物的全套货运单据，等到汇票到期那天，才交付货款。因为只有远期汇票才需要办承兑手续，所以承兑交单条件，只适用于远期汇票的托收。

✐ **根据课文内容回答下列问题：**

1. 什么是"支付"？

2. 买卖双方在谈判时，在支付问题上应当明确什么？

3. 哪些货币常被选为支付工具？为什么？

4. 为什么出口人倾向于使用信用证？

5. 如果按银行信用划分，信用证主要有哪几种？按支付时间划分呢？

6. 什么是即期不可撤销信用证？

7. 为什么国际贸易中较少采用"可撤销信用证"？

8. 什么是"汇票"？

9. "跟单托收"的单指的是什么？

10. 托收这种支付方式对谁比较有利？为什么？

11. 哪一种托收对出口人风险较大？为什么？

12. 汇付一般用于哪些方面？为什么？

✐ **根据意思，给课文划分层次(不是自然段)并写出每个层次的大意。**

生词和用法

商场	shāngchǎng	N.	面积较大，商品齐全的综合商店，或由各种商店组成的大型市场：自选~、豪华~、购物~。 mall; market
遵照	zūnzhào	V.	依照：~规定、~合同、~政策、~指示、~命令；< >违背。　to obey; to comply with; to follow
如数	rúzhù	Adv.	照原来的数目，只修饰动词：~付给、~归还、~到齐。　exactly the number or amount

凭据	píng jù	N.	用作证明的文件或实物；凭证：缺乏~、~不足。
			evidence; proof
待	dài	V.	等待：~机、~命、有~改进、仍~解决。
			to wait; to await
分	fēn	V.	把整体事物变成几个或使连在一起的事物离开：~工、~批、~期、~家、~组；~居、~散、~担、~发、~开、~裂；＜＞合。
			to divide; to separate
		V.	分别、辨别：不~高低、~清是非。
			to differentiate; to distinguish
属	shǔ	V.	隶属；归属	to subordinate to; to belong to
分属	fēn shǔ	V.	分别隶属于。	to be under different authorities
币	bì	N.	货币：钱~、纸~、硬~、人民~、港~、新台~、外~。	money; currency
币值	bìzhí	N.	货币的价值，即货币购买商品的能力。
			currency value
比率	bǐlǜ	N.	两数相比所得的值，也叫比值。
			ratio; rate
金融	jīnróng	N.	指货币的发行、流通和回笼，贷款的发放和收回，存款的存入和提取，汇款的往来等经济活动：~市场、~中心、~资本、~界。
			finance; banking
波动	bōdòng	V.	起伏不定，不稳定：物价~、情绪~、湖水~着；Cf. 变动、改动；＜＞稳定。
			to fluctuate; to undulate
兑换	duìhuàn	V.	用一种货币换另一种：~外币、~率、自由~。
			to exchange; to convert
相对	xiāngduì	Adj.	比较的：~稳定、~地说、~而言；＜＞绝对。
			relatively; comparatively
欧洲	ōuzhōu	N.		Europe

欧元	ōuyuán	N.	从2002年起，通用于德、法、西班牙、意大利、等欧洲国家的货币。Euro
托收	tuōshōu	N.	Collection, one of the payment methods in foreign trade
汇	huì	V.	通过银行、邮电局等把一笔钱从一个地方转到另一个地方。 to remit; to transfer (through a bank or the postal service)
汇付	huìfù	VP	通过银行或邮局把货款寄给卖方。 to remit money as payment
		N.	通过银行或邮局寄给卖方的货款。 remittance
信汇	xìnhuì	NP	进口人将货款交给本地银行，由银行用信件委托出口人所在地银行付款给出口人。 Mail Transfer, 简称M/T
电汇	diànhuì	NP	进口人要求银行用电报委托出口人所在地银行付款给出口人。 Telegraphic Transfer, 简称T/T
票汇	piàohuì	NP	进口人向本地银行购买银行汇票，自行寄给出口人，出口人凭以向汇票上指定的银行取款。 Demand Draft, 简称D/D
应	yìng	Mph.(V.)	满足要求；允许；接受：有求必~、~邀、~聘。 to comply with; to grant 回答：答~、呼~、~承、~对。 to answer; to respond
可靠	kěkào	Adj.	可以信赖依靠的（人）；真实可信的（事）：质量~、为人~、~的消息。 reliable; dependable; trustworthy
双重	shuāngchóng	Adj.	两层；两方面的（多用于抽象事物）：~任务、~标准、~保障、~国籍、~性格。 double; dual; two-fold
保障	bǎozhàng	V./N.	保护；保证（抽象事物，如生命、财产、自由、

权利等），使不受侵犯和破坏：~供给、~安全、
有~。

to ensure; to guarantee; to
safeguard; guarantee; security

乐于	lèyú	V.	对做某件事情感到快乐；~接受、~助人、~参加、~提供；＜＞苦于。

to be delighted in +Disyllabic V.

亦	yì	Adv.	〔书〕＝也，也是：反之~然，~无不可。

also; too

反之亦然	fǎnzhī yìrán	Idm.	反过来也是一样。	the reverse is also true; and vice versa

履行	lǚxíng	V.	实践（自己答应做的或应该做的事）：~义务、~职责、~合同、~诺言。

to fulfil (obligation); to perform
(duty); to keep one's words

颇	pō	Adv.	〔书〕很，相当地：~＋单音节Adj.:~多、~大、~佳、~易；~+VP:~有道理、~感兴趣。

considerably; rather; quite

一经	yìjīng	Conj.	表示只要经过某个步骤或行为，（下文说明就能产生的结果）；一旦。

once; as soon as

未	wèi	Adv.	没有＋V.；还没：~知、~定、~婚、~成年、~能、~完、~曾、~尝；＜＞已。

have not; did not; not yet; not

受益	shòuyì	VO	得到好处，受到利益：~人、~不浅、双方~。

to benefit from; to profit by

片面	piànmiàn	Adj.	单方面的：~决定、~更改、~撤销、~之词、~观点、~性；＜＞全面。

unilateral; one-sided

议付	yìfù	V./N.	to negotiate (through a bank), negotiation

议付银行	yìfùyínháng	N.	指愿意买入或贴现受益人交来跟单汇票的银行。议付银行可以是指定的银行，也可以是非指定的银行，由信用证的条款来规定。

negotiating bank

收取	shōuqǔ	*V.*	收下交来的钱或物：~手续费、~押金、~货款、~保险金；＜＞交付。 to receive; to accept; to take
罕	hǎn	*Adj.*	稀少；不经常出现或发生：希~、~见、~闻、~有；＜＞常。 rare; seldom
汇票	huìpiào	*N.*	由一方开给另一方的无条件的书面支付命令，要求对方立即或在一定时间内支付一定金额给某人或指定的人。 bill of exchange; draft
即期 汇票	jíqī huìpiào	*NP*	规定付款人见票后即需付款的汇票。 sight bill
远期 汇票	yuǎnqī huìpiào	*NP*	规定付款人于未来的一定日期付款的汇票。 time bill
延	yán	*Mph.(V.)*	推迟；拉长：~期、~迟、~长、~展、~误、~续、~伸。 to delay; to extend
延长	yáncháng	*V.*	（在时间或距离上）向长的方面发展：~两天、~寿命、~学制、~线路；＜＞缩短。 to extend; to prolong; to lengthen
利息	lìxī	*N.*	因存款、放款而达到的本金以外的钱：提高~、偿还~。 interest
委托	wěituō	*V.*	请别人代办事情：~办理、~照顾、~收取、接受~、~书。 to entrust; trust
受款人	shòukuǎnrén	*NP*	接受款项的人。 payee
保险单	bǎoxiǎndān	*NP*	保险公司向受保人开具的承保保证。上面载明受保人名称、受保财物、险别、保险期限、保险金额等项目，并附有关于保险公司的责任范围以及保险人和受保人的权利和义务的说明。如果受保财物遭受损失时，保险单是受保人索赔的主要依据，也是保险公司理赔的主要依据。 insurance policy

承兑 交单	chéngduì jiāodān	*NP*	Documents against Acceptance, 简称D/A. 简称
付款 交单	fùkuǎn jiāodān	*NP*	Documents against Payment, 简称D/P.
省	shěng	*V.*	免掉、减去：~去手续、~去两字；＜＞加。 to omit; to leave out
免	miǎn	*V.*	去掉；除去：~税、~费、~试、~检、~票。 to excuse from; to exempt
交纳	jiāonà	*V.*	一方向另一方（通常为政府或组织）按照规定或 契约交付一定数量的金钱或实物：~学费、~押 金、~税款；＜＞收缴。 to pay; to submit
押金	yājīn	*N.*	作为抵押的钱。 deposit; cash pledge
尤其	yóuqí	*Adv.*	表示（在上文提到的方面）更进一步：~突出、~ 重要、~注意、~喜欢、~麻烦、~容易。 particularly; especially
冒	mào	*V.*	不顾（危险、恶劣环境等）：~险、~雨、~着寒 风、~昧。 to risk; to brave
除非	chúfēi	*Conj.*	强调某条件是唯一的先决条件，相当于"只 有"。 only if; only when; unless
库存	kùcún	*N.*	指仓库中现存的现金或物资。 stock; reserve
亟	jí	*Adv.*	〔书〕急迫地：~盼、~欲、~待解决。 urgently; anxiously
滞	zhì	*Mph. (V.)*	不流通，停滞：~销、~留、停~、迟~。 stagnant; sluggish
滞销	zhìxiāo	*V.*	（货物）卖不出去，销路不畅；＜＞畅销。
轻易	qīngyì	*Adv.*	随随便便，轻率地：~决定、~同意；＜＞慎 重。 lightly; rashly
预	yù	*Adv.*	预先、事先：~备、~订、~约、~报、~防、~ 计、~算、~想、~祝、~制、~展、~习、~购、~ 见、~料。 in advance; beforehand

预付	yùfù	V.	预先支付：~货款、~押金、~房租。 pay in advance
保证金	bǎozhèngjīn	NP	为了保证履行某种义务而交纳的一定数量的钱。 cash deposit
垫付	diànfù	V.	暂时代人付钱。 pay for somebody and expect to be paid back later
核对	héduì	V.	审核查对：~事实、~数字、~账目。 to check
无误	wúwù	Adj.	没有差错：核对~、准确~。 error-free; flawless
扣除	kòuchú	V.	从总额中减去：~利息、~手续费、~成本。 to deduct
索偿	suǒcháng	V.	要求偿还。 to claim payment

补充词

代表团	dàibiǎotuán	N.	受委托或指派代表政府、团体办事或表达意见的一组人：代表~、经济~、贸易~。 delegation
均	jūn	Mph.	均匀；相等：平~、~匀。 average; even
审核	shěnhé	V.	审查核定，多用于书面材料或数字材料：~报表、~计划、~预算、~经费。 to audit and verify
赎	shú	V.	用钱财换回抵押品；<>典、当。 to redeem
赎单	shúdān	VO	to redeem the bill of lading
贬值	biǎnzhí	V.	货币购买力下降；价值降低，不带宾语；<>升值。 to devalue
独立自主	dúlìzìzhǔ	VP	一个国家或政权不受别的国家或政权的统治，

			自己做主而存在。	to maintain independence and keep the initiative in one's own hand
现行	xiànxíng	Adj.	现在施行的；现在有效的：~规定、~措施、~做法；＜＞历史。	currently in effect; in operation
实施	shíshī	V.	实行，多指法令、政策、办法等。	to implement; to carry out (policy, plan, regulation)
畜	chù	N.	禽兽，多指家禽，如猪、牛、羊、马等。	domestic animal; livestock
鉴定	jiàndìng	V.	鉴别、确定人或事物的真假好坏：~文物、~质量、技术~、自我~。	to appraise; to examine and determine
吹	chuī	V.	合拢嘴唇用力出气；气体流动；〔口〕夸口、~牛。	to blow; to puff; to boast; to brag
实业	shíyè	N.	工商企业的统称。	industry; business
妥	tuǒ	Adj.	齐备、停当，多用于动词后作补语：备~、办~、谈~、想~。	appropriate; proper
备妥	bèituǒ	VP	准备妥当。	get ready properly
办妥	bàntuǒ	VP	办理妥当。	to get something done properly
如期	rúqī	Adv.	按照期限或时间，多作状语：~开始、~完成、~到达、~举行；＜＞过期。	as scheduled; on schedule
从速	cóngsù	Adv.	尽快；赶紧：~办理、~解决、~安排、~调查。	as soon as possible; without delay

词语例释

一、遵照＋Noun Phrase（＋Verb Phrase）　（to conform to; to Verb in accordance with）

l-2. 同样，在国际贸易中，买方在签订合同后，必须遵照合同的规定，如数、按期向有关银行交付货款，然后才能取得代表货物所有权的凭据，待货物运抵后，再凭各项货运单据提货。

1. 遵照海关的规定，进口汽车都要交纳百分之一百二十的关税。
2. 遵照医生的吩咐，老钱每天都喝少量的酒，吃很多水果。
3. 她没有遵照总经理的指示，轻易就给客户打了八折，结果造成了很大的损失。

动词"遵照"有"依照"的意思，经常与"路线、方针、规定、精神、原则、政策"等名词配合使用，后面多接动词或动词短语。"遵照"多用于书面语，有尊敬的色彩。"按照"可用于口语，也可用于书面，不带尊敬的色彩。"按照"可用在对上级的决定、命令、指示等，也可用于客观规律。

The Verb 遵照 means "to obey, to follow, to accord with". It is often coordinated with Nouns such as 路线、方针、规定、精神、原则、政策 and followed by a Verb or Verb Phrase. 遵照 is mostly used in written Chinese, and has the connotation of respect while 按照 is used in both written and spoken Chinese, and does not have a respectful connotation. 按照 can be used for a decision, an order, or a instruction from the superior or authority, it can be used for an objective law as well.

二、对（someone/something）**而言，**……　（relatively to/compared with someone/something, Clause...)

l-4. 支付，相对卖方"交货"而言——是买方执行合同的具体行动。

1. 相对做生意的买方而言，学生就是老师的顾客。
2. 中国的经济近十年有了很大的发展，但是相对发达国家而言，其人均生产总值还是相当低的。

3. 不少人都以为坐飞机很危险，其实<u>相对</u>开车<u>而言</u>，事故率还要低。

这个短语，相当于口语的"对……来说"（第六课"词语例释"一），表示某种判断是针对某人某物作出的。

> This short phrase is equivalent to the colloquial expression 对……来说 (see 词语例释、一 in Lesson 6), indicating a certain judgement is made toward a certain person or certain thing.

三、 应……的要求/邀请，Subject +Verb　（at the request/invitation of）

l-15. 信用证是银行应进口人（买方）的要求，开给出口人（卖方）的一种保证承担付款责任的凭证。

1. 因天气的关系，<u>应</u>卖方的<u>要求</u>，买方同意对方延迟十天装运。
2. <u>应</u>中国政府的<u>邀请</u>，英国经济贸易代表团上个月访问了北京。
3. <u>应</u>"空中巴士"公司的<u>邀请</u>，亚洲各大航空公司都派代表参观了在法国巴黎举行的航空展览。

语素"应"有动词的性质，表示"回答、允许、接受"等意思，常与其他词构成合成词或固定词组，如：应邀、答应、呼应、有求必应等。多用于书面语。

> The morpheme 应 is a Verb in nature, meaning 回答、允许、接受, etc. It is often associated with other words to form words or set phrases, such as in 应邀、答应、呼应、有求必应, and is primarily used in written Chinese.

四、 一方面……，另一方面……　（on the one hand..., on the other hand...）

l-18. 对卖方而言，信用证是收取货款的一种双重保障：<u>一方面</u>有买方对支付货款的承诺，<u>另一方面</u>有开证银行（一般为进口地银行）以自己的信用对付款作出的保证。

1. 对买方来说，托收比较有利，<u>一方面</u>可以省去开信用证的手续，另一方面又不必给开证银行交付押金。

2. 他决定选"商贸汉语"这门课，<u>一方面</u>学一些有关进出口贸易的基本知识，<u>另一方面</u>提高自己的汉语水平。

3. 现代社会的妇女比男的忙多了，她们<u>一方面</u>要工作赚钱，<u>另一方面</u>又要照顾家庭。

连词"一方面"连接并列的两种相互关系或一个事物的两个方面，常用在介词词组或分句中间，构成"一方面……（另）一方面……"的格式，后面常用副词"又、也、还"等呼应。"一方面"侧重表示并存的两个方面，时间可有先后。"一边……一边、一面……一面"侧重同时进行的两个动作。

The Conjunction 一方面 links two parallel relations or the two aspects of an issue. It is usually used in Prepositional Phrases or clauses, forming the pattern 一方面……（另）一方面……, which often correlated with the Adverbs 又、也 or 还. While the focus of 一方面 is on the two aspects that coexist and may follow a time sequence, 一边……一边 and 一面……一面 emphasize the two actions take place simultaneously.

五、 乐于＋Disyllabic Verb/Polysyllabic Verb Phrase　(to be delighted to Verb)

l-21. 因此，采用信用证支付，既安全又迅速，大多数出口人都<u>乐于</u>接受。

1. 这种运动大多数青少年都<u>乐于</u>参加。

2. 假如贵方对此技术感兴趣，本公司<u>乐于</u>提供有关的资料。

3. 我们将十分<u>乐于</u>见到你们的新产品早日上市。

动词"乐于"表示对做某件事情感到快乐，不单独作谓语，须跟动词性质的双音节或多音节词语作宾语。可与"乐于"配合使用的双音节动词有：

The Verb 乐于 indicates that it is a pleasure to do something. It does not function as a Predicate itself and has to be followed by a disyllabic Verb or Verb Phrase as its Object. The following Verbs are commonly used together with 乐于:

帮助、支持、关心、服务、提供、了解、介绍、说明、解释、回答、讨论、办理、负责、安排、进行、加强、发展、处理、执行、寻找、前往、改进、学习、参加、接受、告知、遵守、合作。

六、 颇＋Monosyllabic Adj./Polysyllabic Verb Phrase （rather; quite; considerably...）

l-24. 信用证的种类<u>颇</u>多，……

　　1. 这艘轮船速度<u>颇</u>快，三天后即可抵达目的港。

　　2. 她设计的服装<u>颇</u>有特色，在时装界也<u>颇</u>有影响。

　　3. 本人对贵方的产品<u>颇</u>感兴趣，但若要立即定购则<u>颇</u>有困难。

　　副词"颇"有"很"的意思，可跟"有一些、有点"连用，使程度稍降。"颇"多用于书面语，可与"颇"配合使用的单音节形容词有：佳、多、大、高、长、远、深、快、新、易、难、贵、硬、紧、急、冷、热、重等。

The Adverb 颇 is similar to 很 and can be tuned down to some extent by using 有一些、有点. It is mostly used in written Chinese to modify monosyllabic Adjectives such as 佳、多、大、高、长、远、深、快、新、易、难、贵、硬、紧、急、冷、热、重.

　　双音节形容词常与"颇为"配合使用，如：

When modifying a disyllabic Adjective, 为 usually goes after 颇. The following are some disyllabic Adjectives commonly used with 颇为:

　　重要、麻烦、清楚、容易、困难、方便、详细、小心、稳定、普遍、有利、安全、危险、客观、有效.

　　"颇"也可以用来修饰多音节词组，如：

颇 can be used to modify polysyllabic phrases also, for example:

颇＋有意义、有影响、有名气、有特色、有道理、有吸引力、有竞争性、感兴趣、具规模、费心思、知内情、负责任等。

七、（Subject 1）一经＋Disyllabic Verb，Subject 2＋Verb Phrase （once Subject 1..., Subject 2＋VP.. ）

l-26. 不可撤销信用证是指信用证<u>一经</u>开出，在有效期内，未经受益人（一般为出口人）或有关当事人的同意，开证行不得片面修改或撤销已开出的信用证。

1. 此药品<u>一经</u>开启，必须立即服用，否则两小时后失效。
2. 合同<u>一经</u>签订，双方都不可反悔。
3. 这个新产品<u>一经</u>试验成功，马上就投入生产。

副词"一经"用于双音节动词前面，强调只要经过某个过程或行动，就会产生相应的效果。主要用在承接复句的前一分句中，后一分句常用"就、便"等呼应。

The Adverb 一经 is placed before a disyllabic Verb to emphasize that there will be some kind of result accordingly once an action is taken or it has undergone certain process. It is primarily used in the first clause of a Successive Complex Sentence, and 就 or 便 are usually used in the second clause.

八、 连同＋Noun Phrase, ＋Verb Phrase （together with...; along with...）

l-37. 托收方式是出口人在装运货物后，先填写托运委托书，开具汇票，然后把委托书和汇票，<u>连同</u>全套货运单据送交出口地托收银行，再通过它在进口地的分行或代理银行，向进口人收取货款。

1. 客户已将使用手册、说明书，<u>连同</u>设计图纸，全部带走了。
2. 美元、英镑、马克、法郎、日元，<u>连同</u>港币，在中国都被视为币值比较稳定的外币。
3. 与我们有业务关系的银行，<u>连同</u>贵行，一共有八家。

介词"连同"表示"包括、算上"的意思，多连接"把"字句的并列宾语，有时后面可跟"一起、一道"等。常用于书面语。

The Preposition 连同 is meant "including; together with". It links up the parallel Objects of the 把 structure and sometimes followed by 一起 or 一道, and is often used in the written language.

九、 除非……，否则……　　（unless..., otherwise...）

l-49. 除非是资信良好的老客户，或者是为了推销有大量库存、亟待处理的滞销商品，<u>否则</u>一般都不会轻易同意使用"承兑交单"这种支付方式。

1. <u>除非</u>你有充分的凭据，<u>否则</u>他不会承认。

2. 对方一定要用托收方式支付。<u>除非</u>我们降价百分之十，<u>否则</u>她不订货。

3. <u>除非</u>出口人同意，开证行<u>才</u>会修改不可撤销信用证，<u>否则</u>不可能片面修改这样的信用证。

连词"除非"强调某条件是唯一的先决条件，相当于"只有"的意思，常跟"才、否则、不然、要不"等配合。注意"除非"和"只有"的区别："除非"有时是从反面强调不能缺少某个唯一条件，语气较重；"只有"是从正面提出某个唯一条件，语气较轻。"除非"可用在"是……"前，如：

除非是你才这样想。

"只有"后一般都不跟"是……"。

The Conjunction 除非 emphasizes that certain condition is the sole prerequisite, and is about the same as 只有 in meaning. It is normally associated with 才、否则、不然、要不, etc. Note the differences between 除非 and 只有: Sometimes 除非 stresses the consequence from the negative side that a specific condition is indispensable, and that the tone is more serious, while 只有 simply states that something is the only condition and the tone is milder. In addition, while it is possible for 除非 to be placed before 是……, such as in: 除非是你才这样想. This is not the case for 只有.

词义辨析

一、 波动　更动　变动

　　"动"字的基本意思之一，就是改变原来的位置或状态，与"静"相对。"波动"是不及物动词，不带宾语，强调事物像水波一样起伏动荡，很不稳定，多用于描述情绪、价格等。"更动"是及物动词，相当于"改、改动"的意思，但一般指较小的改动，如文字、次序、日期等。"变动"既是及物动词，又是不及物动词，可带也可不带宾语。"变动"主要指"改变、变化"的意思，使用范围较广，可用于计划、题目、日期等较小的方面，也可指一些大的社会现象。

One of the basic meanings of 动 is "to change the original position or state". It is the antonym of 静. As an Intransitive Verb, 波动 does not take any Object. It emphasizes the fluctuation or instability such as mood or price, moving up and down like waves. However, 更动 is a Transitive Verb. It is similar to 改 and 改动 in meaning, but normally refers to modification, or minor changes, such as wording, order, or date. 变动 can be both transitive and intransitive, with or without taking an Object. It means "to change, to alter", and is used in wider scope. It can refer to small things such as a plan, topic, and schedule, or more significant social phenomena.

二、 省　节省　免

　　动词"省"的一个意思，是"节约、省俭"，跟"费"字相对。"省"常带宾语或补语，也可受程度副词修饰，如：省钱、省力、省时间、省事、她过日子很省（省得很）。"省"的另一个意思，是"免掉、减去"，例如：

The Verb 省 can mean "to save, be frugal". It is the opposite of the character 费. It usually takes an Object or a Complement, and is possible to be modified by an Adverb of Degree. For example, 省钱、省力、省时间、省事、她过日子很省（省得很）. Another meaning of 省 is "to omit, leave out", as in the following,

这两个字不能<u>省</u>。

这样可以<u>省</u>一道手续。

"节省"表示使可能被耗费的东西尽量少耗费，少花甚至不花。常带宾语或补语，多用在"人力、物力、财力、精力、物质、时间、能源"等方面。

节省 indicates the effort of spending as less as possible, trying to be economical. It usually takes an Object or a Complement, and is often associated with Nouns such as 人力、物力、财力、精力、物质、时间、能源.

"免"有"除掉、去掉"的意思，多与单音节名词组成动宾词组，例如：免费、免票、免税、免礼、免职等。用于主题 - 评论句时，常带助词"了"，如：

免 means "to exempt, relieve, remit", and normally takes a monosyllabic Noun to form a Verb Object Construction as in 免费、免票、免税、免礼、免职, etc. When it is used in a Topic-Comment Sentence, 免 usually goes with 了, for example,

请客的事，我看就免了吧。

另外，"免"还有"避免"的意思，须带宾语，多用于"以免/ 难免/ 免得＋双音节动词或动词短语"的句式，例如：你们还是早一点走好，以免迟到。

In addition, 免 can also mean "避免 (avoid)". It must take an Object and is primarily used in the pattern 以免/难免/免得＋Disyllabic Verb/Verb Phrase, for example,

你们还是早一点走好，以免迟到。

三、待　等待　亟待

动词"待"作"等待、等候"解时，含有"较长时间地等"的意味，一般不单独使用而较多位于副词后双音节动词前，构成像"尚待解决、有待提高、且待分解"等词组，常用于书面语。其主语一般是事物很少是人，只有在文言或戏剧中，有"待我细说"等用法。

When the Verb 待 is interpreted as "wait, await, expect", it has a connotation of "waiting for quite some time". Normally, it is not used alone but usually follows an Adverb and before a disyllabic Verb, forming a phrase such as 尚待解决、有待提高、且待分解, etc. It is mostly used in written Chinese, and its Subjects are things instead of human in general. Only in literary Chinese or opera, things like 待我细说 is heard occasionally.

"等待"表示不采取行动，直到期望的人或事物、情况出现。"等候"除了用于具体的人和事外，还可用于抽象的名词，如"等待时机、等待机会、等待这一伟大时刻的到来"等。

等待 indicates "not taking any actions until the emergence of the person, thing, or situation that is expected". In addition to words referring to specific people or things, it can also be used before abstract nouns such as 等待时机, 等待机会, or 等待这一伟大时刻的到来, etc.

副词"亟"是"急迫地"的意思。与动词"待"结合，就是"急迫地等待"。"亟待"多用于书面语，后面常跟双音节动词，如：亟待解决、亟待调查清楚。

The Adverb 亟 signifies "urgently, anxiously". When it is associated with 待, it means "to wait anxiously". It is used primarily in written Chinese, and is followed by disyllabic verbs such as 亟待解决, 亟待调查清楚.

四、 延长　延期　延续

"延"的基本意思是"拉长、伸长、(往后)推迟"的意思。动词"延长"强调线性或持续性的加长，多用于道路、队伍等条形事物的长度或时间、寿命、活动等的延伸发展，可带宾语。"延期"表示把原定的日期向后推迟，可与其他动词连用，如：

The essential meaning of 延 is "to extend, to stretch, to postpone". The Verb 延长 emphasizes linear or duration prolongation, and is primarily used for the length of things such roads, queues or extension/development of time, life span, activities, etc. It can take an Object. 延期 indicates "to defer, put off, postpone" a date set before. It can go together with other Verbs, for example,

运动会因雨<u>延期</u>。

卖方来电，要求<u>延期</u>三天装船。

交易会<u>延期</u>举行。

"延续"指按照原来的样子继续或延长下去，多用于状态、事件或情况，常带补语但不可带宾语。例如：

延续 refers to the continuation or lasting of a state, event, or situation as it is. It often takes a Complement but not an Object. Here are some examples,

这种情况还会<u>延续</u>下去。

谈判<u>延续</u>了五个多小时。

语法

一、承接复句　Successive Complex Sentences

各个分句按时间顺序，叙述连续的动作或先后方式的事件，这种复句叫承接复句。承接复句的各分句有时可不用关联词语，只靠排列的次序组成。例如：

In a Successive Complex Sentence, each clause describes one action or one event in a series of actions or events, according to the chronological order. Sometimes, the clauses in a Successive Complex Sentence do not need to use any Connectives, simply relying on their sequencing. For example:

他扔下电话，穿上衣服，飞快地跑了出去。

汽车走着走着，忽然"轰"的一声，停在那儿不动了。

但是，更多的时候，承接复句是用以下的关联词语来连接各个分句的：

However, in most of the cases, the following are used to join the clauses in Successive Complex Sentences:

1. 开始/首先/起先

2. 接着/跟着/然后/后来/继而/随后

3. 就/便/才/再/又

4. 一……就……/一经……就……

5. 于是 (乎)

6. 最后/终于

下面是一些使用关联词语的承接复句的例子：

Here are some sentences that use Connectives to link up clauses:

1. 开始很多人都觉得没有什么希望了，后来大家一起想办法，终于
   把船开了回来。

2. 今天我们开会，先请马总经理讲话，然后请刘副经理谈谈亚洲市
   场的情况，最后讨论一下明年的工作计划。

3. 还盘，指的是交易的一方在接到一项发盘以后，不能完全同意发
   盘的条件，但仍有兴趣进行交易，为了进一步洽商，于是针对该
   发盘的内容提出不同的建议。

4. 小梁每天一起床就去跑步。

二、 标点符号(2)标号   Punctuation (II)

汉语的标点符号主要分为两大类：一类叫"点号"，即在第四课介绍
过的句号、问号、叹号、逗号、顿号、分号和冒号；另一类叫"标号"。
常用的标号有引号、括号、破折号、省略号、着重号、连接号、间隔号
和书名号等。

There are two categories of punctuation marks in Chinese. One is called
diǎnhào , namely, those introduced in Lesson Four, including Full Stop, Question
Mark, Exclamation Mark, Comma, Listing Mark, Semicolon, and Colon; the
other category is named **biāohào**, which includes Quotation Marks, Brackets,
Dash, Ellipses, Mark of Emphasis, Linking Mark, Separation Dot, and Punctuation
Mark for the Title of a Book or an Article.

（一）引号 " "　Quotation Marks

引号由前引号和后引号组成。引号标明文中直接引用别人的原话（没有经过任何改动），即所谓的直接引语，为的是把引语和作者自己的话区别开来。转述别人的话，或经过改动、不太确切的，叫"间接引语"，一般不用引号。引用成语、俗语等，可以用也可以不用引号，如例 2。句中需要特别强调或有特殊含义的词语，也要用引号。如例 4：

Quotation Marks consist of two parts, a beginning quote mark and an ending quote mark. Quotation Marks are used to show a passage by others in origin (without any modification) has been cited, that is, a "direct quote". Quotation Marks serve the purpose to distinguish the writer's own words from others. When one reports other's remarks, when one uses quotes with some modification, or when the quote is not very accurate, these are "indirect quotes". Normally, indirect quotes do not require Quotation Marks. As for quoting Idioms, or Common Sayings, it is optional to use or not to use Quotation Marks, just as it is shown in Example 2. Sometimes, when words or phrases that need to be stressed, or they bear some special meaning, Quotation Marks are to be used, as in Example 4.

1. "我又不是你老师，问我干什么？"小华不耐烦地对弟弟说。
2. 这就是俗话所说的"讨价还价"，在进出口业务中，叫做"价格谈判"。
3. 发虚盘时，一般都要加上"以我方最后确认为准"的条件，以避免发生误解和引起不必要的争议或纠纷。
4. 因此，所谓"虚"和"实"都是以发盘人是否明确表示愿意对其发盘承担签订合同的法令责任而言的。

要注意引文末尾标点的使用：如果引用的是一句完整的话，原来的标点不变，句末的标点要放在引号内，如例 1。如果引文是作者自己的话的一部分，引文末尾(即后引号前)不加标点，而应该根据全句(不仅是引文)的需要，在后引号后面加上适当的标点符号，如例 3。一般情况下，都是使用双引号(" ")。如果引语内还要用引号，外面一层用双引号，里面一层用单引号（' '），如例 5：

Note the correct use of punctuation at the end of a quotation: If the quote is a complete sentence, the original punctuation marks in the quote remain unchanged, and the one that appears at the end of the quote should go before the ending Quotation Mark (see Example 1). However, if the quote is part of the writer's own words, no punctuation mark is needed after that quote and right before the ending Quotation Mark. Whatever punctuation is to use after that depends on the circumstance and the need of the entire sentence rather than the quote itself (see Example 3 please). In normal situation, Double Quotation Marks (" ") are used. However, if there is another quote within a quote, Single Quotation Marks (' ') are used for the inside quote and Double Quotation Marks are for the embedding quote. For example:

5. 他笑了笑，说："经理，您不是叫我们'要尽量节省'吗？"

(二) 括号（ ） Parentheses

括号由两部分组成，即前括号和后括号。括号标明文中注释性的话。当括号内的话注释句子中某些词语时，括号连同注释语要紧跟在被注释的词语后面，如例 1。如果括号里的注释语本身有标点，其末尾（即后括号前）的标点要省去，见例 2。

当括号内的话注释整个句子、或对全句作补充说明时，后括号要在被注释的句子之外。如果注释语本身有标点，保持原样，不作改动，如例 3。

Parentheses appear in pairs, with one goes at the front, and one goes in the back. Parentheses mark the interpretative remarks in a text. When the words within Parentheses explain a certain word or phrase in a sentence, the Parentheses, along with the explanation, must follow immediately the word or phrase to be explained as shown in Example 1. If there is punctuation in the explanation, the one appears at the end, that is, the punctuation before the closing Parenthesis should be deleted. This is illustrated in Example 2.

When the remarks within a pair of Parentheses interpret an entire sentence, or when they function as a supplementary explanation, the closing Parenthesis should be placed outside the explanatory remarks. If there are any punctuation marks within those remarks, keep them as they are, as shown in Example 3.

1. 有约束力的发盘 (实盘) 是指发盘人明确地、肯定地表达了签订合同的意图。

2. 贵方寄来的样品 (真丝手帕两款：编号 SP306 和 SP541；全棉绣花桌布三款：编号 ZB107、ZB129 及 ZB188) 均已收到。

3. 十分遗憾，我们至今仍未收到贵方的信用证 (今天已是四月二十八日，离装运期仅五天。) 。请接函后，立即回复并告知信用证何时可开达我方。

(三) 破折号——　Dash

破折号标明行文中注释说明的语句，表示话题的转变 (如例 2) 或声音的延长 (如例 3) 等。破折号和括号的用法不同：破折号引出的解释说明是正文的一部分，不可以省略；括号里的解释说明不是正文，只是解释，省略后不一定影响全句的意思。

Dash marks the annotation in a piece of writing, including the turning of a topic or a prolongation of sound, etc. The use of a Dash differs from the use of Brackets in that a Dash introduces an note, which is part of the main text and cannot be omitted, while remarks within Brackets are explanations or supplements. The latter is not a critical part of the main text, and its omission may not affect the integrity of the meaning of a sentence.

1. 买方在签订合同后，必须遵照合同的规定，如数、按期向有关银行交付货款，然后才能取得货物所有权的凭据——提单。

2. "今天真热啊！——你什么时候回国？"朱明对正在看电视的林文说。

3. "呜——"火车开动了。

4. 根据权限的大小，代理可以分为以下的三种：
   ——总代理；
   ——独家代理；
   ——一般代理。

(四) 省略号…… Ellipsis

省略号标明文中省略了的部分。常见的省略有两种：一是引文的省略 (如例 1)，二是列举的省略 (如例 2)。注意汉语的省略号是六个圆点 (……)，不是英语的三个圆点 (…)。

Ellipsis indicates the omission of certain words or phrases in writing. There are two types of omission in general: one is the omission of quote such as in example 1; the other is the omission of the listed items. Please note that ellipsis in Chinese is six round dots instead of three dots in English.

1. 她轻轻地唱着："大海啊，大海……"
2. 春天来了，公园里的花开了，有红的，有黄的，有白的……

省略号还可以表示说话人因为激动、害怕、或者边说边想，说话时断断续续、吞吞吐吐。如：

Ellipsis can also signify that the speaker hesitates or speaks disjointedly because of excitement, fear, or searching for words in speaking. For instance:

3. "我……我……错了，我……对不起……你们"他流着眼泪说。
4. 那……那好像……好像是……去年八月底的一个晚上。

(五) 着重号 . Mark of Emphasis

着重号标明文中强调的词语，要求读者特别注意。着重号标在所强调的词语下方。例如：

The Mark of Emphasis highlights the words or phrases to be stressed, drawing the attention of readers. It is located beneath the word or phrase to be emphasized. Look at these examples:

1. 修辞是追求最佳表达效果的运用语言的艺术。
2. 事业是干出来的，不是吹出来的。

(六) 连接号— **Linking Mark**

连接号的作用是把意义相关的词语如时间、地点、数目等联系起来。连接号在文中一般占一个字的位置。

The Linking Mark functions to link up words that are relevant in meaning, such as time, place, number, etc. to show the span, range, or scope. A Linking Mark takes up the space of one character in a text.

1. 鲁迅(1881—1936)年，原名周树人，浙江绍兴人。　　（时间）
2. 往返纽约—波士顿的班机每小时都有。　　　　　　（地点）
3. 今天少云，气温23 —27摄氏度。　　　　　　　　（数量幅度）
4. 中国最近向美国订购了五架新型的波音—777客机。（型号）

(七) 间隔号·　**Separation Dot**

间隔号表示某些民族人名中各部分的分界，月份和日期的分界，或书名与篇章之间的分界。例如：

The Separation Dot shows the division of each part of the names of people who are non-Han nationalities, a specific date and the month, or the title of a book and the title of one of its chapters. For instance:

1. 马克·吐温是美国的著名作家。
2. 他们是在五·四青年节的晚会上认识的。
3. 我刚从图书馆借来了这本《中国大百科全书·语言文字》。

(八) 书名号《　》 **Punctuation Mark for the Title of a Book or a Title of an Article**

书名号标明书名、篇名、报刊名等。如果书名号里还有书名号，外面一层用双书名号（《　》），里面一层用单书名号（〈　〉）。例如：

This Punctuation Mark is unique in Chinese, which marks titles of books, chapters, journals, etc. If there is another title within a title, the double marks (《　》) are used for the one that embeds another title, while the single marks (〈　〉) are used for the embedded title.

1. 老师送了一本《汉英词典》给我。

2. 今天我们学了鲁迅的短篇小说《孔乙己》。

3. 这些信息都可以在《人民日报·海外版》上找到。

4. 她经常看中文版的《读者文摘》。

5. 你看过最新一期《〈红楼梦〉研究辑刊》吗？

标号的位置　The Positioning of the Punctuation Marks

引号、括号、书名号的前半部分不出现在一行的末尾，后半部分不出现在一行的开头。破折号和省略号都占两个字的位置，中间不断开。连接号和间隔号一般占一个字的位置。着重号标在汉字的下边。

Quotation Marks, Parentheses, and the Punctuation Marks for the Title of a Book or an Article appear in pairs. Thus the first half of them does not go at the end of a line, and the second half of them does not appear at the beginning of a line. A Dash, and an Ellipsis takes up respectively the space of two characters, and there is no disjunction in between. In general, a Linking Mark, and a Separation Dot occupies one character in space individually. The Mark of Emphasis goes beneath the word or phrase it emphasizes.

修辞

篇章　Composition

篇章，广义上来说，就是指首尾完整的一篇文章。段落（自然段）、段组和意义段都是篇章的构件。

篇章的组织要求前后连贯，条理清楚，完整周密，使整篇文章成为一个有机的统一体，主题得到完满的表现。要达到这些要求，必须处理好下面的几个问题：

In a broad sense, a composition is a complete piece of writing. Paragraphs, groups of paragraphs, and Thematic Sections are all components of a composition.

The organization of a composition requires coherence, clarity and unity, to weave the essay into an organic entity so that the theme can be presented successfully. In order to achieve all these, the following should be handled with care.

一、　叙述角度的问题

为了保证文章前后连贯、意义联系密切、主题集中明确，叙述角度一般应该统一。在表述时必须谨慎确定叙述角度，不宜随意变换。叙述角度包括三方面的内容：一是叙述的着眼点，也就是陈述对象，讲的是谁或什么的问题；二是叙述的立足点，即以什么作为出发点，站在什么时间、什么地点上说话的问题；三是叙述的人称，即以什么身份讲话的问题。

1. Narrative Perspectives

The *narrative perspective* should be, in general, consistent in an essay so that it can maintain focus in its theme, coherence in meaning, and cohesion in organization. Careful consideration must be given to the selection of a *narrative perspective*, which should not be changed arbitrarily. Narrative perspectives include three things: a) who or what is to be about, b)when and where the narrative is made, and c) from what angle the author chooses to write — as the first person, the second person, or the third person.

首先，关于叙述对象问题。就句子来说，句子的主语就是陈述对象——主语不同，陈述对象也不同。但是，段落的陈述对象不完全等于甚至不等于句子的陈述对象，而段组、意义段、整篇文章的陈述对象也互不等同。总的来说，下一重的陈述对象必须服从上一重的。也就是说，句子的陈述对象要服从段落的，段落的要服从段组或意义段的，而意义段的又必须服从全文的。这样才能保证叙述角度的统一，才不致影响文章的前后连贯，影响主题的明确集中。

First of all, it is what topic the composition is to be about. In a sentence, the Subject of the sentence is something the sentence is going to say about, something for the predicate to describe. When the Subject of a sentence changes, the intended topic is switched accordingly. However, the topic of a paragraph is not identical to, sometimes even different from, the Subject of a sentence. The topic of a groups of paragraphs, of a Thematic Section, or of an essay, may differ from one another. In general, the topic of a stratum at a lower level must be in concord with the one at a higher level. In other words, what a sentence is going to talk about must be congruent with the topic of a paragraph, the topic of a paragraph must be consistent with the idea of a Thematic Section, and the idea of a Thematic Section must conform with the theme of the essay. Only in this way can a composition maintain a consistent motif. Only in this way can unity and coherence be achieved.

其次是立足点的问题。在一般情况下，说话者所站的位置是说话的此时此地。但是在追述过去，展现未来或想象中的情景时，则有站在当时的"此时此地"说话，或站在"过去"、"未来"、"想像中"的"彼时彼地"说话的可能。在这种情况下，如果分不清是站在"此时此地"还是"彼时彼地"说话，随意转换立足点，就会影响意思的完整统一。

The second issue is the standing point of narration. In most cases, the time and the place where the speaker is located is considered when and where the narrative is made. However, when one recounts the past, or looks forward to the future, or describes an imagined situation, it is possible for him or her to speak either in the sense of "here and now", that is, at the moment and in the place where the remarks are made, or in the sense of "there and then", namely, in "the past", in "the future" or in an "imagined situation". Under such circumstances, if the writer fails to maintain a consistent foothold, and jumps from standing point to standing point, it is rather difficult to achieve unity and coherence.

第三就是人称，即以什么身份说话的问题。记叙性、议论性的文章，有的用第一人称，有的用第三人称，只有少数文章用第二人称。人称通常是一致的，但有时也可根据需要变换。这种情况在小说、诗歌等文艺作品中比较常见，公文信件、说明文、政论文等则较为罕见。

Thirdly, it concerns what status the writer chooses to use, as the first person, the second person, or the third person. In narrative, or commentary writings, sometimes the first person is used, and sometimes the third person is used. The second person is rarely used. The use of Person in a composition is usually quite consistent, but occasionally there may be some exceptions, depending on the situation. This is more common in novels, poems or other literary works, but it is quite uncommon in official documents, business letters, expositions, or political essays, etc.

二、層次的劃分和安排問題

　　層次是文章的結構單位。整篇文章的層次是意義段，意義段的層次是段落或段組，而段落的層次是句子或句群。層次又是文章內容的表現次序。層次的劃分和安排是貫穿整篇文章的問題：篇章有篇章的層次，意義段有意義段的層次，段落又有段落的層次。

2. The Determination and Arrangement of Strata

　　Strata are structural components of an essay. Thematic Sections are essential strata in a composition, so are paragraphs in a thematic section, and sentences in a paragraph. Strata are also representing sequence of contents in a composition. The determination and arrangement of strata are a matter that concerns the entire essay: there are strata in a composition of its own, so does strata in a Thematic Section of its own, and the same is true to a paragraph.

　　層次的劃分主要有以下的幾種方法：

1. 按時間順序或事物發展的階段來劃分。
2. 按結構空間或事物的組成部分、空間位置來劃分。
3. 按事物的不同側面，如人物的精神品質、材料的不同性質、支持中心論點的不同論據等來劃分。
4. 按事物的整體或部分關係來劃分。

　　The following are common ways to determine strata in writing compositions:

1. Determination according to chronological order or the developmental stages of events.
2. Determination according to the structural space, or the component parts of

objects, or the geographical location.

3. Determination according to the different aspects of things, such as personal characters, various natures of materials, different supporting evidences for the arguments.

4. Determination according to the relation of the part and the whole within an object.

　　层次的划分要正确反映客观事物的内在联系，要科学和讲究逻辑。注意不要把本来属于同一层次的内容硬拆成两层，也不要互相插乱，把不同层次的内容混在同一个层次里。

The determination of strata should reflect accurately the mutual relations among factors within things. It should be scientific and logical. We must be cautious not to separate ideas that belong to the same stratum from each other and put them arbitrarily into different strata, and not randomly blend ideas that belong to different stratum into one paragraph or one part.

　　层次的安排是要解决把哪个层次放在什么位置才恰当的问题：哪个层次先说，哪个层次后说，怎样才能做到条理清楚，层次分明。例如按时间顺序叙述，一般时间在先的先说，时间在后的后说。但有时为了需要，也可用倒叙、插叙等方法。又如按结构空间或事物的不同侧面叙述或论说，既可由近而远，由表及里，又可由远而近，由里及外。论说文可以由主及次，由论点到论据，或者反过来，由次及主，由论据再到论点等等。事务文体的公文、信件，多数都有一定的惯用格式。不管哪种方法，层次的安排都要根据文体的要求和客观事物的内在联系来确定，才能有效地把意思表达清楚。

The arrangement of strata deals with the problem how to place the right stratum in its own position. That is: which part should be mentioned first, which one goes next, how to make it properly-organized with unity and coherence. For example, if things are arranged according to chronological order in an essay, in general, whatever happens first is to be mentioned first, and whatever happened later is to be mentioned next. However, writing techniques such as flashback, or narration interspersed with flashback may be used occasionally when it is necessary. Likewise, when discussing or arguing in accordance with the structural space or different aspects of things, it is possible to proceed from outward to inward, from immediateness to remoteness gradually, or vice versa. As for expository writing, reasoning can be either inductive or deductive. Arguments can be presented from less significant to more significant, or conversely, from the most important points to the least important argument. Official documents, business letters usually have their own formats or conventions, which are pretty consistent. Regardless of what way is used, the arrangement of strata and the organization of ideas must be determined by the due requirements of the particular style as well as the inter-relations among factors involved in the particular matter or object. Only in this way, ideas can be presented effectively and clearly.

三、 衔接问题

　　衔接是把文章的各部件连接成为有机的统一体的方法。衔接包括段落、意义段内部的连接，段落与段落、意义段与意义段的之间的连接。

3. The Linkage

The Linkage tries to synthesize all parts of a composition into an organic entirety. It includes connections within a paragraph, or a Thematic Section, and connections between paragraphs, and between Thematic Sections.

　　连接从所接的语义范围来说，可分为总体衔接和局部衔接。总体衔接涉及所连接单位的全部语义；局部衔接只涉及所连接单位的部分语义。局部衔接大多是上下句子、句群，或紧邻的段落、意义段之间的衔接。当衔接的语义包含了上下层次的全部内容时，就是总体衔接。

The Linkage can be divided into *holistic linkage and partial linkage* in terms of the scope of ideas to be connected. While *holistic linkage* involves all the ideas in each part of the essay, *partial linkage* involves specific ideas related to a part of an essay. *Partial linkage* usually connects adjacent sentences, groups of sentences, or links up paragraphs, and Thematic Sections next to each other. When linkages deals with the joining of all contents across a higher and a lower stratum, it is *holistic linkage*.

衡接从所接语义关系的性质来说，可分为顺接和逆接。顺接就是所连接的单位，后面的意思顺着前面的意思说；逆接就是后面的单位不顺着前面的意思说，而是朝着相反的方向或转向其他的方面说。这种情况大致与句子之间的"转折"关系相同，差别只是在段落或意义段之间更大的范围而已。

Linkage may be considered as *regular linkage* and *inverse linkage* in terms of the relations of ideas between the parts involved. By *regular linkage*, it is meant that the idea of the unit to be connected goes along in the same direction with the ideas of its previous parts. *Inverse linkage*, conversely, connects a part of text the idea of which takes an opposite direction, or diverts from the original arguments in the previous sections of the essay. Such linkage, by and large, is similar to an Adversative Complex Sentence in relation between its clauses. The only difference is that *inverse linkage* involves a larger part of an essay; connecting paragraphs or Thematic Sections.

从位置上来说，衡接又可分为交接和呼应。交接用于上下两个层次紧邻交界之处，呼应则用于前后层次非紧邻连接的地方。

Linkage may be labeled as joining or echoing, depending on the position where the connection actually is. Joining is usually used in the boundary between two strata whereas echoing is used to connect elements that are not adjacent in a text.

从方式来说，衡接主要有意合和关联两种。意合就是相关的结构单位靠语义关系自然组合，没有用另外的语言手段把它们衡接起来。关联就是用关联词语把段落或意义段连结起来，其用法基本上与各种复句表述的逻辑关系相近或者相同。除了关联词语外，同义词、近义词或重复相同的词语或句子，以及各种辞格，也都可以作为衡接的手段。

Association in meaning and conjunction are the two dominant ways of linkage. Association in meaning refers to the relevant parts in an essay that cohere together simply by ideas, without using any linguistic mechanism. Conjunction, as its name suggests, relies on Connectives to link up paragraphs or Thematic Sections, which is similar to the ways that clauses are joined in

Complex Sentences. In addition to correlatives, the use of synonyms, or the use of repetition of the same word, phrase, or sentence, and the application of various methods in Chinese rhetoric（辞格）, can achieve the same purpose.

四、 照应问题

　　照应是使篇章完整周密的重要方法。凡是前面提到的，后面应有着落；后面写的，前面应有交待。这样前后互相呼应，就容易取得平衡。不然的话，前面提到的，后面没有着落，就不完整。比如，前面说一共有四点，可是要是只说了两点就没有下文了，所提的"四点"有两点就是多余的。相反，如果后面写到的而前面却没有必要的交待，就会令人觉得突然，不好理解。除了注意内容上的前后照应外，还要注意风格、语体上的协调。比如事务语体的文章，要求庄重严肃，一般不用口语词汇，更不用方言俚语，不用排比、设问等句式，也不用比喻、拟人等辞格。

4. Coalescence

　　Coalescence is critical to the completion and thoroughness of a composition. Whatever has been mentioned previously, there must be a follow-up; whatever is to be elaborated later in an essay, a foreshadowing needs to be provided. In this way, an essay is well organized and there is coherence among parts. Otherwise, the essay will be incomplete in contents. For instance, if four items have been mentioned at the beginning, yet only two of them are presented. The remaining two will be superfluous. On the contrary, if no necessary introduction is given first but later, the same idea is to be presented somewhere in the text, its occurrence then may startle readers and may cause difficulty for comprehension. In addition to contents, attention must be paid to the consistence of style and genre also. For example, business writing is usually formal and serious, colloquial words are seldom used, let alone slang and vulgarisms. Some sentence types such as parallelism and rhetorical questions are nor used either, nor are some writing techniques such as metaphor or personification.

练习

一、 用线将意思相同的词和词语连起来：

一个一个地发给   开汇票

一家人分开生活，不住在一起   人民币

不是一次，而是在不同时间把钱付完   预付

把运输的费用交给某人   汇款

给现钱，不是用支票或其他手段付款   纸币

交给银行寄发   预购

不是本国自己发行使用的钱   分期付款

中国法定的货币   交付运费

由国家银行或政府指定银行发行的纸制货币   外币

通过银行或邮局寄钱   付邮

卖方给买方发出的书面命令，要求在指定时间

交付一定的金额   用现金支付

事情发生或进行之前   预计

没有收到货物以前就付款   分居

预先订货或购买   分发

事情发生前计算、计划或推测   预先

二、 用括号里的词或词组改写下列句子，但不改变其基本意思，必要时可对词序作一定的调整：

1. 根据贵方来信的指示，还没有兑换的外币，都已存入银行了。

   （遵照；未）

2. 和本国的公司比较起来，我们更愿意与外国公司合作。

   （相对……而言；乐于）

3. 学校接受了全体老师和学生的要求，在图书馆安装了的电子设备，现在带书包进出图书馆都不用检查了。（应……要求；免）

4. 近年来，人民币与美元的兑换率都相当稳定，没有出现大幅度的升
   降。　　　　　　　　　　　　　　　　　　　　（颇为；波动）

5. 承兑交单是一种风险较大的支付方式，因为汇票一承兑以后，买方
   即可取得代表货物所有权的货运单据，所以在进出口业务中较为少
   用。　　　　　　　　　　　　　　　　　　（一经……就；罕）

6. 四月已到，急着要交个人所得税，请将本人的存款，还有利息，电
   汇到以下的地址。　　　　　　　　　　　　　　（亟待；连同）

7. 只有出现特殊情况，她才会这样做，要不然她不会随便地把她的信
   用卡号码告诉别人。　　　　　　　　（除非……否则……；轻易）

8. 这件事请进口地的东方银行代替办理比较好，一来他们可以与进口
   商直接联系，二来这家银行跟我们有多年的业务关系，非常可靠。
   　　　　　　　　　　　　　　（委托；一方面……另一方面……）

三、 选择最合适的词填空：

1. 该轮的启航日期如有什么＿＿＿＿＿＿，请来电告知。
   a. 波动　　　　　b. 更动　　　　　c. 变动

2. 老师说这封信写得不错，她只＿＿＿＿＿＿了几个词句。
   a. 波动　　　　　b. 更动　　　　　c. 变动

3. 上个星期日元和美元的兑换率＿＿＿＿＿＿得很厉害。
   a. 波动　　　　　b. 更动　　　　　c. 变动

4. 在正式的商业信函里，这几个字不能＿＿＿＿＿＿。
   a. 省　　　　　　b. 节省　　　　　c. 免

5. 很多人出国的时候都喜欢去＿＿＿＿＿＿税商店买些东西。
   a. 省　　　　　　b. 节省　　　　　c. 免

6. 我厂生产的再生包装材料可以帮助贵方_____大量的资金，并且有利于环境保护。

   a. 省　　　　　b. 节省　　　　　c. 免

7. 这次事故的原因还有_____查明。

   a. 待　　　　　c. 等待　　　　　d. 亟待

8. 她耐心地_____，终于把这批库存的滞销产品卖出去了。

   a. 待　　　　　c. 等待　　　　　d. 亟待

9. 明天就是交货期了，可是这批货还在仓库里，_____组织装运。

   a. 待　　　　　c. 等待　　　　　d. 亟待

10. 最近，汽油的价格一直在下跌，这种情况可能还会_____两周左右。

   a. 延长　　　　　b. 延期　　　　　c. 延续

11. 请通知大家，原定在星期六举行的毕业晚会因雨_____。

   a. 延长　　　　　b. 延期　　　　　c. 延续

12. 这次展览十分成功。因为有很多人还没有参观，最后只好再_____三天。

   a. 延长　　　　　b. 延期　　　　　c. 延续

四、 找出本课和第二、第八课课文中所有的承接复句。

五、 根据下面的示意图，用承接复句叙述"信用证支付的一般程序"。

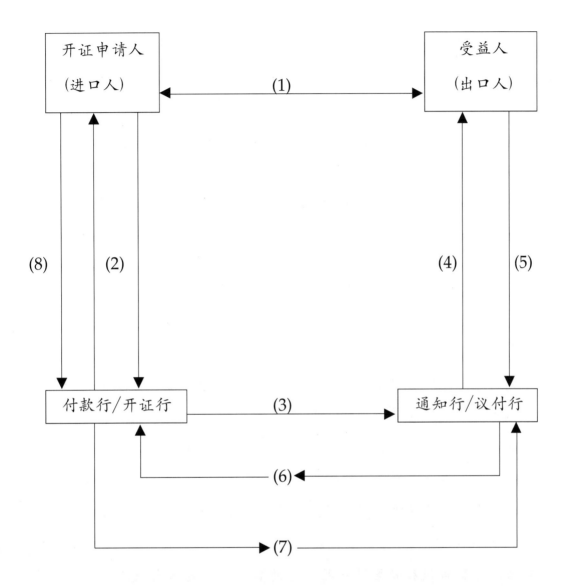

(1) 进出口人在贸易合同中，规定采用信用证方式支付。

(2) 进口人向当地银行提出申请，填写开证申请书，依照合同填写各项规定和要求，并交纳押金或提出其他保证，请银行(开证行)开证。

(3) 开证行根据申请书内容，向出口人(受益人)开出信用证，并寄交出口人所在地银行、分行或代理行(统称通知行)。

(4) 通知行核对印鉴无误后，将信用证交给出口人。

(5) 出口人审核信用证与合同相符后，按信用证规定装运货物，并备齐各项货运单据，开出汇票，在信用证有效期内，送请当地银行(议付行)议付。

(6) 议付行按信用证条款审核单据无误后，按照汇票金额扣除利息，把货款垫付给出口人，同时将汇票和货运单据寄开证行(或其指定的付款行)索偿。

(7) 开证行(或其指定的付款行)核对单据无误后，付款给付款行。

(8) 开证行通知进口人付款，进口人付款赎单。

六、 在适当的地方给下面的句子加上正确的标点符号：

1. 一九四九年后　中国建立了独立自主的商品检验机构　中华人民共和国商品检验局简称　商检局

2. 列入我国　现行实施检验商品种类表　内的出口商品　主要是传统的大宗商品　质量不稳定和影响人畜健康的商品

3. 我国除对进出口商品实施法定检验外　商品检验局还接受办理对外贸关系人　买方卖方　承运人　托运人或保险人　申请的其他鉴定工作

4. 他也有　汉英词典　可是用得不多　因为他有一本　活字典　他的中国女朋友

5. 清凉　牌电风扇是名牌产品　它的名气确实是吹出来的

七、 根据本课修辞部分关于"篇章"的说明，回答下面的问题：

1. 第九课全文的陈述对象是什么？第二、第三个段落(自然段)的陈述对象又是什么？

2. 第八课第二、第四个段落(自然段)的陈述对象是什么？为什么第十四五行、第二十一行的句子都用了被动句？它们的陈述对象又是什么？

3. 这两课的立足点在哪儿？也就是说作者是站在什么位置上说话的？这两课用的是第几人称？

4. 第九课的层次是按什么安排的？第二课呢？

5. 第九课各段落或意义段之间的衔接是顺接还是逆接？第七课的第一、第二个段落（自然段）之间呢？

6. 第九课从第十五行起一直到末尾，各段落和意义段之间是怎样衔接的？是意合还是关联？第二、第三个段落（自然段）之间呢？

八、 把下列句子翻译成汉语：

1. At the invitation of the U.S government, the Chinese Economic and Business [i.e. "trade"] Delegation will visit the United States next month. On the one hand, the two parties are pleased to witness the development of economic exchanges between China and the U.S. in recent years; on the other hand, the delegation is going to negotiate with the U.S. officials on some important issues concerning trade and tariff which demand prompt solutions.

2. Relative to other foreign currencies, U.S. dollar is considerably stable. Although the money [i.e. "financial"]market often fluctuates, it is seldom to see U.S. dollar devalue to a large extent. Unless there occurs huge problems in the U.S. economy; otherwise, the U.S. dollar will remain very reliable. Therefore, I never exchange a large sum of U.S. dollars with Japanese Yen rashly. I don't want to take the risk.

3. Sea Star Company asked [i.e. "entrust"] us to receive the payment of their commodities. Following the instructions of our client, after the buyer makes the payment for the goods, you should give him/her the Bill of Lading, along with other relevant documents, once you have checked [i.e. "undergone the process of checking"] and (found) no error. Then, deduct the service charge and send the money to the seller by Telegraphic Transfer.

九、 商业信函练习五

　　按照中文传统式商业信函的格式，以进口商马虎的名义，给出口商胡图写一封信，要求延期付款。内容必须包括下列几点：

1. 说明具体的是哪一笔交易，包括合同号、订单号、什么货物、货款总额、汇票号码及承兑日期 (即进口商<u>马虎</u>本来应该在哪一天按照哪个合同的规定付给出口商<u>胡图</u>多少钱)。

2. 找一个容易让人相信同时又容易令人同情的理由，说明没有办法按期承兑汇票，请求出口商同意延期 30 天付款。

3. 对这件事情深表遗憾，希望对方谅解。请对方尽快回复 (说明是否同意)，并感谢对方的帮助。

文化与商贸背景知识

✎ 中国银行简介

中国银行是国家指定的外汇专业银行，其主要任务包括：办理一切贸易和非贸易外汇的国际结算；办理国际银行之间的存款和进出口贸易的信贷；经营外币存款和外汇人民币的存款业务；办理华侨汇款和国际汇兑；经营外汇，包括黄金买卖以及一切国际银行业务。

中国银行的总行设在北京，在国内各城市、口岸设有上百个分行，并在国外的新加坡、香港、东京、纽约、旧金山、洛杉矶、多伦多、伦敦、卢森堡等地开设了分行。中国银行已经同全世界一百五十多个国家和地区的一千多家银行建立了业务关系。根据英国《银行家》杂志 1997 年公布的排名，在全世界一千多家大银行中，以核心资本计算，中国银行名列第十五位；以总资产计算，中国银行名列世界第二十四位。

✎ 汇票

(一) 汇票的含义

汇票是由一方开给另一方的无条件的书面支付命令，要求对方立即或在一定时间内支付一定金额给某人或其指定的人。

汇票的当事人有：

1. 出票人(Drawer)——即签发汇票的人，在进出口业务中，通常是出口人或出口地银行。

2. 受票人(Drawee)——即汇票的付款人，在进出口业务中，通常是进口人或其指定的银行。

3. 受款人(Payee)——即领汇票所规定金额的人，在进出口业务中，通常是出口人本人或其指定的银行。

(二) 汇票的种类

汇票主要可分为以下几种：

1. 光票 (Clean Bill) 和跟单汇票 (Documentary Bill)——出票人开出的汇票没有附带任何货运单据，称为光票；相反，如果开出的汇票附有货运单据(如提单、发票、保险单) 等，称为跟单汇票。国际贸易中的汇票大多数是跟单汇票。

2. 即期汇票 (Sight Bill) 和远期汇票 (Time Bill)——汇票上规定收到汇票后立即付款 (见票即付) (Pay ...at sight) 是即期汇票。反之，如果汇票上规定在将来的一定日期付款的，是远期汇票。远期汇票一般有三种：

甲、付款人见票后若干天付款，如30天、60天、90天、120天等 (At ... days sight)；

乙、出票和若干天付款 (At...days after date of draft)；

丙、指定的日期付款或指定在提单签发后若干天付款 (At ...days after date of B/L)。

✏ **商业信函**(5)

香港乐延有限公司：

<u>我方××××年3月6日第97号合同</u>

按上述合同规定：这些货物分批装运，我方应在4月30日前装运全部货物的半数，其余的将在5月内装运；同时，贵方的不可撤销即期信用证亦应于4月15日前开达我方。

目前，我方第一批货物已经备妥，亟待装船。然而，十分遗憾，贵方有关信用证至今仍未开到，以致我方难以按计划如期组织装运。根据船期消息，如果贵方能在本月25日前将信用证开达我方，我们将尽力合作，如期装运该货物总数的百分之五十。希接函后从速办理，以便我方能按时交货。这样对于双方顺利履行合同以及今后的合作都是有利的。我们相信贵方定能在近日内将信用证办妥。

亟盼早日回复。

美国大同实业公司

××××年4月18日

✏ **汇票、信用证**

F 14

凭
Drawn under

信用证或购买证第
L/C or A/P No.

日期
dated

付
By drawer

号
凭

急

年 月 日
年 月 日

按
Payable with interest @ ____ % ____

号码
No.

汇票全额
Exchange for

见票
At ____ sight of this FIRST of Exchange (Second of exchange being unpaid)

中国, 广州, Kwangchow, China.

年 月 日 197

后（本汇票之副本未付）付

或其指定人

pay to the order of

金额
the sum of

此致
To

No. 汇票号

Exchange for USD 小写金额

At 到期日：填入时间 sight of this **Second** of Exchange

(**First** of the same tenor and date unpaid), pay to the Order of 受款人：填入付款行，e.g. Bank of China, Head office the sum of

US DOLLARS 大写金额 Only

Drawn under 开证行名称 L/C No. ------ DATED ----（开证日期）.

To 付款行（开证行）名称及地址

BeiJing Aug. 22, 1997 开证日期及出票地

东方科学仪器进出口公司

THE ORIENTAL SCIENTIFIC INSTRUMENTS
IMPORT AND EXPORT CORPORATION

出票人手签

Authorized Signature

中国工商银行
THE INDUSTRIAL AND COMMERCIAL BANK OF CHINA

OFFICE: BEIJING MUNICIPAL BRANCH
ADDRESS:

TELEX: 22752/22847
SWIFT: TEL:3479734
FAX:

信用证通知书
Notification of Documentary Credit

7 日 1 月 1997年
DAY--MONTH--YEAR

To: 致: THE ORIENTAL SCIENTIFIC INSTRUMENTS I/E CORP.	WHEN CORRESPONDING PLEASE QUOTE OUR REF.NO 如有接洽，请注明我行编号	T9701009

Issuing Bank 开证行 KRUNG THAI BANK PUBLIC COMPANY LTD. BANGKOK	Transmitted to us through 转递行

L/C No.信用证号 A139710002	Dated 开证日期 97/01/03	Amount 金额 USD28,998.00

Shipment Date 装期	Expiry date 效期	Charges 费用 ☒ 受益人 ☐ 申请人 ☐

Dear Sirs, 迳启者:
We have pleasure in advising you that we have received from the a/m bank a(n)
兹通知贵司，我行收自上述银行

(X)telex/swift issuing 电传开立   ( )uneffective   未生效

( )pre—advising of 预先通知   ( )mail confirmation of 证实书

(X)original 正本   ( )duplicate   副本

letter of credit, contents of which are as per attached sheet(s).

This advice and the attached sheet(s) must accompany the relative documents when presented for negotiation.
信用证一份，现随附通知，贵司交单时，请将本通知书及信用证一并提示。
(X)Please note that this advice does not constitute our confirmation of the above L/C nor
does it convey any engagement or obligation on our part.
本通知书不构成我行对此信用证之保兑及其它任何责任。
( )Please note that we have added our confirmation to the above L/C, negotiation is
restricted to ourselves only.
上述信用证已由我行加具保兑，并限向我行交单。

Remarks: 备注 :

This L/C consists of   sheet(s), including the covering letter and attachment(s).
本信用证连同面函及附件共   页。
If you find any terms and conditions in the L/C which you are unable to comply with and / or any
error(s), it is suggested that you contact applicant directly for necessary amendment(s) so as
to avoid any difficulties which may arise when documents are presented.
如本信用证中有无法办到的条款及 / 或错误，请迳与开证申请人联系
进行必要的修改，以排除交单时可能发生的问题。

Yours faithfully,
For THE INDUSTRIAL AND COMMERCIAL
BANK OF CHINA
中 国 工 商 银 行

中国工商银行
THE INDUSTRIAL AND·COMMERCIAL BANK OF CHINA   ①

OFFICE:BEIJING MUNICIPAL BRANCH
ADDRESS:

TELEX: 22752/22847
SWIFT: 修 改 通 知 书
TEL:3479734   Notification of Amendment   3 日   2 月1997年
FAX: DAY--MONTH--YEAR

To: 致 : · THE ORIENTAL SCIENTIFIC INSTRUMENTS I/E CORP.	WHEN CORRESPONDING PLEASE QUOTE OUR REF.NO 如有接洽，请注明我行编号 → T9701009-1
Issuing Bank 开证行 KRUNG THAI PUBLIC COMPANY LTD.,BANGKOK	Transmitted to us through 转递行
L/C No. 信用证号 A139710002	Amendment No. 修改次数 1
L/C dated 开证日期 97/01/03	Amendment dated 修改日期 97/01/17

Dear Sirs, 迳启者

We have pleasure in advising you that we have received from the a/m bank a(n)
兹 通 知 贵 司，我 行 自 上 述 银 行 收 到 一 份
(X) telex/swift of   电修改   ( ) uneffective   未生效的修改
(X) original   正本修改   ( ) duplicate   副本修改

amendment to the captioned L/C, contents of which are as per attached sheet(s).
内 容 见 附 件
This amendment should be attached to the captioned L/C advised by us,otherwise, the beneficiary
will be responsible for any consequences arising therefrom.
本修改须附于有关信用证，否则，贵公司须对因此而产生的后果承担责任。
If you don't raise an objection within 7   working days the amendment will be considered to be accepted.
如贵司在   个工作日内不提出异议，将视为接受此修改。

Remarks:备注:

This amendment consists of   sheet(s),including the covering letter and attachments.
本 修 改 连 同 面 函 及 附 件 共   页 。

Yours faithfully,
For THE INDUSTRIAL AND COMMERCIAL
BANK OF CHINA
中 国 工 商 银 行

致: **交通银行**
TO: **BANK OF COMMUNICATIONS**

不可撤销信用证申请书 APPLICATION FOR IRREVOCABLE DOCUMENTARY CREDIT	信用证号码 Credit Number	日期 Date

請貴行用 Please establish　□ by airmail　□ by brief cable　□ by full cable/swift （ 如開証金額超過美元十萬或等價其他貨幣，請貴行以詳電開發此信用証）	按照下述項目開發不可撤銷信用証 : an irrevocable Credit as follows: (If amount of Credit is over USD100,000.00 or its equivalent value ,please establish the Credit by full cable/swift)

開証申請人 Applicant(名稱及地址　name and address)	受益人 Beneficiary(名稱及地址　name and address)

通知行(如未經填寫則可由貴行選擇) Advising Bank (If left in blank, any correspondent at your option)	金額 Amount(小寫及大寫　In figures and words)

准許/禁止分批裝運 Partial shipments　□ allowed　□ not allowed	有效期限 Expiry Date in the beneficiary's country :

货物由 Shipment/dispatch/taking in charge from/at :

運至 for transportation to :

不得運於 not later than

以貴行/貴行之代理行爲付款人之　　　即期匯票　　　天期匯票
Draft (s) to be drawn on you/your correspondent　□ at sight　□ at( ) day(s) after sight

按發票價值全額付下列單據(除特別註明外，單據一式最少爲二份)，提交我公司支款
for full invoice value of goods accompanied by the following documents (at least in duplicate unless otherwise specified) to be surrendered to me/us against payment.

經簽署發票
■ Signed commercial invoice

運輸單據
■ Transport documents:

海運 (港至港) Shipment to be effected by Sea from Port to Port:

全套潔淨 "已裝船"海運提單作成　　貴行抬頭/空白抬頭，並由發貨人空白背書註明 "運費付訖/運費待付"並通知開証申請人
□ Full set of clean "On Board" ocean Bills of Lading made out to your order / to order and endorsed in blank by the shipper marked "Freight" Prepaid / to Collect" and notify Applicant
　准許/禁止 轉運　Transhipment　□ allowed　　　　□ not allowed

複合運送 (至少包括兩種不同運送方式) Shipment to be effected by Multimodal transport (At least two different modes of transport):

全套一式三份 "已裝載"複合運送單據作成　　貴行抬頭/空白抬頭，並由發貨人空白背書註明 "運費付訖/運費待付"並通知開証申請人
□ Full set 3/3 of clean "On Board"Multimodal transport document made out to your order / to order and endorsed in blank by the shipper marked "Freight Prepaid / to Collect" and notify Applicant
　准許轉運　Transhipment allowed

航空運送 Shipment to be effected by Air:

潔淨空運提單以　　貴行/開証申請人爲收貨人，註明 "運費付訖/運費待付"及通知開証申請人，並列明飛行班次，信用証號碼及實際發貨日期
□ Clean Air Waybill consigned to your Bank / Applicant marked "Freight Prepaid / to Collect" notify Applicant indicating flight number , L/C number and actual dispatch date
　准許轉運　Transhipment allowed

鐵路運送 Shipment to be effected by Railway:

全套潔淨正本鐵路運送單據以　　貴行/開証申請人爲收貨人，註明 "運費付訖/運費待付"並通知開証申請人
□ Full set clean Original Railway Cargo Receipt consigned to your Bank / Applicant marked "Freight Prepaid / to Collect" and notify Applicant
　准許轉運　Transhipment allowed

本地交貨 Local Delivery:

開証申請人簽出及手筆之貨物收據，証明以　　貴行信託人身份已收妥實證正常良好之貨物，並註明信用証號碼，貨物總金額，數量及收貨日期，貨物收據上之開証申請人簽章署與預留　貴行的印鑑相符
□ Cargo Receipt issued and manually signed by the Authorized signatory of Applicant whose signature(s) must comply with that shown in your files showing this L/C number ,total value,quantity and date of receipt of goods and certifying that the goods have been received in good order and condition and in trust for Bank of Communications,Hong Kong.

保險單/保險證由投保人空白背書最少按110%CIF價值投保下列各險:
□ Insurance policy or Certificate for at least 110% of CIF value endorsed in blank by the assured and covering:

　一切險/水漬險/平安險,戰爭險及/或陸上運輸險(此項保險只適用於由國內至香港運輸)
□ All Risks / W.A / F.P.A. War Risks & / or Overland Transportation Risks / Overland Transportation All Risks as per Ocean Marine Cargo Clauses and Ocean Marine Cargo War Risk Clause of PICC / Overland Transportation Cargo Insurance Clauses(Train,Trucks) of PICC (For shipment to be effected from China to Hong Kong only)

　按協會貨運險條款的一切險/水漬險/平安險/航空險，戰爭險，罷工暴動險
□ Institute cargo clauses (A / B / C / Air),Institute War Clauses and Institute Strike Clauses

　其他保險　　　　延續火險 (適用於國內至香港運輸)　　　　裝運中失險 (適用於貨柜運輸)
□ Additional Risks:　□ F.R.E.C. (For shipment to be effected from China to Hong Kong)　□ J.W.O.B. (In case shipment effected by container)
　　　　　　　　　　□ _____

保險單/保險證需註明可在目的地以匯票貨幣索賠
showing claims payable at destination in the same currency as the draft.
請代訂保險投保下列各險:
□ Please cover insurance on our behalf. Risk covered:_____

（請翻後頁 Please turn over..........）

This Credit is subject to the Uniform Customs and Practice for Documentary Credits (1993 Revision),International Chamber of Commerce Publication No.500

☐ 裝箱單 Packing List ☐ 重量單 Weight List

☐ 由 發出及簽署之產地來源証
Certificate of Origin issued and signed by ____________________

☐ 由 發出及簽署之質量及數量証
Certificate of Quality and Quantity issued and signed by____________________

☐ 信用証受益人出具之証明書確認於裝運日後 天內/裝運日前最少 天前已將裝運資料以電報/傳真通知開証申請人
Beneficiary's certificate certifying that shipment details have been advised to applicant by telex / fax within________day(s) after shipment / at least________day(s) before shipment.

☐ 信用証受益人出具之証明書，証明全套單據副本，已以傳真/速遞/快郵/掛號航寄形式，於裝運日後 天內送交開証申請人，並附有關速遞/郵寄收據
Beneficiary's certificate certifying that one set of N/N shipping documents have been sent to Applicant by Fax / DHL / Speed Post / Registered Airmail within________day(s) after shipment and the relative DHL / Postal receipt must be attached thereto.

☐

☒ 信用証受益人致開証銀行之証明書，証明其已接受和 / 或拒絕接受此信用証項下之修改書，並引述有關之修改書號碼，如此信用証從未作出修改，則受益人無需提示此証明書（我公司茲確認此証明書將由貴行保留，不論受益人提交與否，或其提交之証書是否符合信用証要求，將不構成此信用証項下之不符點）
Beneficiary's certificate addressed to Issuing Bank confirming their acceptance and/or non-acceptance of all the amendments made under this Credit quoting the relevant amendment number(s).If this Credit has not been amended ,such Certificate is not required.(We hereby confirm that this Certificate is to be retained by you and whether the Beneficiary presents this Certificate or whether the Certificate presented comply with the terms of this Credit does not form a discrepancy between the documents received by you and those called for by this Credit)

証明裝運/付貨 Evidencing Shipment / Delivery of:

貿易條件CIF / CFR / FOB / LOCAL DELIVERY

其它條款Other terms &conditions:

☐ 貨物提單上註明以貨柜裝載運送
Shipment must be effected in container and Bills of Lading to be so certified.

☐ 保險由最終買家投保
Insurance to be covered by Final Buyer.

☐ 本証金額及貨量 Credit amount and shipment quantity ☐ 以單項目計 for each item 准增減 _____% more or less acceptable

☐ 單據需於裝運日後 天內及信用証有效期內作出提示
Documents must be presented within________day(s)after the date of shipment / delivery but within the validity of the Credit.

☒ 代理行費用包括償付行費用由受益人付，如受益人拒付，則由我公司負責
All your correspondent's charges including Reimbursing Bank charges are for account of Beneficiary,if refused,are for our account.

☐ 其它之條款/單據如附頁，並作爲此信用申請書不可分割的一部
Other terms and conditions/documents as per attached sheet(s) which form an integral part of this Application.

We hereby authorize you to debit our account for whatever money(s) payable to you under this transaction.It is understood that this Application and the opening by you of this Letter of Credit shall be subject in all respects to the terms and conditions contained in the General Security Agreement signed by us.	FOR BANK USE ONLY
	Receiving Date
	Signature Verified By
申請開証人簽章 Signature of Applicant	Terms Checked By
	Approved By
	Prepared By
Tel No. A/C No. Contact Person:	Remark

（本申請書中文英文內容如有差異，以英文爲準）

This Credit is subject to the Uniform Customs and Practice for Documentary Credits (1993 Revision),International Chamber of Commerce Publication No.500

B90 500 x 100 x 1 94.5am.

新华信托储蓄商业银行香港分行

SIN HUA TRUST, SAVINGS & COMMERCIAL BANK, LTD.

INCORPORATED IN CHINA

HONG KONG BRANCH

信 开 OPENED BY MAIL

追加行编号	U
日期19 年 月 日	

致
To Bank of China,
    Peking

日期
Date 9th Nov., 1978.

迳启者
Dear Sirs,

兹开立不得撤销商业信用证 第
We hereby open our Irrevocable Commercial Letter of Credit No. 2083348

受益人
in favour of China National Chemicals I/E Corp., Peking Branch.

开证人
for account of 远仪 Far East Scientific Co.,

汇票金额不得超过
up to an aggregate amount of HK$33,300.—

金额大写
(say) Hong Kong Dollars Thirty Three Thousand and Three Hundred Only. — — — —

— — — — — — — — — — — — — — — — — — —

按 凡装足下列出口货物之发票金额计算
for 100 % of the invoice value relative to the shipment of,

Sulphuric Acid   3,000 Bottles.   @HK$11.10

2500 ml

As per Contract No. 78AP-30.

由 你地
from your port

运亚 香港
to Hong Kong

价格为
CIF Hong Kong

受益人所出之   日期汇票以我行为付款人并附具下列注有"X"标记之单据,
Draft(s) to be drawn at 90 days sight on our bank & accompanied by the following documents, marked "X",

☒ 在签发票一式二份的
    Signed Commercial Invoice in duplicate

☒ 保险单或保险凭证按发票金额加
    Insurance Policy or Certificate for full invoice value plus 10 % 保受下列各险,
                                                            % covering,

     ☐ 全险/基本险/综合险及战争险
        TLO/WA/ALL Risks and War Risks

     ☒ 陆上运输险
        Overland Transportation Risks All Risks & Breakage,

     ☐

☐ 全套洁净"巳装运"海运提单作成我行抬头
    Full set of clean "On Board" ocean Bills of Lading made out to our order
    注明运费付讫通知开证人
    marked freight prepaid notify accountee

☒ 全套运输行所出货物承运收据作成我行抬头注明运费付讫通知开证人
    Full set of Forwarding Agents' Cargo Receipt made out to our order marked freight prepaid notify accountee

☐ 邮包收据载明邮包以我行为收件人并注明本证号数及开证人户名
    Parcel Post Receipt showing parcels addressed to our Bank a/c accountee and marked with this L/C Number

☐ 其他单据
    Other Documents

     ☐ 产地证明书
        Certificate of Origin   ☐

     ☐ 明细重量单
        Detailed Weight List

     ☐ 装箱单
        Packing List

准许/禁止分批装运
Partial shipments are permitted / prohibited

准许/禁止转运
Transhipment is permitted / prohibited

装运日期不得迟于
Shipment(s) must be effected not later than 8th Jan., 1979

本证有效期内不得议价,其有效期在 你地
This L/C is irrevocable and valid in your port   until 8th Jan., 1979 inclusive.

凡兑本证所出之汇票必须载明本证号数及开立日期
Draft(s) so drawn must be inscribed with the number and date of this L/C

其他条款,
Other Conditions,

据此专信用证并按共所列条款开具之汇票向我行提示并于交出本证规定之单据经我行同意对共出票人背书人及善意持有人履行承兑付款责任
We hereby agree with the drawers, endorsers and bona-fide holders of the draft(s) drawn under and in compliance with the terms of this credit that such draft(s) shall be duly honoured on due presentation and delivery of documents as herein specified.

议付银行须注立,兑本证收付之汇票及单据请直迳寄我行
Instructions to Negotiating Bank: The draft(s) and documents taken up under this credit are to be forwarded direct to us by you.

偿付办法 人民币汇票,兑兑我行承兑如若干到期日即记账期,港币汇票,我行于到期日划收帐期。
For Reimbursement, ☒ Draft in RMB¥, Please debit our account upon maturity as indicated in our Advice of Acceptance. Draft in HK$, We shall credit your account upon maturity.

本证根据国际商会1974年修订之第290号
小册跟单信用证统一规则办理
This credit is subject to the Uniform Customs and practice for Documentary credits (1974 Revision). International Chamber of Commerce publication No. 290.

Yours faithfully,

新华信托储蓄商业银行香港分行

For SIN HUA TRUST, SAVINGS & COMMERCIAL BANK, LTD.

HONG KONG BRANCH

第十课

保险

✎ **思考下面的问题，然后带着这些问题去阅读课文：**

一、为什么要对货物进行保险？保险业务与海运有什么关系？

二、海运保险业务主要有哪几类的风险？

三、按责任范围，海洋货物运输保险可以分成哪几个基本险别？哪一种险别的责任范围最大？哪一种最小？

四、被保人在什么情况下、什么时间内可以向保险公司提出索赔？

课文：保险

　　在国际贸易中，货物往往要经过多次装卸、长途运输，才能从卖方交到买方手中。在这个过程中，货物可能会遇到各种风险而遭受损失。为了保障货物在遭受损失后能够得到一定的补偿，买方或卖方会在货物起运之前，向保险公司投保货物运输险。通常，被保人（买方或卖方）会根据需要运输的货物的价值和特点，向保险人（保险公司）投保不同险别的保险，并按照货物的价值交纳一定金额的保险费；保险人承保后，开出保险单，如果所保的货物在运输过程中遭受约定范围内的损失，保险公司将按照保险单的规定和损失的程度，给予被保人经济上的补偿。虽然大多数被保人都知道发生事故的概率比较低，买保险所付的钱很可能是白花的，但是与其靠碰运气不出事，不如花钱买个平安。一旦发生事故，也不至于货物全部损失，血本无归。

　　国际上货运保险业务是随着国际贸易和航海事业的发展而兴旺

起来的。它的发展，又反过来促进了国际贸易和航运事业的发展。
15 由于海洋运输具有运载量大、费用低廉等优点，目前国际贸易大部
分的货物都采用海运，因此，来自海上的风险也就占了首位，而大
多数的保险都与海运有关。

　　在海运保险业务中，风险主要有两类：一类是"海难"；另一
类是"外来风险"。海难包括自然力量造成的灾害和意外原因造成的
20 事故，例如暴风雨、雷电、海啸、船舶搁浅、触礁、沉没、碰撞、
失火、爆炸等。外来风险通常是指由外来原因造成的货物损坏或者
丧失，如偷窃、短量、破碎、受潮等。

　　货物在海运过程中因海难(即"自然灾害"和"意外事故")而遭受
部分或全部损失，叫做"海损"。根据各国海运保险业务的习惯，海
25 损也包括与海陆连接的陆路运输中所发生的损失。海洋货物运输保
险，按照不同的责任范围，分为三个基本险别：平安险、水渍险
和一切险。这三个险别的责任范围，一个比一个广。譬如水渍险，
保险公司负责赔偿的范围就大于平安险——除了平安险的各项责任
外，还负责被保货物由于恶劣气候、雷电、海啸、地震、洪水等自
30 然灾害所造成的损失。投保一切险，不仅包括了平安险和水渍险的
全部责任，而且负责被保货物在运输途中由于某些外来原因所造成
的全部或部分损失，例如偷窃、短量、沾污、破碎、受潮等。然
而，投保一切险并非意味着保险公司将负责赔偿由任何原因引起的
一切货损，是万无一失的。对由于托运人或收货人的过失和故意行
35 为，货物的特性、运输延误和自然损耗等引起的损失，保险公司并
不负赔偿责任。某些特殊风险，如交货不到、拒收、战争、罢工等
并没有包括在一切险的范围内。所以，如果货物有可能遭受这一类
的风险，被保人就需要在投保一种基本险的基础上，加保一种或数
种附加险，如交货不到险、拒收险、战争险、罢工险等。险别不
40 同，保险公司的责任范围大小各异，收取的保险费用也有高低差
别。因此，被保人必须根据货物的性质、包装、运输、装载、季

节、气候以及安全等具体情况全面考虑，选择适当的险别投保，做到既经济又安全。

平安险、水渍险和一切险三种基本险别承保责任的起讫期限，是按照国际保险业中惯用的"仓至仓条款"来计算的。换言之，保险公司的责任，自被保货物运离保险单所注明的发货人的仓库时开始生效，包括正常运输过程中的海上和陆上运输，直至该货物送交保险单所注明的收货人的仓库时为止。如果货物在卸货港从海轮上卸离后而没有运到收货人的仓库，保险责任仍继续有效，但是最长的责任期以60天为限。如果货物卸离海轮60天后仍未运入收货人的仓库，发生问题，保险公司概不负责。

如果被保货物遭受保险责任范围内的损失，被保人有权持有关单据向保险公司提出索赔。根据国际惯例，一般索赔期限为两年。若被保人超过期限要求索赔，保险公司可以不予受理。

✐ 根据课文回答下列问题：

1. 为什么对货物要进行保险？

2. 被保人投保需要做什么？保险人承保后有什么责任？

3. 为什么货运保险业务大多数与海运有关？

4. 海运保险业务主要有哪几类风险？请举例说明。

5. 什么是"海损"？它是否只限于货物在海运过程中的损失？

6. 海运保险包括哪几个基本险别？哪一种险别的责任范围最广？

7. 保险公司承保"一切险"，是否要负责赔偿货物的一切损失？为什么？

8. 险别的责任范围越大意味着什么？应该如何选择适当的险别投保？

9. 基本险别的保险责任起讫期限是怎样计算的？如果货物在卸货港卸离海轮两个月以后发生货损，保险公司是否要负责赔偿？为什么？

10. 在什么情况下可以提出索赔？国际惯例对索赔期限有什么规定？

✐ **根据意思，给课文划分层次(不是自然段)并写出每个层次的大意。**

生词和用法

往往	wǎngwǎng	Adv.	表示某种情况时常存在或经常发生；Cf. 常常。 often; usually
遭	zāo	V.	遇到(不幸或不利的事)：~难、~劫、~受、~遇。 to meet with; to suffer from (disasters, misfortune, etc.)
遭到	zāodào	V.	遇到(不幸或不利等)：~反对、~拒绝、~罚款、~破坏。 to suffer; to encounter; to meet with
补偿	bǔcháng	V./N.	抵消(损失、消耗)；补足(缺欠、差额)。 to compensate; to make up
起运	qǐyùn	V.	(货物)开始运出(多指运往外地)：~时间、~地点。 start shipment
投保	tóubǎo	V.	个人或团体就其生命或财产等向保险公司购买保险服务。 to take out insurance; to ensure
承保	chéngbǎo	V.	保险公司同意负责为个人或团体的生命或财产等提供保险服务：~人、~范围、~通知书。 to accept insurance
予	yǔ	V.	〔书〕给：~以、授~、准~、免~、请~批准。 to give; to grant
给予	jǐyǔ	V.	＝给(用于抽象事物)：~帮助、~支持、~同情、~解决；＜＞不予。 to give; to render
不予	bùyǔ	VP	不给：~批准、~考虑、~办理、~承保；＜＞给予。 not to grant; to refuse
概率	gàilǜ	N.	表示某种事件在同一条件下发生的可能性大小的量，也叫机率。 probability
白	bái	Adv.	徒然；没有效果：~花钱、~跑一趟、~~浪费。 in vain; for nothing

与其	yǔqí	Conj.	用在比较两件事的利害得失而决定取舍，常与"不如、宁可"等连用。
			It's better to ... than...; ... rather than ...
碰运气	pèng yùnqì	VO	试探命运或机会。 to take a chance; to try one's luck
运气	yùnqì	N.	命运：~真好、~不佳。 luck; fate
出事	chūshì	VO	发生事故。 to have an accident; to meet with a mishap
血本	xuèběn	N.	指做生意的本钱。 original capital; principal
归	guī	V.	〔书〕返回：~国、~家。 to go back to; to return
血本无归	xuèběn wúguī	Idm.	损失了全部做生意的本钱；无法收回本钱。 a total loss of the original capital (for doing business)
航海	hánghǎi	N.	驾驶船只在海上航行：~运动、~仪器、~日志、~图。 navigation
航运	hángyùn	N.	水上运输事业的统称，分内河航运，沿海航运，远洋航运：~公司、~保险、~事业。 shipping
兴旺	xīngwàng	Adj.	兴盛、旺盛：日益~、事业~、人丁~、~发达；＜＞萧条。 prosperous; flourishing; thriving
促进	cùjìn	V.	促使发展：~发展、~生产、~技术提高。 to promote; to accelerate; to advance
海难	hǎinàn	N.	发生在海上、造成性命财产损失的灾难。 perils of the sea
外来风险	wàilái fēngxiǎn	NP	由于外来原因引起的风险，如盗窃、雨淋、短量、破碎、受潮、战争、交货不到、拒收等。 Extraneous Risks

灾害	zāihài	N.	由自然或战争所造成的祸害。
			calamity; disaster
意外	yìwài	Adj.	意料之外：感到~、十分~
			unexpected; unforeseen
		N.	意想不到地不幸事件：发生~、出现~。
			accident; mishap
事故	shìgù	N.	意外的（多指生产或工作中发生的）损失或灾祸：责任~、工伤~、医疗~。
			accident; mishap
暴风雨	bàofēngyǔ	NP	大而急的风雨。　　rainstorm; storm; tempest
雷电	léidiàn	N.	一块云接近另一种物体或者带异性电的两块云互相接近时，产生火花放电现象，电光很强，叫做闪电，同时发出强大的响声叫做雷，合称雷电。　　thunder and lighting
海啸	hǎixiào	N.	由海底地震或风暴造成的海面发生险恶巨浪的现象。　　tsunami; seismic sea wave; tidal wave
船舶	chuánbó	N.	＝船只，船的总称。
			ships and boats; shipping
搁浅	gēqiǎn	V.	（船只）进入水浅的地方不能行驶。
			to run aground; to be stranded
触礁	chùjiāo	VO	船只在航行中碰上暗礁。
			to run on rocks; to strike a reef or rock
沉没	chénmò	V.	没入水中；＜＞浮起。
			to sink
碰撞	pèngzhuàng	V.	运动着的物体跟别的物体突然接触碰上。
			to collide; to run into
失火	shīhuǒ	V.	发生火灾。　　to be on fire; to catch fire
爆炸	bàozhà	V.	物体体积急剧膨大，使周围气压发生强烈变化而产生巨大的响声。

			to explode; to blow up; explosion
丧失	sàngshī	V.	〔书〕失去，意义重，多指抽象事物，如：~信心、勇气、能力、主权、立场、理智、人格等；＜＞获得。　　to lose; to forfeit
偷窃	tōuqiè	V.	＝偷，盗窃；用不合法的手段秘密取得，把别人的东西拿走据为已有。　　to steal; theft
破碎	pòsuì	V.	(使)破成碎片；零碎的。　　to smash; to tatter; to break
破碎险	pòsuìxiǎn	NP	Clash and Breakage Risk
受潮	shòucháo	VP	(物体)被潮气渗入。　　to be affected with moisture; to become damp
受潮险	shòucháoxiǎn	NP	Sweating Risk
海损	hǎisǔn	NP	货物在海运过程中受到损失。　　average, marine loss
险别	xiǎnbié	N.	保险的类别。　　(types of) coverage; terms of insurance
平安险	píng'ānxiǎn	NP	Free of Particular Average (F.P.A.)
水渍险	shuǐzìxiǎn	NP	With Particular Average (W.P.A.)
一切险	yīqièxiǎn	NP	All Risks
譬如	pìrú	Conj.	比如。　　for instance; for example
恶劣	èliè	Adj.	很坏：行为~、作风~、环境~ 、天气~；＜＞良好。　　odious; abominable
气候	qìhòu	N.	一定地区里经过多年观察所得到的概括性的气象情况，它与气流、纬度、海拔、地形等有关。　　climate
地震	dìzhèn	N.	由地球内部的变动引起的地壳震动。　　earthquake; seism

洪水	hóngshuǐ	N.	河流因大雨或融雪而引起的暴涨的水流，常常造成灾害。 flood
沾污	zhānwū	V.	因为接触被脏东西附着上。 to contaminate; to be tainted
沾污险	zhānwūxiǎn	N.	Contamination Risk
意味	yìwèi	N.	含蓄的意思；情调；情趣：~深长、~无穷。 meaning; significance
意味着	yìwèizhe	VP	含有某种意义。 to signify; to mean
万无一失	wànwú yīshī	Idm.	绝对不会出差错；形容十分有把握。 no danger of anything going wrong; perfectly safe; no risk at all
托运	tuōyùn	V./N.	委托运输部门运送(行李货物等)：~人、~单、~行李。 to consign for shipment
过失	guòshī	N.	因疏忽而犯的错误：~行为、~责任、~犯罪。 fault; error
延误	yánwù	V.	由于拖延而耽误，多指时间。 to incur loss through delay
损耗	sǔnhào	V.	损失消耗：电能的~、~精力。 to lose; to wear and tear; loss
		N.	货物由于自然原因或运输而造成的消耗损失：合理~、~率。 loss; wear and tear
拒	jù	Mph.(V.)	拒绝；不接受(请求、意见或赠礼等)：~收、~付、~赔。 to reject; to refuse
拒收险	jùshōuxiǎn	NP	Rejection Risk
交货不到险	jiāohuò bùdào xiǎn	NP	Failure to Delivery Risk
战争险	zhànzhēngxiǎn	NP	War Risk
罢	bà	Mph.(V.)	停止：~工、~课、~教、~市、~手、~休。 to stop; to cease

罢工	bàgōng	VO	工人为了实现某种要求或表示抗议而集体停止工作。 to strike; to go on strike
罢工险	bàgōngxiǎn	NP	Strikes Risk
数	shù	Pron.	＝几：~天、~年、~小时、~十种、~笔交易。 several; a few
全面	quánmiàn	Adj.	各个方面的总和：~性、~考虑、~发展、~规划；＜＞片面。 overall; total; comprehensive
讫	qì	Mph.(V.)	(事情)完结：收~、付~、验~；截止：起~；＜＞起。 to end
起讫	qǐqì	V.	开始和终结。 the beginning and the end
仓库	cāngkù	N.	储藏物资的建筑物。 warehouse
仓至仓条款	cāngzhì cāng tiáokuǎn	NP	Warehouse to Warehouse Clause
生效	shēngxiào	V.	发生效力：合同~、立即~、~日期；＜＞失效。 to go into effect; to become effective
海轮	hǎilún	N.	用于远洋航行的轮船。 oceangoing vessel
概	gài	Adv.	一律；~不＋双音节动词(负责、退换、受理)。 all; without exception
索赔	suǒpéi	VP	要求赔偿：~期限、~证书。 to lodge a claim; to claim indemnity
受理	shòulǐ	V.	接受案件，进行审理。 to accept a case

补充词

| 汇率 | huìlǜ | N. | 两种货币相互兑换的比价、比例。 exchange rate |

浮动	fúdòng	V.	若随水漂流、移动；上下变动，不稳定：~汇率、~价格、人心~。 to float; to fluctuate
终止	zhōngzhǐ	V.	结束；停止：~学习、~纠纷；<>开始。 to stop; to end; to terminate
宁可	nìngkě	Adv.	表示在比较两方面的利害得失后选取一方面。 would rather; better
宁肯	nìngkěn	Adv.	宁可。 would rather
宁愿	nìngyuàn	Adv.	宁可；表示希望或意愿时，用宁愿。 would rather
劣	liè	Mph.	坏，不好：恶~、低~、~质、~等；<>优。 bad; inferior; of low quality
报税	bàoshuì	VO	公民履行义务，按期向国家申报交纳个人收入所得税。 to file a tax return
袭击	xíjī	V.	突然打击。 to make a surprise attack; to raid; to hit
泡	pào	V.	把物体较久地放在液体中：~茶、~湿、~坏。 to steep; to soak
湿	shī	Adj.	沾了水或水分较多的；<>干。 damp; wet
兹	zī	N.	〔书〕现在。 now; at present
		Pron.	这；这个。 this
拟	nǐ	V.	打算；想要。 to intend; to plan
临近	línjìn	V.	靠近，接近；须带时间词或处所词作宾语：~春节、~港口。 close to; to approach
恳	kěn	Adv.	真诚，诚恳：~请、~求、~谈。 earnestly; sincerely

词语例释

一、往往 ＋ Verb Phrase （often; usually）

l-1. 在国际贸易中，货物<u>往往</u>要经过多次装卸、长途运输，才能从卖方交到买方手中。

1. 这家银行的工作效率很高，<u>往往</u>在很短的时间内就能将信用证开好。

2. 恶劣的天气<u>往往</u>会造成海难事故。

3. 一种新药，<u>往往</u>要经过多年的试验，才能上市出售。

副词"往往"表示某种情况时常存在或经常发生，只用于到目前为止出现的情况，有一定的规律性，不用于表示主观意愿。"常常"除了可用于过去、现在和将来外，还可以用于主观意愿。用"往往"的句子，要指明与动作有关的情况、条件或结果，而"常常"不受此限制。下面的句子只能用"常常"而不能用"往往"：

The Adverb 往往 indicates that certain things happen or exist frequently and may fall into a pattern. It does not refer to subjective desires, however. 常常 can refer to subjective desires in addition to situations in the past, the present, and the future. Sentences using 往往 should specify the situations, conditions or results relevant to the action, whereas 常常 is not subject to such limitation. The following sentences can only be used with 常常 but not 往往.

她常常跑步。　　　　　　　　　✘ 她往往跑步。

请你以后有空常常来。　　　　　✘ 请你以后有空往往来。

他常常希望有机会到世界各地去旅行。　✘ 他往往希望有机会到世界各地去旅行。

二、不予/ 给予 ＋ Disyllabic/Polysyllabic Verb　（[not]to give; [not]render）

l-9. ……保险人承保后，开出保单，如果所保的货物在运输过程中遭受约定范围内的损失，保险公司将按照保险单的规定和损失的程度，<u>给予</u>被保人经济上的补偿。

l-54. 若被保人超过期限要求索赔，保险公司可以<u>不予</u>受理。

1. 我们的签证申请已寄出一个多月了，但是美国大使馆仍未<u>给予</u>办理。

2. 请你们收到传真后，对有关进行技术合作的条件，立即<u>给予</u>明确的答复。

3. 在过去的十年里，这家银行对我们公司的进出口业务<u>给予</u>了很多的帮助。

4. 这个事故是由于托运人的过失造成的，所以保险公司对他们要求赔偿的要求根本就<u>不予</u>考虑。

"给予"表示把动作或态度加到对方，相当于"给"，多用于书面语，宾语多为动词，如：帮助、爱好、支持、同情、照顾、鼓励、考虑、说明、解释、批准、肯定、解决、处理、办理、答复、赔偿、补偿、通行等。"不予"是给予的否定形式。

　　Similar to 给, 给予 means that an action or an attitude is taken toward the other party, and is primarily used in written Chinese. The Object that follows 给予 is mostly Verbs such as 帮助、爱好、支持、同情、照顾、鼓励、考虑、说明、解释、批准、肯定、解决、处理、办理、答复、赔偿、补偿、通行, etc. 不予 is the negation of 给予.

三、与其……不如……　（would rather; better ... ）

l-10. 虽然大多数被保人都知道发生事故的概率比较低，买保险所付的钱很可能是白花的，但是<u>与其</u>靠碰运气不出事，<u>不如</u>花钱买个平安。

1. 天气这么好，<u>与其</u>在家看电视，<u>不如</u>出去运动运动。

2. 这些滞销货，<u>与其</u>在仓库里放着，还<u>不如</u>低价卖出去。这样不但可以节省开支，还可以加快资金周转。

3. 因为这是我们第一次与贵国做生意，有关装运和保险的手续，<u>与其</u>我们自己办理，<u>不如</u>你们帮忙办理。

"与其……不如……"表示在比较两种客观情况的优劣之后，说话人认为后者比前者好而作出的取舍。当泛指一般情况而上下文很清楚时，可省略全句的主语，如例 1。当前后分句的主语一致时，"与其……不如……"放在主语后，如例 2。当前后分句的主语不同时，主语分别位于"与其"和"不如"后面。

与其……不如…… indicates that after comparing the advantages and disadvantages of two things the speaker makes up his/her mind that the latter is better than the former. When the context is clear and it refers to situations in general, the Subject of the sentence can be omitted, as in Example 1. When the Subjects of the two clauses are identical, 与其……不如…… is placed after the subject. When the subjects of the two clauses are different, the Subjects should follow 与其 and 不如 respectively.

四、 A 随着 B（的 Verb Phrase）而 Verb Phrase　（along with...; accompanied with...)

l-13. 国际上货运保险业务是随着国际贸易和航海事业的发展而兴旺起来的。

1. 中国的进出口总额随着经济的发展而大幅度增加。
2. 人民币与外币的汇率随着国际金融市场的变化而上下浮动。
3. 人类对大自然的认识将随着科学技术的发展而不断加深。

"随着"可跟介词"而"配合，后面跟宾语，构成介宾词组作状语，表示产生某种结果的依据条件。

随着 can work together with 而, and is followed by an Object, forming a Prepositional Phrase to function as an Adverbial. It refers to the condition based on which brings about a certain result.

五、 Subject +Verb Phrase 1, 反过来 Verb Phrase 2　（conversely; in turn; the other way round）

l-15. 它的发展，又反过来促进了国际贸易和航运事业的发展。

1. 中国的经济发展有利于世界的和平与稳定；世界局势的稳定反过

　　　　来又有助于中国的现代化。

　　2. 生产落后，教育水平低是造成人口过多的主要原因之一，而人口
　　　　过多<u>反过来</u>又影响了生产和教育水平的提高。

　　3. 国际经济文化交流增加了各国人民之间的相互了解，这种了解<u>反</u>
　　　　<u>过来</u>又促进了各国之间的经济和文化交流。

　　词组"反过来＋动词"表示某一事物受到另一事物的影响后，回过头
来对原来影响它的事物起某种作用。

　　The phrase 反过来＋Verb is used to show that after being impacted by
another thing, something in turn, has some kind of effect on the thing that
impacted it originally.

六、 Subject 因 Verb Phrase 1 而 Verb Phrase 2 （due to; owing to; because）

l-23. 货物在海运过程中<u>因</u>海难（即"自然灾害"和"意外事故"）<u>而</u>遭受部分
　　　或全部损失，叫做"海损"。

　　1. 经过讨论，我们同意了卖方<u>因</u>受生产能力限制<u>而</u>采用分批装运的
　　　　要求。

　　2. 他托运的行李<u>因</u>（为）超重<u>而</u>受到了罚款。

　　3. 对不起，这种货物，厂商<u>因</u>利润太低<u>而</u>停止生产了。

　　"因"基本上与"因为"意思相同，后面的"而"把表示目的、方式、结
果的成分同前面的原因连接起来。这个句型多用于书面语。

　　因 is basically the same as 因为 in meaning, and 而 links up the elements
expressing purpose, manner, result, etc. with the preceding cause/reason. This
expression is usually used in written Chinese.

七、 A 意味着 B （to signify; to mean; to imply）

l-33. 然而，投保一切险并非<u>意味着</u>保险公司将负责赔偿由任何原因引起
　　　的一切货损，是万无一失的。

　　1. 生产成本的提高<u>意味着</u>价格的上涨，然而价格上涨并非<u>意味着</u>利

润的增加。

2. 科学的发展意味着人类的进步。

3. 大学毕业并非意味着学习的终止。

动词"意味"表示"含有某种意义、标志着、可以理解为……"的意思。后面须加助词"着"再跟主谓词组小句作宾语。

The Verb 意味 means "to have the sense of", "to signify", or "to be considered as". A Particle 着 must be attached to and then followed by a clause as its Object.

八、万无一失　（no danger of anything going wrong; perfectly safe ）

l-34. 然而，投保一切险并非意味着保险公司将负责赔偿由任何原因引起的一切货损，是万无一失的。

1. 大家都非常重视这次试验，为了做到万无一失，对各种设备和仪器进行了反复的检查。

2. 你放心好了，这件事交给她去办理，万无一失。

3. 这件事关系重大，我们必须想一个万无一失的办法，才能动手。

"万无一失"是成语，表示绝对不会出差错，形容十分有把握。可作谓语或定语。

万无一失 is an Idiom which means that there is absolutely no chance to go wrong, and it is a hundred percent certain to happen as planned or predicted. It can be used as a Predicate or an Attributive.

九、换言之　（in other words; that is to say ）

l-45. 平安险、水渍险和一切险三种基本险别承保责任的起讫期限，是按照国际保险业中惯用的"仓至仓条款"来计算的。换言之，保险公司的责任，自被保货物运离保险单所注明的发货人的仓库时开始生效……

1. 这笔交易的价格条款是 F.O.B. 大连。卖方所负的责任，只是在大连港把货物装上船为止。<u>换言之</u>，如果货物装上船后发生什么问题，都应该由买方负责。

2. 这是不可撤销的信用证，未经受益人及有关当事人同意，开证行不得片面修改或撤销。<u>换言之</u>，只有经过卖方和议付行的同意，买方和开信用证的银行才能修改或撤销给卖方开出的信用证。

3. 在国际贸易中，卖方通常在交易前定出一个最低的订货量，叫"起订量"。<u>换言之</u>，买方订货的数量，必须等于或超过起订量。如果低于这个数量，卖方不接受这样的订货。

文言词组"换言之"是口语"换句话说"的意思，常在句中作插入语。

The literary phrase 换言之 is equal to the colloquial expression 换句话说, and is often used as an insertion in a sentence.

十、 自……（起／开始，）至……（为止）   ([starting] from... till [ending at/in]...)

l-46. ……保险公司的责任，<u>自</u>被保货物运离保险单所注明的发货人的仓库时开始生效，包括正常运输过程中的海上和陆上运输，<u>直至</u>该货物送交保险单所注明的收货人的仓库为止。

1. 此信用证的有效期，<u>自</u>本日起，<u>至</u>六月二十日为止。

2. 中国贸促会和各大外贸公司，每年<u>自</u>四月十五日起至四月三十日止，都在广州举办大型的春季交易会。

3. 那家电脑公司给顾客提供了很好的售后服务：<u>自</u>顾客交款提货开始，<u>至</u>电脑不能使用为止，有什么问题他们都负责修理。

介词"自"相当于"从、由"的意思，后接名词，构成介词宾语作状语。"至"是"到"的意思，多用于书面语。"自……至……"即口语"从……到……"的意思，表示事情的起点和终点。注意"自从"和"自"的区别："自从"只表示时间的起点，而"自"可表示时间、处所、系列的起点。"自从"的时间起点是过去的，而"自"则是现在或将来的。另外，"自从"口语书面语都可用，"自"只用于书面语。

The Preposition 自 is similar to 从 or 由 in meaning. It is followed by a

Noun, to form a Prepositional Object as an Adverbial, 至 means the same as 到, and is mostly used in writing. The phrase 自……至…… is the counterpart of spoken Chinese 从……到……, which refers to the starting point and the ending point. Note the differences between 自 and 自从. 自从 indicates the starting point of time only, but 自 refers to the starting point of place, series, in addition to time. While the starting point of 自从 is in the past, the one for 自 is for both the present and the future. Moreover, 自从 can be used in both spoken and written Chinese, 自 is used in writing only.

词义辨析

一、常常 往往 平常 经常

　　这几个词都跟时间有关系，除了"平常"以外，其他的都是副词。"常常"表示次数多，频率高，相隔不久就重现。它可用于描述过去、现在或将来的事情，也可单独修饰动词。

　　副词"往往"表示某种情况时常存在或经常发生，但只用于过去出现的情况，并侧重于其规律性。"往往"不可用于将来，也不可用于主观愿望。下面的句子只能用"常常"而不可用"往往"：

These words all pertain to time. Except 平常, others are Adverbs. 常常 refers to things happening frequently, and recurring at short intervals. It can describe things in the past, at present and in the future. It can modify a Verb directly by itself.

The Adverb 往往 indicates something that existed or happened regularly, but only in the past. Its focus is on the regularity of an action or event. Unlike 常常, 往往 cannot be used in the future, nor can it refer to actions with a subjective desire. In the following sentences, only 常常 is possible but not 往往:

　　希望你今后常常 (✘往往) 来。
　　他常常 (✘往往) 想去中国留学。

另外，"往往"不可单独修饰动词，必须带有其他说明与动作有关的情况、条件或结果的状语，表明在通常情况下怎样或可能怎样。例如：

In addition 往往 cannot modify a Verb directly by itself, and has to go together with other Adverbial that shows some situation related to the action, a condition or a result, indicating what it is like or how it may be under normal circumstances. It is incorrect to say 她往往上街. but it is possible to say,

她往往<u>一个人</u>上街; or 她往往上街<u>都买很多东西</u>。

"平常"作名词，指"在正常的情况下"，相当于"平时"。可位于主语前或后，如：

As a Noun, 平常 refers to "as a rule, ordinarily, in normal times", and is similar to 平时. It can go before or after a Subject of a sentence, as in the following examples,

小刘<u>平常</u>很早起床，今天怎么还在睡觉？
<u>平常</u>小刘都是五点起床。
小刘当了经理以后，还是跟<u>平常</u>一样。

"平常"还可作形容词，表示"普通、不突出"的意思，可以重叠，如：

平常 can also function as an Adjective, indicating "ordinary, nothing special". It can be duplicated, as in 这只是一件<u>平平常常</u>的事情.

这只是一件<u>平平常常</u>的事情。

"经常"强调动作、行为或情况反复出现，经久不断，常有连惯性，并可加后缀，构成名词"经常性"。除了作副词外，还可作形容词，修饰名词，如"这是<u>经常</u>的事"、"经常的工作"、"经常的活动"。

经常 emphasizes the recurrence of an action or situation, with more continuity than interruption. It can become a Noun 经常性 by attaching a suffix. In addition to an Adverb, 经常 can also function as an Adjective to modify Nouns, such as in 这是<u>经常</u>的事, 经常的工作, 经常的活动.

二、 遭　遭受　遭遇　遭到

"遭"有"逢、遇、受到"的意思，多指不幸或不好的事，如：遭殃、遭了灾、遭谋害。动词"遭受"表示"受到(不幸或损害)"，着重指自身受到。只用于贬义而不用于褒义。

"遭遇"作动词时,是"碰上、遇到"的意思,对象一般是不幸、不顺利的事或敌人等。常带宾语或补语,例如:

遭 can mean "to meet with, encounter, to suffer", and usually refers to things unfortunate or negative. For example, 遭殃、遭了灾、遭谋害. The Verb 遭受 indicates "to suffer from (a disaster or lose)", and is used in a derogative sense only.

When 遭遇 functions as a Verb, it means "to encounter, meet with, run up against", and its Objects are misfortune, difficulty, or enemy, etc. It often take an Object or a Complement, for example,

他们在研究新产品的过程中,<u>遭遇</u>了很多困难。

种种灾难,她这辈子<u>遭遇</u>得实在太多了。

另外,"遭遇"还可作名词,表示所遇到的不幸或不顺利的事情,如:

In addition, 遭遇 can be a Noun also, referring to things that are unfortunate or miserable. Here are some examples,

她向大家诉说了自己不幸的<u>遭遇</u>。

他童年的<u>遭遇</u>很悲惨。

虽然及物动词"遭到"也是"碰上、遇到、受到"的意思,而且只用于不幸和不好的事,但"遭到"后面只带双/多音节动词或名词作宾语,不带补语,也不可作名词。例如:

Although the Transitive Verb 遭到 also means "to encounter, to meet with, to suffer", and is used for misfortune or bad things, it can only proceed disyllabic or polysyllabic Verbs or Nouns. It cannot takes a Complement, nor can it be a Noun. Some common examples are:

遭到批评(打击、破坏、虐待、污染、不幸、严重的自然灾害),etc.

三、做　作　造　制

"做"是常用动词,通用于口语和俗白文字。一个很常用的意思就是

"加工、制作 (具体的事物)",如:做饭、做衣服、做家具等。另一个常用的意思是"从事某种工作或活动",如:做生意、做木工、做市场调查工作等。第三个常用的意思是"充当、担任",其宾语多是表示职务或职业的名词,如:做老师、做经理、做老板等。

As a commonly used Verb, 做 is widely used in spoken and informal written Chinese. One of the essential meaning is "to do, process, make (concrete things)", for example, 做饭、做衣服、做家具, etc. Another basic meaning is "to do (some kind of work)", engage in (some activities), such as in 做生意、做木工、做市场调查工作. A third meaning is "to act, to become", and its Objects are usually Nouns indicating some kind of position or profession, for example, 做老师、做经理、做老板, etc.

"作"表示"进行、举行",常以动词作宾语,意思与所带的动词大致相同,但较正式,如:作安排、作决定、作准备、作估计等。"作"的另一个意思是"创作、写作",常见的动宾词组有:作文、作诗、作画、作曲等。"作"还有"假装、把 (A) 当作(B)"的意思,如"装模作样"、"认贼作父"、"作态"等。

作 refers to "to carry out, carry on, conduct" and is often followed by Verbs. The meaning of this "作＋Verb" phrase is similar to the Verb itself, but is more formal. For example, 作安排 (＝安排)、作决定 (＝决定)、作准备、作估计, etc. Another meaning of 作 is "to write, to compose", and the common Verb-Object Constructions are 作文、作诗、作画、作曲, etc. In addition, 作 can also mean "to pretend, to take (A) as (B)". Some common examples are, 装模作样、认贼作父、作态, etc.

"造"作动词时,主要指"制作、建立",多用于比较大的物件或工程,如造船、造飞机、造汽车、造林、造山运动等。"造"还有"凭空假编、虚构、无中生有"的意思,多为贬义,如:造谣、生造、造假、造神等。当表示非天然、人工制成的物品时,都用"人造＋名词",如:人造革、人造冰、人造橡胶、人造卫星等。

As a Verb, 造 means "to make, build". It is primarily for a large machinery or a project, as in 造船、造飞机、造汽车、造林、造山运动(orogenic movement), etc. 造 also means "to fabricate, cook up" and is mostly in a derogative sense, for example, 造谣、生造、造假、造神. When referring to man-made, non-natural things, the Phrase "人造＋Noun" is used. The common terms are, 人造革、人造冰、人造橡胶、人造卫星, etc.

"制"表示"制造、制作"，侧重加工使出成品的操作，多用于书面语，比较正式郑重，如：制图、制版、制表、制药、制革等。

制 means "to make, manufacture". Its emphasis is on the operation to process and produce certain products. It is mostly used in written Chinese and is formal, for example, 制图、制版、制表、制药、制革.

四、做成　造成　制成

这三个动词都带有表示结果的"成"字，即"成为、变成"的意思。它们的区别在于第一个字，也就是动词"做"、"造"、"制"，分别表示以不同的手段，使某种事物或情况变成另一种。

"做成"表示通过加工制作，使某些具体的原材料成为成品，如：把布做成衣服。

These three Verbs share a morpheme 成, which means "to turn into, become", indicating some sort of result. The distinctions of these words lie in their first characters, that is, 做、造 and 制. Each of them show a different means to turn something into another.

做成 indicates to turn some kind of material into a product after processing, as in the sentence, 把布做成衣服.

"造成"主要是指由外界因素而使某种情况出现，有"使产生、使形成"的意思。多用于抽象事物，常带名词、动词或小句作宾语。例如：

The Transitive Verb 造成 refers to "bring about, give rise to, cause", and is mostly used for abstract things. It often takes a Noun, a Verb, or a Clause as its Objects: 造成损失、造成严重的污染、造成很坏的影响、造成产品卖不出去的被动局面, etc.

"制成"指制作、制造成功或成形，多用于较大的具体事物。例如：

制成, on the contrary, means to successfully make something or to produce something, and is usually for large, concrete things, for example,

经过几年的努力，他们自己<u>制成</u>了这台先进的设备。

五、丢失　丧失　失去

"失"字作动词时，有"遗失、亏掉"的意思，与"得"相对。"丢失"含有因疏忽大意而使原有的东西不复存在之意，多用于口语，其对象主要是具体事物，如行李、钱包、护照、钥匙、课本等。

As a Verb, the character 失 is the opposite of 得, meaning "to lose". 丢失 is the disyllabic version of 失, indicating some no longer exists or in possession because of carelessness. It is primarily used in spoken Chinese and the things involved are usually concrete such as 行李、钱包、护照、钥匙、课本, etc.

"丧失"表示因某种原因，使原有的东西无法挽回地失去，不再具有的意思。语义比"丢失"重，多用于书面语。"丧失"的对象多是像主权、立场、人格、信心、勇气、理智等抽象事物。

丧失 means something that one owned or had is lost and cannot be recovered, for whatever reason. It is stronger than 丢失, and is often used in written Chinese. Its Objects are mostly abstract Nouns such as 主权、立场、人格、信心、勇气、理智, etc.

"失去"指因某种情况、某种变化或发展而使原有的人或事物不复存在。通用于口语和书面语，宾语可以是名词或动词，如：失去亲人（孩子、机会、意义、价值、联系、控制）等。

失去 indicates that someone or something is gone because of situation change or situation development. It is generally used in spoken and written Chinese, and its Objects can be either Nouns or Verbs, for example, 失去亲人（孩子、机会、意义、价值、联系、控制）, etc.

语法

一、取舍复句　Complex Sentences of Preference

两个分句表示不同的情况或事物，说话者经过对比后，选取一个而舍弃另一个，这种复句叫做取舍复句。常用的关联词语有：

A Complex Sentence of Preference consists of two clauses, each of which represents a different situation or thing. After a comparison, the speaker prefers one over the other. The commonly used Connectives of Complex Sentences of Preference are:

与其……不如/毋宁……、与其……宁可/宁愿……、宁愿/宁可……也不……、宁可……也（决）不……、宁可/宁愿/宁肯……也要……。

例如：For example:

1. 与其写信，不如给他发电子邮件。
2. 与其多而质量差，宁肯少而质量高。
3. 我宁可今晚不睡觉，也要把这本书看完。
4. 像这样的事情，她宁愿自己动手，也决不去麻烦别人。
5. 很多父母宁肯自己少吃点，少用点，也要把钱省下来让孩子上大学。

　　取舍复句中表示所取的分句，可出现在前，也可在后。例句 (1) 和 (2) 就是舍前取后，而例 (3)、(4) 则相反。有时，也可以只说出取者而隐去舍者，用"宁可……也……"关联的例 (5) 就是这样的句子。取舍复句与选择复句的区别在于前者表示经过比较后作出取舍，而后者只提出可供选择的事项。

The clause represents the preference, and may come at the beginning or at the end of the sentence. While the preferences in Examples (1) and (2) come last, the ones in Examples (3) and (4) come first. In some cases, only the referred option is mentioned, the other is omitted such as in example (5). The distinction between a Complex Sentence of Preference and an Alternative Complex Sentence is that the former makes a choice after comparing the two things, and the latter provides options to choose only.

二、定语 (2)　Attributive (2)

(一) 多项定语　Multiple Attributives

一个名词或名词性质的短语，有时可以同时被几个定语修饰。如：

A Noun or a Noun Phrase, can sometimes be modified by several Attributives simultaneously. For example:

<u>健康</u>、<u>快乐</u>的孩子　　　　　<u>一只</u> <u>大</u> <u>黄</u> 狗
　①　　②　　　　　　　　　　①　②　③

<u>那</u> <u>两个</u> <u>穿西装</u> <u>坐在沙发上</u>的 <u>中国</u> 人
①　②　③　　　④　　　⑤

同时修饰一个中心语的几个定语，叫多项定语。

The Attributives that modify a Head Noun simultaneously are named Multiple Attributives.

(二) 多项定语的排列顺序　The Sequence of Multiple Attributives

照汉语的习惯，多项定语基本上是以从大到小的顺序排列的。离中心语越远的，多数是比较大的单位；离中心语越近的定语，与中心语的关系也越密切。这一点与英语有所不同。例如：

Multiple Attributives are arranged from general to specific by convention in Chinese. Normally, the further away the Attributive from the Head Noun, the larger the unit is; the closer the Attributive is to the Head Noun in distance, so is the relation between the two. This is quite different from English. For example:

上海是 <u>世界</u> <u>最大的</u> <u>城市</u>之一。　Shanghai is one of <u>the largest</u> <u>cities</u>
　　　①　　②　　③　　　　　　　　　　　　③　　　②

<u>in the world</u>.
①

学校　电脑中心　三楼　西边儿　吴老师的　那间　办公室已经关门了。
①　　②　　　③　　④　　　⑤　　　⑥

The office <u>of Professor Wu's</u> in the <u>west wing</u> of the <u>third floor</u> in the
⑥　　　　　　　　⑤　　　　　　　　　④　　　　　　　③

<u>computer center</u> at <u>school</u> has closed already.
②　　　　　　　①

甲、从离中心语最远的修饰语算起，多项定语的排列顺序一般是：

A. Starting from the one that is the furthest away from the Head Noun, the presenting sequence of Multiple Attributives is:

1. 表示所属的名词、代词或短语（表示"谁的"）。
2. 指示代词或数量短语（表示"哪个、多少"）。
3. 主谓短语、动词短语（表示"干什么的、怎么样的"）。
4. 介词短语（表示"与什么有关、对象、目的、方式"）。
5. 表示性质、状态、特征的形容词短语（表示"什么样的"，双音节的多带"的"字）。
6. 表示质料、年龄、职业等的名词（表示"什么"，通常不带"的"字）。

例如：

1. Noun, Pronoun, or Phrase indicating subordination, affiliation (referring to "whose").
2. Demonstrative Pronoun or Phrase of Quantity (referring to "which one" or "how many or how much").
3. Subject and Predicate Clause or Verb Phrase (referring to "doing what" or "how it does").
4. Preposition Phrase (referring to "concerning what", "dealing with what", "for what purpose" or "in what way").
5. Adjective Phrase concerning nature, state, or characteristic (referring to "what type" or "how it is" and disyllabic Adjectives usually with the character of 的).
6. Nouns concerning materials, age, or occupation (referring to "what", usually without the character of 的).

For Example:

〔老人的 那件 新 羊皮〕大衣也弄脏了。
　① 　②　⑤ ⑥

〔老人的 那件 刚买的 新 羊皮〕大衣也弄脏了。
　① 　② 　③ 　⑤ ⑥

〔老人的 那件 刚从百货商店 买来的 新 羊皮〕大衣也弄脏了。
　① 　② 　　④ 　③ 　⑤ ⑥

〔老人的 那件 他儿子刚给他 从百货商店 买来的 新 羊皮〕大衣也弄脏了。
　① 　② 　③ 　④ 　③ ⑤ ⑥

我认识〔这个 教古代汉语的、高高的 青年〕老师。
　② 　③ 　⑤ 　⑥

他开着〔一辆 跟别人借来的 红色的 德国〕跑车。
　② 　④ 　⑤ 　⑥

小冯又看了一遍〔这封 经理修改过的、用电脑打出来的 英文〕信。
　① 　③ 　④ 　⑥

〔她 那双 哭红了的 美丽的 大〕眼睛又亮起来了。
　① ② 　③ 　⑤ 　⑤

乙、 如果是领属关系的多项定语，按下面的顺序排列：

B.　If the Multiple Attributives represent a subordinate relation, they will go
　　in the following order:

名词/代词＋指示代词＋数量词＋中心语
Noun/Pronoun+Demonstrative Pronoun+Quantifier+Head Noun

〔你朋友的　这　几本〕书　我已经看完了。

丙、 如果多项定语是并列关系，可按一定的逻辑顺序 (如时间、地位、
　　等级、重要性或习惯等) 排列。例如：

C.　If the Multiple Attributives represent a parallel relation, they then can be
　　listed according to certain logical order (such as time, status, ranking,
　　significance, or convention). For example:

(时间)　　这几天，他一直在考虑去年生意成功、今年生意失败的原因。

（地位）　会议讨论了全面提高<u>小学、中学、大学的</u>教学质量问题。

（等级）　虽然是同一个牌子的茶叶，质量也有<u>高、中、低的</u>差别。

（重要性）唐老师对每个学生的<u>学习、生活和家庭的</u>情况都非常关心。

（习惯）　她第一次用中文写了一封给<u>爷爷、奶奶、爸爸、妈妈的</u>信。

如果多项定语的地位相等，可以自由排列，如：

If the status of each Attributive is the same, it does not matter which one goes first and which one goes next. For example:

小高、小林、小杨的字都写得不错。

小林、小杨、小高的字都写得不错。

小杨、小高、小林的字都写得不错。

修辞

句式：主动句和被动句　Sentence Forms: Active and Passive Sentences

在主谓句中，如果谓语的中心语是表示行为动作的动词，那么主语和谓语动词之间就存在着"施事"或"受事"的关系：主语是动作的执行者，或者是动作的支配对象。主语是动作执行者的句子叫主动句；主语是动作支配对象的句子叫被动句。例如：

In Subject Predicate Sentences, if the center of the Predicate is an action Verb, the relation between the Subject and the Verb Phrase will be either an "*agent*" or a "*patient*". That is, the Subject of the sentence may be the "executor" of an action, or the "object" to be controlled/affected by an action. While the former is called a Sentence of Active Voice, the latter a Sentence of Passive Voice. For example:

主动句：<u>狗</u>吃了我的作业。

被动句：<u>我的作业</u>被狗吃了。

表示被动的句型主要有下面几种：

The followings are several major patterns that express the sense of "passiveness" in Chinese:

1. 他没按规定停车，结果车被拖走了，还被罚了五十块钱。
2. 小芳的钱都让她的男朋友用光了。　　　　　（口语）
3. 你看，货物都叫雨淋湿了！　　　　　　　　（口语）
4. 门给风吹开了。　　　　　　　　　　　　　（口语）
5. 这个道理已经为无数事实所证明。　　　　　（书面语）
6. "金星"号货轮遭到暴风雨袭击，船体和货物都受到不同程度的损坏。
7. 你方的损失将由保险公司赔偿。

　　当一件事情，既可用主动句表达，又可用被动句表达时，选用哪种句式，就不仅仅是一个语法问题，而且是修辞的问题了。请比较一下与上面的被动句相对应的主动句：

When an idea is expressed, either in Active Voice or Passive Voice, it is not a simple matter of grammar but an issue of rhetoric in regard of which sentence form to use. Let's compare these sentences of Active Voice that mirror the previous ones of Passive Voice:

1a. 他没按规定停车，结果<u>警察(?)</u>把车拖走了，还罚了他五十块钱。
2a. 小芳的<u>男朋友</u>把她的钱都用光了。
3a. 你看，<u>雨</u>把货物都淋湿了！
4a. <u>风</u>把门吹开了。
5a. <u>无数事实</u>已经证明了这个道理
6a. <u>暴风雨</u>袭击了"金星"号货轮，使船体和货物都受到不同程度的损坏。
7a. <u>保险公司</u>将赔偿你方的损失。

　　这几个主动句虽然意思与被动句大致相同，但是它们的句子结构不同，叙述的角度和陈述对象也不同。主动句的话题是施事者，意念的重点是"谁做了什么"；而被动句的话题是受事者，意念的重点是"谁/什么东西被怎么样了"。因此，如果交谈或写作时要把受事者作为话题，作为陈述对象，或者为了强调，突出受事者受到了什么样的处置、影响，就要用被动句。以下是汉语使用被动句的基本条件：

Although these sentences are more or less the same in meaning, their structures differ and the perspective of representation and the object of the argument are different. The topic of an Active Sentence is the *"agent"*, and the focus of the notion is "who did what", whereas the topic of a Passive Sentence is the *"patient"*, and the focus is on "what was done to whom/on what". Hence, when the *"patient"* becomes the topic of a conversation or writing, as the object of an argument, or for the sake of emphasis, to highlight how the *patient/object* is dealt with, what impact it receives, a Passive Sentence must be used. The following are situations when a Passive Sentence is to be used:

1. 强调主语 (受事者) 的遭遇，其结果多数是消极的、不幸的，或不是受事者所希望的。例如：

   To emphasize the misfortunate, negative experience of the sentence subject (patient) and the results are generally negative, unpleasant, or something undesirable. For example:

   a. 她的新衣服给狗弄脏了。

   b. 我们提出的交易条件被对方拒绝了。

2. 突出受事者，不必说出、不愿说出或无法说出施事者时，例如：

   To give prominence to the *patient*, or when it is not necessary, not willing to, or unable to name the *"agent"*, the executor of the action. For example:

   a. 老胡办公室的电脑给偷走了。

   b. 因此，"装运"这个词常被用来代替"交货"的概念，国际贸合同中的"交货条件"也常被称为"装运条件"。

3. 统一前后句子的主语，使语义连贯，语气流畅。试比较下面的两组句子：

   To make the Subject of the previous sentence and the following ones consistent, so as to make the text more coherent in meaning and smoother in its flow. Now compare the two groups of sentences in the following pairs:

甲 a) 他打开门，想看看外面的情况，但刚走了两步，<u>就立刻被风刮倒了</u>。他赶紧扶着墙站起来，跑回屋子里去了。

甲 b) 他打开门，想看看外面的情况，但刚走了两步，<u>风就立刻把他刮倒了</u>。他赶紧扶着墙站起来，跑回屋子里去了。

乙 a) 在一般情况下，装运港要便于货物的装运，所以都<u>由卖方在洽商时提出</u>，经买方同意后确定；目的港要便于货物的接收或转售，所以<u>由买方提出</u>，经卖方同意后确定。

乙 b) 在一般情况下，装运港要便于货物的装运，所以<u>卖方在洽商时提出装运港</u>，经买方同意后确定；目的港要便于货物的接收或转售，所以<u>买方提出目的港</u>，经卖方同意后确定。

这两组句子，如果把 (a) 句的划线部分换成 (b) 句的主动句式，虽然语义差不多，但是因为要变换主语，就显得没有 (a) 句那么的连贯和流畅。

If all the underlined parts of the a) sentences in these two groups are converted into Active Voice such as in the b) sentences, even though the basic meaning remains more or less the same, the flow of the sentences seems to be broken, and the meaning is less coherent. The reason is that the Subjects of these sentences have been changed, and the original focus has been switched.

当然，不是所有的主动句都有相应的被动句式或者都可以转换成被动句式的。下面的句子就很难转换成被动句：

Not all Active Sentences, of course, have their corresponding Passive forms, or are not possible to be turned into Passive. The following sentences are just a few examples:

现在很多人都在学汉语。

✘现在汉语被很多人都在学。　　✘现在汉语在被很多人学 (习)。

小周要买两本关于统计的书。

✘两本关于统计的书要被小周买。　✘两本关于统计的书要被小周(购)买。

由于汉语的被动句多数用于表示对主语(受事者)来说是不利的或受损害的情况，所以它的使用频率要比英语的低得多。一般来说，如果对主语(受事者)来说是有利的或是愉快的，希望其发生的，基本上都不用"被"、"让"、"叫"、"给"或"受"等引起的被动句，而使用在结构和词序上与主动句相同，但在意义上是被动的句式。如：

Since Passive Sentences in Chinese refer to situations that are unlucky, or suffering of the *patient*, they are used much less frequently than their counterparts in English. If it is a situation favorable, pleasant or desirous to the subject of a sentence (*patient*), Passive Sentences with the Particles 被、让、叫、给, or 受 are not used. Instead, those with the same sentence structures and word order as Active Sentences but Passive in meaning are used. For example:

合同打印好了。
✘合同被打印好了。
她的钱包找到了。
✘她的钱包被找到了。
这个工厂的生产成本降低了百分之十。
✘这个工厂的生产成本被降低了百分之十。

另外，如果要说明发生在过去的某件事情是什么人做的、或者事情发生的时间、地点、方式等时，汉语用的是"是……的"句型而不是被动句。例如：

In addition, when we want to specify who was the executor of a past action, or the time, the place, and the manner of a past action, the sentence pattern 是……的 is used rather than the Passive Voice. For instance:

这本书是陈教授翻译的。
✘这本书被陈教授翻译了。
那条高速公路是三年前修建的。
✘那条高速公路三年前被修建了。

因此，学习被动句时，不但要注意被动句的形式，还要懂得使用被动句的场合。知道什么时候该用、什么时候不该用以及为什么要用被动句，了解汉语被动句与英语被动句之间的差别。只有这样，才能准确地表达意思，收到良好的交际效果。

When we learn Passive Sentences in Chinese, therefore, not only should we know their forms, but also the situations of their usage. Only when we know when to use them, when NOT to use them and why, as well as the differences between Chinese and English Passive Sentences, can we accurately express ourselves and communicate effectively in Chinese.

练习

一、 用线将意思相同的词和词语连起来：

保险公司同意为被保人提供保险服务和
负责赔偿的项目和方面　　　　　　　　　　　　　保险人

为某个人或团体当保证人　　　　　　　　　　　　外来风险

保险公司给被保人开的书面证明，表示
在一定范围内如有损失负责赔偿的文件　　　　　　出事率

向另一方收取一定费用，同时向其提供
在一定范围内保险服务的一方　　　　　　　　　　作保

人或交通工具遇到危险　　　　　　　　　　　　　汇率

不顾危险地进行某种活动　　　　　　　　　　　　罢课

有遇到不幸或造成灾难的可能　　　　　　　　　　承保范围

学生为实现某种要求或表示抗议而集体停止上课　　效率

由外来原因如偷窃、雨淋、短量、破碎、受潮等
造成的货损　　　　　　　　　　　　　　　　　　遇险

停止进行某项已经开始了的活动　　　　　　　　　冒险

单位时间内完成的工作量　　　　　　　　　　　　保险单

一个国家的货币兑换其他国家货币的比率　　　　　危险

发生事故与没有发生事故的比例　　　　　　　　　　罢手

二、用括号里的词或词组改写下列句子，但不改变其基本意思，必要时可对词序作一定的调整：

1. 为了避免意想不到的不幸事件发生，保证旅客安全，航空公司规定，从起飞开始到降落为止，旅客都要系安全带。

   （发生意外；自……至……）

2. 我们已经做好了各方面的准备，新安装的两套电脑化设备可以保证绝对不会出现任何问题。　　（万无一失；全面）

3. 社会的经济情况发生变化，房屋的价格也跟着波动。换句话说，经济情况好了，买房子的人就多，房子也就贵了。

   （A 随着 B 而 Verb；换言之）

4. 工人们一起停止工作，表明了工厂的管理有严重的问题。

   （罢工；意味着）

5. 高速公路上出事经常与开车的速度有关，所以开车要小心。有时候就是慢一两分钟也要比为了快一秒钟而冒险好。

   （往往；与其……不如……）

6. 最近海关规定，凡是从英国来的牛肉，一律不让进口。

   （来自；不予）

7. 你教他不会没有效果的。他学会了，其他人也会跟他学，结果对你也是一种帮助。　　（白Verb；反过来）

8. 对因为操作疏忽犯错误而造成的损失，我们一律不负责。

   （过失；概不）

三、选择最合适的词填空：

1. 他_____不复习，要考试了才看书，怎么会考得好呢？

   a. 常常　　　　b.平常　　　　c. 经常　　　　d. 往往

2. 刚开始做生意的人，_____只看到别人做生意赚钱，却很少想到他们也有亏本的时候。
   a. 常常   b. 平常   c. 经常   d. 往往

3. _____老陈都要仔细检查几遍以后才在合同上签字，今天他连看都不看就签了。
   a. 常常   b. 平常   c. 经常   d. 往往

4. 王大明打碎了客户寄来的样品，_____了经理的批评。
   a. 遭到   b. 遭受   c. 遭遇   d. 遭

5. 虽然她_____了很多困难和失败，但是还是坚持下去，终于取得了成功。
   a. 遭到   b. 遭受   c. 遭遇   d. 遭

6. 请放心，保险公司会按照规定，赔偿你们所_____的损失的。
   a. 遭到   b. 遭受   c. 遭遇   d. 遭

7. 这次暴风，给美国南部_____了很大的损失。
   a. 造成   b. 制成   c. 做成

8. 那个精美的盒子，是用玻璃加工_____的。
   a. 造成   b. 制成   c. 做成

9. 银行开信用证就是以最近的信用为进口人_____保，保证承担付款的责任。
   a. 造   b. 制   c. 作   d. 做

10. 中国的_____船工业近年来有了很大的发展。
    a. 造   b. 制   c. 作   d. 做

11. 买保险要看情况和需要，选择适当的险别，才能_____到既经济又安全。
    a. 造   b. 制   c. 作   d. 做

12. 这次意外事故，虽然轮船受到一定的损坏，但是没有造成人员或货物的_____，保险公司未必会赔偿。

    a. 失去　　　　　b. 丢失　　　　　c. 丧失

13. 通过海关的保证，他们把_____了的两箱货物找回来了。

    a. 失去　　　　　b. 丢失　　　　　c. 丧失

14. 因为老是重复同样的活动，孩子们很快就_____兴趣了。

    a. 失去　　　　　b. 丢失　　　　　c. 丧失

四、 找出课文里的取舍复句。

五、 用取舍复句完成下列对话：

1. 我们就是少赚点儿钱，也不能违约。

        （宁可……也决不……）

2. 你自己随便找药吃不是个办法，应该赶快去看医生才行。

        （与其……还不如……）

3. 很多人怕自己报税会出错，所以都愿意花几十块甚至几百块钱请别人报税而不想花几小时自己填税表。

        （宁肯……也不……）

4. 我们还是自己租船订舱吧，这比请卖方帮忙办理便宜些。

        （与其……倒不如……）

5. 我觉得就是多花一些钱，住得离学校近一点儿，也比每天坐两小时的公共汽车好。

        （与其……宁可……）

6. 哪怕把牛奶倒掉，让水果蔬菜烂掉，他们都不希望农副产品价格下跌。　　　　（宁愿……也不……）

六、 按照例子，把下面各组句子改写成一句合乎汉语习惯、有多项定语的长句：

    例：　他是一位教授。

他是老教授。

他很有经验。

他教了三十多年汉语了。

他是一位教了三十多年汉语、很有经验的老教授。

1. 我们已经收到了信息。

   你们给我们提供这些信息。

   这些是关于贵国贸易惯例的信息。

2. 这是一份价格表。

   这是彩色价格表。

   这是用电脑打印的价格表。

   这是我们公司的价格表。

3. 她不认识那个人。

   那个人是他们银行的副经理。

   那个人负责进出口业务。

   那个人有很多白头发。

   那个人对人很客气。

   那个人五十多岁。

4. 他们把工厂建在一个地方。

   他们把工厂建在山上。

   他们把工厂建在没有什么人去的地方。

   这个工厂试验新产品。

5. 几个朋友都在准备考试。

   他们是小张的好朋友。

   他们在准备汉语水平考试。

   汉语水平考试下星期举行。

6. 两个学生在政府部门找到了工作。

   两个女学生找到了工作。

刚从中国留学回来的学生找到了工作。

工作是翻译工作。

我们系的学生找到了工作。

7. 进口商选择了那个港口。

那个港口比较小。

那个港口离产地不远。

那个港口是新的。

那个港口有集装箱码头。

8. 这些产品受到了欢迎。

这些产品是中国的。

这些是轻工产品。

这些产品设计新颖、美观大方。

大家热烈欢迎这些产品。

七、 先用"被、受、由"或"是……的"在适当的地方填空，如可能的话，再把被动句改为主动句，然后比较改动前后句式和意思的异同：

这批货物_____天宁公司从香港进口，_____中国远洋运输公司的"黄山"号货轮装运_____。根据合同规定，保险_____买方自己负责办理。在装运时，即发现有六箱货物_____盗。在运输途中，"黄山"号遭到了暴风雨的袭击，有五分之一的货物_____潮，其中八箱_____海水泡湿，货轮也_____到一定的损坏。这个事故_____到了买方的严重关注，检查结果已_____送到了保险公司。目前，这个事件仍在_____调查中。

八、 把下列句子翻译成汉语：

1. According to the stipulations of the contract, the seller is responsible for the safety of the goods from the time it has been transported from the warehouse till loaded on board of the ship. In other words, if there is any damage to the

goods caused by loading, the seller will render compensation. However, once the goods have been loaded on board, it is the buyer or the insurer who will bear the responsibility. If any damage or loss has happened to the goods during shipment or after its arrival of the destination port, the seller is not responsible at all.

2. Mail order and direct marketing has been thriving along with the development of science and technology. They often utilize television to advertise. Quite a lot of people think that it would be better to buy inexpensive goods by making phone calls than waiting for a sale and going to stores. Yet, buying things in this way is not necessarily risk-free at all. Sometimes, whether you will get what you like is a matter of luck [i.e. "also depends on trying one's luck"].

3. Two years ago, the regulation of increasing the speed (limit) on freeways began to go into effect. This regulation has been opposed by many people. To them, increasing the speed means more mishaps and accidents. More accidents mean an increase of auto-insurance premiums. To some insurance companies, the increase in auto-insurance premiums means more profit. However, they have forgot one thing [i.e. "one point"]: if more people have suffered from accidents, they will, in turn, ask for more compensation.

九、 商业信函练习六

按照中文商业信函<u>新型通用式</u>的格式，把下面的信翻译成中文：

The People's Insurance Company of China
Guangzhou Branch
137 Changti ["Long (river) bank" literally]
Guangzhou, China

                                    May 3, 1999

Big Apple Farm Produce Corporation
49 126 Street, Suite 57-D
Flushing, NY 11358
USA

Dear Sirs,

From your letter of April 28th, we are pleased to note that you plan to insure with us 5, 000 cartons of Litchi which will be shipped from Guangzhou to New York.

We would like to inform you that the current rate for the proposed shipment against All Risks is at 110% of the total value of the invoice, subject to PICC's Ocean Marine Cargo Clauses, details of which you can find in our enclosed copies.

If our rate is not higher than what you expected, please fax us the necessary information about your shipment so that we can issue the policy immediately.

                            Yours truly,

                            Wuxian Bao
                            [literally "guarantee no risks"]
                            Manager

文化与商贸背景知识

📎 宴请

中国人热情好客，也很讲究吃喝，因此，设宴招待客人是社会交际的一项主要内容。

当外商到达中方公司所在地进行洽谈，或交易达成后，或客人要回国，作为主人的中方常常会设宴招待客商，表示欢迎、祝贺或者欢送。同时，中国人也很重视"礼尚往来"。作为客人的外商，不能总是"被动地"受邀请去赴宴，所以也要在适当的时机回请对方，以表示尊敬和谢意。

正式的宴会，大都由负责设宴的一方事先点好菜并安排好座位，因而客人一到，就可由服务员带到预定的座位上。正式的宴会一般都安排了主人和主宾讲话、祝酒。这时候，所有参加宴会的人都应该停止进餐。有时候参加宴会人比较多，就有几张、甚至几十张餐桌。主人和主宾坐的一桌就是主桌，其他餐桌都要依主桌行事：主桌祝酒，其他桌也要起立祝酒；主桌没有祝酒，其他桌不可自己先起立祝酒或者串桌敬酒。

开始进餐时，主人多数都会客气地说"没有什么菜，请不要客气"，或"菜不太好，请大家吃饱"等，并且招呼客人动手先吃。如果你是客人，可以说"您先请"，或者说"谢谢主人的盛情，我先吃，失礼了"。

在吃饭的过程中，中方主人常常会用自己的筷子给客人夹菜，同时请客人"多吃一点儿，不要客气"。作为客人，你可以说"不客气，我自己来"或"多谢多谢，自便好了"。另外，每吃一道菜时，都应该讲一两句赞美的话，如"非常好吃"、"实在太好了"等等，借以表示感谢。当看到自己不喜欢或不习惯吃的菜时，可以向给你夹菜的中方主人或服务员表示谢绝。有时宴会上有度数较高的白酒，中国人也常会请别人"干杯"。如果你喝不惯烈酒，可以夸奖对方"海量"、"好酒量"。同时谦虚地表示自己"酒量有限"、"甘拜下风"，或者婉言谢绝。千万不要不自量力，或者喝得太急、太猛，以免失态、失礼。如果你先吃完，而同桌还有人没有吃完，应该说一声"请慢用"或"失陪了"等关照的话。相反，如果同桌大多数人都已用餐完毕，自己就要尽快吃完，以配合大家的节奏。

宴会是双方进行广泛交谈的好机会。在进餐的初、中期，如果你是主人，可以向客人的来访表示欢迎；如果你是客人，可以感谢主人的热情接待，谈谈自己到此地访问的感想等。此外，拉拉家常，谈谈旅游、娱乐、体育、音乐、电影等，更能增进相互了解，消除商务谈判时的紧张。和日本人一样，中国人也很注意"宴会效用"，常常把宴会上的交谈当作谈判桌上谈判的延续。他们往往会在宴会的中、后期，逐渐地把话题引向业务谈判的内容上去。所以，不管你是主方还是客方，在宴会上都要保持清醒的头脑，对业务上的事情要认真考虑，不要作出随便的承诺。

✐ 商业信函(6)

中国人民保险公司：

　　兹有总金额为300,000美元的精美瓷器150箱，拟由天津新港通过海运，运往美国旧金山。现装船日期定为5月22日，敬请贵公司将你们的险别及其保险范围、保险率、办理手续函告我方。由于此批货物为易碎品，请顺告知，我方应投平安险、水渍险还是一切险？

　　因装船期已临近，为不致延误装运，恳请速来函答复，以便我方能尽快办理保险手续，按期发货。如能满足我方要求，则感激之至。

中国陶瓷进出口总公司
唐山分公司
××××年4月18日

✐ 保险单、运输险投保单、投保清单、保险条款

中保财产保险有限公司
The People's Insurance (Property) Company of China, Ltd.

总公司设于北京　　　　　　　一九四九年创立
Head Office BEIJING　　　　　Established in 1949

发票号码: INVOICE NO.	保险单 INSURANCE POLICY	保险单号表 POLICY NO. BJ01/　BJ01A/OM19701-0755

被保险人:
Insured: THE ORIENTAL SCIENTIFIC INSTRUMENTS IMPORT AND EXPORT CORPORATION

中保财产保险有限公司（以下简称本公司）根据被保险人的要求，由被保险人向本公司缴付约定的保险费，按照本保险单承保险别和背面所载条款与下列特款承保下述货物运输保险，特立本保险单。

THIS POLICY OF INSURANCE WITNESSES THAT THE PEOPLE'S INSURANCE (PROPERTY) COMPANY OF CHINA,Ltd. (HEREINAFTER CALLED "THE COMPANY") AT THE REQUEST OF THE INSURED AND IN CONSIDERATION OF THE AGREED PREMIUM PAID TO THE COMPANY BY THE INSURED, UNDERTAKES TO INSURE THE UNDERMENTIONED GOODS IN TRANSPORTATION SUBJECT TO THE CONDITIONS OF THIS POLICY AS PER THE CLAUSES PRINTED OVERLEAF AND OTHER SPECIAL CLAUSES ATTACHED HEREON.

标记 MARKS & NOS	包装及数量 QUANTITY	保险货物项目 DESCRIPTION OF GOODS	保险金额 AMOUNT INSURED
N/M	ONE SET	GOLD PLATING LINE	USD31,897.00
		B/L NO.: COSU2707000	

总 保 险 金 额:
TOTAL AMOUNT INSURED UNITED STATES DOLLARS THIRTY-ONE THOUSAND EIGHT HUNDRED AND NINETY-SEVEN AND 80/100 ONLY.

保费 PREMIUM AS ARRANGED	费率 RATE AS ARRANGED	装载运输工具 PER CONVEYANCE S.S.	BY SHIP " SONG HE V.110 "

开航日期
SLG. ON OR ABT. AUG.26,1997 As per B/L 起运
FROM TIANJIN 至
TO BANGKOK

承保险别
CONDITIONS COVERING ALL RISKS AS PER OCEAN MARINE CARGO CLAUSES OF

THE PEOPLE'S INSURANCE COMPANY OF CHINA DATED 1/1/81

所保货物，如遇出险，本公司凭本保险单及其他有关证件给付赔款，如发生本保险单项下负责赔偿的损失或事故，应立即通知本公司下述代理人查勘。

CLAIMS, IF ANY, PAYABLE ON SURRENDER OF THIS POLICY TOGETHER WITH OTHER RELEVANT DOCUMENTS. IN THE EVENT OF ACCIDENT WHERE BY LOSS OR DAMAGE MAY RESULT IN A CLAIM UNDER THIS POLICY IMMEDIATE NOTICE APPLYING FOR SURVEY MUST BE GIVEN TO THE COMPANY'S AGENT AS MENTIONED HEREUNDER.

CCIC (THAILAND) COMPANY LIMITED 22 SOI PIPA 2. CONVENTROAD SILOM, BANGRAK BANGKOK 10120 THAILAND TEL : (00662)-2385272,2336090 TELEX : 22235 CCICTH FAX : (00662)-2385273

中保财产保险有限公司
The People's Insurance (Property) Company of China,Ltd.
The People's Insurance C
of China

赔款偿付地点
CLAIM PAYABLE AT/IN BANGKOK, THAILAND (IN USD)

日期
DATE AUG.07, 1997

出单公司地址
ADDRESS OF ISSUING OFFICE ROOM 1106-1113, TOWER B, BEIJING COFCO PLAZA, NO.8, JIANGUOMENNEI AVENUE, BEIJING CHINA

中国人民保险公司
THE PEOPLE'S INSURANCE COMPANY OF CHINA

总公司设于北京　　一九四九年创立
Head Office: PEKING　　Established in 1949

发票号码　　　　　保险单　　　　保险单号次
Invoice No.　　INSURANCE POLICY　　Policy No.

中　国　人　民　保　险　公　司　（以　下　同　称　本　公　司）
This Policy of Insurance witnesses that The People's Insurance Company of China (hereinafter called
报　　据
"The Company"), at the request of ....
（以　下　同　称　被　保　险　人）　的　要　求，由　被　保　险　人　向　本　公　司　缴　付　约　定
(hereinafter called the "Insured") and in consideration of the agreed premium paying to the Company by the
的　保　险　费，按　照　本　保　险　单　承　保　险　别　和　背　面　所　载　条　款　与　下　列
Insured, undertakes to insure the undermentioned goods in transportation subject to the conditions of this Policy
特　款　承　保　下　述　货　物　运　输　保　险，特　土　本　保　险　单。
as per the Clauses printed overleaf and other special clauses attached hereon.

标　记 Marks & Nos.	包装及数量 Quantity	保险货物项目 Description of Goods	保险金额 Amount Insured

总　保　险　金　额：
Total Amount Insured:
保　费　　　　　　费率　　　　　　装载运输工具
Premium　as arranged　Rate　as arranged　Per conveyance S.S.
开　行　日　期　　　　　　　　　　　　　　　　　至
Slg. on or abt.　　　　　from　　　　　　to
承保险别
Conditions

所保货物，如送出险，本公司凭本保险单及其他有关证件给付赔款。
Claims, if any, payable on surrender of this Policy together with other relevant documents.
所保货物，如发生本保险单项下负责赔偿的损失或事故，
In the event of accident whereby loss or damage may result in a claim under this Policy immediate notice ap-
应立即通知本公司下述代理人查勘。
plying for survey must be given to the Company's Agent as mentioned hereunder:

中国人民保险公司广州分公司
THE PEOPLE'S INSURANCE CO. OF CHINA
KWANGCHOW BRANCH

赔款偿付地点
Claim payable at ....
日　期　　　　　广　州
DATE .... Kwangchow
地址：中国广州长堤137号
Address: 137 Changtei, Kwangchow, China.
Cables: 42001 Kwangchow.

中 國 保 險 公 司

香 港 分 公 司

CHINA INSURANCE CO., LTD.

HONG KONG BRANCH: INTERNATIONAL BUILDING, 15TH FLOOR, 141, DES VOEUX ROAD, CENTRAL, HONG KONG.

TEL. 5465077   TELEX: 61433 ZHONG HX   FAX: 5434947

九龍支公司:
電話：332 3467 傳真：770 3580
荃灣支公司:
電話：414 4131 傳真：416 0045
元朗支公司:
電話：475 0402 傳真：474 9500

眼睆支公司:
電話：341 6387 傳真：343 9349
屯門支公司:
電話：664 1383 傳真：567 0799
沙田支公司:
電話：695 9331 傳真：695 9927

運輸險投保書
MARINE INSURANCE APPLICATION

請出具
PLEASE ISSUE   保單 POLICY ☐   暫保單 COVER NOTE ☐   內容如下 AS PER FOLLOWING PARTICULARS.

日期
Date: _____

保戶名稱
Assured: _____

過 戶
Held to the order of _____

保險金額
Sum Insured: _____

船名／運輸工具
Vessel or Conveyance: _____   開航日期 Sailing on: 日 月 年

航程 由
Voyage: From _____   至 To _____

何處轉船
With Transhipment at _____   賠款地點 Claim payable at: _____

保品：
Subject-matter Insured: _____   L.C. / Order No. _____

嘜 頭 MARKS & NUMBERS	貨物名稱及數量 QUANTITY & DESCRIPTION OF GOODS	包 裝 PACKING

保險條件
Terms: _____

暫保單號碼
Declaring Cover Note No.: | NMC _____

需要正單（   ）份 及副本（   ）份
（   ) main policy & duplicates; & (   ) copies required.

地址
Address: _____

電話
Telephone: _____   聯絡人： _____

Applicant's Signature

此欄由本公司專用 FOR OFFICE USE ONLY			
Policy No.	Clause Code	Rate	Premium
Card No.			
A/C No.	Discount:		Examiner:

中 国 人 民 保 险 公 司
The People's Insurance Company of China
Head Office

运 输 险 投 保 单
Application for Transportation Insurance

被 保 险 人
Assured's Name

兹 有 下 列 物 品 拟 向 中 国 人 民 保 险 公 司 投 保 :
1 nsurance is required on the following commodities :

标 记 Marks & Nos.	包装及数量 Quantity	保险货物项目 Description of goods	保险金额 Amount insured

装 载 运 输 工 具
Per conveyance

开 航 日 期　　　　　　　　　　　　　　　提单号码
Slg. on/abt. _____　　　B/L No. _____
自　　　　　　　　　　　　　　　　　　至
Form _____　　　　　　to _____

　　请 将 要 保 的 险 别 标 明
please indicate the Conditions &./or
Special Coverage :

备 注:
Remarks :

投保人(签名盖章)　　　　　　　　　　电 话
Name/Seal of Proposer : _____　　Telephone No : _____

地 址　　　　　　　　　　　　　　　　日 期
Abbress : _____　　　　Date : _____

本 公 司 自 用 FOR OFFICE USE ONLY

费 率　　　　　　　保 费　　　　　　　　　　经办人
Rate _____　　Premium _____　　By _____

投保清单

Details of Goods Insured

项目 Descriptions of Goods	数量 Quantity	金额 Amount	项目 Descriptions of Goods	数量 Quantity	金额 Amount

中国人民保险公司
海洋运输货物保险条款

一九八一年一月一日修订

一、责任范围
本保险分为平安险、水渍险及一切险三种。被保险货物遭受损失时，本保险按照保险单上订明承保险别的条款规定，负赔偿责任。

（一）平安险

本保险负责赔偿：

1. 被保险货物在运输途中由于恶劣气候、雷电、海啸、地震、洪水自然灾害造成整批货物的全部损失或推定全损。当被保险人要求赔付推定全损时，须将受损货物及其权利委付给保险公司。被保险货物用驳船运往或运离海轮的，每一驳船所装的货物可视作一个整批。

推定全损是指被保险货物的实际全损已经不可避免，或者恢复、修复受损货物以及运送货物到原订目的地的费用超过该目的地的货物价值。

2. 由于运输工具遭受搁浅、触礁、沉没、互撞、与流冰或其他物体碰撞以及失火、爆炸意外事故造成货物的全部或部份损失。

3. 在运输工具已经发生搁浅、触礁、沉没、焚毁意外事故的情况下，货物在此前后又在海上遭受恶劣气候、雷电、海啸等自然灾害所造成的部份损失。

4. 在装卸或转运时由于一件或数件整件货物落海造成的全部或部份损失。

5. 被保险人对遭受承保责任内危险的货物采取抢救、防止或减少货损的措施而支付的合理费用，但以不超过该批被救货物的保险金额为限。

6. 运输工具遭遇海难后，在避难港由于卸货所引起的损失以及在中途港、避难港由于卸货，存仓以及运送货物所产生的特别费用。

7. 共同海损的牺牲、分摊和救助费用。

8. 运输契约订有"船舶互撞责任"条款，根据该条款规定应由货方偿还船方的损失。

（二）水渍险

除包括上列平安险的各项责任外，本保险还负责被保险货物由于恶劣气候、雷电、海啸、地震、洪水自然灾害所造成的部份损失。

（三）一切险

除包括上列平安险和水渍险的各项责任外，本保险还负责被保险货物在运输途中由于外来原因所致的全部或部分损失。

二、除外责任
本保险对下列损失不负赔偿责任：

（一）被保险人的故意行为或过失所造成的损失。

（二）属于发货人责任所引起的损失。

（三）在保险责任开始前，被保险货物已存在的品质不良或数量短差所造成的损失。

（四）被保险货物的自然损耗、本质缺陷、特性以及市价跌落、运输延迟所引起的损失或费用。

（五）本公司海洋运输货物战争险条款和货物运输罢工险条款规定的责任范围和除外责任。

三、责任起讫
（一）本保险负"仓至仓"责任，自被保险货物运离保险单所载明的起运地仓库或储存处所开始运输时生效，包括正常运输过程中的海上、陆上、内河和驳船运输在内，直至该项货物到达保险单所载明目的地收货人的最后仓库或储存处所或被保险人用作分配、分派或非正常运输的其他储存处所为止。如未抵达上述仓库或储存处所，则以被保险货物在最后卸载港全部卸离海轮后满六十天为止。如在上述六十天内被保险货物需转运到非保险单所载明的目的地时，则以该项货物开始转运时终止。

（二）由于被保险人无法控制的运输延迟、绕道、被迫卸货、重行装载、转载或承运人运用运输契约赋予的权限所作的任何航海上的变更或终止运输契约，致使被保险货物运到非保险单所载明目的地时，在被保险人及时将获知的情况通知保险人，并在必要时加缴保险费的情况下，本保险仍继续有效，保险责任按下列规定终止：

　　1．被保险货物如在非保险单所载明的目的地出售，保险责任至交货时为止，但不论任何情况，均以被保险货物在卸载港全部卸离海轮后满六十天为止。

　　2．被保险货物如在上述六十天期限内继续运往保险单所载原目的地或其他目的地时，保险责任仍按上述第（一）款的规定终止。

四、被保险人的义务

　　被保险人应按照以下规定的应尽义务办理有关事项，如因未履行规定的义务而影响保险人利益时，本公司对有关损失，有权拒绝赔偿。

　　（一）当被保险货物运抵保险单所载明的目的港（地）以后，被保险人应及时提货，当发现被保险货物遭受任何损失，应即向保险单上所载明的检验、理赔代理人申请检验，如发现被保险货物整件短少或有明显残损痕迹应即向承运人、受托人或有关当局（海关、港务当局等）索取货损货差证明。如果货损货差是由于承运人、受托人或其他有关方面的责任所造成，并应以书面方式向他们提出索赔，必要时还须取得延长时效的认证。

　　（二）对遭受承保责任内危险的货物，被保险人和本公司都可迅速采取合理的抢救措施，防止或减少货物的损失，被保险人采取此项措施，不应视为放弃委付的表示；本公司采取此项措施，也不得视为接受委付的表示。

　　（三）如遇航程变更或发现保险单所载明的货物、船名或航程有遗漏或错误时，被保险人应在获悉后立即通知保险人并在必要时加缴保险费，本保险方继续有效。

　　（四）在向保险人索赔时，必须提供下列单证：

　　保险单正本、提单、发票、装箱单、磅码单、货损货差证明、检验报告及索赔清单。如涉及第三者责任，还须提供向责任方追偿的有关函电及其他必要单证或文件。

　　（五）在获悉有关运输契约中"船舶互撞责任"条款的实际责任后，应及时通知保险人。

五、索赔期限

　　本保险索赔时效，从被保险货物在最后卸载港全部卸离海轮后起算，最多不超过二年。

中 国 人 民 保 险 公 司
海 洋 运 输 货 物 战 争 险 条 款

一九八一年一月一日修订

一、责任范围

本保险负责赔偿：

（一）直接由于战争、类似战争行为和敌对行为、武装冲突或海盗行为所致的损失。

（二）由于上述（一）款引起的捕获、拘留、扣留、禁制、扣押所造成的损失。

（三）各种常规武器，包括水雷、鱼雷、炸弹所致的损失。

（四）本条款责任范围引起的共同海损的牺牲、分摊和救助费用。

二、除外责任

本保险对下列各项不负赔偿责任：

（一）由于敌对行为使用原子或热核制造的武器所致的损失和费用。

（二）根据执政者、当权者、或其他武装集团的扣押、拘留引起的承保航程的丧失和挫折而提出的任何索赔。

三、责任起讫

（一）本保险责任自被保险货物装上保险单所载起运港的海轮或驳船时开始，到卸离保险单所载明的目的港的海轮或驳船时为止。如果被保险货物不卸离海轮或驳船，本保险责任最长期限以海轮到达目的港的当日午夜起算满十五天为限，海轮到达上述目的港是指海轮在该港区内一个泊位或地点抛锚、停泊或系缆，如果没有这种泊位或地点，则指海轮在原卸货港或地点或附近第一次抛锚、停泊或系缆。

（二）如在中途港转船，不论货物在当地卸货与否，保险责任以海轮到达该港或卸货地点的当日午夜起算满十五天为止，俟再装上续运海轮时恢复有效。

（三）如运输契约在保险单所载明另外以外的地点终止时，该地即视为本保险目的地，仍照前述（一）款的规定终止责任，如需运往原目的地或其他目的地时，在被保险人于续运前通知保险人并加缴保险费的情况下，可自装上续运的海轮时重新有效。

（四）如运输发生绕道，改变航程或承运人运用运输契约赋予的权限所作的任何航海上的改变，在被保险人及时将获知情况通知保险人，在必要时加缴保险费的情况下，本保险仍继续有效。

注：本条款系海洋运输货物保险条款的附加条款，本条款与海洋运输货物保险条款中的任何条文有抵触时，均以本条款为准。

第十一课

合同

✍ **思考下面的问题，然后带着着这些问题去阅读课文：**

一、什么是合同？为什么要签订合同？

二、合同的基本格式包括哪些部分？每部分有些什么内容？

三、出口业务的合同基本上有哪几种？它们有什么不同？

四、谁负责制作合同？制作合同时要注意什么？

五、合同什么时候开始生效？在这以前和以后，双方要做什么？

课文：合同

买卖双方经过口头或函电洽商，就各项交易条件取得一致意见后，交易就算达成。但是，这样的协议未必具有足够的法律约束力——万一日后某一方反悔，或对某些问题有不同的解释，争议就很难避免。常言道："空口无凭，立字为据"指的就是这个道理。因此，在进出口业务中，一般都要求买卖双方把各自在某一笔交易中具体的权利和义务以及双方商定的条件，以书面的形式固定下来，以便互相监督，各自执行，即使出现争议，也有据可查。这种对双方都有约束力的法律性文件，就是"合同"，有时也叫做"合约"或"契约"。

书面合同的基本格式可分为约首、本文和约尾三个组成部分。约首就是合同的首部，包括合同的名称、合同编号、签约日期和签约地点、买卖双方的名称和地址，以及序言等内容。合同序言一般表示双方订立合同的意愿和执行合同的保证、合同对双方都具有法

律约束力等。本文是合同的主体。它明确规定了买卖双方的权利和
15 义务。这些权利和义务在合同中，又详细体现为各项交易条件或条
款。约尾是指合同的尾部，包括合同文字的效力、份数、附件的效
力以及双方签字等。

尽管各个公司的书面合同格式各异，但一般说来，出口业务的
合同基本上有两种形式，即销售合同和成交确认书或销售确认书。
20 销售合同的内容比较全面，包括商品的名称、品质、规格、价格、
数量、包装、交货期、装运港和目的港、运输标志、支付方式、商
品检验、保险、异议索赔、仲裁、不可抗力等条件。除了对双方的
权利义务和各项交易条件作出明确的规定以外，合同对发生争议如
何处理等问题，也有详细的说明。因此，这种形式的合同，一般适
25 用于大宗商品或成交金额较大的交易。

成交(销售)确认书是一种简式合同，内容较为简单。成交确认
书一般包括买卖双方的权利义务以及所有的交易条件，如商品名
称、品质、规格、价格、数量、包装、交货期、装运港和目的港、
运输标志、支付方式、商品检验、保险等等，但是对于异议索赔、
30 仲裁、不可抗力等条款，一般不予列入。成交确认书经过双方签字
后，也具有销售合同的同等效力。这种形式的合同，多数适用于金
额不大，批数较多的土特产品和轻工产品，或者是已订有代理、包
销等长期协议的交易。

国际贸易中的合同多数由卖方制作，叫做“销售合同”，但有时
35 也可由买方制作。买方制作的合同，叫做“订购合同”或“购货合
同”。

合同的制作是一件严肃而细致的工作，制作时必须注意以下的
问题。首先，合同是个有机整体，各个条款之间应该前后呼应，相
互衔接，保持一致，不应出现互相矛盾的内容。比如，商品名称，
40 如果出现在各个条款中，就必须前后一致，不能使用不同的名称。

　　　标明单价、总值的货币必须相同。如果价格条件为 F.O.B. 或
C. & F.，在保险条款中应注明"保险由买方自理"。如果价格条件是
C.I.F.，不仅应注明由卖方投保，而且对投保金额、险别等都要详细
说明。其次，合同的各个条款要订得具体、完善，文字则要简练、
明确，切忌使用模棱两可的文字和词句。　　　　　　　　　　　　45

　　　合同制作完毕，必须经过严格核对，确认与谈判协议无误后，
才能由双方主管人员签字。合同一经签署，便立即生效，成为约束
双方的法律文件。此后，双方各持正本一份，副本若干份，作为自
己执行合同和监督对方履约的依据。对于合同的各项条款，任何一
方都要共同遵守，严格执行，不得单独修改其内容。无论哪方，如　50
无合法原因，不履行或不完全履行自己的义务，就是违约，必须承
担违约的法律责任。因此，"重合同，讲信用"是国际贸易的一条基
本原则，买卖双方都必须以严肃认真的态度对待合同。

✐ 根据课文内容回答下列问题：

1. 什么是合同？

2. 为什么要订立合同？

3. 合同的基本格式如何？每部分包括什么内容？

4. 销售合同包括哪些内容？它主要适用于什么交易？

5. 什么是成交确认书？它跟销售合同有什么不同？

6. 合同一般哪方制作较多？这种合同叫什么合同？

7. 买方可否制作合同？这种合同叫什么？

8. 制作合同必须注意什么问题？

9. 在合同上签字以前，双方应当做些什么？

10. 合同什么时候开始生效？生效后的合同有什么作用？

11. 如果一方不履行或不完全履行合同上规定的业务，会有什么后果？

✏ **根据意思，给课文划分层次 (不是自然段) 并写出每个层次的大意。**

生词和用法

万一	wànyī	Conj.	表示可能性极小的假设 (多用于不如意的事)。
			just in case; if by any chance
		N.	指可能性极小的意外变化：以防~。
			contingency; eventuality
解释	jiěshì	V./N.	分析阐明；说明某事的含义、原因、理由等：~课文、~法律、~误会、作~。
			to explain; to interpret; interpretation
常言	chángyán	N.	习惯上常说的像谚语、格言之类的话。
			common saying
道	dào	V.	说；用语言表达：~白、能说会~、~喜、~谢、~歉。
			to say; to talk; to speak
空口无凭	kōngkǒu wúpíng	Idm.	单凭嘴说而没有真凭实据。
			There is no record for an oral promise.
立字为据	lìzì wéi jù	Idm.	开立文书作为凭据。
			To prepare a document as evidence.
有据可查	yǒujù kě chá	Idm.	有凭据可以查对。
			There is documented record for investigation.
约	yuē	N.	约定的事，共同订立、需要共同遵守的条文：合~、条~、公~、契~、守~、履~、商~、失~、违~。
			pact; agreement; treaty; contract
合约	héyuē	N.	合同 (多指条文比较简单的)。
			contract
契约	qìyuē	N.	证明出售、抵押、租赁等关系的文书。
			contract; charter

序言	xùyán	N.	序文，写在文件或著作正文之前的段落或文章。 preface; forward
主体	zhǔtǐ	N.	事物的主要部分：~工程、~结构、文章的~。 main part; principle part
效力	xiàolì	N.	事物所产生的有利作用：~很大、没有~、失去~、发生~。 effect; authenticity
体现	tǐxiàn	V./N.	某种性质或现象在一事物上具体表现出来。 to embody; to reflect; embodiment
附件	fùjiàn	N.	随同主要文件一同制定或发出的文件。 appendix; annex
检验	jiǎnyàn	V.	检查验看：商品~、质量~、~标准。 to inspect; to examine
异议	yìyì	N.	不同的意见：提出~、没有~、独持~。 objection; dissent
仲裁	zhòngcái	V./N.	双方争执不决时，由第三者调解裁决：进行~、~法庭、~机构、~协定。 to arbitrate; arbitration
不可抗力	bùkěkànglì	N.	在当时的条件下，人力所不能抵抗的破坏力，如洪水、地震等自然灾害，因不可抗力而产生的损害，依法律不追究民事责任。 irresistible force; force majeure; Acts of God
同等	tóngděng	Adj.	等级或地位相同：~地位、~效力、~学历、~重要、~对待。 of the same class, rank, or status; on an equal basis
包销	bāoxiāo	V.	一方与另一方订立合同，专门负责把有关商品包下来销售。 to be the sole agent for a product of a firm
制作	zhìzuò	V.	制定文书； to draw up or prepare (a contract, document); 制造(比较精细的物件，如仪器、家具、陶瓷、

工艺品等）。Cf. 制造
to make; to manufacture

严肃	yánsù	Adj.	（作风、态度等）认真：~地指出、~的批评、~检查；＜＞马虎。 serious; earnest; solemn
细致	xìzhì	Adj.	精细周密；多指做事或思考问题的态度：~地分析、~地核对、~的工作；＜＞粗略。 careful; meticulous; painsticking
有机	yǒujī	Adj.	指事物构成的各部分互相关联协调，而具有不可分的统一性，就象一个生物体一样：~联系、~结合、~体；＜＞无机。 organic
整体	zhěngtǐ	N.	全体，一个事物的全部：~利益、~观念；＜＞局部。 whole; entirety
呼应	hūyìng	V.	不带宾语，一呼一应，相互通气；指文章或戏剧情节前后呼应。 to act in coordination with each other; to work in concert with
衔接	xiánjiē	V.	事物互相连接：前后~、相互~。 to cohere; to link up; to join
矛盾	máodùn	V.	言语行动相互抵触：自相~、前后~。 to contradict; to conflict
		Adj.	contradictory
		N.	形容对立的事物互相排斥的状态。 contradiction
完善	wánshàn	Adj.	齐备而美好；设备~；＜＞简陋。 perfect
		V.	使完备而变得美好：~生产责任制、~实验条件。 to perfect
简练	jiǎnliàn	Adj.	简洁精练，多指语言文字：力求~、~的文字。 terse; succinct

切忌	qièjì	V.	切实避免或防止，一般带动词作宾语： must guard against; to avoid by all means
完毕	wánbì	V.	〔书〕完结：准备~、工作~、装运~、检验~。 to finish; to complete; to end
签署	qiānshǔ	V.	在重要文件上签字：~合同、~命令、~提单 to sign
正本	zhèngběn	N.	文书或文件的正式的一份；＜＞副本。 original (of a document)
副本	fùběn	N.	文件正本以外的其他本。 duplicate; transcript; copy
履行	lǚxíng	V.	实现，用于自己答应做或应该做的事，常带宾语或补语：~合同、~义务、~诺言。 to fulfil; to carry out
履约	lǚyuē	VO	〔书〕做约定的事，不带宾语：按时~；＜＞违约。 to keep a promise; to carry out a contract
遵守	zūnshǒu	V.	依照规定行动，不违背：~纪律、~秩序、~时间、~协议；＜＞违反。 to observe; to abide by; to comply with
重	zhòng	V.	重视：尊~、敬~、看~、~男轻女、~合同。＜＞轻 to lay stress on; to attach importance to
讲	jiǎng	V.	讲求；重视某一方面并设法使它实现，满足要求：~究、~效率、~质量、~速度、~信用。 to tress; to pay attention to
对待	duìdài	V.	以某种态度或行为加之于人或事。 to treat; to approach; to handle

补充词

首脑	shǒunǎo	N.	领导人，为首的人或机关等：~会议、~人物。 head; chief
吃惊	chījīng	VO	受惊；不带宾语，可拆开：吃了一惊。 to be startled; to be shocked
勇敢	yǒnggǎn	Adj.	不怕危险和困难，有胆量。 brave
坚强	jiānqiáng	Adj.	强有力，不怕各种打击摧残；常指意志、组织等。 strong; firm; staunch
器官	qìguān	N.	生物体中具有某种独立生理机能的部分：发音~、感觉~、呼吸~、消化~。 organ; apparatus
捐	juān	V.	捐助，献出，一般用于钱财、生命等，多带宾语：~款、~血、~助、~献。 to contribute; to donate;
官员	guānyuán	N.	担任一定级别职务的政府工作人员：政府~、外交~、海关~。 officer; official
散漫	sǎnmàn	Adj.	随随便便，不守纪律；＜＞严谨。 undisciplined; careless and sloppy
纪律	jìlù	N.	政府、机关、军队、团体制定的、要求其成员必须遵守的规章、条文：遵守~、违反~、~严明。 discipline
（长）矛	chángmáo	N.	古代的一种兵器，柄长，一端装有青铜或铁制的枪头。 lance; spear; pike;
盾（牌）	dùnpái	N.	古代用来防护身体，遮挡刀箭的牌状武器。 shield
刺（穿）	cìchuān	VP	穿入、插入。 to stab; to penetrate; to pierce
骄傲	jiāo'ào	Adj.	自以为了不起，看不起别人，含贬义；自豪，引以为荣，含褒义。＜＞虚心、谦虚

			proud; arrogant
锋利	fēnglì	*Adj.*	刀具、武器的刀口薄或头子尖，容易切进或刺入物体。 sharp
抵触	dǐchù	*V.*	冲突、对立，常用"相、互相"等作状语：互相~、发生~。 to conflict; to contradict
业余	yèyú	*Adj.*	工作、学习以外的：~爱好、~时间。＜＞专业 spare time; amateur
体校	tǐxiào	*N.*	专门训练青少年运动员的体育学校：业余~。 school of physical education
训练	xùnliàn	*V./N.*	通过有计划、有步骤的培养，使具备某种技能或特长。 to train; to drill
勤学苦练	qín xué kǔ liàn	*VP*	勤：做事尽力，不偷懒；表示勤奋学习，刻苦练习。 to study diligently and train hard
胳膊	gēbo	*N.*	人肩膀以下手腕以上的部份。 arm
教练	jiàoliàn	*V.*	训练别人使掌握某种技术。 to coach
		N.	从事教练工作的人：篮球~、游泳~、主~。 coach
一举	yījǔ	*Adv.*	表示经过一次行动就能做到：~成功、~打破记录。 with one action; instantly
冠军	guànjūn	*N.*	体育运动等竞赛中的第一名：世界~、全国~、乒乓球~。 champion
记录	jìlù	*N.*	在一定时间、一定范围内记载下来的最好成绩：世界~、亚洲~、打破~、创造新~、保持~。 record

词语例释

一、就 Noun Phrase + Verb Phrase （with regard to; concerning; on）

l-1. 买卖双方经过口头或函电洽商，就各项交易条件取得一致意见后，交易就算达成。

1. 中美两国首脑就双方共同关心的问题进行了广泛的讨论。
2. 经过反复谈判，买卖双方终于就支付方式和装运时间达成了一致意见。
3. 就价格而言，美国车普遍低于日本车，但是就质量而言，日本车一般都高于美国车。

介词"就"引出分析、讨论、研究或处理的对象或范围。"就"可在主语前，有停顿。

The Preposition 就 introduces the object or the scope of a question to analyze, to discuss, to study or to deal with. 就 can occur before the Subject of the sentence with a pause.

二、万一 （just in case; if by any chance）

l-3. 但是，这样的协议未必具有足够的法律约束力——万一日后某一方反悔，或对某些问题有不同的解释，争议就很难避免。

1. 这是一笔金额非常大的交易，一定要核对清楚。万一有什么错误，我们都负不起这个责任。
2. 我看还是投保一切险比较好，万一出现什么问题，也不会血本无归。
3. 你还是把这些药带上吧，万一谁生病了，也不用到处去找医生。

"万一"可作副词，也可作连词，表示可能性极小的假设，多用于不希望发生的事情。

万一 can function as an Adverb or a Conjunction, indicating a hypothesis that has a very little chance of realization. It is mostly used for things that are undesirable.

三、 体现 （to embody; to incarnate; to reflect）

l-15. 这些权利和义务在合同中，又详细<u>体现</u>为各项交易条件或条款。

1. 张小姐在签合同前，反复核对各项条款，<u>体现</u>了她对工作认真负责的精神。

2. 我方的行动<u>体现</u>了希望通过协商解决问题的良好愿望。

3. 老师这样做，<u>体现</u>了她对你们的关心和爱护。

　　"体现"着重于抽象意义，间接表现人的精神或事物的性质等，常带"精神、作风、决心、品质、关心、爱护、愿望、特色、传统"等作宾语。"表现"指人或事物直接表露自身的神情、精神或性质变化等。

The Verb 体现 emphasizes the abstract meaning, and indirectly shows the vitality or energy of a person, or the nature of things. It usually takes these abstract Nouns as its Objects: 精神、作风、决心、品质、关心、爱护、愿望、特色、传统. A synonymous Verb 表现 also refers to human beings and things, but it primarily refers to the expression, the look, or the change of nature demonstrated directly by a person or an object.

四、 如何 ＋ Disyllabic Verb （how; how to）

l-24. 除了对双方的权利义务和各项交易条件作出明确的规定以外，合同对发生争议<u>如何</u>处理等问题，也有详细的说明。

1. 公司主管们正在开会研究<u>如何</u>减少装卸过程中货损的问题。

2. 有些商人总是说他们的商品<u>如何如何</u>好，别人的商品<u>如何如何</u>差，其实有时候一点儿根据也没有。

3. 很久没有联系了，不知近况<u>如何</u>？

　　代词"如何"，相当于"怎样、怎么样"的意思，多用于书面语，常带谓语或状语。"如何"后面的动词多为双音节动词，试比较：如何办理/处理/解决？＝＞怎么办？

　　如何 is a Pronoun, which is similar to 怎样 or 怎么样 in meaning. It is normally used in written Chinese, and often takes a Predicate or Adverbial. The

Verb follows 表现 is a disyllabic one, in general. Compare the following: 如何办理/处理/解决？＝＞怎么办？

五、 适用于 （to suit; to be applicable to）

l-25. 因此，这种形式的合同，一般适用于大宗商品或成交金额较大的交易。

1. 这种大型的高性能电脑适用于科研单位，并不适用于个人。
2. 汇付这种支付方式一般只适用于收付佣金，样品费或履约保证金等。
3. 我认为你们的教学方法既适用于大学，也适用于中小学。

动词"适用"是"适合使用"的意思，可受程度副词"很、非常"等修饰。作谓语可带宾语或补语。表示对象时，要用介词"于"连接名词性词语。

The Verb 适用 means "something is suitable for certain use" and can be modified by Adverbs such 很 or 非常. When it functions as a Predicate, it may take an Object or a Complement. The Preposition 于 is used to link up a Noun Phrase as the target to be involved.

六、 较为＋Disyllabic Adjective （rather; comparatively more...）

l-26. 成交（销售）确认书是一种简式合同，内容较为简单。

1. 本人这段时间的工作较为繁忙，所以未能及时复信。
    （Cf. 比较忙，✗较为忙）
2. 尽管那个工厂的设备较为陈旧，但他们的产品质量还是相当不错的。 （Cf. 比较旧，但✗较为旧）
3. 新收到的说明书内容较为丰富，大概要七八天才能翻译完。
    （Cf. 比较多，但✗较为多）

副词"较为"的意思相当于"比较"，但只修饰双音节形容词。因此，单音节形容词于"较为"连用时，要改为意思相同或相近的双音节词，

如：难——困难、忙——繁忙、旧——陈旧、慢——缓慢，多——丰富
(内容)、好——优越(条件)等。

Similar to 比较 in meaning, but the Adverb 较为 modifies disyllabic Adjectives only. Hence, when monosyllabic Adjectives are associated with 较为, they have to change to disyllabic synonyms such as in the following examples: 难——困难、忙——繁忙, 旧——陈旧、慢——缓慢, 多——丰富(内容)、好——优越(条件).

七、对于Noun Phrase/Verb Phrase （to; as to; in relation to; with regard to）

l-29. 成交确认书一般包括买卖双方的权利义务以及所有的交易条件，如商品名称、品质、规格、价格、数量、包装、交货期、装运港和目的港、运输标志、支付方式、商品检验、保险等等，但是对于异议索赔、仲裁、不可抗力等条款，一般不予列入。

1. 对于"海王"号货轮失火的具体情况，保险公司还不太了解。

2. 对于你们的市场调查报告，刘经理有些不同的看法。

3. 这是工人们对于减少生产事故的几点建议。

介词"对于"表示人、事物、行为之间的对待关系。多跟名词组合，也可跟动词或小句组合。"对于"可在主语前，有停顿，也可用在主语后。"对于"后面的名词可为动作的承受者，如句 (1)。"对于"后面的名词或动词也可以指涉及的事物，如例 (2)。"对于……"后面的短语可加"的"修饰名词或动词，如例 (3)。"对于"与介词"对"的某些用法相同，但"对于"不能用在助动词和副词后，下面的句子只能用"对"，不能用"对于"：

The Preposition 对于 indicates the attitude, opinion, and mutual relation between people, things or behaviors. It is associated mostly with Nouns, but may go together with a Verb, or a short sentence. 对于 can precede the Subject of a sentence, with a pause, and may follow the Subject. The Noun after 对于 can be the Object of an action, such as in Example (1). The Noun or the Verb after 对于 can refer to the thing involved, such as in Example (2). The character 的 may be added to the phrase after 对于 to modify a Noun or a Verb, as in Example (3). Some of the usage of 对于 is similar to that of the Preposition 对, but 对于 cannot be used before an Auxiliary Verb or an Adverb. The following sentences only apply to 对 but not 对于:

我们很快会对这件事作出处理的。✗我们很快会对于这件事作出处理的。

大家对这件事都很关心。　　　　✗大家对于这件事都很关心。

另外，表示人与人之间的关系，或动作的对象时，也只能用"对"：

In addition, when referring to relations among people, or the object/target of an action, 对 is the only option as illustrated below:

我们对你完全信任。　　　　✗我们对于你完全信任。

老师对我很热情。　　　　　✗老师对于我很热情。

她对你说了些什么？　　　　✗她对于你说了些什么？

八、 Adjective 1 而 Adjective 2 （Adjective 1 and/yet Adjective 2）

l-37. 合同的制作是一件严肃而细致的工作，制作时必须注意以下的问题。

1. 合同是有法律约束了的文件，必须订得简练而明确。
2. 练习要少而精，才能取得好的效果。
3. 知错而不改，是永远也不会有进步的。

　　连词"而"可连接两个并列的形容词，表示互相补充，相当于"又"的意思，如例 (1)。"而"也可以连接意思相反的形容词或动词，表示转折，意思同"然而、但是、却"，如例 (2) 和例 (3)。

　　The Conjunction 而 connects two parallel Adjectives, making them complement each other. It is equal to 又 in meaning, as shown in Example (1). It can connect two antonymous Adjectives or Verbs, indicating an adversative relation. In such case, it is the same as 然而、但是、却 semantically, as shown in Examples (2) and (3).

九、 不仅……而且/也/连…… （not only ... but also... /even... ）

l-43. 如果价格条件是 C.I.F. ，<u>不仅</u>应注明由卖方投保，<u>而且</u>对投保金额、险别等都要详细说明。

1. 我们的新产品<u>不仅</u>在性能上达到了规定的技术指标，在质量上<u>也</u>超过了进口的名牌产品。

2. 酒后开车<u>不仅</u>是个人的问题，<u>而且</u>是关系到大家生命安全的问题。

3. 水渍险<u>不仅</u>包括了平安险的责任范围，<u>连</u>由于恶劣气候、雷电、海啸、地震、洪水等自然灾害所造成的损失，也负责赔偿。

　　连词"不仅"用法与"不但"相同，用在递进复句前一分句，后一分句用"而且、也、反而"等配合。"不仅"常用在"是……"前，也可说"不仅仅"。

　　不仅 is a Conjunction and its usage is similar to 不但. It is used in the first clause of a Progressive Complex Sentence, and is coordinated with 而且、也、反而 in the second clause. 不仅 often occurs in front of 是……, and can be reduplicated as 不仅仅.

十、 Disyllabic Verb/Noun ＋完毕 （to finish; to complete; to end ）

l-46. 合同制作<u>完毕</u>，必须经过严格核对，确认与谈判协议无误后，才能由双方主管人员签字。

1. 货物已经装运<u>完毕</u>，下午就可以启航。

2. 请用传真通知我方，货运单证是否已准备<u>完毕</u>。

3. 会议仍未<u>完毕</u>，不得离开会场。

　　"完毕"表示"完了、结束"的意思，是不及物动词，不带宾语，不能带"着、过"，多用于书面语。"完毕"前的动词为双音节动词，"吃、喝、看、玩、睡、来、走、做"等单音节动词不能与"完毕"组合。

　　The Intransitive Verb 完毕 means 完了、结束, and does not take any Object. It cannot be associated with the Aspect Particles such as 着 or 过. 完毕 is primarily for written Chinese, and the Verbs precedes it should be disyllabic. Monosyllabic Verbs such as 吃、喝、看、玩、睡、来、走、做 are simply not use together with 完毕.

词义辨析

一、对于　关于　至于

　　"对于"是介词，表示人和事物，或事物之间的关系，用以引进动作的对象，或表示事物的关联，多跟名词、动词或小句组合。例如：

　　对于 is a Preposition which indicates the relationship between human and things, or the inter-relation between things. It is primarily used to introduce an Object or target of an action, or the connection between things. It is usually associated with a Noun, a Verb, or a Clause, for example,

　　我不同意你对于这个问题的看法。＝对于这个问题，我不同意你的看法。

　　这种药对于治疗心脏病很有帮助。＝对于治疗心脏病，这种药很有帮助。

　　对于他的要求，我们还没有答应。＝我们还没有答应他的要求。

　　"对于"一般不用来表示人与人之间的关系，也没有"向、朝"的意思。下面的句子都不能用"对于"：

　　In general, 对于 does not refer to inter-personal relations, nor does it mean "facing, toward". It cannot be used in the following sentences,

　　她对同学很关心。

　　我们公司从仓库正对着码头。

　　"关于"也是介词。英语的翻译，有时也与"对于"相同，但"关于"主要表示关联和涉及的某种事物，而"对于"则是指出动作的对象。比较下面的句子：

　　关于 is also a Preposition. Its English translation is quite similar to 对于, which can be "with regard to, concerning". However, 关于 primarily indicates something the action involved or related to, whereas 对于 introduces the Object of an action. Compare the following sentences,

关于这个问题，你可以跟小张联系。

对于这个问题，我们要尽快解决。

"关于"作状语时，只能位于句首，而"对于"可放在句首，也可在主语的后面。例如：

When 关于 functions as an Adverbial, it can only appear at the beginning of the sentence. However, 对于 can go either at the beginning of the sentence, or after the Subject, as in the following examples,

关于非洲市场，我了解得不多。✗我关于非洲市场了解得不多。

对于他的做法，大家都很有意见。＝大家对于他的做法都很有意见。

另外，"关于"有提示性质，可以直接作书名或文章的标题，而"对于"必须在末尾加上名词，才能作书名或标题。比较下面两个意思相同的标题：

In addition, 关于 can be used in a title of a book or an article, directly before the subject-matter. When 对于 is used as part of a book or article title, a Noun has to be added to the end of the title. Compare the following,

关于如何提高教学质量　对于如何提高教学质量的建议

"至于"作介词时，用于引进另一个话题，表示另提一件事或一种情况。"至于"还可作动词，表示事情发展到某种程度，后面多带动词或动词性短语，常用于否定句或反问句。例如：

As a Preposition, 至于 is to introduce a new topic, indicating a change of topic, meaning "as for" in English. 至于 can serve as a Verb also, indicating to a certain extent. It is usually followed by a Verb or Verb Phrase, and used in Negation or Rhetorical Questions. For example,

这篇文章生词虽然多，但是还不至于看不懂。(否定) (Negation)

要是早点去看大夫，哪至于病成这样？(反问) (Rhetorical Question)

二、表示　表现　表明　体现

"表示"作动词，是指通过语言行动显示出某种思想、感情、态度等，可带动词作宾语，如：表示欢迎（感谢、支持、同情、关心、赞赏）等。此外，"表示"还可作名词，指显示出某种思想、感情、态度的言语、动作或神情，例如：

The Verb 表示 refers to show one's ideas, feelings, attitude, etc. through language or action. It can take another Verb as its Object, such as 表示欢迎（感谢, 支持, 同情, 关心, 赞赏）. Moreover, it can also function as a Noun, indicating the expression of some ideas, feelings, or attitude, etc., for example,

这是一种友好的表示。

动词"表现"有两种意思。一个是指显现出来的意思，是个中性词，强调用言语、行为、形象或其他形式显出内在的本质、特点、状况、思想、感情或内容。在这点上，意思与"表示"相近，但"表现"所带的宾语，一般都是名词，而很少是动词。"表现"还有一个贬义的意思，就是"故意显示自己的长处"，如：他老是喜欢在女生面前表现自己的大方。"表示"没有这层意思。

The Verb 表现 can mean two things. One is "to show, display, manifest", and it is a neutral term. Its focus is on displaying the nature, characteristics, state, ideas, feelings, content, etc. through language, action, image or other means. It is similar to 表示 in this sense. However, the Objects of 表现 are generally Nouns, and rarely Verbs. There is another meaning for 表现, "to show off", which is derogative in Chinese: 他老是喜欢在女生面前表现自己的大方. 表示 does not have such meaning.

"表明"是"明白表示"的意思，常带名词宾语，如"决心、态度、观点"等。"表明"也可带小句作宾语，例如：

As it suggests, 表明 means "to oindicate explicitly, to show clearly". It often takes Nouns like 决心, 态度, 观点 as its Object. In addition, 表明 can also take a Clause as its Object, for example,

他用行动<u>表明</u>他对错误的认识是深刻的。

"体现"表示某种抽象的、概括的意义，如人的思想、精神、风格或事物的性质特点等，间接地在另一种事物上具体地显现出来。而"表现"则指人或事物直接显现自己的思想、感情、状况、变化、性质等。

> 体现 means "to embody", that is, showing something, usually with an abstract sense such as ideology, spirit, style, nature or characteristics via something else indirectly. On the contrary, 表现 refers to something that displays itself more directly.

三、履行　执行　进行

这三个动词都含有"行"字，表示"做、办、从事某项活动"的意思，常见的例子有"试行、行个方便、行不通、行医"等。"履行"侧重于实践自己答应做的或应该做的事情，常带"合同、义务、职责、诺言、条约"等名词作宾语。

> These three Verbs all contain the character 行, which means "to do, handle, engage in certain activity". The common examples are 试行、行个方便、行不通、行医, etc. 履行 emphasizes to carry out, or practice things one promised or obligated to do. Its Objects are 合同,义务,职责,诺言,条约, etc.

"执行"表示实施上级布置、颁布或已规定的事项，常带宾语或补语，多用于"政策、法令、方针、计划、命令、合同、规定"等。另外，也可作动词"负责、监督"等的宾语。

> 执行 indicates to implement decisions or regulations announced or stipulated by the authorities or superior. It usually takes an Object or a Complement, and is used mostly with Nouns such as 政策,法令,方针,计划,命令. Sometimes, it can also be the Object of Verbs like 负责,监督, etc.

"进行"强调从事持续性的，比较正式、严肃的活动，不可用于像"吃饭、睡觉、玩"这样的日常生活小事。"进行"常跟双音节动词搭配使用，而这些动词的后面不可再带宾语。例如：

进行 emphasizes to engage in or carry out activities that are formal and last a certain duration, but not with trivial daily matters such as 吃饭, 睡觉, 玩, etc. Moreover, 进行 should go with disyllabic Verbs, which cannot take an Object any more, for example,

我们要对这件事进行调查。（✘进行查）

大家决定对学习有困难的同学进行帮助（✘进行帮助学习有困难的同学）。

四、严重　严肃　严格

"严"字有"程度深、厉害"和"严厉、严格"的意思。形容词"严重"表示程度深、影响大、情势危急，一般不用于好的方面。除了作定语和谓语以外，"严重"还可作状语，以下是一些常见的用法：

The character 严 can mean "serious" and "severe, strict". The Adjective 严重 indicates that someone or something is pressing or possibly in danger, with a high degree or grave impact, usually not used in a positive sense. Besides functioning as Attributive and Predicate, 严重 can be Adverbial, too. Here are some of its common usages:

严重的问题；病情很严重；喝酒严重(地)影响了他的学习和健康。

"严肃"也是形容词，它的一个意思是指神情或气氛使人觉得敬畏，例如：

严肃 is an Adjective. One of its meanings refers to the solemnity, seriousness of a person's look or an atmosphere, for example,

黄经理是个严肃的人，平常极少开玩笑。

另一个意思是指人在作风、态度方面认真，例如：

The other meaning is being serious, conscientious in doing things, as in the sentence:

我们必须严肃对待这个问题。

"严格"可作形容词，表示在遵守制度或掌握标准时认真，不放松，强调不降低标准。常与"要求、检查、执行、区分、遵守、掌握、训练"

等动词搭配，可以用来对自己，也可以用来对别人。"严格"还可作及物动词，须带宾语，表示"严格执行、不放松，使严格"。例如：严格纪律；严格考试制度；严格质量检查。

When 严格 is an Adjective, it means "demanding total obedience or observance (of rules) or following guidelines, without lowering the standard." It is usually associated with Verbs such as 要求, 检查, 执行, 区分, 遵守, 掌握, 训练. It can be used for oneself, and to others as well. In addition, 严格 can function as a Transitive Verb that takes an Object, which means "to enforce strictly", for example, 严格纪律, 严格考试制度, 严格质量检查, etc.

语法

一、复句小结　A Summary of Complex Sentences

汉语的复句分为两大类：联合复句和偏正复句。联合复句中的各个分句在语法上是平等的，不互相修饰或互相说明；偏正复句中的两个分句，一个是偏句，一个是正句，偏句起修饰、限制作用，正句被偏句修饰或限制。

There are two main categories of Complex Sentences in Chinese: *Coordinate Complex Sentences and Subordinate Complex Sentences*. All clauses in a *Coordinate Complex Sentence* are equal in terms of grammar function, and they do not modify or illustrate each other. There are normally two clauses in a *Subordinate Complex Sentence*, one being the main clause, and the other the subordinate clause. While the subordinate clause functions to modify or restrict its main clause, the main clause is subject to the modification or restriction of its subordinate clause.

按照各个分句与分句之间的逻辑关系，联合复句可再分为选择、并列、解说、递进和承接等类型；偏正复句又可细分为因果、条件、目的、转折、假设和取舍等类型。下面是各种类型的复句以及常用的关联词语。

According to the logical relations between clauses, **Coordinate Complex Sentences** can be categorized as *Alternative, Coordinative, Elaborative, Progressive,* and *Successive* several types. **Subordinate Complex Sentences**, similarly, may be divided into such categories as *Cause and Effect*, *Condition*, *Purpose*, *Adversative*, *Hypothesis*, and *Preference*. The following is a summary of various types of Complex Sentences and the frequently used Connectives:

二、分句主语和人称代词的隐现　The Absence and Presence of Clausal Subjects and Personal Pronouns

(一)分句主语的隐现　The Absence or Presence of Clausal Subjects

一个复句可以有两个或两个以上的分句。由于汉语里主语与谓语之间结构上的联系比较松散，不像英语那样，每个分句基本上都要有一个主语，在某些情况下，特别是几个分句有同一个主语时，某些分句的主语就可隐去。这样做不但不会影响句子的意思，反而更合乎汉语的习惯。在几个分句有同一个主语的复句中，主语可以在前一个分句中出现（例1），也可以在后一个分句中出现（例2），甚至可以只在中间的分句出现（例3）。请看下面的句子：

A Complex Sentence may consist of two or more clauses. As the tie between the Subject and the Predicate in a Chinese sentence is relatively loose in structure, unlike its English counterpart that each simple sentence requires a Subject, in some cases, some clausal Subjects can be absent, especially when several clauses share an identical Subject. Such absence, instead of causing ambiguity or misunderstanding, is much more idiomatic, and conforms to Chinese practice. When a Subject is shared by several clauses in a Complex Sentence, it can be present in the first clause as in Example 1. It can also appear in the last clause, as in the case of Example 2. It can still be placed in the middle clause. Please look at these sentences:

1. 以前她觉得汉语非常难，后来认识了几个中国朋友，每天都跟他们一起聊天，现在她的汉语已经说得很流利了。

2. 尽管在运输过程中遇到了很多困难，经过大家的共同努力，我们还是按时安全地把货物运到了目的港。

3. 为了保证旅客们的安全，空中小姐在飞机起飞前，都要逐个座位检查，请旅客们把安全带系好。

当然，相同的主语也可以同时出现在复句的各个分句里。这样主要是为了强调主语，达到一定的修辞效果。例如：

Of course, it is possible for an identical Subject to be present in all the clauses in a Complex Sentence. This is primarily to highlight the Subject of the sentence, and to achieve some kind of rhetorical effect. For example:

复句的类型及常用关联词语

类型	关系	关 联 词 语
联 合 复 句	选择	或，或者……或者……，(是)……还是……，不是……就是……，要么……要么……，要就是……要就是……
	并列	也，又，还，则，而，同时，既……又……，也……也……，是……不是……，不是……而是……，一方面……一方面……
	解说	即，即是说，也就是说，换言之，换句话说，比方说，例如，譬如，比如；……，有的……，有的……；第一……，第二……；一是……，二是……，三是，
	递进	而且，并且，更，甚至，进而，不但(不仅，不只，不光，不单)……而且(还，也，又)……，别说(不用说)……就是(连)……，不但不(没)……反而……尚且……何况(更不用说)……；……，甚至于(乃至于)……；
	承接	开始，首先，接着，跟着，继而，然后，后来，就，便，才，再，于是(乎)，最后，终于

偏正复句	因果	因为……所以……，由于……因此……，由于……所以……，因此，因而，之所以……是因为……，……以致……，既然……就（那么，也，总，则）……	
	条件	只有……才……，只要……就……，除非……才……，无论（不论，不管）……都（也，还，总是）……，一旦……就……	
	目的	为，为了，为着，为了……起见……，……以……，……以便……，……以免……，……免得（省得）……，	
	转折	虽然（尽管）……但是（可是，然而，却，而）……，……但（但是，可是，不过，只是，就是，然而，却，而）……	
	假设	如果（要是，假如，倘若，假若）……那就（就，便，那么）……，若……则……，如果（要是，假如）……那就（就，那么）……，要不是……就……，万一……也（就）……，即使（纵然，哪怕，就算）……也（还）……	
	取舍	与其……不如（毋宁，宁可，宁肯，宁愿）……，宁可（宁肯，宁愿）……也不……	

4. 时间就是金钱，时间就是生命。

5. 我们不但善于破坏一个旧世界，我们还将善于建设一个新世界。

　　复句中各个分句的主语不同，一般都要逐一列出。但是如果语境清楚，关系明确，不会引起误解时，某个分句的主语也可以隐去。通常来说，隐去的成分基本上是后面分句的主语，而同时又是前一分句的宾语或定语。这种句子在口语里用得比较多。例如：

When the Subjects in the clauses differ from each other, they should normally be present. However, if the context is clear, the relation of each part is unambiguous, and will not cause any misunderstanding, the Subject of certain clause may be absent. Normally, the omitted element is the Subject of a second clause while in the meantime, the Object or the Attributive of the preceding clause. This type of sentences is quite common in spoken Chinese. For instance:

6. 我看了一下<u>进口的产品</u>，（进口的产品）质量不怎么样，（进口的产品）说不定还没有我们的好呢。

（隐去的部分在前一分句里作宾语。）

7. 小方的新电脑很好，可以打中文，不过今天（小方）没带来。明天叫他带来，帮你打一下就行了。

（隐去的部分在前一分句里作定语。）

（二）人称代词的隐现　The Absence or Presence of Personal Pronouns

汉语的人称代词无论在句子还是篇章中，和英语比起来，出现的频率都低一些。在下列情况下，按汉语的习惯，一般都可隐去。

Chinese Personal Pronouns, compared with English ones, are used less frequently no matter whether in sentences or in discourse. They can be absent in the following situations:

1、在单句中，当人称代词作人或事物的定语，尤其是表示身体部位、衣着服饰、物品工具的领属或从属关系时，往往隐去。如：

1. Personal Pronouns are usually absent when they function as an Attributive of a Noun Phrase referring to human beings or objects in single sentences, particularly body parts, dress and adornment, objects or tools that belong to, or subordinate to a person or a thing. For example:

妈妈说："去，先洗洗（你的）手再吃！"

他戴上了（他的）帽子，一句话也没说就走了。

糟糕！我忘了带（我的）飞机票了。

2、前面已经提及的事物（尤其是主题评论句中），如果用人称代词在后面的小句（评论部份）中作宾语复指，一般也隐去。如：

2. When a Personal Pronoun functions as an Object in an upcoming clause referring to a matter that has been mentioned previously, it is often absent, particularly in Topic-Comment Sentences. For instance:

> 哪儿有人咬狗的，我不信（它）。
>
> 那本书我昨天见过，可是没拿（它）。
>
> 索赔的问题你放心吧，保险公司会解决（它）的。

3、含有两个分句的复句，如果后一分句的人称代词指的是前一分句的主语，这个人称代词也常隐去。如：

3. In a Complex Sentence that consists of two clauses, if the Personal Pronoun in the second clause refers back to the Subject in the first clause, this Pronoun is often absent. For example:

> <u>林小宁</u>虽然还不太明白，可是（她）没有继续问下去。
>
> <u>老余</u>一喝酒（他）就喜欢说话。
>
> 你<u>黄广财</u>今天有新房子了，（你）也有新汽车了，（你）还想要什么？

4、在同一段落，特别是同一话题链里，人称主语基本上按照"名词→人称代词→隐去代词（零形式）"的方向，逐步简化和抽象化。如：

4. Within the same paragraph, especially in the same topic chain, Personal Pronouns tend to gradually become simpler and abstract as the topic chain or paragraph develops, following a pattern from "Noun to Pronoun, and then to the zero form of Pronoun (absence)". Such a pattern is observed in the paragraph below:

> 著名作家<u>老舍</u>先生每天要写一两千字到两三千字，在家的时间，<u>他</u>都给了这一至三千字。<u>他</u>静静地吸烟，然后写；（他）静静地喝茶，又写；（他）静静地擦桌子，还写；（他）静静地浇花，继续写；（他）静静地看画，写，写，写……（他的）思想变成了文字。

汉语的代词看起来很容易，因为语义比较简单，而且在其他语言中基本上都有对应词。但是，代词的功能不仅在单句，更重要的是在篇章，在于句子与句子之间的相互连接和照应。因此，学习汉语代词，应注意从篇章着眼，阅读时留意代词与其前后名词或短语的相互关系，注意对比汉语和英语的差别，这样才能真正掌握汉语代词的正确用法。

Chinese Pronouns seem to be very easy not only because they are semantically simple, but also because they basically have their counterparts in other languages. However, the function of pronouns is more on the discourse level than on sentence level, in the co-reference and coherence between clauses and sentences. Therefore, when learning Chinese Pronouns, we should focus on the discourse level when reading, and pay more attention to the mutual relations between a Pronoun and the Nouns or Noun Phrase before or after it. Meantime, we should compare and contrast the Pronoun usage of both Chinese and English so as to know how to use Chinese Pronouns properly.

修辞

句式：肯定句与否定句　Sentence Forms: Affirmative and Negative

从正面表述某种情况或肯定的看法，句子的主要成分没有"不"、"没（有）"、"非"、"无"等否定词的陈述句，是肯定句。从反面表述某种情况或否定的看法，句子的主要成分含有"不"、"没（有）"、"非"、"无"等否定词的陈述句，是否定句。

A Declarative Sentence that states a fact or an opinion from the positive perspective and contains no negation word such as 不、没（有）、非, or 无 in its main sentence elements, is an *Affirmative Sentence*. Contrarily, a sentence states a fact or an opinion from the negative perspective and contains negation word such as 不、没（有）、非, or 无 in is main sentence elements, is a *Negative Sentence*.

有的时候，同一事物或同一意思可以有肯定句来表示，也可以用否定句来表示。试比较下面的句子：

Sometimes, the same thing or idea can be expressed either with an *Affirmative Sentence* or a *Negative Sentence*. Now compare these pairs of sentences:

1a) 我*同意*报虚盘。　　　　1b) 我*不反对*报虚盘。

2a) 他们的生意*失败了*。　　　2b) 他们的生意*没有成功*。

3a) 她这样做*是有道理的*。　　3b) 她这样做*不是没有道理的*。

这三组句子，意思大致相同，但是相对而言，肯定句的 a)句语义较重，语气也强一些；否定句的 b)句，语义稍轻，语气也弱一些。因此，这种语义轻重、语气强弱的差别，就使肯定句和否定句具有一定的修辞作用。一般来说，肯定句观点明确，态度鲜明，语气强烈；否定句观点比较灵活，甚至有所"保留"，语气也比较委婉缓和。

The meaning of each pair of the above sentences is more or less the same. However, the *Affirmative Sentences* in group a), relatively speaking, carry more weight in meaning and sound more forceful, whereas the *Negative Sentences* seem less powerful and the tone sounds milder. Such differences in terms of the power in meaning and firmness in speaking tone, therefore, may *equip Affirmative and Negative sentences* with certain rhetorical function. *Affirmative Sentences*, in general, are more explicit in meaning, with a clear-cut stand, and firm in the speaking tone. *Negative Sentences*, on the flip side, are less explicit or flexible in meaning, and at times, may show some reservation. The tone of a *Negative Sentence* may also be tactful and milder.

但是有的句子连续使用两个否定词，构成"不……不……"、"没有……不……"、"无不……"、"非……不可"等句型，就是双重否定句。双重否定句可以比肯定句的语义更重，语气更强。例如：

Nonetheless, when two negation words are used consecutively in a sentence, forming patterns like 不……不……、没有……不……、无不……、非……不可, it is double negation. Compared with a regular *Affirmative Sentence*, a sentence with double negation can be even more powerful in meaning and firmer in its tone. For example:

4a) 从前线回来的人说到白求恩，*没有*一个人*不佩服*，*没有*一个

　　人<u>不</u>为他的精神所感动。　　（毛泽东《纪念白求恩》）

5a) 我<u>非</u>学会用电脑<u>不可</u>。

6a) 凡是事业上成功的人，<u>无不</u>经过一番努力。

　　如果把这三个句子改为肯定句，无论是语义或语气都不如原来的句子：

If these sentences are turned into regular *Affirmative Sentences*, they are no match of the original sentences both in meaning and the speak tone.

4b) 从前线回来的人说到白求恩，每个人都佩服，每个人都为他的精神所感动。

5b) 我一定要学会用电脑。

6b) 凡是事业上成功的人，都经过一番努力。

　　但是，有些双重否定句，特别是表示推辞、或刻意表示公正时，却比肯定句的语气委婉一些。试比较下面的句子：

Occasionally, some sentences with double negation may sound more tactful than a regular *Affirmative Sentence*, particularly when the speaker tries to refuse or tries to be fair. Compare the following sentences:

7a) 我<u>不是不</u>想帮忙，不过实在是没有时间。

7b) 我想帮忙，不过实在是没有时间。

8a) 当然，他也<u>不是没有</u>错误。

8b) 当然，他也有错误。

　　这里，肯定句 b)句的意思就比较直接，语气就不如双重否定的 a)句那么委婉。

In these cases, the *Affirmative Sentences* are more direct in meaning and less tactful or gentle in the tone of speech.

　　在书面语中，同一个意思，如果先用肯定句从正面说，然后再用否定句从反面说，这种互相衬托，反复表达的方法，可以加强语气，突出语义而避免单调的重复。例如：

In written Chinese, if an idea is first expressed in *Affirmative Sentences* from the positive perspective, and then restated in the negative form, a emphatic effect can be achieved, showing a firm stand, yet avoiding simple repetitions. For example:

我们要的是广泛的、符合大多数人的利益的真自由，不是狭隘的、只让少数人为所欲为的假自由。

我们不应该肯定自己的一切，只应该肯定正确的东西；我们也不应该否定自己的一切，只应该否定错误的东西。

了解肯定句和否定句的修辞作用，恰当地使用这两种句式，就可以更有效地表达意思，收到更好的效果。

Knowing the rhetorical functions of *Affirmative Sentences* and *Negative Sentences*, knowing when and how to use these two sentence forms, will definitely enable us to express ourselves more effectively, and achieve better results in communication in Chinese.

练习

一、用线将意思相同的词或词语连起来：

履行合同上规定的义务	效力
国家与国家签订的有关政治、军事、经济或文化方面的权利和义务的文书	签证
违背了共同拟订的条款或预约	签字
双方或多方当事人依法订立的有关权利和义务的协议	能力
收件人收到公文信件后在单据上签字，表示已收到	合约
一国主管机关在本国或外国公民所持的护照或旅行文件上签注、盖印表示准其出入本国国境	履约
在文件。单据上写上自己的名字，表示负责	违约
一种事物所产生的有利的作用	物力

指可供使用的物资　　　　　　　　　　　　　　　条约

指能做好某项工作或事情的才能、力量或条件　　　签收

二、 用括号里的词或词组改写下列句子，但不改变其基本意思，必要时可对词序作一定的调整：

1. 保险公司对"财神"号货轮搁浅的事故，进行了三个月的调查，向轮船公司提出了不同的意见。　　　　　　　（就⋯⋯，异议）

2. 你最好把这些文件复印几份，以后如果真的发生什么意外，也有凭据可以查对。　　　　　　　　　　　　　（万一，有据可查）

3. 医生通常都不给小孩开这种药，因为它只适合成年人使用。

　　　　　　　　　　　　　　　　　　　　　（一般，适用于）

4. 大家对这个工艺品展览都很感兴趣，因为它把中国的民族特色充分具体地表现出来了。　　　　　　　　　（对于，体现）

5. 工业发达国家都很关心怎样解决亚洲的金融危机问题。这不但关系到亚洲的经济发展，而且影响到世界金融的稳定。

　　　　　　　　　　　　　　　　（如何，不仅⋯⋯也⋯⋯）

6. 下星期开会，恐怕比较困难，我们不可能在这么短时间内把资料准备好。　　　　　　　　　　　　　　　（较为，完毕）

7. 小马是个又聪明又用功的工人。他学了不到两个星期，就可以自己一个人操作这台机器了。　　　　　　（⋯⋯而⋯⋯，单独）

三、 选择最合适的词填空：

1. 董事长的英语是不错，_____他的法语嘛，我真的不清楚。

　　a. 对于　　　　　b. 关于　　　　　c. 至于

2. _____海洋运输保险业务，老程有比较深入的研究。

　　a. 对于　　　　　b. 关于　　　　　c. 至于

3. 我每天都看电视，可是却没听到_____日本最近发生地震的消息。

a. 对于   b.关于   c.至于

4. 在那次事故中，她_____得十分勇敢、坚强。

a. 表示   b.表明   c.表现

5. 他们把死去的儿子的器官捐给了意大利的病人，_____了他们对
   人类伟大的爱。

a. 表示   b.表明   c.表现

6. 高先生来信_____他有兴趣进口我们的产品。

a. 表示   b.表明   c.表现

7. 交纳个人所得税，是每个公民都应该_____的义务。

a. 履行   b.执行   c.进行

8. 海关官员上船检查，任何人不得妨碍他们_____任务。

a. 履行   b.执行   c.进行

9. 经过洽商，双方决定今后要在生产和销售方面_____更广泛的合
   作。

a. 履行   b.执行   c.进行

10. 别看他平时喜欢开玩笑，工作的时候可_____啦。

a. 严重   b.严肃   c.严格

11. 这批货物在装卸过程中受到了_____的损坏。

a. 严重   b.严肃   c.严格

12. 美国政府对于药物的进口有非常_____的规定。

a. 严重   b.严肃   c.严格

四、 找出本课课文中的各种复句。

五、 改正下列句子的错误并指出它们是什么类型的复句。

1. 他特别喜欢向人显示自己的画，不管你没有兴趣，他都要拿给你
   看。

2.　这次谈判，她不但学会了很多东西，而且总经理也改变了对她的看法。

3.　经过几年的努力，老孙最后学会说英语、看英文报纸了。

4.　因为合同是关于买卖双方具体的权利和义务、以及交易条件的法律性文件，因此合同的制作是一件严肃而细致的工作。

5.　尽管大楼里到处都写着"请勿吸烟"，却他们还在办公室里抽烟。

6.　除非你们再交百分之二十的进口税，就海关放行。

7.　签订合同以前，必须仔细检查，以便错误。

8.　这批货不能按时运抵目的港，由于货轮在海上遇到了台风。

9.　无论是海洋运输或者联合运输，这类货物都应该投保"水渍险"，为了安全起见。

10.　给在中国的朋友写信，也慢也费时间，可是打国际长途电话又太贵，如果我实在有事要跟他们联系，宁可传真。

六、 按照汉语的习惯，删去下列句子中多余的主语或人称代词：

1. 高荣骑他的自行车不小心，结果他摔断了他的腿。

2. 既然大家都累了，大家就休息一下吧。

3. 开始她想学日文，后来她又想学法文，最后她还是选了西班牙文。

4. 老师要不是关心你们，老师就不会这么批评你们了。

5. 卫元元不管多么忙，他每天都会去医院看一下那个老人。

6. 我们投保了一切险，我们也投保了罢工险，所以我们相信保险公司一定会赔偿我们的损失。

7. 除非保险公司在索赔期限内收到被保人的索赔要求，保险公司才会按规定赔偿损失。

8. 她一紧张她就抓她的头发。

9. 现在他们做他们的练习的时候，他们都不用笔，他们只用他们的电脑了。

10. 你就是再有钱，你也买不到聪明和幸福。

七、 找出下面短文中隐去了的人称代词：

1. 从前，有一个人在大街上卖长矛和盾牌。他举起手中的盾，大声地说："这盾牌非常坚固，无论什么东西都不能刺穿。"接着，又举起手中的矛，骄傲地说："这长矛非常锋利，不管什么东西，都能刺穿。"这时，有人问："如果拿这矛，去刺这盾，那将会怎么样呢？"卖长矛和盾牌的人听了，没话可说，只好红着脸走了。这就是成语"自相矛盾"的故事，表示一个人说话、办事前后互相抵触。

2. 小庄今年二十岁，上海人，现在清华念大学。从五岁起就喜欢游泳，天天吵着爸爸带她去泡水，不到两个月就学会了游泳。上中学以后，小庄进了业余体校。她勤学苦练，每天一放学就跑去游泳馆，一练就是四五个小时。有时候累得胳膊都抬不起来，还是坚持训练。在著名教练李坚强的指导下，技术提高得非常快。十五岁那年参加了全国运动会，一举夺得了两项冠军，并破了一项亚洲记录。

八、 把下列句子的划线部份改写成否定句或双重否定句，但不改变其基本意思，然后比较一下改写前后两种句式在语义和语气上的异同：

1. 今年的天气有一点儿<u>反常</u>，都十二月了还这么暖和。

2. 虽然她这次比赛会遇到很多困难，但是拿第一名也<u>是可能的</u>。

3. 马小姐的那辆汽车恐怕<u>很贵</u>吧。

4. 我也<u>知道</u>这样做的后果，可他是经理，<u>我只好听他的</u>。

5. 到了现在这种情况，就是经验丰富的老船长也<u>很难有什么办法</u>了。

6. 你去图书馆，<u>一定</u>会找得到老陈的。

7. <u>只有</u>经过失败，<u>才会</u>取得成功。

8. 每一个商人都想赚钱，这是肯定的。

9. 那样说也可以，不过太正式，有点像书面语了。

10. 这个句型非常重要，你们一定要记住才行。

九、 把下列句子翻译成汉语：

1. We would rather have repetitive negotiations with the opposite side on [i.e. "with regard to"] the price before the conclusion of a deal than breaking the contract afterwards. Once a contract is signed [i.e. "finished signing"], we will strictly abide by it and conscientiously carry it out. By doing so, it embodies our principle of "laying stress on contract, and valuing one's credit".

2. This medicine is suitable for male patients only. As for female patients, it may not have the equal effect. At present, there is neither (scientific) a theory nor an empirical [i.e. "experimental"] evidence to prove it is effective for women. If by any chance there occurs any problem, the insurance company will not bear any responsibility.

3. Teenagers [i.e. "youth and juvenile"] are rather [i.e. "comparatively more"] undisciplined. To educate teenagers how to observe discipline is a job of patience and meticulousness. We should treat this job with (an attitude of) seriousness and conscientiousness.

文化与商贸背景知识

✐ 中国人的面子

　　中国是一个讲礼仪，但更讲面子的民族。"面子"对中国人来说是非常重要的。有一定身份或地位的人，更是注重自己的面子，很怕"丢面子"。因为丢了面子就意味着失去了这个身份或地位应有的威望和尊严。如果有人在公众场合当面向朋友提出批评，指责其过失，就会被认为很不给面子，被批评者就会觉得丢了面子，下不了台。如果客人当着主人的面，对其家人评头品足，对其家事说三道四，即使客人说的都是事实，主人也会觉得没有面子，内心一定会责怪客人不"留点面子"。有时，人们为了面子，就是能力有限或财力不足，也要"打肿脸充胖子"。

中文的"面子"有两重意思：一是体面、光荣，即个人的名誉、成就、钱财等所造成的影响和威望；二是情面，也就是与亲戚朋友之间的情分和关系。譬如某人(甲)认识很多朋友，在一些重要部门(特别是政府的部门)有很多"关系"，很有影响，要办什么事情都很方便，这样的人就会被认为很有面子。如果(乙)是甲的好朋友，请他帮忙办一件事情，甲觉得乙也有些面子或值得帮忙，于是就委托丙去办这件事。虽然(丙)根本就不认识乙，但是因为看在甲的面子上，所以就帮了乙的忙。假如事情办好了，那么，丙就觉得这件事为自己争了面子(证明了自己的能力)，同时也为甲争了面子(认识自己并且委托自己办这件事，证明了甲的威望或影响)。而乙的朋友们也会觉得乙很有面子，因为他有关系、有办法能办成这样的事情。相反，假如甲不肯帮忙，乙就觉得甲不给自己面子；或者甲答应了并且也叫了丙帮忙，但是丙却没把事情办成或者办坏了。这样，丙就会觉得自己不但很没有面子，而且也丢了甲的面子。因为事情没办成，乙在朋友面前，也没有什么面子。因此，可以说，中国人在相互交往中，整天就为了自己或别人的面子，纠缠在关系网中。

和中国人打交道、做生意，也要注意面子的问题。比如在主人面前，尤其是在年纪比较大、地位比较高的人面前，不要随便批评中国或有关单位的事情。另外，在业务洽谈时，也要注意与对方谈判人员个人和业务的关系，不要让对方觉得自己在谈判时丢了面子。比如一笔生意，对方很希望谈成而你的公司却认为这笔生意不值得谈时，最好能找个比较合适的理由，让对方向他们的上级有个交待。这样也许可以维持对方公司对他们的信任，保存他们的面子。这就是所谓的"买卖不成仁义在"。又如，你有意购买对方的商品，但是发现其产品不如其他的同类产品时，也无须为了使对方降价而过分直率地批评甚至贬低其产品。如果谈判时让对方觉得丢了面子，那么就算这次谈判你赢了，但后面的交易环节也不一定会是很顺利的，很可能会留下不良的后果，影响到今后的交易。商业谈判是相互协商讨论的过程，不可能不听取对方的意见，了解对方的意愿和想法。因此，有时在保证自己利益的同时，也要设身处地为对方着想，说话要留有余地，顾全其面子。在坚持原则的同时，措辞可以温和点。要尽量减少紧张气氛，消除对抗情绪。这样成功的可能性就会大一些。

✐ **合同、订购合同、成交确认书**

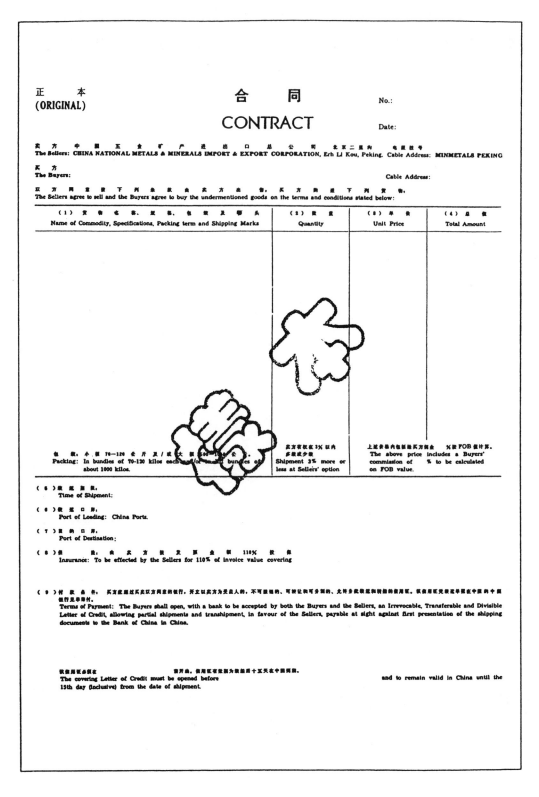

正　本
(ORIGINAL)

合　同
CONTRACT

No.:

Date:

卖　方　中国五金矿产进出口总公司　北京二里沟　电报挂号
The Sellers: CHINA NATIONAL METALS & MINERALS IMPORT & EXPORT CORPORATION, Erh Li Kou, Peking. Cable Address: **MINMETALS PEKING**

买　方
The Buyers: 　　　　　　　　　　　　　　　　　　　　　　Cable Address:

以　方　同　意　按　下　列　条　款　由　卖　方　出　售，买　方　购　进　下　列　货　物：
The Sellers agree to sell and the Buyers agree to buy the undermentioned goods on the terms and conditions stated below:

（1）货物名称、规格、包装及唛头 Name of Commodity, Specifications, Packing term and Shipping Marks	（2）数量 Quantity	（3）单价 Unit Price	（4）总值 Total Amount
包装：小捆 70－120 公斤 及／或大捆 500 公斤左右。 Packing: In bundles of 70-120 kilos each and/or in bundles of about 1000 kilos.	卖方有权在 3% 以内多装或少装。 Shipment 3% more or less at Sellers' option	上述货物内包括给买方佣金　％按 FOB 值计算。 The above price includes a Buyers' commission of 　% to be calculated on FOB value.	

（5）装运期限：
Time of Shipment:

（6）装运口岸：
Port of Loading: China Ports.

（7）目的口岸：
Port of Destination:

（8）保　险：由　买　方　按　发　票　金　额　110% 投　保
Insurance: To be effected by the Sellers for 110% of invoice value covering

（9）付款条件：买方应通过买卖双方同意的银行，开立以卖方为受益人的、不可撤销的、可转让和可分割的、允许分批装运和转船的信用证。该信用证凭卖方单据在中国的中国银行见单即付。
Terms of Payment: The Buyers shall open, with a bank to be accepted by both the Buyers and the Sellers, an Irrevocable, Transferable and Divisible Letter of Credit, allowing partial shipments and transhipment, in favour of the Sellers, payable at sight against first presentation of the shipping documents to the Bank of China in China.

该信用证须在装运　前开出，信用证须有效期为装运期后十五天在中国到期。
The covering Letter of Credit must be opened before 15th day (inclusive) from the date of shipment.　　　　　　and to remain valid in China until the

（ 10 ）单据。卖方应向议付银行提供已装船清洁提单、发票、装箱单/重量单，如果本合同按 CIF 条件，应再提供可转让的保险单或保险凭证。
Documents: The Sellers shall present to the negotiations bank, Clean On Board Bill of Lading, Invoice, Packing List/Weight Memo, and Transferable Insurance Policy or Insurance Certificate when this Contract is made on CIF basis.

（ 11 ）装 运 条 件。
Terms of Shipment:

1. 载 运 船 只 由 卖 方 安 排，允 许 分 批 装 运 并 允 许 转 船。
   The carrying vessel shall be provided by the Sellers. Partial shipments and transhipment are allowed.

2. 装 运 于 货 物 装 船 后，卖 方 应 将 合 同 号 码、品 名、数 量、船 名、装 船 日 期 以 电 报 通 知 买 方。
   After loading is completed, the Sellers shall notify the Buyers by cable of the contract number, name of commodity, quantity, name of the carrying vessel and date of shipment.

（ 12 ）品质和数量/重量的异议与索赔。货到目的口岸后，买方如发现货物品质及/或数量/重量与合同规定不符，除属于保险公司及/或船公司的责任外，买方可以凭双方同意的检验机构出具的检验证明书向卖方提出异议。品质异议须于货到目的口岸之日起30天内提出，数量/重量异议须于货到目的口岸之日起15天内提出。卖方应于收到异议后30天内答复买方。
Quality/Quantity Discrepancy and Claim:
In case the quality and/or quantity/weight are found by the Buyers to be not in conformity with the Contract after arrival of the goods at the port of destination, the Buyers may lodge claim with the Sellers supported by survey report issued by an inspection organization agreed upon by both parties, with the exception, however of those claims for which the insurance company and/or the shipping company are to be held responsible. Claim for quality discrepancy should be filed by the Buyers within 30 days after arrival of the goods at the port of destination, while for quantity/weight discrepancy claim should be filed by the Buyers within 15 days after arrival of the goods at the port of destination. The Sellers shall, within 30 days after receipt of the notification of the claim, send reply to the Buyers.

（ 13 ）人力不可抗拒。由于人力不可抗拒事故，使卖方不能在本合同规定期限内交货或者不能交货，卖方不负责任。但卖方必须立即以电报通知买方。如买方提出要求，卖方应以挂号函向买方提供中国国际贸易促进委员会或有关机构所出具的发生事故的证明文件。
Force Majeure: In case of Force Majeure, the Sellers shall not be held responsible for late delivery or non-delivery of the goods but shall notify the Buyers by cable. The Sellers shall deliver to the Buyers by registered mail, if so requested by the Buyers, a certificate issued by the China Council for the Promotion of International Trade or any competent authorities.

（ 14 ）仲　　　裁。凡因执行本合同或与本合同有关事项所发生的一切争执，应由双方通过友好方式协商解决。如果不能取得协议时，则应提交被告国家根据被告国仲裁机构的仲裁规则进行仲裁。仲裁决定是终局的，对双方有同等约束力。仲裁费用除非另有规定外，均由败诉一方负担。
Arbitration: All disputes in connection with this Contract or the execution thereof shall be settled by negotiation between two parties. If no settlement can be reached, the case in dispute shall then be submitted for arbitration in the country of defendant in accordance with the arbitration regulations of the arbitration organization of the defendant country. The decision made by the arbitration organization shall be taken as final and binding upon both parties. The arbitration expenses shall be borne by the losing party unless otherwise awarded by the arbitration organization.

（ 15 ）备　　　注。
Remarks:

卖　　方
Sellers:
中 国 五 金 矿 产 进 出 口 总 公 司
CHINA NATIONAL METALS & MINERALS
IMPORT & EXPORT CORPORATION

买　　方
Buyers:

订 购 合 同
PURCHASE CONTRACT

合同号码,
CONTRACT NO.:

北 京
PEKING

买 方,
The Buyers: CHINA NATIONAL CHEMICALS IMPORT & EXPORT CORPORATION, Erh Li Kou, Peking.   Telex: 22043 CHEMI CN PEKING
Cable: "SINOCHEM" PEKING

卖 方,
The Sellers:

兹经买卖双方同意按照以下条款由买方购进由卖方售出以下商品,
This Contract is made by and between the Buyers and the Sellers; whereby the Buyers agree to buy and the Sellers agree to sell the under-mentioned goods subject to the terms and conditions as stipulated hereinafter:

(1)商品名称及规格,
    Name of Commodity and Specification:

(2)数 量,
    Quantity:

(3)单 价,
    Unit Price:

(4)总 值,
    Total Value:

(5)包 装,
    Packing:

(6)生产国别及制造厂商,
    Country of Origin & Manufacturer:

(7)付款条件, 买方于交易达成后
    使用以下规定条款由中国银行。
    Terms of Payment: After conclusion of business, the Buyers shall open with the Bank of China,   , an irrevocable letter of credit in favour of the Sellers payable at the issuing Bank against presentation of the shipping documents as stipulated under Clause 3 (A) of the Terms of Delivery of this Contract after departure of the carrying vessel. The letter of credit shall remain in force till the 15th day after shipment.

(8)保   险,由买方负责,
    Insurance: To be covered by the Buyers.

(9)装 运 时 间,
    Time of Shipment:

(10)装 运 口 岸,
     Port of Loading:

(11)目 的 口 岸,
     Port of Destination:

(12)装 运 唛 头,
     Shipping Mark(s):

每件货物上应明确刷明目的口岸、件号、毛重及净重及尺码、大概尺寸列明右边(如易燃品及/或易爆货物,应按照惯例在各件货物上明显刷出其惯用及标准之标准解释说明),
On each package shall be stencilled conspicuously: port of destination, package number, gross and nett weights, measurement and the shipping mark shown on the right side. (For dangerous and/or poisonous cargo, the nature and the generally adopted symbol shall be marked conspicuously on each package).

(13)其 他 条 款, (A)本合同按照本合同规定之买卖(即卖买)之规定条款,按买卖双方各方合同之不可分割条件。(B)本合同以中文及英文两种文字书写,两种文字均有各款具有同等效力。
     Other terms: (a) Other matters relating to this Contract shall be dealt with in accordance with the Terms of Delivery as specified overleaf, which shall form an integral part of this Contract. (b) This Contract is made out in Chinese and English, both versions being equally authentic.

(14)附 加 条 款, (本合同其他条件如与以下条款如有抵触时,以附加条款为准。)
     Supplementary Condition(s) (Should any other clause in this Contract be in conflict with the following Supplementary Condition(s), the Supplementary Condition(s) should be taken as final and binding.):

卖   方   买   方
THE SELLERS   THE BUYERS

交 货 条 款
TERMS OF DELIVERY

1. 装 运 条 件:

凡用一级贸易条件，卖方应在本合同第（9）条规定之时限内，将货物由装运口岸直接船运到中国口岸，在未经买方同意前，中途不得转船。货物不得用悬挂买方不能接受之国家的旗帜的船只装载，亦不得在本合同第（11）条规定之口岸前，不得停靠台湾省及其附近口岸。

For C & F Terms: The Sellers shall ship the goods within the time as stipulated in Clause (9) of this Contract by a direct vessel sailing from the port of loading to China Port. Transhipment en route is not allowed without the Buyers' consent. The goods should not be carried by vessels flying the flags of the countries not acceptable to the Buyers. The carrying vessel shall not call or stop over at the port/ports of Taiwan Province and the port/ports in the vicinity of Taiwan Province prior to her arrival at the port of destination as stipulated in the Clause (11) of this Contract.

凡用船上交货：

(A) 装运本合同货物的船只，由买方或买方租船代理人中国租船公司（地址：北京，二里沟，电报挂号：ZHONGZU PEKING）洽订船位。卖方应负责将本合同第（9）条规定的货物于买方所通知的船只及约定的日期内装上约定的船只。

The shipping space for the contracted goods shall be booked by the Buyers or the Buyers' shipping agent, China National Chartering Corporation (Address: Erh Li Kou, Peking. Cable Address: ZHONGZU PEKING). The Sellers shall undertake to load the contracted goods on board the vessel nominated by the Buyers on any date notified by the Buyers, within the time of shipment stipulated in the Clause (9) of this Contract.

(B) 买方船期前10—15天，应将本合同号码、船名、船只预计到达日期、装运数量及经船代理人的名称，以便卖方可予通知船舶代理人及交货准备之装船，卖方应将装上船只实况及时用电通知买方。如因某种缘故买方有必要更换船只或原定之船只到达装货港较预计日期提前或推迟时，买方或其船舶代理人应及时通知卖方，卖方亦应与中租代理保持密切联系。

10-15 days prior to the date of shipment, the Buyers shall inform the Sellers by cable of the contract number, name of vessel, ETA of vessel, quantity to be loaded and the name of shipping agent, so as to enable the latter to contact the shipping agent direct and arrange the shipment of the goods. The Sellers shall cable in time the Buyers of the result thereof. Should, for certain reasons, it become necessary for the Buyers to replace the named vessel with another one, or should the named vessel arrive at the port of shipment earlier or later than the date of arrival as previously notified to the Sellers, the Buyers or their shipping agent shall advise the Sellers to this effect in due time. The Sellers shall also keep close contact with the agent of Zhongzu.

(C) 如买方所订之船只到达装货港后，卖方不能按买方所通知之时限内将约定货物装船，则空舱费及滞期费等一切费用和由此而发生的后果均由卖方负担。但若船只撤离或所定之船只提前或推迟到达装货港时，在卖方并未得到及时通知停止交货（如货物于下列代码通知之装船日期较晚装运，则可计算货物存港费用）内，卖方于装货港存储保险费从第16天起计算，上述损失应由买方负担。但属不可抗力者除外。卖方仍应负责于装货船只到达装货港时立即将货物自负风险及费用装船，上述费用凭正本单据核实后支付。

Should the Sellers fail to load the goods, within the time as notified by the Buyers, on board the vessel booked by the Buyers after its arrival at the port of shipment, all expenses such as dead freight, demurrage, etc., and consequences thereof shall be borne by the Sellers. Should the vessel be withdrawn or replaced or delayed eventually or the cargo be shut out, etc., and the Sellers are not informed in good time to stop delivery of the cargo, the calculation of the loss for storage expenses and insurance premium thus sustained at the loading port shall be based on the loading date notified by the agent to the Sellers (or based on the date of the arrival of the cargo at the loading port in case the cargo should arrive there later than the notified loading date). The above-mentioned loss is to be calculated from the 16th day after expiry of the free storage time at the port should be borne by the Buyers with the exception of Force Majeure. However, the Sellers still undertake to load the cargo immediately upon the carrying vessel's arrival at the loading port at their own risks and expenses. The payment of the afore-said expenses shall be effected against presentation of the original vouchers after being checked.

2. 装船通知，货物装运完毕后，卖方应即将合同号码、货物名称、数量、发票价值、毛重、船名、开船日期及到达口岸，由于卖方不将上述装船通知以电报及时通知买方致使买方不能及时投保时，则由此而发生的一切损失均由卖方负担。

Advice of Shipment: Immediately after completion of loading of goods on board the vessel the Sellers shall notify the Buyers by cable of the contract number, name of goods, quantity or weight loaded, invoice value, name of vessel, port of shipment, sailing date and port of destination. Should the Buyers be made unable to arrange insurance in time owing to the Sellers' failure to give the above mentioned advice of shipment by cable, the Sellers shall be held responsible for any and all damage and/or loss attributable to such failure.

3. 装 运 单 据:

(A) 卖方凭下列单据向付款银行议付货款：

(a) 填写通知目的口岸中国对外贸易运输公司分公司的全套洁净、空白抬头的全式已装船的海运提单（如系用C & F条件，应注明运费付讫字样，如系用船上交货则注明运费到付字样）。 (b) 已签署的发票五份，注明合同号码及装运唛头。 (c) 注明大纲码装箱单/或重量单2份。 (d) 本交货条款第5条规定的由工厂出具的品质及数量或重量证明书1份。 (e) 本交货条款第2条规定的装船电知买方的电报副本一份。

The Sellers shall present the following documents to the paying bank for negotiation of payment: (a) Full set of clean on board, "freight prepaid" for C & F Terms or "freight to collect" for FOB Terms, ocean Bills of Lading, made out to order and blank endorsed, notifying the Branch of China National Foreign Trade Transportation Corporation at the port of destination. (b) Five copies of signed invoice indicating contract number and shipping marks. (c) Two copies of packing list and/or weight memo with indication of measurement. (d) One copy each of the certificate of quality and quantity or weight, as stipulated in the Clause 5 of the Terms of Delivery. (e) One duplicate copy of the cable advice of shipment, as stipulated in the Clause 2 of the Terms of Delivery.

(B) 卖方须于装船后，立即将提单，发票和装箱单1份航寄买方在目的口岸的收货代理人即中国对外贸易运输公司的分公司。

The Sellers shall despatch, in care of the carrying vessel, two copies of duplicates of Bill of Lading, Invoice and Packing List to the Buyers' receiving agent, the Branch of China National Foreign Trade Transportation Corporation at the port of destination.

(C) 船在装运后立即将上述单据副本航寄买方一份，及两份寄交目的口岸中国对外贸易运输公司分公司。

Immediately after the departure of the carrying vessel, the Sellers shall airmail one set of the duplicate documents to the Buyers and two sets to the Branch of China National Foreign Trade Transportation Corporation at the port of destination.

4. 危险品使用说明：凡属危险品及/或有毒物品，卖方必须提供有关说明书，说明其危险或有毒性质，运输、储存及装卸注意事项，以及发生意外时之应急和急救措施。卖方应将说明书连同其他装运单据航空邮寄买方及目的口岸的中国对外贸易运输公司的分公司各3份。

Dangerous Cargo Instruction Leaflets: For dangerous and/or poisonous cargo, the Sellers must provide instruction leaflets stating the hazardous or poisonous properties, transportation, storage and handling remarks, as well as precautionary and first-aid measures and measures against fire. The Sellers shall airmail, together with other shipping documents, three copies each of the same to the Buyers and the Branch of China National Foreign Trade Transportation Corporation at the port of destination.

5. 商品检验：双方同意以制造厂出具的品质及数量或重量证明书作为向付款银行议付货款单据的一部分，但商品的品质及数量或重量的检验应按照下列规定办理：

(A) 一般商品：货物运抵目的口岸内容如经中国商品检验局复验后，如发现品质或数量或重量与本合同规定不符时，除属于保险公司或船方负责者外，买方于货物到达目的口岸后90天内，凭中国商品检验局出具的检验证明书向卖方提出退货或索赔。因退货或索赔引起的一切费用（包括检验费）及损失均由卖方负担。在此情况下，凡属于检验机构可以检验的，买方可以在索赔货物同时，将索赔货物的样品寄交卖方。

For General Cargo: In case the quality, quantity or weight of the goods be found not in conformity with those stipulated in this Contract after re-inspection by the China Commodity Inspection Bureau within 90 days after arrival of the goods at the port of destination, the Buyers shall return the goods to or lodge claims against the Sellers for compensation of losses upon the strength of Inspection Certificate issued by the said Bureau, with the exception of those claims for which the insurers or owners of the carrying vessel are liable. All expenses (including inspection fees) and losses arising from the return of the goods or claims should be borne by the Sellers. In such case, the Buyers may, if so requested, send a sample of the goods in question to the Sellers, provided that sampling is feasible.

(B) 医用药品：凡运往中国的医用药品受中华人民共和国药事法所约束。不准不合格医用药品运往中国。双方合同议定凡本类合同货物之质量应以中国商品检验局检验为准，该局于货物到达目的口岸后90天内检验货物并将检验结果作为最后依据并对双方具有约束力。卖方应将所有不合格医用药品收回，偿还买方货物之价值以及由于退货而发生的一切损失如运费、储存费、保险费、利息、检验费用等。如中国商品检验局于货物运抵目的口岸后90天内检验发现质量或数量/重量与本合同不符，买方有权根据中国商品检验局出具之检验证明向卖方提出索赔。

For Pharmaceuticals: Pharmaceuticals imported into China are subject to laws and regulations of the People's Republic of China. Disqualified pharmaceuticals are prohibited to be imported. It is mutually agreed that for the quality of the contracted goods in this category, the Inspection Certificate issued by the China Commodity Inspection Bureau after inspecting the goods within 90 days from the date of arrival at the port of destination shall be taken as final and binding upon both parties. The Sellers shall take back all the disqualified goods and compensate the Buyers for the value of the goods plus all losses sustained due to return of the cargo, such as freight, storage charges, insurance premium, interest, inspection charges, etc. Should the quantity/weight be found not in conformity with those stipulated in this Contract after inspection by the China Commodity Inspection Bureau, the Buyers shall have the right to claim against the Sellers for compensation of losses within 90 days after the arrival of the goods at the port of destination on the basis of the Inspection Certificate issued by the said Bureau.

6. 人力不可抗拒：由于一般公认的人力不可抗拒原因致使卖方不能交货或延迟交货，在此情况下卖方不负责任。但卖方必须立即电告买方并在事故发生后15天内航空邮寄买方事故发生所在地之主管政府机关或商会所出具的证明此类事故的证明书，除人力不可抗拒原因而不能交货或延迟交货外，卖方应赔偿由此而直接引起买方的一切损失及费用。如果人力不可抗拒原因延续到90天以上时，买方有权撤销合同或合同中未交货部分。

Force Majeure: The Sellers shall not be held responsible for late delivery or non-delivery of the goods owing to generally recognized "Force Majeure" causes. However, in such case, the Sellers shall immediately cable the Buyers the accident and airmail to the Buyers within 15 days after the accident, a certificate of the accident issued by the competent government authorities or the chamber of commerce which is located at the place where the accident occurs as evidence thereof. With the exception of late delivery or non-delivery due to "Force Majeure" causes, in case the Sellers fail to make delivery within the time as stipulated in the Contract, the Sellers should indemnify the Buyers for all losses and expenses incurred to the latter directly attributable to late delivery or failure to make delivery of the goods in accordance with the terms of this Contract. If the "Force Majeure" cause lasts over 90 days, the Buyers shall have the right to cancel the Contract or the undelivered part of the Contract.

7. 仲裁，一切因执行本合同所发生与本合同有关之争执，应通过友好协商解决，如双方协商不能取得协议时，应提交中国国际贸易促进委员会对外贸易仲裁委员会，根据该会仲裁程序暂行规定进行仲裁。仲裁地点在中国北京，仲裁裁决是终局的，对双方均有约束力。仲裁费用除非仲裁委员会另有决定外，均由败诉一方负担。

Arbitration: All disputes in connection with this Contract or the execution thereof shall be amicably settled through negotiation. In case no settlement can be reached between the two parties, the case under dispute shall be submitted to the Foreign Trade Arbitration Commission of the China Council for the Promotion of International Trade for arbitration. The arbitration shall take place in Peking, China and shall be executed in accordance with the Provisional Rules of Procedure of the said Commission and the decision made by the Arbitration Commission shall be accepted as final and binding upon both parties. The fees for arbitration shall be borne by the losing party unless otherwise awarded.

成交确认书

（　）字第＿＿＿＿＿号

日　期＿＿＿＿＿

卖方　中国纺织品进出口总公司广东省分公司　　　　　签约地点：

地　址　广州市延安二路255号　　　　　　电报挂号 "CANTEX"　0093　电话31999

买方＿＿＿＿＿＿＿＿＿＿＿＿＿＿＿＿＿＿＿＿＿

地　址＿＿＿＿＿＿＿＿＿＿＿＿＿＿＿　电报挂号＿＿＿＿＿　电话＿＿＿＿＿

兹经买卖双方同意成交下列商品订立条款如下：

(1) 品　号	(2) 商品名称、规格	(3) 数量	(4) 单价	(5) 金额	(6) 装运期

上列数量内可包括20%以内的剩余

数量及总值均得有		总　值	

(7)装运口岸和目的地：自

(8)付款条件：买方应按本确认书规定装运期开始一天的前　　　天开到凭见票　　　付款的、足额的保兑的、不可撤销的、允许转让的信用证。信用证应规定数量和金额允许有　%的增减。信用证的议付有效期应规定在最后装运期后至少10天在出运口岸到期。信用证应规定允许分批装运和转运。

(9)保　险：由卖方按发票金额110%投保水渍险一种(如陆运，则投保陆上运输险)如来证加列其他附加险，则可由卖方代为投保，保费由买方负担。

(10)包　装：按卖方一般出口包装。

(11)装船标记：除另有约定者外概按卖方一般出口装船标记刷唛。

(12)花色及规格：买方必须在规定装运期开始一天的前　　　天将花色（或规格）寄达卖方。

(13)商品品质：本确认书所售丝及绸缎的品质按照中华人民共和国商品检验局关于输出入商品检验标准的规定按卖方一般出口品质。

(14)异议索赔：如买方不按本确认书规定的期限内将花色（及规格）寄达及将信用证开达卖方，卖方有权撤销本确认书或逾期交货，买方应负赔偿卖方由此遭受的一切损失。

买　方　　　　　　　　　　　卖　方

东 方 科 学 仪 器 进 出 口 集 团 公 司
THE ORIENTAL SCIENTIFIC INSTRUMENTS IMPORT & EXPORT GROUP

售 货 确 认 书
SALES CONFIRMATION

中国·北京三里河路52号
No.52,San Li He Road
Beijing 100864,China
Tel: 2614983
Fax: 2614399

To Messrs:
S.C.WORKS CO. LTD.
10/10-11 CHAROEN KRUNG RD..
    BANGKOK 10200

编号
No.   970EB64098TH
日期
Date. Aug 11, 1997

兹确认售予你方下列货品，其成交条款如下：
Dear Sirs,
We hereby confirm having sold to you the following goods on the terms and conditions as specified below:

(1) 货物名称及规格，包装及装运唛头 Name of Commodity and Specification, Packing and Shipping Mark	(2) 数量 Quantity	(3) 单位 Unit	(4) 单 价 Unit Price	(5) 合计金额 Amount

(6) 装 运 期 限   收到可以转船及分批装运之信用证 90天内装出。
    Date of shipment: ■ Within 90 days after receipt of L/C allowing transhipment and partial shipment.
            □

(7) 装 运 口 岸   (8) 到 达 口 岸
    Port of Loading: TIANJIN   Port of Destination: BANGKOK

(9) 付 款 条 件   开给我方100%不可撤回即期付款及可转让可分割之信用证，并须注明可在上述装运日期后15天内在中国议付
              有效。
    Terms of Payment: ■ By 100% Confirmed, Irrevocable, Transferable and Divisible Letter of Credit to be availabl
              by sight draft to remain valid for negotiation in China until the 15th day after the aforesai
              Time of Shipment.
            □

(10) 保 险   按中国保险条款，保全险及兵险。(不包括罢工险)
    Insurance: ■ Covering all risks and war risk only (excluding S.R.C.C.) as per the China Insurance Clauses.
            由客户自理。
            □ To be effected by the buyer.
            □

备 注
REMARKS:
(1) 买方须于 97.03.26 前开到本批交易的信用证(或通知售方进口许可证号码)，否则，售方有权：不经通知取消本确认书，或接受买
    方对本约执行的全部或一部，或对因此遭受的损失提出索赔。
    The Buyer shall have the covering Letter of Credit reach the Seller (or notify the Import License Number) before
    97.03.26 failing which the Seller reserves the right to rescind without further notice,or to accept whole or any
    part of the Sales Confirmation not fulfilled by the Buyer, or to lodge a claim for losses thus sustained, if any.
(2) 品质／数量异议：如买方提出索赔，凡属品质异议须于货到目的口岸之日起 7 天内提出，凡属数量异议须于货到目的口岸之日
    起 7 天内提出，对所装货物所提任何异议属于保险公司、轮船公司、其他有关运输机构或邮递机构所负责者，售方不负任何责任。
    QUALITY/QUANTITY DISCREPANCY: In case of quality discrepancy, claim should be filed by the Buyer within 7 after
    the arrival of the goods at port of destination; while for quantity discrepancy,claim should be filed by the Buyer
    within 7 after the arrival of the goods at port of destination. It is understood that the Seller shall not be
    liable for any for which the Insurance Company, Shipping Companuy,other transportation organization or Post Office
    are liable.
(3) 本确认书内所述全部或部分商品，如因人力不可抗拒的原因，以致不能履约或延迟交货，售方概不负责。
    The Seller shall not be held for failure or delay in delivery of the entire lot or a portion of the goods under
    this Sales Confirmation in consequence of any Force Majeure incidents.
(4) 其他 Other clause:

买买确认签署   东 方 科 学 仪 器 进 出 口 集 团 公 司
Confirmed by   THE ORIENTAL SCIENTIFIC INSTRUMENTS IMP. & EXP. GROUP

第十二课

索赔

✎ **思考下面的问题，然后带着这些问题去阅读课文：**

一、什么时候会引起争议？什么是"索赔"和"理赔"？

二、国际贸易中的索赔主要有哪几种？

三、什么是"不可抗力"？

四、索赔和理赔分别要注意哪些问题？

五、在什么情况下双方会把争议提交仲裁结构裁决？

课文：索赔

　　一项贸易合同签订以后，在其执行过程中，牵涉的部门是多方面的。除了买卖双方以外，还有运输部门和保险公司。由于进口商或出口商委托运输公司运送货物，承运人不但是这笔交易的有关当事人，而且他们与托运人签发的装运单据对双方都是有法律约束力的合同。同样，因为进口商或出口商对货物向保险公司进行了投保，保险人不但是这笔交易的有关当事人，他们与投保人共同签订的保险书也是对双方都有法律约束力的合同。如果任何一方的工作出现某种过失，就会有意或无意地造成违约，引起争议。 5

　　所谓"违约"，是指签约的一方认为另一方未能全部或部份履行合同规定的责任和义务。所谓"争议"，是指由此而引起有关当事人之间的纠纷。为了弥补由一方违约而造成另一方的经济损失，受损害的一方(通常是买方或卖方)往往会向应负责任的一方提出赔偿的要求，这就是"索赔"；责任方对受损方提出的索赔要求进行处理， 10

这就是"理赔"。因此，索赔和理赔是一个问题的两个方面。

15　　　国际贸易中引起索赔的原因很多，但概括起来，主要可分为贸易索赔、运输索赔和保险索赔三种。

　　　贸易索赔又分买方违约和卖方违约两种。属于买方违约的情况主要有：在 F.O.B. 的条件下，不按合同规定如期派船接货；不按期开立信用证；无理拒收货物；不按合同规定支付或拒绝支付货款

20　等。属于卖方违约的情况主要有：不按合同规定的交货期交货或拒不交货；所交货物的品质、规格或数量与合同规定不符；货物包装不良以及由此产生的货损；错发错运；提供的运输单据种类、份数不足等。

　　　运输索赔是指轮船公司对承运货物在运输途中遭受的损失负有

25　向货主赔偿的责任。运输索赔通常包括下列情况：货物未按期运抵，货物遗失，搬运不当造成货损，货物数量少于提单所注明的数量，改变航线而造成货物在途中受损等。

　　　如果被保险的货物在运输途中，发生了保险公司承保范围内（如自然灾害、意外事故等）规定的残损，投保人可持保险单据及其

30　他必要的有关证件（如商检证明书等）向保险公司索赔。这就是保险索赔。

　　　一旦发现违约，受损的一方应根据事实，分清责任，明确索赔对象是卖（买）方、运输部门还是保险公司。有时违约并不是因为某一当事人的过失，而是由于水灾、火灾、地震、海啸等自然灾害，

35　或像战争、罢工等意外事故。这些都是当事人不能预料，也无法采取预防措施的，在国际贸易上称为"不可抗力"。在这种情况下，当事人可以免除赔偿的责任。

　　　索赔和理赔都有一定的时间限制，叫做"索赔期限"。关于这一点，在合同上一般都有所说明。如果一方过了有效期限才提出索

40　赔，另一方可以不予理赔。一般商品的索赔期限，通常在货物抵达

目的地后30到45天；机器设备等则可在抵达目的地后60天或更长时间。按照国际惯例，责任方在收到索赔后，应迅速组织调查，并在45天内予以回复。

索赔时，受损方应根据损失的内容和程度，客观、冷静地向责任方提出索赔。同时，要提供充份的证据，如货损检验证明、船长签署的货物短损证明、以及提单、保险单、商业发票等。叙述事实要简洁清楚，实事求是。引用合同中的条款或证明文件，应绝对准确，注意前后一致，切忌自相矛盾。说理要充份，语气既要坚定有力，一针见血，又要婉转客气，不失礼貌。提出赔偿要求或解决办法要具体明确，不可含糊其辞。

责任方在理赔时，应当抓紧调查，及时处理。要着眼于保持今后的业务来往，同时要站在对方的处境替对方设想，做到公平、合理。该赔的就赔，不该赔的则拒赔，但要充份说明理由。遇到不合理的要求，应礼貌地指出，据理力争。语气要郑重、强硬，但不要给人蛮横无理的感觉。

无论索赔还是理赔，都要以相互谅解、友好协商的态度来解决问题。但很难排除有时会出现"公说公有理，婆说婆有理"，双方各执一词，意见相持不下的局面。在这种情况下，双方可以将争议提交仲裁结构。通常在合同中都有明确规定的仲裁条款，以便双方在无法通过协商解决争议时，由双方同意的第三者或仲裁结构出面裁决。

✐ 根据课文内容回答下列问题：

1. 在执行贸易合同时，除了买卖双方外，还涉及哪些当事人？为什么？

2. "违约"和"争议"的定义是什么？

3. 交易的一方遭受损失后，一般会采取什么行动？这种行动叫做什么？

4. 什么是"理赔"？它跟"索赔"是什么关系？

5. 国际贸易中的索赔主要有哪几种？

6. 卖方什么时候可以向买方提出索赔？

7. 在什么情况下，买方可以向卖方索赔？

8. 运输部门在什么情况下要向交易的一方赔偿？

9. 什么是"保险索赔"？

10. 责任方在什么情况下可以免除索赔责任？为什么？

11. 索赔时应该注意什么？理赔呢？

12. 当双方无法通过协商解决他们之间的争议时，应该怎么办？

✎ **根据意思，给课文划分层次（不是自然段）并写出每个层次的大意。**

生词和用法

牵涉	qiānshè	V.	同一件事情涉及、关联到其他人或事情，常带宾语或补语。　to involve; to drag in
当事人	dāngshìrén	NP	跟事情有直接关系的人；指参加法律诉讼的一方，如原告、被告。 person (or party)involved/concerned; party (to a lawsuit)
弥补	míbǔ	V.	把不够的对方补足（常带宾语，对象一般限于有缺陷、损失、空白、不足等）：~过失、~不足、~损失。　to make up; to remedy
概括	gàikuò	V.	把事物的共同点归结在一起，总括；（带宾语或补语）：~全文、~大意、~一下。 to summarize; to generalize
		Adj.	简单扼要：~地说一下。 briefly
遗失	yíshī	V.	由于疏忽而丢失（可带宾语或补语）：~车票、~已久。　to lose

残损	cánsǔn	*Adj.*	残缺破损。	incomplete; broken, damaged
免除	miǎnchú	*V.*	免去、除掉（可带宾语或补语）：～职务、～责任、～水患。	to remit; to excuse; to exempt
冷静	lěngjìng	*Adj.*	沉着而不感情用事：头脑～、～地思考；＜＞激动。	calm; sober; cool-headed
叙述	xùshù	*V.*	写出或说出事情的前后经过（可带宾语或补语）：～情况、～清楚、～一下。	to narrate; to recount
实事求是	shíshì qiúshì	*Idm.*	实事：客观存在的一切事物；求：研究、探索；是：客观事物的内部联系和发展规律。表示从实际情况出发，不夸大，不缩小，正确地对待和处理问题。	to be true to the fact; to seek truth from facts; to be practical and realistic
引用	yǐnyòng	*V.*	用别人说过的话或做过的事作为根据。	to quote; to cite
绝对	juéduì	*Adv.*	(1)完全、一定：～满意、～准确；＜＞相对。(2)用在否定词前面，表示完全否定。这样用与"决"相通：～没问题、～不可能。	absolutely
自相矛盾	zìxiāng máodùn	*Idm.*	矛：进攻敌人用的长刺击武器；盾：保护自己的盾牌。比喻自己的言行前后互相抵触。	to be self-contradictory
说理	shuōlǐ	*V.*	说明道理：～斗争、～的文章。	to argue; to reason things out
语气	yǔqì	*N.*	(1)说话的口气：～很硬、商量的～。	tone (in speech);
			(2)表示陈述、疑问、祈使、感叹等分别的语法范畴。	mood (in grammar)
坚定	jiāndìng	*Adj.*	稳固确定，不因外来影响而动摇，多指立场、主张、意志等；＜＞犹豫。	

firm; staunch; steadfast

一针 见血	yī zhēn jiàn xiě	Idm.	表示言辞直截了当，简明而切中要害。 to pierce to the truth with a single pertinent remark; to hit the nail on the head.
婉转	wǎnzhuǎn	Adj.	(1)说话温和、曲折而不失本意：~拒绝、~地批评、说话很~；＜＞直率。 mild and indirect; tactful; (2)(指歌声、乐曲声或鸟叫声)圆转柔和、抑扬动听。 (of sounds) sweet and agreeable
含糊其辞	hánhúqící	VP	说话意思含混，使人不好理解。 to talk ambiguously
抓紧	zhuājǐn	V.	紧紧地抓住，不放松，可带宾语：~时间、~工作、~调查、~学习；＜＞放松。 to firmly grasp; to pay close attention to
着眼	zhuóyǎn	VO	从某方面观察、考虑(可带宾语或补语)：~于未来、~点。 to have something in mind; to view from the angle of
处境	chǔjìng	N.	所处的环境，面临的情况(多指不利的)：~困难、~危险。 (unfavorable) situation; plight
设想	shèxiǎng	V.	(1)着想；考虑(不带宾语)：为别人~、周密地~。 to have consideration for; to give thought to (2)假想，想象：后果很难~、不堪~。 to imagine
协商	xiéshāng	V.	为取得一致意见而共同商量(可带补语，可重叠)：平等~。 to consult; to talk things over
公平	gōngpíng	Adj.	处理事情合情合理，不偏袒哪一方：买卖~、~交易、~竞争、太不~了！ fair; impartial

据理力争	jùlǐlìzhēng	VP	依据道理，极力争辩，决不妥协让步。 To argue strongly on one's ground.
郑重	zhèngzhòng	Adj.	严肃认真：~的态度、~声明；＜＞轻率。 serious; solemn; earnest
强硬	qiángyìng	Adj.	强而有力，不肯退让的：~的对手、~的要求、态度很~；＜＞温和。 strong; tough; unyielding
蛮横	mánhèng	Adj.	态度粗暴，不讲道理：态度~、~无理。 rude and unreasonable; peremptory
谅解	liàngjiě	V.	了解实情后原谅或消除意见 (可带宾语) to gain forgiveness from; to understand; to make allowance for
排除	páichú	V.	除掉；消除，多指故障、困难等，可带宾语或补语：~干扰、~困难、~这种可能性。 to remove; to eliminate; to rule out
公说公有理， 婆说婆有理 gōng shuōgōng yǒu lǐ póshuōpóyǒulǐ		Idm.	双方都说自己有道理。 Both parties claim to be right.
各执一词	gèzhíyīcí	VP	各自坚持一种说法，形容意见不统一。 Each sticks to one's own position
相持 不下	xiāng chíbùxià	VP	双方互不相让，坚持对立 (不带宾语，可带补语)。 To be locked in a stalemate
局面	júmiàn	N.	一段时间内事情的形势和状态：新~、安定的~、打开~。 situation; aspect; phase
裁决	cáijué	V.	考虑并做出决定，可带动词作宾语：~纠纷、~争议。 to rule; to adjudicate

补充词

虚心	xūxīn	Adj.	不自以为是，能够接受别人的意见；＜＞骄傲。modest
贷款	dàikuǎn	VO	一方借钱给另一方；或向另一方借钱。to loan money; to provide a loan
亏欠	kuīqiàn	V.	在财物或感情上欠人家的。to be indebted
照顾	zhàogù	V.	特别关心，给予优待：~老人、~孩子、~病人。to take care
耕地	gēngdì	N.	可耕作种植农作物的土地。cultivated land
留情	liúqíng	V.	做事说话都注意到照顾情面，比较宽容：手下~、毫不~。to show mercy or forgiveness
直率	zhíshuài	Adj.	爽直坦率，言语行动没有顾忌；＜＞委婉。frank; candid; straightforward
切中	qièzhòng	V.	（言论或办法）正好击中（某种弊病）：~要害、~时弊。to hit (the mark)
要害	yàohài	N.	人体上致命的部位；比喻重要、关键的部份。vital part; critical point
不堪	bùkān	Aux.	不能（多用于不好或不愉快的方面）：~入耳、~回首、~设想。cannot bear
夸大	kuādà	V.	说的超过事实原有的程度，含贬义，常带宾语：~事实、~个人作用；＜＞缩小。to exaggerate; to overstate
争端	zhēngduān	N.	引起争执的事由：国际~。controversial issues; dispute
主题	zhǔtí	N.	文艺作品中通过具体艺术形像表现出来的中心思想；泛指文章的中心思想。theme; the main idea

苦功	kpdgōng	N.	刻苦的功夫，常作"下、练"的宾语。
			hard work; painstaking effort
热乎乎	rèhūhū	Adj.	形容热和，表示对别人的热情感到温暖、满意。
			warm
涌	yǒng	V.	水或云气冒出来。 to gush; to pour
辛苦	xīnkǔ	Adj.	身心劳苦。 tired; exhausted
		V.	使身心劳苦。 to fatigue; to tire
申明	shēnmíng	V.	郑重地说明、解释或辩白，常带宾语：~理由、~主张、~立场。 to declare; to state
将近	jiāngjìn	Adv.	表示时间或数量上接近，用在动词、表示时间或数量的名词前：~完成、~半年、~50人。
			close to; nearly; almost
抱怨	bàoyuàn	V./N.	心里不满，埋怨，常带宾语或补语。
			to complain; complaint

词语例释

一、Subject 向 Somebody +Verb （to; from; toward）

l-5. 同样，因为进口商或出口商对货物向保险公司进行了投保，保险人不但是这笔交易的有关当事人，他们与投保人共同签订的保险书也是对双方都有法律约束力的合同。

1. 她常常虚心向别人请教，所以进步很快。
2. 我向你保证，这批货一定能按期运抵目的港。
3. 由于现在的利率很低，所以不少人都向银行贷款买房子。

介词"向"引进动作的对象，跟指人的名词、代词组合，只用在动词前。

The Preposition 向 introduces the Object toward which an action is directed. It is associated with a Personal Noun or Pronoun, and is placed before a Verb only.

二、弥补 （to make up; to remedy）

l-11. 为了<u>弥补</u>由一方违约而造成另一方的经济损失，受损害的一方（通常是买方或卖方）往往会向应负责任的一方提出赔偿的要求，这就是"索赔"。

1. 我们要多学习别人的经验，来<u>弥补</u>自己的不足。
2. 他因为太忙，没有时间跟孩子在一起，所以就给孩子买很多东西，想<u>弥补</u>自己对孩子的亏欠。
3. 这些国家只想到经济发展而不重视环境保护，结果造成了不可<u>弥补</u>的损失。

动词"弥补"表示补偿不足的地方，作谓语，可带像"损失、不足、亏损、欠缺、缺陷、过失、错误、短处、亏欠"等宾语。"弥补"也可以作定语，如例 (3)。

The Verb 弥补 indicates "to make up the insufficient, or to mend a loss or a mistake". It functions as a Predicate and can take an Object such as 损失、不足、亏损、欠缺、缺陷、过失、错误、短处、亏欠. It can also serve as an Attribute, such as in Example (3).

三、在……下 （under the circumstances of; on condition of）

l-18. 属于买方违约的情况主要有：<u>在</u>F.O.B. 的条件<u>下</u>，不按合同规定如期派船接货；……

l-34. <u>在</u>这种情况<u>下</u>，当事人可以免除赔偿的责任。

1. <u>在</u>老师的帮助<u>下</u>，同学们的中文水平都有了很大的提高。
2. <u>在</u>医生和护士的精心治疗照顾<u>下</u>，小亮的伤很快就好了。
3. 中国<u>在</u>只占全世界耕地面积百分之七的情况<u>下</u>，养活了十二亿人，实在是不简单！

在＋动词/名词短语＋下，用在动词或主语前，说明条件或情况。

The phrase 在＋Verb/Noun Phrase＋下 is used before the Verb or the Subject of a sentence to show the condition or situation that leads to a certain result.

四、 自相矛盾 （to be self-contradictory）

l-44. 引用合同中的条款或证明文件，应绝对准确，注意前后一致，切忌自相矛盾。

1. 如果把这位总统前前后后说过的话作一个比较，就会发现有很多地方是自相矛盾的。
2. 当别人指出他的观点自相矛盾时，他却一点儿也不脸红。
3. 刚才你说这是免费的，现在又要我们付钱，不是自相矛盾吗？

成语"自相矛盾"可作谓语、定语或状语，比喻自己的言行前后互相抵触。

The idiom 自相矛盾 can function as a Predicate, an Attributive or an Adverbial. It is used as a metaphor to show that one's actions or words contradict with each other.

五、 一针见血 （to hit the nail on the head）

l-44. 说理要充份，语气既要坚定有力，一针见血，又要婉转客气，不失礼貌。

1. 那个孩子虽然年纪小，但是他一针见血地指出了问题：国王并没有穿衣服！
2. 刘小姐刚才的发言真是一针见血，毫不留情。
3. 他是个直率的人，说话不多，可是常常能一针见血，切中要害。

成语"一针见血"表示说话、写文章直截了当，切中要害，常作谓语或状语。

The idiom 一针见血 indicates that one speaks or writes in a straightforward manner, which pierces to the truth with a single pertinent remark. It is similar to the English idiom "to hit the nail on the head". It is often used as a Predicate or an Adverbial.

六、 抓紧 （to firmly grasp; to pay close attention to）

l-46. 责任方在理赔时，应当<u>抓紧</u>调查，及时处理。

1. 我们必须<u>抓紧</u>教育工作，才能使孩子们适应21世纪的竞争。
2. 如果不<u>抓紧</u>解决这个问题，到时候所有的电脑都会有问题。
3. 现在还有二十分钟，请大家<u>抓紧</u>时间。

这是个动补结构，意思是"紧紧抓住，毫不放松"，后面可跟宾语。动词和补语之间可插入"得、不"或程度副词"很、非常"等。如：

This is a Verb-Resultative Compound, meaning "to grasp firmly and do not let go". It may take an Object. The Infix 得 and 不 can be inserted in between 抓 and 紧 to form a Potential Complement, so can Adverbs such as 很 or 非常 to form a Complement of Degree. Please see these examples:

他对学习<u>抓</u>得很<u>紧</u>。

由于前一段时间对质量<u>抓</u>得不够<u>紧</u>，这个公司的产品销售受到了一定的影响。

七、 着眼 （to see from the angle of）

l-46. 要<u>着眼</u>于保持今后的业务来往，同时要站在对方的处境替对方设想，做到公平、合理。

1. 进行科学研究要从大处<u>着眼</u>，从小处着手。
2. 他们<u>着眼</u>于未来，在组织球队时就挑选年纪比较小的运动员。
3. 编写高年级的教材，应该<u>着眼</u>于提高学生的阅读能力和写作能力。

"着"有"使接触到别的事物"的意思，如："着手（动手、开始做）、着笔（用笔、下笔）、着眼"等。动词"着眼"表示从某方面观察、考虑，作谓语，可带宾语或补语。前面多有介词短语"从……"，后面可跟"于"引进宾语。

着 bears the meaning of "to enable to contact other things" and is often placed before certain body parts or a stationary. For instance, 着手 (to set about something; to start doing), 着笔 (to start writing), or 着眼, etc. The Verb 着眼 indicates to observe or to consider from certain perspective. It serves as a Predicate, and may take an Object or a Complement. There is a Prepositional Phrase 从……before 着眼 which is followed by 于 to introduce the Object of the sentence.

八、 设想 （to have consideration for; to give thought to）

l-47. 要着眼于保持今后的业务来往，同时要站在对方的处境替对方设想，做到公平、合理。

1. 我们不能只看到当前的利益，应该为子孙后代设想。
2. 政治家总是叫老百姓替国家设想，那么为什么国家就不替老百姓设想呢？
3. 彭太太说："请你替我设想设想，我一天到晚工作，回家还得做饭管孩子，哪儿有时间运动啊？"

动词"设想"表示"着想、考虑"的意思，作谓语，不带宾语，前面常有"为、替"等介词引进对象。另外，"设想"还有"想象、假想"的意思，作谓语，不带宾语。如：

The Verb 设想 means "to think" or "to give consideration to". It is used as a Predicate without an Object. It usually follows a Prepositional Phrase starting with 为 or 替, which introduces the Object. In addition, 设想 also means "to imagine" or "to suppose", which functions as an Intransitive Verb without taking an Object, neither. For example:

事情并不像你设想的那么简单。

中国已经有这么多人了，如果不控制人口的增长，后果将不堪设想。

当表示"想象、假想"时，"设想"还可以作名词，如：

It can also be a Noun when it means 想象 or 假想, for example:

请谈谈你们的<u>设想</u>。

这只是我个人的<u>设想</u>。

九、局面 （situation; phase）

l-52. 但很难排除有时会出现"公说公有理，婆说婆有理"，双方各执一词，意见相持不下的<u>局面</u>。

1. 老洪当了总经理以后，公司的出口贸易很快就打开了新<u>局面</u>。
2. 经过二十年的经济改革以后，中国终于开始改变了贫穷落后的<u>局面</u>。
3. 大家都不知道金融市场这种不稳定的<u>局面</u>还会持续多久。

"局面"表示一个时期内事情的形势和状态，所指的事情可以是世界性的，也可以是其中的某一个方面的情况。

局面 refers to a situation or a state in a specific period of time. The things it refers to may be of world significance, or may be just one specific aspect of a situation.

词义辨析

一、了解　理解　谅解

在这三个动词中，"解"字是"明白、懂得"的意思。"了解"表示知道得很清楚，而且比知道的程度深。可带宾语或补语，也可被副词修饰，对象多指人或事的具体情况。例如：正确了解、深入了解、很了解、非常了解、最了解、了解得很。"知道"则不可这样用。"了解"的另一个意思，是"打听、调查"。例如：

The character 解 means "to understand, to know". 了解 indicates to know someone or something thoroughly, in a much higher degree than 知道. It can take an Object or a Complement, and be modified by an Adverb as well, for example, 正确了解、深入了解、很了解、非常了解、最了解、了解得很.

However, 知道 cannot be modified by an Adverb. There is another usage of 了解, that is "to find out, inquire". Here are two examples,

请你去<u>了解</u>(＝打听)一下。

先<u>了解</u>(＝调查)清楚以后再说。

"理解"与"了解"的意思大致相同。指事时,侧重在理性上懂得、领悟;指人时,表示有同感,能够把自己放在对方的处境去考虑问题,对象多是心情、处境、想法等。

理解 is similar to the meaning of 了解, to some extent. When referring to things, its focus is on rational comprehension. When it refers to human beings, it emphasizes that one can put him/herself in the position of another person, somewhat similar to "empathy". Its Objects are mostly 心情、处境、想法, etc.

"谅"是"宽容、不责备、原谅"的意思。"谅解"表示在了解事情的真相后,原谅或消除意见。可带或不带宾语,如:

谅 means "to tolerate, not reproach, forgive". 谅解 indicates that one forgives or clears up any negative opinions after knowing the fact. It does not require to take an Object all the time, for example,

我<u>谅解</u>你的难处,但希望你以后不要瞒着我。

你们应该相互<u>谅解</u>,搞好关系。

二、争吵 争论 争议

"争"字的基本意思之一,是"争执、争论"。这三个动词,翻译成英语,都可以是 argue/dispute,它们之间的区别,主要在"争"字后面的词素。"争吵"侧重于"吵",即因意见不合而大声争辩,互不相让,而且不一定是很理性的。"争吵"不可带宾语,但可带补语,如:争吵得很厉害;争吵起来;争吵了一会儿。

One of the basic meaning of 争 is "to argue, quarrel". When translated into English, these three Verbs can all be "argue, dispute". Their differences, to a large extent, lie in the characters that follow 争 respectively. The emphasis of 争吵 is on 吵, which means "squabble", quarrel loudly and may not necessarily be rational. It cannot take an Object, but is possible to go with a Complement, as in the following, 争吵得很厉害、争吵起来、争吵了一会儿, etc.

"争论"强调各自表达自己的看法，进行比较理性的、一般不带偏见的争辩和讨论。"争论"可带宾语或补语，例如：

争论 stresses that each party discusses and debates over different opinions, which may be emotional but is usually rational and civilized. It can take either an Object or a Complement, for example,

他们一直在<u>争论</u>这件事，而且有时候<u>争论</u>得很激烈。

"争议"是书面语，一般用于比较大的事情或比较有意义的问题，着重在以商议的方式来进行争论。常作"有、值得、发生、引起"等动词的宾语。

争议 is a word of written language, and is usually used for serious matters, things with significance. Its meaning leans more toward "confer", with the hope to reach a compromise or solution through controversy. Although it is a Verb, it often follows other Verbs such as 有、值得、发生、引起, etc.

三、 坚持　保持　相持　支持

"持"字有"拿着、握着、保住、守住、支持、对抗"等意思。"坚持"表示坚决保持、持续进行、不改变、不放弃，多指在困难的情况下，主意坚定，坚决执行自己的意见和继续原有的行动，不改变立场、观点。其对象主要是"真理、方针、立场、原则、主张、意见、工作、学习、锻炼"等。

The character 持 has multiple meanings, such as "holding, retain, keep, support, confront". 坚持 means "to persist in, persevere, insist on", and refers to remaining faithful to something, upholding an idea or continuing an on-going action, usually under difficult situations. Its Objects are primarily 真理、方针、立场、原则、主张、意见、工作、学习、锻炼, etc.

"保持"表示维持(现状)，使原有事物继续存在，保持不变，不消失或减弱。所带的宾语，多数是名词，如"传统、习惯、荣誉、成绩"等，如果是动词，基本上都是不带宾语或补语的双音节动词，如"联系、中立、警惕、不变"等。

保持 is "to maintain", that is, to keep something in existence at the same level or in the same status. Its Objects are mostly Nouns, such as 传统、习惯、荣誉、成绩. Sometimes, it can be followed by Verbs such as 联系、中立、警惕、不变, but they are basically disyllabic Intransitive Verbs that do not take an Objects or a Complement.

"相持"指相互对持，坚持对立、互不相让。"相持"不带宾语，但可带补语，如：双方相持不下；他们已经相持了好一段时间了。

相持 indicates that two parties are locked in a stalemate, or each sticks to his/her own gun, not willing to yield. It cannot take an Object, but is possible to take a Complement, for example, 双方相持不下, 他们已经相持了好一段时间了.

"支持"是及物动词，常带宾语或补语。一个意思是在精神道义上给予鼓励或在钱财、物质或人力等方面给予赞助，例如：感谢你们对我们的大力支持。

另一个意思是勉强维持、支撑，多指在困难、不顺利的情况下，例如：

The Transitive Verb 支持 often takes an Object or a Complement. The first meaning is "to support", as in the sentence 感谢你们对我们的大力支持. Another meaning is "to hold out, sustain barely", which usually refers to unfavorable, difficult situations, for example,

她几天没睡觉，已经快支持不住了。

语法

一、多重复句　Multiple-Layer Complex Sentences

与英语相比，汉语句子延伸的范围比较大，逻辑关系也比较复杂。

有时候一个复句可以包含几个分句，而某个分句本身就是一个复句。换言之，这个作为分句的复句又含有自己的分句。这种含有多层次、逻辑关系复杂的复句，叫多重复句。让我们先看看下面的例子：

The scope of a Chinese sentence, compared with the English one, is much larger and the logical relations of its elements can be much more complicated. Sometimes, a Complex Sentence may contain several clauses, and one of which can be another Complex Sentence. In other words, as part of a Complex Sentence, a clause may contain its own clauses. Such sentences that have multiple layers, and complicated logical relations are called **Multiple-Layer Complex Sentences**. Let's first look at these examples:

1. 如果价格条件是 C.I.F.，‖ 不仅应该注明由卖方投保，‖ 而且应对投
   ①   ②   ③

   保金额、险别等都要详细说明。

2. 还盘，指的是交易的一方在接到一项发盘以后，‖ 不能完全同意该
                                    ①   ②

   发盘的条件，‖ 但仍有兴趣进行交易，‖ 为了进一步洽商，‖ 于是
            ③   ④

   针对该发盘的内容提出不同的建议。
   ⑤

3. 由于市场的供求关系，‖ 商品的供应量对市场价格影响很大：‖ 若
        ①   ②

   供过于求，‖ 价格就会下跌；‖ 若供不应求，‖ 则会上涨。
   ③   ④   ⑤   ⑥

例 (1) 是一个二重复句。所谓二重复句，是句子中的某个分句 (至少是其中的一个分句，也可能是各个分句) 本身是一个简单型的复句形式，也就是说，这个分句还包含着自己的分句。例 (1) 由两个大分句组成。前一个大分句用关联词"如果"表示一种假设关系。后一个大分句又由②③两个小句组成，它们之间是一种递进关系，关联词是"不但……而且……"。这样，整个句子就有两个层次的逻辑关系：假设下面是递进，所以是二重复句。

Example (1) is a Double-Layer Complex Sentence. By Double-Layer Sentence, it is meant that within a Complex Sentence, one of the clauses (at least one clause, may be every single one) is itself a Complex Sentence structurally. That is, this clause contains a clause of its own. Example (1) consists of two major clauses. The first one uses a Connective 如果 to indicate a relation of hypothesis. The second one consists of two minor clauses, ② and ③, which form a progressive relation by using the Connectives 不但……而且……. Accordingly, there are two layers of logical relations in the whole sentence: a progressive relation beneath a hypothesis. Thus, it is a Double-Layer Complex sentence.

例 (2) 是一个三重复句。所谓三重复句，是句子中的某个分句 (至少是其中的一个分句) 本身是一个二重复句。也就是说，这个分句自己有两个 (或者是两个以上的) 分句，其中的一个分句是个复句并且含有另外的分句。例 (2) 由两个大分句①和③组成。前后两大分句由关联词"但"连接，是一种转折关系。前一大分句包含小句①和②，不用关联词而靠语序表示承接关系。后一大分句包含三个小句③④⑤，关系也较为复杂。其中③和⑤是承接关系，关联词是"于是"；而④和⑤又是一个用关联词"为了"连接的目的复句。因此，整个句子就有三个层次：首先是转折关系，然后在第二个大分句中又是一层承接关系 (③和⑤)。再下来是在这层关系下包含的目的关系，所以这是一个三重复句。

Example (2) is a Triple-Layer Complex Sentence. By Triple-Layer Complex Sentence, it is meant that within a Complex Sentence, one of the clauses (at least one) is itself a Double-Layer Complex Sentence. In other words, this cause contains two (or more than two) clauses, and one of which is a Complex Sentence that has its own clauses. Example (2) consists of two major clauses ① and ③ which are connected with the Conjunction 但, indicating a adversative relation. There are two minor clauses (① and ②) in the first major clause. The logical relation between them is a successive one; and is signified by word order instead of using of any Connectives. There are three minor clauses, ③,④ and ⑤ in the second major clause, and their relations are quite complicated. Among these three minor clauses, ③ and ⑤ are a Complex Sentence with a successive relation, using 于是 as their Connective. The clauses ④ and ⑤ are another Complex

Sentence of purpose which uses 为了 as a Connective . Hence, there are three layers of logical relations in the entire sentence: first is an adversative relation, then is a successive one with clauses ③ and ⑤ in the second major clause, followed by a Complex Sentence of Purpose embedded underneath itself. Therefore, this is a Triple-Layer Complex Sentence.

例 (3) 是一个四重复句。所谓四重复句，是句子中的某个分句 (至少是其中的一个分句) 本身是一个三重复句。也就是说，这个分句至少有两个分句组成，其中之一是一个二重复句——它的分句又含有另外一个复句。例 (3) 一共有四层。整句由①②两个大分句组成，两者用关联词"由于"连接，是一种因果关系。②作为整个句子的后一大分句，又含有③④⑤⑥四个小句，通过冒号连接，表示属于并列复句的一种总分关系。小句③④和⑤⑥中间有一个分号，因而是一种并列关系。而③和④之间，⑤和⑥之间都是一种假设关系。由此可见，整个句子共有四个层次：因果——总分——并列——假设，所以是个四重复句。

Example (3) is a Quadruple-Layer Complex Sentence. Similar to the previous ones, a Quadruple-Layer Complex Sentence refers to one clause (at least one) of a Complex Sentence is itself a Triple-Layer Complex Sentence. That is, this clause consists of at least two clauses and one of which is a Double-Layer Complex Sentence —its clause contains another Complex Sentence. There are four layers of logical relations in Example (3) altogether. The entire sentence is composed of two major clauses ① and ②, which are connected with a Conjunction 由于, forming a cause and effect relationship. As the second major clause of the whole sentence, clause ② contains four minor clauses, which are ③④⑤⑥ respectively. They are then connected together by a colon, indicating these are parallel subsets of a general category. Between the two pairs of minor clauses ③④ and ⑤⑥, is a semi-colon, which shows that they are Coordinative Complex Sentences. Further down a level, it is a relation of hypothesis between ③④, so is the one between clauses ⑤ and⑥. Therefore, four layers of logical relations are observed in this sentence: cause and effect, general to specific, coordinative, and hypothesis. It is a typical example of Quadruple-Layer Complex Sentence.

多重复句，根据其复杂程度，可以有六七重之多，但大致上都跟以上的例子差不多，一层一层递加罢了。学会分析多重复句，对于准确理解原文的意思，提高阅读能力，有着深刻的现实意义。只要掌握了正确的方法，了解分句与分句之间，句子与句子之间的相互关系，注意关联词语的使用，就不会因为句子长、层次多、关系复杂而不知所云，或者只看到局部的意思而产生误解。

The number of layers of Multiple-Layer Complex Sentences can increase, depending on the complexity of the logical relations within a particular sentence. No matter how complicated a sentence can be, it basically follows the same fashion as shown in the above examples, just adding more layers of relations, step by step. It is very practical to learn how to analyze Multiple-Layer Complex Sentences because it helps us to understand correctly the exact meaning of the original authentic text, and to improve our reading comprehension. As long as we learn the right way, and be able to understand the relations between various clauses and sentences, and pay attention to the use of Connectives, we will not be confused by lengthy sentences with multiple-layers and complicated logical relations. We will less likely misinterpret the entire text nor simply to rely on our partial understanding.

分析多重复句，首先要有全局观念，从总体上识别直接构成整个复句的主要分句。然后辨析分句的结构层次和相互关系，再由表及里，从大到小，找出这些分句中包含的下一层分句的界限。要根据关联词的特点，确定各分句之间的逻辑关系。对没有或省略了关联词语的分句，要结合上下文，看能否加上合适的关联词语，使分句之间的关系逐步显露出来。

When we analyze Multiple-Layer Complex Sentences, we must first have an overall point of view, and be able to identify, as a whole, the major clauses that directly make up the entire sentence. Then we can analyze the structural layers of the clauses and their mutual relations, moving from the surface to the deeper structure, from the general to the more specific elements, and gradually find out the boundaries between the clauses and the minor ones beneath them. We should determine the logical relations between clauses according to the traits of the Connectives. As for those clauses that do not have Connectives or whose Connectives have been omitted, we should read and look into the context carefully, and see whether certain Connectives can be added so that the correct logical relation between clauses can be revealed.

二、 紧缩复句 Contracted Complex Sentences

紧缩复句是以类似单句的形式来表达复句内容的特殊复句。所谓 "紧"，就是"紧凑"——分句之间的语音停顿(或书面上的逗号)取消了， 整个句子虽然有两个甚至更多的谓语，但是在形式上却像是一个单句的 谓语部份。所谓"缩"，就是"缩略"——复句中原有的某些成份，特别是 某些关联词语省略了。例如：

Contracted Complex Sentences are special ones that express ideas conveyed by regular Complex Sentences, in the forms similar to simple sentences. The so-called *Contracted Complex Sentences* are both compact and condensed. First, the pause in speaking (or the punctuation in writing) is cancelled. Second, some of the elements in the original Complex Sentences are omitted, particularly certain Connectives. Although a Contracted Complex Sentence may have two or even more Predicates, it looks, at least in its form, much more like the predicate of a Simple Sentence. For example:

1. （要是）你去我就去。   〔假设复句〕
2. （这些东西就是）再便宜我也不买。   〔让步假设复句〕
3. （因为）她看见你忙，（所以）就没进来。   〔因果复句〕
4. （无论）我怎么看也看不明白。   〔条件复句〕
5. （虽然）他七十多岁（了，但是）还每天跑步呢！〔转折复句〕

紧缩复句是在长期使用中形成的一些固定格式，是不能随意生造 的。下面是比较常见的一些紧缩复句的类型和例子：

Contracted Complex Sentences are some fixed structures that have been formed in language use for many years. They are not coined arbitrarily at will. The following are some types of *Contracted Complex Sentences* commonly found in Chinese:

1A. 紧缩假设复句　Contracted Complex Sentences of Hypothesis

a) （如果/要是）……就……

喜欢<u>就</u>拿走吧。
想去<u>就</u>早点去。

b) （如果/要是）不……（就）不/别……
　　＝＞非……不可

买不起<u>就</u>别买。
她上街不花钱<u>就</u>不舒服。＝＞
她上街不花钱<u>就</u>不行。＝＞她
上街<u>非</u>花钱<u>不可</u>。
你不努力学习<u>就</u>不行。＝＞你
<u>非</u>努力学习<u>不可</u>。

c) （如果/要是）又……（又）……

我不说<u>又</u>能把我怎么样？
<u>又</u>没有地址<u>又</u>没有电话，怎么
跟她联系？

d) （如果/要是）……还……

我不相信你，<u>还</u>会告诉你吗？
明年有空，我<u>还</u>要去北京。

e) （如果/要是）……再……

出了事<u>再</u>想办法。
有意见以后<u>再</u>提。

1B. 紧缩让步假设复句　Contracted Complex Sentences of Concessive Hypothesis

f) （就是/即使）……也……

想睡<u>也</u>没时间睡。
董事长有时候<u>也</u>要听他的。

g) （就是/即使）不……也……

走<u>不</u>动<u>也</u>得走。
<u>不</u>买<u>也</u>要付钱？

h) （就是/即使）……再……也

风险<u>再</u>大<u>也</u>不怕。
<u>再</u>忙<u>也</u>要吃饭啊。

i) （就是/即使）……又……

你有钱<u>又</u>有什么了不起？
我们迟到了<u>又</u>怎么样？

j)　（就是/即使）……还……   请我<u>还</u>不去呢！

　　　　　　　　　　　　　　　　　　　　这几块钱有什么用？买瓶水<u>还</u>
　　　　　　　　　　　　　　　　　　　　得三块呢。

k)　（就是/即使）……都……   这孩子走<u>都</u>走不稳，还想跑。

　　　　　　　　　　　　　　　　　　　　他二年级的课文<u>都</u>看不懂，更
　　　　　　　　　　　　　　　　　　　　不用说看报了。

2. 紧缩因果复句　Contract Complex Sentences of Cause and Effect

a)　（因为）……就/便……   母亲不放心，<u>就</u>一直在门口等
　　　　　　　　　　　　　　　　　　　　着。

　　　　　　　　　　　　　　　　　　　　我觉得不错，<u>就</u>多买了几个。

b)　（既然）……就/便……   你们已经知道了，<u>就</u>不必再问
　　　　　　　　　　　　　　　　　　　　了。

　　　　　　　　　　　　　　　　　　　　是学生<u>就</u>要做作业。

3. 紧缩条件复句　Contracted Complex Sentences of Condition

a)　（只要）……就/便……   你看完说明书<u>就</u>知道了。

　　　　　　　　　　　　　　　　　　　　有汽车<u>就</u>得买保险。

b)　（只要）一……就……   <u>一</u>吃药<u>就</u>没事了。

　　　　　　　　　　　　　　　　　　　　他<u>一</u>喝酒<u>就</u>脸红。

c)　（无论）……也/都……   我怎么说<u>也</u>没用。

　　　　　　　　　　　　　　　　　　　　什么时候<u>都</u>要注意节约。

d)　（只有）……才……   这些书老师<u>才</u>能借。

　　　　　　　　　　　　　　　　　　　　学过三年汉语的学生<u>才</u>能上这
　　　　　　　　　　　　　　　　　　　　门课。

4. 紧缩转折复句　Contracted Adversative Complex Sentences

a)　（虽然……但是）又……   他想赚大钱，<u>又</u>怕冒风险。

小钟觉得这样做有问题，<u>又</u>不好意思反对，只是站在一边不说话，<u>也</u>不动手。

b) （虽然……但是）还……　　　　货已经备好，<u>还</u>没有装运。

我走了，<u>还</u>会记住你们的。

c) （虽然还不/没……）就……　　　　<u>还</u>不到六月<u>就</u>已经这么热了。

方亮<u>还</u>没毕业<u>就</u>找到工作了。

d) （虽然……但是……）反而……　　昨天下了一场大雨，<u>反而</u>更热了。

电视、电脑降价了，买的人<u>反而</u>少了。

紧缩复句的特点： Some characteristics of Contracted Complex Sentences:

1. 紧缩复句用字不多，结构紧凑，内容丰富，表意精炼，一般多用于口语。

   Contracted Complex Sentences use fewer words, and are compact in structure. They have substantial information, and are concise in meaning, and thus are generally used in spoken Chinese.

2. 紧缩复句多数是偏正复句，表示的逻辑关系以假设、让步、因果、条件、转折等关系居多。

   Contracted Complex Sentences are mostly subordinate complex ones. The logical relations expressed are primarily of hypothesis, concession, cause and effect, and adversative, etc.

3. 紧缩复句与语境关系非常密切，因为关联词语的省略，很多时候要靠上下文才能确定其逻辑关系。有时一个紧缩复句可填上不同的关联词语，但意思完全不同。例如：

   The use of *Contracted Complex Sentences* is closely related to the context. Because of the omission of Correlatives, oftentimes, the logical relation is determined by the context. Sometimes, it is possible to insert various Connectives to a *Contracted Complex Sentence*, resulting in different meaning. For instance:

> （如果）你去，我们就不去了。   〔假设〕
>
> （只要）你去，我们就不去了。   〔条件〕
>
> （因为）你去，（所以）我们就不去了。   〔因果〕

4. 紧缩复句省略的关联词语，基本上是连词，如"因为……所以……"、"如果"、"无论"、"只有"、"即使"等。像"就"、"也"、"又"、"还"、"都"、"才"等关联副词，一般都予以保留。当然也有一些紧缩复句是完全不用关联词语的。如：

The omitted Connectives in contracted sentences are conjunctions in general, such as 因为……所以……、如果、无论、只有、即使, just listing a few of them. Adverbs such as 就、也、又、还、都、才, however, are basically kept. Some *Contracted Complex Sentences*, of course, do not need any Connectives. These are a few examples:

> 〔假设〕   （要是）不买（就）拉倒。
>
>   （如果）丢了怎么办？
>
> 〔条件〕   （只要）你有多少，我（就）买多少。
>
>   钱是我的，我爱给谁（就）给谁！
>
> 〔因果〕   （因为）他病了，（所以）没有来。
>
>   （因为）下大雨，（所以）不去了。
>
> 〔转折〕   （虽然）好看（不过）不好用。
>
>   （虽然）吃力（可是）不讨好。

修辞

句式：常式句与变式句　Sentence Forms: Regular and Inverted Sentences

按照汉语的一般语序规律构成的句子，叫常式句；为一定修辞目的而改变常规语序的句子，叫变式句。

Sentences that follow the normal word order in Chinese are *Regular Sentences*; sentences that deviate from the norm of *Regular Sentence* form in order to achieve certain rhetorical effect are called *Inverted Sentences*.

一、强调谓语的变式句　Inverted Sentences Emphasizing the Predicate

汉语主谓句的正常语序，一般是主语在前，谓语在后。但是，有时为了强调谓语所表述的内容，可以改变主语和谓语的语序，用谓语在前，主语在后的变式句表达。例如：

The normal word order of Chinese sentences is, in general, that the Subject goes first, then the Predicate next. However, in some cases, this word order can be reversed, that is, by placing the Predicate before the Subject, so as to emphasize what is expressed in the Predicate. For instance:

別了，<u>再见在火线中吧</u>，我的"哥哥"！　（殷夫《写给一个哥哥的信》）

<u>出来吧</u>，你们！

<u>搞什么名堂</u>？这个家伙。

主谓语变式句多数用在祈使句或疑问句。在主语和谓语之间往往有明显的语音停顿，书面上用逗号或问号隔开。这样既可以突出谓语，也明确了变序条件下的主谓关系。

The inversion of Subject and Predicate is mostly used in Imperative Sentences, or Interrogative Sentences. There is usually a noticeable pause in speaking between the Subject and the Predicate, and is separated by a comma or a Question Mark in writing. It can, in this way, highlight the Predicate and clarify the relation of Subject and Predicate when the normal word order has changed.

二、强调宾语的变式句　Inverted Sentences Emphasizing the Object

汉语句子的话题，基本上都是由主语来充当的。但是有时为了修辞的需要，也会把宾语提前来充当句子的话题，使强调的语气更为突出。例如：

In Chinese, the Subject of a sentence usually serves as the topic of that sentence also. Sometimes, for the sake of rhetoric, it is possible to move the object up front and make it the topic of the sentence, to further emphasize its significance. For example:

北京是美丽的，我知道，因为我不但是北京人，而且到过欧美，看见过许多西方的名城。　　　　　　　　　　　（老舍《我热爱新北京》）

鸟的天堂里没有一只鸟，我不禁这样想。（巴金《鸟的天堂》）

"风景如画"这意义，我日前在绍兴从中深刻地体会到。

（许钦文《鉴湖风景如画》）

三、 强调定语或状语的变式句　Inverted Sentences Emphasizing the Attributive or Adverbial

汉语的定语或状语在常式句都是在中心语前面。如果把定语或状语放在中心语后面，就形成了修饰语后置的变式句，也可以收到突出、强调的修辞效果。如：

As a rule, Chinese modifiers such as Attributive or Adverbial are placed before the Head Phrase to be modified. When an Attributive or Adverbial switched position with the thing it modifies, an inverted sentence is formed. In doing so, it can also achieve the effect of emphasis. Note the following examples:

〔定语后置〕　她一手提著竹篮，内有一个破碗，空的；……

（鲁迅《祝福》）

道里纯粹不是中国味。街上满眼是俄国人，走着的，坐着的；……　　　　　　　　（朱自清《西行通讯》）

〔状语后置〕　如果我能够，我要写下我的悔恨和悲哀，为子君，为自己。　　　　　　　　　　　（鲁迅《伤逝》）

他们从山上带下来平安与快乐在他们心里，他们又带来许多好看的百合花，在空着的篮里，在头巾里，在用山草结成的包里。　　　　　（李广田《山之子》）

四、 强调偏句的变式句 Inverted Sentences Emphasizing the Subordinate Clause

汉语里的偏正复句，多数的语序比较固定，基本上是从句在前，主句在后。也就是说，作为全句语义重心所在的正句，一般都位于偏正复句的后半部份。特别是像表示因果、条件、目的、假设、让步、转折关系的偏正复句，更是遵从时间顺序，先提原因或条件，再讲结果或结论，先提出目的，再讲为达到目的而采取的行动等。但是，有时为了强调从句的内容，也可以把表示原因、条件、目的等从句，与主句交换位置，构成变式的偏正复句。如：

The word order of Subordinate Complex Sentences in Chinese is quite consistent, generally with the subordinate clause going first, then the main clause. In other words, as the focus of the entire sentence, the main clause is normally situated at the second part of a sentence. Subordinate Complex Sentences, particularly those representing a logical relation of *Cause and Effect, Condition, Purpose, Hypothesis, Concession, or Adversative*, usually follow a chronological order. That is, a cause/reason or condition is mentioned first, then a result or a conclusion is presented; or a purpose is stated prior to the introduction of the action that will lead to the achievement of that purpose. However, sometimes when it is necessary to highlight the cause/reason, condition, or purpose, the main clause may change position with its subordinate clause, resulting in inverted sentences as in the following:

〔因果〕 这只是我自己心情改变罢了，<u>因为我这次回乡，本没有什么好心绪</u>。 (鲁迅《故乡》)

〔条件〕 我好像做了一场大梦。满园的创伤使我的心仿佛又给放在油锅里煎熬。这样的煎熬是不会有终结的，<u>除非我给自己过去十年的苦难生活作了总结，还清了心灵上的欠债</u>。 (巴金《小狗包弟》)

〔假设〕 抗战以来八九年教书生活的经验，使我整个的否定了我们的教育。我不知道我还能继续支持这样的生活多久，<u>如果我真是有廉耻的话</u>！

（闻一多《八年的回忆与感想》）

〔目的〕　　不过，我还是用原稿去印单行本，<u>为是保存原来面貌</u>。

（老舍《福星集》）

〔转折〕　　北方的早春又是那么寒冷，我不愿意滞留在阴晦而冰冷的车站里，只好决定进城，<u>虽然时间那么样早</u>。

（杨朔《昨日的临汾》）

练习

一、　用线将意思相同的词和词语连起来：

因为疏忽而犯的错误　　　　　　　　　　　　遗失

没有代价地、白白消耗或失去的东西　　　　说理

开始动手做某件事情　　　　　　　　　　　着笔

因为损坏或遗失别人的东西，用钱来补偿　　赔偿

合乎常情，合乎事理　　　　　　　　　　　道理

因为疏忽而丢失东西　　　　　　　　　　　过失

用钱或物补偿自己给别人造成的损失　　　　赔款

开始动笔、下笔写东西　　　　　　　　　　着眼

事情或论点的根据、理由、情理　　　　　　赔本

向别人行礼，表示认错、道歉　　　　　　　着想

做生意引起资金、本钱的亏损　　　　　　　损失

说明道理　　　　　　　　　　　　　　　　赔礼

从某方面观察、考虑　　　　　　　　　　　合情合理

为某人或某事的利益考虑　　　　　　　　　着手

二、　用括号里的词或词组改写下列句子，但不改变其基本意思，必要时可对词序作一定的调整：

1. 请你根据实际情况，不夸大、不缩小，把事故的过程说出来。

（实事求是，叙述）

2. 这些纠纷都是由于翻译的英语水平不高造成的。今后我们应当着眼于如何提高他们的英语水平。　　　　　　（引起，从……去考虑）

3. 家长们的要求是完全合理的，可是谁有办法补偿学生的时间损失呢？　　　　　　　　　　　　　　　　　（绝对，弥补）

4. 这件事很难说没有提交仲裁的可能，因为目前双方都坚持自己的说法，互不相让。　　　　　　　　（排除……可能性，各执一词）

5. 我们都要学习她的这种精神，时时、处处都为大家的利益着想。

（A向B+Verb，设想）

6. 既然这件事情涉及到总经理，他一定会依据道理，极力争辩。

（牵涉，据理力争）

三、 选择最合适的词填空：

1. 保险公司在接到索赔要求后，要立即组织调查，＿＿＿＿＿＿损失的情况。

a. 谅解　　　　b. 理解　　　　c. 了解　　　　d. 误解

2. 虽然这是小何的过失，但是她老老实实地承认了错误，得到了大家的＿＿＿＿＿＿。

a. 谅解　　　　b. 理解　　　　c. 了解　　　　d. 误解

3. 这句话太长了，意思不好＿＿＿＿＿＿，最好把它改短一点。

a. 谅解　　　　b. 理解　　　　c. 了解　　　　d. 误解

4. 提出的索赔要求必须具体明确，不可含糊其辞，否则会引起＿＿＿＿＿＿。

a. 谅解　　　　b. 理解　　　　c. 了解　　　　d. 误解

5. 老陆和太太结婚几十年了，可是从来没有＿＿＿＿＿＿过。

a. 争议　　　　b. 争吵　　　　c. 争端　　　　d. 争论

6. 已经十一点多了，他们还在热烈地_____着那个电影的主题。

    a. 争议   b. 争吵   c. 争端   d. 争论

7. 万一双方发生_____，合同上对如何处理也有详细的说明。

    a. 争议   b. 争吵   c. 争端   d. 争论

8. 爸爸要他学电脑，他却要学历史，两个人_____了好久，最后还是爸爸让步了。

    a. 相持   b. 坚持   c. 支持   d. 保持

9. 如果没有你们的_____和帮助，我们就不可能取得成功。

    a. 相持   b. 坚持   c. 支持   d. 保持

10. 即使是冬天，还有不少人_____每天跑步。

    a. 相持   b. 坚持   c. 支持   d. 保持

四、 找出第十一、第十二课课文中所有的多重复句。

五、 把下面的每组句子连接起来，使之成为合乎逻辑的多重复句：

    例：因为我是你们的老师，所以我应该帮助你们。
        如果你们有困难，我应该帮助你们。 ⟶

            因为我是你们的老师，所以，如果你们有困难，我应该帮助你们。

1. 虽然他不想去南方，但是他还是去了。
   妈妈也不希望他去南方，但是他还是去了。

2. 无论有多大的风险，他们都决心把实验继续做下去。
   他们决心把实验继续做下去，并且取得最后的成功。

3. 为了帮助遭受水灾的人们，〔很多人〕都积极捐了款。
   不但城里的工人、职员、个体户捐了款，而且乡下的农民、老人、小孩也捐了款。

4. 要是你们不想做，请尽快告诉我们。

或者〔要是你们〕不能做，请尽快告诉我们。

请尽快告诉我们，免得大家都等着。

5. 尽管这家公司目前还比较小，但是很有发展前途。

因为他们的产品技术先进，所以很有发展前途。

只要他们不断提高产品的质量，就很有发展前途。

6. 要学好中文，一是要多练习，二是要注意学习方法。

只有经常练习，才能不断有所提高。

不但要肯下苦功，还要懂得怎样学习，提高学习效率。

7. 虽然轮船公司应该赔偿货物在运输途中遭受的损失，但是，……可以免除赔偿的责任。

如果损失是自然灾害造成的，那么当事人可以免除赔偿的责任。

或者〔如果损失是〕意外事故造成的，那么当事人可以免除赔偿的责任。

当事人可以免除赔偿的责任，因为这些都是当事人不能预料和事先采取预防措施的。

8. 事情不一定像她说的那么严重，所以不必太紧张。

由于台风昨天才到达那个地区，所以不必太紧张。

另外"和平"号走的航线也在那个地区的边上，所以不必太紧张。

即使遇到这样的台风，"和平"号也不会有什么问题。

"和平"号不会有什么问题，因为这是一条设备先进的新船。

因为这是一条设备先进的新船，所以不必太紧张。

六、 删去可省略的关联词语，把下面的句子变成紧缩复句：

1. 你既然觉得电视没有意思，就把它关了吧。

2. 不管我怎么叫，他都不起床。

3. 只要质量好，价钱贵一点儿也没关系。

4. 双方只有冷静地说理协商，才能公平合理地解决问题。

5. 如果过了有效期限才提出索赔，对方可以不予受理。

6. 即使你可以一时欺骗某些人，你能永远欺骗所有的人吗？

7. 我宁愿自己去打工也不要他的钱。

8. 因为飞机晚点了，所以大家只好在飞机场耐心地等待。

七、 移动划线部分，适当地调整关联词语或标点符号，把下列的常式句改写成变式句：

1. <u>老大爷</u>，您辛苦了！

2. <u>我想</u>，嗨！她也够累的了。

3. 突然，一种<u>热乎乎的</u>感觉涌上他的心头。

4. <u>因为这是他签的第一份合同</u>，所以他把合同看了又看。

5. <u>如果真是那么容易的话</u>，为什么他们不自己做呢？

6. <u>不管谁先动手</u>，打人就是不对！

7. <u>为了让她多睡一会儿</u>，我没有叫醒她。

8. <u>尽管环境和条件都很重要</u>，要学好最后还是要靠自己。

八、 把下列句子翻译成汉语：

1. When facing the rude and unreasonable boss, she was very calm. She spoke with a firm and forceful tone, and pierced to the truth with a single pertinent remark [revealing] that his words were self-contradictory.

2. At that time, if Clinton could seize the opportunity, and recount the whole story [i.e. "the process"] true to the facts, (and) admit his mistakes to the American people, it was possible that he could have gained the forgiveness and understanding of the people. This problem might also have been solved fairly and rationally. As he only has had his reputation [i.e. "face"] in his mind, the political damage that this mistake caused is unmendable.

3. A situation like this has been lasting for some time already. Since each party sticks to his own words, and their opinions are locked in a stalemate, their attitude is getting tougher and tougher. Under such circumstances, it is absolutely impossible to solve the problem through consultation.

九、 商业信函练习七

用传统式的格式，把下面的信翻译成汉语，注意婉辞的正确使用：

China National Cereals, Oils and Foodstuffs
Import and Export Corporation
Dalian Branch
General Manager
Bao Zi
789 Youtiao Road
Dalian, China

May 16, 2003

Kellogg Cereals Company, Ltd.
Sales Department
Executive Manager
Ben McDonald
55 Hamburger Street
New York, NY 12345
USA

Dear Mr. McDonald:

30,000 Metric Tons of Flour per M/V "Rainbow"
Our Contract No. 7906MF

Your shipment of 30,000 metric tons of flour per M/V "Rainbow" arrived at Dalian yesterday. With much regret, we inform you that the actual weight of the goods is 29,953 metric tons only, which does not agree with the original quantity specified in your invoice.

We are enclosing Inspection Report No. DL 641 issued by the Dalian Commodity Inspection Bureau, who certifies that the quantity is 29,953 metric tons, a shortage of 47 metric tons. Such a shortage has exceeded the overload/underloading range as stipulated in our Contract No. 7906MF. Therefore, we lodge a claim against you for shortage in weight of 47 metric tons as follows:

F.O.B. Value of the Goods	US$14,100.00
Freight	$ 5,200.00
Insurance Premium	$ 470.00
Inspection	$ 893.50
Total	US$20663.50

We hope that this matter will receive your best attention and are looking forward to your prompt response.

Yours Sincerely,

Bao Zi

文化与商贸背景知识

婉辞

人们在交谈时，有时为了避免失礼或不愉快，往往会用婉转含蓄的话来暗示或代替本来要说的话。这种不直接说出本意，不太刺激，使语气和缓、轻松一些的话语，就是婉辞。

婉辞可用于口语，也可用于书面语。比如，在生活上，为了避免说"死"字，中国人习惯用"过去了"、"老了"、"走了"等说法，或者更文雅些，说"逝世"、"长眠"、"作古"等。又如，在公众场合或在别人家里作客，要上厕所，可以说去"净手"、"更衣"、"方便一下"、甚至"上一号"。说别人胖了，用"发福了"来代替；说别人瘦了，用"苗条了"。

在政治经济方面，尤其是新闻媒体的报导，也常用一些比较温和、中性的字眼。例如，把身体有缺陷、或智力有问题的人，叫"残疾人"、"残障人士"或"弱智人士"，称"失败"为"失利"，"落后"为"后进"，"失业"叫做"待业"，"解雇"叫做"下岗"。另外，像"市场疲软(萧条)"、"经济困难(危机)"、"让利(降价)出售"、"调价(涨价)"等，都是一些比较委婉的说法。

在外贸、外交等场合，有时不想直接对某件事情表态，说话留有余地，也常用婉辞。如："无可奉告"(不能告诉你)、"谢绝参观"(不让看)、"再研究研究"(这件事可能行也可能不行)等。

✎ 商业信函 (7)

××××年5月8日

光华贸易公司：

<u>第PK258号合同项下的300箱瓷器</u>

　　由"巨人"号货轮运来的我方上述合同项下的300箱瓷器前天下午已抵达旧金山。我们遗憾地向你方申明，将近六分之一的货物受损，其中有的已完全破碎。

　　随函附上由美国加州公平检验公司出具的第495号检验报告。从此检验报告中，贵方可看到，货损很可能是由于包装设计不合理和包装材料太差所致。这次事故我方损失实在太大，因此，我们不得不向贵方提出索赔15 000万美元（包括检验费），详情请见所附索赔清单。

　　希望贵方从速处理此事，并尽快予以回复。

美国蓝天厨房用具有限公司

美国加州

蓝天厨房用具有限公司

经理先生：

<u>第PK258号合同项下的300箱瓷器</u>

贵方5月8日的索赔函及附件已收悉。对于这一不幸事件，我方深表同情。假如此事确实属我方责任，本公司愿意按规定赔偿。然而，必须指出，我方一贯重视产品的质量和包装，对贵方这批订货的包装和我们以往的处理并无两样。同时，这批瓷器的包装设计已使用多年，极少听到抱怨。因此，我们认为，货物如此严重的破损是由于运输过程中的野蛮装卸造成的。另外，第PK258号合同项下的这些货物是在F.O.B.条件下成交的，轮船公司是贵方自己联系的，所以，对于你们提出的索赔，十分遗憾，我方实在难以负任何责任。

我们建议贵方立即与轮船公司联系，了解有关装卸和搬运的具体情况。如果这批货物已投保了破碎险，请向保险公司提出索赔。

我们真诚地希望此事能得到妥善的解决，并期望今后继续与贵公司合作。

光华贸易公司

××××年5月12日

例释词语表

A

按 NP+VP	according to; in the light of	L-6, p.226

B

便于＋V.	easy to; convenient for	L-7, p.278
并非……而是……	instead of; rather than	L-8, p.321
不得＋VP	not allowed to; prohibited from	L-3, p.96
不仅……而且……	not only...but also...	L-11, p.479
（才/就）不致＋VP	not in such a way to; not likely to	L-6, p.227

C

称为/称作	to be called as	L-2, p.53
驰名中外	to be renowned at home and abroad	L-5, p.187
除非……否则……	unless...otherwise...	L-9, p.379
此外	besides; in addition; moreover	L-1, p.15

D

打……折（扣）	to give (somebody) a discount	L-6, p.225
代替	to substitute; to replace	L-8, p.321
得不偿失	the loss outweighs the gain	L-6, p.223
对……而言	relative to/compared with someone/something	L-9, p.374
对……来说	for/to somebody/something	L-6, p.222
对于	as for; in relation to; with regard to	L-11, p.477

E

Adj.1 而 Adj.2	to be Adj.1 and/yet Adj. 2	L-11, p.478

F

凡是……都……	every single one; all;	L-3, p.100
反过来	conversely; in turn; the other way round	L-10, p.427
反之	conversely; on the contrary	L-3, p.97
否则	otherwise; if not.., or else...	L-3, p.97

G

各自＋V.	each; respectively	L-4, p.140
关系到	to be significant to; to affect; to matter to	L-6, p.223

| 取决于 | to depend on; to hinge on | L-4, p.140 |
| 却 | but; yet; whereas | L-4, p.139 |

R

然而	but; yet; however	L-7, p.274
任何……都/也	any; whatever; whichever; whoever	L-1, p.11
日益	with each passing day; increasingly	L-7, p.279
如何＋V	how; how to	L-11, p.475
如同	to be like; to be similar	L-3, p.92
若……就/则	if...then...	L-6, p.224

S

涉及（到）	to involve; to relate to	L-8, p.322
（替/为……）设想	to have consideration for; to give thought to	L-12, p.521
A使B＋V	to make/cause someone to do something	L-7, p.276
始终	from beginning to end; always	L-4, p.138
是……而不是……	it is...but not...; instead of; rather than	L-4, p.142
是否	whether; if	L-3; p.101
适用于	to suit; to be applicable for;	L-11, p.476
受到＋V	to receive; to subject to; to suffer from	L-8, p.323
算	to be counted as; to be considered as	L-8, p.320
随着	along with; in pace with	L-7, p.278
A随着B而V	along with; accompanied with	L-10, p.427

T

讨价还价	to bargain; to haggle	L-4, p.139
体现	to embody; to reflect	L-11, p.475
通过	through; by means of	L-1, p.14
同时	at the same time; in the meantime	L-4, p.141

W

Disyllabic V+ 完毕	to finish; to complete; to end	L-11, p.479
往往	often; usually	L-10, p.425
万无一失	no danger of anything going wrong	L-10, p.429
万一	just in case; if by any chance	L-11, p.474
未必	not necessarily; may not	L-2, p.59
为……所V	to be Verb+ed [by somebody]	L-5, p.187
无论……都/也	no matter...; regardless	L-2, p.59

X

（跟/与）……相反	opposite to; contrary to	L-2, p.60
相应（地）＋V	corresponding; relevant; accordingly	L-4, p.141
A向B＋V	to; toward; from	L-12, p.517

Y

一般来说	generally speaking; in general	L-4, p.143
一旦……就……	once...than..; when ever..., will/would...	L-3, p.95
一方面……（另）一方面	on the one hand..., one the other hand...	L-9, p.375
一经VP	once; whenever	L-9, p.378
一针见血	to hit the nail on the head	L-12, p.519
以便	so as to; so that; in order that	L-1, p.12
以NP＋V	to use/take NP to VP	L-3, p.92
VP1以VP2	in order to; in order that	L-3, p.93
以免	so as to avoid; so as not to	L-5, p.189
以……为……	to take...as...	L-5, p.189
义不容辞	to be duty-bound; to have a unshirkable duty	L-8, p.320
意味着	to signify; to imply	L-10, p.428
因而	therefore; hence	L-3, p.98
因……而……	due to; owing to	L-6, p.225
因VP1而VP2	due to; owing to; because	L-10, p.428
应……要求/邀请	at the request/invitation of	L-9, p.375
Adj. 于	more/less than (in comparison)	L-6, p.224
于是	thus; therefore; as a result	L-2, p.58
（给/不）予	(not) to give; (not) to render	L-10, p.425
与其……不如……	would rather...than...; better...	L-10, p.426
A与B相符/不符	(not) to conform/congruent with	L-5, p.190
由somebody＋V	to be Verb+ed by somebody	L-3, p.94
有利于	to be favorable to; to be advantageous to	L-7, p.279
有助于	to be conducive to; to contribute to	L-1, p.15
允许	to allow; to permit	L-8, p.324

Z

在……基础上	on the basis of; based on	L-7, p.276
在……下	under the circumstances of; on condition of	L-12, p.518
则	then; whereas	L-1, p.13
占	to constitute; to account for; to make up	L-8, p.322
知己知彼	to know oneself and one's opponent well	L-1, p.13

A（是）指B	to be referred to; to indicate; to mean	L-3, p.95
只有……才……	only and if only...then...	L-2, p.55
只要……就……	as long as/so long as...then...	L-5, p.186
至于	as for; as to	L-5, p.188
抓紧 ＋V	to firmly grasp; to pay close attention to	L-12, p.520
着眼	to see from the angle/prospect of	L-12, p.520
自……（起/开始）至………（为止）		
	(starting) from...till (ending at)...	L-10, p.430
自相矛盾	to be self-contradictory	L-12, p.519
遵照	to conform to; in accordance with	L-9, p.374
作为	as...; being...	L-2, p.56
（对……有/起到……）作用		
	to play a role in...	L-7, p.277

词汇表

安排	ānpái	V. /N.	to arrange; to plan; arrangement	4*
安全	ānquán	Adj./N.	safe; secure; safety; security	8
安装	ānzhuāng	V.	to install	5
岸	àn	N.	shore, coast	4
按	àn	Prep.	according to	4
盎斯	àngsī	MW	ounce	6
罢	bà	Mph.(V.)	to stop; to cease	10
罢工	bàgōng	VO	to strike; to go on strike	10
罢工险	bàgōngxiǎn	NP	Strikes Risk	10
白	bái	Adv.	in vain; for nothing	10
百分比	bǎifēnbǐ	N.	percentage	6
拜访	bàifǎng	V.	〔敬辞〕to pay a visit to; to call on (somebody)	1
颁发	bānfā	V.	to issue, to grant	2x
办理	bànlǐ	V.	to conduct; to handle	4
办妥	bàntuǒ	VP	to get something done properly	9x
半职	bànzhí	Adj.	part-time; half-time (employee)	2x
磅	bàng	MW	pound	6
包	bāo	N./V.	bag; sack; to wrap	7
包	bāo	MW	a measure word	7
包括	bāokuò	V.	to include; to consist of	1
包销	bāoxiāo	V.	to be the sole agent for a product of a firm	11
包装	bāozhuāng	N./V.	packing; package; to pack	2

---

* This refers to the number of the Lesson in which the term appears in its "生词和
用法" section. That with an "x" indicates that the term appears in the "补充词"
section.

保护	bǎohù	*V./N.*	to protect; protection	7
保留	bǎoliú	*V.*	to reserve, to keep back (one's opinion)	2
保险	bǎoxiǎn	*V./N./Adj.*	to insure; insurance	4
保险单	bǎoxiǎndān	*NP*	insurance policy	8x
保障	bǎozhàng	*V.*	to ensure; to guarantee; to safeguard;	7x
		N.	guarantee; security	9
保证	bǎozhèng	*V./N.*	(to) guarantee	1
保证金	bǎozhèng jīn	*NP*	cash deposit	9
暴风雨	bàofēngyǔ	*NP*	rainstorm; storm; tempest	
报关	bàoguān	*VO*	to declare something at the Customs	4
报价	bàojià	*N./VO*	(to) offer	2
报价单	bàojiàdān	*NP*	quotation sheet	3
报刊	bàokān	*N.*	newspapers and periodicals; journals	1
报税	bàoshuì	*VO*	to file a tax return; to declare customs duty	10x
抱怨	bàoyuàn	*V. N.*	to complain; complaint	12x
爆炸	bàozhà	*V.*	to explode; to blow up; explosion	10
备	bèi	*Mph.(V.)*	to provide, to be prepared to; be ready to	2x
备妥	bèituǒ	*VP*	get ready properly	9x
奔驰	Bēnchí	*Pr. N.*	Mercedes Benz	5
奔驰	bēnchí	*V.*	to run quickly; to speed; to gallop	5
奔腾	Bēnténg	*N.*	Pentium	8x
奔腾	bēnténg	*V.*	to gallop; to surge forward	8x
笔	bǐ	*MW/ N.*	a measure word for things related to money	2
比率	bǐlǜ	*N.*	ratio; rate	9
币	bì	*N.*	money; currency	9
必不可少	bì bù kě shǎo	*Idm.*	indispensable; essential; necessary	2

避免	bìmiǎn	V.	to avoid; to refrain from	3
必要	bìyào	Adj./N.	indispensable; necessary	1
币值	bìzhí	N.	currency value	9
编号	biānhào	V./N.	to number; serial number	3x
贬斥	biǎnchì	V.	to denounce	3x
贬值	biǎnzhí	V.	to devalue	9x
辨别	biànbié	V.	to distinguish; to differentiate	3
变动	biàndòng	V./N.	to change; alternation	1
便于	biànyú	Adj.	easy to; convenient for	7
标明	biāomíng	V.	to mark clearly; to indicate properly	4
标志	biāozhì	N./V	sign; mark; symbol; to symbolize	5
表达	biǎodá	V.	to express	3
别	bié	Mph.(N.)	categorization; distinction	4
波动	bōdòng	V.	to fluctuate; to undulate	9
玻璃	bōlí	N.	glass	6
博士	bóshì	N.	Doctor of Philosophy; Ph. D.	2x
补偿	bǔcháng	V./N.	to compensate; to make up	10
补充	bǔchōng	V.	to replenish; to supplement	6x
不一定	bù yīdìng	Adv.	not necessarily; not definitely	2
不堪	bùkān	Aux.	cannot bear	12x
不可抗力	bùkě kànglì	N.	irresistible force; force majeure; Acts of God	11
部门	bùmén	N.	department; section	1
不胜	bùshèng	Adv./V.	very much; deeply; cannot bear	5x
不予	bùyǔ	VP	not grant; to refuse	10
不致	bùzhì	VP	not result in; not incur	6

裁决	cáijué	V.	to rule; to adjudicate	12
材料	cáiliào	N.	data; material	1
财务	cáiwù	N.	financial affairs	2x
采用	cǎiyòng	V.	adopt; to use; to utilize	3
参考	cānkǎo	V.	to refer to; for reference; to consult	5
参赞	cānzàn	N.	counselor	1x
残损	cánsǔn	Adj.	incomplete; broken, damaged	12
仓库	cāngkù	N.	warehouse	10
仓至仓条款	cāngzhìcāng tiáokuǎn	NP	Warehouse to Warehouse Clause	10
操作	cāozuò	V.	to operate	5
差别	chābié	N.	only; sole	4
差异	chāyì	N.	difference; divergence; diversity	6
查收	cháshōu	VP	please find (in a letter); to receive	8x
产地	chǎndì	N.	place of production; place of origin	5
长度	chángdù	N.	length	6
(长)矛	chángmáo	N.	lance; spear; pike	11x
常言	chángyán	N.	saying	11
厂商	chǎngshāng	N.	manufacturers and companies	1
畅销	chàngxiāo	Adj. /V.	a booming sale; to sell briskly	7x
超出	chāochū	V.	to exceed; to surpass	6
超额	chāo'é	V.	to go beyond the quota; to surpass the target	6
超级市场	chāojí shìchǎng	NP	supermarket	7
潮	cháo	Adj.	damp; moist	7
撤销	chèxiāo	V.	to cancel; to revoke	5

陈列	chénliè	V.	to display; to exhibit	7
沉没	chénmò	V.	to sink	10
称谓	chēngwèi	N.	appellation; title	4x
承	chéng	V.	to undertake; to contract	8
承保	chéngbǎo	V.	to accept insurance	10
成本	chéngběn	N.	cost	4
承担	chéngdān	V.	to bear, to undertake	2
承兑交单	chéngduì jiāodān	NP	Documents against Acceptance, 简称D/A.	9
成分	chéngfèn	N.	component; composition; ingredient	5
成功	chénggōng	Adj./N.	to succeed; success	1
承诺	chéngnuò	V./N.	promise to undertake; acceptance of offer	2
成千上万	chéng qiān shàng wàn	Idm.	thousands and thousands; countless, numerous	4x
程序	chéngxù	N.	procedure; sequence	2
承运人	chéng yùnrén	NP	a contractor of shipping	8
承载	chéngzài	V.	to bear the weight of	7
吃惊	chījīng	VO	to be startled; to be shocked	11x
持	chí	V.	to hold; to grasp	2x
驰名	chímíng	V.	well-known, renowned	5
驰名中外	chímíng zhōngwài	Idm.	renowned at home and abroad	5
持续	chíxù	V.	to continue; to sustain	5x
持证	chízhèng	VO	to be certified; to have a license (to engage in certain job)	2x
充分	chōngfèn	Adj.	sufficient	1

出口	chūkǒu	N./V.	export	1
出入	chūrù	N.	Discrepancy; difference	6
出事	chūshì	VO	to have an accident; to meet with a mishap	10
出售	chūshòu	V.	to sell	2
除非	chúfēi	Conj.	only if; only when; unless	9
储存	chǔcún	V.	to store; to stockpile; to save	6
处境	chǔjìng	N.	(unfavorable) situation; plight	12
处理器	chǔlǐqì	N.	processor (of a computer)	8x
畜	chù	N.	domestic animal; livestock	9x
触礁	chùjiāo	VO	to run on rocks; to strike a reef or rock	10
船舶	chuánbó	N.	ships and boats; shipping	10
船期	chuánqī	NP	sailing date	8
传统	chuántǒng	N.	tradition	5
传真	chuánzhēn	N.	fax, facsimile	1
吹	chuī	V.	to blow; to puff; to boast; to brag	9x
纯正	chúnzhèng	Adj.	pure; unadulterated	6x
刺 (穿)	cì (chuān)	VP	to stab; to penetrate; to pierce	11x
赐复	cìfù	V.	to favor a reply	5x
从事	cóngshì	V.	to engage in (doing sth.)	1
从速	cóngsù	Adv.	as soon as possible; without delay	9x
促	cù	V.	to urge; to promote	6
促进	cùjìn	V.	to promote; to accelerate; to advance	10
错过	cuòguò	V.	to miss; to let slip	8
打	dá	MW	dozen	6
达成	dáchéng	V.	to reach (agreement)	2
大方	dàfang	Adj.	natural and poised; unaffected	7

大连	Dàlián	Pr.N.	A harbor city in Liaoning Province in northeastern China.	8
大使	dàshǐ	N.	ambassador	1
大使馆	dàshǐguǎn	N.	embassy	1
大宗	dàzōng	Adj. N.	a large amount; a large quantity of	4
袋	dài	N. /MW	sack; bag; pocket; a measure word	7
待	dài	V.	to wait; to await	9
代表	dàibiǎo	N./V.	representative; to represent	1
代表团	dàibiǎotuán	N.	delegation	9x
贷款	dàikuǎn	VO	to loan money; to provide a loan	12x
代理	dàilǐ	V.N.	to act as an agent (or proxy, procurator)	8
代理人	dàilǐrén	N.	agent	8
代替	dàitì	V.	to substitute; to replace; to take the place of	8
代销	dàixiāo	VP	to sell on a commission basis	8x
单独	dāndú	Adv.	alone; by oneself; on one's own	5
单据	dānjù	N.	payment document; documents attesting to the giving or receiving of money, goods, etc.	8
单位	dānwèi	N.	unit	4
当面	dāngmiàn	Adv.	to somebody's face; in someone's presence.	1
当事人	dāngshìrén	NP	person (or party) involved/concerned; party (to a lawsuit)	12
盗	dào	V.N.	to steal; to rob; theft	7
道	dào	V.	to say; to talk; to speak (literary)	11
道义	dàoyì	N.	morality and justice	8x
得不偿失	débù chángshī	Idm.	the loss outweighs the gain	6
等待	děngdài	V.	to wait; await	6x

低廉	dīlián	*Adj.*	inexpensive; cheap	8
抵	dǐ	*Mph.(V.)*	to arrive	4
抵触	dǐchù	*V.*	to conflict; to contradict	11x
递	dì	*V.*	to hand over; to pass; to give	3
递盘	dìpán	*VO*	to bid	3
地位	dìwèi	*N.*	status; position	5
地域	dìyù	*N.*	region; district; territory	4
地震	dìzhèn	*N.*	earthquake; seism	10
地址	dìzhǐ	*N.*	address	1
电报	diànbào	*N.*	telegram	3
电风扇	diànfēngshàn	*N.*	electric fan	5x
垫付	diànfù	*V.*	pay for somebody and expect to be paid back later	9
电汇	diànhuì	*NP*	Telegraphic Transfer, 简称 T/T	9
电器	diànqì	*N.*	electric appliance	6
电子邮件	diànzǐ yóujiàn	*NP*	eletronic mail; e-mail	3
调查	diàochá	*V./N.*	to investigate; investigation	1
跌	diē	*V.*	to fall; to drop	6
订	dìng	*V.*	to conclude; to draw up; to agree on	2
定	dìng	*V.*	fixed; formulated	3
锭	dìng	*N.*	ingot	7
订舱	dìngcāng	*VO*	to book shipping space	4
订立	dìnglì	*V.*	to conclude, to make (a contract)	2
董事长	dǒng shìzhǎng	*N.*	president /chairperson of the board of directors	1x

动向	dòngxiàng	N.	trend; tendency	1
独立自主	dúlì zìzhǔ	VP	to maintain independence and keep the initiative in one's own hand	9x
盾 (牌)	dùnpái	N.	shield	11x
短	duǎn	Mph.(V.)	to lack; to be less	6
短量	duǎnliàng	N. /VO	shortage (of amount)	10
短装	duǎnzhuāng	VP N.	underload	6
对待	duìdài	V.	to treat; to approach; to handle	
对方	duìfāng	N.	the other party；＜＞我方	1
兑换	duìhuàn	V.	to exchange; to convert	9
对象	duìxiàng	N.	target; object; partner	1
额	é	Mph.(N.)	a specified number or amount	4
恶劣	èliè	Adj.	odious; abominable	10
发挥	fāhuī	V.	to bring into play; to give free rein to	7x
发盘	fāpán	VO	to offer	2
发票	fāpiào	N.	invoice; Commercial Invoice	3
法律	fǎlǜ	N.	law	1
繁	fán	Adj.	numerous; miscellaneous; many and diverse	2
繁多	fánduō	Adj.	various	6
繁琐	fánsuǒ	Adj.	tedious; with trivial details	6
反复	fǎnfù	Adv./V.	repetitively; again and again	2
反悔	fǎnhuǐ	V.	to go back on one's words	3
反映	fǎnyìng	V.	to reflect; to mirror	5
反之	fǎnzhī	Conj.	conversely; on the contrary	3
反之亦然	fǎnzhī yìrán	Idm.	the reverse is also true; and vice versa	9
范围	fànwéi	N.	scope; range	1

方	fāng	N.	part; party	2
方式	fāngshì	N.	mode; way; fashion	2
防	fáng	V.	to prevent; to guard against; to resist; anti-; -proof	7
纺织	fǎngzhī	V.N.	spinning and weaving	6
纺织品	fǎngzhīpǐn	N.	textile; fabric	6
费	fèi	N.	fee; cost	4
费用	fèiyòng	N.	expenses; cost; expenditure	4
分	fēn	Mph.(N.)	branch; division	2x
分	fēn	V.	to divide; to separate; to differentiate; to distinguish	9
分属	fēn shǔ	V.	to be under different authority	9
分配	fēnpèi	V. /N.	to distribute; to allot; to assign	7
分批	fēnpī	VP	in batches; lots; in turns	8
分析	fēnxī	V./N.	to analyze; analysis	1
粉丝	fěnsī	N.	vermicelli made from bean starch, etc.	5
锋利	fēnglì	Adj.	sharp	11x
风险	fēngxiǎn	N.	to suffer; to incur (a disaster or a loss)	4
奉告	fènggào	V.	to inform; to let other's know	8x
否	fǒu	Adv.Partcl.	not	3
否则	fǒuzé	Conj.	otherwise	3
浮动	fúdòng	V.	to float; to fluctuate	10x
幅度	fúdù	N.	range; score; extent	6
符合	fúhé	V.	to accord with; to conform with	5
腐	fǔ	Adj.	rotten; putrid; stale	7
副	fù	Adj.	deputy; vice; assistant	1x

副本	fùběn	N.	duplicate; transcript; copy of original document	11
负担	fùdān	V./N.	to bear; burden	4
附加	fùjiā	V.	to add; to attach	2
附件	fùjiàn	N.	appendix; annex	11
付款 交单	fùkuǎn jiāodān	NP	Documents against Payment, 简称D/P.	9
附上	fùshang	VP	to attach; to add	1
副修	fùxiū	VP/N.	to minor in (an area of study /a subject)	2x
附言	fùyán	N.	postscript	4x
富有	fùyǒu	V.	to be rich in; full of	5x
复杂	fùzá	Adj.	complicated; complex	2
负责	fùzé	V./Adj.	to be responsible for; be in charge of	1
该	gāi	Pron.	this	3
改	gǎi	V.	to change; to revise; to alter; to correct	3
概	gài	Adv.	all; without exception	10
概括	gàikuò	V./Adj.	to summarize; to generalize; briefly	12
概率	gàilù	N.	probability	10
概念	gàiniàn	N.	concept	8
盖章	gàizhāng	V.	to seal; to stamp (with a seal)	3x
感激	gǎnji	V.	feel grateful; to feel indebted	5x
赶紧	gǎnjǐn	Adv.	In a hurry; lose no time; quickly	4x
钢材	gāngcái	N.	steel products; steels; rolled steel	7
钢铁	gāngtiě	N.	iron and steel	6
港口	gǎngkǒu	N.	port; harbor	1
高温	gāowēn	Adj. N.	high temperature	5x
高雄	Gāoxióng	Pr.N.	A harbor city in southern Taiwan	8

告	gào	V. Mph.(V.)	to declare, announce (of the status of something); to make known	8
胳膊	gēbo	N.	arm	11x
搁浅	gēqiǎn	V.	to run aground; to be stranded	10
格式	géshì	N.	form; pattern	3
各执一词	gè zhí yī cí	VP	Each sticks to one's own position	12
耕地	gēngdì	N.	cultivated land	12x
更改	gēnggǎi	V.	to revise; to change; to alter	3
公说公有理，婆说婆有理	gōng shuō gōng yǒu lǐ, pó shuō pó yǒu lǐ	Idm.	Both parties claim to be right	12
公布	gōngbù	V.	to promulgate; to publish; to announce	5
供货	gōnghuò	VO	supply of goods	3
公斤	gōng jīn	MW	kilogram	6
功能	gōngnéng	N.	function	2
公平	gōngpíng	Adj.	fair; impartial	12
供求	gōngqiú	N.	supply and demand	1
公升	gōngshēng	MW	liter	6
公司	gōngsī	N.	company; corporation	1
工艺品	gōngyìpǐn	N.	handicraft article	5
购	gòu	Mph. (V.)	to buy	2
构成	gòuchéng	V.	to constitute; to form; to compose	8
购买	gòumǎi	V.	to purchase; to buy	2
谷类	gǔlèi	N.	grain; cereal	6
鼓励	gǔlì	V.	to encourage; to urge	6

固定	gùdìng	*Adj./V.*	fixed; regular; to fix; to regularize	3
固体	gùtǐ	*N.*	solid	7x
关税	guānshuì	*N.*	customs duty; tariff	1
官员	guānyuán	*N.*	officer; official	11x
关注	guānzhù	*V.*	to pay close attention to	5
管理	guǎnlǐ	*V./N.*	to manage, to administer, to run, to look after	2x
管制	guǎnzhì	*V./N.*	to control	1
冠军	guànjūn	*N.*	champion	11x
惯例	guànlì	*N.*	convention; usual practice	1
罐头	guàntou	*N.*	canned food	5
广泛	guǎngfàn	*Adj.*	extensive; wide-ranging	5
广告	guǎnggào	*N.*	advertisement; commercial	1
归	guī	*V.*	to go back to; to return	10
规程	guīchéng	*N.*	rules; regulations	5
规定	guīdìng	*V./N.*	to stipulate; to set rules and regulation; rules	1
规格	guīgé	*N.*	specifications; standards	2
国际	guójì	*Adj.*	international	1
国境	guójìng	*N.*	national territory	1x
过程	guòchéng	*N.*	process; course	2
过失	guòshī	*N.*	fault; error	10
海关	hǎiguān	*N.*	Customs Service	1x
海轮	hǎilún	*N.*	oceangoing vessel	10
海难	hǎinàn	*N.*	perils of the sea	10
海损	hǎisǔn	*NP*	average	10
海啸	hǎixiào	*N.*	tsunami; seismic sea wave; tidal wave	10
海洋	hǎiyáng	*N.*	seas and oceans	8

函	hán	N.	letter; mail	3
含糊	hánhú	Adj.	Ambiguous; vague	3
含糊其辞	hánhú qící	VP	to talk ambiguously	12
含量	hánliàng	N.	content	5
含义	hányì	N.	meaning; implication	2
罕	hǎn	Adj.	rare; seldom	9
罕见	hǎnjiàn	Adj.	rare; seldom seen	5x
航海	hánghǎi	N.	navigation	10
航空	hángkōng	V./N	to aviate; to fly	8
航运	hángyùn	N.	shipping	10
毫	háo	Adv.	in the least; (not) at all	3
好家伙	hǎo jiāhuo	Intjn.	(for exclamation) good lord; good heaven	4x
号	hào	VO	to number	11
号码	hàomǎ	N.	number (of phone or room, etc.)	1
核对	héduì	V.	to check	9
合格	hégé	Adj.	qualified	2x
合计	héjì	V.	to add up to; to amount; total	3x
合理	hélǐ	Adj.	reasonable; rational	3x
合同	hétóng	N.	contract	2
合约	héyuē	N.	contract	11
合作	hézuò	V./N.	to cooperate	1
洪水	hóngshuǐ	N.	flood	10
后果	hòuguǒ	N.	consequence	3
呼应	hūyìng	V.	to act in coordination with each other; to work in concert with	11

互利	hùlì	*Adj.*	mutually beneficial; of mutual benefit	5x
华丽	huálì	*Adj.*	magnificent; gorgeous	7
环节	huánjié	*N.*	link; component	2
还盘	huánpán	*VO*	to counter offer	2
换算	huànsuàn	*V. N.*	to convert; conversion	6
化学	huàxué	*N.*	chemistry; chemical	5
汇	huì	*V.*	to remit; to transfer (through a bank or postal service)	9
汇付	huìfù	*VP/N.*	to remit money as payment; remittance	9
汇率	huìlǜ	*N.*	exchange rate	10x
汇票	huìpiào	*N.*	bill of exchange; draft	9
货币	huòbì	*N.*	money; currency	4
货柜	huòguì	*N.*	container	7
货损	huòsǔn	*NP*	damage or loss of goods	7
货物	huòwù	*N.*	commodity; goods	4
货源	huòyuán	*N.*	source or supply of goods	6
即	jí	*V.*	that is; i.e.	2
基本	jīběn	*Adj.*	basic; fundamental; essential	2
稽查	jīchá	*V.*	to check; to audit; to examine	2x
基础	jīchǔ	*N.*	base; basis; foundation	1
机构	jīgòu	*N.*	organization	1x
机会	jīhuì	*N.*	opportunity; chance	1
基金会	jījīnhuì	*N.*	foundation	2x
积极	jījí	*Adj.*	positive; active; vigorous	7
机械	jīxiè	*N.*	machinery; mechanical	5
亟	jí	*Adv.*	urgently; anxiously	9

集合	jíhé	V.	to gather; to assemble	7
即期 汇票	jíqī huìpiào	NP	sight bill	9
即使	jíshǐ	Conj.	to indicate; to refer to	3
集装箱	jízhuāngxiāng	N.	container	7
给予	jǐyǔ	V.	to give; to render	10
际	jì	Mph.(Adj)	inter-	1
计量	jìliàng	V.	to measure; to calculate	4
记录	jìlù	N.	record	11x
纪律	jìlù	N.	discipline	11x
技能	jìnéng	N.	skill	2x
技术	jìshù	N.	technology; technique	5
计算	jìsuàn	V.	to calculate; to compute; to count	6
加仑	jiālún	MW	gallon	6
家用 电器	jiāyòng diànqì	NP	electric appliance	5x
假若	jiǎruò	Conj.	if	8
价格	jiàgé	N.	price	2
价格表	jiàgé biǎo	NP	price list	3
价值	jiàzhí	N.	value	4
坚定	jiāndìng	Adj.	firm; staunch; steadfast	12
坚固	jiāngù	Adj.	solid; firm; sturdy	7
坚强	jiānqiáng	Adj.	strong; firm; staunch	11
简练	jiǎnliàn	Adj.	terse; succinct	11
检验	jiǎnyàn	V.	to inspect; to examine	11
鉴定	jiàndìng	V.	to appraise; to examine and determine	9x

建立	jiànlì	V.	to establish; to set up	1
建议	jiànyì	V./N.	to suggest; suggestion	2
将近	jiāngjìn	Adv.	close to; nearly; almost	12x
讲	jiǎng	V.	to tress; to pay attention to	11
奖励	jiǎnglì	N./V.	award; reward	2x
奖学金	jiǎngxuéjīn	N.	scholarship	2x
降低	jiàngdī	V.	to reduce; to lower; to cut down	4
骄傲	jiāo'ào	Adj.	proud; arrogant	11x
交付	jiāofù	V.	to pay; to hand over; to deliver	4
交货	jiāohuò	VO	to deliver (goods); delivery	2
交货不到险	jiāohuò bùdàoxiǎn	NP	Failure to Delivery Risk	10
交纳	jiāonà	V.	to pay; to submit	9
交易	jiāoyì	N.	deal; transaction; trade	1
狡猾	jiǎohuá	Adj.	crafty; cunning; sly	3x
教练	jiàoliàn	V./N.	to coach; coach	11x
金融	jīnróng	N.	finance; banking	9
金属	jīnshǔ	N.	metal	6
谨	jǐn	Adv.	sincerely; solemnly	8x
仅仅	jǐnjǐn	Adv.	only; merely	3
尽量	jǐnliàng	Adv.	to the best of one's ability; as far as possible	4
进出口	jìnchūkǒu	NP	＝进口＋出口 import and export	1
进口	jìnkǒu	N./V.	import	1
进行	jìnxíng	V.	to conduct; carry out ; carry on	1
经济	jīngjì	N./Adj.	economy; economical	1
经理	jīnglǐ	N.	manager	1x

经历	jīnglì	N./V.	experience; to experience	2x
精美	jīngměi	Adj.	exquisite; elegant	7
精细	jīngxì	Adj.	delicate; exquisite; with great detail	6x
经销	jīngxiāo	V.	to deal in; to sell	5x
经营	jīngyíng	V.	to deal in/with; to manage	1
竞争	jìngzhēng	V./N	to compete; competition	3x
阶段	jiēduàn	N.	stage; phrase; period	2
接洽	jiēqià	V.	to consult with; to take up the matter with	2
接收	jiēshōu	V.	to receive	8
结构	jiégòu	N.	structure; composition	5
结合	jiéhé	V.	to combine; to joint	5
洁净	jiéjìng	Adj.	clean	8x
节省	jiéshěng	V.	to save up; to economize	4
解释	jiěshì	V./N.	to explain; to interpret; interpretation	11
纠纷	jiūfēn	N.	dispute; controversy	3
均	jūn	Adv.	all	5x
均	jūn	Mph.	average; even	9x
局面	júmiàn	N.	situation; aspect; phase	12
局势	júshì	N.	situation	8
据	jù	Prep.	according to; on the ground of	2
拒	jù	Mph.(V.)	to reject; to refuse	10
具备	jùbèi	V.	to possess; to have	3
距离	jùlí	N./V.	distance; to be away from	4
据理力争	jù lǐ lì zhēng	VP	to argue strongly on one's ground	12
拒收	jùshōu	VP	refuse to accept	6

拒收险	jùshōuxiǎn	NP	Rejection Risk	10
具体	jùtǐ	Adj.	specific; concrete	2
具有	jùyǒu	V.	to possess; to have; to be of (certain quality)	2
捐	juān	V.	to contribute; to donate	11x
绝	jué	Adj.	extreme; most	7
绝对	juéduì	Adv.	absolutely	12
开端	kāiduān	N.	beginning; start	5x
开启	kāiqǐ	V.	to open	7
开支	kāizhī	V./N.	to pay (expenses); expenditure	4
考虑	kǎolù	V.	to consider; to think	5x
可靠	kěkào	Adj.	reliable; dependable; trustworthy	9
克	kè	MW	gram	6
客观	kèguān	Adj.	objective	5
客户	kèhù	N.	client; customer	1
恳	kěn	Adv.	earnestly; sincerely	10x
肯定	kěndìng	V./Adj.	intention; intent	3
空口无凭	kōngkǒu wúpíng	Idm.	There is no record for an oral promise	11
空调机	kōngtiáojī	N.	air conditioner; air conditioning	5x
口	kǒu	N.	opening; mouth; entrance	1
口岸	kǒu àn	N.	port	1x
口头	kǒutóu	N.	oral; verbal	2
空…格	kòng...gé	VO	to indent ...spaces	4x
扣除	kòuchú	V.	to deduct	9
苦功	kǔgōng	N.	hard work; painstaking effort	12x
库存	kùcún	N.	stock; reserve	6x

夸大	kuādà	V.	to exaggerate; to overstate	12x
会计	kuàijì	N.	accounting; accountant	2x
会计师	kuàijìshī	N.	accountant	2x
款	kuǎn	N.	a sum of money; fund	8
矿砂	kuàngshā	N.	mineral ore	5
亏欠	kuīqiàn	V.	to be indebted	12x
捆	kǔn	V.	to tie; to bind; to bundle up; bundle;	7
		MW	a measure word	
扩大	kuòdà	V.	to extend, to enlarge	7
缆	lǎn	N.	hawser; mooring rope; cable	6
乐于	lèyú	V.	to be delighted in + Disyllabic V.	9
雷电	léidiàn	N.	thunder and lightening	10
冷静	lěng jìng	Adj.	calm; sober; cool-headed	12
厘米	límǐ	MW	centimeter	6
礼物	lǐwù	N.	gift; present	4x
例	lì	Mph.(N.)	example; instance	1
立方	lìfāng	MW	cube; cubic	6
利润	lìrùn	N.	profit	4
力图	lìtú	V.	to try hard to; to strive for	4
利息	lìxī	N.	interest	9
力争	lìzhēng	V.	to do all one can to, to strive for	4
立字为据	lìzì wéi jù	Idm.	to prepare a document as evidence	11
联合	liánhé	V./Adj.	to join, to unite, joint, united	8
联合运输	liánhé yùnshū	V./N.	through transport, through traffic, coordinated transport	8

联系	liánxì	V.	to contact; to be in touch	1
良好	liánghǎo	Adj.	good; favorable; positive	1
粮食	liángshí	N.	grain; cereals; food	6
了解	liǎojiě	V.	to find out; to understand	1
量	liàng	N.	quantity; amount; volume	6
谅解	liàng jiě	V.	to gain forgiveness from; to understand; to make allowance for	12
劣	liè	Mph.	bad; inferior; of low quality	10x
临近	línjìn	V.	close to; to approach	10x
零售	língshòu	V.	retail	3x
领事	lǐngshì	N.	consul	1x
领事馆	lǐngshìguǎn	N.	consulate	1x
留情	liúqíng	V.	to show mercy or forgiveness	12x
流通	liútōng	V./N.	to circulate; circulation	7
龙口	Lóngkǒu	Pr. N.	A place in Shandong Province, China well-known for producing mungbean noodles	5
陆路	lùlù	N.	land route	8
鹿特丹	Lùtèdān	Pr.N.	Rotterdam (Netherlands)	8
伦敦	Lúndūn	Pr.N.	London	8
轮椅	lúnyǐ	N.	wheel-chair	7x
裸	luǒ	Adj.	(nude cargo) bare; naked	7
裸装	luǒzhuāng	VP	goods loaded on means of transportation without any cover	7
旅游	lǚyóu	V./N.	to travel; to tour	2x
铝	lǚ	N.	aluminum	7
履行	lǚxíng	V.	to fulfil (obligation); to perform (duty); to keep one's words; to carry out	9

履约	lǚyuē	VO	to keep a promise; to carry out a contract	11
绿豆	lǜdòu	N.	mungbean	5
码	mǎ	MW	yard	6
蛮横	mánhèng	Adj.	rude and unreasonable; peremptory	12
满	mǎn	Adj.	full; filled; packed	4x
矛盾	máodùn	V./Adj.	to contradict; to conflict; contradictory;	11
		N.	contradiction	
冒	mào	V.	to risk; to brave	9
贸易	màoyì	N./V.	trade	1
煤炭	méitàn	N.	coal	6
美观	měiguān	Adj.	beautiful; artistic	7
蒙	méng	V.	to receive; to meet with	5x
弥补	míbǔ	V.	to make up; to remedy	12
米	mǐ	MW	meter	6
米制	mǐzhì	N.	the metric system	6
密封	mìfēng	VP	to seal up; to seal hermetically	8x
秘书	mìshū	N.	secretary	2x
棉花	miánhua	N.	cotton	5
免	miǎn	V.	to excuse from; to exempt	9
免除	miǎnchú	V.	to remit; to excuse; to exempt	12
面积	miànjī	N.	area; space	6
名称	míngchēng	N.	name; title	3
名目	míngmù	N.	names of things; items	6
名牌	míngpái	N.	brand-name; famous (product)	5
名片	míngpiàn	N.	business card	1
明确	míngquè	Adj./V.	clear and definite	3

模棱两可	móléng liǎngkě	Idm.	to probe; to explore	3
某	mǒu	Pron.	certain; some	2
木材	mùcái	N.	timber; lumber	6
目的港	mùdìgǎng	NP	port of destination	4
目录	mùlù	N.	catalog; list	1
乃至	nǎizhì	Conj.	even; to the extent of; even go so far as to	7
耐克	Nàikè	Pr. N.	Nike	5
内	nèi	Mph.(N.)	to set a limit; to restrict	3
内在	nèizài	Adj.	inherent; intrinsic	5
尼龙	nílóng	N.	nylon	7
拟	nǐ	V.	to intend; to plan	10x
宁可	nìngkě	Adv.	would rather; better	10x
宁肯	nìngkěn	Adv.	would rather	10x
宁愿	nìngyuàn	Adv.	would rather	10x
欧元	Ōuyuán	N.	Euro	9
欧洲	Ōuzhōu	N.	Europe	9
排除	páichú	V.	to remove; to eliminate; to rule out	12
牌号	páihào	N.	brand	5
盘	pán	N.	price or condition in trading	2
泡	pào	V.	to steep; to soak	10x
赔偿	péicháng	V.	to compensate; reparation	5
碰运气	pèng yùnqì	VO	to take a chance; to try one's luck	10
碰撞	pèngzhuàng	V.	to collide; to run into	10
批	pī	MW	batch; lot; group	8
批发	pīfā	V.	wholesale	3x

譬如	pìrú	*Conj.*	for instance; for example	10
片面	piànmiàn	*Adj.*	unilateral; one-sided	9
票汇	piàohuì	*NP*	Demand Draft, 简称 D/D	9
品	pǐn	*Mph.(N.)*	article; product	5
品名	pǐnmíng	*N.*	name of commodity	3x
品质	pǐnzhì	*N.*	quality; (moral) character	2
乒乓球	pīng pāngqiú	*N.*	ping pong ball; table-tennis	5
凭	píng	*V./Prep.*	to rely on; to depend on	5
平安险	píng'ānxiǎn	*NP*	Free of Particular Average (F.P.A.)	10
平等	píngděng	*N. /Adj.*	equality; equal	7x
平方	píngfāng	*MW*	square	6
凭据	píngjù	*N.*	evidence; proof	9
颇	pō	*Adv.*	considerably; rather; quite	9
破碎	pòsuì	*V.*	to smash; to tatter; to break	10
破碎险	pòsuìxiǎn	*NP*	Clash and Breakage Risk	10
普遍	pǔbiàn	*Adj.*	common; popular	8
蒲式耳	pǔshì'ěr	*MW*	bushel	6
期限	qīxiàn	*N.*	allotted time; time limit; deadline	3
其	qí	*Pron.*	his; her; its; their; him; her; them	2
清除	qīngchú	*V.*	to clear away with; to eliminate	6
旗袍	qípáo	*N.*	a close-fitting dress for women with high neck and slit skirt	4x
启航	qǐháng	*VP*	to set sail	8x
起讫	qǐqì	*V.*	the beginning and the end	10
起首	qǐshǒu	*N.*	the beginning of a letter or a document	4x

企业	qǐyè	N.	enterprise	2x
起运	qǐyùn	V.	start shipment	10
讫	qì	Mph.(V.)	to end	10
器官	qìguān	N.	organ; apparatus	11x
气候	qìhu	N.	climate	10
气体	qìtǐ	N.	gas	6
契约	qìyuē	N.	contract; charter	11
洽	qià	Mph.(V.)	to consult with; to discuss	2
洽商	qiàshāng	V.	to discuss; to consult with	2
洽谈	qiàtán	V.	to talk something over with somebody; to hold a talk with somebody	1
签	qiān	V.	to sign (one's name)	2
签订	qiāndìng	V.	to conclude and sign (a contract or treaty)	2
牵涉	qiānshè	V.	to involve; to drag in	12
签署	qiānshǔ	V.	to sign	11
强硬	qiángyìng	Adj.	strong; tough; unyielding	12
切忌	qièjì	V.	must guard against; to avoid by all means	11
切中	qièzhòng	V.	to hit (the mark)	12x
勤学苦练	qínxué kǔ liàn	VP	to study diligently and train hard	11x
青岛	Qīngdǎo	Pr. N.	A coastal city in Shandong Province, China famous for its beer. It was used to be named "Tsingtao"	5
倾向	qīngxiàng	V.	to be inclined to	4
轻易	qīngyì	Adv.	lightly; rashly	9
情况	qíngkuàng	N.	circumstances; situation	1
取得	qǔdé	V.	to obtain; to acquire; to achieve	1

取决	qǔjué	V.	to decide upon (after discussion)	4
权利	quánlì	N.	right	2
全面	quánmiàn	Adj.	overall; total; comprehensive	10
缺少	quēshǎo	V.	to lack; to be short of	3
确	què	Mph(Adj.)	firm; definite; accurate; true	3
却	què	Adv.	but; yet; however; whereas	4
确定	quèdìng	V./Adj.	to finalize; to define; to fix	2
确切	quèqiè	Adj.	exact; precise	3
确认	quèrèn	V.	to confirm; to affirm; to acknowledgy	3
然而	rán'ér	Conj.	however; nevertheless; but; yet	7
燃料	ránliào	N.	fuel	8x
热乎乎	rèhūhu	Adj.	warm	12x
任何	rènhé	Adj.	any; whichever; whatever	1
任务	rènwù	N.	task; assignment; mission	8
日常	rìcháng	Adj.	Day-today; everyday; daily	3
日益	rìyì	Adv.	day by day; increasingly	7
容	róng	V.	to hold; to contain	6
容积	róngjī	N.	volume; capacity	6
荣誉	róngyù	N.	honor; credit	2x
如	rú	Prep.	in compliance; according to	6
如期	rúqī	Adv.	as scheduled; on schedule	9x
如数	rúshù	Adv.	exactly the number or amount	9
如同	rútóng	V.	once; someday	3
若	ruò	Conj.	if	6
若干	ruògān	Pron.	a certain number or amount; several	7
散	sǎn	Adj.	scattered, fall apart	6

散漫	sǎnmàn	Adj.	undisciplined; careless and sloppy	11x
散装	sǎnzhuāng	VP	bulk, in bulk	6
丧失	sàngshī	V.	to lose; to forfeit	10
色泽	sèzé	N.	color and luster	5
商标	shāngbiāo	N.	trade mark	5
商场	shāngchǎng	N.	mall; market	9
商定	shāngdìng	V.	to decide upon (after discussion)	4
商会	shānghuì	N.	chamber of commerce	1
商品	shāngpǐn	N.	commodity; goods	1
商务	shāngwù	N.	commercial affairs; business affairs	1
设备	shèbèi	N.	equipment; facilities	5
涉及	shèjí	V.	to involve; to relate	8
设计	shèjì	V.N.	(to) design; (to) plan	5
慎重	shènzhòng	Adj.	cautious; careful	6
设想	shèxiǎng	V.	to have consideration for; to give thought to to imagine	12
申明	shēnmíng	V.	to declare; to state	12x
深圳	Shēnzhèn	N.	a city in Guangdong Province near Hong Kong, one of special economic zones in China	2x
审核	shěnhé	V.	to examine and verify	9x
审计	shěnjì	V./N.	to audit	2x
生物	shēngwù	N.	living objects; organism	5
生物学	shēngwù xué	N.	biology	5
生效	shēngxiào	V.	to go into effect; to become effective	10
生意	shēngyì	N.	trade; business	1
省	shěng	V.	to omit; to leave out	9

湿	shī	*Adj.*	damp; wet	10x
失火	shīhuǒ	*V.*	to be on fire; to catch fire	10
实	shí	*Adj.*	true; real; factual	2
识别	shíbié	*V.*	to distinguish; to discern; to identify	7
实际	shíjì	*Adj./N.*	real; practical; reality	2
实盘	shípán	*N.*	offer with engagement; firm offer	2
实施	shíshī	*V.*	to implement; to carry out (policy, plan, regulation)	9x
实事求是	shíshì qiúshì	*Idm.*	to be true to the fact; to seek truth from facts; to be practical and realistic	12
实现	shíxiàn	*V.*	to realize; to materialize	7
实业	shíyè	*N.*	industry; business	9x
石油	shíyóu	*N.*	petroleum	6
始终	shǐzhōng	*Adv./ N.*	from beginning to end	4
适	shì	*Mph(Adj.)*	suitable; fit; -able	1
视	shì	*Mph.(V.)*	revision; change; alter	3
市场	shìchǎng	*N.*	market	1
适当	shìdàng	*Adj.*	suitable, appropriate	1
事故	shìgù	*N.*	accident; mishap	8x
市民	shìmín	*N.*	Residents of a city; citizens	4x
试探	shìtàn	*V.*	to probe; to explore	3
视为	shìwéi	*VP*	to be considered as; treated as	3
事务所	shìwùsuǒ	*N.*	a (law/accounting) firm	2x
事先	shìxiān	*Adv.*	in advance; beforehand; prior	6
适销	shìxiāo	*N./Adj.*	salable; marketable	1
适应	shìyìng	*V.*	to suit; to fit; to adapt	7

事由	shìyóu	N.	the matter concerned; content	4x
收取	shōuqǔ	V.	to receive; to accept; to take	9
首	shǒu	N./Adj.	head; first; chief	8
手段	shǒuduàn	N.	means; measure; method	7
首脑	shǒunǎo	N.	head; chief	11x
首先	shǒuxiān	Adv.	first of all	1
手续	shǒuxù	N.	procedures; formalities	4
首要	shǒuyào	Adj.	of first importance	8
手织	shǒuzhī	VP	hand-knitting	6x
售	shòu	V.	to sell	2
受潮	shòucháo	VP	to be affected with damp; to become damp	10
受潮险	shòu cháoxiǎn	NP	Sweating Risk	10
受款人	shòu kuǎnrén	NP	payee	9
受理	shòulǐ	V.	to accept a case	10
受益	shòuyì	VO	to benefit from; to profit by	9
书面	shūmiàn	N.	written; in writing	2
赎	shú	V.	to redeem	9x
赎单	shúdān	VO	to redeem the bill of lading	9x
属	shǔ	V.	to subordinate to; to belong to	9
署名	shǔmíng	V./N.	to sign; signature	4x
属下	shǔxià	VP	to subordinate to; under	8x
属于	shǔyú	V.	to belong to; to be part of	2
数	shù	Pron.	several; a few	10
数量	shùliàng	N.	amount; quantity; number	2

数码	shùmǎ	N.	number; figure; digital	5
术语	shùyǔ	N.	terminology; technical terms	4
双重	shuāngchóng	Adj.	double; dual; twofold	9
水渍险	shuǐzìxiǎn	NP	With Particular Average (W.P.A.)	10
说理	shuōlǐ	V.	to argue; to reason things out	12
说明	shuōmíng	V./N.	to explain; to illustrate; explanation; illustration	1
说明书	shuōmíngshū	NP	manual	1
硕士	shuòshì	N.	Master (degree)	2x
丝绸	sīchóu	N.	silk; silk cloth	4x
俗语	súyǔ	N.	common saying; proverb	4
塑料	sùliào	N.	plastic	8x
随着表	suízhebiǎo	Prep.	along with; in the wake of; in pace with	7
损耗	sǔnhào	V./N	to lose; to wear and tear; loss	10
损失	sǔnshī	V./N.	to lose; loss	5
索	suǒ	Mph.(V.)	to ask for; to demand	2x
		N.	thick rope; cable	6
索偿	suǒcháng	V.	to claim payment	9
索赔	suǒpéi	VP	to lodge a claim; to claim indemnity	10
所谓	suǒwèi	Adj.	so-called	2
所有权	suǒyǒuquán	N.	ownership	8
贪心	tānxīn	Adj./N.	greedy; avaricious; greed; avarice	3x
谈判	tánpàn	V./N.	to negotiate; negotiation	2
讨价还价	tǎojià huánjià	Idm.	to bargain; to haggle	4
套	tào	MW	set; a set of (document, furniture, garment, etc.)	6

		V.	to cover with; to encase	8x
套语	tàoyǔ	N.	set phrase; polite formula of a letter or document	4x
特产	tèchǎn	N.	local specialty; famous product of a country or a place	5
特色	tèsè	N.	distinguishing feature; characteristic	5
特殊	tèshū	Adj.	special; particular	5
特征	tèzhēng	N.	characteristic; feature; trait	5
提单	tídān	N.	bill of lading	8
提供	tígōng	V.	to supply; to furnish	1
体积	tǐjī	N.	volume; bulk	6
体现	tǐxiàn	V./N.	to embody; to reflect; embodiment	11
体校	tǐxiào	N.	school of physical education	11x
天津	Tiānjīn	Pr.N.	One of the four municipalities directly under the Central Government in China, about 100 kilometers to the Southeast of Beijing	8
天然	tiānrán	Adj.	natural	5
填写	tiánxiě	V.	to fill out (a form)	3x
条件	tiáojiàn	N.	condition	1
条款	tiáokuǎn	N.	clause; article	4
条例	tiáolì	N.	rules; regulations	1
停车	tíngchē	VO	to park a car; to stop; to pull up	4x
停车场	tíngchē chǎng	NP	parking lot; garage	4x
通过	tōngguò	Prep./V.	through; by means of;　to pass through	1
偷窃	tōuqiè	V./N.	to steal; theft	10
同等	tóngděng	Adj.	of the same class, rank, or status; on an equal basis	11

投	tóu	V.	to throw; to cast; to put in	2
投保	tóubǎo	V.	to take out insurance; to ensure	10
投保人	tóubǎorén	N.	the insured party	8x
投石 问路	tóushí wènlù	Idm.	to throw a stone to test the situation for safety before making a move (usually at night)	2
桶	tǒng	N./MW	barrel; bucket; pail; drum; a measure word	7
统一	tǒngyī	V./Adj.	to unify; unified	5
突出	tūchū	Adj./V.	outstanding; prominent; to give prominence to; to highlight	7
途径	tújìng	N.	(mostly used in analogy) way; channel	1
图样	túyàng	N.	pattern; drawing	5
图纸	túzhǐ	N.	blueprint; drawing	5
土产	tǔchǎn	N.	local product	5
土特产	tǔtèchǎn	N.	土产＋特产：special local products	5
团体	tuántǐ	N.	group; organization	5
推荐	tuījiàn	V.	to recommend	1
推销	tuīxiāo	V.	push the sale; to promote sales; to peddle; to market	7
托盘	tuōpán	N.	tray	7
托收	tuōshōu	N.	collection, one of the payment methods in foreign trade	9
托运	tuōyùn	V./N.	to consign for shipment	10
妥	tuǒ	Adj.	appropriate; proper	9x
外地	wàidì	N.	part of the country other than where one lives	4x
外观	wàiguān	N.	outward appearance; exterior	5
外界	wàijiè	N.	outside; the outside or external would	7

外来风险	wàilái fēngxiǎn	NP	extraneous risks	10
外资	wàizī	N.	foreign capital; foreign investment	2x
完备	wánbèi	Adj.	complete; perfect	3
完毕	wánbì	V.	to finish; to complete; to end	11
完善	wánshàn	Adj./V.	perfect; to perfect	11
完整	wánzhěng	Adj.	complete; integrated	3
婉转	wǎnzhuǎn	Adj.	mild and indirect; tactful; (of sounds) sweet and agreeable	12
万无一失	wàn wú yī shī	Idm.	no danger of anything going wrong; perfectly safe; no risk at all	10
万一	wànyī	Conj./N	just in case; if by any chance	11
往来	wǎnglái	N.	come and go; contact	1
网络	wǎngluò	N.	network	7x
往往	wǎngwǎng	Adv.	often; usually	10
违	wéi	Mph.(V.)	to violate; to disobey	3
维修	wéixiū	V.	to maintain; service	5
唯一	wéiyī	Adj.	only; sole	4
违约	wéiyuē	VO	to break a contract; to violate a treaty	3
委托	wěituō	V.	to entrust; trust	9
未	wèi	Adv.	have not; did not; not yet; not	9
未必	wèibì	Adv.	not necessarily; may not	2
味觉	wèijué	N.	sense of taste	5
文件	wénjiàn	N.	document; file; mailes	3
稳定	wěndìng	Adj./V.	stable; steady; to stabilize	5
无论	wúlùn	Conj.	no matter what/how; regardless	2
无声	wúshēng	VO	silent; noiseless	7

无误	wúwù	Adj.	error-free; flawless	9
务	wù	Mph.(N.)	matter; business	1
物	wù	Mphh.(N.)	object; thing	4
误会	wùhuì	V./N.	to misunderstand; misunderstanding	6
误解	wùjiě	V./N.	misunderstanding	3
物理	wùlǐ	N.	physics; physical	5
悉	xī	Mph.(V.)	to know; to learn; to be informed	8x
吸引	xīyǐn	V.	to attract; to lure	3x
袭击	xíjī	V.	to make a surprise attack; to raid; to hit	10x
细致	xìzhì	Adj.	careful; meticulous; pain-sticking	11
衔接	xiánjiē	V.	to cohere; to link up; to join	11
险别	xiǎnbié	N.	(types of) coverage; terms of insurance	4
限	xiàn	V./N.	conversely; on the contrary	3
现货	xiànhuò	N.	merchandise on hand	5x
现行	xiànxíng	Adj.	currently in effect; in operation	9x
限于	xiànyú	V.	to be limited to	2
限制	xiànzhì	V./N	to restrict; to place or impose restriction; to confine; limit; restriction	8
箱	xiāng	N./MW	box; case; trunk	7
相持不下	xiāngchí bùxià	VP	to be locked in a stalemate	12
相对	xiāngduì	Adj.	relatively; comparatively	9
相反	xiāngfǎn	Adj./Conj.	opposite; on the contrary	2
相互	xiānghù	Adv.	mutual; each other; reciprocal, (less common than 互相)	2
相应	xiāngyìng	V./Adv.	to correspond; corresponding; accordingly	4
详细	xiángxì	Adj.	detailed; minute	5

想像力	xiǎngxiànglì	NP	imagination	7x
享誉全球	xiǎngyù quánqiú	Idm.	to enjoy fame all over the world	6x
项	xiàng	MW	Measure Word for things classified by items	1
橡胶	xiàng jiāo	N.	rubber	5
象征	xiàngzhēng	V.	to symbolize; to signify; to stand for	8
		N.	symbol; emblem; token	
销	xiāo	V.	to sell; to market	7
消费	xiāofèi	V./N.	to consume; consumption	7
销路	xiāolù	N.	market; sale	6
销售	xiāoshòu	V./N.	to sell; to market	1
小册子	xiǎo cèzi	N.	brochure; pamphlet	1
小额	xiǎo é	Adj./ N.	a small amount	4
小麦	xiǎomài	N.	wheat	5
效果	xiàoguǒ	N.	effect; result	7
效力	xiàolì	N.	effect; authenticity	11
效率	xiàolù	N.	efficiency	7
携带	xiédài	V.	to carry; to take along	7
协会	xiéhuì	N.	association; society	2x
协商	xiéshāng	V.	to consult; to talk things over	12
协议	xiéyì	V./N.	to agree upon; to reach an agreement	6
辛苦	xīnkǔ	Adj./V.	tired; exhausted; to fatigue; to tire	12x
欣然	xīnrán	Adv.	joyfully; with pleasure	8x
信汇	xìnhuì	NP	Mail Transfer, 简称M/T	9
信任	xìnrèn	V.	to trust; to have confidence in	6x
信息	xìnxī	N.	information	1

信誉	xìnyù	N.	credit and reputation; prestige	5
兴旺	xīngwàng	Adj.	prosperous; flourishing; thriving	10
形式	xíngshì	N.	form; shape	2
形式发票	xíngshì fāpiào	NP	pro-forma invoice	3
形态	xíngtài	N.	form; shape	5
行为	xíngwéi	N.	behavior; action; deed	2
形形色色	xíngxíng sèsè	Adj.	of every hue; of all forms	6
性能	xìngnéng	N.	function; performance	5
性质	xìngzhì	N.	nature; characteristic	2
修改	xiūgǎi	V.	to modify; to alter; to change	2
虚	xū	Adj.	false; nominal	2
虚盘	xūpán	N.	offer without engagement	2
虚伪	xūwěi	Adj.	hypocritical; dishonest; false	3x
虚心	xūxīn	Adj.	modest	12x
叙述	xùshù	V.	to narrate; to recount	12
序言	xùyán	N.	preface; forward	11
选择	xuǎnzé	V./N.	to select; to choose	1
削减	xuējiǎn	V.	to reduce; to cut down	6
学历	xuélì	N.	education; record of formal schooling	2x
学士	xuéshì	N.	Bachelor (degree)	2x
血本	xuèběn	N.	original capital; principal	10
血本无归	xuèběn wúguī	Idm.	a total loss of the original capital (for doing business)	10
询	xún	Mph.(V.)	to ask about; to inquire	2
询盘	xúnpán	VO	to in quire	2

询问	xúnwèn	V.	to inquire; to ask about	5x
训练	xùnliàn	V./N.	to train; to drill	11x
迅速	xùnsù	Adj.	rapid; fast; swift	8
押金	yājīn	N.	deposit; cash pledge	9
言	yán	Mph(N/V)	words; remarks; to say; to speak	3
延	yán	Mph.(V.)	to delay; to extend	9
延长	yáncháng	V.	to extend; to prolong; to lengthen	9
严格	yángé	Adj.	strict; rigorous	6
严肃	yánsù	Adj.	serious; earnest; solemn	11
延误	yánwù	V.	to incur loss through delay	10
羊毛衫	yáng máoshān	NP	woolen sweater	6x
邀请	yāoqǐng	V.	to invite	3
要害	yàohài	N.	vital part; critical point	12x
液体	yètǐ	N.	liquid	6
业务	yèwù	N.	business; profession	1
业余	yèyú	Adj.	spare time; amateur	11x
一针见血	yīzhēn jiànxiě	Idm.	to pierce to the truth with a single pertinent remark; to hit the nail on the head	12
一般	yībān	Adj.	general(ly), ordinal(ly)	2
一旦	yīdàn	Adv./N.	once; someday	3
一经	yījīng	Conj.	once; as soon as	9
一举	yījǔ	Adv.	with on action; instantly	11x
依据	yījù	N.	(on the) basis of; foundation; evidence	5
一切险	yīqièxiǎn	NP	All Risks	10
一时	yīshí	Adv. /N.	For a while; temporarily	3

一致	yīzhì	Adj.	identical; the same; unanimous (in opinion, view, etc.)	2
遗憾	yíhàn	Adj./N.	to be regretted; regretful; regret	6x
仪器	yíqì	N.	instrument; apparatus	3x
遗失	yíshī	V.	to lose	12
意	yì	Mph.(N.)	equivocal; ambiguous	3
异	yì	Mph.(Adj)	different; other; another	5
溢	yì	Mph.(V.)	to overflow; to spill	6
亦	yì	Adv.	also; too	9
义不容辞	yì bù róng cí	Idm.	to be duty bound; to have an unshirkable duty	8
议付	yìfù	V./N.	to negotiate (through a bank), negotiation	9
议付银行	yìfù yínháng	N.	negotiating bank	9
意见	yìjiàn	N.	opinion; point of view	2
意图	yìtú	N.	intention; intent	3
意外	yìwài	Adj./N	unexpected; unforeseen; accident; mishap	10
意味	yìwèi	N.	meaning; significance	10
意味着	yìwèizhe	VP	to signify; to mean	10
义务	yìwù	N.	responsibility, duty, obligation	2
意向	yìxiàng	N.	intention; purpose	1
意义	yìyì	N.	meaning; sense; significance	7
异议	yìyì	N.	objection; dissent	11
意愿	yìyùn	N.	desire; wish; aspiration	3
溢装	yìzhuāng	VP/N.	overload	6
因素	yīnsù	N.	factor; element	8
英寸	yīngcùn	MW	inch	6

引用	yǐnyòng	V.	to quote; to cite	12
应	yìng	Mph.(V.)	to comply with; to grant; to answer; to respond	9
涌	yǒng	V.	to gush; to pour	12x
勇敢	yǒnggǎn	Adj.	brave	11x
优点	yōudiǎn	N.	merit; advantage; virtue	8
优惠	yōuhuì	Adj.	favorable	3x
优良	yōuliáng	Adj.	excellent	5
优美	yōuměi	Adj.	beautiful; graceful	6x
尤其	yóuqí	Adv.	particularly; especially	9
邮政	yóuzhèng	N.	postal service	8
有竞争力	yǒu jìng zhēnglì	Adj. P.	competitive	3x
有吸引力	yǒu xī yǐnlì	Adj. P.	attractive	3x
有关	yǒuguān	Adj.	related; relevant	1
有机	yǒujī	Adj.	organic	11
有据可查	yǒujù kěchá	Idm.	there is documented record for investigation	11
有限	yǒuxiàn	Adj.	limited; finite	3
有效	yǒuxiào	Adj.	valid; effective	2
有意	yǒuyì	VO	to intend; be inclined to	2
有助于	yǒuzhùyú	VP	to be conducive to; to be helpful to	1
愚蠢	yúchǔn	Adj.	stupid; foolish	3x
于是	yúshì	Conj.	hence; therefore; as a result	2
予	yǔ	V.	to give; to grant	10
允许	yǔnxǔ	V.	permit; allow	8
与其	yǔqí	Conj.	it's better to ... than...; ... rather than ...	10

语气	yǔqì	N.	tone (in speech); mood (in grammar)	12
预	yù	Adv.	in advance; beforehand	9
预报	yùbào	V. N.	to forecast; to predict	5x
预付	yùfù	V.	pay in advance	9
预计	yùjì	V.	to estimate; to calculate in advance	5x
源	yuán	Mph.(N.)	source; cause	6
远期	yuǎnqī	N.	long term	5x
远期汇票	yuǎnqī huìpiào	NP	time bill	9
约	yuē	N.	pact; agreement; treaty; contract	11
约束	yuēshù	V.	to restrain; to keep in bound	2
约束力	yuēshùlì	NP	the power to constrain; constraints	3
运气	yùnqì	N.	luck; fate	10
运输	yùnshū	V./N.	to transport; transportation; carriage	1
运载	yùnzài	V./.N.	to carry, to deliver; to load; carriage; delivery	8
杂志	zázhì	N.	magazine	1
灾害	zāihài	N.	calamity; disaster	10
再生	zàishēng	VP	to resurrect; to recycle and regenerate	8x
赞扬	zànyáng	V.	to praise; to commend	3x
遭	zāo	V.	to meet with; to suffer from (disasters, misfortune, etc.)	10
遭到	zāodào	V.	to suffer; to encounter; to meet with	10
遭受	zāoshòu	V.	to suffer; to incur (a disaster or a loss)	4
造型	zàoxíng	N.	design; shape; modeling; figure	5
则	zé	Adv.	but; on the other hand	1
责任	zérèn	N.	responsibility	2

沾污	zhānwū	V.	to contaminate; to be tainted	10
沾污险	zhānwūxiǎn	N.	Contamination Risk	10
展览	zhǎnlǎn	V./N.	to display; to exhibit; exhibition	1
展销	zhǎnxiāo	V./N.	show; commodity exhibition	7
展销会	zhǎnxiāohuì	N.	An exhibition fair; a trade show	4x
占	zhàn	V.	to make up; to account for; to occupy	8
战争险	zhànzhēngxiǎn	NP	War Risk	10
张家口	Zhāngjiākǒu	Pr. N.	A city in Hepei Province, China famous for producing mungbean	5
涨	zhǎng	V.	to rise; to go up	6
掌握	zhǎngwò	V.	to know well; to control	1
障碍	zhàng' ài	N./V.	obstacle; obstruction; to hinder; to obstruct	6
照顾	zhàogù	V.	to take care	12x
针对	zhēnduì	V.	to be directed against (at); to pinpoint at	2
争端	zhēngduān	N.	controversial issues; dispute	12x
争取	zhēngqǔ	V.	to trive for; to attempt to gain	3
征收	zhēngshōu	V.	to levy ; to collect; to impose (taxes)	1x
争议	zhēngyì	V./N.	to dispute; dispute	3
折扣	zhékòu	N.	discount	6
整体	zhěngtǐ	N.	whole; entirety	11
震	zhèn	V.N.	to shock; to shake; shock; quake	7
正本	zhèngběn	N.	original (of a document)	11
证书	zhèngshū	N.	certificate	2x
正文	zhèngwén	N.	the body of a letter or article	4x
政治	zhèngzhì	N./Adj.	politics; political	8

郑重	zhèngzhòng	*Adj.*	serious; solemn; earnest	12
知己 知彼	zhī jǐ zhī bǐ	*Idm.*	to know oneself and one's opponents well	1
支付	zhīfù	*V./N.*	to pay; payment	2
执	zhí	*Mph.(V.)*	to hold; to grasp	2
直达	zhídá	*V.*	through traffic; nonstop	8
值得	zhídé	*V.*	to be worth; to deserve	4
直接	zhíjì	*Adj./Adv.*	direct; immediate	1
直率	zhíshuài	*Adj.*	frank; candid; straightforward	12x
职务	zhíwù	*N.*	position; title	4x
执行	zhíxíng	*V.*	to carry out; to implement	2
直销	zhíxiāo	*V.*	direct marketing; to sell directly	7x
指	zhǐ	*V.*	to indicate; to refer to	3
指标	zhǐbiāo	*N.*	target; index	5
指定	zhǐdìng	*V.*	to appoint; to assign (person in charge, time, place, etc.)	7
指示	zhǐshì	*V./N*	to instruct; to give directions; instructions	8x
质	zhì	*Mph. (N.)*	nature; characteristic; quality	5
致	zhì	*V.*	to send; to express	5x
滞	zhì	*Mph.(V.)*	stagnant; sluggish	9
质地	zhìdì	*N.*	quality of a material; texture	6x
制定	zhìdìng	*V.*	to formulate; to lay down	5
制度	zhìdù	*N.*	system	1
质量	zhìliàng	*N.*	quality	5
滞销	zhìxiāo	*V.*	slow sale, sluggish sale	9
制作	zhìzuò	*V.*	to draw up or prepare (a contract, document); to make; to manufacture	11

中性	zhōngxìng	Adj.	neutral	7
终止	zhōngzhǐ	V.	to stop; to end; to terminate	10x
周转	zhōuzhuǎn	N./V	to turn over; to circulate	6
种类	zhǒnglèi	N.	variety; kind; type	5
重	zhòng	V.	to lay stress on; to attach importance to	11
仲裁	zhòngcái	V./N.	to arbitrate; arbitration	11
重量	zhòngliàng	N.	weight	6
诸多	zhūduō	Num.	a good deal of ; a lot of (to modify abstract nouns only)	8
逐步	zhúbù	Adv.	step by step; progressively	6
逐渐	zhújiàn	Adj.	gradual; gradually	6x
主动	zhǔdòng	Adj.	initiative	2
主管	zhǔguǎn	N./V.	chief executive officer; person in charge; to take charge of; to be responsible for	5x
主计员	zhǔjìyuán	N.	chief accountant	2x
主任	zhǔrèn	N.	director (of a branch/department)	2x
主题	zhǔtí	N.	theme; the main idea	12x
主体	zhǔtǐ	N.	main part; principle part	11
主修	zhǔxiū	VP/N.	to major in; to specialized in (a major/subject)	2x
驻	zhù	V.	to stay; to be stationed	1
助理	zhùlǐ	Adj./N.	assistant	2x
注明	zhùmíng	VP	to give clear indication of; to specify	7
祝颂	zhùsòng	V.	to express good wishes or praise	4x
祝颂语	zhùsòngyǔ	N.	expressions of good wishes or praise in letters or documents	4x
注重	zhùzhòng	V.	to lay stress on; to pay attention to; to attach importance to	7

抓紧	zhuājǐn	V.	to firmly grasp; to pay close attention to	12
专门	zhuānmén	Adj.	special; specialized	7
专攻	zhuāngōng	VP	to concentrate on; to specialized in (a major)	2x
专业	zhuānyè	N.	specialization; major (at college)	2x
转船	zhuǎnchuán	VO	to transship; transshipment	8
转售	zhuǎnshòu	V.	to resell	8
赚	zhuàn	V.	to make profit; to make money; to gain	4
装潢	zhuānghuáng	V./N	to decorate; decoration; packaging	7
装卸	zhuāngxiè	V.	to load and unload	4
装运	zhuāngyùn	V./N.	to load; to ship; loading; shipment	2
装运港	zhuāngyùngǎng	NP	port of loading	4
追订	zhuīdìng	VP	to place an additional order	6x
着眼	zhuóyǎn	VO	to have something in mind; to view from the angle of	12
兹	zī	N./Pron.	now; at present; this	10x
资金	zījīn	N.	capital; fund	6
资信	zīxìn	N.	assets and credit	1
自然	zìrán	Adv./Adj.	naturally; of course	2
自我	zìwǒ	Prep/Adv.	self (+disyllabic V.) indicating a self-directed action toward oneself	1
自相矛盾	zìxiāng máodùn	Idm.	to be self-contradictory	12
宗	zōng	MW	A Measure Word for 心事、交易、货物、款项、案件，etc.	4
总	zǒng	Adj.	chief; head; general	1x

总裁	**zǒngcái**	*N.*	president/chairman (of a party, a company); director general (of a board)	1x
组合	**zǔhé**	*V./N.*	to make up; to compose	7
组织	**zǔzhī**	*V./N.*	to organize; organization	4
遵守	**zūnshǒu**	*V.*	to observe; to abide by; to comply with	11
遵照	**zūnzhào**	*V.*	to obey; to comply with; to follow	9
做工	**zuògōng**	*N.*	workmanship	6x

翻译练习答案

第一课

1. 经过充分的市场调(查)研(究)，我们发现中国是我们产品的适销市场，另外，上海港的条件也不错。我们选择了中国的大同公司作为我们的交易对象。这样有助于我们的商品出口。

2. 任何公司想与美国公司建立业务关系，都可以直接与美国驻华大使馆商务处联系。他们可以提供关于有兴趣和中国做生意的美国公司的各种资料，例如：有关厂商的地址、电话号码和传真号码。除此以外，他们也准备了一些小册子和商业报刊，以便大家了解美国的贸易惯例和法律制度。

3. 首先让我自我介绍一下。我是马天明，中国轻工进出口公司广东分公司的销售经理。我是通过你们多年的客户金先生得到有关你们公司的信息的。我们很有兴趣跟你们做生意，并且希望今后能发展合作关系。

第二课

1. 如果一方有意出售，另一方同意购买，而双方对所有的交易条件都取得了一致意见，交易就可以达成，于是，签订合同就是一个必不可少的环节。在国际贸易中，这叫做"接受"。

2. 合同的内容包括商品的名称、品质、规格、价格、支付方式、数量、包装、装运、交货期等等。作为一项法律文件，合同具有一定的约束力。签订合同后，无论发生什么事情，任何一方都必须执行，不可修改其内容。

3. 只有买方承诺付款，卖方才可交货。从银行提供的信息来看，买方还没付款。与你说的相反，责任应该属于买方，不存在我方不执行合同的问题。

第三课

1. 总经理一旦决定出售某种商品，就会明确地、毫不含糊地表达她的

意图。有时候即使知道可能会有严重的后果，她也不会改变(她的)
计划。

2. 这个合同少了一项内容，因而是不完整的。我们不知道卖方是否能
   在三天内修改合同，否则我们不能签约，只好撤销这个合同。

3. 请不要误解我的意思，报"虚盘"是指我们不想马上成交。凡是我一
   时不能确定价钱是否是最合适的时候，我就报虚盘。这样，我可以
   掌握主动，以避免不必要的麻烦。

4. 口头接受，如同书面接受，都会被视为有效的承诺，因此都有同样
   的法律约束力。无论是买方还是卖方，一旦接受了交易条件，都不
   能反悔。

第四课

1. 保险始终是高利润的生意。无论什么时候，都有人要旅行，都有货
   物需要运输，因此都有发生危险的可能。一般来说，办理保险手续
   并不复杂，同时，也不必讨价还价，所以很多人都买了不同险别的
   保险。

2. 既然这些货物都同时到达目的港，我倾向于一起组织装运，可是她
   却要各自安排租船订舱。当然，这样对支付运费可能比较方便，但
   是费用也会相应提高。解决问题的唯一办法，是我们坐下来再谈
   判。

3. 一般来说，喜欢讨价还价的人都比较注意节省(开支)。真正懂得节
   省的人和喜欢讨价还价的人的差别是：前者需要的时候才买，而不
   是东西便宜就买。也就是说，他们是否买取决于需要而不是价钱。
   我觉得这种做法值得学习。

第五课

1. 他们的是名牌产品，我们的新产品一时难以和他们的竞争。但是，我
   们的新产品设计合理，结构独特，操作方便，维修简单。凭着它的高
   性能和优良品质，我相信这个新产品一定会成为驰名中外的产品。

2. 这是个特殊情况。保险公司始终都十分关注你们所遭受的损失。只要我们调查清楚，就会赔偿你们的损失。至于赔偿多少，我们将以我们的调查结果为依据。当然，我们也会参考你们和其他方面提供的资料。一旦把我们的调查和其他信息结合起来，我们就会有一个比较客观、详细的了解。那时候，我们就可以向你们公布结果了。

3. 这些所谓的工艺品的造型既没有现代特色又与我们的传统不符，如果（它们）单独展出，你根本就不知道是什么东西。我认为它们不会为本地人所欢迎。你最好撤销这个展览以免没有人来参观。

第六课

1. 目前，电脑已经供过于求，而且价格一直下跌。很多电脑商为了促销，给顾客打九折或者八折，有的甚至以低于成本的价格出售。如果这些电脑卖不出去，电脑商还得找地方储存，那时候，真是得不偿失。

2. 世界上有各种各样的计量单位。对很多人来说，不同计量制度的转换不但繁琐，而且容易有出入。例如，铁矿和钢铁产品都是按重量计算的。但是，如果按英制计算，一吨相当于2,240磅；如果按美制计算，一吨则只有2,000磅。这就不可避免地造成误解。因此，越来越多国家都在逐步采用米制。

3. 香烟的进口关系到人们的身体健康，我们必须慎重考虑。政府一方面鼓励人们少抽烟或者不抽烟，另一方面对香烟的进口有严格的规定。我们不应该为了赚钱而冒险。

第七课

1. 随着市场情况的变化，我们决定在不提高成本的基础上扩大生产规模。我们将提高工作效率作为主要手段，使产量增加一倍。

2. 汽车的设计越来越美观，而竞争则日益紧张。这样的竞争有利于提高产品质量和降低价格。可以说，市场经济在这里起着决定性的作用。

3. 这种电脑便于携带，容易操作。很多人经常带着它们去工作、开会、乃至于去旅行，看起来这些人的生活已经离不开电脑了。然而，有一个问题，那就是这些电脑都没有防盗功能。

第八课

1. 保证旅客的安全是我们义不容辞的责任。（这样的）天气根本就不允许我们开船。我们关心的首要问题并非错过飞机而是你们的安全。假如轮船遭到什么危险，不但我们联合运输公司的名声大受影响，而且你们的生命也会有危险。

2. 这种电脑价格低廉，性能稳定，基本上不受任何限制。它结合了各种先进的技术，因此很受欢迎。它已经迅速代替了进口的名牌产品，占今年销售总额的四分之三。它是个成功的象征。

3. 对外贸易比一般的生意复杂得多。它涉及银行、运输、海关、商检和其他很多部门，所以，所有权属于政府的进出口公司占了85%以上。这家公司并非属于政府而是属于容先生和他的儿子，它可以算是中国最大的私人公司了。

第九课

1. 应美国政府的邀请，中国经济贸易代表团下个月将访问美国。一方面双方都乐于见到中美两国之间最近几年经济交流的发展，另一方面，代表团将和美国官员一起讨论一些亟待解决的有关贸易和关税的问题。

2. 相对其他外币而言，美元是相当稳定的。虽然金融市场经常波动，但是很少见到美元大幅度贬值。除非美国经济出现重大问题，否则美元还是非常可靠的。因此，我从来不轻易以大量的美元兑换日元，我不想冒险。

3. 海星公司委托我们代收货款。遵照客户的指示，在买方支付货款后，一经查核无误，你就把提货单连同其他有关单据一起交给买方。然后扣除手续费，再把钱电汇给卖方。

第十课

1. 按照合同的规定，货物自运离仓库起到装上货轮为止，卖方应对货物的安全负责。换言之，如果货物因装船而受到任何损坏，卖方将予以赔偿。但是，货物一旦装上船后，买方或承保人应对货物的安全负责。如果货物在运输途中或到达目的港后有任何损失，卖方概不负责。

2. 邮购和直销随着科技的发展而兴旺起来。他们经常利用电视做广告。很多人都觉得，与其等商店打折去商店买东西，不如打电话买便宜的东西。然而，这样买东西也不是万无一失的，有时候能否买到你想买的东西也要靠碰运气。

3. 两年前，提高高速公路速度限制的规定开始生效。这个规定受到很多人的反对。对他们来说，提高速度意味着更多的意外和事故，更多的事故意味着保险费的增加。对一些保险公司来说，汽车保险费的增加意味着更高的利润。但是他们忘了一点：如果越多人出事，他们会反过来索取更多的赔偿。

第十一课

1. 我们宁可在成交以前就价格与对方进行反复谈判，也不在成交后违约。合同一旦签订完毕，我们就严格遵守，认真执行。这样做体现了我们"重合同、讲信用"的原则。

2. 这种药只适用于男性病人，对于女性病人不一定有同等效力。目前不仅没有科学理论而且没有实验资料证明这种药对妇女有效，万一出了什么问题，保险公司将不负任何责任。

3. 青少年较为散漫。教育青少年遵守纪律是一项耐心而细致的工作。我们应该以严肃而认真的态度来对待这项工作。

第十二课

1. 面对蛮横无理的老板，她非常冷静。她用坚定有力的语气，一针见血地指出他的话是自相矛盾的。

2. 那时候，如果克林顿抓紧时机，实事求是地叙述整个事情的经过，向美国人民承认错误，他是有可能得到人民的谅解的。这个问题也可能得到公平合理的解决。由于他只着眼于自己的面子，这个错误造成的政治损失是不可弥补的。

3. 这种局面已经持续了一段时间了。由于双方各执一词，意见相持不下，而且态度越来越强硬。在这种情况下，通过协商解决问题是绝对不可能的。